Handbook of Evidence-based Psychotherapies
A Guide for Research and Practice

Handbook of Evidence-based Psychotherapies

A Guide for Research and Practice

Edited by

Chris Freeman
Cullen Centre, Royal Edinburgh Hospital
and
Mick Power
Clinical and Health Psychology, University of Edinburgh

John Wiley & Sons, Ltd

Other Wiley Editorial Offices

John Wiley & Sons Inc., 111 River Street, Hoboken, NJ 07030, USA

Jossey-Bass, 989 Market Street, San Francisco, CA 94103-1741, USA

Wiley-VCH Verlag GmbH, Boschstr. 12, D-69469 Weinheim, Germany

John Wiley & Sons Australia Ltd, 42 Mc Dougall Street, Milton, Queensland 4064, Australia

John Wiley & Sons (Asia) Pte Ltd, 2 Clementi Loop #02-01, Jin Xing Distripark, Singapore 129809

John Wiley & Sons Canada Ltd, 6045 Freement Blvd, Mississauga, ONT, L5R 4J3

Wiley also publishes its books in a variety of electronic formats. Some content that appears
in print may not be available in electronic books.

Anniversary Logo Design: Richard J. Pacifico

Library of Congress Cataloging-in-Publication Data

Handbook of evidence-based psychotherapies : a guide for research
    and practice / edited by Chris Freeman and Mick Power.
        p.   cm.
    ISBN-13: 978-0-471-49820-9 (alk. paper)
    ISBN-10: 0-471-49820-3 (alk. paper)
    1. Psychotherapy—Handbooks, manuals, etc.   2. Evidence-based
medicine—Handbooks, manuals, etc.   I. Freeman, Chris.   II. Power, Michael J.
    [DNLM: 1. Mental Disorders—therapy.   2. Psychotherapy—methods.   3. Evidence-Based Medicine.
WM420 H23128   2007]
RC455.2.E94H3622   2007
616.89′14—dc22   2006022727

British Library Cataloguing in Publication Data

A catalogue record for this book is available from the British Library

ISBN-13   978-0-471-49820-9 (ppc)
ISBN-10   0-471-49820-3 (ppc)

Typeset in 10/12pt Times by TechBooks Electronic Services, New Delhi, India
Printed and bound in Great Britain by Antony Rowe, Chippenham, Wiltshire
This book is printed on acid-free paper responsibly manufactured from sustainable forestry
in which at least two trees are planted for each one used for paper production.

Contents

Part III   Conclusions

About the Editors

Chris Freeman is a consultant psychiatrist and psychotherapist based at the Cullen Centre in the Royal Edinburgh Hospital and is also a senior lecturer in the Department of Psychiatry at the University of Edinburgh. He established the South of Scotland Training Programme in Cognitive Behaviour Therapy and has published widely in the areas of eating disorders and psychological therapies.

Mick Power is Professor of Clinical Psychology at the University of Edinburgh and an honorary consultant clinical psychologist at the Royal Edinburgh Hospital. He is the co-founder of the journal *Clinical Psychology and Psychotherapy* and has previously edited handbooks of mood disorders and of cognition and emotion. His main interest is in the application of theories of cognition and emotion to the understanding of psychological disorders.

Contributors

Michael Barkham, School of Psychology, University of Leeds, Leeds, UK.

Aaron T. Beck, Center for Cognitive Therapy, University of Pennsylvania, Philadelphia, USA.

Kathryn L. Bleiberg, Weill Medical College of Cornell University, New York, USA.

Tom M. Brown, Department of Psychiatry, NHS, Glasgow, UK.

Alan Carr, Department of Psychology, University College Dublin, Dublin, Eire.

Fiona Cathcart, St Columba's Hospice, Edinburgh, UK.

Katherine Cheshire, Lynebank Hospital, Fife, UK.

Rob Durham, Department of Psychiatry, University of Dundee, Dundee, UK.

Paul Emmelkamp, Department of Clinical Psychology, University of Amsterdam, Amsterdam, The Netherlands.

Winnie Eng, College of Staten Island, City University of New York, New York, USA.

Peter Fisher, Division of Clinical Psychology, University of Liverpool, Liverpool, UK.

Chris Freeman, Cullen Centre, Royal Edinburgh Hospital, Edinburgh, UK.

Nick Heather, School of Psychology and Sport Sciences, Northumbria University, Newcastle, UK.

Richard G. Heimberg, Department of Psychology, Temple University, Philadelphia, USA.

J.H. Kamphuis, Department of Clinical Psychology, University of Amsterdam, Amsterdam, The Netherlands.

Willem Kuyken, School of Psychology, University of Exeter, Exeter, UK.

Ken Laidlaw, Section of Clinical and Health Psychology, University of Edinburgh, Edinburgh, UK.

Roslyn Law, Cullen Centre, Royal Edinburgh Hospital, Edinburgh, UK.

Stan Lindsay, Department of Psychology, Institute of Psychiatry, London, UK.

William R. Lindsay, Department of Psychology, University of Abertay, Dundee, UK.

Katharine Logan, Cullen Centre, Royal Edinburgh Hospital, Edinburgh, UK.

Siobhan MacHale, Department of Psychiatry, St John's Hospital, Livingston, UK.

Sharon Y. Manning, Behavioral Tech Research Inc. USA.

Frank Margison, Gaskell Psychotherapy Centre, Manchester, UK.

John C. Markowitz, Weill Medical College of Cornell University, New York, USA.

John McLeod, Department of Couselling, University of Abertay, Dundee, UK.

Jane Morris, Young People's Unit, Royal Edinburgh Hospital, Edinburgh, UK.

Mick Power, Section of Clinical and Health Psychology, University of Edinburgh, Edinburgh, UK.

Mark C. Ramm, Orchard Clinic, Royal Edinburgh Hospital, Edinburgh, UK.

N. Sanjay Kumar Rao, The County Hospital, Durham, UK.

Stanley J. Renwick, Care Principles, York, UK.

Jan Scott, Section of Psychological Therapies, Institute of Psychiatry, London, UK.

John Spector, Shrodells Psychiatric Unit, Watford General Hospital, Watford, UK.

Peter Sturmey, Department of Psychology, City University of New York, New York, USA.

Douglas Turkington, Royal Victoria Infirmary, Newcastle Upon Tyne, UK.

E. Vedel, Department of Clinical Psychology, University of Amsterdam, Amsterdam, The Netherlands.

David A. Winter, Department of Psychology, University of Hertfordshire, Hatfield and Barnet, Enfield and Haringey NHS Trust, UK.

Preface

There has never been a greater interest in evidence-based psychotherapies. Therapists more than ever wish to evaluate their clinical practice and develop their skills using such evidence in a self-reflective manner; healthcare managers want the best supported practices for psychological therapies run in a cost-efficient way and our patients and clients themselves surely also want some reassurance that there may be some support for the practices that they may be subjected to at times when they are likely to be in considerable distress.

So why might there be problems with such a noble cause? Since at least the early 1950s the general area of psychotherapy has been beset by a considerable degree of inflammatory accusation and counter-accusation that at times has felt like a religious war. The politics of established psychotherapies versus newcomers vying for position has seen considerable polarisation around the issue of which therapy tries to monopolise science while accusing other therapies of being non-scientific. All therapies, of course, are capable of using the practices of the scientific method in order to establish an evidence base and to amend, adapt and alter practices accordingly. This scientific approach is possible whatever the extreme claims of individual practitioners from the different psychotherapies might reflect. Psychoanalysis is neither more nor less capable of being evaluated than is behaviour therapy.

The main issues for the current volume are therefore, first, to accept that there is a need for an evidence base for the psychotherapies but, second, to cast a highly critical eye on many of the assumptions about the collection of that evidence base and to be critical of the so-called evidence base itself. We have therefore asked our contributors not simply to sing the praises of their preferred approach nor to over-state the strength of the relevant evidence base but rather to maintain a critical and honest stance regarding the strengths and weaknesses of the claimed evidence. We have also sandwiched the overview of psychological therapies and the disorder-by-disorder reviews between an introductory chapter that provides a critical starting point or perspective from which to approach the subsequent chapters and a concluding chapter that provides a critical framework for the evaluation of approaches to the evidence base together with a way forward for the future.

Our hope therefore is that the challenges that face the philosophical and practical issues of the concept and collection of evidence in psychotherapy are all debated in this volume in a manner that will be useful and enlightening to everybody involved in research on or the delivery of psychotherapy. We hope, too, that our clients and patients may also benefit from these debates for otherwise our efforts will be hollow.

Chris Freeman and Mick Power

PART I

Overview of Therapies

CHAPTER 1

Introduction

Mick Power
University of Edinburgh, UK
and
Chris Freeman
Royal Edinburgh Hospital, UK

INTRODUCTION

There has been a recent surge of interest in evidence-based medicine, which has led one or two sceptics to question what medicine was based on before. The answer is, of course, that medicine has always been based on 'evidence' but maybe not on evidence as we now know it. There was always 'evidence' that the world was flat (you just had to look at the Earth), that the sun rotated around the Earth (you just had to look at the sun moving through the sky) and that blood letting was an effective form of treatment for maladies (some patients did actually recover who might otherwise have died). In a world where we seek to confirm rather than disprove our beliefs there is always evidence to be cited in favour of multiple and contradictory viewpoints. Given the ambiguous nature of evidence, therefore, one of the key questions for a book such as this has to be a consideration of the concept of evidence itself. What counts as evidence? Do different approaches take different views of what counts as evidence? What of apparently contradictory sets of evidence? How can such contradictions be resolved or explained?

There is now a major growth industry in medicine that examines the nature of evidence and draws evidence together in order to produce expert clinical guidelines for the treatment and management of all possible disorders. Most of this work draws on quantitative and qualitative methods for the assessment and grading of evidence in addition to methods for combining evidence across studies. Earlier evidence review methods were of a qualitative nature but there are now quantitative review methods, for example in the forms of meta-analyses and mega-analyses (see later) that allow the combination of evidence from different studies. The increasingly influential Cochrane reviews (named after the epidemiologist, Archie Cochrane, in particular for his influential 1972 book) categorise evidence from different studies into levels: high-quality meta-analyses and randomised controlled trials (RCTs), case-control or cohort studies, case reports or case series, and expert opinion.

Handbook of Evidence-based Psychotherapies: A Guide for research and practice.
Edited by C. Freeman & M. Power. Copyright © 2007 John Wiley & Sons, Ltd.

Cochrane reviews and other clinical guideline groups (such as the SIGN groups in Scotland and the NICE groups in England) pool together all published studies that satisfy basic inclusion criteria, but thereby suffer from the *publication bias* problem that positive results are more likely to be submitted and accepted for publication than are negative results. It is possible to estimate the extent of this bias based on the standard error of published findings (see, for example, Begg & Mazumdar, 1994), although this is rarely done when such reviews are carried out. However, an equally important issue that keeps many psychotherapists awake at night is whether or not the RCT view of evidence is the appropriate one for psychotherapy. Although RCTs provide the gold standard for evidence in many areas of medicine, a number of the requirements for a high-quality RCT are difficult to meet in psychotherapy research. For example, although in theory patients and raters in pharmacotherapy trials may be blind as to whether the person is in the placebo group or the active drug group of the trial, it is nearly impossible to blind patients (and therefore raters) about which arm of a psychotherapy trial they are in. Part of the purpose of this chapter and a number of subsequent chapters will therefore be to consider some of the limitations of the current evidence-based approach to avoid uncritical acceptance of a flawed and complex evidence base while also avoiding the need for its complete rejection.

EVIDENCE AND PSYCHOTHERAPIES

One of the classic and most destructive uses of evidence was in Eysenck's (1952) claim that psychodynamic psychotherapy was no more effective than leaving people to recover spontaneously. Apart from the controversy that Eysenck sparked, he also led to a generation of psychotherapy researchers determined to improve the science of psychotherapy outcome research, subsequent summaries of which argued that Eysenck had considerably over-estimated rates of spontaneous recovery and under-estimated psychotherapy change (for example, Luborsky, Singer & Luborsky, 1975; Smith & Glass, 1977). These research efforts focussed primarily on analyses of the immediate outcome of therapy and, by-and-large, led to the conclusion that all therapies were equally effective because of the operation of 'common factors' such as the therapeutic relationship. Although there is some truth in such a conclusion, and there is no question of the importance of a positive therapeutic relationship in relation to outcome (Hubble, Duncan & Miller, 1999), the chapters in this book will testify that such a conclusion must be significantly qualified in relation to specific disorders and different individuals.

One of the issues that any account of the psychotherapies must deal with and explain is the continued development of new psychotherapies; perhaps the focus on common factors may partly explain this continued development, but nevertheless it provides an enormous challenge if the evidence base is to keep pace with the rate of development even simply in terms of the number of new approaches. Herink (1980) documented over 250 varieties of therapy. This number had increased to about 400 by the early 1990s (Norcross & Goldfried, 1992) and the latest estimates put the number at about 500. Indeed, somewhere in California there is probably another therapy being christened at this very moment. The question that must be asked of this diversity is whether 500 different therapies need to operate by 500 different mechanisms, or whether, alternatively, there exist common factors that can offer some unification of the diverse theories and practices that occur under the label 'psychotherapy'. These common factors might apply irrespective of whether or not the therapies or therapists are effective, so a more specific question must also be asked: 'Does the *good* cognitive therapist share anything in common with the *good* behaviour therapist or the *good* dynamic psychotherapist?' There is, in fact, a growing belief that, whatever the brand name, good therapeutic practice cuts across the artificial boundaries that therapies place around themselves in order to appear distinct from their competitors.

Some of the impetus for the exploration of integrative approaches to psychotherapy has arisen from the failure of many studies of the effectiveness of different therapies to find significant differences in outcome, as noted above. Stiles, Shapiro & Elliott (1986) have labelled this the paradox of 'outcome equivalence contrasted with content non-equivalence'. That is, it is clear from analyses of the content of therapy sessions that therapists of different persuasions do different things in therapy that are broadly consistent with the type of therapy to which they adhere (De Rubeis *et al.*, 1982; Luborsky *et al.*, 1985). Stiles, Shapiro & Elliott (1986) further argue that outcome equivalence applies not only to areas such as depression but also to areas where 'clinical wisdom' might suggest otherwise; for example, such wisdom would suggest that behavioural and cognitive-behavioural methods are more effective than other forms of therapies for the treatment of phobias. However, the evidence for this proposal arises from analogue studies with sub-clinical populations (primarily students), but they argued that it is less clear-cut from clinical trials.

The current book will provide an important update on issues such as whether or not all therapies really are equal and whether it really does not matter what the content of therapy is because outcomes are very much the same. We hope to show that, although this conclusion has some truth, in particular in its focus on the need for a positive therapeutic relationship, at the level of specific psychological disorders that range from simple phobias to severe psychoses there is evidence of differential effectiveness of therapies – that some things help and that some things do not.

EXAMPLES OF THE EVIDENCE BASE

The subsequent chapters in this book will provide numerous specific examples of studies that provide evidence one way or another for the use of particular therapies with particular disorders, but it is worth considering one or two such studies briefly, then considering one or two of the meta-analyses and mega-analyses in order to illustrate some of the more general points that we wish to make about the evidence base.

One of the most famous and most expensive therapy outcome studies was the National Institute of Mental Health (NIMH) Treatment of Depression Collaborative Research Program, which will be considered in order to illustrate the problems that have arisen from the general failure to find differential effectiveness of therapy outcome (see Elkin *et al.*, 1989; Elkin, 1994) but also to illustrate other issues about the evidence base. This trial was the largest of its kind ever carried out. There were 28 therapists working at three sites; eight therapists were cognitive-behavioural, 10 were interpersonal therapists, and a further 10 psychiatrists managed two pharmacotherapy conditions, one being imipramine plus 'clinical management', the second being placebo plus 'clinical management'. Two-hundred-and-fifty patients meeting the criteria for major depressive disorder were randomly allocated between the four conditions. The therapies were manualised and considerable training and supervision occurred both before and throughout the trial by leading authorities for each therapy (see Shaw & Wilson-Smith, 1988, for a detailed account of this process). Elkin *et al.* (1989) reported that all four groups improved approximately equally well on the main symptom outcome measures. Perhaps the most surprising result was the extent of the improvement in the placebo-plus-clinical management group, which substantially outperformed control groups in most other studies, although a *post hoc* analysis showed that it was less effective for patients with more severe depressive disorders. Imber *et al.* (1990) have further shown that there were no specific effects of treatments on measures such as the Dysfunctional Attitude Scale on which, for example, the cognitive therapy condition would have been expected to make more impact than the other treatments. In summary, the NIMH trial illustrates that although it has been important to test treatment effectiveness, the simple comparison of outcome of treatment is the most expensive and least informative way in which to approach the issue.

To move now to an example of meta-analysis, we will start with the Robinson *et al.* (1990) study, which has been widely cited and is the most influential meta-analysis in the area of depression. Robinson *et al.* identified 58 trials of a comparison of psychological therapies and a further 15 trials of psychological therapy versus pharmacotherapy that were published between 1976 and 1986. The statistical combination of these studies gave an effect size of 0.73 for psychotherapy versus control (as a reminder, an effect size significantly greater than zero shows a positive benefit, with an effect size of >0.7 being considered to be a large effect). Other comparisons revealed a benefit of cognitive therapy over non-CBT therapies of 0.47, and of other cognitive-behavioural therapies over non-CBT therapies of 0.27. This meta-analysis has often been quoted as showing a distinct small-to-moderate benefit of cognitive and cognitive behavioural approaches over psychodynamic approaches in the treatment of depression. However, there are a considerable number of qualifications to this apparently straightforward conclusion. First, only nine of the 58 trials were based on standard clinical recruitment, with 50 % of trials recruiting participants through the media, 25 % of trials being student based, and with only 35 % having inclusion criteria for clinical depression. In addition, most of the studies reported only post-treatment data without follow-up data being included. Although more recent studies and more recent meta-analyses (such as Gloaguen *et al.*, 1998) generally have stricter inclusion criteria and include follow-up data, it is important to note the limitations of many of the earlier studies and the earlier meta-analyses.

A second type of approach for combining quantitative data has begun to appear – this is the so-called *mega-analysis* in which case-level data from several studies are combined in order to provide statistical power for more sophisticated analyses. For example, Thase *et al.* (1997) combined data from six different studies to give a total of 795 participants who had received cognitive behaviour therapy or interpersonal psychotherapy alone or combined with an anti-depressant. Their analyses showed that there is a benefit for combined drug-psychotherapy treatment for more severe levels of depression, but for mild to moderate levels of depression there was no advantage for combined treatment.

SOME BENEFITS OF THE EVIDENCE-BASED THERAPY (EBT) APPROACH

The examples presented so far illustrate that the evidence-based approach is fraught with more pitfalls than might at first be apparent. Qualitative and quantitative data analyses to date have provided few categorical assertions that do not require caution and careful interpretation. In psychotherapy, the evidence-based approach should therefore be seen as more of a method to aid the asking of questions than as a source of answers. It is a method fraught with its own problems. We can, however, begin to draw together and examine criteria for the evidence-based approach.

The American Psychological Association Task Force (American Psychological Association, 1995; see also Crits-Cristoph, 1996) proposed a set of criteria for evidence-based therapies (or 'empirically validated treatments' in their parlance), which are a useful starting point. The Task Force proposed that for a treatment to be well-established it should:

(1) Have at least two good between-group design experiments demonstrating efficacy in one or more of the following ways:
   A. Superior to pill or psychological placebo or to another treatment
   B. Equivalent to an already established treatment in experiments with adequate statistical power (about 30 per group). OR
(2) Have a large series of single-case design experiments (N >= 9) demonstrating efficacy. These experiments must have:
   A. Used good experimental designs and
   B. Compared the intervention to another treatment as in 1)A.

These overall criteria were additionally qualified by a requirement for the use of treatment manuals, that the client groups should be very clearly described and that the benefits should be found by at least two different teams.

The Task Force also spelled out criteria for 'probably efficacious treatments' as follows:

(1) There should be two experiments showing the treatment is more effective than a waiting-list control group. OR
(2) One or more experiments meeting the Well-Established Treatment criteria above but only from one team rather than two or more. OR
(3) A small series of single-case design experiments (N >= 3) otherwise meeting Well-Established Treatment Criteria but again only from one team rather than two or more.

These APA guidelines provide a useful starting point for categorising evidence into different types and grades. However, the use of the term 'experiments' throughout may seem either odd or even aversive to many psychotherapists, as if their patients were being treated as rats running through mazes (although therapy, in imitation of life, may seem like that sometimes!). The criteria reveal the influence of the American behaviour therapy tradition with its focus on quasi-experimental single case designs (for example, so-called ABA, ABBA, ABCA designs) but, apart from the language, the criteria overlap with the Cochrane review criteria that were summarised earlier. That is, the best quality evidence from a 'good between-group design' is considered to come from a randomised controlled trial, although the APA guidelines give more weight to single-case quasi-experimental designs than do the Cochrane criteria.

A second clear benefit of the evidence-based approach is the continued examination of the therapeutic relationship, client variables, therapist variables, and other common factors in relation to therapy process and outcome. The traditional approach to such common factors is best summarised in the series of handbooks that have been edited over the years by Garfield and Bergin (for example, Garfield & Bergin, 1978, 1986; Lambert, 2004) and which have exhaustively detailed research into therapist factors, client factors, and therapy factors. Work on therapist factors was best exemplified by research into client-centred therapy (Rogers, 1957) and the proposed trinity of warmth, empathy, and genuineness (Truax & Carkhuff, 1967), which every therapist was supposed to possess. However, the early optimism that characterised this work eventually led to the realisation that even 'ideal' therapists had patients with whom they did not get on well and that the presence of these therapist factors in themselves was not sufficient for therapeutic change. As Stiles, Shapiro & Elliott (1986, p. 175) concluded: 'The earlier hope of finding a common core in the therapist's personal qualities or behaviour appears to have faded.'

Work on client variables has in the past been characterised by the examination of atheoretical lists of sociodemographic and personality variables (see, for example, Garfield, 1978), from which it has been possible to conclude very little. In a re-examination of this issue, Beutler (1991) concluded that there still has been no development in our understanding of client variables. Following a summary of some of the major variables that might be examined, Beutler (1991, p. 229) also pointed out that: 'There are nearly one and one-half million potential combinations of therapy, therapist, phase, and patient types that must be studied in order to rule out relevant differences among treatment types.'

Fewer than 100 methodologically sound studies have been carried out to test these possible interactions! There are, however, some promising leads from investigations of client attitudes and expectations that provide a more sophisticated view of such variables. For example, Caine and his colleagues (Caine, Wijesinghe & Winter, 1981) found that the type of model that clients had of their problems (for example, medical versus psychological) and the direction of their main interests ('inner-directed' versus 'outer-directed') predicted drop-out rates and outcome in therapy.

Work on specific therapy factors has also run aground on the problems of finding any differential effects (for example, Stiles, Shapiro & Elliott, 1986). Some of these problems were outlined earlier, when the pattern of outcome equivalence of psychotherapies for a range of disorders was outlined. As we hope this book will demonstrate, there are beginning to be advances in this area, which should continue in the future, for example with the use of so-called 'dismantling', in which one or more of the putative 'active' ingredients of a therapy are dropped in some of the conditions, and the manualisation of therapies combined with measures of treatment adherence, which ensure that something like the therapy in question is actually taking place. However, as the NIMH Collaborative Depression study demonstrated (see above), the fact that some therapists did extremely well and some not so well irrespective of the type of therapy demonstrates that therapy factors will only emerge in interaction with other therapist and client variables rather than as main effects. A specific example of this point comes from the Sheffield Psychotherapy Project carried out by David Shapiro and his colleagues. The analyses of this project published initially showed an advantage for prescriptive (cognitive-behavioural) therapy over exploratory (psychodynamic) therapy in the treatment of stressed managers. However, a later reanalysis (Shapiro, Firth-Cozens & Stiles, 1989) found that this advantage was true for one of the principal therapists involved in the study, but the second therapist was equally effective with both types of therapy. In an interesting conclusion, Shapiro, Firth-Cozens & Stiles (1989, p. 385) turned the initial question of which brand of therapy is better than which other brand on its head, as follows: 'The present findings are broadly consistent with the clinical lore that each new therapist should try different approaches to find the one in which he or she is most effective.'

The notion of the importance of the alliance between therapist and patient arose early in the psychoanalytic literature. Freud (1912) viewed it as the healthy part of the transference, a proposal that was later extended by other psychoanalytic writers. Carl Rogers (1957) also focused on the importance of the therapeutic relationship, although the client-centred view is different to the psychoanalytic. The diverse influences on the origins of the concept and the growing awareness of its importance in cognitive-behaviour therapies (Safran & Segal, 1990) make it a cosmopolitan concept that has the advantage that therapists of different orientations can begin to talk to each other because of a shared language, but the disadvantage that they might mistakenly think they are talking about the same thing! Fortunately, this problem is surmountable. As Wolfe & Goldfried (1988, p. 449) stated: 'The therapeutic alliance is probably the quintessential integrative variable because its importance does not lie within the specifications of one school of thought.'

In order to understand the concept, the three factors proposed by Bordin (1979) provide a reasonable starting point; namely, that there should be a bond between the therapist and the patient, that there should be an agreement on goals, and that there should be an agreement on tasks. In addition, the work of Jerome Frank (1973, 1982) provides a more general framework from which to view both the therapeutic relationship and the whole question of common factors in psychotherapy. To quote: 'The efficacy of all procedures . . . depends on the establishment of a good therapeutic relationship between the patient and the therapist. No method works in the absence of this relationship' (Frank, 1982, p. 15).

Frank goes on to describe a number of shared components that help to strengthen the relationship with the patient and which help the patient to have more positive expectations. Two of these components are:

- *A confiding relationship.* The patient should be able to trust and talk to the therapist about painful issues without feeling judged. These issues may be ones that the patient is revealing for the first time. This feature of confiding is not of course unique to therapeutic relationships, but is a characteristic of any confiding relationship (Power, Champion & Aris, 1988). One of the problems that has been identified in poor therapeutic relationships is that the confiding and expression of negative feelings by the patient is responded to with hostility by the therapist; the outcome of such therapy is often unsuccessful (Henry, Schacht & Strupp, 1986) and, hence, the emphasis now is on the establishment of a positive therapeutic relationship between therapist and client.
- *A rationale.* Patients should be provided both with a framework within which to understand their distress together with an outline of the principles behind the therapy and what treatment might involve from a practical point of view. Failure to provide such a rationale may leave the patient mystified or anxious, with misconceptions about what might or might not happen and, as a consequence, the risk of dropping out of therapy prematurely. The cognitive-behaviour therapies are particularly strong on providing such rationales; for example, *Coping with Depression* and *Coping With Anxiety* booklets are typically handed to patients after one or two sessions of cognitive therapy as a homework assignment. Fennell & Teasdale (1987) reported that a positive response to the *Coping With Depression* booklet was a good indicator of positive outcome in cognitive therapy.

One of the points that must also be dealt with in therapy is the likelihood, as in real life, of the development of 'misalliances'. Some of these misalliances may be temporary and resolvable if dealt with, whereas others may for example require referral on to another agency or other drastic action. As a starting point from which to consider misalliances, we can consider again Bordin's (1979) three components of the therapeutic alliance, that is, the bond, the goals, and the tasks, all or any of which can be implicated in a misalliance. It is well recognised that it is more difficult to develop an alliance with some patients than others; thus, the extension of cognitive therapy into work with personality disorder individuals has helped to heighten awareness of the therapeutic relationship amongst cognitive therapists together with a re-examination of a number of related psychodynamic issues (Beck, Freeman & Davis, 2004; Linehan, 1993). Less intractable misalliances occur when, for example, the patient attends therapy in order to appease someone else such as a spouse or partner or professional such as a GP, or the patient expects physical treatment rather than psychotherapy, or is attending because of a court order, and so on. Through careful discussion of the relevant issues the therapist should be able to identify these types of misalliances. Even when a satisfactory alliance has been established the painful work of therapy can lead to 'ruptures' (for example, Gaston *et al.*, 1995); for instance, a behavioural exposure session that goes wrong and becomes too anxiety provoking can lead to a setback in the relationship that needs to be addressed before the therapeutic work is continued.

These points on some advantages and benefits of the evidence-based approach highlight the fact that the development of criteria for different grades of evidence and the continued exploration of therapeutic relationship, therapist, client, common, and specific factors in therapy process and outcome is of major benefit to the area. Nevertheless, there are a number of important warnings that have been hinted at throughout this chapter, and to which we return in the next section.

EVIDENCE-BASED THERAPY: SOME WARNINGS

There are a number of points and warnings about the evidence-based approach that we would like to flag up, whilst mindful of the fact that these points (and others) will also be considered in many of the subsequent chapters.

- Any EBT can be done *ineffectively*. Just because a practitioner claims to be doing an EBT this does not guarantee that the therapy is being carried out effectively. Ineffectiveness can, of course, arise for a variety of reasons that may relate to therapist factors, client factors, the therapeutic relationship, the manner of the intervention, and factors outside of therapy such as negative life events. The lessons of the NIMH collaborative depression programme discussed earlier (Elkin, 1994) showed that there was considerable variation in the way that cognitive behaviour therapy was carried out across the three sites at which the eight therapists were based, despite the extensive training and ongoing supervision of the therapists by a leading therapist (see Shaw & Wilson-Smith, 1988). These 'site' differences can be more accurately interpreted as individual therapist differences.
- Any 'non-evidence based' therapy can be carried out *effectively*. Think of your favourite non-EBT and somewhere there is a practitioner who is doing the therapy very effectively. On average, the evidence base tends to show that doing something is better than doing nothing at all; that is, only rarely is a therapy shown to be worse than the control condition (though there have been one or two exceptions to this rule, as in the case of doing interpersonal therapy with drug/alcohol problems). The fact that the evidence base highlights the importance of the therapeutic relationship irrespective of therapeutic model emphasises the fact that sometimes the therapeutic relationship may be enough to bring about positive change (Okiishi *et al.*, 2003). Ultimately, we are all in the business of psychotherapy and

thereby share much in common (Power, 2002), although we often criticise most those we are closest to.

- All therapists have treatment failures no matter how effective they are. While many therapists hide in embarrassment from such failures there is often as much to be learned from failure as there is from treatment successes. Freud's (1905) famous treatment failure, the case of *Dora,* provided him with the opportunity to develop the concept of transference to include both negative as well as positive transference. The careful consideration of such failures can be used to explore the limits of any therapeutic system and its attendant theoretical premises (Foa & Emmelkamp, 1983). The evidence also shows that therapeutic benefits may continue after the end of therapy, that even though a therapeutic intervention may appear to be a failure or non-beneficial immediately post-treatment, sometimes benefits continue to develop. A dramatic example of such gains was documented in a recent study of cognitive behavioural therapy versus interpersonal therapy for bulimia; preliminary findings based on post-treatment data showed a significant advantage of cognitive behavioural therapy over interpersonal therapy, but follow-up data showed continued gains in the interpersonal therapy condition such that by 18 months both treatments were equally effective (Agras *et al.*, 2000). These findings further emphasise the need for long-term follow-up data before firm conclusions can be reached about the impact of therapy. The main point is that therapies and therapists can have powerful effects on clients, both for good and for bad. A further example of this can be seen in the divisive debate about false memories and therapy (Davies & Dalgleish, 2001); the evidence suggests that some vulnerable individuals may be prone to the creation of false memories of experiences such as sexual abuse or alien abduction under the influence of therapy, just as other individuals may recover true memories of repressed abuse (Power, 2001). The careful evaluation of evidence is necessary in therapy just as it is in the comparison between therapies.

- The issue of therapy *efficacy* versus therapy *effectiveness* has been highlighted in a number of recent discussions (for instance, Bower, 2003). To reiterate the main points: studies of therapy efficacy are typically RCTs carried out in specialist research centres by the originators of a specific variety of therapy. In contrast, studies of therapy effectiveness refer to how clinical practitioners work with therapy in everyday practice. In order to understand therapy process and outcome, it is essential to have information for both efficacy and effectiveness; thus, major limitations occur, as summarised earlier, in the interpretation of therapy efficacy data because of the highly selective inclusion and exclusion criteria for participants that do not reflect everyday clinical practice; because of therapist allegiance effects, especially in earlier RCTs in which some therapists apparently carried out treatments that they did not believe in (for example, behaviour therapists claiming to do psychoanalytic psychotherapy); and because of the need to address issues such as subjects dropping out, longer term follow-up, and the importance of adaptations of therapy (for example, number of sessions, spacing of sessions, and integrative content) in everyday situations. There is now a considerable drive to establish effectiveness studies, for example, through the coordination of practice research networks (for example, Barkham & Mellor-Clark, 2003), which establish networks of practitioners who then use common assessment tools and methods with which to evaluate their routine clinical practice.

- It is now well-recognised that therapists do not always do what they claim to be doing, hence the need for supervision, taping, and review of therapeutic interventions when these are to form part of the evidence base. An interesting addendum to this observation comes from a study reported by Goldsamt *et al.* (1992), which consisted of a content analysis of a video produced to illustrate the therapeutic approaches of Beck (Beckian cognitive therapy), Meichenbaum (Meichenbaum's form of cognitive-behavioural therapy) and Strupp (psychodynamic therapy). In this video, these three well-known therapists each interview the same patient, named 'Richard', in order to illustrate their therapeutic approaches. The results of the content analyses showed unexpectedly that Meichenbaum and Strupp were more similar to each other than they were to Beck, rather than finding the predicted similarity between Beck and Meichenbaum; thus, whereas Meichenbaum and Strupp both tended to focus on the patient's impact on other people, Beck focused more on the impact that other people had on the patient. The moral is, in re-emphasis of what has long been well known in the therapy literature, that the purported differences in therapy should not be based on what therapists say they do but rather on what they actually do; the contrast can be considerable (cf. Sloane *et al.*, 1975).

These five points are meant to illustrate that reading the evidence base for psychological therapies is far from straightforward and is a more complex process than many would wish.

SUMMARY OF ISSUES AND CONCLUSIONS

In summary, there is a rapidly increasing number of therapies and it is suggested that they share a number of common factors or basic underlying principles. One of the puzzles that has arisen from the vast amount of psychotherapy outcome research is the general lack of differential effectiveness of treatments despite their technical diversity. As discussed above, one of the most dramatic examples of this effect is the NIMH multimillion dollar production in which the least 'active' of all the treatments, the placebo plus clinical management condition, performed as well as the other conditions overall. Results such as these point to the operation of powerful common factors and individual therapist effects. Nevertheless, we hope that the following chapters will illustrate that a conclusion that all therapies are equal for all problems is a misinterpretation of the data. As evidence-based research moves beyond the outcome question and begins to examine therapy process and predictors of outcome using sophisticated multivariate statistical techniques, then the evidence base will begin to reflect the sophistication of clinical expertise.

REFERENCES

Agras, W.S., Walsh, T., Fairburn, C.G. *et al.* (2000). A multicenter comparison of cognitive-behavioral therapy and interpersonal psychotherapy for bulimia nervosa. *Archives of General Psychiatry, 57*, 459–466.

American Psychological Association (1995). *Task Force on Psychological Intervention Guidelines.* Washington, DC: American Psychological Association.

Barkham, M. & Mellor-Clark, J. (2003). Bridging evidence-based practice and practice-based evidence: Developing a rigorous and relevant knowledge for the psychological therapies. *Clinical Psychology and Psychotherapy, 10*, 319–327.

Beck, A.T., Freeman, A. & Davis, D.D. (2004). *Cognitive Therapy of Personality Disorders* (2nd edn). New York: Guilford Press.

Begg, C.B. & Mazumdar, M. (1994). Operating characteristics of a rank correlation test for publication bias. *Biometrics, 50*, 1088–1101.

Beutler, L.E. (1991). Have all won and must all have prizes? Revisiting Luborsky *et al.*'s verdict. *Journal of Counselling and Clinical Psychology, 59*, 226–232.

Bordin, E.S. (1979). The generalizability of the psychoanalytic concept of the working alliance. *Psychotherapy: Theory, Research, and Practice, 16*, 252–260.

Bower, P. (2003). Efficacy in evidence-based practice. *Clinical Psychology and Psychotherapy, 10*, 328–336.

Caine, T.M., Wijesinghe, D.B.A. & Winter, D.A. (1981). *Personal Styles in Neurosis: Implications for Small Group Psychotherapy and Behaviour Therapy.* London: Routledge & Kegan Paul.

Cochrane, A. (1972). *Effectiveness and Efficiency: Random Reflections on Health Services.* London: The Nuffield Provincial Hospitals Trust.

Crits-Cristoph, P. (1996). The dissemination of efficacious psychological treatments. *Clinical Psychology: Science and Practice, 3*, 260–263.

Davies, G.M. & Dalgleish, T. (2001). *Recovered Memories: Seeking the Middle Ground.* Chichester: Wiley.

De Rubeis, R.J., Hollon, S.D., Evans, M.D. & Bemis, K.M. (1982). Can psychotherapies for depression be discriminated? A systematic investigation of cognitive therapy and interpersonal therapy. *Journal of Consulting and Clinical Psychology, 50*, 744–756.

Elkin, I. (1994). The NIMH Treatment of Depression Collaborative Research Program: Where we began and where we are. In A.E. Bergin & S.L. Garfield (eds), *Handbook of Psychotherapy and Behavior Change* (4th edn). New York: Wiley.

Elkin, I., Shea, M.T. & Watkins, J.T. *et al.* (1989). National Institute of Mental Health Treatment of Depression Collaborative Research program. *Archives of General Psychiatry, 46*, 971–982.

Eysenck, H.J. (1952). The effects of psychotherapy: An evaluation. *Journal of Consulting Psychology, 16*, 319–324.

Fennell, M.J.V. & Teasdale, J.D. (1987). Cognitive therapy for depression: Individual differences and the process of change. *Cognitive Therapy and Research, 11*, 253–271.

Foa, E.B. & Emmelkamp, P.M.G. (1983) (eds). *Failures in Behavior Therapy.* New York: Wiley.

Frank, J.D. (1973). *Persuasion and Healing* (2nd edn). Baltimore: Johns Hopkins University Press.

Frank, J.D. (1982). Therapeutic components shared by all psychotherapies. In J.H. Harvey & M.M. Parks (eds), *Psychotherapy Research and Behavior Change.* Washington, D.C.: American Psychological Association.

Freud, S. (1905). Fragment of an analysis of a case of hysteria ('Dora'). In J. Strachey (ed.), *The Standard Edition of the Complete Psychological Works of Sigmund Freud*, Vol. 7. London: Hogarth Press.

Freud, S. (1912). On beginning the treatment. In J. Strachey (ed.), *The Standard Edition of the Complete Psychological Works of Sigmund Freud*, Vol. 12. London: Hogarth Press.

Garfield, S.L. (1978). Research on client variables in psychotherapy. In S.L. Garfield & A.E. Bergin (eds), *Handbook of Psychotherapy and Behavior Change: An Empirical Analysis* (2nd edn). New York: Wiley.

Garfield, S.L. & Bergin, A.E. (1978) (eds). *Handbook of Psychotherapy and Behavior Change: An Empirical Analysis* (2nd edn). New York: Wiley.

Garfield, S.L. & Bergin, A.E. (1986) (eds). *Handbook of Psychotherapy and Behaviour Change* (3rd edn). New York: Wiley.

Gaston, L., Goldfried, M.R., Greenberg, L.S., *et al.* (1995). The therapeutic alliance in psychodynamic, cognitive-behavioral, and experiential therapies. *Journal of Psychotherapy Integration, 5*, 1–26.

Gloaguen, V., Cottraux, J., Cucherat, M. & Blackburn, I.M. (1998). A meta-analysis of the effects of cognitive therapy in depressed patients. *Journal of Affective Disorders, 49*, 59–72.

Goldsamt, L.A., Goldfried,, M.R., Hayes, A.M. & Kerr, S. (1992). Beck, Meichenbaum, and Strupp: Comparison of three therapies on the dimension of therapist feedback. *Psychotherapy, 29*, 167–176.

Henry, W.P., Schacht, T.E. & Strupp, H.H. (1986). Structural analysis of social behaviour: Application to a study of interpersonal process in differential psychotherapeutic outcome. *Journal of Consulting and Clinical Psychology, 54*, 27–31.

Herink, R. (1980). *The Psychotherapy Handbook.* New York: Meridian.

Hubble, M.A., Duncan, B.L. & Miller, S.D. (1999). *The Heart and Soul of Change: What Works in Therapy.* Washington, DC: American Psychological Association.

Imber, S.D., Pilkonis, P.A., Sotsky, S.M. *et al.* (1990). Mode-specific effects among three treatments for depression. *Journal of Consulting and Clinical Psychology, 58*, 352–359.

Lambert, M.J. (2004) (ed.). *Bergin and Garfield's Handbook of Psychotherapy and Behavior Change* (5th edn) New York: Wiley.

Linehan, M.M. (1993). *Cognitive-Behavioral Treatment of Borderline Personality Disorder.* New York: Guilford.

Luborsky, L., McLellan, A.T., Woody, G.E. *et al.* (1985). Therapist success and its determinants. *Archives of General Psychiatry, 42*, 602–611.

Luborsky, L., Singer, B. & Luborsky, L. (1975). Comparative studies of psychotherapies: Is it true that 'everyone has won and all must have prizes'? *Archives of General Psychiatry, 32*, 995–1008.

Norcross, J.C. & Goldfried, M.R. (1992) (eds). *Handbook of Psychotherapy Integration.* New York: Basic Books.

Okiishi, J., Lambert, M.J., Nielsen, S.L. & Ogles, B.M. (2003). Waiting for supershrink: An empirical analysis of therapist effects. *Clinical Psychology and Psychotherapy, 10*, 361–373.

Power, M.J. (2001). Memories of abuse and alien abduction: Close encounters of a therapeutic kind. In G.M. Davies & T. Dalgleish (eds), *Recovered Memories: Seeking the Middle Ground.* Chichester: Wiley.

Power, M.J. (2002). Integrative therapy from a cognitive-behavioural perspective. In J. Holmes & A. Bateman (eds), *Integration in Psychotherapy: Models and Methods.* Oxford: Oxford University Press.

Power, M.J., Champion, L.A. & Aris, S.J. (1988). The development of a measure of social support: The Significant Others (SOS) Scale. *British Journal of Clinical Psychology, 27*, 349–358.

Robinson, L.A., Berman, J.S. & Neimeyer, R.A. (1990). Psychotherapy for the treatment of depression: A comprehensive review of controlled outcome research. *Psychological Bulletin, 108*, 30–49.

Rogers, C.R. (1957). The necessary and sufficient conditions of therapeutic personality change. *Journal of Consulting Psychology, 21*, 95–103.

Safran, J.D. & Segal, Z.V. (1990). *Interpersonal Process in Cognitive Therapy.* New York: Basic Books.

Shapiro, D.A., Firth-Cozens, J. & Stiles, W.B. (1989). The question of therapists' differential effectiveness: A Sheffield Psychotherapy Project Addendum. *British Journal of Psychiatry, 154*, 383–385.

Shaw, B.F. & Wilson-Smith, D. (1988). Training therapists in cognitive-behaviour therapy. In C. Perris, I.M. Blackburn & H. Perris (eds), *Cognitive Psychotherapy: Theory and Practice.* Berlin: Springer-Verlag.

Sloane, R.B., Staples, F.R., Cristol, A.H. *et al.* (1975). *Psychotherapy Versus Behaviour Therapy.* Cambridge, MA.: Harvard University Press.

Smith, M.L. & Glass, G.V. (1977). Meta-analysis of psychotherapy outcome studies. *American Psychologist, 32*, 752–760.

Stiles, W.B., Shapiro, D.A. & Elliott, R. (1986). Are all psychotherapies equivalent? *American Psychologist, 41*, 165–180.

Thase, M.E., Greenhouse, J.B., Frank, E. *et al.* (1997). Treatment of major depression with psychotherapy or psychotherapy-pharmacotherapy combinations. *Archives of General Psychiatry, 54*, 1009–1015.

Truax, C.B. & Carkhuff, R.R. (1967). *Toward Effective Counselling and Psychotherapy: Training and Practice.* Chicago: Aldine.

Wolfe, B.E. & Goldfried, M.R. (1988). Research on psychotherapy integration: recommendations and conclusions from an NIMH workshop. *Journal of Consulting and Clinical Psychology, 56*, 448–451.

CHAPTER 2

Cognitive Therapy

Willem Kuyken
University of Exeter, UK
and
Aaron T. Beck
University of Pennsylvania, USA

INTRODUCTION

Cognitive therapy is a system of psychotherapy that (1) is based on a cognitive theory of personality and psychopathology with solid empirical foundations for its basic tenets, (2) sets out principles and strategies of practice that emerge from practice, theory and research and (3) has been subjected to outcome studies that attest to its efficacy and effectiveness with a broad range of disorders and populations (Figure 2.1). There are several main forms of cognitive-behavioural therapy. Those with an established pedigree include Aaron T. Beck's cognitive therapy (Beck *et al.*, 1979), Albert Ellis' rational-emotive therapy (Ellis, 1962), Don Meichenbaum's cognitive-behavioural modification (Meichenbaum, 1977) and Arnold Lazarus's multi-modal therapy (Lazarus, 1989). These approaches tend to have more commonalities than differences and differences tend to be of emphasis rather than content. This chapter focusses on a form of cognitive therapy developed by Professor Aaron T. Beck in the 1970s.

We first describe the cognitive theory that underpins cognitive therapy. The practice of cognitive therapy is described and illustrated through a case example. We then outline the areas in which cognitive therapy has been applied and briefly summarise its evidence base. Finally, we set out future directions.

THE COGNITIVE MODEL

At the heart of cognitive therapy lies a deceptively simple idea. Perceptions of ourselves, the world and the future shape our emotions and behaviours. What and how people think profoundly affects their emotional well being. As Shakespeare's Hamlet put it '... is nothing either good or bad, but thinking makes it so ...' From this principle comes the idea that if we evaluate and modify any dysfunctional thinking, we can profoundly affect our emotional

Handbook of Evidence-based Psychotherapies: A Guide for research and practice.
Edited by C. Freeman & M. Power. Copyright © 2007 John Wiley & Sons, Ltd.

Empirically Grounded Clinical Interventions

Figure 2.1 Factors involved in the development of evidence-based cognitive therapy. Salkovskis (2002). Reprinted with permission.

wellbeing. Enduring changes occur when people are able to modify dysfunctional beliefs and learn healthier and more adaptive beliefs.

This central feature of cognitive therapy is based on two broader assumptions. First, that a broader bio-psycho-social context is implicated in the development and maintenance of emotional disorders. Cognitive therapy theorists and researchers have themselves emphasized different biological factors (Gilbert, 1984; Beck, 1999) and social factors (Gotlib & Hammen, 1992). Biological and social theories of emotional disorders are not seen as competing theories, but rather as complementary theories operating at different levels of analysis with different points of focus. Second, even though a client's presenting problems arise in a bio-psycho-social context, the client's perspective and agency are seen as the main

Table 2.1 Typical belief content among people diagnosed with a range of emotional disorders

Emotional disorder	Typical thought content
Depression	Negative view of the self, the world and the future
Generalised anxiety disorder	Fear of physical or psychological danger
Panic disorder	Fear of imminent physical or psychological disaster
Eating disorder	Fear of being physically unattractive, out of control
Hypochondriasis	Concern about serious insidious medical disorder
Anti-social personality disorder	I have been unfairly treated and am entitled to my fair share by whatever means it takes
Medical disorders, where patients report significant degrees of pain	This pain is intolerable and there is nothing I can do to control it

Table 2.2 Cognitive distortions

Distortion	Example
All-or-nothing thinking: the person sees things in black-and-white categories.	'My performance is not perfect, so I must be a total failure.'
Overgeneralisation: the person sees a single negative event as a never-ending pattern of defeat.	'I'm always messing up everything.'
Mental filter: the person picks out a single negative detail and dwells on it exclusively, so that perceptions of all of reality become darkened.	People notice that they have put on a few pounds and think, 'I am overweight, I am horrible', ignoring other parts of their life – that they have a nice smile, people like them, they are holding down a job or raising a family.
Fortune telling: the person makes negative predictions about the future without realising that the predictions may be inaccurate.	'I'll never get a job or have a relationship.'
Emotional reasoning: the person assumes that negative emotions necessarily reflect the way things are.	'I feel hopeless, therefore thing are hopeless.'
Shoulds, musts, and oughts: people try to motivate themselves with shoulds and shouldn'ts, as if they had to be whipped and punished before they could be expected to do anything.	'I shouldn't sit here, I should clean the house.'
Personalisation: people see themselves as the cause of some negative external event, for which they are in reality not primarily responsible.	For example, if someone yells at you, you might think 'I did something wrong', but maybe the other person is having a bad day or has a bad temper.

focus in cognitive therapy. Cognitive theory takes into account the broadest range of factors that can help understand why a client presents with a particular set of problems, and then focusses on how the client has shaped this through a process of making sense of their lives. A powerful illustration is the work of Victor Frankl, a survivor of Auschwitz who went on to describe how he was able to draw meaning from his experience and how this process enabled him to survive Auschwitz and its aftermath (Frankl, 1963).

Cognitive theory has been continually developed as research examines its basic tenets. The most enduring descriptions of cognitive theory of emotional disorders propose that schema interact with situations through processes of selective attention and inference, thereby generating individual emotional reactions (Beck, 1976). These schemata are conceptualised as relatively stable, so that similar situations will tend to produce similar emotional reactions because the same schema are being activated. In people at risk for emotional disorders, these predisposing maladaptive schemata lie dormant and become activated only in the presence of schema-triggering situations. Each emotional disorder is characterised by a particular set of unique schemata: the content specificity hypothesis (Table 2.1). Across emotional disorders, a range of cognitive distortions drive processes of selective attention and maladaptive inference (Table 2.2).

In recent reformulations, cognitive theory has been articulated as a theory primarily of the maintenance of emotional disorders, For example, for depression it has been proposed that schema become activated only during the onset and course of emotional disorders (Miranda & Persons, 1988). In the case of depression, schema are described as comprising a particular triad of negative beliefs about the self, the world and the future, and that a depressed person sees a large array of situations in a schema-congruent way. Once activated, schema-congruent processes trigger a stream of negative ruminative automatic thoughts (e.g., 'My partner will be angry that I have achieved nothing today') that are congruent with underlying core beliefs (e.g., 'I am a loser') and dysfunctional assumptions (e.g., 'If I take on challenges, I will fail'). This relationship between triggers that activate underlying schema, core beliefs, dysfunctional assumptions, negative automatic thoughts and emotional, behavioural and somatic reactions has become the conceptual basis for cognitive therapy (Figure 2.2).

A generation of researchers has empirically examined cognitive theories of emotional disorders. This research has examined the basic cognitive dimensions of personality and psychopathology, idiosyncratic processing and memory and the role of cognitive factors in diathesis-stress models. It is beyond the scope of this chapter to review this literature but we note several significant developments to cognitive theories of emotional disorders (see Beck, 1996; Power & Dalgleish, 1997; Teasdale & Barnard, 1993). First, they introduce a more integrative model of emotional disorders, explicitly drawing in cognitive, motivational, behavioural and physiological response systems. This suggests that cognitive products such as images, thoughts, and ruminative thinking may be powerfully shaped by reciprocal processing in physiological, emotional and behavioural response cycles. Second, reformulated cognitive theories move away from linear processing models to parallel modular processing models. Cognitive, motivational and behavioural systems operate simultaneously and cognitive products (such as thoughts, images, memories, plans) can emerge in awareness as a product of these systems. These models are postulated as a potentially more complete explanation of how an individual adapts to changing circumstances, tackling the complexity, predictability, regularity and uniqueness of normal and abnormal reactions. These more integrative and complex theories are only just being subjected to research and interested readers are referred to Beck (1996) and Dalgleish & Power (1998).

THE PRACTICE OF COGNITIVE THERAPY

Several features distinguish cognitive therapy, regardless of the client's problem area, the therapy format, or the client's age or ability.

Cognitive Therapy Focusses on Cognition and Behaviour

The cognitive model of emotional disorders is central to every aspect of cognitive therapy: the formulation, intervention planning and change processes. Thus, the therapist seeks to understand the client's presenting problems in terms of maladaptive beliefs and behaviours and develops an intervention plan that will effect changes in the presenting problems through changes in beliefs and behaviours. When successes and difficulties are encountered in the therapeutic process these are formulated in terms of maladaptive beliefs and behaviours, and therapy proceeds accordingly.

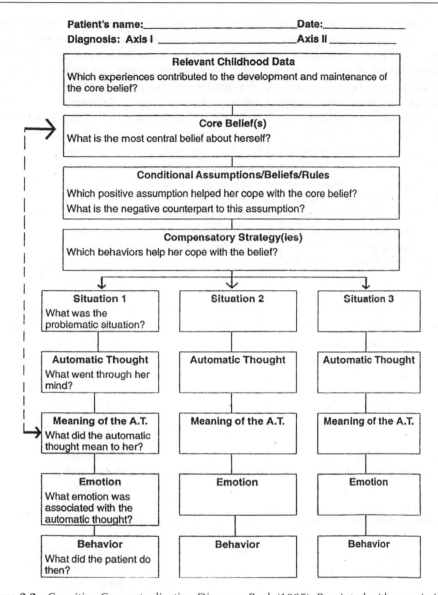

Patient's name:_____ **Date:**_____
Diagnosis: Axis I _____ **Axis II** _____

Relevant Childhood Data

Which experiences contributed to the development and maintenance of the core belief?

Core Belief(s)

What is the most central belief about herself?

Conditional Assumptions/Beliefs/Rules

Which positive assumption helped her cope with the core belief?

What is the negative counterpart to this assumption?

Compensatory Strategy(ies)

Which behaviors help her cope with the belief?

Situation 1	**Situation 2**	**Situation 3**
What was the problematic situation?		
Automatic Thought	**Automatic Thought**	**Automatic Thought**
What went through her mind?		
Meaning of the A.T.	**Meaning of the A.T.**	**Meaning of the A.T.**
What did the automatic thought mean to her?		
Emotion	**Emotion**	**Emotion**
What emotion was associated with the automatic thought?		
Behavior	**Behavior**	**Behavior**
What did the patient do then?		

Figure 2.2   Cognitive Conceptualization Diagram. Beck (1995). Reprinted with permission.

Cognitive Therapy is Based on a Cognitive Formulation of the Presenting Problems

Cognitive therapy distils cognitive theories of emotional disorders to the understanding of particular cases through the case formulation method. A skilled cognitive therapist aims to understand presenting problems in terms of cognitive theory while maintaining the 'essence' of the presenting problems for a particular individual. To the scientist-practitioner cognitive therapist, individualised case formulation is the heart of good practice (Tarrier & Calam,

2002). The process of clinical formulation has been described as ' . . . the linchpin that holds theory and practice together' (Butler, 1998), serving as a clinical tool that practitioners use as a framework for describing and explaining the problems that individuals may present with in cognitive therapy (Bieling & Kuyken, 2003). A case formulation should guide treatment and serve as a marker for change and as a structure for enabling practitioners to predict beliefs and behaviours that might interfere with the progress of therapy. It guides the practitioner in planning and delivering the right intervention, in the right way at the right point towards the collaboratively agreed goals for therapy. It can help therapists make sense of complex, multi-faceted presenting problems. Therapists can use formulation to anticipate and plan for difficulties in therapy, and thereby reduce drop-out rates. Finally it can increase empathy for clients, by making sense of what otherwise appear 'difficult-to-understand' behaviours (such as self-injury or anti-social behaviours).

There have been several attempts to provide individualised case-formulation systems firmly based in cognitive theory that can be used by cognitive therapist in day-to-day practice and in treatment process and outcome research (J.S. Beck, 1995; Greenberger & Padesky, 1995; Linehan, 1993; Muran & Segal, 1992; Needleman, 1999; Persons, 1993). For example, the J.S. Beck (1995) case formulation approach uses the client's developmental history and several prototypical problematic situations to identify problematic core beliefs, dysfunctional assumptions and maladaptive compensatory strategies. Developmental experiences, core beliefs, conditional assumptions and compensatory strategies are related to each other in understandable ways. In brief, adverse developmental experiences (for example, an intensely and enduringly critical parent) lead to maladaptive core beliefs (such as 'I am no good') with subsidiary beliefs (such as 'If I am upbeat and bubbly at all times, no one will figure out that I am really no good') that are compensated for by a range of behavioural strategies ('In all my interactions I will try to be as upbeat as possible') (Figure 2.2).

Cognitive Therapy Aims to Enable Clients to Identify, Evaluate and Respond to Maladaptive Thoughts, Beliefs and Behaviours

The change process in cognitive therapy involves clients learning to recognise how their thoughts, feelings and behaviours are related to one another and how they are implicated in the presenting difficulties. Clients then go on to learn how to actively evaluate and respond to maladaptive thoughts and behaviours. Early phases of cognitive therapy involve the therapist in an active and educative role; middle phases involve much more of a joint problem-solving stance with later stages involving clients essentially 'running their therapy'. Placing the client in this active role of evaluating problematic patterns of thought and behaviour serves the parallel functions of increasing a sense of hope and mastery.

Cognitive Therapy Draws on a Wide Range of Cognitive and Behavioural Techniques to Change Thinking, Beliefs, Emotions and Behaviours

The development of cognitive therapy over several decades has drawn on other therapeutic modalities, the extensive accumulated clinical expertise of cognitive therapists, increasingly sophisticated and fine-tuned theory and a large body of research. This has led to the development of a wide range of cognitive and behavioural therapeutic strategies on which a cognitive therapist can potentially draw. The main cognitive approaches involve teaching clients to be able to identify, evaluate and challenge cognitive distortions (such as all-or-nothing thinking) and maladaptive beliefs ('I have to be upbeat and bubbly at all times to be liked'). The main behavioural approaches involve increasing positively reinforcing behaviours (for example, behaviours that are pleasurable and generate a sense of mastery in people diagnosed with depression) and extinguishing or replacing negative behaviours (such as 'safety behaviours' that maintain a fear in people diagnosed with an anxiety disorder).

The interventions selected will depend on the client, the nature of the difficulties, the goals, the therapeutic relationship, previous experience of therapy and the therapist's expertise. The cognitive case formulation provides a rationale for selecting interventions from this increasingly large and complex array (Needleman, 1999) and the focus of the work is provided by the nature of the difficulties. For example, for people diagnosed with depression, initial work often focusses on behavioural activation (Beck *et al.*, 1979).

Cognitive Therapy is Based on Active Collaboration

From the first meeting the client and therapist engage in a process of 'collaborative empiricism' (J. Beck, 1995). This involves working together to identify the primary presenting problems, generating goals for therapy, selecting interventions and planning ways to avoid relapse. The therapist takes an active stance, supporting the client in working towards the therapy goals. Cognitive therapists are active and comfortable with structuring therapy sessions and the therapy process. When this collaboration is successfully established, the therapist and client work like a scientific partnership, approaching the client's problems together as a scientist approaches a scientific problem. Thoughts, beliefs and behaviours become hypotheses for testing, the basis for experiments to evaluate their basis in reality and their pragmatic value. This guided discovery process aims to develop good problem-solving skills and ultimately healthier ways of thinking and behaving.

A Good Therapeutic Relationship is Necessary but Not Sufficient for Effecting Change

Cognitive therapists, like other therapists, aim to provide an empathic, warm, genuine and respectful context in which to work. Given the focus of cognitive therapy, they should be particularly skilled at seeing the world from their clients' perspective (accurate empathy) while holding a realistic perspective in the face of what may be quite distorted thinking. Cognitive therapists explicitly model a hopeful, collaborative and problem-solving stance.

For clients with significant interpersonal problems, which are manifest in the therapeutic relationship, therapists might work to examine the beliefs and behaviours that underpin the relationship difficulties.

Cognitive Therapy Tends to be Short to Medium Term

Cognitive therapy typically involves 16 to 20 meetings, although brief versions have been developed for particular circumstances (Bond & Dryden, 2002) and longer versions are sometimes indicated (Beck, Freeman & Davis, 2003). Cognitive therapy aims to alleviate distress in the short term and give people the skills to make long-term changes for themselves.

Cognitive Therapy Focusses on Current Problems and is Goal Oriented

Cognitive therapists work with clients to identify and prioritise problems that the client is currently experiencing and to identify mutually agreed goals. The primary therapeutic work is then working with the client on these problems towards these goals, reviewing the problem and goal list on a regular basis. Cognitive therapists work strategically, planning several steps ahead, anticipating the stages of change that will enable a client to achieve his or her goals and the likely obstacles.

Sometimes, the current problem is a historical problem. For example, a client might find it difficult to begin working on homework assignments because a previous experience of therapy led to the belief that 'this won't help'. Until this belief is examined in the light of the previous experience the client might well be unable to progress.

Cognitive Therapy is Structured

Cognitive therapy has evolved a structured format that enables the therapist and client to work in the most efficient and effective way. The structure remains constant throughout therapy making therapy more transparent and understandable for both therapist and client.

Having outlined what distinguishes cognitive therapy, we aim to convey a sense of how cognitive therapy proceeds in practice. We will outline a typical therapy session, as well as a typical progression for therapy as a whole. We will conclude with a case example, illustrating this process. The interested reader is referred to J. Beck (1995) for a comprehensive overview of cognitive therapy in practice.

COGNITIVE THERAPY IN PRACTICE

A typical *cognitive therapy session* involves checking how the client has been doing, re-viewing the previous session, setting an agenda, working through the agenda items, setting homework, reviewing/summarising the session and eliciting feedback. It begins with the therapist and client negotiating an agenda or list of topics that they agree to work on in that session. This involves ensuring the agenda is manageable, prioritising the items and linking them to the therapy goals. The therapist will usually ask the client for a brief synopsis of the time since they last met and as far as possible will try to enable a linking of both positive and negative experiences to thoughts and behaviours. For example, a client who reports feeling less depressed may go on to link this to returning to work and having less time to ruminate. A session would then review the homework from the previous session, again seeking to link progress or lack of progress to the therapy goals. For example, an adolescent female client with borderline personality traits may have a goal of having more control over her rapid and distressing mood cycles. Her homework involved identifying the thoughts at the beginning of a mood cycle over the course of a week and labelling these as one of a range of cognitive distortions. In the review of the homework, it became clear that all-or-nothing thinking was a characteristic of almost all the rapid mood cycling.

The session then moves on to the further agenda items. As they work through the items, the therapist and client seek to examine how the issues can be understood in terms of the cognitive formulation and how the issues relate to the therapeutic goals. Once there is a hypothesis about how the issue can be meaningfully understood, an appropriate intervention can be suggested. This is done collaboratively, with the therapist setting out the rationale and proceeding where there is a clear basis for collaboration. With the example of the adolescent client with borderline traits, an agenda item might well be conflict with a friend. Through collaborative empiricism, it emerged that the client's behaviour was based on mind reading the motives for her friend's behaviour. This provides the basis for socialising to the cognitive model and the beginnings of thought challenging. As the therapist and client work through the agenda items, the therapist makes use of frequent capsule summaries. These serve to ensure therapist and client agree about what has been said, provide a chance to review the session as it proceeds and build a strong therapeutic relationship.

At the end of the session, the therapist asks the client for a summary of the session (for example, 'What do you think you can take away from today's session that might be useful to you?'). The therapist and client agree homework that will move the client on towards his or her goals and solve any anticipated difficulties with the homework. Finally, the therapist asks for any feedback, both positive and negative, on the session (for example, 'What did you like and not like about how today went so that we can ensure next time things are working well for you?').

A *typical cognitive therapy* might comprise three phases. The first involves ensuring a sound therapeutic relationship, socialising the client to cognitive therapy and establishing the problem/goal list. The therapist aims for some improvements very early (preferably in the first session), to build a sense of hope about the therapeutic process. The second phase involves identifying and evaluating the client's thoughts and behaviours that are involved in maintaining the presenting problems. As appropriate, client and therapist work together to challenge maladaptive thought patterns (for example, all-or-nothing thinking) and develop more adaptive ways of thinking. Similarly, maladaptive behaviours (such as avoidance) are identified, evaluated and alternative behaviours are tried out. The third and final phase of therapy focusses on relapse prevention. The goal of cognitive therapy is to enable clients to 'become their own cognitive therapists', anticipating problematic situations, challenging their maladaptive thinking in these situations and experimenting with new and more adaptive ways of thinking and behaving. The therapist increasingly assumes the role of consultant to the 'client cognitive therapist', reviewing what *the client learned* in therapy, reinforcing the client's effective problem solving, supporting the client in preparing for setbacks and supporting the client with learning effective problem-solving skills. Sessions tend to become less frequent and are discontinued as the client and therapist have confidence that the therapeutic goals have substantively been attained and the client has the cognitive and behavioural skills to manage both everyday and anticipated future problems. The cognitive formulation of the client's presenting problems should enable a good prediction of what future difficulties are most likely to prove problematic. This is used to rehearse how the client might manage these difficulties and thereby prevent future relapse if these difficulties occur.

The Structure of Cognitive Therapy: Behavioural Techniques, Cognitive Techniques and Homework

Cognitive therapy is made up of a range of therapeutic approaches (Figure 2.3).

The first class of therapeutic approaches focus on the client's behaviour. The rationale is that for some people behaviour monitoring, behavioural activation and behavioural change can lead to substantive gains. For example, people with more severe depression often become withdrawn and inactive, which can feed into and exacerbate depression. They withdraw and then label themselves as 'ineffectual', fuelling the depression. By focussing on this relationship and gradually increasing the person's sense of daily structure and participation in masterful and pleasurable activities the person can take the first steps in combating depression (Beck *et al.*, 1979). Other behavioural strategies include scheduling pleasurable activities, breaking down large tasks (such as finding employment) into more manageable graded tasks (buying a newspaper with job advertisements, preparing a resume . . .), teaching relaxation skills, desensitising a person regarding feared situations, role playing and assertiveness training. Recent adaptations to cognitive therapy for depression suggest that the changes in behavioural contingencies may be particularly important in treating severe and recurrent depression (McCullough, 2000).

The second class of therapeutic approaches focus on the client's automatic thoughts and beliefs. Automatic thoughts intervene between situations and emotional reactions and have an automatic, repetitive and uncontrolled quality. Cognitive techniques are designed to increase clients' awareness of these thoughts, challenge them by evaluating their basis in reality, and providing more adaptive and realistic alternative thoughts. The Dysfunctional Thought Record is used as a primary tool for developing this skill (Table 2.3). In enabling clients to learn this skill, the therapist acts as a teacher, adapting his or her style depending on the client's response. Some clients find this process easy to learn and make significant gains very quickly, whereas for others it is more difficult.

In cognitive theory dysfunctional assumptions ('If I put my needs first, others will dislike me') and core beliefs (e.g. 'I am unlikeable') underlie automatic thoughts and are the next focus of cognitive interventions. Careful questioning about and exploration of the client's unrealistic and maladaptive beliefs is carried out to examine if beliefs are based in reality and to correct the distortions and maladaptive beliefs that perpetuate emotional distress. The joint exploration of the person's beliefs engenders a spirit of guided discovery, in which maladaptive constructions of reality are gradually uncovered. By discovering maladaptive meanings ascribed to experiences, life can take on a 'new meaning', more geared to reality and the person's satisfactions and goals in life. This process opens the relationship between the person's maladaptive beliefs, feelings and behaviour. For example, the man who believed 'I must always put others needs above mine' found that he often felt guilty and resentful. As a consequence he would try even harder to meet the needs of his co-workers, family and friends, to the point that he became exhausted, lost sight of his own goals and needs, and became depressed. A broad range of cognitive techniques has evolved to facilitate this cognitive work (J. Beck, 1995; Greenberger & Padesky, 1995). For example, core beliefs like 'I am unlikeable' can be evaluated and replaced with more adaptive core beliefs ('I am basically OK and likeable') through Socratic questioning, examining advantages and disadvantages of the old and new core beliefs, acting 'as if' the new core beliefs were true, using coping cards, developing metaphors, subjecting the beliefs to tests across the

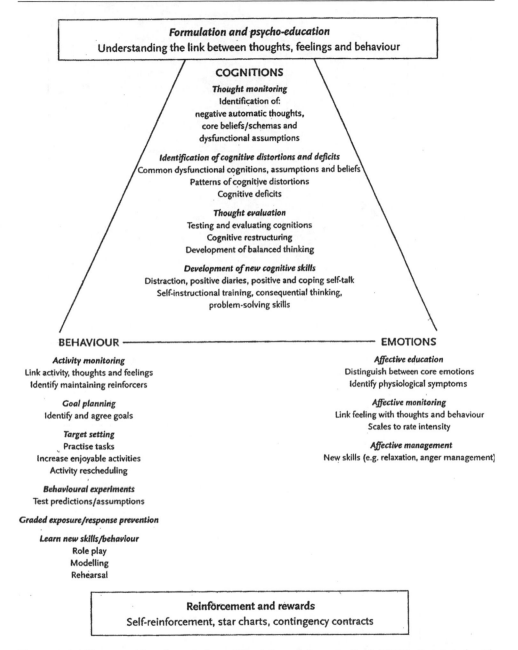

Figure 2.3 The cognitive therapist's toolkit. Adapted from Stallard (2002). Reprinted with permission.

person's life history and reconstructing associated memories and images (see J. Beck, 1995).

For many clients, automatic images or picture, rather than thoughts, are powerfully associated with emotions and behaviours. Images are central to many anxiety disorders,

Table 2.3 Dysfunctional thought record. Beck et al (1979). Reprinted with permission

Daily record of thoughts and feelings
Name _____
Week ending _____

Date	The situation *What were you doing or thinking about?*	Emotion *What did you feel? How bad was it (0–100)?*	Automatic thoughts *What exactly were your thoughts? How far did you believe each of them (0-100 %) ?*	Rational response *What are your rational answers to the automatic thoughts? How far do you believe each of your rational responses right not?*	What was the outcome? *How do you feel (0–100)? What can you do now?*

such as post-traumatic stress disorder (PTSD), social phobia and panic disorder. Images are handled in similar ways but instead of verbally evaluating and challenging images, more visual techniques are used (J. Beck, 1995).

The third range of approaches takes place between therapy sessions as homework assignments. Homework is an essential element of cognitive therapy, aimed at building understanding and coping skills throughout the week, increasing self-reliance and rehearsing adaptive cognitive and behavioural skills. Homework moves the discussions in session from abstract, subjective discussion of issues to real day-to-day experiences. The therapist acts as coach, guiding and debriefing the client from week to week. Homework assignments are designed collaboratively, are tailored to the individual, are set up as no-lose propositions and may range from the therapist suggesting a relevant book to the person agreeing to undertake a long procrastinated assignment (such as telephoning a friend to resolve an area of unspoken conflict), while monitoring the thoughts and images that come to mind in preparing for the assignment (for example, 'the friend will be angry towards me'). As therapy progresses, the client takes on more responsibility for setting and reviewing the homework. Several therapy process-outcome studies suggest that homework is perceived as helpful and contributes significantly to change in cognitive therapy (Burns & Nolen-Hoeksema, 1991; Burns & Spangler, 2000; Detweiler & Whisman, 1999).

We have described the practice of cognitive therapy by outlining the components that together distinguish it, by describing a typical cognitive therapy session, by detailing the main phases of therapy and briefly outlining some of the most common cognitive and behavioural techniques. A case example follows to illustrate cognitive therapy.

CASE EXAMPLE

Thomas was a 68-year-old married man, diagnosed with Parkinson's disease four years previously. As a consequence of the disease he had become uncertain and fearful of others' reactions to him in professional and social situations and had increasingly avoided such situations. This had profoundly affected his self-concept; he was experiencing many features of depression.

A cognitive formulation of Thomas's presenting problems suggested that, at a core level, central to his sense of self, Thomas had assimilated the belief that his acceptability as a person was conditional on being respected and regarded as competent in all domains and at all times. His career as a carpenter and his retirement interests involved fine motor skills that had been essentially lost through the progression of the Parkinson's disease.

The onset and progression of the Parkinson's disease had activated Thomas's beliefs about his acceptability as a person as conditional on being respected and regarded as competent, because it had compromised his competence in what he believed were key areas. He had begun to doubt his self-worth and acceptability; as he put it, 'people will think I am at the end of the pier ["a lesser person"] if they know about the Parkinson's disease.' Because Thomas tried to 'camouflage' the disease and its impact on him from friends and family, he had started to avoid many social situations. This had in turn maintained the social fears and exacerbated his depression by disabling opportunities to establish whether his beliefs were true: whether people would in fact 'write him off'.

Thomas attended 16 therapy meetings over eight months. Initially meetings were weekly, but later meetings were biweekly and then monthly. The steps in cognitive therapy were:

(1) education about social anxiety, depression and the cognitive model to normalise Thomas's experience, (2) diary keeping of thoughts, feelings and behaviour across a range of upsetting situations to help Thomas further understand his beliefs and their role in his psychological difficulties, (3) reducing avoidance of feared situations in graded homework assignments and (4) testing and challenging hypothesised conditional and core beliefs.

In terms of his presenting problems, Thomas responded well to cognitive therapy's pragmatic 'here-and-now' approach. Thomas identified the following strategies from cognitive therapy as helpful in managing his social anxiety: (1) the solicitous use of self-disclosure, (2) 'what-if' thinking (asking yourself 'What would be so terrible if the feared consequences really did happen?'), and (3) 'the head-on approach' (confronting fears head-on, in a shameless, bold manner). Armed with these strategies, Thomas attended a series of social engagements (giving a speech at a colleague's leaving party, visiting former colleagues, several Christmas parties) to test the basis of his beliefs in reality. On each occasion, his fear was not substantiated. In fact, on several occasions Thomas was taken aback by how warmly his friends and colleagues welcomed him. Thomas drew on a boxing metaphor and said that he felt 'better able to cope with difficult situations, because I can beat my negative thinking to the punch.' He stated that he no longer avoided social situations and, for the most part, depression featured less prominently. However, the progression of his Parkinson disease presented considerable challenges, and Thomas over several years attended 'booster sessions' to help him maintain his psychological health as best as possible while his physical health deteriorated.

TRAINING AND SUPERVISION IN COGNITIVE THERAPY

Our experience of observing skilled cognitive therapists suggests the metaphor of a swan. Above the water, it seems that the swan is composed and at one with its surroundings. However, the strength of the river's current and the nearby weirs suggest that the swan is continually taking stock of its environment and working hard beneath the water's surface. Similarly, skilled cognitive therapists are constantly formulating and reformulating clients' problems, maintaining a good working therapeutic relationship, considering the best available intervention options, modelling hope and effective problem solving and anticipating what might happen as the therapy progresses.

Developing these skills requires training and supervision. Our experience suggests several goals for cognitive therapy trainers and supervisors. A first goal is to develop therapists' formulation skills, so that interventions have a clear rationale (Bieling & Kuyken, 2003; Needleman, 1999). Novice therapists often use cognitive therapy techniques without a clear basis in a cognitive formulation of the person's presenting problems. Learning formulation skills involves learning the technical aspects of a case formulation system, the cognitive theories that underpin it and having a good understanding of how this relates to the client's personal world. A second goal is to enable trainees to develop skills in collaborative empiricism. Trainees are encouraged to learn how to work with their clients to formulate hypotheses, carry out experiments, note and analyse the outcome of experiments, and through this process facilitate client cognitive and behavioural change. When done well this is facilitative, Socratic and clearly related to client change. When done badly it can look and sound like the trainee is 'beating his or her formulation into a person' (Padesky, 1993). Third, a very common mistake in novice therapists is focussing overly on the cognitive therapy techniques and neglecting the therapeutic relationship, which can be at the cost of compromised therapeutic outcomes (Castonguay *et al.*, 1996). Fourth, we would suggest that therapists begin training with simpler cases working towards more complex presentations as their knowledge and skills develop. Clients with complex, co-morbid and personality difficulties present therapeutic challenges for the most experienced therapists. Moreover, the change process is likely to be more sporadic and protracted (Roth & Fonagy, 1998), and requires a further layer of formulation difficulties around the change process and skills in managing therapeutic change (Leahy, 2001). Fifth, as cognitive therapy has expanded to include more and more applications across more and more service settings, the content of any cognitive therapy training programme has similarly expanded. Training in the main cognitive therapy manuals, such as *Cognitive Therapy of Depression* (Beck *et al.*, 1979), should remain core to any training programme. Once this basic competency is achieved, we would suggest that the general therapy skills outlined above enable the development of transferable skills to other populations and settings. Continuing professional development, particularly supervision, will support this transfer of knowledge and skills.

Like most training in evidence-based psychological therapies, cognitive therapy training involves a combination of reading core cognitive therapy texts, didactic teaching, clinical demonstrations and supervised clinical practice. Cognitive therapy training has a long lineage dating back to small groups of training therapists working with A.T. Beck at the Centre for Cognitive Therapy at the University of Pennsylvania in the 1970s. The first cognitive therapy treatment manual, *Cognitive Therapy of Depression* (Beck *et al.*, 1979) arose from this process. This seminal text set the standard for the many that have followed addressing different population and service settings. There are excellent texts that try to make fully explicit what is involved in cognitive therapy (J.S. Beck, 1995; Greenberger & Padesky, 1995; Leahy & Dowd, 2002; Needleman, 1999), and texts relating to cognitive therapy for a range of emotional problems (for example, Beck *et al.*, 1979; Beck & Emery with Greenberg, 1985; Beck, Freeman & Davis, 2003; Chadwick, Birchwood & Trower, 1996; Heimberg & Becker, 2002; McCullough, 2000; Morrison, 2002; Segal, Williams, & Teasdale, 2002).

Basic cognitive therapy training is increasingly a part of professional training for psychologists, psychiatrists, psychiatric nurses and other mental health professionals. The extent and depth of this training will depend on the professional training programme, but would normally enable these professionals to use principles from cognitive therapy in their clinical practice on qualification. Intermediate cognitive therapy programmes tend to be aimed at qualified psychological practitioners who wish to develop their cognitive therapy practice. Advanced cognitive therapy training programmes aim for specialist cognitive therapy knowledge and skills that enable a practitioner to use cognitive therapy with clients with complex presentations and across a range of specialist settings. They also enable graduates to take on cognitive therapy teaching and supervision roles. Advanced programmes tend to be international or national training programmes (two examples are the Beck Institute for Cognitive Therapy and Research, Philadelphia and the Center for Cognitive Therapy, Newport Beach, California). There are intermediate and advanced cognitive therapy training programmes in many countries, and as more and more clinicians go through advanced training programmes the network of available teachers and supervisors widens.

Cognitive therapy supervision has a distinctive flavour, mirroring some of the distinguishing characteristics of cognitive therapy (Padesky, 1996). The aim of cognitive therapy supervision is to ensure that cognitive therapists are effective cognitive therapists. That is to say, the supervisee's practice is informed by the cognitive model, carries the distinguishing hallmarks of cognitive therapy, and enables clients to work towards their goals. The supervisor and supervisee work collaboratively in an individualised yet structured way. Supervision normally includes: attention to the supervisees' individual goals, theory-practice linking, formulation, intervention planning, education about specific techniques and interventions, generalisation of skills learned to other cases and other issues, as requested (for example, research, teaching, supervision). Cognitive therapy supervision relies on having audio or video tapes of the supervisee's therapeutic work as the basis for discussion and direct feedback. Role playing is commonly used to try alternatives to the approach adopted in the taped session or to rehearse issues that are anticipated in upcoming therapy sessions. As with cognitive therapy, effective supervision relies on a good relationship and relies on the supervisor modelling an interested, empathic, hopeful and problem-solving stance.

Cognitive therapy trainers have advocated that training, like therapy, should be evidence-based and lead to agreed and demonstrable outcomes. Therapist adherence to the core characteristics of cognitive therapy and to the treatment manuals has in some studies been linked to improved outcomes suggesting the importance of trainers ensuring that trainee therapists demonstrate these core competencies. The Cognitive Therapy Scale (Barber, Liese & Abrams, 2003) was developed for this purpose, and sets out the specific competencies that therapists must demonstrate. Cognitive therapy supervisors and trainers regularly use this scale to assess and provide feedback to trainees. There is enough evidence to suggest that it is a reliable and valid measure of therapist competence (Dobson, Shaw & Vallis, 1985). The interested reader is referred to Padesky (1996) for more detailed description of models of cognitive therapy training and supervision.

COGNITIVE THERAPY: AREAS OF APPLICATION

The last few decades have seen cognitive therapy adapted for mood, anxiety, personality, eating and substance misuse disorders. As well as these formal psychiatric disorders, cognitive therapy has been adapted for relationship problems and the psychological aspects of a range of medical disorders. Most recently cognitive therapy has been applied to the problem of anger generally and its manifestations in conflict specifically, while colleagues, mainly in England, have applied cognitive therapy to people with psychosis. A thorough review of these applications is beyond the scope of this chapter, but a brief overview is provided for the main areas of application. Interested readers may wish to follow up the references describing these adaptations and the following excellent reviews of evidence-based psychotherapies (Compas *et al.*, 1998; De Rubeis & Crits-Cristoph, 1998; Fonagy *et al.*, 2002; Kazdin & Weisz, 1998; Rector & Beck, 2001).

Cognitive Therapy for Affective Disorders

The first full description of a cognitive therapy format was cognitive therapy for depression (Beck *et al.*, 1979). There have been numerous randomised clinical trials that support the efficacy and effectiveness of cognitive therapy for depression, across a variety of clinical settings and populations (for review, see Clark, Beck & Alford, 1999; De Rubeis & Crits-Cristoph, 1998; Dobson, 1989; Robinson, Berman & Neimeyer, 1990). In outpatient trials, effect sizes are considerable compared to no treatment controls, with about half of the intent-to-treat patients showing full recovery (Hollon & Shelton, 2001). Some studies suggest cognitive therapy has particular relapse prevention effects (see, for example, Evans *et al.*, 1992). More recently there have been important developments for recurrent and severe depression (McCullough, 2000) and for the prevention of depression relapse in individuals at high risk by virtue of their history of recurrent depression (Jarrett *et al.*, 2001; Segal, Williams & Teasdale, 2002). Extensive clinical expertise has been invested in the development of cognitive therapy for bipolar disorder (Basco & Rush, 1996; Newman *et al.*, 2002) but it would be premature to comment on the emerging outcome literature (for example, Lam *et al.*, 2000) although preliminary studies suggest that cognitive therapy may prove to be an efficacious psychotherapy for people diagnosed with bipolar disorder. A large scale trial is currently under way in the US.

Cognitive Therapy for Anxiety Disorders

Cognitive therapy has been adapted for the full range of anxiety disorders: generalised anxiety disorder (Beck & Emery with Greenberg, 1985); panic disorder (Clark, 1986; Craske & Barlow, 2001); social phobia (Heimberg & Becker, 2002) and obsessive-compulsive disorder (Frost & Steketee, 2002; Salkovskis, 1985). For generalised anxiety disorder, Chambless & Gillis (1993) computed effect sizes across five studies in which cognitive therapy was compared with one of several control conditions: non-directive therapy (Borkovec & Costello, 1993) or waiting list (Butler *et al.*, 1987, 1991). Substantial effect sizes (1.5–2) at post-test and follow up suggest that cognitive therapy is an efficacious intervention for generalised anxiety disorder. A review of 12 trials of cognitive therapy for panic suggested that 80 % of patients achieved full remission at the end of treatment (Barlow & Lehman, 1996). De Rubeis & Crits-Christoph (1998) reviewed 11 outcome studies of cognitive therapy for panic disorder. Overall, their review suggests cognitive therapy to be efficacious with high proportions of clients with panic, although effects in some studies were less impressive for more avoidant clients. In their review of the literature relating to social phobia, De Rubeis & Crits-Christoph (1998) conclude that there is evidence that the behavioural components of treatment (exposure) lead to clinically significant and enduring change, but the evidence for the additional benefits of cognitive restructuring is weak or not robust across practitioners. However, there is evidence that the cognitive interventions serve a role in the maintenance of gains derived from exposure (Barlow & Lehman, 1996).

Cognitive therapy for obsessive-compulsive disorder is comparatively understudied, and the limited outcome research suggests cognitive therapy produces clinical significant change at termination in the majority of clients, (Emmelkamp, Visser & Hoekstra, 1988; Freeston *et al.*, 1997) with six-month follow ups suggesting the maintenance of gains in at least one study (Emmelkamp, Visser & Hoekstra, 1988).

Cognitive therapy for PTSD typically involves exposure to traumatic memories, behavioural 'stress inoculation' training and cognitive restructuring (Foa & Rothbaum, 1997; Resick & Schnicke, 1992). While there is considerable controversy about which of these elements is effective, there is evidence that as a whole cognitive therapy leads to clinically significant improvements in PTSD symptomatology (Devilly & Spence, 1999; Foa *et al.*, 1999; Marks *et al.*, 1998).

Cognitive Therapy for Personality Disorders

The 1990s saw several developments of cognitive therapy for personality disorders. Beck, Freeman & Davis (2003) adapted traditional cognitive therapy for each of the DSM-IV personality disorders. Layden *et al.* (1993) developed a more in depth adaptation for borderline personality disorder, and Linehan (1993) developed a more integrative behavioural-cognitive Zen Buddhist approach for this client group. Meanwhile, Young developed a schema-focussed cognitive therapy for personality disorders, which emphasises the importance of underlying schema change in this group (Young, 1994; Young, Klosko, & Weishaar, 2003). Several preliminary effectiveness studies suggest that these approaches produce significant symptom changes in people diagnosed with personality disorders (Kuyken *et al.*, 2001, Linehan *et al.*, 1999; Linehan, Heard & Armstrong, 1993). It is premature to comment on whether these are evidence-based interventions although several large-scale trials are currently under way.

Cognitive Therapy for Eating Disorders

Only more recently has cognitive therapy been adapted for eating disorders (Vitousek, 1996). In their review of eight outcome studies, Compas *et al.* (1998) concluded that cognitive therapy for bulimia nervosa meets criteria for an efficacious approach, although effectiveness research suggests that on average only 55 % are in full remission at follow up. A recent multi-site study has broadly replicated these findings (Agras *et al.*, 2000). It is premature to comment on cognitive therapy for anorexia nervosa as, although several adaptations have been suggested (Vitousek, Watson & Wilson, 1998), there is very limited research attesting to its efficacy or effectiveness to date.

Cognitive Therapy for Substance Misuse

There is a large body of research on psychosocial interventions for substance misuse, but cognitive therapy for substance abuse disorders is a more recent development (Beck *et al.*, 1993; Marlatt & Gordon, 1985; Thase, 1997) and to date the evidence base for cognitive therapy as a preferred treatment choice is weak. The largest study in this area assigned 1 726 people with alcohol-abuse problems to cognitive therapy, a facilitated 12-step programme or motivational interviewing. Improvements were observed in all groups but, contrary to the study's hypotheses, there was no evidence that treatment matching improved outcomes or that any one intervention achieved improved outcomes (Allen *et al.*, 1997). Evidence for cognitive therapy's evidence base with other substance abuse problems is decidedly mixed.

Cognitive Therapy for Psychosis

The last decade has seen an exciting development in cognitive therapy approaches for psychosis (Chadwick, Birchwood, & Trower, 1996; Fowler, Garety, & Kuipers, 1995; Morrison, 2002). While outcome research in this area is limited, a range of efficacy and effectiveness studies suggests that cognitive therapy is efficacious in the treatment of positive symptoms and that changes are maintained at follow-up (Garety *et al.*, 1994; Kuipers *et al.*, 1998; Rector & Beck, 2001; Tarrier *et al.*, 1993).

Cognitive Therapy in Health Psychology Settings

A cognitive model of stress examines the role of beliefs in illness and proposes that a person's beliefs about illness determine both emotional reactions to illness/health and to health behaviours (Beck, 1984; Pretzer, Beck & Newman, 1989). This formed the basis for forms of cognitive therapy for a range of problems in health psychology and behavioural medicine, including pain, HIV/AIDS, cancer, heart disease and health-related behaviours like exercise and smoking. For example, a link has been established between anger and hostility and coronary heart disease (Emmelkamp, & Van Oppen, 1993). Cognitive therapy to reduce anger and hostility therefore suggests a way of reducing the rates of heart disease. R. Beck and Fernandez (1998) analysed 50 studies, over two decades, incorporating 1 640 angry subjects treated with cognitive therapy. Using meta-analysis, it was found that cognitive therapy had a mean-effect size of 0.70, which indicated that the average individual treated with cognitive therapy had a better outcome than 76 % of untreated subjects in terms of anger reduction.

Cognitive Therapy for Different Populations and in Different Settings

Given the common features of cognitive therapy and these widely differing areas of application, it is not surprising that cognitive therapy has evolved in several different formats to ensure it is acceptable and effective to a range of groups of people (children, adolescents, adults, older adults and people with learning disabilities), in different therapy formats (self-help, individual, couples, families, groups, organisations) and across different levels of service delivery (primary, secondary and tertiary care).

There is increasing interest in cognitive therapy for children, in part because the approach appears acceptable to children and adolescents and pragmatic in these service settings (Friedberg & McClure, 2001). A comprehensive review of the outcome literature for children and adolescents suggests that cognitive therapy is effective for generalised anxiety, simple phobias, depression and suicidality (Fonagy *et al.*, 2002; Kazdin & Weisz, 1998). As with adult populations, the evidence base is particularly compelling for depression (Lewinsohn & Clarke, 1999). Cognitive therapy has been adapted for older adults (Laidlaw *et al.*, 2003) and for people with learning disabilities and mental retardation (Kroese, Dagnan & Loumides, 1997).

Cognitive therapy has been disseminated most effectively through a range of self-help books, most notably David Burns' (1989) *Feeling Good Handbook* and Greenberger & Padesky's (1995) *Mind Over Mood*. There is some evidence that this format is effective for individuals with depression (Jamison & Scogin, 1995). More recently computerised and Web-based versions of cognitive therapy have been developed. Essentially this involves delivering cognitive therapy via an interactive computer interface, either on a PC, through the Web, or in some cases through automated telephone systems. The UK National Institute for Clinical Excellence has reviewed the evidence base for this approach, concluding that computer-aided delivery of cognitive therapy may have potential as an option in certain groups of clients, and it may be most suitably delivered as part of a stepped care protocol. It concluded that the evidence base was limited and further research is indicated. It remarked that computerised approaches potentially increase flexibility for clients about the rate and timing of therapy, overcome client-therapist relationship problems, but might present problems of literacy, cultural background and acceptability of the format to a broad group of potential clients.

Individual cognitive therapy is the most common format, although couples, family, groups and organisational consultancy formats have also been developed. In individual therapy it is common to involve spouses, friends, parents or others, either as informants or as people who can help the client change (see Baucom *et al.*, 1998). Cognitive couple therapy has been shown to be acceptable and effective in depression in one spouse, chronic interpersonal problems, and marital problems (Baucom *et al.*, 1998; Dattilio & Padesky, 1990; Epstein & Baucom, 1989). Cognitive therapy in group format has been shown to be acceptable and effective for depression (Robinson, Berman & Neimeyer, 1990) and social phobia (Heimberg *et al.*, 1993).

Twenty-five years of increasingly sophisticated research suggests that cognitive therapy is effective to a clinically significant degree for a majority of patients with a variety of presenting problems in a range of populations and settings. An evidence-based conclusion is that cognitive therapy is a treatment of choice for people diagnosed with depression, generalized anxiety, panic, bulimia nervosa, psychosis and a range of somatoform disorders. More recently, preliminary outcome studies suggest cognitive therapy is a promising intervention for people diagnosed with personality disorders and substance misuse, but further research is indicated.

FUTURE DIRECTIONS

We predict that the period to 2030 will see a range of exciting developments in cognitive therapy research and practice. In the area of outcome research, the most obvious area for advancement is where promising initial research suggests that cognitive therapy may prove to be an evidence-based approach: personality disorders, anorexia nervosa and substance misuse. Here efficacy and effectiveness research is urgently needed to establish whether people with these complex mental health problems can be helped through cognitive therapy. Similarly, psychotherapy outcome research is needed to examine how cognitive therapy fares when it is adapted to different populations (for example, older adults) and to different service settings (such as primary care).

In a climate of managed health care, evidence-based practice and practice guidelines, researchers, practitioners and policy makers are increasingly asking the question 'What works best for whom?' Beyond the comparative outcome studies, this sets the stage for increasingly interesting psychotherapy process and psychotherapy process outcome research. The mechanisms by which cognitive therapy is effective are not well understood, and this research will inform practice and health-care policy. The stepped care approach to planning services and interventions is likely to be important here, as we become increasingly knowledgeable about what works for whom and through what mechanism. Cognitive therapy is amenable to contemporary stepped care approaches, whereby clients are assessed and offered increasingly specialised, intensive and complex interventions based on an algorithm of clinical need and optimal cost-effectiveness. Using the range of cognitive therapy approaches, steps might graduate from bibliotherapy to computer-based approaches, to brief psycho-educational approaches in primary care, to brief group approaches in secondary care to more in depth and extended individual or group cognitive therapy in either secondary or tertiary care.

The recent focus on primary and secondary prevention of emotional disorders is welcome and there is much mileage in building on initial successes (see, for example, Jaycox *et al.*, 1994; Segal, Williams & Teasdale, 2002). The acceptability of cognitive therapy to many children and adolescents and to people with recurrent mental health problems combined with an increasing acknowledgement that primary and secondary prevention are high priority health-care areas suggests we are likely to see much innovative and important work in this area.

Cognitive therapy is established as a mainstream psychotherapy of choice and training; supervision and accreditation are areas that require further development that extends and builds on existing best practice. There is an increasing body of cognitive therapy practitioners and researchers who are well placed to continue this work.

REFERENCES

Agras, S.W., Walsh,T., Fairburn, C.G. *et al.* (2000). A multi-center comparison of cognitive-behavioral therapy and interpersonal psychotherapy for bulimia nervosa. *Archives of General Psychiatry, 57*, 459–466.

Allen, J.P., Mattson, M.E., Miller, W.R., *et al.* (1997). Matching alcoholism treatments to client heterogeneity: Project MATCH posttreatment drinking outcomes. *Journal of Studies on Alcohol, 58*, 7–29.

Barber, J.P., Liese, B.S. & Abrams, M.J. (2003). Development of the Cognitive Therapy Adherence and Competence Scale. *Psychotherapy Research, 13*, 205–221.

Barlow, D.H. & Lehman, C.L. (1996). Advances in the psychosocial treatment of anxiety disorders. *Archives of General Psychiatry, 53*, 727–735.

Basco, M.R. & Rush, A.J. (1996). *Cognitive-behavioral Therapy for Bipolar Disorder*. New York: Guilford.

Baucom, D.H., Shoham, V., Mueser, K.T. *et al.* (1998). Empirically supported couple and family interventions for marital distress and adult mental health problems. *Journal of Consulting and Clinical Psychology, 66*, 53–88.

Beck, A.T. (1976). *Cognitive Therapy and the Emotional Disorders*. New York: Meridian.

Beck, A.T. (1984). Cognitive approaches to stress. In R.L. Woolfolk & C. Lehrer (eds), *Principles and Practice of Stress Management* (pp. 255–305). New York: Guilford Press.

Beck, A.T. (1996). Beyond belief: A theory of modes, personality and psychopathology. In P.M. Salkovskis (ed.), *Frontiers of Cognitive Therapy* (pp. 1–25). New York: Guilford Press.

Beck, A.T. (1999). Cognitive aspects of personality disorders and their relation to syndromal disorders: A psycho-evolutionary approach. In C.R. Cloninger (ed.), *Personality and Psychopathology* (pp. 411–429). Washington, DC: American Psychiatric Press.

Beck, A.T. & Emery, G. with Greenberg, R.L. (1985). *Anxiety Disorders and Phobias: A Cognitive Perspective*. New York: Basic Books.

Beck, A.T., Freeman, A. & Davis, D. (2003). *Cognitive Therapy of Personality Disorders* (2nd edn). New York: Guilford.

Beck, A.T., Rush, A.J., Shaw, B.F. & Emery, G. (1979). *Cognitive Therapy of Depression*. New York: Guilford Press.

Beck, A.T., Wright, F.D., Newman, C.F. & Liese, B.S. (1993). *Cognitive Therapy of Substance Abuse*. New York: Guilford Press.

Beck, J.S. (1995). *Cognitive Therapy: Basics and Beyond*. New York: Guilford Press.

Beck, R. & Fernandez, E. (1998). Cognitive-behavioral therapy in the treatment of anger: A meta-analysis. *Cognitive Therapy and Research, 22*, 63–74.

Bieling, P.J. & Kuyken, W. (2003). Is cognitive case formulation science or science fiction? *Clinical Psychology Science and Practice, 10*, 52–69.

Bond, F.W. & Dryden, W. (eds) (2002). *Handbook of Brief Cognitive Behaviour Therapy.* Chichester: Wiley.

Borkovec, T.D. & Costello, E. (1993). Efficacy of applied relaxation and cognitive behavioral therapy and the treatment of generalized anxiety disorder. *Journal of Consulting and Clinical Psychology, 61*, 611–619.

Burns, D.D. (1989). *The Feeling Good Handbook: Using the New Mood Therapy in Everyday Life.* New York: HarperCollins.

Burns, D.D. & Nolen-Hoeksema, S. (1991). Coping styles, homework compliance, and the effectiveness of cognitive-behavioral therapy. *Journal of Consulting and Clinical Psychology, 59*, 305–311.

Burns, D.D. & Spangler, D.L. (2000). Does psychotherapy homework lead to improvements in depression in cognitive behavioral therapy or does improvement lead to increased homework compliance? *Journal of Consulting and Clinical Psychology, 68*, 46–56.

Butler, G. (1998). Clinical formulation. In A.S. Bellack & M. Hersen (eds), *Comprehensive Clinical Psychology* (pp. 1–24). New York: Pergammon Press.

Butler, G., Cullington, A., Hibbert, G. *et al.* (1987). Anxiety management for persistent generalised anxiety. *British Journal of Psychiatry, 151*, 535–542.

Butler, G., Fennell, M., Robson, P. & Gelder, M. (1991). Comparison of behaviour therapy and cognitive behaviour therapy in the treatment of generalized anxiety disorder. *Journal of Consulting and Clinical Psychology, 59*, 167–175.

Castonguay, L.G., Goldfried, M.R., Wiser, S. *et al.* (1996). Predicting the effect of cognitive therapy for depression: A study of unique and common factors. *Journal of Consulting and Clinical Psychology, 64*, 497–504.

Chadwick, P., Birchwood, M. & Trower, P. (1996). *Cognitive Therapy of Delusions, Voices, and Paranoia.* New York: Wiley.

Chambless, D.L. & Gillis, M.M. (1993). Cognitive therapy of anxiety disorders. *Journal of Consulting and Clinical Psychology, 61*, 248–260.

Clark, D.A., Beck, A.T. & Alford, B.A. (1999). *Scientific Foundations of Cognitive Theory and Therapy of Depression.* New York: Wiley.

Clark, D.M. (1986). A cognitive approach to panic. *Behaviour Research and Therapy, 24*, 461–470.

Compas, B.E., Haaga, D.A.F., Keefe, F.J. *et al.* (1998). Sampling of empirically supported psychological treatments from health psychology: Smoking, chronic pain, cancer, and bulimia nervosa. *Journal of Consulting and Clinical Psychology, 66*, 89–112.

Craske., M.G. & Barlow, D.H. (2001). Panic disorder and agoraphobia. In D.H. Barlow (ed.), *Clinical Handbook of Psychological Disorders: a Step-by-step Treatment Manual* (3rd edn; pp. 1–59). New York: Guilford Press.

Dalgleish. T. & Power, M.J. (eds) (1998). *Handbook of Cognition and Emotion.* New York: Wiley.

Dattilio, F.M. & Padesky, C.A. (1990). *Cognitive Therapy with Couples.* Sarasota: Professional Resources Exchange, Inc.

De Rubeis, R. J. & Crits-Christoph, P. (1998). Empirically supported individual and group psychological treatments for adult mental disorders. *Journal of Consulting and Clinical Psychology, 66*, 37–52.

Detweiler, J.B. & Whisman, M.A. (1999). The role of homework assignments in cognitive therapy for depression: Potential methods for enhancing adherence. *Clinical Psychology: Science and Practice, 6*, 267–282.

Devilly, G.J. & Spence, S.H. (1999). The relative efficacy and treatment distress of EMDR and a cognitive-behaviour trauma treatment protocol in the amelioration of posttraumatic stress disorder. *Journal of Anxiety Disorders, 13*, 131–157.

Dobson, K. (1989). A meta-analysis of the efficacy of cognitive therapy for depression. *Journal of Consulting and Clinical Psychology, 57*, 414–419.

Dobson, K., Shaw, B. & Vallis, T. (1985). Reliability of the quality of cognitive therapy. *British Journal of Clinical Psychology, 24*, 295–300.

Ellis, A. (1962). *Reason and Emotion in Psychotherapy*. New York: Lyle Stuart.

Emmelkamp, P. M. & Oppen, P. van (1993). Cognitive interventions in behavioral medicine. *Psychotherapy and Psychosomatics, 59*, 116–130.

Emmelkamp, P.M., Visser, S. & Hoekstra, R.J. (1988). Cognitive therapy and exposure in vivo in the treatment of obsessive-compulsives. *Cognitive Therapy and Research, 12*, 103–114.

Epstein, N. & Baucom, D.H. (1989). Cognitive-behavioral marital therapy. In A. Freeman & K.M Simon (eds), *Comprehensive Handbook of Cognitive Therapy* (pp. 491–513). New York: Plenum Press.

Evans, M.D., Hollon, S.D., De Rubeis, R.J. *et al.* (1992). Differential relapse following cognitive therapy and pharmacotherapy for depression. *Archives of General Psychiatry, 49*, 802–808.

Foa, E.B., Dancu, C.V., Hembree, E.A. *et al.* (1999). Comparison of exposure therapy, stress inoculation training, and their combination for reducing posttraumatic stress disorder in female assault victims. *Journal of Consulting and Clinical Psychology, 67*, 194–200.

Foa, E.B. & Rothbaum, B.O. (1997). *Treating the Trauma of Rape*. New York: Guilford Press.

Fonagy, P., Target, M., Cottrell, D. *et al.* (2002). *What Works for Whom? A Critical Review of Treatments for Children and Adolescents*. New York: Guilford.

Fowler, D., Garety, P. & Kuipers, E. (1995) *Cognitive Behaviour Therapy for Psychosis: Theory and Practice*. New York: Wiley.

Frankl, V. E. (1963). *Man's Search for Meaning*. New York: Pocket Books.

Freeston, M.H., Ladouceur, R., Gagnon, F. *et al.* (1997). Cognitive-behavioral treatment of obsessive thoughts: A controlled study. *Journal of Consulting and Clinical Psychology, 65*, 405–413.

Friedberg, R. & McClure, J. (2001). *Clinical Practice of Cognitive Therapy with Children and Adolescents: The Nuts and Bolts*. New York: Guilford Press.

Frost., R.O., & Steketee, G. (eds). (2002). *Cognitive Approaches to Obsessions and Compulsions: Theory, Assessment, and Treatment*. Elmont, NY: Pergamon Press.

Garety, P., Kuipers, L., Fowler, D. *et al.* (1994). Cognitive behavioural therapy for drug resistant psychosis. *British Journal of Medical Psychology, 67*, 259–271.

Gilbert, P. (1984). *Depression: From Psychology to Brain State*. London: Lawrence Erlbaum.

Gotlib, I.H., & Hammen, C.L. (1992). *Psychological Aspects of Depression: Toward a Cognitive Interpersonal Integration*. Chichester: Wiley.

Greenberger, D. & Padesky, C.A. (1995). *Mind over Mood: Change How You Feel by Changing the Way You Think*. New York: Guilford Press.

Heimberg, R.G., & Becker, R.E. (2002). *Cognitive-behavioral Group Therapy for Social Phobia*. New York: Guilford Press.

Heimberg, R.G., Salzman, D.G., Holt, C.S. *et al.* (1993). Cognitive-behavioral group treatment for social phobia: Effectiveness at five-year follow-up. *Cognitive Therapy and Research, 17*, 325–339.

Hollon, S.D. & Shelton, R.C. (2001). Treatment guidelines for major depressive disorder. *Behaviour Therapy, 32*, 235–258.

Jamison, C. & Scogin, F. (1995). The outcome of cognitive bibliotherapy with depressed adults. *Journal of Consulting and Clinical Psychology, 63*, 644–650.

Jarrett, R.B., Kraft, D., Doyle, J. *et al.* (2001). Preventing recurrent depression using cognitive therapy with and without a continuation phase: A randomized clinical trial. *Archives of General Psychiatry, 58*, 381–388.

Jaycox, L.H., Reivich, K.J., Gillham, J. & Seligman, M.E.P. (1994). Prevention of depressive symptoms in school children. *Behaviour Research and Therapy, 32*, 801–816.

Kazdin, A.E. & Weisz, J.R. (1998). Identifying and developing empirically supported child and adolescent treatments. *Journal of Consulting and Clinical Psychology, 66*, 19–36.

Kroese, B., Dagnan, D. & Loumides, K. (1997). *Cognitive-behaviour Therapy for People with Learning Disabilities*. London: Routledge.

Kuipers, E., Fowler, D., Garety, P. *et al.* (1998). London-East Anglia randomised controlled trial of cognitive behaviour therapy for psychosis: III. Follow-up and economic evaluation at 18 months. *British Journal of Psychiatry, 173*, 61–68.

Kuyken, W., Kurzer, N., De Rubeis, R.J. *et al.* (2001). Response to cognitive therapy in depression: The role of maladaptive beliefs and personality disorders. *Journal of Consulting and Clinical Psychology, 69*, 560–566.

Laidlaw, K., Thompson, L.W., Gallagher-Thompson, D. & Dick-Siskin, L. (2003). *Cognitive Behaviour Therapy with Older People*. New York: Wiley.

Lam, D.H., Bright, J., Jones, S. *et al.* (2000). Cognitive therapy for bipolar illness – a pilot study of relapse prevention. *Cognitive Therapy and Research, 24*, 503–520.

Layden, M.A., Newman, C.F., Freeman, A. & Morse, S.B. (1993). *Cognitive Therapy of Borderline Personality Disorder.* Needham Heights, MA: Allyn & Bacon.

Lazarus, A. (1989). *The Practice of Multimodal Therapy: Systematic, Comprehensive, and Effective Psychotherapy.* Baltimore, MD: Johns Hopkins University Press.

Leahy, R.L. (2001). *Overcoming Resistance in Cognitive Therapy*. New York: Guilford Press.

Leahy, R.L. & Dowd, T.E. (eds) (2002). *Clinical Advances in Cognitive Psychotherapy: Theory and Application*. New York: Springer.

Lewinsohn, P.M. & Clarke, G. N. (1999). Psychosocial treatments for adolescent depression. *Clinical Psychology Review, 19*, 329–342.

Linehan, M.M. (1993). *Cognitive-behavioral Treatment of Borderline Personality Disorder*. New York: Guilford Press.

Linehan, M.M., Heard, H.L & Armstrong, H.E. (1993). Naturalistic follow-up of a behavioral treatment for chronically parasuicidal borderline patients. *Archives of General Psychiatry, 50*, 971–974.

Linehan, M.M., Schmidt, H., Dimeff, L.A. *et al.* (1999). Dialectical behaviour therapy for patients with borderline personality disorder and drug-dependence. *American Journal on Addictions, 8*, 279–292.

Marks, I., Lovell, K., Noshirvani, H. *et al.* (1998). Treatment of posttraumatic stress disorder by exposure and/or cognitive restructuring: A controlled study. *Archives of General Psychiatry, 55*, 317–325.

Marlatt, A. & Gordon, J. (1985). *Relapse Prevention: Maintenance Strategies in the Treatment of Addictive Behaviors*. New York: Guilford Press.

McCullough, J.P. (2000). *Treatment for Chronic Depression: Cognitive Behavioral Analysis System of Psychotherapy*. New York: Guilford Press.

Meichenbaum, D. (1977). *Cognitive-behaviour Modification: An Integrative Approach*. New York: Plenum Press.

Miranda, J. & Persons, J.B. (1988). Dysfunctional attitudes are mood-state dependent. *Journal of Abnormal Psychology, 97*, 76–79.

Morrison, A. (2002). *A Casebook of Cognitive Therapy for Psychosis*. New York: Brunner-Routledge.

Muran, J.C. & Segal, Z.V. (1992). The development of an idiographic measure of self-schemas: An illustration of the construction and use of self-scenarios. *Psychotherapy, 29*, 524–535.

Needleman, L.D. (1999). *Cognitive Case Conceptualisation: A Guidebook for Practitioners*. Mahwah, NJ: Lawrence Erlbaum.

Newman, C.F., Leahy, R.L., Beck, A.T. *et al.* (2002). *Bipolar Disorder: A Cognitive Therapy Approach*. Washington DC: American Psychological Association.

Oppen, P. van., De Haan, E., Balkom, A.J.L.van *et al.* (1995). Cognitive therapy and exposure in vivo in the treatment of obsessive compulsive disorder. *Behaviour Research and Therapy, 33*, 379–390.

Padesky, C.A. (1993). *Socratic Questioning: Changing Minds or Guiding Discovery?* Keynote address at the European Congress of Behavioural and Cognitive Therapies.

Padesky, C.A. (1996). Developing cognitive therapist competency: Teaching and supervision models. In P.M. Salkovskis (ed.), *Frontiers of Cognitive Therapy* (pp. 266–292). New York: Guilford Press.

Persons, J.B. (1993). Case conceptualization in cognitive-behaviour therapy. In K.T. Kuehlwein & H. Rosen (eds), *Cognitive Therapy in Action: Evolving Innovative Practice* (pp. 33–53). San Francisco: Jossey-Bass.

Power, M.J. & Dalgleish, T. (1997). *Cognition and Emotion: From Order to Disorder*. Hove: Psychology Press.

Pretzer, J.L., Beck, A.T. & Newman, C. (1989). Stress and stress management: A cognitive view. *Journal of Cognitive Psychotherapy: An International Quarterly, 3*, 163–179.

Rector, N.A. & Beck, A.T. (2001). Cognitive behavioral therapy for schizophrenia: An empirical review. *Journal of Nervous and Mental Diseases, 198*, 278–287.

Resick, P.A. & Schnicke, M.K. (1992). Cognitive processing therapy for sexual assault victims. *Journal of Consulting and Clinical Psychology, 60*, 748–756.

Robinson, L.A., Berman, J.S. & Neimeyer, R.A. (1990). Psychotherapy for the treatment of depression: A comprehensive review of controlled outcome research. *Psychological Bulletin, 108*, 30–49.

Roth, A., & Fonagy, P. (1998). *What Works for Whom: A Critical Review of Psychotherapy Research*. New York: Guilford Press.

Salkovskis, P.M. (2002). Empirically grounded clinical interventions: cognitive-behavioural therapy progresses through a multi-dimensional approach to clinical science. *Behavioural and Cognitive Psychotherapy, 30*, 3–9. Cambridge: Cambridge University Press.

Segal, Z., Williams, J.M.G. & Teasdale, J.D. (2002). *Mindfulness-based Cognitive Therapy for Depression: A New Approach to Preventing Relapse*. New York: Guilford Press.

Stallard, P. (2002). *Think Good – Feel Good: A Cognitive Behaviour Therapy Workbook for Children and Young People*. Chichester: John Wiley & Sons, Ltd.

Tarrier, N., Beckett, R., Harwood, S. *et al.* (1993). A trial of two cognitive-behavioural methods of treating drug-resistant residual psychotic symptoms in schizophrenic patients: I. Outcome. *British Journal of Psychiatry, 162*, 524–532.

Tarrier, N. & Calam, R. (2002). New developments in cognitive-behavioural case formulation. Epidemiological, systemic and social context: an integrative approach. *Behavioural and Cognitive Psychotherapy, 30*, 311–328.

Teasdale, J.D. & Barnard, P. J. (1993). *Affect, Cognition, and Change: Remodeling Depressive Thought*. Hove: Erlbaum.

Thase, M. (1997). Cognitive-behavioral therapy for substance abuse disorders. In L.J. Dickstein, M.B. Riba & J.M. Oldham (eds), *American Psychiatric Association Review of Psychiatry*, (Vol. 16, pp. I-45–I-72). Washington, DC: American Psychiatric Press.

Vitousek, K. (1996). The current status of cognitive-behavioral models of anorexia nervosa and bulimia nervosa. In Salkovskis, P.M. (ed.), *Frontiers of Cognitive Therapy* (pp. 383–418). New York: Guilford Press.

Vitousek, K., Watson, S. & Wilson, G.T. (1998). Enhancing motivation for change in treatment-resistant eating disorders. *Clinical Psychology Review, 18*, 391–420.

Young, J. (1994). *Cognitive Therapy for Personality Disorders: A Schema-focused Approach* (revised edition). Sarasota, FL: Professional Resource Press.

Young, J., Klosko, J. & Weishaar, M.E. (2003). *Schema Therapy: A Practitioner's Guide*. New York: Guilford Press.

CHAPTER 3

Interpersonal Psychotherapy and Depression

Kathryn L. Bleiberg and John C. Markowitz

Weill Medical College of Cornell University, USA

Interpersonal psychotherapy (IPT) is a time-limited (12–16 sessions), diagnosis-targeted, empirically tested treatment. Relative to most psychotherapies, it has been carefully studied but, until recently, used primarily in research settings and not widely used in clinical practice. The success of IPT in the treatment of outpatients with major depression has led to its testing for an expanded range of diagnostic indications. Furthermore, it has grown from being a treatment used by research therapists into an increasingly popular treatment approach for clinicians in private practice.

The increasing focus on the empirical grounding of treatments and growing economic pressures on treatment accord greater stature to treatments like IPT. This has been reflected not only in a growing interesting in clinical training in IPT but in treatment guidelines from several countries and professional organizations. A local example is *What Works for Whom?* based on a report commissioned for the National Health Service of the English Department of Health (Roth & Fonagy, 1996) The rising international interest among researchers and community clinicians led to the organization of the First International Conference of Interpersonal Psychotherapy, held in June 2004 in Pittsburgh, Pennsylvania. The conference provided an opportunity for clinicians to learn more about IPT and its adaptations.

This chapter is intended for clinicians in the United Kingdom who are interested in exploring IPT as one of the available evidence-based interventions for mood and other disorders. Readers should also know that there is a British Interpersonal Psychotherapy Society as well as an international one (http://www.interpersonalpsychotherapy.org/). This chapter provides a brief overview of IPT for clinicians. For greater depth of discussion, the reader is referred to the IPT manual (Weissman, Markowitz & Klerman, 2000).

BACKGROUND

Klerman, Weissman and colleagues developed IPT as a treatment arm for a pharmacotherapy study of depression. They recognized that many outpatients in clinical practice received

Handbook of Evidence-based Psychotherapies: A Guide for research and practice.
Edited by C. Freeman & M. Power. Copyright © 2007 John Wiley & Sons, Ltd.

talking therapy as well as medication and felt that their study would gain face validity by including both modalities. Yet they had no idea what was actually practised in the surrounding offices in New England – as indeed we have little grasp of what is presumably eclectic psychotherapy practice in the community today. Being researchers, they developed a psychotherapy based on research data, as well as to some degree on existing interpersonal theory.

Interpersonal therapy is based on principles derived from psychosocial and life events research into depression, which has demonstrated relationships between depression and complicated bereavement, role disputes (such as bad marriages), role transitions (and meaningful life changes) and interpersonal deficits. Life stressors can trigger depressive episodes in vulnerable individuals and conversely depressive episodes compromise psychosocial functioning, leading to further negative life events. In contrast, social supports protect against depression. Interpersonal therapy theory borrows from the post-World War II work of Adolph Meyer, Harry Stack Sullivan (1953), as well as the attachment theory of John Bowlby and others. Sullivan, who popularized the term 'interpersonal', emphasized that life events occurring after the early childhood years influenced psychopathology. This idea, which seems commonplace enough today, was radical in an era dominated by psychoanalysis, when the focus was almost exclusively on early childhood experiences. Interpersonal therapy uses this principle for practical, not aetiological practical purposes. Interpersonal therapists do not presume to know the *cause* of a depressive episode, whose aetiology is presumably multifactorial, but instead pragmatically use the connection between current life events and onset of depressive symptoms to help patients understand and combat their episode of illness.

TREATMENT WITH IPT

Interpersonal therapists use a few simple principles to explain the patient's situation and illness. These are simple enough for dysphoric patients with poor concentration to grasp them. First, they define depression as a *medical illness*, a treatable condition that is not the patient's fault. This definition displaces the burdensome guilt of the depressed patient from the patient to her illness, making the symptoms ego-dystonic and discrete. It also provides hope for a response to treatment. The therapist uses ICD-10 or DSM-IV (American Psychiatric Association, 1994) criteria to make the mood diagnosis, and rating scales such as the Hamilton Depression Rating Scale (HDRS) (Hamilton, 1960) or Beck Depression Inventory (BDI) (Beck, 1978) to assess symptoms.

Indeed, the therapist temporarily gives the patient the 'sick role' (Parsons, 1951), which helps the patient to recognize that he or she suffers from a common mood disorder with a predictable set of symptoms – not the personal failure, weakness, or character flaw that the depressed patient often believes is the problem. The sick role excuses the patient from what the illness prevents him or her from doing, but also obliges the patient to work *as* a patient in order to ultimately recover the lost healthy role. I am told that in the United Kingdom (unlike the United States), clinicians hear the term 'sick role' as tainted term associated with long-term psychiatric disability. This is not at all its IPT connotation. On the contrary, the sick role is intended as a temporary role, coincident with the term of a time-limited treatment, to relieve self-blame while focusing the patient on a medical diagnosis. The time limit and brief duration of IPT, and the IPT therapist's frequent encouragement of the patient to take social risks and improve his or her situation, guard against regression and passivity.

A second principle of IPT is to focus the treatment on an interpersonal crisis in the patient's life, a *problem area* connected to the patient's episode of illness. By solving an interpersonal problem – complicated bereavement, a role dispute or transition – the IPT patient can both improve his or her life situation and simultaneously relieve the symptoms of the depressive episode. Since randomized controlled outcome studies have repeatedly validated this coupled formula, IPT can be offered with confidence and optimism similar to that accompanying an antidepressant prescription. This therapeutic optimism, while hardly specific to IPT, very likely provides part of its power in inspiring the patient.

Interpersonal therapy is an eclectic therapy, using techniques seen in other treatment approaches. It makes use of the so-called common factors of psychotherapy (Frank, 1971).

These include building a therapeutic alliance, helping the patient feel understood (through use of a medical disease model and relating mood to event), facilitation of affect, a rationale for improvement (if you fix your situation, your mood should improve), support and encouragement, a treatment ritual, and success experiences (*viz.*, actual life changes). Beyond this, its medical model of depressive illness is consistent with pharmacotherapy (and makes IPT highly compatible with medication in combination treatment). Interpersonal therapy shares role playing and a 'here-and-now' focus with cognitive behaviour therapy (CBT), and addresses interpersonal issues in a manner marital therapists would find familiar. It is not its particular techniques but its overall strategies that make IPT a unique and coherent approach.

Although IPT overlaps to some degree with psychodynamic psychotherapies, and many of its early research therapists came from psychodynamic backgrounds, IPT meaningfully differs from them. Unlike psychodynamic psychotherapies, IPT focuses on the present, not the past; the IPT therapist relates current symptoms and interpersonal difficulties to recent life events, not to childhood experiences. Interpersonal therapy focuses on real-life change rather than self-understanding and on building social skills rather than character change. It employs a medical model approach to psychoeducation about depression rather than a conflict-based approach. The IPT therapist takes a more active stance than the psychodynamic therapist and avoids exploration of the transference and dream interpretations (Markowitz, Svartberg & Swartz, 1998). Interpersonal therapy is like CBT in that it is a time-limited treatment targeting a syndromal constellation (such as major depression). However, IPT is much less structured, assigns no explicit homework, and focuses on affect and interpersonal problem areas rather than automatic thoughts. Interpersonal therapy emphasizes that depression is a medical illness, whereas CBT describes depression as a consequence of dysfunctional thought patterns.

Each of the four IPT interpersonal problem areas has discrete, if somewhat overlapping, goals for therapist and patient to pursue. Interpersonal therapy techniques help the patient to pursue these interpersonal goals. The therapist repeatedly helps the patient relate life events to mood and other symptoms. These techniques include an *opening question,* which elicits an interval history of mood and events; *communication analysis*, the reconstruction and evaluation of recent, affectively charged life circumstances; *exploration of patient wishes and options,* in order to pursue these goals in particular interpersonal situations; *decision analysis*, to help the patient choose which options to employ; and *role playing*, to help patients prepare interpersonal tactics for real life. The reformulation of cases using an IPT focal problem area often makes difficult cases more manageable both for patient and clinician.

Interpersonal therapy deals with current interpersonal relationships, focusing on the patient's immediate social context rather than on the past. The IPT therapist attempts to intervene in depressive symptom formation and social dysfunction rather than enduring aspects of personality. It is, in any case, difficult to assess personality traits accurately when confounded by the state changes of an Axis I disorder such as a depressive episode (Hirschfeld *et al.*, 1983). Interpersonal therapy builds new social skills (Weissman *et al.*, 1981), which may be as valuable as changing personality traits.

Phases of Treatment

Acute IPT treatment has three phases. The *first phase*, usually lasting one to three sessions, involves diagnostic evaluation, obtaining a thorough psychiatric history, and setting the treatment framework. The therapist reviews symptoms, gives the patient a diagnosis the patient as depressed by standard criteria (such as ICD-10), and gives the patient the sick role. ('You have an illness called major depression which is treatable . . . it is not your fault.')

The psychiatric history includes the *interpersonal inventory*, which is not a structured instrument but a careful review of the patients' past and current social functioning and close relationships, their patterns and mutual expectations. The therapist should gain a sense of who the patient is with other people, how he or she interacts with them, and how relationships may have contributed to or have been altered by the depressive episode. Depressed patients frequently have difficulty in asserting their needs, confronting others or getting angry effectively, and taking social risks. Changes in relationships close to the onset of symptoms are elucidated: for example, the death of a loved one (potential complicated bereavement), children leaving home (a role transition), or worsening marital strife (a role dispute). The interpersonal inventory provides a framework for understanding the social and interpersonal context in which the depressive symptoms occur and should lead to a treatment focus.

The therapist assesses the need for medication, based on symptom severity, past illness history, treatment response, and patient preference, then provides psychoeducation by discussing the constellation of symptoms that define major depression, their psychosocial concomitants and what the patient may expect from treatment. The therapist next links the depressive syndrome to the patient's interpersonal situation in a formulation (Markowitz & Swartz, 1997) centred on one of four interpersonal problem areas: (1) *grief*; (2) *interpersonal role disputes*; (3) *role transitions*; or (4) *interpersonal deficits*. With the patient's explicit acceptance of this formulation as a focus for further treatment, therapy enters the middle phase.

Any formulation necessarily simplifies a patient's complex situation. It is important, however, to keep depression treatment focused on a simple theme that even a highly distractible depressed patient can grasp. When patients present with multiple interpersonal problems, the goal of formulation is to isolate one or at most two salient problems that are related (either as antecedent or consequence) to the patient's depressive episode. More than two foci make the treatment unfocused. Choosing the focal problem area requires clinical acumen, although research has shown IPT therapists agree in choosing such areas (Markowitz *et al.*, 2000), and patients seem to find the foci credible.

In the *middle phase*, the IPT therapist follows strategies specific to the chosen interpersonal problem area. For *grief* – complicated bereavement following the death of a loved one – the therapist encourages the catharsis of mourning and, as that affect is released, helps the patient find new activities and relationships to compensate for the loss. For *role disputes*, which are overt or covert conflicts with a spouse, other family member, co-worker, or close friend, the therapist helps the patient explore the relationship, the nature of the dispute, whether it has reached an impasse, and available options to resolve it. Should these options fail, therapist and patient may conclude that the relationship has reached an impasse and consider ways to change or live with the impasse or to end the relationship. Patients with depression tend to have difficulty asserting themselves, which makes it difficult for them to resolve interpersonal conflicts. The IPT therapist helps the patient to consider ways to more effectively communicate thoughts and feelings and role-plays potential interactions with the patient.

A *role transition* is a change in life status defined by a life event: beginning or ending a relationship or career, a geographic move, job promotion or demotion, retirement, graduation, or diagnosis of a medical illness. Even a much-wanted new role such as getting married or having a child may be accompanied by unforeseen sense of loss. The patient learns to manage the change by mourning the loss of the old role while recognizing positive and negative aspects of the new role he or she is assuming, and taking steps to gain mastery over the new role. Frequently the new role, while undesired, is discovered to have previously unseen benefits. *Interpersonal deficits,* the residual fourth IPT problem area, is reserved for patients who lack one of the first three problem areas: that is, patients who report no recent life events. The category is poorly named, and really means that the patient is presenting without the kind of defining recent life event on which IPT usually focuses. Not surprisingly, patients whose treatment focuses on interpersonal deficits generally have worse outcomes in IPT than patients whose treatment focuses on one of the other problem areas. In an effort to improve the identification and potentially the treatment of patients with interpersonal deficits, Andrade, Frank and Swartz in Pittsburgh are developing a system to reclassify the category into sub-types of deficits. Interpersonal deficits recognizes that the patient is usually quite socially isolated, defines the patient as lacking social skills, including having problems in initiating or sustaining relationships, and helps the patient to develop new relationships and skills. Some, or indeed most, patients who might fall into this category in fact suffer from dysthymic disorder, for which separate strategies have been developed (Markowitz, 1998).

Interpersonal therapy sessions address current, 'here-and-now' problems rather than childhood or developmental issues. Each session after the first begins with the question: 'How have things been since we last met?' This focuses the patient on recent mood and events, which the therapist helps the patient to connect. The therapist provides empathic support for the patient's suffering but takes an active, non-neutral, supportive and hopeful stance to counter depressive pessimism. The therapist elicits the options that the patient has to make positive changes in his or her life in order to resolve the focal interpersonal problem, options that the depressive episode may have kept the patient from seeing or exploring fully. Simply understanding the situation is insufficient: therapists stress the need for patients to test these options in order to improve their lives and simultaneously treat their depressive episodes. It can be seen why this focus on interpersonal functioning might build social skills and lead the patient to make meaningful life changes in a relatively brief treatment interval.

The *final phase* of IPT occupies the last few sessions of acute treatment (or the last months of a maintenance phase). Here the therapist's goal is to build the patient's newly regained sense of independence and competence by having him or her recognize and consolidate therapeutic gains. The therapist anchors self-esteem by elucidating how the patient's depressive episode has improved because of the changes the patient has made in his or her life situation and in resolving his interpersonal problem area ('Why do you think you're feeling so much better?... It's impressive what you've accomplished!') – at a time when the patient had felt weak and impotent. The therapist also helps the patient to anticipate depressive symptoms that might arise in the future, and their potential triggers and remedies. Relative to psychodynamic psychotherapy, IPT de-emphasizes termination, which is simply a graduation from successful treatment. The therapist helps the patient see the sadness of parting as a normal interpersonal response to separation, distinct from depressive feelings. If the patient has not improved, the therapist emphasizes that it is the treatment that has failed, not the patient and that alternative effective treatment options exist. This is analogous to a failed pharmacotherapy trial; if one treatment fails, it is the illness rather than the patient who is resistant and thankfully other treatment options remain. Patients who have a successful acute response, but whose multiple prior depressive episodes leave them at high risk for recurrence, may contract for maintenance therapy as acute treatment draws to a close. Another strength of IPT is that its maintenance form, like its acute format, has also demonstrated efficacy in rigorous trials.

INTERPERSONAL THERAPY FOR UNIPOLAR MOOD DISORDERS: EFFICACY AND ADAPTATIONS

The history of IPT has been a sequence of manual-based clinical trials, often adapting IPT to the particular psychosocial problems and needs of the target treatment population.

Acute Treatment of Major Depression

The first acute study of IPT was a four-cell, 16-week randomized trial comparing IPT, amitriptyline (AMI), combined IPT and AMI, and a non-scheduled control treatment for 81 outpatients with major depression (DiMascio et al., 1979; Weissman et al., 1979). Amitriptyline more rapidly alleviated symptoms, but at treatment completion there was no significant difference between IPT and AMI in symptom reduction. Each reduced symptoms more efficaciously than the control condition, and combined AMI-IPT was more efficacious than either active monotherapy. One-year follow-up found that many patients remained improved after the brief IPT intervention. Moreover, IPT patients had developed significantly better psychosocial functioning at one year, whether or not they received medication. This effect on social function was not found for AMI alone, nor was it evident for IPT immediately after the 16-week trial (Weissman et al., 1981).

The ambitious, multi-site National Institute of Mental Health Treatment of Depression Collaborative Research Program (NIMH TDCRP) (Elkin et al., 1989), randomly assigned 250 outpatients with major depression to 16 weeks of IPT, CBT, or either imipramine (IMI) or placebo plus clinical management. Most subjects completed at least 15 weeks or 12 sessions. Mildly depressed patients (17-item HDRS score <20) showed equal improvement in all treatments. For more severely depressed patients (HDRS >20), IMI worked fastest and most consistently outperformed placebo. Interpersonal therapy fared comparably to IMI on several outcome measures, including HDRS, and was superior to placebo for more severely depressed patients. The great surprise of this study was that CBT was not superior to placebo (albeit not significantly worse than IPT or IMI) among more depressed patients. Reanalysing the NIMH TDCRP data using the Johnson-Neyman technique, Klein & Ross (1993) found 'medication superior to psychotherapy, [and] the psychotherapies somewhat superior to placebo . . . particularly among the symptomatic and impaired patients' (Klein & Ross, 1993, p. 241), and 'CBT relatively inferior to IPT for patients with BDI scores greater than approximately 30, generally considered the boundary between moderate and severe depression' (Klein & Ross, 1993, p. 247).

Shea *et al.* (1992) conducted an 18-month naturalistic follow-up study of TDCRP subjects and found no significant differences in recovery among remitters across the four treatments. Twenty-six per cent of IPT, 30 % of CBT, 19 % of imipramine, and 20 % of placebo subjects who had acutely remitted remained in remission 18 months later. Among acute remitters, relapse over the year and a half was 33 % for IPT, 36 % for CBT, 50 % for imipramine (medication having been stopped at 16 weeks), and 33 % for placebo. The authors concluded that 16 weeks of specific treatments were insufficient to achieve full and lasting recovery for many patients.

Hoencamp and colleagues (JCM personal communication, 1996, 2002) in the Hague are completing a study of IPT versus nefazodone, alone and in combination, for acute treatment of major depression.

Maintenance Treatment

Interpersonal therapy was first developed and tested in an eight-month, six-cell study (Klerman *et al.*, 1974; Paykel *et al.*, 1975). In today's parlance this study would be considered a 'continuation' treatment, as the concept of maintenance antidepressant treatment has lengthened. One-hundred-and-fifty acutely depressed women outpatients who responded (with >50 % symptom reduction) to between four and six weeks of AMI were randomly assigned to receive eight months of weekly IPT alone, AMI alone, placebo alone, combined IPT-AMI, IPT-placebo, or no pill. Maintenance pharmacotherapy prevented relapse and symptom exacerbation, whereas IPT improved social functioning (Weissman *et al.*, 1974). Effects of IPT on social functioning were not apparent for six to eight months, and combined psychotherapy-pharmacotherapy had the best outcome.

Two studies in Pittsburgh, Pennsylvania have assessed longer antidepressant maintenance trials of IPT. Frank *et al.* (1990, 1991a), studied 128 outpatients with severe recurrent depression. Patients were initially treated with combined high dose imipramine (>200 mg/day) and weekly IPT. Responders remained on high dosage medication while IPT was tapered to a monthly frequency during a four-month continuation phase. Patients remaining remitted were then randomly assigned to three years of either:

- ongoing high dose imipramine plus clinical management;
- high dose imipramine plus monthly IPT;
- monthly IPT alone;
- monthly IPT plus placebo; or
- placebo plus clinical management.

High-dose imipramine, with or without maintenance IPT, was the most efficacious treatment, protecting more than 80 % of patients over three years. In contrast, most patients on placebo relapsed within the first few months. Once-monthly IPT, although less efficacious than medication, was statistically and clinically superior to placebo in this high-risk patient population. Reynolds and colleagues (1999) essentially replicated these maintenance findings in a study of geriatric patients with major depression comparing IPT and nortriptyline.

The modal depressed patient is a woman of childbearing age, and many depressed pregnant or nursing women prefer to avoid pharmacotherapy. Frank and colleagues' finding of an 82-week survival time without recurrence with monthly maintenance IPT alone would suffice to protect many women with recurrent depression through pregnancy and nursing without medication. Further research is needed to determine the relative efficacy of IPT to newer medications such as selective serotonin reuptake inhibitors, as well as the efficacy of more-frequent-than-monthly doses of maintenance IPT. A study is under way in Pittsburgh comparing differing doses of maintenance IPT for depressed patients.

Geriatric Depressed Patients

Interpersonal therapy was initially used as an addition to a pharmacotherapy trial of geriatric patients with major depression to enhance compliance and to provide some treatment for the placebo control group (Rothblum et al., 1982; Sholomskas et al., 1983). Investigators noted that grief and role transition specific to life changes were the prime interpersonal treatment foci. These researchers suggested modifying IPT to include more flexible duration of sessions, more use of practical advice and support (for example, arranging transportation, calling physicians); and recognizing that major role changes (such as divorce at age 75) may be impractical and detrimental. The six-week trial compared standard IPT to nortriptyline in 30 geriatric depressed patients. Results showed some advantages for IPT, largely due to higher attrition from side effects in the medication group (Sloane, Stapes & Schneider, 1985).

Reynolds et al. (1999) conducted a three-year maintenance study for geriatric patients with recurrent major depression in Pittsburgh using a combination of IPT and high-dose nortriptyline in a design similar to the Frank et al. (1990) study. The IPT manual was modified to allow greater flexibility in session length under the assumption that some elderly patients might not tolerate 50-minute sessions. The authors found older patients needed to address early life relationships in psychotherapy in addition to the usual 'here-and-now' IPT focus. This study corroborated the maintenance results of Frank and colleagues, except that in this geriatric trial combined treatment had advantages over pharmacotherapy alone as well as psychotherapy alone.

It is notable that both the Frank et al. (1990) and Reynolds et al. (1999) studies used unusually high doses (maintenance of acute levels, rather than a dosage taper) of antidepressant medications, while employing the lowest ever (albeit only ever) monthly maintenance dosage of a psychotherapy. Thus, it is easy to misinterpret the comparison of high-dose tricyclic antidepressants to low-dose IPT-M in these studies. Had the tricyclics been lowered comparably to the reduced psychotherapy dosage, as had been the case in earlier antidepressant medication maintenance trials, recurrence in the medication groups might well have been greater. There were no precedents for dosing maintenance psychotherapy, for which the choice of a monthly interval for IPT-M was reasonable, and indeed somewhat clinically beneficial. For less severely recurrent major depression, or at somewhat higher IPT doses, how might maintenance IPT fare?

Depressed Adolescents (IPT-A)

Mufson, Moreau & Weissman (1993) modified IPT to address developmental issues of adolescence. In adapting IPT to this population, they added a fifth problem area and potential focus: the single parent family. This interpersonal situation appeared frequently in their adolescent treatment population and actually reflected multiple wider social problems in an economically deprived, high crime and drug-filled neighbourhood. Other adaptations included family and school contacts. The researchers completed a controlled 12-week clinical trial comparing IPT-A to clinical monitoring in 48 clinic-referred, 12- to 18-year-old patients who met DSM-III-R criteria for major depressive disorder. Thirty-two patients completed the protocol (21 IPT-A, 11 controls). Patients who received IPT-A reported significantly greater improvement in depressive symptoms and social functioning, including interpersonal functioning and problem-solving skills (Mufson, Weissman & Moreau, 1999). Mufson is completing a follow-up trial of IPT-A in a large-scale effectiveness study in school-based clinics and is also piloting it in a group format for depressed adolescents.

Rossello and Bernal compared 12 weeks of randomly assigned IPT (n = 22), CBT (n = 25), and a waiting-list control condition (n = 24) for adolescents ages 13 to 18 in Puerto Rico who met DSM-III-R criteria for major depression, dysthymia, or both. The investigators did not use Mufson's IPT-A modification. Both IPT and CBT were more efficacious than the waiting list in improving adolescents' self-rated depressive symptoms. Interpersonal therapy was more efficacious than CBT in increasing self-esteem and social adaptation. (Rossello & Bernal, 1999).

Depressed HIV-Positive Patients (IPT-HIV)

Recognizing that medical illness is the kind of serious life event that might lend itself to IPT treatment, Markowitz et al. (1992) modified IPT for depressed HIV patients (IPT-HIV), emphasizing common issues among this population including concerns about illness and death, grief and role transitions. A pilot open trial found that 21 of the 24 depressed patients responded. In a 16-week controlled study, 101 subjects were randomized to IPT-HIV, CBT, supportive psychotherapy (SP), or IMI plus SP (Markowitz et al., 1998). All treatments were associated with symptom reduction but IPT and IMI-SP produced symptomatic and functional improvement significantly greater than CBT or SP. These results recall those of more severely depressed subjects in the NIMH TDCRP study (Elkin et al., 1989). Many HIV-positive patients responding to treatment reported improvement of neurovegetative physical symptoms that they had mistakenly attributed to HIV infection.

Depressed Primary Care Patients

Many depressed individuals are willing to accept medical treatment but not mental health treatment. Schulberg and colleagues compared IPT to nortriptyline for depressed ambulatory medical patients in a primary care setting (Schulberg et al., 1993; Schulberg & Scott, 1991). Interpersonal therapy was integrated into the routine of the primary care centre. For example, nurses took vital signs before each session and if patients were medically hospitalized, IPT was continued in the hospital when possible.

Patients with current major depression (n = 276) were randomly assigned to IPT, nortriptyline, or primary care physicians' usual care. They received 16 weekly sessions followed by four monthly sessions of IPT (Schulberg et al., 1996). Depressive symptoms improved more rapidly with IPT or nortriptyline than in usual care. About 70 % of treatment completers receiving nortriptyline or IPT recovered after eight months, compared to 20 % in usual care. This study had an odd design for treatment in the United States in bringing mental health treatment into medical clinics, but might inform treatment in the United Kingdom, where a greater proportion of antidepressant treatments are delivered in primary care settings.

Conjoint IPT for Depressed Patients with Marital Disputes (IPT-CM)

It is well established that marital conflict, separation and divorce can precipitate or complicate depressive episodes (Rounsaville et al., 1979). Some clinicians have feared that individual psychotherapy for depressed patients in marital disputes can lead to premature rupture of marriages (Gurman & Kniskern, 1978). To test and address these concerns, Klerman and Weissman developed an IPT manual for conjoint therapy of depressed patients with marital disputes (Klerman & Weissman, 1993). Both spouses participate in all sessions and treatment focuses on the current marital dispute. Eighteen patients with major depression linked to the onset or exacerbation of marital disputes were randomly assigned to 16 weeks of either individual IPT or IPT-CM. Patients in both treatments showed similar improvement in depressive symptoms but patients receiving IPT-CM reported significantly better marital adjustment, marital affection and sexual relations than did individual IPT patients (Foley et al., 1989). These pilot findings require replication in a larger sample and with other control groups.

Antepartum/Postpartum Depression

Pregnancy and the postpartum period are times of heightened depressive risk for patients who may wish to avoid pharmacotherapy. Spinelli & Endicott (2003) compared 16 weeks of IPT to a weekly parenting education control programme in a group of 38 antepartum women with major depression. Pregnancy is deemed a role transition that involves the depressed pregnant woman's self-evaluation as a parent, physiological changes of pregnancy, and altered relationships with the spouse or significant other and with other children. 'Complicated pregnancy' has been added as a fifth potential interpersonal problem area. Session timing and duration are adjusted for bed rest, delivery, obstetrical complications, and child care, and postpartum mothers may bring children to sessions. As with depressed HIV-positive patients, therapists use telephone sessions and hospital visits as necessary (Spinelli, 1997). The IPT group showed significantly greater improvement of depression than the parent education control programme. O'Hara et al. (2000) compared 12 weeks of IPT to a waiting list for 120 women with postpartum depression. The IPT group showed greater improvement than the waiting-list control group on measures of depression and social adjustment.

Klier et al. (2001) adapted IPT to a 9 week, 90-minute group format and treated 17 women with postpartum depression. Scores on the 21-item Ham-D fell from 19.7 to 8.0, suggesting efficacy. In a still more intriguing study, Zlotnick *et al.* (2001) treated 37 women at risk for postpartum depression with either four 60-minute sessions of an IPT-based group approach or usual treatment. This preventive application resembles a group form of interpersonal counselling (Klerman *et al.*, 1987), a simplified version of IPT. Six of 18 women in the control condition, but none of 17 in the interpersonal group, developed depression after three months postpartum.

Dysthymic Disorder (IPT-D)

Interpersonal therapy was modified for dysthymic disorder, a disorder whose chronicity does not fit the standard IPT model. This adaptation also may provide a better fit for dysthymic patients without acute life events who previously would have been put in the interpersonal deficits category of acute IPT. IPT-D encourages patients to reconceptualize what they have considered lifelong character flaws as ego-dystonic, chronic mood-dependent symptoms: as chronic but treatable 'state' rather than immutable 'trait'. Therapy itself was defined as an 'iatrogenic role transition', from believing oneself flawed in personality to recognizing and treating the mood disorder. Markowitz (1994, 1998) openly treated 17 pilot subjects with 16 sessions of IPT-D, of whom none worsened and 11 remitted. Based on these pilot results, a comparative study of 16 weeks of IPT-D alone, SP, sertraline plus clinical management, as well as a combined IPT/sertraline cell, has been completed at Weill Medical College of Cornell University.

Browne *et al.* (2002) in Hamilton, Canada treated more than 700 dysthymic patients in the community with either 12 sessions of standard IPT over 4 months, sertraline for two years, or their combination. Patients were followed for two years. Based on an improvement criterion of at least a 40 % reduction in score of the Montgomery-Asberg Depression Rating Scale (MADRS) at one year follow-up, 51 % of IPT-alone subjects improved, fewer than the 63 % taking sertraline and 62 % in combined treatment. On follow-up, however, IPT was associated with significant economic savings in use of health care and social services. Combined treatment was thus most cost effective, as efficacious as sertraline alone but less expensive.

In a comparison of medication to combined treatment, Feijò de Mello *et al.* (2001) randomly assigned 35 dysthymic outpatients to moclobemide with or without 16 weekly sessions of IPT. Both groups improved but with a non-significant trend for greater improvement on the Ham-D and MADRS in the combined treatment group.

Subsyndromally Depressed Hospitalized Elderly Patients

Recognizing that subthreshold symptoms for major depression impeded recovery of hospitalized elderly patients, Mossey *et al.* (1996) conducted a trial using a modification of IPT called interpersonal counselling (IPC) (Klerman *et al.*, 1987). Seventy-six hospitalized patients over age 60 with subsyndromal depression were randomly assigned to either 10 sessions of IPC or usual care (UC). A euthymic, untreated control group was also followed. Three-month assessment showed non-significantly greater improvement in depressive symptoms and on all outcome variables for IPC relative to UC, whereas controls showed mild symptomatic worsening. In the IPC and euthymic control groups, rates of rehospitalization were similar and significantly less than the subsyndromally depressed group receiving usual care. After 6 months the IPC group showed statistically significant improvement in depressive symptoms and self-rated health as compared to the UC group. The investigators felt 10 sessions were not enough for some patients, and that maintenance IPC might have been useful.

Other Applications

The success of IPT in treating unipolar mood disorders has led to its expansion to treat other psychiatric disorders. Frank and colleagues in Pittsburgh have been assessing a be- haviourally modified version of IPT as a treatment adjunctive to pharmacotherapy for bipolar disorder. Further, IPT is increasingly being applied for a range of non-mood disorders. There are intriguing applications of IPT as treatment for bulimia (Agras et al., 2000; Fairburn et al., 1993; Wilfley et al., 1993, 2000) and anorexia nervosa; social phobia (Lipsitz et al., 1999), posttraumatic stress disorder, borderline personality disorder and other conditions. Life events, the substrate of IPT, are ubiquitous, but how useful it is to focus on them may vary from disorder to disorder. There have been two negative trials of interpersonal therapy for substance disorders (Carroll, Rounsaville & Gawin, 1991; Rounsaville et al., 1983), and it seems unlikely that an outwardly focused treatment such as IPT would be useful for such an internally focused diagnosis as obsessive compulsive disorder. In the continuing IPT tradition, clinical outcome research should clarify the question of its utility. Interpersonal therapy is also being modified for use in other formats, for example as group therapy (Klier et al., 2001; Wilfley et al., 1993, 2000; Zlotnick et al., 2001) and as a telephone intervention. Weissman (1995) developed an IPT patient guide with worksheets for depressed readers that may be used in conjunction with IPT.

In summary, IPT is one of the best tested psychotherapies, particularly for mood disorders, where it has demonstrated efficacy as both an acute and maintenance monotherapy and as a component of combined treatment for major depressive disorder. It appears to have utility for other mood and non-mood syndromes, although evidence for most of these is sparser. Monotherapy with either IPT or pharmacotherapy is likely to treat most patients with major depression successfully, so combined treatment should probably be reserved for more severely or chronically ill patients (Rush & Thase, 1999). How best to combine time-limited psychotherapy with pharmacotherapy is an exciting area for future research: when is it indicated, in what sequence and for which patients.

Comparative trials have begun to reveal moderating factors that predict treatment outcome. The NIMH Treatment of Depression Collaborative Research Program, which compared IPT and CBT, suggested factors that might predict better outcome with either IPT or CBT. Sotsky and colleagues (1991) found that depressed patients with low baseline social dysfunction responded well to IPT, whereas those with severe social deficits (prob- ably equivalent to the 'interpersonal deficits' problem area) responded less well. Greater symptom severity and difficulty in concentrating responded poorly to CBT. Patients with greater initial severity of major depression and impaired functioning responded best to IPT and to imipramine. Imipramine worked most efficaciously for patients with difficulty functioning at work, reflecting its faster onset of action. Patients with atypical depression responded better to IPT or CBT than to imipramine or placebo (Shea et al., 1999).

Barber & Muenz (1996) studied TDCRP completers and found IPT more efficacious than CBT for patients with obsessive personality disorder, whereas CBT fared better for avoidant personality disorder. This finding did not hold for the intent-to-treat sample. Biological factors, such as abnormal sleep profiles on EEG, predicted significantly poorer response to IPT than for patients with normal sleep parameters (Thase *et al.*, 1997). Frank *et al.* (1991) found that psychotherapist adherence to a focused IPT approach may enhance outcome. Moreover, sleep EEG and adherence, the first a biological and the latter a psychotherapy factor, had additive effects in that study. Replication and further elaboration of these predictive factors deserve ongoing study.

Another exciting development is the use of neuroimaging studies to compare IPT and pharmacotherapy outcomes. Martin *et al.* (2001) in Sunderland, using SPECT, found that IPT and venlafaxine had overlapping but also differing effects on right posterior cingulate (IPT), right posterior temporal (venlafaxine), and right basal ganglia activation (both treatments). Brody *et al.* (2001) in Los Angeles reported slightly different but roughly analogous findings using PET scanning of patients treated with IPT and paroxetine.

TRAINING

Until very recently, IPT was delivered almost entirely by research study therapists. As the research base of IPT has grown and it has become included in treatment guidelines, there has been a growing clinical demand for this empirically supported treatment. Interpersonal therapy training is now increasingly included in professional workshops and conferences, with training courses conducted at university centres in the United Kingdom, Canada, continental Europe, Asia, New Zealand and Australia in addition to the United States. Interpersonal therapy is taught in a still small but growing number of psychiatric residency training programmes in the United States (Markowitz, 1995) and has been included in family practice and primary care training. It was not, however, included in a recent mandate for psychotherapy proficiency of US psychiatric residency programmes.

There has been no formal certificate for IPT proficiency and no accrediting board. When the practice of IPT was restricted to a few research settings this was not a problem, as one research group taught another in the manner described above. As IPT spreads into clinical practice, issues arise about standards for clinical training and questions of competence and accreditation gain greater urgency. Training programmes in IPT are still not widely available, as a recent US Surgeon General's report noted (Satcher, 1999). Many psychiatry residency and psychology training programmes still focus exclusively on long-term psychodynamic psychotherapy or on CBT. In these programmes, too, the lack of exposure to time-limited treatment has been noted (Sanderson & Woody, 1995).

The principles and practice of IPT are straightforward. Yet any psychotherapy requires innate therapeutic ability and IPT training requires more than reading the manual (Rounsaville *et al.*, 1988; Weissman, Rounsaville & Chevron, 1982). Therapists learn psychotherapy by practising it. Interpersonal therapy training programmes are generally designed to help already experienced therapists refocus their treatment by learning new techniques, not to teach novices psychotherapy. This makes sense, given its development as a focal research therapy: IPT has never been intended as a universal treatment for all patients, a conceptualization of psychotherapy that in any case seems naively grandiose in the modern era.

Until there is a formal certification process, we recommend that clinicians interested in learning IPT follow the training guidelines for researchers. Interpersonal therapy candidates should have a graduate clinical degree (MD, PhD, MSW, RN), several years of experience conducting psychotherapy, and clinical familiarity with the diagnosis of patients they plan to treat. The training developed for the TDCRP (Elkin *et al.*, 1989) became the model for subsequent research studies. It included a brief didactic programme, review of the manual, and a longer practicum in which the therapist treated two or three patients under close supervision monitored by videotapes of the sessions (Chevron & Rounsaville, 1983). Rounsaville *et al.* (1986) found that psychotherapists who successfully conducted an initial supervised IPT case often did not require further intensive supervision, and that experienced therapists committed to the approach required less supervision than others (Rounsaville *et al.*, 1988). Some clinicians have taught themselves IPT using as the IPT manual (Klerman *et al.*, 1984) and peer supervision to guide them. For research certification as well as for training in the community, we recommend at least two or three successfully treated cases with hour-for-hour supervision of taped sessions – not a lot to ask to learn a psychotherapy well (Markowitz, 2001). When first learning IPT, the first two to three cases should be patients with acute major depression. Only after mastering the basics of IPT for major depression, should clinicians attempt one of the adaptations of IPT.

Challenges for Clinicians

Learning any new psychotherapy requires some adjustment. Conforming to the technical requirements of IPT – limited number of sessions, taping sessions for supervision and doing serial symptom measurement – may be challenging for clinicians in private practice who have not provided psychotherapy in the controlled setting of a research study or manualized time-limited treatment. Psychodynamic psychotherapists have the challenges of learning to take a more active stance, offering more direct advice and redirecting a patient to the focal problem area as needed rather than allowing for free association; of focusing on the present instead of the past; and of adhering to the structure of the sessions. Conversely, the therapist used to a cognitive or behavioural approach has to adapt to working with less structure; the IPT therapist facilitates discussions about interpersonal events that occur between sessions as opposed to reviewing written homework assignments or teaching specific behavioural techniques. Furthermore, the IPT therapist facilitates the expression of affect sometimes resulting in having to tolerating strong affect in the treatment room; this represents a significant shift for the CBT therapist who is used to eliciting thoughts rather than feelings.

Differential Therapeutics

As a clinician, when might you think of using IPT? As a psychiatrist decides which antidepressant medication to prescribe based on a patient's symptom constellation and research findings, so too should clinicians consider when to use IPT. The research to date supports that IPT works best for depressed patients who face distressing life events ranging from medical illness to job and relationship changes and conflicts. Patients with interpersonal deficits who report no recent life events or changes will probably fare better in CBT. Interpersonal therapy may also work well for patients with anxiety and personality disorders who report recent life events, but research is in these areas, although promising, is still in the early stages. Interpersonal therapy may be a good option for patients who want to augment their medication treatment with psychotherapy; given that IPT and pharmacotherapy share the medical model of depressive illness, IPT seems like a good fit, although further research in this area is needed. Additional moderating factors that predict treatment outcome in clinical trials were described earlier in the research section of this chapter.

The educational process for IPT in clinical practice requires further study. We do not know, for example, what levels of education and experience are required to learn IPT, or how much supervision an already-experienced psychotherapist is likely to require. The International Society for Interpersonal Psychotherapy (ISIPT) is currently debating how best to set standards for clinical practice of IPT, which doubtless varies from country to country. Recent meetings of the ISIPT indicated that the United Kingdom has advanced farther in developing specific guidelines for IPT training than elsewhere in the world and some countries are adopting the standards developed in the United Kingdom. Interpersonal therapy therapists in Britain have agreed on four-level set of accreditation standards for clinical training and practice that are essentially equivalent to those for researchers (Appendix A). These rigorous standards should ensure high quality of IPT in the United Kingdom.

APPENDIX A: IPT UNITED KINGDOM NETWORK: ACCREDITATION STANDARDS

Level A-IPT Interest

- Available for health care professionals who are interested in IPT. This will provide an overview in the form of an introductory training course lasting two days or more.
- Wider groups rather than just clinical staff working in mental health may express interest in IPT.

Level B-Basic Training as IPT Therapist

- Trainees should have read the IPT manual and have attended a recognized training course of 2–4 days.
- Supervision is offered at the discretion of the supervisor.
- Supervisees should have previous clinical training with a good knowledge of mood disorders.
- The first case using IPT should be in the treatment of major depression and the second case should be depression, dysthymia, adolescent depression or bulimia/binge eating disorder.
- Each trainee should be supervised for a minimum of two cases on the model. Supervision should be provided by a recognized supervisor, i.e. through ISIPT or UKIPTSIG.
- All sessions should be recorded (video/audio) and a minimum of three tapes from each case selected at random by the supervisor for formal review e.g. using the IPT Competency Scale. A minimum of 12 out of 16 sessions per case will be supervised. Supervision can be individual or in group format, but each trainee should receive at least four hours of supervision for each case. In group supervision, trainees will have the opportunity to discuss their own cases for four hours. The two cases should preferably be in two different focal areas.

- A satisfactory supervisor's report should be provided when the above criteria are met, e.g. 'x has attended an introductory course in IPT and has achieved a satisfactory standard in two supervised cases.'

Level C-CPD for IPT Therapists

- Therapists should carry an IPT caseload – at least two cases a year.
- Interpersonal therapists should receive ongoing supervision, at least monthly. This may be individual, peer group or via the telephone.
- Therapists are recommended to attend conference/courses regarding IPT developments.

Level D – Recommendations for Becoming IPT Supervisor/Trainer

- To have achieved a level A, B and continue level C.
- To have a minimum of 10 supervised cases, preferably with two cases in each focal area.
- This supervision may be an individual or group, and includes the two or three cases in level B.
- Supervisors would be required to be a member of a network of supervisors. It is proposed that regional groups be established and meet at least twice a year.
- Supervisors must attend an introductory supervisor's workshop before providing supervision. It is proposed that existing supervisors will run such workshops twice yearly.
- Attendance at conferences/courses is recommended as in Level C.
- Supervisors should be prepared to keep their IPT clinical and supervisory skills active by supervising at least two trainings per year and keeping Level C activity for clinical work.

ACKNOWLEDGEMENTS

Adapted from Markowitz, J.C. (2004). Interpersonal Psychotherapy. In M. Power (ed.), *Mood Disorders: A Handbook of Science and Practice* (pp. 183–200). Chichester: Wiley. Appendix A is reprinted with permission from Chris Freeman MD, IPT UK Network.

REFERENCES

Agras, W.S, Walsh, B.T., Fairburn, C.G. *et al.* (2000). A multicenter comparison of cognitive-behavioral therapy and interpersonal psychotherapy for bulimia nervosa. *Archives of General Psychiatry, 57,* 459–466.

American Psychiatric Association (APA) (1994). Diagnostic and Statistical Manual of Mental Disorders (DSM-IV) (4th edn). Washington, DC: American Psychiatric Association.

Barber, J.P. & Muenz, L.R. (1996). The role of avoidance and obsessiveness in matching patients to cognitive and interpersonal psychotherapy: Empirical findings from the Treatment for Depression Collaborative Research Program. *Journal of Consulting and Clinical Psychology, 64,* 951–958.

Beck, A.T. (1978) *Depression Inventory.* Philadelphia, PA: Center for Cognitive Therapy.

Beck, A.T., Rush, A.J., Shaw, B.F. & Emery, G. (1979). *Cognitive Therapy of Depression.* New York: Guilford.

Blom, M.B.J., Hoencamp, E. & Zwaan, T. (1996). Interpersoonlijke psychotherapie voor depressie: een pilot-onderzoek. *Tijdschrift voor Psychiatrie, 38*, 398–402.

Brody, A.L., Saxena, S., Stoessel, P. *et al.* (2001). Regional brain metabolic changes in patients with major depression treated with eiteher paroxetine or interpersonal therapy: Preliminary findings. *Archives of General Psychiatry, 58*, 631–640.

Brown, C., Schulberg, H.C., Madonia, M.J. *et al.* (1996). Treatment outcomes for primary care patients with major depression and lifetime anxiety disorders. *American Journal of Psychiatry, 153*, 1293–1300.

Browne, G., Steiner, M., Roberts, J. *et al.* (2002). Sertraline and/or interpersonal psychotherapy with patients with dysthymic disorder in primary care: A 6-month comparison with longitudinal 2-year follow-up of effectiveness and costs. *Journal of Affective Disorders, 68*, 317–330.

Carroll, K.M., Rounsaville, B.J. & Gawin, F.H. (1991). A comparative trial of psychotherapies for ambulatory cocaine abusers: Relapse prevention and interpersonal psychotherapy. *American Journal of Drug and Alcohol Abuse, 17*, 229–247.

Chevron, E.S. & Rounsavillle, B.J. (1983). Evaluating the clinical skills of psychotherapists: A comparison of techniques. *Archives of General Psychiatry, 40*, 1129–1132.

Depression Guideline Panel (1993). *Clinical Practice Guideline. Depression in Primary Care*, Volumes 1–4. Rockville, MD: US Department of Health and Human Services, Agency for Health Care Policy and Research.

DiMascio, A., Weissman, M.M., Prusoff, B.A. *et al.* (1979). Differential symptom reduction by drugs and psychotherapy in acute depression. *Archives of General Psychiatry, 36*, 1450–1456.

Elkin, I., Shea, M.T., Watkins, J.T. *et al.* (1989). National Institute of Mental Health treatment of depression collaborative research program: General effectiveness of treatments. *Archives of General Psychiatry, 46*, 971–982.

Fairburn, C.G., Jones, R., Peveler, R.C. *et al.* (1993). Psychotherapy and bulimia nervosa: Longer-term effects of interpersonal psychotherapy, behavior therapy, and cognitive behavior therapy. *Archives of General Psychiatry, 50*, 419–428.

Fairburn, C.G., Norman, P.A., Welch, S.L. *et al.* (1995). A prospective study of outcome in bulimia nervosa and the long-term effects of three psychological treatments. *Archives of General Psychiatry, 52*, 304–312.

Feijò de Mello, M., Myczowisk, L.M. & Menezes, P.R. (2001). A randomized controlled trial comparing moclobemide and moclobemide plus interpersonal psychotherapy in the treatment of dysthymic disorder. *Journal of Psychotherapy Practice and Research, 10*, 117–123.

Foley, S.H., Rounsaville, B.J., Weissman, M.M. *et al.* (1989). Individual versus conjoint interpersonal psychotherapy for depressed patients with marital disputes. *International Journal of Family Psychiatry, 10*, 29–42.

Frank, E. (1991a). Interpersonal psychotherapy as a maintenance treatment for patients with recurrent depression. *Psychotherapy, 28*, 259–266.

Frank, E. (1991b). *Biological Order and Bipolar Disorder.* Presented at the meeting of the American Psychosomatic Society, Santa Fe, NM, March.

Frank, E., Kupfer, D.J., Perel, J.M. *et al.* (1990). Three-year outcomes for maintenance therapies in recurrent depression. *Archives of General Psychiatry, 47*, 1093–1099.

Frank, E., Kupfer, D.J., Wagner, E.F. *et al.* (1991). Efficacy of interpersonal psychotherapy as a maintenance treatment of recurrent depression. *Archives of General Psychiatry, 48*, 1053–1059.

Frank, E., Shear, M.K., Rucci, P. *et al.* (2000a). Influence of panic-agoraphobic spectrum symptoms on treatment response in patients with recurrent major depression. *American Journal of Psychiatry, 157*, 1101–1107.

Frank, E., Swartz, H.A. & Kupfer, D.J. (2000b). Interpersonal and social rhythm therapy: Managing the chaos of bipolar disorder. *Biological Psychiatry, 48*, 593–604.

Frank, E., Swartz, H.A., Mallinger, A.G. *et al.* (1999). Adjunctive psychotherapy for bipolar disorder: Effects of changing treatment modality. *Journal of Abnormal Psychology, 108*, 579–587.

Frank, J. (1971). Therapeutic factors in psychotherapy. *American Journal of Psychotherapy, 25*, 350–361.

Gurman, A.S. & Kniskern, D.P. (1978). Research on marital and family therapy: Progress, perspective, and prospect. In S.B. Garfield & A.B. Bergen (eds), *Handbook of Psychotherapy and Behavior Change* (pp. 817–902). New York: John Wiley & Sons.

Hamilton, M. (1960). A rating scale for depression. *Journal of Neurology, Neurosurgery and Psychiatry, 25*, 56–62.

Hirschfeld, R.M.A., Klerman, G.L., Clayton, P.J. *et al.* (1983). Assessing personality: effects of the depressive state on trait measurement. *American Journal of Psychiatry, 140*, 695–699.

Karasu, T.B., Docherty, J.P., Gelenberg, A. *et al.* (1993). Practice guideline for major depressive disorder in adults. *American Journal of Psychiatry (Supplement) 150*, 1–26.

Klein, D.F. & Ross, D.C. (1993) Reanalysis of the National Institute of Mental Health treatment of depression collaborative research program general effectiveness report. *Neuropsychopharmacology, 8*, 241–251.

Klerman, G.L. (1990). Treatment of recurrent unipolar major depression disorder. *Archives of General Psychiatry, 47*, 1158–1162.

Klerman, G.L., Budman, S., Berwick, D. *et al.* (1987). Efficacy of a brief psychosocial intervention for symptoms of stress and distress among patients in primary care. *Medical Care, 25*, 1078–1088.

Klerman, G.L., DiMascio, A., Weissman, M.M. *et al.* (1974). Treatment of depression by drugs and psychotherapy. *American Journal of Psychiatry, 131*, 186–191.

Klerman, G.L. & Weissman, M.M. (1993). *New Applications of Interpersonal Psychotherapy.* Washington, DC: American Psychiatric Press.

Klerman, G.L., Weissman, M.M., Rounsaville, B.J. & Chevron, E.S. (1984). *Interpersonal Psychotherapy of Depression.* New York: Basic Books.

Klier, C.M., Muzik, M., Rosenblum, K.L. & Lenz, G. (2001). Interpersonal psychotherapy adapted for the group setting in the treatment of postpartum depression. *Journal of Psychotherapy Practice and Research, 10*, 124–131.

Kocsis, J.H., Frances, A.J., Voss, C. *et al.* (1988). Imipramine treatment for chronic depression. *Archives of General Psychiatry, 45*, 253–257.

Lipsitz, J.D., Fyer, A.J., Markowitz, J.C. & Cherry, S. (1999). An open trial of interpersonal psychotherapy for social phobia. *American Journal of Psychiatry, 156*, 1814–1816.

Malkoff-Schwartz, S., Frank, E., Anderson, B.P. *et al.* (2000). Social rhythm disruption and stressful life events in the onset of bipolar and unipolar episodes. *Psychological Medicine, 30*, 1005–1016.

Markowitz, J.C. (1994). Psychotherapy of dysthymia. *American Journal of Psychiatry, 151*, 1114–1121.

Markowitz, J.C. (1995). Teaching interpersonal psychotherapy to psychiatric residents. *Academic Psychiatry, 19*, 167–173.

Markowitz, J.C. (1998). *Interpersonal Psychotherapy for Dysthymic Disorder.* Washington, DC: American Psychiatric Press.

Markowitz, J.C. (2001). Learning the new psychotherapies. In M.M. Weissman (ed.) *Treatment of Depression: Bridging the 21st Century* (pp. 281–300). Washington, DC: American Psychiatric Press.

Markowitz, J.C., Klerman, G.L., Perry, S.W. *et al.* (1992). Interpersonal therapy of depressed HIV-seropositive patients. *Hospital and Community Psychiatry, 43*, 885–890.

Markowitz, J.C., Kocsis, J.H. & Fishman, B. (1998). Treatment of HIV-positive patients with depressive symptoms. *Archives of General Psychiatry, 55*, 452–457.

Markowitz, J.C., Leon, A.C., Miller, N.L. *et al.* (2000). Rater agreement on interpersonal psychotherapy problem areas. *Journal of Psychotherapy Practice and Research, 9*, 131–135.

Markowitz, J.C., Svartberg, M. & Swartz, H.A. (1998). Is IPT time-limited psychodynamic psychotherapy? *Journal of Psychotherapy Practice and Research, 7*, 185–195.

Markowitz, J.C. & Swartz, H.A. (1997). Case formulation in interpersonal psychotherapy of depression. In T.D. Eels (ed.), *Handbook of Psychotherapy Case Formulation* (pp. 192–222). New York: Guilford Press.

Martin, S.D., Martin, E., Rai, S.S. *et al.* (2001). Brain blood flow changes in depressed patients treated with interpersonal psychotherapy or venlafaxine hydrochloride. *Archives of General Psychiatry, 58*, 641–648.

Mossey, J.M., Knott, K.A., Higgins, M. & Talerico, K. (1996). Effectiveness of a psychosocial intervention, interpersonal counseling, for subdysthymic depression in medically ill elderly. *Journal of Gerontology, 51A(4)*, M172–M178.

Mufson, L., Moreau, D. & Weissman, M.M. (1993). *Interpersonal Therapy for Depressed Adolescents.* New York, Guilford Press.

Mufson, L., Weissman, M.M., Moreau, D. & Garfinkel, R. (1999). Efficacy of interpersonal psychotherapy for depressed adolescents. *Archives of General Psychiatry, 56*, 573–579.

O'Hara, M.W., Stuart, S., Gorman, L.L. & Wenzel, A. (2000). Efficacy of interpersonal psychotherapy for postpartum depression. *Archives of General Psychiatry, 57*, 1039–1045.

Parsons, T. (1951). Illness and the role of the physician: a sociological perspective. *American Journal of Orthopsychiatry, 21*, 452–460.

Paykel, E.S., DiMascio, A., Haskell, D. & Prusoff, B.A. (1975). Effects of maintenance amitriptyline and psychotherapy on symptoms of depression. *Psychological Medicine, 5*, 67–77.

Reynolds, C.F. III, Frank, E., Perel, J.M. *et al.* (1999). Nortriptyline and interpersonal psychotherapy as maintenance therapies for recurrent major depression: a randomized controlled trial in patients older than fifty-nine years. *Journal of the American Medical Association, 281*, 39–45.

Rossello, J. & Bernal, G. (1999). The efficacy of cognitive-behavioral and interpersonal treatments for depression in Puerto Rican adolescents. *Journal of Consulting and Clinical Psychology, 67*, 734–745.

Roth, A. & Fonagy, P. (1996) *What Works for Whom? A Critical Review of Psychotherapy Research.* New York: Guilford.

Rothblum, E.D., Sholomskas, A.J., Berry, C. & Prusoff, B.A. (1982). Issues in clinical trials with the depressed elderly. *Journal of the American Geriatric Society, 30*, 694–699.

Rounsaville, B.J., Chevron, E.S., Weissman, M.M. *et al.* (1986). Training therapists to perform interpersonal psychotherapy in clinical trials. *Comprehensive Psychiatry, 27*, 364–371.

Rounsaville, B.J., Glazer, W., Wilber, C.H. *et al.* (1983). Short-term interpersonal psychotherapy in methadone-maintained opiate addicts. *Archives of General Psychiatry, 40*, 629–636.

Rounsaville, B.J., O'Malley, S.S., Foley, S.H. & Weissman, M.M. (1988). The role of manual-guided training in the conduct and efficacy of interpersonal psychotherapy for depression. *Journal of Consulting and Clinical Psychology, 56*, 681–688.

Rounsaville, B.J., Weissman, M.M., Prusoff, B.A. & Herceg-Baron, R.L. (1979). Marital disputes and treatment outcome in depressed women. *Comprehensive Psychiatry, 20*, 483–490.

Rush, A.J. & Thase, M.E. Psychotherapies for depressive disorders: A review. In M. Maj & N. Sartorius (eds), *Depressive Disorders: WPA Series Evidence and Experience in Psychiatry* (pp. 161–206). Chichester: John Wiley & Sons.

Sanderson WC, Woody S (1995). Manuals for empirically validated treatments: a project of the task force on psychological interventions. *Clinical Psychologist, 48*, 7–11.

Satcher, D. (1999). *Surgeon General's Reference: Mental Health: A Report of the Surgeon General.* Rockville, MD: US Department of Health and Human Services.

Schulberg, H.C., Block, M.R., Madonia, M.J. *et al.* (1996). Treating major depression in primary care practice. *Archives of General Psychiatry, 53*, 913–919.

Schulberg, H.C. & Scott, C.P. (1991). Depression in primary care: treating depression with interpersonal psychotherapy. In C.S. Austad & W.H. Berman (eds), *Psychotherapy in Managed Health Care: The Optimal Use of Time and Resources* (pp. 153–170). Washington, DC: American Psychological Association.

Schulberg, H.C., Scott, C.P., Madonia, M.J. & Imber, S.D. (1993). Applications of interpersonal psychotherapy to depression in primary care practice. In G.L. Klerman & M.M. Weissman (eds) New Applications of Interpersonal Psychotherapy (pp. 265–91). Washington, DC: American Psychiatric Press.

Seligman, M.E.P. (1995). The effectiveness of psychotherapy: The Consumer Reports study. *American Psychologist, 12*, 965–974.

Shea, M.T., Elkin, I., Imber, S.D. *et al.* (1992). Course of depressive symptoms over follow-up: findings from the National Institute of Mental Health Treatment for Depression Collaborative Research Program. *Archives of General Psychiatry, 49*, 782–794.

Shea, M.T., Elkin, I., & Sotsky, S.M. (1999). Patient characteristics associated with successful treatment: outcome findings from the NIMH Treatment of Depression Collaborative Research Program. In D.S. Janowsky (ed.) *Psychotherapy Indications and Outcomes* (pp. 71–90). Washington, DC: American Psychiatric Press.

Sholomskas, A.J., Chevron, E.S., Prusoff, B.A. & Berry C (1983). Short-term interpersonal therapy (IPT) with the depressed elderly: Case reports and discussion. *American Journal of Psychotherapy, 36*, 552–566.

Sloane, R.B., Stapes, F.R. & Schneider, L.S. (1985). Interpersonal therapy versus nortriptyline for depression in the elderly. In G.D. Burrows, T.R. Norman & L. Dennerstein (eds). *Clinical and Pharmacological Studies in Psychiatric Disorders* (pp. 344–346). London, John Libbey.

Sotsky, S.M., Glass, D.R., Shea, M.T. *et al.* (1991). Patient predictors of response to psychotherapy and pharmacotherapy: Findings in the NIMH treatment of depression collaborative research program. *American Journal of Psychiatry, 148*, 997–1008.

Spinelli, M. (1997). *Manual of Interpersonal Psychotherapy for Antepartum Depressed Women (IPT-P)*. Available through Dr Spinelli, Columbia University College of Physicians and Surgeons, New York.

Spinelli, M. & Endicott, J. (2003). Controlled clinical trial of interpersonal psychotherapy versus parenting education program for depressed pregnant women. *American Journal of Psychiatry, 160*, 555–562.

Stuart, S. & O'Hara, M.W. (1995). IPT for postpartum depression. *Journal of Psychotherapy Practice and Research, 4*, 18–29.

Stuart, S., O'Hara, M.W. & Blehar, M.C. (1998). Mental disorders associated with childbearing: report of the biennial meeting of Marce Society. *Psychopharmacology Bulletin, 34*, 333–338.

Sullivan, H.S. (ed) (1953). *The Interpersonal Theory of Psychiatry*. New York: W.W. Norton.

Thase, M.E., Fava, M., Halbreich, U. *et al.* (1996). A placebo-controlled, randomized clinical trial comparing sertraline and imipramine for the treatment of dysthymia. *Archives of General Psychiatry, 53*, 777–784.

Thase, M.E., Buysse, D.J., Frank, E. *et al.* (1997). Which depressed patients will respond to interpersonal psychotherapy? The role of abnormal EEG profiles. *American Journal of Psychiatry, 154*, 502–509.

Weissman, M.M. (1995). *Mastering Depression: A Patient Guide to Interpersonal Psychotherapy*. Albany, NY: Graywind Publications. Currently available through The Psychological Corporation, Order Service Center, P.O. Box 839954, San Antonio, TX 78283-3954. Tel. 1-800-228-0752. Fax 1-800-232-1223.

Weissman, M.M., Klerman, G.L., Paykel, E.S. *et al.* (1974). Treatment effects on the social adjustment of depressed patients. *Archives of General Psychiatry, 30*, 771–778.

Weissman, M.M., Klerman, G.L., Prusoff, B.A. *et al.* (1981). Depressed outpatients: Results one year after treatment with drugs and/or interpersonal psychotherapy. *Archives of General Psychiatry, 38*, 52–55.

Weissman, M.M., Markowitz, J.C. & Klerman, G.L. (2000). *Comprehensive Guide to Interpersonal Psychotherapy*. New York: Basic Books.

Weissman, M.M., Prusoff, B.A., DiMascio, A. *et al.* (1979). The efficacy of drugs and psychotherapy in the treatment of acute depressive episodes. *American Journal of Psychiatry, 136*, 555–558.

Weissman, M.M., Rounsaville, B.J. & Chevron, E.S. (1982). Training psychotherapists to participate in psychotherapy outcome studies: Identifying and dealing with the research requirement. *American Journal of Psychiatry, 139*, 1442–1446.

Wilfley, D.E., Agras, W.S., Telch, C.F. *et al.* (1993). Group cognitive-behavioral therapy and group interpersonal psychotherapy for the nonpurging bulimic individual: a controlled comparison. *Journal of Consulting and Clinical Psychology, 61*, 296–305.

Wilfley, D.E., MacKenzie, R.K., Welch, R.R. *et al.* (2000). *Interpersonal Psychotherapy for Groups*. New York: Basic Books.

Zlotnick, C., Johnson, S.L., Miller, I.W. *et al.* (2001). Postpartum depression in women receiving public assistance: Pilot study of an interpersonal-therapy-oriented group intervention. *American Journal of Psychiatry, 158*, 638–640.

CHAPTER 4

Behaviour Therapy

P.M.G. Emmelkamp, E. Vedel and J.H. Kamphuis
University of Amsterdam, The Netherlands

INTRODUCTION

Behaviour therapy can be defined in various ways. Some behaviour therapists view behaviour therapy as 'the application of learning theories' whereas others (cognitive behaviour therapists) emphasize cognitive change. There are also behaviour therapists who view behaviour therapy as the application of findings from controlled research into clinical treatment procedures. These proponents of the so-called experimental-clinical approach do not exclusively base themselves on learning theories or cognitive theories.

It is of note that the distinction between cognitive and behaviour therapy procedures is rather artificial. Behaviour therapists often integrate cognitive and behavioural methods in their clinical practice. For didactic purposes, however, the editors chose to cover the cognitive approach and the behavioural approach in separate chapters. One should keep this decision in mind when reading this chapter further.

Although behaviour therapy and behaviourism appear to be strongly related, the relationship between these two movements is far from unequivocal. Behaviourism is an important movement in experimental psychology, originating at the start of the twentieth century. The American psychologist Watson is usually considered the 'father' of behaviourism, although it seems more likely that he functioned as a catalyst or charismatic leader of a larger societal movement (Kanfer, 1990). The onset of behaviour therapy, however, was much later and did not occur until the 1950s. Behaviour therapy started in response to the operative psychodynamic view of problem behaviour. The discontent with the then-prevailing – notoriously unreliable – psychodiagnostic assessment and the effects of psychotherapy was another important impetus.

In 1952, the British psychologist Hans Eysenck caused a major stir with his empirical review claiming that the effects of traditional psychotherapy did not exceed those of no treatment at all. As an effective alternative, Eysenck (1952) mentioned behaviour therapy based on modern learning theory. At the time, only a few British psychologists and psychiatrists were experimenting with this method, following the South African psychiatrist Joseph Wolpe. A similar development occurred more-or-less simultaneously in the United States. While Wolpe and the British group based themselves predominantly on classical

Handbook of Evidence-based Psychotherapies: A Guide for research and practice.
Edited by C. Freeman & M. Power. Copyright © 2007 John Wiley & Sons, Ltd.

conditioning principles, in the United States the emphasis was on the application of operant conditioning principles in the treatment of dysfunctional behaviour. In 1963, Eysenck
established the journal *Behaviour Research and Therapy,* which to this day is the leading
journal in behaviour therapy.

CLINICAL ASSESSMENT

Clinical assessment plays an important part in behaviour therapy. It is critical in arriving at a
clear definition of the problem behaviour and in evaluating the effects of treatment. Several
modalities of assessment can be distinguished. In addition to interviewing the patient the
most important methods are: self-report using questionnaires, self-monitoring of behaviour
by the patient and behavioural observation by others. Before embarking on treatment, the
therapist uses the collected information to conduct a thorough analysis of the problem
behaviour and associated problems.

Questionnaires, Self-monitoring and Observation of Behaviour

Questionnaires are often useful to generate a first impression of the problem behaviour. Depending on the problem behaviour (for example, anxiety, depression, substance abuse) the
therapist can select from a number of questionnaires that collect domain-specific information. When the domain is depression, the therapist can administer the Beck Depression
Inventory (Beck *et al.,* 1996), which is developed to assess the behavioural manifestations of depression, as well as for example the Pleasant Events Schedule (MacPhillamy &
Lewinsohn, 1976), which aims to assess to what extent the patient still initiates pleasant
activities that may serve as reinforcers. In regards to substance use disorders, the Time Line
Follow-Back (TLFB) method gives a good impression of the quantity and frequency of
drinking/drug taking during the past six months, as well as more detailed information on
pattern of substance use (Sobell, Toneatto & Sobell, 1994). For a comprehensive review of
behavioural assessment in addiction see Emmelkamp & Vedel (2006).

When the therapist and patient have determined what behaviour needs to change, it can
be useful to have the patient complete a self-monitoring diary to elucidate the conditions
under which the behaviour occurs. Such diary registrations can illuminate crucial associations between problem behaviour and critical events (antecedents and consequences of the
problem behaviour). It is important to tailor the registration forms to the individual needs
of the patient. In general, during the self-monitoring phase, patients are asked to record
date and time, the situation they are in, their emotion and its intensity, the presence of any
physical sensations, their automatic thoughts and the occurrence of the problem behaviour.
In contrast to cognitive therapy, where diaries are used as a means of changing cognitions,
in behaviour therapy diaries are used as an assessment instrument to enhance the problem
analysis (see Figure 4.1) and the evaluation of treatment. In this respect, it can also be useful
to monitor behaviour by using counters. This type of behavioural assessment is particularly
useful with high-frequency behaviours, such as tics and obsessions.

Observing behaviour can generate important information. For example, a visit to the play-
ground during break can generate valuable information about a child that does not interact
with its peers. Teachers can perform such behavioural observations, provided they receive

DIARY FORM

SITUATIO N (Were am I, with whom and what is happening?):   Date and time: *02-05-02, 19.55*

I'm at the supermarket. It's crowded because it's nearly closing time. At the checkout there are seven people in front of me.

PHYSICAL SENSATIONS

O chest pain or discomfort	O numbness or tingling sensations
● sweating	● chills or hot flushes
O trembling or shaking	● pounding hart, accelerated heart rate
● sensation of shortness of breath or smothering	O derealization, feelings of unreality
O feeling of choking	O ....
O nausea	
● feeling dizzy or lightheaded	

EMOTION (anxious, sad, happy, angry): Intensity of the emotion (0–100)

Anxious!!!   95
(After leaving the supermarket I felt sad and cried)   60

AUTOMATIC THOUGHTS
(What thoughts were associated with the emotion mentioned above? What thoughts caused you to feel like this in this situation?)

If I'm not out of this supermarket soon, I'll faint.
If I faint, nobody will help me and I might even die.
If I faint, people will think I'm crazy or stupid.

BEHAVI OUR (What did you do when you started feeling like that?):

I parked the shopping trolley in a corner of the supermarket, left all the groceries in it and I just got out of the supermarket as quickly as I could.

Figure 4.1   Diary form: a tool for self-monitoring problem behaviour.

specific instructions about what to observe, thereby precluding interpretations. Another example concerns patients with compulsive behaviours. It can be helpful to have patients perform the compulsive behaviours in their natural environment (usually at home) in the presence of the therapist. These observations often provide the therapist with a much clearer understanding of both the problem behaviour and specific triggering stimuli.

In addition to *in vivo* observations, as described above, it can be useful to role-play problematic past situations. An example may clarify this point. Albert is a patient who is afraid of conflict and arguments but claims not to avoid these situations. During conflict role-play Albert indeed does not avoid arguments. However, when expressing criticism Albert becomes visibly tense and immediately takes back his critical comments, which in turn reduces his tension. Role-play especially can be informative in regards to interpersonal problems.

Problem Analysis

Before starting treatment, it is imperative to conduct a thorough analysis of the problems. This is not identical to arriving at a formal diagnosis. Two patients may satisfy the criteria of a particular DSM-IV diagnosis, but a careful analysis might reveal that patient A would benefit more from method X whereas patient B would likely benefit more from method Y. Problem analysis is indispensable for constructing a treatment plan. In this context, it is useful to distinguish a micro-analysis from a macro-analysis (Emmelkamp, 1982).

A micro-analysis or functional behaviour analysis analyses the behaviour within a certain problem domain. The key questions that the therapist attempts to answer are the following. What are the situations in which the behaviour occurs? Which responses (emotional, physiological, cognitive, overt behaviour) occur? What are the consequences of the behaviour? For an illustration of a micro-analysis we refer the reader to Figure 4.2.

When conducting a macroanalysis, the therapist charts the various problem domains while seeking possible connections between the problems. For instance, a patient may be depressed and also experience marital distress. It is of importance to ascertain whether the depression is associated with the marital problems, or whether these are two independent problem areas. If there is a connection between the depression and the marital problems, the therapist should examine the nature of the relation. If the marital distress is fundamental to the depression it may be appropriate to direct early treatment efforts to improving the relationship. With some patients the relation is reversed; the depression causes the marital distress. In this latter case it is not useful to first address the distress. For an illustration of a macroanalysis we refer the reader to Figure 4.3.

BEHAVIOUR THERAPY: CLINICAL PRACTICE

This section first discusses the therapeutic relationship. Next, a number of common behavioural therapy procedures are reviewed. Given space limitations, we limit the discussion to a number of operant techniques and the most important types of exposure, relaxation and aversion therapy. In addition, we present social skills training, problem-solving training and communication training. For a more comprehensive review, we refer the reader to Emmelkamp (2004)

The Therapeutic Relationship

There are some common misconceptions regarding the nature of the therapeutic relationship in behaviour therapy. It is often thought of as distant, one sided and somewhat authoritarian. Arguably, behaviour therapists themselves are partly responsible for this prejudice as they – in contrast to psychodynamic therapists and experientially oriented therapists, for example – pay scarce attention to the therapeutic relationship in their published work. However, most behaviour therapists recognize the importance of a strong treatment alliance and invest time and effort in establishing a cooperative relationship.

There is currently ample literature demonstrating that 'Rogerian' concepts such as warmth and empathy are also characteristic of the therapeutic relationship in behaviour therapy.

However, in contrast to other therapy schools, these variables are not thought of as merely facilitative for the therapeutic process. In behaviour therapy these concepts are thought of as significant situational variables in the promotion of a learning process and changing problem behaviour. This conceptualization implies that not every patient needs equal amounts of warmth, empathy, structuring, support and so forth. Relevant aspects can also differ from one phase of therapy to the next. Diagnosis and functional analysis (microanalyses and macroanalyses) can contribute to an informed decision regarding a productive relational style. The patient's comportment in the therapeutic alliance is another factor for the therapist to consider when choosing a relational style.

As in other therapies, the behaviour therapist may be faced with phenomena such as resistance or transference. Their perceived significance and the way they are dealt with by the behaviour therapist, however, differ from the way in which psychodynamic therapists perceive and act. When a patient displays resistance, for instance by being consistently late, or by avoiding specific subjects, being taciturn or overly talkative, the therapist will examine what factors might elicit such behaviours (Wright & Davis, 1994). The therapeutic stance regarding resistance is thus, in fact, quite similar to how other problem behaviours are regarded and approached. Making use of his observations and, if needed, additional probing, the therapist will attempt to formulate a functional analysis of the resistance behaviour. As a result, the therapist may learn that the behaviours are better understood by other factors than by the initial impression of treatment resistance. Consider the patient who often looks out of the window and is generally taciturn. On closer inspection it may turn out that these behaviours only occur when the therapy session takes place at the end of a gruelling workday.

Sometimes the patient may resist the (initially) agreed upon treatment objective:

> Arnold openly discusses a multitude of problems that bother him, cooperatively registers his problem behaviours (panic attacks), but consistently sabotages his homework assignments. The first session he forgot his assignments, the second session the neighbour visited, and the third session he spent five minutes on the scheduled exercise instead of the agreed upon 90 minutes. When something like this happens, the therapist should collaboratively re-examine the problem analysis with the patient. In this case it demonstrated that Arnold thought that the treatment approach was far too simplistic for his problems. How were a couple of homework assignments going to cure him of his anxiety attacks that had been haunting him for more than 10 years?

In other instances, assumed negative effects of treatment may explain the treatment resistance:

> A 46 year-old woman suffered from social anxiety and agoraphobia. Initially, treatment (exposure *in vivo*) appeared to be going smoothly, but as the exercises progressed treatment halted. The patient started cancelling appointments and when she did show up she had not completed the assignments. In view of the initial smooth progress, the therapist hypothesized that the stagnation might have to do with fears associated with definitive improvement of the complaints. Inquiry revealed that the patient dreaded having to go back to work for her father, whom she described as an authoritarian man whom she felt unable to stand up to. As a result of this discussion, the functional analysis and treatment plan were revised and patient and therapist agreed to include assertiveness training as part of the treatment.

The therapeutic style should be markedly different with a dependent patient versus a patient with clear narcissistic or paranoid features (Velzen & Emmelkamp, 1996). When working with a dependent phobic patient at the start of treatment, it may be advisable to enquire by telephone how the homework assignments are coming along. With a narcissistic patient, however, the therapist would be advised to refrain from this as it may reinforce the narcissistic tendency to demand excessive attention. The same applies for the paranoid patient as this patient may interpret the therapist's good intentions as doubts as to whether he or she is completing the homework assignments. Note that later in therapy one should fade out the telephone inquiries with the dependent patient as well, as these calls may end up reinforcing the undesired dependent behaviours.

There are some general features that characterize the therapeutic relationship in behaviour therapy:

- The patient is treated as a competent person who will (learn to) maximally contribute (1) to the examination of factors that may have caused or maintained the problem behaviour and (2) to the design of strategies for therapeutic change.
- The therapist and patient collaboratively determine the objectives of treatment. Patients have usually tried a number of strategies to remedy their problem with various degrees of success. The therapist is advised to pay heed to these previous self-directed efforts.
- In behaviour therapy the therapist spends considerable time and attention to non-technical elements such as increasing motivation, explaining the therapeutic model, and introducing techniques and homework assignments.

Schindler's (1988) research shows that the first sessions are crucial for the subsequent progress in therapy. The most important dimension is 'support' – a collective term for such divergent therapeutic intervention as giving positive feedback, reassurance and encouragement and positive reframing. Research by Ford confirms that these expressions of support are pivotal at the start of treatment (Ford, 1978). During the later stages of therapy the patient attaches less importance to the non-specific support and becomes more involved in events outside of therapy (see also Raue & Goldfried, 1994).

BEHAVIOUR THERAPY TREATMENT PROCEDURES

It is difficult to categorize behaviour therapy techniques according to the nature of the involved learning processes. A particular technique may seem to be based on operant conditioning but often other learning processes are (implicitly) involved as well. Nevertheless, under the heading 'operant techniques' we will cover a number of procedures that lean heavily on operant conditioning. The token economy and self-control procedures are discussed, respectively.

Operant Techniques

The basic underlying principle of operant techniques is quite simple: their aim is to reinforce desired behaviour while undesired behaviour is extinguished or punished. A prime example of a (usually inpatient) treatment based on operant principles is the token economy. In a token economy, the therapist distributes so-called tokens for occurrences of desired behaviour (like for example brushing teeth, being timely, conducting a conversation, cleaning the room) with the aim to reinforce this behaviour. Tokens are chips that function as secondary reinforcers. The patient can exchange the tokens for various objects (such as money or sweets) and favours (such as a walk outside the clinic or watching television). The main advantage of tokens is that they can be handed immediately following the desired behaviour. Undesired behaviours (like crying, staying in bed all day, arguing) do not generate tokens, which causes these behaviours – according to the principle of extinction – to extinguish. The direct application of reward and punishment was shown to be effective in a wide variety of patient categories, including children with behavioural problems, schizophrenics and mentally disabled people. Nevertheless, the practical utility of tokens remains paramount.

An important study by Paul & Lentz (1977) documented the random assignment of nearly 100 chronic psychiatric patients to a token economy unit, a milieu therapy unit, or a traditionally organized unit (Paul & Lentz, 1977). The token economy unit was most effective, resulting in more discharges and less prescriptions of medication than in each of the other units. Despite its demonstrated efficacy, the interest in token economies has strongly waned over the past years. This may be partly attributed to the dramatic decrease in the average length of stay of inpatient units and the associated development of ambulatory rehabilitation programmes less suitable for the establishment of token economies.

In the field of substance-abuse treatment research, token economies (voucher-based incentives) are regarded as a promising treatment intervention (Higgens, Alessi & Dantona, 2000). Biochemically verified abstinence from recent drug use is rewarded with vouchers exchangeable for retail items meeting a predetermined therapeutic goal. This voucher-based incentive is often combined with an intensive behavioural treatment known as the community reinforcement approach (CRA) developed by Hunt & Azrin (1973). In their overview of research on the voucher-incentive approach, Higgens, Alessi and Dantona (2000) conclude it to be effective in the treatment of cocaine dependence and a promising treatment intervention regarding other substance-use disorders (alcohol, marijuana, nicotine and opioid dependence). However, the effectiveness of this type of intervention has been tested mainly in specialized research clinics and its usefulness in everyday drug-abuse treatment practice remains to be seen (Emmelkamp & Vedel, 2006).

The behaviour therapy approach to depression is based on the assumption that depressive symptoms originate from a deficit of reinforcement for constructive and pleasant behaviours and that depression will remit to the extent the reinforcement of those behaviours increases (Lewinsohn, 1975). Behavioural approaches attempt to change behaviour in order to secure an increase of positive reinforcers. According to this view, depressive cognitions (like, for example, 'I am worthless') are the result of depressed mood and these cognitions change as a result of changing behaviour and the increase of reinforcers.

Treatments derived from Lewinsohn's theory encourage the patient to participate in constructive and pleasurable activities. Activities that patients used to enjoy but ceased doing are now scheduled as homework assignments. Activities are ordered in a hierarchical fashion. Less challenging activities are scheduled first; more challenging activities follow later on in treatment. A number of studies have investigated whether this reinforcement of pleasant and constructive activities would, by itself, lead to a decrease in negative affect. The evidence demonstrated that the increase in pleasant activities indeed gave rise to mood improvement (Emmelkamp 1994). Another way to achieve reinforcement from social interactions is social skills training, which is discussed later.

Rehm (1977) proposed a self-control model for depression that offers a framework for integrating the cognitive and behavioural models (Rehm, 1977). Rehm endorses the importance of reinforcement in depression but posits that reinforcement is not limited to external sources. People can also reinforce themselves, independent of their environment. According to Rehm, the depressed mood and inactivity of depressed patients is the result of negative self-evaluations, reinforcement deficits and excessive self-punishment. Self-reinforcement and self-punishment can take place in behaviour and in thought. His self-control programme for depression consists of six weeks' training in self-registration, self-evaluation and self-reinforcement. Patients are required to complete diaries to register the positive activities they carry out each day (self-registration). During the self-evaluation phase, the therapist emphasizes realistic goal setting. Patients have to select specific and achievable sub-goals and they are subsequently required to judge their progress on a numerical scale (self-evaluation). Next, they receive instructions how to reward themselves when they achieve one of the sub-goals (self-reinforcement). This programme has been shown to be effective with mild to moderately depressed patients, although it is not clear which ingredients of the programme are critical for the observed effects (Emmelkamp 1994).

Exposure

Exposure is a general term for various procedures that have in common that patients are exposed to situations that elicit tension and anxiety and that they are inclined to avoid or flee the situation (Van Hout & Emmelkamp, 2002). Traditionally there were two principal ways in which exposure might take place:

- *in vitro,* or in imagination, in which the patient imagines himself in the anxiety-eliciting situation (also referred to as imaginal exposure);
- *in vivo,* or in reality, in which the patient is in effect exposed to the anxiety-eliciting situation.

It is often difficult to motivate the patient to confront the feared situation. When this happens, the therapist may employ modelling procedures: i.e. the therapist (or another person) may demonstrate the desired approach behaviours in the feared situation.

Two procedural forms of exposure-based treatments can be distinguished:

- Gradual or self-guided exposure. The patient controls the exposure by determining when s/he progresses to the next situation of a higher (threat or anxiety) level.
- Flooding and prolonged exposure *in vivo*. The therapist controls the extent and duration of the exposure.

A short vignette of a dog-phobic patient may clarify the above distinctions. In gradual exposure, therapist and patient collaboratively construct a hierarchy of fear-eliciting situations that the patient usually avoids. These situations are ranked from easy/not challenging to (very) difficult/challenging. An example of an easy item might be 'watching a picture of a puppy' whereas an example of a difficult item might be 'being alone in a room with a Rottweiler'. When the first situation is successfully mastered – the patient experiences no fear – the next step in the hierarchy is confronted, until finally the entire fear hierarchy is completed.

During flooding, the therapist confronts the patient with the most challenging (fear-provoking) situations right away. In our case, this means that the patient is required to be in a room alone with the Rottweiler. The objective is to have the patient habituate to the fear, which allows for the extinction of the fear response.

Flooding *in vivo* is sometimes also referred to as 'prolonged exposure *in vivo*', where 'prolonged' refers to the extended time interval required to achieve habituation. The exposure interval, during which no escape or avoidance is allowed, can last up to two hours. Prolonged exposure *in vivo* is generally the most successful exposure treatment.

However, it can be difficult or impossible to conduct exposure *in vivo* sessions for individuals with some complaints. Imaginal exposure and to some extent virtual-reality exposure (VRE) can then be useful alternatives. Virtual-reality exposure integrates real-time computer graphics, body tracking devices, visual displays, and other sensory inputs to immerse individuals in a computer-generated virtual environment. A number of VR case studies have reported on fear of flying, acrophobia, claustrophobia, spider phobia, and agoraphobia. Moreover, recent controlled studies provide substantial empirical support that VR exposure is at least as effective as exposure *in vivo* treatment for patients with acrophobia (Emmelkamp *et al.*, 2001; Emmelkamp *et al.*, 2002; Krijn *et al.*, 2004) and fear of flying (Krijn, Emmelkamp & Olafsson, 2004).

A modification of the basic principle of exposure is the exposure with response prevention paradigm. This mode of exposure is regularly applied in the treatment of problem behaviours in which certain stimuli elicit maladaptive coping behaviours (for example, drinking/drug use in substance use disorders, vomiting and excessive exercising in bulimia nervosa, and compulsions in obsessive-compulsive disorders).

Exposure is also the underlying principle of behaviour therapies that are focused on the processing of negative experiences, such as those used in post-traumatic stress and complicated bereavement. As a hierarchical presentation of salient stimuli is often not feasible, flooding is most typically used with these problems. Although exposure *in vivo* can be an important component of the treatment, imaginary exposure is typically most central to the treatment of these problems. The efficacy of exposure-based treatments among war veterans and victims of other trauma (such as rape) has been adequately documented (Emmelkamp, 2004; Rothbaum *et al.*, 2000). Exposure for post-traumatic stress can also be conducted by means of writing assignments and treatment may even be applied through the Internet (Lange *et al.*, 2003). The effects of exposure-based bereavement therapy are less convincing as yet (Sireling & Cohen, 1988).

Drug-taking and drinking behaviour are strongly cue and context specific and cue-exposure treatment (CET) is regarded as 'probably efficacious' by Chambless & Ollendick (2001). However, Conklin & Tiffany (2002) are less optimistic and conclude in their meta-analyses that there is no consistent evidence for the efficacy of cue exposure in the treatment of substance-use disorders. When the treatment goal is moderation of drinking rather than abstinence, results are also inconclusive. Sirtarthan *et al.* (2001) compared a moderation goal-orientated CET with cognitive-behaviour therapy in a population of non-dependent alcohol-abusing patients and found a significant decrease in alcohol consumption at post-treatment and at follow-up. Heather *et al.* (2000) found moderation goal oriented CET as effective as behavioural self-control training.

Relaxation

Exposure-based treatment may sometimes be accompanied by additional elements. In systematic desensitization, relaxation is added to the exposure to the anxiety-eliciting situation. Relaxation is not essential for successful exposure however. Relaxation exercises focus on the physiological component of anxiety and tension. The patient learns, first in the therapist's office and later at home, to relax various muscle groups progressively. It is essential that the patient first learns to recognize tension in the different muscle groups. Accordingly, he can apply the relaxation effectively when the early signs of tension manifest themselves.

In behaviour therapy, relaxation exercises are applied much more widely than merely as a component of systematic desensitization. Relaxation training has been an important component of various treatments, most notably in the treatment of generalized anxiety disorder. Relaxation training can also be useful in treating tension headaches and disturbed sleep.

Aversion Therapy

Aversion therapy includes a variety of specific techniques based on both classical and operant conditioning paradigms. Aversion therapy used to be widely employed in the treatment of alcohol abuse/ dependence, but is currently more of historical interest. With aversive conditioning in alcohol-dependent subjects a noxious stimulus (UCS) is paired with actual drinking (CS) or with visual or olfactory cues related to drinking, with the aim of establishing a conditioned aversion for drinking. A variety of aversive stimuli have been used, the most popular of which were electric shocks and nausea- or apnea-inducing substances. Covert sensitization is a variant of aversive conditioning wherein images (for example of drinking situations or of deviant sexual stimuli) are paired with imaginal aversive stimuli (for example a scene in which the patient vomits all over himself). It is called 'covert' because neither the undesirable stimulus nor the aversive stimulus is actually presented, except in the imagination. 'Sensitization' refers to the intention to build up an avoidance response to the undesirable stimulus. Aversion therapy has been ethically controversial and research has not supported its efficacy (Emmelkamp & Kamphuis 2002).

Social Skills Training

According to Liberman (1988) the following skills are necessary to display socially competent behaviour:

- accurate perception of the social situation;
- translation of the perception into a plan of action;
- the execution of the behaviour with adequate verbal and non-verbal behaviour.

In social skills training, patients learn to be more effective in expressing their emotions and to assert themselves. The training can be conducted in individual and group format. In addition to verbal assertiveness the training covers non-verbal aspects of assertiveness, like voice pitch, posture and eye contact.

Social skills training may target (change in) the following behaviours: making a request, refusing a request, expressing a personal opinion, expressing criticism, responding to criticism, asserting oneself. Over the course of repeated role-play the patient learns to perform these behaviours in a more adequate fashion. Key techniques used by the therapist include modelling, feedback, and behavioural rehearsal. The patient is gradually shaped into effective execution of the required skills. Homework assignments include the registration of (naturally occurring) difficult social situations and, later in therapy, the deliberate practice of the instructed skills in selected difficult social situations.

Social skills training has demonstrated its efficacy in treating patients with social phobia (Mersch, *et al.*, 1991; Stravinsky & Armado, 2002). However, patients with other problems can also benefit from social skills training as a component of their treatment. For example, several lines of evidence support the importance of skills training for alcoholics. Among an inpatient group of alcohol-dependent patients in Norway, the effect of social skills training was compared to a (non-treatment) control group (Erikson *et al.*, 1986). At one year follow-up, patients who had received social skills training had consumed significantly less alcohol and had worked more days than the control patients. Further, studies indicate that alcoholics'coping skills are inferior to the coping skills of non-alcoholics in situations that commonly pose a risk of relapse, such as family conflicts and parties in which there is a pressure to drink (Monti & Rohsenow, 1999). In addition, a substantial number of patients who relapsed reported frustrating situations in which they were unable to express their anger adequately, prior to their relapse (Marlatt, 1996). Social skills training now is a central component of various relapse prevention programmes (Emmelkamp & Vedel, 2006; Monti & Rohsenow, 1999).

Lewinsohn & Hoberman (1982) proposed the hypothesis that a social skills deficit may be responsible for the deficit in social reinforcement that a depressed person experiences. A number of studies demonstrated that social skills training not only leads to improved social skills but also to improved mood (Emmelkamp, 1994).

Social skills training was also an effective part of the treatment among chronic psychiatric patients and schizophrenics. It led to improvements in both behavioural assessments and behaviour at the clinic (Dilk & Bond, 1996; Heinssen, Liberman & Kopelowicz, 2000; Penn & Mueser, 1996). Generally, social skills training led to significant improvements in social skills on role-play tests, but not on psychopathology. The question remains to what extent the acquired behaviours generalize to outside the psychiatric setting. Social skills training certainly does not represent a panacea for schizophrenia (Emmelkamp, 2004).

Problem-solving Skills Training

Problem-solving skills training (D'Zurilla, 1986) has a heavy psycho-educational emphasis: executed according to a fixed number of steps and applicable across a wide array of problems. The steps are:

1. Problem orientation, during which patients explore their personal attitude towards problems. The most important aspects are that the patients learn to recognize their negative feelings as signals of problems and learn to distinguish between problems over which one can exert personal control (such as arguments) versus those where one can not (such as cancer).
2. Problem definition, during which the patient and therapist clarify ambiguous references to the problem and define a goal.
3. Brainstorming, during which the patient and therapist generate as many different solutions as possible, without critical appraisal or censure.
4. Choice. A systematic appraisal of advantages and disadvantages is discussed for each solution. The patient selects the most effective option.
5. Execution, during which the patient executes the selected solution and evaluates its effect.

This training is a highly useful component in a number of behaviour therapeutic methods across a variety of problem areas. To illustrate, many depressed patients are characterized by deficient problem-solving skills (Nezu, 1987) and there is evidence that problem-solving training contributes to mood improvement among depressives. Problem-solving training is also an important part of communication training among couples with relationship distress (Emmelkamp et al., 1988). Favourable results were also reported when problem-solving training was added to exposure in vivo in the treatment of agoraphobic patients (Kleiner et al., 1987). Likewise, among schizophrenic patients, problem-solving training was shown to be an important supplement to social skills training (Hansen, 1985).

Communication Training

The main objective of communication training is to teach couples how to improve their communication. Partners receive training in skills that enable them to talk to one another more effectively. The following skills are instructed in a structured fashion: active listening, expression of empathy, expression of emotion, and assertiveness. When the partners have adequately mastered these skills they can apply them when discussing their specific relationship issues. The therapist also applies the systematic problem-solving training as part of the course. Modelling, feedback, shaping and role playing are specific techniques used in communication training. Prior to formulating the treatment plan, the therapist will make a functional analysis of the relationship problems. A number of studies have demonstrated the efficacy of behavioural communication training among couples with relationship distress (Emmelkamp, 1988).

Relationship distress between partners can give rise to a dramatic increase in the risk of clinical depression. About half of the women who are in treatment for depression report marital difficulties. In some cases individual therapy for the depressed patient is inadequate and needs to be supplemented with treatment efforts focused on the relationship issues.

Three controlled studies examined the effect of couple's therapy (communication training) on depression (Beach & O'Leary, 1992; Emanuels-Zuurveen & Emmelkamp 1996; Jacobson et al., 1991). There was no overall difference in mood improvement between patients in the individual cognitive behavioural therapy versus those in couple's therapy but relationship improvement was significantly higher among patients in couple's therapy. These findings suggest that depressed patients with marital difficulties are better served by couple's therapy than by individual cognitive behavioural therapy. Moreover, the additional benefit in terms of relationship improvement can be an important factor in the prevention of relapse.

CASE DESCRIPTION

The many aspects of the behaviour change process discussed above are illustrated in the following case description of an alcohol-dependent depressed female (Vedel & Emmelkamp, 2004). As illustrated below, the clinician should view a case formulation as a working model, one that is open to revision due to new evidence.

Present Complaints

Dianne (52 years old, married, no children) increasingly called her husband Mick at work, sometimes several times a day, complaining of being lonely and craving for a drink. Sometimes Mick would stop work and go to his wife to support her. When together with her husband, Dianne had been able to control her drinking but she now also started drinking during the times Mick was at home.

Dianne had been drinking excessively for the past four years, between 12 and 24 units a day (mostly beer and wine), for several days in a row. After a number of days she then would collapse (too sick to drink) for two days after which she would resume drinking. Besides drinking, Dianne complained about feeling depressed, not being able to structure her day, having difficulty sleeping and eating, having sore muscles, being lonely, feeling guilty and worthless, being on edge all the time, not being able to control her worrying, and having occasional panic attacks. Until 1994 Dianne worked as a community nurse and did not drink much. Due to some reorganization the workload increased, which led to severe burnout. Dianne stopped working and the frequency and the quantity of her drinking increased. She started drinking at home on a daily basis and took tranquilizers (Oxazepam).

During 1998, Dianne was admitted for detoxification (one-week hospitalization) and subsequently treated in a day-care programme at an addiction treatment facility. She kept on drinking; however, her depressive and anxiety symptoms only increased and her relationship with Mick deteriorated.

When we first saw Dianne and Mick in 2000, Dianne had just started using Acamprosate (an anti-craving drug) prescribed by her general practitioner. Dianne was also suffering from depressive symptoms, uncontrollable worrying and situational panic attacks. Dianne had a score of 31 on the Beck Depression Inventory (BDI) (Beck *et al.*, 1961), which is considered rather severe. In view of the fact of a possible substance-related artefact we postponed diagnosing major depression and generalized anxiety disorder. Dianne did not meet the criteria for panic disorder.

Dianne had partly started drinking because of feeling anxious and depressed but her drinking had also made her more anxious and depressed. Using the International Personality Disorder Examination (IPDE) (Loranger, 1999), a semi-structured diagnostic interview, Dianne was diagnosed as having an avoidant and obsessive-compulsive personality disorder.

Mick and Dianne each had their own apartment during the week; during the weekends and holidays Mick stayed at Dianne's place. Preparing for his upcoming retirement, Mick was now going to move in with Dianne.

Marital Adjustment

According to the Maudsley Marital Satisfaction Questionnaire (MMQ) (Arrindell, Emmelkamp & Bast, 1983). Mick was clearly more negative about their relationship than Dianne as is evident from the fact that Mick had a score of 42 while Dianne had a score of 20 on marital dissatisfaction. The Level of Expressed Emotion (LEE) (Cole & Kazarian, 1988) showed that Mick experienced little emotional support from his wife. Dianne was more positive, finding Mick supportive in some areas. To establish if there was any form of violence or fear of violence, verbal or physical abuse, we used the Conflict Tactics Scale (CTS) (Straus, 1979) and interviewed both partners. In the past year Dianne had hit her

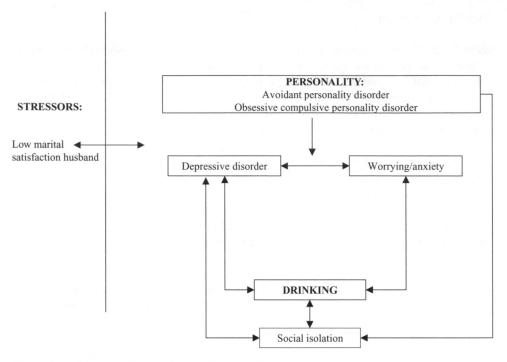

Figure 4.2 Macro analyses of Dianne's complaints.

husband twice while being drunk; in one of these instances Mick had hit her back. Both part-ners agreed this had been an isolated incident and were convinced there would be no future violence.

Macroanalysis

Concerning Dianne, there were four major related and intertwining issues: her drinking, her depressive mood, her anxious symptoms and marital problems. In addition, Dianne met criteria for both the avoidant personality disorder and the obsessive-compulsive personality disorder.

  Many of Dianne's symptoms (such as sleeping difficulties, muscle tension, poor con-centration and low self-esteem) could be accounted for by each of the four problem areas discussed above. We decided to focus our attention on Dianne's drinking as a first step. In general – even with severe comorbid conditions – targeting the drinking problem is the treatment of choice. There is no evidence that, if the patient is not able to control his or her alcohol consumption, targeting other pathology cooccurring with alcohol dependence will be effective and should be considered as a first choice for treatment.

Prioritization of Treatment Strategies

Behavioural couple therapy (BCT) is as effective as individual CBT not only with alcohol abuse but also with depression and anxiety disorders (Emmelkamp & Vedel, 2002). Because of Mick's early retirement and the consequences this was going to have on their relationship, and taking into account their overall low marital satisfaction, we decided to offer Dianne and her husband BCT, focusing on the drinking problem as well as their relationship. If still needed, the spouse-aided therapy for alcohol abuse could be supplemented by spouse-aided therapy for depression or anxiety. Because Dianne had already started using Acamprostate, we agreed that she would continue using the anti-craving agent during the course of our treatment.

Course of Treatment and Assessment of Progress

Initially, Dianne and Mick's treatment followed a BCT manual (Emmelkamp & Vedel, 2006).

The first two sessions were used for psycho-education, explaining the treatment rationale and introducing the sobriety trust contract. We agreed upon abstinence rather than moderation as the treatment goal.

As for the sobriety trust contract; each day at a specific time, in order to prevent the couple arguing about her drinking behaviour throughout the day, Dianne was to initiate a brief discussion with Mick and reiterate her intention not to drink. Dianne was then to ask Mick if he had any questions or fears about possible drinking that day and answer the questions in an attempt to reassure him. Mick was not to mention past or possible future drinking beyond that day.

Behavioral Analysis (Microanalysis)

In order to obtain more information about Dianne's drinking pattern, we asked her to keep a diary. Every time she felt the urge to drink she had to write down where she was (situation), what her feelings were (emotions), what she was thinking or seeing (cognitions or images) and any physical sensations she might be experiencing. She was also asked to rate (1–10) the amount of craving she had experienced, which appeared to be highly related to fluctuations in her depressed mood. The diary was used to identify high-risk situations and to detect seemingly irrelevant decisions that sometimes cumulated into high-risk situations (for example, not getting out of bed in the morning or skipping a planned trip to the supermarket).

Using the daily recordings mentioned above, we introduced the behavioural analysis as a framework of hypotheses with respect to antecedents and consequences of (drinking) behaviour. It was important, during this first phase, to show Dianne and Mick the loop in which Dianne had caught herself; the consequences of her drinking (such as feeling bad about oneself) also being a reason for her to start drinking. During this phase, we also addressed Mick's part in his wife's drinking behaviour. We wanted to decrease those of Mick's behaviours that triggered or rewarded drinking and to increase behaviours that triggered or rewarded non-drinking. For example, it was explained to the couple, that, although acting out of concern, Mick's tendency to come home when Dianne complained about feeling lonely increased the frequency of phone calls and her dependency upon him.

Increasing Positive Interactions

From session two onwards we also tried to increase positive interaction between the couple. We wanted to shift Dianne and Mick's attention from recording only one another's negative behaviours (attentional bias), to also being able to recognize positive behaviours. As a

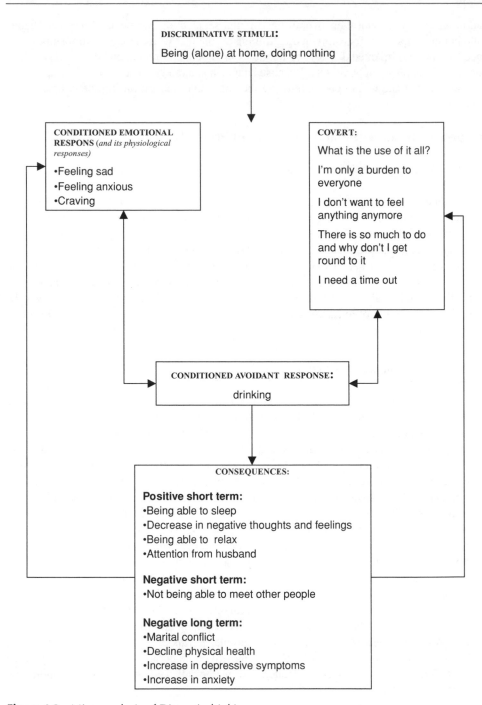

Figure 4.3   Microanalysis of Dianne's drinking.

homework assignment we asked both of them to write down pleasant or positive behaviours that they had observed in each other (for example, asking how the day was or getting up to make some coffee). We also attempted to increase the number of positive behaviours of Dianne and Mick. Trying to identify possible pleasant activities, we asked the couple to talk about pleasant things they did together during the time they were dating each other. In the case of Dianne and Mick they liked going out for dinner and going to the movies. We asked them to take turns in planning comparable pleasant activities.

Identifying High-risk Situations

Using Dianne's diary we identified the most important high-risk situations: staying at home alone and feeling sad or worrying about household chores. We introduced different ways of coping with craving, the two most important being getting involved in some distracting activity and talking about it with someone who can support you.

During these first weeks Dianne was relatively successful in remaining abstinent. Sometimes she would lapse into a one-day drinking episode but the next day she would be able to restrain herself from further drinking. Much time was spent relabelling these 'failures'. Rather then focusing on failure we tried to shift attention to the antecedents that had made Dianne drink in the first place (adding them to the behavioural analysis) and which thoughts/actions had helped her the next day to restrain herself.

Management of Depressed Mood

Although Dianne's sleeping and eating improved to some extent, her worrying lessened and her panic attack disappeared, Dianne kept on feeling sad and low on energy. Thus, the probable diagnosis of general anxiety disorder was not confirmed; however, the diagnosis of depressive disorder was reaffirmed. Therefore after seven sessions of alcohol treatment, the manual *Spouse-aided Therapy with Depressive Disorders* (Emanuels-Zuurveen & Emmelkamp, 1997) was incorporated into Dianne and Mick's treatment programme.

Inactivity being one of Dianne's most salient high-risk situations, we introduced activity training as an intervention to tackle negative mood as well as her drinking problem. Activation training is a fairly common behavioural technique in treating depression, derived from Lewinson's theory of depression. We encouraged Mick to help his wife in organizing her week: combining basic daily activities (like getting dressed in the morning), taking care of neglected activities (such as cleaning up the bedroom) and increasing the amount of pleasant activities (listening to music, going out for a cup of coffee with a friend). Given Dianne's social anxiety, a gradual approach was used in having her engage in social situations.

Communication Training

Communication training was introduced from session nine onwards. During this training both partners' personalities became more salient, this may be due to the fact the drinking and depressive symptoms had lessened. In addition, we addressed assertiveness, not only because of Dianne's social anxiety but also because both partners found it difficult to express disapproval and make a request. During these sessions it became clear that Mick had great difficulty handling Dianne's preoccupation with details and her reluctance to delegate tasks unless he submitted to exactly her way of doing things. We had the couple express their expectations about the future and about their (renewed) relationship toward one another. We found it important to address realistic goal setting, especially because Dianne had very high expectations about Mick moving in with her.

In order to enhance her social support network, we encouraged Dianne to start to visit her old friends again, since she had been neglecting these contacts in the past few years. We also encouraged Dianne to start thinking about working again. She enrolled in a volunteer working programme and started as a hostess in a hospital.

Relapse Prevention

During the final stages of the treatment much time was spent planning for emergencies and coping with future (re)lapses. Dianne and Mick designed their own personal (re)lapse-prevention manual using problem-solving techniques. Different alternatives were discussed like Dianne talking about her craving with Mick, Mick being allowed to confront Dianne with high-risk behaviours (for example, not getting out of bed in the morning) and expressing his concern about the matter, and reintroducing the sobriety trust contract.

Evaluation

At the end of treatment (19 sessions, during a 7-month period) Dianne had been abstinent for two-and-a-half months and no longer met criteria for major depressive disorder: her BDI score dropped to 10, which is considered to be within the normal range. Dianne's confidence in controlling her drinking increased (SCQ). Results show Dianne to be confident about remaining abstinent even when depressed or sad. She was still convinced she would not be able to limit her drinking after one or two drinks.

During the course of the treatment Mick's marital dissatisfaction decreased from 41 to 22 (MMQ). Dianne's score did not change significantly. At post-treatment both partners were near the cut-off point differentiating martially distressed from non-martially distressed couples. The LEE showed Mick to experience more emotional support from his wife compared to the situation before treatment. Dianne seemed to find Mick somewhat less supportive then before treatment.

SUMMARY AND CONCLUSIONS

Exposure therapies are the treatment of choice in adult specific phobia, social phobia, agoraphobia, and obsessive-compulsive disorder (Emmelkamp, 2004) and have also been found quite effective in phobic children (Nauta *et al.*, 2003). Studies of the behavioural treatment of depression have come to a standstill due to the rise of cognitive therapy in this area but the lack of further research into the behavioural treatment of depression is not justified by the data. There are still a number of important issues that need to be addressed. For example, we have no idea why cognitive therapy, behavioural interventions, IPT and pharmacotherapy work equally well with depressed patients, although various researchers provide various theoretical explanations. Unfortunately, to date there is no evidence that either cognitive or behavioural theories explain the improvements achieved with these various treatment procedures.

In the area of substance abuse the interest has moved away from aversive procedures into multifaceted self-control programmes. One of the promising areas for future research is relapse prevention. The results of studies that investigated coping skills programmes to prevent relapse look promising. Another new area that looks promising is spouse-aided therapy as illustrated in the case described above.

Although behaviour therapists have been very productive in evaluating the efficacy of various techniques, relatively little attention has been devoted to the therapeutic process. It is, however, becoming increasingly clear that the quality of the therapeutic relationship may be influential in determining success or failure of behavioural therapies, although well-controlled studies in this area are rare. It is a common misconception that behaviour therapists are 'unempathic' and apply only techniques.

There are marked differences between therapy as conducted in outcome studies and therapy in clinical practice, where it is usually adapted to the individual needs of the patient. For example, clinicians emphasize the importance of the functional behaviour analysis. However, research into the value of the functional behaviour analysis is almost lacking. In a study by Emmelkamp, Bouman & Blaauw (1974) in patients with obsessive-compulsive disorder and a study by Schulte *et al.* (1992) in patients with phobias standardized treatment (exposure and response prevention) proved as effective as idiosyncratic treatment based on a functional behavioural analysis. It seems that the standardized treatment protocols developed over the years have not yet been beaten by an individualized behavioural treatment.

REFERENCES

Beach, S.R.H. & O'Leary, K.D. (1992). Treating depression in the context of marital discord: Outcome and predictors of response of marital therapy versus cognitive therapy. *Behavior Therapy, 23*, 507–528.

Beck, A.T. Steer, A. & Brown, G.K. (1996). *Manual for Beck Depression Inventory-II*. San Antonio, TX: Psychological Corporation.

Chambless, D.L., Ollendick, T.H. (2001) Empirically supported psychological interventions: Controversies and evidence. *Annual Review of Psychology, 52*, 685–716.

Clark, D.M. & Salkovskis, P.M. (1994). A comparison of cognitive therapy, applied relaxation and imipramine in the treatment of panic disorder. *British Journal of Psychiatry, 164*, 759–769.

Conklin, C.A., Tiffany, S.T. (2002). Applying extinction research and theory to cue-exposure addiction treatments. *Addiction, 97*, 155–167.

Dilk, M.N. & Bond, G.R. (1996). Meta-analytic evaluation of skills training research for individuals with severe mental illness. *Journal of Consulting and Clinical Psychology, 64*(6), 1337–1346.

Donahoe, C.P. & Driesenga, S.A (1989). A review of social skills training with chronic mental patients. In M. Hersen, R.M. Eisler & P.M. Miller (eds), *Progress in Behavior Modification*. New York: Academic Press.

D'Zurilla, T.J. (1986). *Problem-solving Therapy: A Social Competence Approach to Clinical Intervention*. New York: Springer.

Emanuels-Zuurveen, L. & Emmelkamp, P.M.G. (1996). Individual behavioural-cognitive therapy versus marital therapy for depresson in maritally distressed couples. *British Journal of Psychiatry, 169*, 181–188.

Emmelkamp, P.M.G. (1982). *Phobic and Obsessive-compulsive Disorders: Theory, Research and Practice*. New York: Plenum.

Emmelkamp, P.M.G. (1994). Behavior therapy with adults. In A. Bergin & S. Garfield (eds), *Handbook of Psychotherapy and Behavior Change*. New York: Wiley.

Emmelkamp, P.M.G. (2004). Behavior therapy with adults. In M. Lambert (ed.), *Bergin and Garfield's Handbook of Psychotherapy and Behavior Change* (5th edn). Wiley: New York, pp. 393–446.

Emmelkamp, P.M.G., Bouman, T. & Blaauw, E. (1994). Individualized versus standardized therapy: A comparative evaluation with obsessive-compulsive patients. *Clinical Psychology and Psychotherapy, 1*, 95–100.

Emmelkamp, P.M.G., Bruynzeel, M., Drost, L. *et al.* (2001). Virtual reality treatment in acrophobia: A comparison with exposure in vivo. *CyberPsychology and Behavior, 4*, 335–340.

Emmelkamp, P.M.G. & Kamphuis, J.H. (2002). Aversion relief. In M. Hersen and W. H. Sledge (eds), *Encyclopedia of Psychotherapy*, Vol. 1 (pp. 139–143). New York: Academic Press.

Emmelkamp, P.M.G., Krijn, M., Hulsbosch, L. *et al.* (2002). Virtual reality treatment versus exposure in vivo: a comparative evaluation in acrophobia. *Behaviour Research and Therapy, 40*, 509–516.

Emmelkamp, P.M.G., Van der Linden – Van den Heuvell, C. *et al.* (1988). Cognitive and behavioral interventions: A comparative evaluation with clinically distressed couples. *Journal of Family Psychology, 1*, 365–377.

Emmelkamp, P.M.G & Vedel, E. (2002). Spouse-aided therapy. In M. Hersen & W. Sledge (eds), *The Encyclopedia of Psychotherapy*, Vol. 2 (pp. 693–698). New York: Academic Press.

Emmelkamp, P.M.G. & Vedel, E. (2006). *Evidence-based Treatment of Alcohol and Drug Abuse: A Practitioner's Guide to Theory, Research and Treatment*. New York: Routledge/Taylor & Francis.

Erikson, L., Björnstad, S. & Götestam, K.G. (1986). Social skills training in groups of alcoholics: One year treatment outcome for groups and individuals. *Addictive Behaviors, 11*, 309–329.

Eysenck, H.J. (1952). The effects of psychotherapy: An evaluation. *Journal of Consulting Psychology, 16*, 319–324.

Ford, J.D. (1978). Therapeutic relationship in behavior therapy: An empirical analysis. *Journal of Consulting and Clinical Psychology, 46*, 1302–1314.

Halford, W.K. & R. Haynes (1991). Psychosocial rehabilitation of chronic schizophrenic patients: Recent findings on social skills training and family psychoeducation. *Clinical Psychology Review, 11*, 23–44.

Hansen, D.J., St Lawrence, J.S. & Guistoff, K.A. (1985). Effects of interpersonal problem-solving training with chronic aftercare patients on problem-solving component skills and effectiveness of solutions. *Journal of Consulting and Clinical Psychology, 53*, 167–174.

Heather, N., Brodie, J., Wale, S. *et al.* (2000) A randomized controlled trial of moderation-oriented cue exposure. *Journal of Studies on Alcohol, 61*, 561–570.

Heinssen, R., Liberman, R.P. & Kopelowicz, A. (2000). Psychosocial skills training for schizophrenia: lessons from the laboratory. *Schizophrenia Bulletin, 26*, 21–45.

Higgins, S.T., Alessi, S. & Dantona, R.L. (2000). Voucher-based incentives: A substance abuse treatment innovation. *Addictive Behaviors, 27*, 887–910.

Hogarty, G.E., Jorna, C.M., Reiss, D.J. *et al.* (1986). Family psychoeducation, social skills training and maintenance chemotherapy in the aftercare treatment of schizophrenia. *Archives of General Psychiatry, 43*, 633–642.

Hunt, G.M. & Azrin, N.H. (1973). A community-reinforcement approach to alcoholism. *Behaviour Research and Therapy, 11*, 91–104.

Jacobson, N.S., Dobson, K., Frusetti, A.E. *et al.* (1991). Marital therapy as a treatment for depression. *Journal of Consulting and Clinical Psychology, 59*, 547–557.

Kanfer, L. (1990). History of behavior modification. In A.S. Bellack & M. Hersen and A.E. Kazdin (eds), *International Handbook of Behavior Modification and Therapy*. New York: Plenum.

Kleiner, L., Marshall, W.L. & Spevack, M. *et al.* (1987). Training in problem-solving and exposure treatment for agoraphobics with panic attacks. *Journal of Anxiety Disorders, 1*, 219–238.

Krijn, M., Emmelkamp, P.M.G., Biemond, R. *et al.* (2004a). Treatment of acrophobia in virtual reality. The role of immersion and presence. *Behaviour Research and Therapy, 42*, 229–239.

Krijn, M., Emmelkamp, P.M.G. & Olafsson, R. (2004b). Virtual reality exposure therapy in anxiety disorders. *Clinical Psychology Review, 24*, 259–281.

Lange, A., Rietdijk, D., Hudcovicova, M. *et al.* (2003). INTERAPY. A controlled randomized trial of the standardized treatment of posttraumatic stress through the Internet. *Journal of Consulting & Clinical Psychology, 71*, 901–909.

Lewinsohn, P.M. (1975). The behavioral study and treatment of depression. In M. Hersen, R.M. Eisler & Miller, P.M. (eds), *Progress in Behavior Modification*. New York: Academic Press.

Lewinsohn, P M. and Hoberman, H.M. (1982). Depression. In A.S. Bellack, M. Hersen & A.E. Kazdin. *International Handbook of Behavior Modification and Therapy*. New York: Plenum.

Liberman, R.P. (1988). Social skills training. In R.P. Liberman. *Psychiatric Rehabilitation of Chronic Mental Patients*. Washington: American Psychiatric Press.

Liberman, R.P., Mueser, K.T. & Wallace, C. J. (1986). Social skills training for schizophrenic individuals at risk for relapse. *American Journal of Psychiatry, 143*, 523–526.

MacPhillamy, D.J. & Lewinsohn, P.M. (1976). *Manual for the Pleasants Event Schedule*. Portland, OR: University of Oregon.

Marlatt, G.A. (1996). Taxonomy of high-risk situations for alcohol relapse. *Addiction, 91*, 37–49.

Mawson, D., Marks, I. & Ramm, E. *et al.* (1981). Guided mourning for morbid grief: A controlled study. *British Journal of Psychiatry, 138*, 185–193.

Mersch, P.P.A., Emmelkamp, P.M.G., Bogels, S.M. *et al.* (1991). Social phobia: Individual response patterns and the long-term effect of behavioral and cognitive interventions. A follow-up study. *Behaviour Research and Therapy, 27*, 421–434.

Monti, P.M. & Rohsenow, D.J. (1999). Coping-skills training and cue-exposure therapy in the treatment of alcoholism. *Alcohol Research and Health, 23*, 107–150.

Nauta, M.H., Scholing, A., Emmelkamp, P.M.G. & Minderaa, R.M. (2003). Cognitive-behavioural therapy for anxiety disordered children in a clinical setting: No surplus value of a cognitive parent training. *Journal of the American Academy of Child & Adolescent Psychiatry, 42*, 1270–1278.

Nezu, A.H. (1987). A problem-solving formulation of depression: A literature review and proposal of a pluralistic model. *Clinical Psychology Review, 7*, 121–144.

Öst, L.G. & Westling, B.E. (1995). Applied relaxation versus cognitive behaviour therapy in the treatment of panic disorder. *Behaviour Research and Therapy, 33*, 145–158.

Paul, G.L. & Lentz, R.J. (1977). *Psychosocial Treatment of Chronic Mental Patients: Milieu Versus Social-learning Programs*. Cambridge: Harvard University Press.

Penn, D. & Mueser, K.T. (1996). Research update on the psychosocial treatment of schizophrenia. *American Journal of Psychiatry, 153*, 607–617.

Ramsay, R. (1979). Bereavement. *Trends in Behaviour Therapy*. New York: Academic Press.

Raue, P.J. & Goldfried, M.R. (1994) The therapeutic alliance in cognitive-behavior therapy. In A.O. Horvath & Greenberg, L.S. (eds), *The Working Alliance: Theory, Research, and Practice* (pp. 131–152). New York: Wiley.

Rehm, L.P. (1977). A self-control model of depression. *Behavior Therapy, 8*, 787–804.

Rothbaum, B.O., Meadows, E.A., Resick, P. *et al.* (2000). Cognitive-behavioral therapy. In E.B. Foa, T.M. Keane & M.J. Friedman. *Effective Treatments for PTSD*. New York: Guilford Press.

Schindler, L. (1988). Client-therapist interaction and therapeutic change. In P.M.G. Emmelkamp (ed.), *Fresh Perspectives on Anxiety Disorders*. Amsterdam: Swets & Zeitlinger.

Schulte, D., Kunzel, R., Pepping, G. & Schulte-Bahrenberg, T. (1992). Tailor-made versus standardized therapy of phobic patients. *Advances in Behaviour Research and Therapy, 14*, 281–294.

Sireling, L., Cohen, D. *et al.* (1988). Guided mourning for morbid grief: A controlled replication. *Behavior Therapy, 19*, 121–132.

Sobell, L.C., Toneatto, T. & Sobell, M.B. (1994). Behavioral assessment and treatment planning for alcohol, tobacco, and other drug problems: Current status with an emphasis on clinical applications, *Behavior Therapy, 25*, 533–580.

Stravinsky, A. & Amado, D. (2000). Social phobia as a deficit in social skills. In S.G. Hofman & P.M. DiBartolo (eds), *From Social Anxiety to Social Phobia: Multiple Perspectives*. Boston: Allya & Bacon.

Van Hout, W.J.A.J. & Emmelkamp, P.M.G. (2002). Exposure in vivo. In M. Hersen & W. Sledge (eds), *The Encyclopedia of Psychotherapy*, Vol. I (pp. 761–768). New York: Academic Press.

Vedel, E. & Emmelkamp, P.M.G. (2004). Behavioral couple therapy in the treatment of a female alcohol dependent patient with comorbid depression, anxiety and personality disorders. *Clinical Case Studies, 3*, 187–205.

Velzen, C. & Emmelkamp, P.M.G. (1996). The assessment of personality disorders: Implications for cognitive and behavior therapy. *Behaviour Research and Therapy*, 34, 655–668.

Wright, J.H. & Davis, D. (1994). The therapeutic relationship in cognitive-behavioral therapy: Patient perceptions and therapist responses. *Cognitive and Behavioral Practice, 1*, 25–45.

CHAPTER 5

Dialectical Behaviour Therapy (DBT)

Sharon Y. Manning
South Carolina Center for DBT, USA

THE THEORETICAL BASIS FOR DBT

When Marsha Linehan is asked to tell the story of her development of dialectical behaviour therapy (DBT) she says that she did not set out to invent a theoretical orientation for the treatment of borderline personality disorder (BPD). Linehan was treating suicidal clients, attempting to use standard behaviour therapy with them. However, it was not successful for many of the clients. They would present at an individual psychotherapy session with one problem, such as panic disorder and Linehan would choose an empirically supported treatment for that problem. When the clients returned for the next session they would not have completed the prescribed homework because other problems would have surfaced. Linehan realized that standard treatments were not working because the problems of the clients changed from session to session and moment to moment. Her laboratory developed DBT from an attempt to find a means of prioritizing the multiple problems presented by clients who engaged in non-suicidal self-injurious behaviors, as well as attempts to help clients and therapists to regulate emotion in the presence of intense emotional suffering (Linehan, 1993a,b).

Dialectical behaviour therapy was developed in a clinical laboratory lab where all of Linehan's and, later in the development of the treatment, her students' therapy sessions were videotaped. The sessions were independently coded with each therapist response being labelled as helpful or not helpful. Over time, the method of balancing acceptance of clients at a given moment while pushing them to change behaviours that were dysregulated was identified as being a dialectical practice. This chapter will describe the dialectical underpinnings of DBT because dialectics is one characteristic that distinguishes DBT from other cognitive-behavioural therapies. A discussion of the structure of the treatment, including its modalities, will be followed by an overview of the current research on DBT.

Handbook of Evidence-based Psychotherapies: A Guide for research and practice.
Edited by C. Freeman & M. Power. Copyright © 2007 John Wiley & Sons, Ltd.

THE DIALECTICAL UNDERPINNINGS OF DBT

Dialectics has two definitions. One defines dialectics in terms of the method of argumentation by which two opposing views are synthesized and the truths of each position are verified to the point that neither has to completely give up its position. The second definition of dialectics is the philosophy that two polarities (the thesis and the antithesis) are merged into a synthesis.

Dialectics pervades DBT. Dialectics is seen in the biosocial theory of the development and maintenance of BPD. Clients with BPD are born with an extreme emotional vulnerability. This vulnerability is manifested in three different ways. The first is an extreme sensitivity to emotional stimuli. People with BPD often experience emotions in response to stimuli that do not trigger emotions, or as intense emotions in others. The second characteristic of emotion vulnerability is an extreme reactivity of emotion. The intensity of emotional experiencing of people with BPD is higher than that of others. Finally, people who are emotionally vulnerable take longer to return to a baseline emotional state than others. Emotional vulnerability, therefore, means that the vulnerable person experiences emotions easily, reacts strongly and then does not recover from the emotions quickly. However, emotional vulnerability alone is not enough to cause one to develop BPD. The second factor in the etiology of BPD is the invalidating environment. The invalidating environment is one that pervasively (frequently and independent of context) communicates to children that their behaviours (thoughts, feelings, actions) do not make sense in some way, or are unreasonable and/or pathological. The invalidating environment has often been defined as one that has physical or sexual abuse, but can also be having a parent who for some reason is not present (either physically or emotionally), or being reared in a family where children are expected to be perfect. The biosocial theory of the etiology and maintenance of BPD postulates that BPD develops from a transaction of the emotionally sensitive child with the invalidating environment. The environment invalidates the child and the child becomes increasingly emotionally sensitive in response to the environment. Then, of course, the environment responds to the child by invalidating more and the child becomes more dysregulated. The dialectic inherent in the biosocial theory is that it takes both polarities (the emotional hard wiring of the child and the environment) to result in BPD, not only one pole.

Dialectics is used by DBT therapists to balance the treatment through acceptance of clients at a given moment and to provide a means of changing their lives. In order to bring about behavioural change, DBT uses problem solving as a main treatment technique. DBT is a cognitive-behavioral treatment that analysizes and finds solutions for problem behaviors. However, emotionally sensitive clients, like those with BPD, have difficulty tolerating problem-solving strategies and can become dysregulated by the process of the change strategies. Therefore, behaviour therapy is balanced by validating clients where they are at that moment. When asked to engage in moment-by-moment analysis of dysfunctional behaviour, severe, multi-problem clients often become extremely dysregulated and the result is behaviour such as attacking the therapist (usually verbally) or leaving the session (either through dissociation or by actually leaving the therapy office). Validation is the highlighting of some piece of the client's reality as making sense, being wise or being understandable at that particular moment. A key to validation is finding that grain of wisdom in the client's responses without validating invalid behaviour. For example, a therapist could validate emotion associated with the experience of being rejected without validating the urge to suicide (an invalid response to rejection). The balance of validation and problem solving (the dialectic of acceptance and change) is the primary dialectic of DBT. All other aspects of the treatment are either acceptance based or change based. The DBT therapist seeks to keep balance in all styles, so as not to push clients unreasonably or to accept clients without trying to help them facilitate change in their lives.

STRUCTURING THE TREATMENT IN DBT

Dialectical behaviour therapy consists of four primary treatment stages with pre-commitment occurring prior to beginning each stage. Currently, the main body of research on DBT is on what is called Stage 1 DBT. The first stage of DBT is usually one year of treatment designed to get the client's behaviours under control. Clients in Stage 1 are usually engaging in severely out of control behaviours. They are suicidal, engaging or having the urges to engage in non-suicidal self-injurious behaviours, are substance abusing, binging and/or purging, criminal behaviour, gambling, and engaging in out of control, impulsive behaviours. Once the clients' behaviours are under control, they move into Stage 2 of DBT. In Stage 2, the behaviours are under control, but the clients' level of misery is still extremely high. Usually, Stage 2 is some form of structure exposure based treatment, usually for trauma. Because the out of control behaviours that lead clients into Stage 1 DBT are usually to avoid or escape misery and trauma cues, it is imperative that these issues be addressed. If they are not adequately treated, there is a danger that the client may revert to Stage 1 behaviours to escape the misery. Stage 3 is treatment for a single problem (depression, anxiety, panic) or issue (marital, vocational, chronic pain). Stage 4 is treatment for the desire to feel completeness and joy. Stage 4 DBT is currently only conceptual but may involve a therapist, a spiritual advisor or a teacher of some kind. This chapter focuses mainly on Stage 1 DBT because all of the current research, except a single study of Stage 3 treatment for binge eating disorder (Telch, Agras & Linehan, 2000) has been conducted on severely disordered Stage 1 clients. Prior to beginning any stage of DBT, the client is asked to commit to the treatment. The commitment requires orientation to the upcoming treatment, role induction and deciding upon the goals of the stage of treatment. Prior to beginning Stage 1 DBT, the client is considered to be in the pre-treatment stage. This stage requires orientation to the treatment with an emphasis on commitment to the goals of the treatment (working on life-threatening behaviours, attending the treatment and not dropping out) and the client's personal goals. Even though the stages of DBT are ordered, clients rarely progress through the treatment in a linear fashion. Clients may return to Stage 1 if needed. This sometimes occurs when clients are in Stage 2 or 3 and there is a life event (death of a partner) that leads to a return to behavioural dyscontrol.

Because of the body of research on Stage 1 DBT, most clients enter into the treatment in Stage 1. As stated, clients in Stage 1 are currently engaging a myriad of dysfunctional, out of control behaviours either because of their emotional dysregulation (their relationships are chaotic, their ability to concentrate is impaired or their anger is out of control) or because they are engaging in behaviours to regulate their intense emotions – such as cutting in order to escape or avoid emotional pain. Prior to beginning any stage of DBT treatment the client and the DBT therapist decide and agree upon goals for the treatment. These goals are incorporated into a treatment hierarchy. In Stage 1 DBT, the primary targets (those addressed in the stage and by the individual psychotherapists) are, first, to reduce life-threatening behaviours (parasuicidal, suicidal, assaultive, homicidal behaviours). Clients are told that keeping them alive is the highest priority in the treatment. The second target is to decrease therapy-interfering behaviours (behaviours on the part of the therapist, such as missing appointments, beginning the session late, taking calls during session, or on the part of the client, such as non-compliance, coming late, missing appointments) that reduce the motivation of the other party to continue in the therapy. Addressing problems in the relationship head on and immediately, reduces therapist and client burnout and dropout. The third Stage 1 target addresses other quality of life issues, such as substance abuse, eating-disordered behaviours, marital difficulties, vocational issues or high-risk sexual behaviour. While reducing the targeted behaviours, clients work to enhance their capabilities, and therefore maintain a reduction in the targeted behaviours by learning new behaviours in skills training.

An examination of the research demonstrates that DBT has now been modified for a variety of different treatment settings and populations. However, the majority of the research has been on DBT as an outpatient programme. Dialectical behaviour therapy was intended to be a comprehensive treatment and thus seeks to perform five functions through its modes:

- enhancing capabilities;
- improving motivation;
- generalization to the natural environment;
- structuring the environment and
- enhancing and improving therapist abilities and motivations to treat the clients.

Enhancing Capabilities

The first function of comprehensive DBT is to enhance the capabilities (called skills in DBT) of the clients. This is the function of the skills training mode. Clients often do not engage in skilful behaviours because such behaviours are not in their repertoires In order to engender behavioural change, clients must learn new, functional behaviours while as increasing the generalization of existing functional behaviours. The *Skills Training Manual for Treating Borderline Personality Disorder* (Linehan, 1993b) is the handbook for skills training. The manual comes complete with lesson plans, and reproducible handouts and homework sheets for patients.

In standard outpatient DBT, skills training is provided in a group that meets for two hours to two-and-a-half hours weekly. The skills training group is a psychoeducational group that focuses on skills acquisition (the teaching of new skills), strengthening (rehearsal with feedback of new skills along with reinforcing the use of new skills) and generalization (practising skilful behaviour outside of the group). The target hierarchy for skills training is not the same as the primary target hierarchy of the treatment. Skills trainers do not address life-threatening behaviours in group. If a client presents with suicidal ideation the skills trainers coach the client on skills to be used while accessing the primary (individual) therapist. The targets of skills training are

- reducing therapy-destroying behaviours – behaviours that will end the group (everyone quits) or cause the programme to be disbanded;
- increasing skills acquisition – for example learning new behaviours; and
- reducing therapy-interfering behaviours – those that interfere with the teaching/learning of new skills.

It is important to note that teaching new, skilful behaviour has a higher priority than dealing with behaviours such as coming late, not doing homework or doodling. Groups attended by emotionally dysregulated clients are often full of such behaviours and addressing each behaviour as it occurs reduces the time available to teach new behaviours. Only those that interfere with everyone's learning and the teaching are handled.

It takes 24 weeks to teach every skill in DBT; they are taught in eight-week modules. Stage 1 DBT requires clients to commit to one year of treatment, so each skill is taught twice. Core mindfulness skills increase knowing of self and decrease identity confusion and cognitive dysregulation (attention difficulties, dissociation, paranoia) through attentional control and becoming fully present in one's life. They are so integral to using other skills that they are taught as the first two weeks of each eight-week module. The distress tolerance skills reduce impulsivity and suicidal or parasuicidal behaviours by increasing ability to tolerate crises without engaging in behaviours that ultimately make greater problems in living and by acceptance of reality as it is without trying to change it. The interpersonal skills decrease chaotic relationships and fears of abandonment by meeting needs while protecting the relationship and increasing a sense of self-respect. The emotion-regulation skills reduce mood lability, problems with anger and anxiety by balancing the experiencing of emotion and by changing unwanted/unneeded emotions. Self-management skills do not make up a specific module but are woven into skills training whenever possible. Self-management skills are defined as 'the attempt to control, manage, or otherwise change one's own behavior, thoughts, or emotional responses to behavior' (Linehan, 1993a, p. 152). Whenever the opportunity arises, skills trainers teach clients principles of reinforcement, contingency clarification and management, goal setting, relapse prevention and chain analysis in order to train patients in managing their own lives.

Improving Motivation

The second function of comprehensive DBT is to improve motivation, which is generally targeted in the individual psychotherapy in standard DBT. Each DBT patient is assigned a primary therapist who coordinates all aspects of the treatment – skills training, pharmocotherapy (if available) and case management. In outpatient DBT the primary therapist is also the individual psychotherapist and meets with the client weekly for one hour. The individual psychotherapist is charged with all of the crisis management and targeting of life-threatening behaviours. The DBT individual therapist examines behaviours to determine what either interfered with engaging in functional behaviour or what caused the client to engage in functional behaviour. This involves an in-depth behavioural chain analysis that examines the emotions, actions and cognitions involved in a problem behaviour. The chain analysis is conducted whenever the client engages in behaviours that are targeted in the hierarchy and helps to determine the function of the behaviour. After the problem behaviour, vulnerability factors and precipitating events are defined, the chain of events (including thoughts, feelings, body sensations and actions) that leads from the precipitating event through the problem behaviour to the consequences and after effects are assessed with solutions woven into the analysis. Special attention is given to whether the problem behaviour is respondent, operant or both.

The psychotherapist uses basic problem-solving strategies with the clients' problems. Problems are analysed, solutions are generated and the client's commitment to engage in the behaviours necessary to solve the problem is obtained. Often, clients are reticent to engage in problem solving or new behaviours because of the emotions that interfere (fear, guilt, shame). The psychotherapist uses informal exposure treatment to reduce the emotions that are blocking adaptive behaviours and then prompts the client to act in the opposite way to the urge associated with the emotions. The individual psychotherapist improves the motivation of the client through cognitive modification procedures namely contingency clarification (highlight the if-then relationships in the client's life) and cognitive restructuring (finding and changing the non-dialectical thinking styles, the judgmental thoughts and the dysfunctional descriptions that are prevalent in the client's thinking).

Generalization to the Natural Environment

A third function of comprehensive DBT is to generalize skilful behaviour from the clinic to the natural environment of the client. In standard outpatient DBT, generalization is addressed by telephone consultation. Multi-problem clients often have difficulty asking for help when it is needed. They either are so fearful of requesting help that they inhibit the behaviour or they can ask for help but do so in a manner that others consider to be demanding or abusive. Consequently, clients often end up in hospitals or emergency rooms when they could have engaged in skilful behaviours and avoided the crisis. One reason for telephone consultation is that it allows clients to practise using skilful means to access needed help. A second reason is to generalize skills learned in the skills training group to their everyday lives. Clients can often verbalize intellectual understanding of skills in the DBT clinic. However, when they get out into their own environment, situations that require skills cue strong emotions. High emotional arousal impedes cognitive processing so their ability to use the new information (skills) decreases. Telephone consultation allows clients to obtain skills coaching and moves the treatment out of the clinic and into their lives. Clients have access to the primary therapist to solve problems about which skills to use in real-life situations. The third reason for telephone consultation is to allow clients to address and solve rifts in the therapeutic relationship. Often clients leave sessions and begin to ruminate on conflict with their individual psychotherapist. Telephone consultation provides a means for clients to 'attend to the relationship' with their psychotherapist without having to wait until the next session.

Structuring the Environment

The fourth function of a comprehensive DBT is to structure the environment, which in standard outpatient DBT is the precise structuring of the clinic to ensure that the behaviours that are targeted for increase through the treatment are reinforced and the behaviours that the treatment is attempting to extinguish are not being reinforced. The role of the administrator in a DBT clinic is to ensure that the clinic itself does not punish target-relevant behaviour and reinforce maladaptive behaviour (for example the clinic might provide extra attention for ongoing suicidal crises and withdraw attention upon improvement).

Case-management issues are also addressed through structuring the environment. DBT favors teaching the client to intervene in his/her own behalf (consultation-to-the-patient strategies) over intervening for them whenever possible. Unless the outcome of the intervention is more important than the client's loss of learning, the therapist will coach and practice with the client how to talk with others. Dialectical behaviour therapists do not provide information to others, including other professionals. Clients are encouraged to speak for themselves whenever they are capable of doing so. Therefore, DBT therapists coach clients on how to interact with their environments whenever possible. For example, the DBT therapist does not contact a client's physician and make suggestions for medications or medical interventions. Instead, the DBT coaches clients on how to ask the physician for whatever it is that they want. Of course, there are times when environmental intervention is necessitated. These times are generally when the outcome is more important that the learning of skilful behaviour by the client or if there is an imminent risk to the client or someone else.

Enhancing Therapists' Capabilities and Motivation

The final function that is addressed in DBT is the enhancement of therapists' capabilities and motivation to treat multiply diagnosed clients. As stated earlier, Linehan saw the necessity of treating the therapists who are subjected to the intense emotional misery and out of control behaviours of a difficult to treat population. This is addressed through a weekly meeting of the therapists involved in all modes of the treatment. The therapist consultation team is not a standard treatment team. Therapists who treat high-risk clients need support from their peers in order to reduce burnout or falling out of the treatment – engaging in iatrogenic behaviours or not doing DBT. The therapist consultation team meets once weekly for one to two hours depending upon the setting. The team meeting is attended by anyone who is providing any mode of DBT. Only those therapists who are engaged in the treatment come to the meeting; there are no visitors. In a nutshell, the therapist consultation team meeting is the application of the therapy to the therapists. Each therapist has the opportunity to bring up problems with a client and ask for support, guidance, input, or whatever the therapist feels is needed. The team's role is to balance validating the difficulty of treating the patient while pointing out when the therapist is falling out of the treatment, being reinforced for providing ineffective treatment or being punished for providing effective treatment. Although supervision and consultation are often deemed ancillary in other treatments, in DBT the consultation team is a mandated mode of treatment regardless of whether DBT is being structured as a comprehensive or a component programme.

Comprehensive DBT can be modified for different settings. For example, an inpatient unit may decide to provide a comprehensive treatment, meeting all criteria through the different modes in the treatment. Capabilities can be enhanced on an inpatient unit through psychopharmacology, patient education and through skills training. Motivation on an inpatient unit is often improved by conjoint psychopharmocology and milieu treatment. Discharge planning with an emphasis on skills used for relapse prevention also supports the function of generalization as well as milieu, staff acting as skills coaches for clients on an inpatient or partial hospitalization unit. The environment in an inpatient unit is structured through the structuring of the administrative hierarchy as well as through family therapy and family education or accessing vocational/financial support through social work services. Finally, in an inpatient DBT programme, therapists' capabilities and motivation are usually enhanced through the DBT consultation team. In intensive outpatient programmes, partial hospitalization programmes and other acute programmes, skills training is streamlined to focus on the crisis skills and those skills needed to prevent relapse and recidivism. In forensic programmes telephone consultation is not a viable option for generalization to the natural environment, but staff on the unit or peers are often trained to be skills coaches.

EDUCATION AND TRAINING IN DBT

Currently there is no research on minimal or optimal training level to provide DBT although there is evidence that DBT can be applied in community mental health settings (Hawkins & Singha, 1998; Mental Health Center of Great Manchester, New Hampshire, 1998). It is recommended that DBT psychotherapists have graduate training and most non-research oriented programmes have master's level therapists as well as doctoral level therapists. Hawkins & Singha (1998) also found that community clinicians could demonstrate content proficiency regardless of education or behavioural background. The *Skills Training Manual for Treating Borderline Personality Disorder* (Linehan, 1993b) does not indicate any minimum education or training level required for the provision of the skills training. At this point, there is no research that examines the relationship between the training or educational level of those who are using the workbook as trainers on the one hand and behavioural outcomes on the other. Skills training groups currently vary: some have two doctoral level or medically trained therapists, some one doctoral level and one master's level clinician and some programmes are using one cotherapist in the group who is a paraprofessional. Currently, accreditation of DBT programmes as well as certification of individual practitioners is being developed. These credentials will require minimum standards of education and licensure as well as training and supervision in DBT.

RESEARCH IN DBT

Recent research in DBT indicates that it is effective in the treatment of multi-disordered clients. Linehan *et al.* (1991) completed the first randomized controlled trial for chronically suicidal females who met criteria for borderline personality disorder in an outpatient clinic and compared DBT with community-based 'treatment as usual' (TAU) after 12 months of treatment. The subjects who were in the DBT condition demonstrated statistically significant reductions in suicidal and non-suicidal self-injurious behaviours during the treatment year, fewer inpatient hospitalization days and improvement on global and social adjustment. Retention in treatment was greater for the subjects in the DBT condition at the conclusion of the study (83 % versus 47 %). Dialectical behaviour therapy subjects also demonstrated significant improvements in reducing anger. All subjects improved over time on depression, hopelessness and suicide ideation (Linehan *et al.*, 1994). Koons *et al.* (2001) conducted a six months study at an outpatient women's clinic for the Veteran's Administration in Durham, NC. The Koons *et al.* study was six months in duration as opposed to the Linehan *et al.* (1991) study, which was one year in duration. The participants in the Koons *et al.* study met criteria for BPD but recent non-suicidal self-injurious behaviour was not controlled. Participants in the DBT protocol had a statistically significant reduction in suicidal ideation, hopelessness, depression and anger compared with TAU at six months.

In response to criticism that the original research on DBT did not control for level of expertise by the TAU condition, Linehan et al (2006) conducted a study testing DBT versus treatment in the community by therapists identified by their peers as being expert clinicians in nonbehavioural treatments. The community treatment by experts condition (CTBE) provided supervision and consultation comparable to the DBT therapists. The DBT condition was again associated with better outcomes than the control condition (CTBE).

DBT clients were 50% less likely to engage in suicide attempts, had a significant decrease in hospitalization, and medical interventions across suicidal behaviours and non-suicidal self-injurious behaviours. DBT clients were less likely to drop out of treatment.

Since the original Linehan *et al.* (1991) research, studies have been carried out on modifications of DBT. Linehan *et al.* (1999) adapted DBT for women who met criteria for BPD and for substance abuse. The original comprehensive DBT programme was modified to include drug replacement therapy when necessary. Urinalyses were conducted at each therapy session. The treatment targets were modified to treat substance abuse specific difficulties, such as problems with attaching to the therapy and the therapists. Case-management strategies were developed to target substance abuse related problems (financial, housing, etc). In addition, the skills training group was split into two components: a one-on-one skills coaching (homework review) group and the teaching group. Self-report and urinalysis data demonstrated that the DBT clients had a statistically significant reduction in illicit drug use compared to the TAU and an increase in global and social functioning at follow-up. As in earlier studies, the clients in the DBT condition had a higher retention in treatment.

Miller, Rathus & Linehan (2006) have adapted DBT for adolescents and have pilot data comparing DBT to TAU for adolescents. Unlike earlier studies with adults, 22% of the population studied included males. The population was adolescent so clients were not required to meet criteria for BPD, however each client did meet three or more criteria for BPD. The programme was modified for 12 weeks of individual psychotherapy with twice-weekly meetings. The skills training group was completed as a multi-family group with parents/caregivers in attendance. The pilot data for the programme suggests differences in inpatient hospitalizations. The retention of clients in the DBT programme was also higher than those in the TAU (DBT 62 % versus TAU 13 %).

One of the questions that is prevalent for treatments that are developed in clinic labs is whether or not they can be applied to other mental health settings. Currently, there are on-going outcome studies being conducted in mental health systems. There is some preliminary evidence that DBT can be learned and applied in public community mental health settings. Hawkins & Singha (1998) evaluated 109 clinicians who were trained in DBT in as part of a community mental health initiative. The clinicians were tested for conceptual knowledge and mastery. The study showed that prior education and training in behaviour therapy did not affect ability to learn and even master DBT content. Another community mental health initiation, the Mental Health Center of Greater Manchester, New Hampshire, implemented DBT successfully and received the American Psychiatric Association Gold Achievement Award in the category of a small community-based programme. The program used an integrated DBT programme which demonstrated clinical changes for clients and cost savings for the system (Psychiatric Services, 1998). These studies indicate that DBT can generalize from academic and research settings into community mental health settings.

There have been two studies that have examined the efficacy of DBT skills training group with no individual DBT psychotherapy. Telch *et al.* (2000) used DBT for binge-eating disorders. The content of the skills training group was modified and chain analyses were conducted in the group. The number of binge-eating episodes and the days when binging occurred decreased. The DBT condition also reported lower scores on measures of weight and eating concerns. In another study Lynch *et al.* (2003) examined DBT group skills and scheduled telephone coaching sessions and antidepressant medication. The group targets were modified to treat elderly depression. At a six-month follow-up, 73 % of medication plus DBT patients were in remission compared with 38 % of the medication patients, a significant difference. The DBT clients showed significant differences in maladaptive Pleasing Others (a targeted behaviour).

CONCLUSION

This chapter introduced DBT as an empirically supported treatment for those clients who have multiple, severe disorders. The treatment is multifaceted and involves five modes to address the functions needed to help suicidal clients. The chapter described the theory of dialectics and its place in the treatment. It is predominantly dialectics, the balancing of acceptance and change, which sets the treatment apart from other cognitive-behavioural treatments. Dialectical behaviour treatment is relatively new – its first study was published in 1993. More study is needed to analyse what makes DBT effective and to further determine its efficacy. Modifications have been created and studied and more are currently being researched. However, at this point, DBT is a treatment worthy of consideration for severely disordered populations.

REFERENCES

Hawkins, K.A. & Singha, R. (1998). Can clinicians master the conceptual complexities of dialectical behavior therapy? An evaluation of a State Department of Mental Health training program. *Journal of Psychiatric Research, 32,* 379–384.

Koons, C.R., Robins, C.J., Bishop, G.K. *et al.* (2001). Efficacy of dialectical behavior therapy in women veterans with borderline personality disorder. *Behavior Therapy, 32,* 371–390.

Linehan, M.M. (1993a). *Cognitive-behavioral Treatment of Borderline Personality Disorder.* New York: Guilford Press.

Linehan, M.M. (1993b). *Skills Training Manual for Treating Borderline Personality Disorder.* New York: Guilford Press.

Linehan, M.M., Armstrong, H.E., Suarez, A. *et al.* (1991). Cognitive-behavioral treatment of chronically parasuicidal borderline patients. *Archives of General Psychiatry, 48,* 1060–1064.

Linehan, M.M., Comtois, K.A., Murray, A.M., Brown, M.Z., Gallop, R.J., Heard, H.L., Korslund, K.E., Tutek, D.A., Reynolds, S.K., & Lindenboim, N. (2006). Two year randomized controlled trail and follow-up of dialectical behavior therapy vs therapy by experts for suicidal behaviors and borderline personality disorder. *Archives of General Psychiatry, 63,* 47–56.

Linehan, M.M., Schmidt., H.L., Dimeff, L.A. *et al.* (1999). Dialectical behavior therapy for patients with borderline personality disorder and drug-dependence. *American Journal on Addictions, 8,* 279–292.

Linehan, M.M., Tutek, D.A., Heard, H.L. & Armstrong, H.E. (1994). Interpersonal outcome of cognitive-behavioral treatment for chronically suicidal borderline patients. *American Journal of Psychiatry, 151,* 1771.

Lynch, T.R., Morse, J.Q., Mendelson, T., & Robins, C.J. (2003) Dialectical behavior therapy for depressed older adults: a randomized pilot study. *American Journal of Geriatric Psychiatry. 11,* 1–13.

Mental Health Center of Greater Manchester, New Hampshire (1998). Integrating dialectical behavioral therapy into a community mental health program. *Psychiatric Services, 49,* 1338–1340.

Miller, A. L, Rathus, J. H. & Linehan, M. M. (2006). *Dialectical Behavior Therapy with Suicidal Adolescents.* New York: Guilford Press.

Telch, C.F., Agras, W.S. & Linehan, M.M. (2000). Group dialectical behavior therapy for binge-eating disorder. A preliminary uncontrolled trial. *Behavior Therapy, 31,* 569–582.

CHAPTER 6

Eye Movement Desensitisation and Reprocessing (EMDR)

John Spector

Watford General Hospital, UK

INTRODUCTION

Eye movement desensitisation and reprocessing (EMDR) was originated and developed by Dr Francine Shapiro and introduced into the professional and clinical world with her seminal randomised control study in 1989 (Shapiro, 1989). At that time it was introduced as 'eye movement desensitisation'. Shapiro (1991) added the word 'reprocessing' to the title to emphasise the cognitive and information processing elements central to the procedure. Shapiro has been well aware of the problems generated by naming the procedure after eye movements (Shapiro, 2002). Eye movements have been only one form of bilateral stimulation used and bilateral stimulation is itself only one component of a number of components making up the procedure. Whilst a few components are unusual, most components are recognisable from other well known therapies but all are arranged in a unique order. Although EMDR procedures have been standardised since 1991, there has been some evolution in ideas about the theoretical underpinnings of EMDR since 1989, in the light of clinical and research findings. Such evolution is a hallmark of evidence-based practice, which should adapt and evolve in response to new findings.

Eye movement desensitisation and reprocessing was originally designed to treat traumatic or 'dysfunctional' memories and experiences and their psychological consequences, and the procedure has mainly been used in the treatment of post traumatic stress disorder (PTSD). However, there have been increasing reports over the years in the scientific literature on the use of EMDR to treat, for example, test anxiety (Maxfield & Melnyk, 2000), personality disorders (Fensterheim, 1996), gambling (Henry, 1996), work performance (Foster & Lendl, 1996), dysmorphophobia (Brown, McGoldrick & Buchanan, 1997), panic disorder (Goldstein & Feske, 1994), pain (Hekmat, Groth & Rogers, 1994), grief (Sprang, 2001) and

Handbook of Evidence-based Psychotherapies: A Guide for research and practice.
Edited by C. Freeman & M. Power. Copyright © 2007 John Wiley & Sons, Ltd.

a wide range of experientially based disorders (Manfield, 1998; Zabukovec *et al.*, 2000). Shapiro (2001, 2002) describes EMDR as an integrative approach, which

- facilitates resolution of memories
- desensitises stimuli that trigger present distress as a result of second-order conditioning
- incorporates adaptive attitudes skills and behaviours for enhanced functioning.

There were only six randomised controlled studies across *all* psychological treatments for PTSD from 1980 when the diagnosis of PTSD entered DSM-III up until 1992 (Solomon, Gerrity & Muff, 1992). Although the publication of Shapiro's seminal 1989 study initially attracted little attention, this changed after the publication by Joseph Wolpe of a successful case using EMD procedures (Wolpe & Abrams, 1991). These events precipitated the publication of over 100 case studies and, at the time of writing, 20 randomised controlled studies, on EMDR and PTSD alone. This amounts to significantly more research into EMDR than for any other single psychological or psycho-pharmacological approach to PTSD and provides a strong basis on which evidence can be adjudged.

Eye movement desensitisation and reprocessing has been controversial, particularly in its early years, although much of the controversy may be based on misreading or misunderstanding (Perkins & Rouanzoin, 2002). For example (Rosen *et al.*, 1999; Herbert *et al.*, 2000) have attacked EMDR as being promoted as a 'one-session cure'. Shapiro (2002) has pointed out that even in her 1989 seminal paper she stated that 'it must be emphasised that the EMD procedure as presented here serves to desensitise the anxiety related to traumatic memories, not to eliminate all PTSD related symptomatology and complications, nor to provide coping strategies to victims.' In fact some 13 years after the introduction of EMDR there seems to be a growing consensus that, for 'simple'(one-off) trauma, EMDR, although a highly efficient procedure, averages out at around three to five longish treatment sessions (Shapiro, 2001; Van Etten & Taylor, 1998). There has also been much debate about the utility of the eye movement component of EMDR, and about the theoretical basis of EMDR, both of which will be addressed in separate sections in this chapter. Suffice it to say that whatever the merits of the criticisms of EMDR, it has been an astoundingly successful therapeutic procedure in terms of the research interest and publications generated in a relatively short period of time and in terms of the tens of thousands of clinicians across the world who have trained in the procedure. As adherence amongst clinicians has grown, and as the evidence base has grown, this has been reflected in wide acceptance in evidence-based guidelines. It has been acknowledged as effective in the treatment of PTSD by independent reviewers for the American Psychological Association (APA) (Chambless *et al.*, 1998) and by the American Department of Veteran Affairs and Department of Defense (2004). It has been designated an effective psychotherapy for PTSD in the practice guidelines of the International Society for Traumatic Stress Studies (Chemtob, Tolin & Van der Kolk, 2000; Shalev *et al.*, 2000) and it is recommended UK by the National Institute for Clinical Excellence (NICE, 2005), as one of only two empirically supported treatments of choice for adult PTSD, as well as in a number of other international guidelines on the management of PTSD.

THE EMDR PROCEDURE

Shapiro (1999) describes the eight phases of EMDR treatment. The first of these phases is 'client history and treatment planning'. The history taking is undertaken with the same degree of thoroughness that any good mental health clinician would employ when considering a client for psychotherapy. Particular emphasis will be placed on the nature of the client's psycho-pathology and the client's suitability for EMDR. Contraindications such as suicidal ideation, organic problems that could interfere with processing, and motivational issues, are assessed. Secondary gain factors accruing from the psycho-pathology are identified and may be addressed in the treatment plan. Suitable targets are identified for processing in the treatment phase. Such targets for processing or reprocessing are usually traumatic events or disturbing incidents seminal in the clients presenting problems. Present stimuli that trigger emotional disturbance in the client will also be targeted, as well as anticipated future situations that could elicit disturbance. The EMDR assessor will be particularly listening out for examples of trauma or critical incidents in clients' histories, as well as paying particular attention to the words clients use to describe themselves in relation to others and the world in general. These self-referential beliefs will give clues as to negative and positive cognitions in the assessment phase.

Phase two is called the 'preparation' phase. During this phase the emphasis is on establishing an appropriate therapeutic relationship, educating the client with regard to the effects of trauma and around reasonable expectations of EMDR, and teaching the client self control techniques. The use of metaphor is usually introduced at this stage to facilitate the creation of a manageable 'distance' for clients to reconnect with their traumatic material. This is part of a 'mindfulness' process (Teasdale, 1999) deliberately aimed at helping clients become their own observers. Emphasis is placed in the preparation phase on creating a sense of control and safety in clients, and in this regard clients are taught the use of a 'stop signal' to use if they wish to stop the procedure at any time, and also a 'safe place' is elicited and elaborated with the use of bilateral stimulation. This 'safe place' may be returned to from time to time during the procedure to give the client a sense of wellbeing and control.

The third phase is named the 'assessment' phase. During this phase the first memory to be reprocessed is targeted. A visual image or picture that represents the worst part of the traumatic memory is elicited. Next a negative belief or cognition associated with the identified picture is elicited. This negative belief needs to be meaningful in the present as well as in the old memory. Next a positive or preferred belief or cognition is elicited that the client would like to be able to believe. This positive belief is then rated on the 'validity of cognitions' (VOC) scale (Shapiro, 1989), which is a seven point semantic differential scale from disbelief to full belief. The emotions associated with the targeted memory are identified and the disturbance level in relation to the traumatic incident is rated on the SUD scale (Wolpe, 1958). Finally physical sensations and their location in relation to the targeted traumatic memory are elicited.

Each stage of this assessment stage is very deliberate. Traumatic memories may be held in any one of three modalities – visual in the form of visual memories and images, cognitive in the form of disturbing or negative thoughts in relation to the trauma and sensory in the form of physical sensations associated with the trauma. The EMDR assessment protocol is designed to tap into any one and all of these modalities in order that all traumatic feeder channels are accessed for reprocessing. Furthermore during this assessment protocol, the client is progressively brought into closer and closer connection with the whole traumatic experience, and it is only after the visual image, the negative and positive cognition, and the emotions associated with the trauma have been elicited that the disturbance levels (SUDS) is measured at maximal intensity. Finally the elicitation of a positive cognition is designed to point up the possibility to the client of irrationality in the negative belief and create an expectation of adaptive change. Identification of the physical sensations associated with the trauma is vital in that for some clients the physical sensory element may store the memory of the trauma most powerfully and be most closely connected to affective responses. Sometimes in EMDR clients are asked simply to notice their physical sensations as a means of facilitating processing or avoiding being overwhelmed by disturbing images or thoughts.

The next three phases of EMDR involve bilateral stimulation usually by means of sets of eye movements but possibly by auditory or tactile stimulation. Phase four is called the 'de-sensitisation phase'. To commence, clients are asked to focus on the visual image, negative belief, and associated physical sensations around the trauma, while following the eye move-ments but they are also instructed to just *notice* their experience and are informed that things may change. This injunction to just 'notice' their experience – a kind of 'mindfulness' – facilitates typically a free associative process across sets of eye movements in which the client will move in and out of exposure to the disturbing traumatic target. Sometimes un-expected material may arise, but all the clients experiences are accepted as associated in some way with the reprocessing and desensitising process, and as long as new information is appearing and there is *movement* of information, the desensitisation phase is kept going. Occasionally where clients get stuck or 'loop' (keep returning to the same material without reprocessing it), then an intervention called 'cognitive interweave' is used to introduce func-tional information into the clients' awareness to 'jump start' the reprocessing. However, in general one of the remarkable aspects of EMDR is that the therapist largely stays out of the desensitisation process and allows the client's adaptive and instinctive movement of informa-tion from dysfunctional to functional to occur spontaneously and naturally. Movement away from the traumatic target during EMDR desensitisation and reprocessing is *not* considered avoidance, but rather an essential part of 'cleaning out' feeder channels to those targets. De-sensitisation and reprocessing are continued until the targeted traumatic material no longer causes any disturbance at all, as measured on the SUDS scale, which will be down to 0.

Phase 5 is the 'installation' phase, during which the positive cognition is now paired with the original traumatic image, and belief in the positive cognition is strengthened with successive sets of bilateral stimulation and measured on the VOC scale. This phase finishes when the positive belief is rated 6, or ideally 7, on the VOC scale.

Phase 6 is the 'body scan' phase, in which clients mentally scan their bodies for any remaining physical signs of disturbance that may need reprocessing.

Phase 7 is the 'closure' phase, during which clients are re-introduced to self-control techniques and the safe place to give them a sense of wellbeing at the end of the session. In this phase the client is instructed as to keeping a diary of experiences following the session and up until the next session.

The final eighth phase is the 're-evaluation' phase where additional targets for reprocess-ing may be elicited.

THE THEORETICAL BASIS OF EMDR

Shapiro (1993, 1995, 2001) calls the model that guides the use of EMDR the adaptive information processing (AIP) model. She emphasises that it is just that – a model – and may be modified in the light of further experimental and clinical findings. The model uses the terminology of neuro-physiological information processing introduced by Bower (1981) and Lang (1979). The model begins by suggesting that there appears to be an innate and adaptive neurologically based information processing system within all of us that allows experience to be used constructively by the individual in an integrative way. However, with severe psychological trauma, an imbalance occurs in the nervous system caused possibly by changes in neuro-transmitters and hormonal changes. The result is that the information acquired from the trauma is not adaptively processed but is maintained within the system neurologically in all its disturbing state. This disturbing material can then be triggered by a variety of internal and external cues, resulting in the well-known symptoms of post traumatic stress disorder, such as flashbacks, nightmares and hyper-vigilance.

Shapiro suggests that under the AIP model, the procedural elements of EMDR stimulate a neuro-physiological process that facilitates information processing. The mechanism by which this activation of facilitation occurs may include:

- An effect of the client's dual focusing of attention as he simultaneously attends to the present stimuli and the past trauma.
- Changes in the neurological state of the brain, caused perhaps by the effects of neuronal bursts or the induction of a neurobiological state similar to that of REM sleep.
- De-conditioning caused by a relaxation response.

It is suggested that, with each set of bilateral stimulation, disturbing information is moved at an accelerated rate further along the appropriate neuro-physiological pathways until it is adaptively resolved.

Shapiro posits both a psychological and a neurobiological basis for accelerated information processing as a result of bilateral stimulation. The psychological explanation, she suggests, is related to dual attention focusing: 'Specifically, the information processing mechanism may be activated when attention is elicited by, or focused on, the external cues. The simultaneous focus on the traumatic memory may cause the activated system to process the dysfunctionally stored material' (Shapiro, 2001). Dual attention focusing as an important facilitator of EMDR effectiveness is given extra support by Lee *et al.* (2006).

The neurobiological explanation relates to her own hypothesis and those of others (such as Stickgold, 2002) that the eye movements themselves may induce an altered brain state that modifies the behaviour of the information processing system and that other rhythmical movements or repeated stimulation could have similar effects (auditory and tactile).

The theory also incorporates the concept of 'memory networks', which are a series of channels where related memories, thoughts, images, emotions and sensations are stored and linked to one another. In EMDR each channel is 'cleaned out' by reprocessing all the dysfunctionally stored material connected to the traumatic target (or 'node'). The reprocessing is done during each set of eye movements (or other stimulae), where images, thoughts and emotions complete a shift in their progress towards greater therapeutic resolution.

Shapiro argues that there are a number of critical elements to the AIP model:

- That traumatic material is represented by dysfunctional information that is physiologically stored and that can be accessed and transformed. She argues that this is consistent with other researchers' views on, for example, declarative and non-declarative memory (Brewin, 1989; Brewin, Dalgleish & Joseph, 1996; Stickgold, 2002). Shapiro suggests that after EMDR traumatic memories may shift from being held primarily and dysfunctionally in non-declarative memory to appropriate storage in declarative memory. Certainly, work by Van der Kolk, Burbridge & Susuki (1997) using position emission topography (PET) scanning of the brains of PTSD patients before and after three sessions of EMDR shows the marked asymmetry in lateralisation of the traumatised brains appears to be corrected and it is suggested that these changes reflect a more realistic differentiation between real and perceived threat, and the reduction in hyper-vigilance.

- The second element is an information processing system that is intrinsic and adaptive. This belief is the basis of EMDR's client-centred model, which assumes that the client's shifting cognitions and affect during EMDR treatment will move optimally with minimal therapist intrusion.
- Concomitant with the transformation in disturbing information in EMDR is a shift in cognitive structure and self-reference. This leads spontaneously to new more self-enhancing behaviours.
- A final element is that the AIP model and the EMDR procedure produce rapidity in the transformation of disturbing traumatic material generally in much less time than has been traditionally thought. Shapiro (2001) suggests that 77 % to 90 % of civilian PTSD is eliminated within three 90 minute sessions.

A number of authors have speculated further and elaborated on the possible theoretical basis of EMDR, including McCulloch & Feldman (1996), Armstrong & Vaughan (1996) ('facilitation of an investigatory/orienting response'), Bergman (1995) ('re-synchronisation of hemispheric activity'), Stickgold (2002) ('the induction of a neuro-biological state similar to REM sleep optimally configured to support cortical integration of traumatic memories into general semantic networks').

Sweet (1995), building on the work of Foa and her colleagues, suggests that several areas are critical to emotional processing: exposure to the traumatic fear ('the conditioned stimulus'); the fear/arousal response; the cognitive or meaning aspects of the experience to be activated – all preferably to be activated simultaneously; moreover, corrective physiological and cognitive information must be introduced, leading to habituation and re-attribution. Sweet found EMDR alone amongst therapies reviewed to contain all these elements.

Hyer & Brandsma (1997) suggest that EMDR works because it involves the curative components of other packages in one package. Lipke (1996) sets out the stages in the EMDR procedure, highlighting the influence of already known therapeutic activities, but also pointing out the unique arrangement of these activities in EMDR: Boudewyns & Hyer (1996) suggest that the EMDR procedure contains five components of therapy necessary for change. Firstly, EMDR is a non-directive and phenomenological method. Secondly, it emphasises movement of information or processing. Successful information processing results in adaptive integration of previously held information and emotions as new or associated information is accessed in a process that has been labelled 'desensitisation using free association'. Thirdly, the clients are facilitated in becoming their own observers of their experiences as they make contact with the trauma – strengthening the observing ego – a kind of mindfulness. Fourthly, an important position is given to cognition by highlighting negative and positive anchoring cognitions. Cognitive reattribution is a vital part of EMDR processing, together with affective and physiological habituation and shift. Fifth is the 'now' processing, with the emphasis on affect and sensations.

Welch & Beere (2002) synthesise neurobiological and psychological explanations for EMDR's effectiveness. The authors set out three interrelated hypotheses with predictions stemming from their model. Firstly, they suggest that EMDR both intensifies and reduces arousal – that EMDR is a 'mood state activator'. The process by which this occurs is explained by the other two hypotheses. The second hypothesis is that the bilateral movements in EMDR lead to bilateral stimulation of the cerebral hemispheres, and here the authors point out that much research has demonstrated lateralisation effects in PTSD. This bilateral stimulation facilitates a reconnection of the two hemispheres. The third hypothesis is that the constricted and avoidant attention in PTSD sufferers is altered through the EMDR procedure, allowing the patient to begin attending to the internal processing of the trauma.

OUTCOME RESEARCH IN EMDR

There are currently, at the time of writing, 20 randomised controlled (RCTs) in EMDR and PTSD, (not including follow-up RCTs) and also four meta-analyses. This is a considerable outcome research base in a relatively short period of 17 years since the seminal paper on EMDR and represents a considerably greater research interest in this area than in any other single approach to PTSD, whether psychological or pharmacological. Although some of the earlier studies were criticised for lacking methodological rigour (Lohr, Tolin & Lilienfeld, 1998), later studies have by-and-large adhered to 'the gold standard' criteria of Foa & Meadows (1997) – random selection, standard treatment delivery, objective standardised measures, and clear inclusion and exclusion rules for clients (diagnostic criteria). Of the 20 RCTs, two are comparisons with waiting list or delayed treatment controls, three are component analyses, and 15 are treatment comparisons. Of the treatment comparisons, eight are comparisons with variations of exposure treatments. Only one of the treatment comparisons yields a negative result for EMDR against its treatment comparison (Taylor *et al.*, 2003).

Treatment Comparisons

This research in EMDR can be viewed as having two phases. The first phase from Shapiro's seminal 1989 paper up until 1998 was characterised by research examining whether EMDR was an effective psychotherapeutic procedure for post traumatic stress disorder, and the contribution of its various elements, especially eye movements. The second phase from 1999 largely accepted EMDR as an effective treatment for PTSD (Foa, 2000) and now focused on research comparing the effectiveness and efficiency of EMDR directly with variations of exposure. Maxfield & Hyer (2002) rate most of this research according to the 'gold standard' of research (Foa & Meadows, 1997) and according to the degree of treatment fidelity.

1989–98

This phase of research into EMDR in its first decade was stimulated by the *Shapiro (1989)* publication outlining the procedure and its successful use with a mixed group of PTSD clients. Its merit lies in its originality, but few conclusions may be drawn from it because of design flaws including no blind assessors, unclear sample definition, and diagnostic assessment, limited use of standardised measures and a control treatment that was not the equivalent of a properly conducted flooding procedure.

Vaughan et al. (1994) was the first study to compare EMDR with an exposure treatment (image habituation training) and also applied muscle relaxation. All treatments led to significant decreases in PTSD symptoms over those on a waiting list but with greater reductions in the EMDR group across all measures, and with significantly greater reductions for intrusive memories. This study used blind assessors and reliable and standardised measures.

However, there were no psychophysiological measures and 22 % of subjects failed a strict definition of PTSD.

Marcus, Marquis & Sakai (1997) showed EMDR producing significantly greater improvements over a standard care treatment group on measures of PTSD, depression and anxiety. Standard care treatment embraced a variety of psychotherapies. *Marcus et al. (2004)* found EMDR superiority was maintained at three- and six-month follow-ups. *Carlson et al. (1998)* showed EMDR to be significantly more effective that a biofeedback assisted relaxation group and a wait list control. These results were largely maintained at three-month follow up and this is important because this is one of the only studies of combat veterans (chronic, complex trauma) where sufficient treatment was provided to demonstrate treatment effects. *Scheck, Schaeffer & Gillette (1998)* compared EMDR with an 'active listening' approach with improvements for both groups but with the EMDR group showing significantly greater improvements on all PTSD related, anxiety, depression, and self-esteem scales.

Two randomised controlled studies (RCTs) compared EMDR to wait list or delayed treatment controls. *Wilson, Becker & Tinker (1995)* demonstrated significant improvements in the EMDR treatment group across all measures and maintained at three months follow up. However, only 46 % of subjects fitted a PTSD classification and there were no psychophysiological measures. *Wilson et al. (1997)* found that improvements with EMDR were largely maintained at 15 months follow-up. *Rothbaum (1997)* in a well controlled study compared female rape victims treated with EMDR to those on a wait list control. Results showed that after EMDR 90 % of the participants no longer met full criteria for PTSD and subjects treated with EMDR improved significantly more on PTSD and depression than wait-list controls.

There were three component analysis RCTs in this research phase up until 1998. *Renfrey & Spates (1994)* compared EMDR to the procedure with visual attention held static. No significant differences were found between treatment conditions, although Renfrey and Spates acknowledged 'an observed tendency for the two treatment conditions that involved eye movements to appear more efficient'. *Pitman et al. (1996)* compared normal EMDR with a control group where eyes were static and subjects were instructed instead to tap their fingers rhythmically while the therapist used alternating hand movements mimicking the normal EMDR procedure. There were no significant differences between treatment conditions although Pitman *et al.* commented on the speed of improvements in the EMDR procedure in relation to their imaginal flooding procedure described in the same journal edition. *Wilson et al. (1996)* compared EMDR to the procedure with eyes held static and to EMDR with eye movements replaced by alternative thumb tapping. Only the eye movement group showed complete desensitisation to anxiety as measured by SUDS and psychophysiological measures.

From 1999 Onward

This second phase of research into EMDR was characterised by direct comparisons of EMDR with other treatments, mainly exposure therapies.

Rogers et al. (1999) was a well controlled study comparing EMDR and exposure, paying particular attention to process issues such as speed, ease of application, comfort for the client, and safety. Twelve Vietnam veterans were given EMDR or exposure over one extended session with both groups showing improvements, but with EMDR showing greater positive changes on within session SUDS levels and on self monitored severity of intrusive recollections. However, sample size was small and only one session of treatment was examined.

Edmond et al. (1999) assigned 59 adult female survivors of childhood sexual abuse randomly either to EMDR, eclectic therapy or a delayed treatment group. On every outcome measure the EMDR participants scored significantly better than controls after six sessions of treatment.

Ironson et al. (2002) compared EMDR to prolonged exposure (PE) in 22 community-based PTSD victims. Both treatments produced significant reductions in PTSD and depression symptoms at the end of treatment and at three months follow up. However, seven out of 10 subjects had 70 % reduction in PTSD symptoms after three sessions in the EMDR group, compared with two out of 12 with PE, with a significantly lower dropout rate in the EMDR group. However sample size was small and assessors not entirely blind.

Lee et al. (2002) compared EMDR with stress inoculation training (SIT) plus prolonged exposure in 24 randomly assigned PTSD subjects. There were no significant differences between EMDR and SIT plus PE on global measures post treatment, except for significant improvement on intrusion symptoms in the EMDR group, and EMDR showed significantly greater improvement on trauma and distress measures at three months follow up. Sample size again was low and assessors not blind to treatment assignment.

Power, McGoldrick & Brown (2002). This study is the largest comparison of EMDR and exposure so far, with the longest follow up. It has also been published as a study for the Scottish Home and Health Department. It involved the random assignment of 105 PTSD patients to EMDR, exposure plus cognitive restructuring, or a wait-list control. The EMDR and ECR groups both demonstrated significant clinical gains over the wait-list control, with no significant differences in effectiveness between the treatment groups. The EMDR was, however, significantly more efficient than the ECR, with patients in the EMDR group receiving a mean of 4.2 sessions in comparison with a mean of 6.4 sessions for the exposure group. The statistical analysis in this study was however open to criticism and termination of treatment was to some extent left to clinical judgement.

Taylor et al. (2003) in a well controlled study was the only randomised study to show exposure statistically superior to EMDR on two subscales (out of ten). However the exposure group did include therapist assisted *invivo* exposure in addition to imaginal exposure and one hour of daily homework. The EMDR group used only standard sessions and no homework.

Rothbaum et al. (2005). This study evaluated the relative efficacy of prolonged exposure and EMDR compared to a no-treatment wait list control, for rape victims. Improvement in PTSD was significantly greater in both the PE and EMDR group than the wait list group. PE and EMDR didn't differ in effectiveness but Rothbaum points out that 'EMDR seemed to do equally well despite these exposure and no homework.'

Treatment Comparisons Based on EMDR with Children

Three randomised controlled studies (Chemtob *et al.*, 2002; Jabghaderi *et al.*, 2004; Soberman *et al.* 2002) support growing evidence for the effectiveness of EMDR in the treatment of children with PTSD.

Meta-analyses

Van Etten & Taylor (1998) was a meta-analysis of all treatments for PTSD, which indicated that behaviour therapy, SSRIs, and EMDR were the most effective forms of treatment. They also specified that EMDR appeared to be the 'more efficient' form of therapy, given that EMDR necessitated one third the amount of time to achieve its effects compared to outcomes reported in behaviour therapy research.

Davidson & Parker (2001) in a meta-analysis covering a smaller number of studies, examined EMDR with a variety of populations and measures. Eye movement desensitisation and reprocessing was found to be effective, but not superior to other exposure techniques, and no incremental effect of eye movements was noted when EMDR was compared with the same procedure without them.

Maxfield & Hyer (2002) in a meta-analysis of all PTSD outcome studies with EMDR found studies with greater scientific rigour yielded larger effect sizes, and that there was a significant correlation between effect size and treatment fidelity.

Bradley et al. (2005) in a meta-analysis of studies on psychotherapy for PTSD between 1980 and 2003 found that EMDR and cognitive behaviour therapy were both effective treatments for PTSD, and were equally effective.

Conclusion

Research findings thus far suggest that EMDR is an effective psychotherapy, a conclusion in accordance with a number of regulatory bodies such as the American Psychological Association (APA), the International Society for the Study of Trauma and Stress (ISTSS), and the National Institute for Clinical Excellence (NICE, 2005) for the British Department of Health. Results in randomised controlled comparison studies overwhelmingly show an effect for EMDR with a trend towards greater efficiency when compared to traditional exposure procedures. However, there is controversy around the role of eye movements or bilaterality, around whether EMDR can be construed as a variant of exposure therapy and around the theoretical basis for EMDR.

CONTROVERSIES IN EMDR

Eye movement desensitisation and reprocessing has been controversial since its introduction in 1989. Initially, some of the criticism may have been provoked by the impression that EMDR was being advanced as 'a one-session cure' (Herbert *et al.*, 2000; Lohr *et al.*, 1998). Shapiro (2002) has responded vigorously to such criticisms. Nevertheless, these critics persisted with the view that EMDR was in some way being 'oversold' together with criticisms of the theoretical basis of EMDR as being unsubstantiated and untestable, criticisms focusing on the role of eye movements and, up until recently, doubts about the effectiveness of EMDR, although there are few now who continue to claim that EMDR is not effective, and the argument has shifted more to whether EMDR is effective simply because of its exposure components.

Proponents of EMDR have argued that some of the polarity in views on EMDR have arisen because studies indicating less good results for EMDR have been those conducted with poor fidelity to proper EMDR procedures (Maxfield & Hyer, 2002), and with only one to three sessions of treatment applied to complex multiply traumatised client groups.

This section will set out particular areas of controversy around EMDR.

Is EMDR a Power Therapy?

Rosen *et al.* (1998) describe EMDR as a 'power therapy' (Figley, 1997), and group it together with therapies such as thought field therapy (Callahan, 1995), trauma incident reduction (Gerbode, 1989), and emotional freedom techniques (Craig, 1997). Rosen *et al.* say: 'These Power Therapies appeal to popular healthcare models with an emphasis on tapping energy points.' Poole, De Jongh & Spector (1999), however, respond that the theoretical foundations of these procedures linked together have no common ground whatsoever. Eye movement desensitisation and reprocessing incorporates well-established therapeutic principles of exposure, cognitive restructuring and self-control procedures, and should be viewed as part of an overall treatment process, rather than a 'one-off' treatment method. They also point out that none of the other procedures mentioned had been evaluated by any properly controlled randomised studies, whereas EMDR had been evaluated by several.

How Valid is the Theoretical Basis for EMDR?

Rosen *et al.* (1998) criticise the theoretical basis of EMDR as unsubstantiated. Poole, De Jongh & Spector (1999) address this criticism by pointing out that Shapiro's 'accelerated information processing model' is just that – a model – which may evolve in the light of new findings over time. They argue that this is no different from Wolpe's early theory of reciprocal inhibition to explain the effects of behaviour therapy being superseded by other more cogent models in the light of new knowledge and research. Criticisms of reciprocal inhibition as an explanatory theory did not undermine the effectiveness of systematic desensitisation, and Poole *et al.* argue that nor do criticisms of Shapiro's model undermine the effectiveness of EMDR.

More recent developments of theory, such as Stickgold (2002) and Welch & Beere (2002), develop Shapiro's theory and the latter case provides testable hypotheses.

Are Eye Movements Necessary?

Rosen *et al.* (1998) cite Lohr, Tolin & Kleinknecht (1998) that eye movements add nothing to treatment outcome. However, three out of five studies drawn on by Lohr *et al.* for their conclusions actually provide some *support* for the role of eye movements in EMDR in the reduction of reports of symptoms (Lohr, Kleinknecht & Tolin, 1995; Lohr, Tolin & Kleinknecht, 1996; Montgomery & Ayllon, 1994). For example, Lohr, Kleinknecht & Tolin (1995): 'Only when the eye movement was added, was there a substantial reduction of SUD ratings.' Montgomery and Ayllon (1994) concluded from their study that: 'The addition of saccadic eye movements to the treatment package resulted in the significant decreases in self reports of distress previously addressed.'

As noted in multiple reviews, such as Chemtob *et al.* (2000), Feske (1998), Spector & Read (1999), the results concerning the importance of eye movements in EMDR are inconclusive. However, of particular interest in this debate are the results of independent researchers (Andrade, Kavanagh & Baddely, 1997) (a study now replicated by Van den Hout *et al.* (2001), and Kavanagh *et al.* (2001)), showing that eye movements significantly reduce the vividness of emotive and traumatic imagery. Studies by Kuiken *et al.* (2002) indicating that eye moments facilitate attentional orienting, and studies by Christman *et al.* (2003) indicating that eye moments enhance the retrieval of episodic memory, are highly relevant to the eye movement debate.

Are EMDR Effects Just Exposure Effects?

The debate about whether EMDR is an effective procedure has now moved on, with its critics now suggesting that EMDR is simply a variant of exposure combined with inconsequential eye movements (Herbert *et al.*, 2000; Lohr *et al.*, 1999; McNally, 1999; Rosen *et al.*, 1998). However, Boudewyns & Hyer (1996) point out: 'In strict exposure therapy, the use of many (EMDR treatment components) is considered contrary to (exposure) theory.' Shapiro (1999) points out that, beside eye movements, EMDR contains the additional elements of the creation and dismissal of traumatic imagery, cognitive restructuring, alignment of sensory input related to the targeted trauma, sequential targeting of information, and dosed short exposure. The unique element of free association that determines the route of the client's reprocessing is central to the procedure and very different from sustained exposure, which clearly calls for prolonged, uninterrupted, and undistracted stimulus exposure (Marks *et al.*, 1998; Foa *et al.*, 1999). In this regard, the EMDR procedures would be considered avoidant. According to a strict exposure definition, EMDR should sensitise rather than desensitise its recipients: 'Continuous stimulation in neurons and immune and endocrine cells tends to dampen responses, and intermittent stimulation tends to increase them' (Marks *et al.*, 1998). The use of short bursts of exposure to the traumatic material in EMDR contrasts sharply with the expected minimum of 25 to 100 uninterrupted minutes recommended for exposure procedures (Foa *et al.*, 1999).

An interesting study by Lee *et al.* (2006) investigated whether improvements in EMDR were more consistent with traditional exposure ('reliving effects') or dual focus of attention ('distancing effects'). The evidence was that the improvements were more consistent with dual focus of attention (distancing) effects, pointing up an essential difference between EMDR and cognitive behavioural therapies.

Critics of EMDR need to address the central question of how a procedure so apparently *alien* to traditional exposure can produce effective and efficient results.

Is EMDR More or Less Effective and Efficient Than Exposure/CBT?

Until 1998 critics of EMDR suggested that claims for its effectiveness were based on comparisons with non-effective therapies, rather than CBT/exposure therapies being demonstrated as effective. There was some truth to this criticism in that the only genuine comparison with CBT/exposure therapy up until 1998 was in the Vaughan *et al.* (1994) study, in which EMDR was compared with image habituation training (an exposure variant) with some minor advantages for EMDR especially in reducing intrusions.

However, since 1998, seven studies have directly compared EMDR with exposure (Ironson *et al.*, 2002; Jaberghaderi *et al.* 2004; Lee *et al.*, 2002; Power *et al.*, 2002; Rogers *et al.*, 1999; Rothbaum *et al.*, 2005; and Taylor *et al.*, 2003).

These studies have all been reported on in the 'outcomes' section. If all the direct comparisons with exposure studies, are included, a clear trend is emerging. With the exception of the Taylor *et al.* (2003) study, all of the other studies show EMDR to be roughly equal in effectiveness with exposure therapies, with a slight trend towards greater efficiency for EMDR (Ironson *et al.*, 2002; Power *et al.*, 2002). The Power *et al.* study, which is the largest comparison so far with the longest follow up, indicates EMDR was about 50 % faster in achieving its results (a mean of 4.2 sessions, in comparison with a mean of 6.4 sessions for exposure therapy).

CONCLUSION

Overall, EMDR appears to be an effective and efficient therapeutic procedure for the treatment of civilian PTSD. Evidence for its utility in treating complex and multiple trauma is less convincing, although when sufficient treatment time is given (in excess of the three sessions so commonly applied) for this difficult group (see, for example, Carlson *et al.*, 1998; Marcus *et al.*, 1997) EMDR appears to have some effectiveness. Evidence for EMDR's effectiveness for problems other than PTSD is not yet extensive or rigorous enough to draw firm conclusions.

Developments in the theoretical basis of EMDR are becoming more interesting, cogent and testable. However, theory has developed *post hoc* from clinical findings and no direct link between theory and clinical practice and observations has been as yet conclusively proven.

The role of eye movements or bilateral stimulation remains controversial, although the much replicated work of Andrade *et al.* (1997), demonstrating that eye movements do have specific effects in reducing the vividness of emotional imagery in traumatised persons, may be relevant to this debate, as may the studies of Cristman *et al.* (2003) and Kuiken *et al.* (2002) suggesting particular benefits for eye moments.

It is clear that EMDR is an amalgam of different therapeutic elements, of which eye movements or bilateral stimulation are just one element. Other than having evidence that the procedure in its totality is effective and efficient, we still do not know which elements are the most therapeutically potent, although Shapiro (2002) gives some guidelines as to how future research might elucidate some of these questions.

Finally, there is some evidence from direct comparisons between EMDR and exposure for the treatment of PTSD that EMDR and exposure are roughly equal in effectiveness, with some evidence for greater efficiency in EMDR.

REFERENCES

Andrade, J., Kavanagh, D. & Baddely, A. (1997). Eye movements and visual imagery: A working memory approach to the treatment of post-traumatic stress disorder. *British Journal of Clinical Psychology, 36*, 209–223.

Armstrong, M.S. & Vaughan, K. (1996). An orienting response model of eye movement desensitisation. *Journal of Behaviour Therapy and Experimental Psychiatry, 27*(1), 21–32.

Bergmann, U. (1998). Speculations on the Neurobiology of EMDR. *Traumatology, 4*(1).

Boudewyns, P.A. & Hyer, L.A. (1996). Eye movement desensitisation and reprocessing (EMDR) as treatment for Post Traumatic Stress Disorder (PTSD). *Clinical Psychology and Psychotherapy, 3*, 185–195.

Boudewyns, P.A., Stwertka, S.A., Hyer, L.E. *et al.* (1993). Eye movement desensitization and reprocessing: A pilot study. *Behaviour Therapist, 16*, 30–33.

Bower, G.H. (1981). Mood and memory. *American Psychologist, 36*, 129–148.

Bradley, R., Greene, J., Russ, E. *et al.* (2005). A multidimensional meta-analysis of psychotherapy for PTSD. *American Journal of Psychiatry, 162*(2), 214–227.

Brewin, C.R. (1989). Cognitive change processes in psychotherapy. *Psychological Review, 96*, 379–394.

Brewin, C.R., Dalgleish, T. & Joseph, S. (1996). A dual representational theory of post-traumatic stress disorder. *Psychological Review, 103*, 670–686.

Brown, K.W., McGoldrick, T. & Buchanan, R. (1997). Body dysmorphic disorder: Seven cases treated with eye movement desensitization and reprocessing. *Behavioural and Cognitive Psychotherapy, 25*, 203–207.

Callahan, R. (1995). *Five Minute Phobia Cure.* Wilmington, DE: Enterprise.

Carlson, J. Chemtob, C., Rusnak, K. *et al.* (1998). Eye movement desensitation and reprocessing (EMDR) treatment for combat-related Post Traumatic Stress Disorder. *Journal of Traumatic Stress, 2*, 3–24.

Chambless, D.L., Baker, M.J., Baucom, D.H. *et al.* (1998). Update on empirically validated therapies. *Clinical Psychologist, 51*, 3–16.

Chemtob, C.M., Nakashima, J., Carlson, J.G. (2002). Brief-treatment for elementary school children with disaster-related PTSD: a field study. *Journal of Clinical Psychology, 58*, 99–112.

Chemtob, C.M., Tolin, D.F., Van der Kolk, B.A. & Pitman, R.K. (2000). Eye movement desensitization and reprocessing. In E.B. Foa, T.M.Keane & M.J. Friedman (eds) *Effective Treatments for PTSD: Practice Guidelines from the International Society for Traumatic Stress Studies* (pp. 139–155 and 333–335). New York: Guilford Press.

Craig, G. (1997). *Six Days at the VA: Using Emotional Freedom Therapy* (videotape). Available from Gary Craig, 1102 Redwood Blvd, Novato CA94947.

Cristman, S., Garvey, K., Propper, R. *et al.* (2003). Bilateral eye movements enhance the retrieval of episodic memories. *Neuropsychology, 17*, 221–229.

Davidson, P.R. & Parker, K.C. (2001). Eye movement desensitization and reprocessing (EMDR): A meta-analysis. *Journal of Consulting and Clinical Psychology, 69*(2), 305–316.

Department of Veterans Affairs and Department of Defense (2004). *Clinical Practice Guideline for the Management of Post-traumatic Stress.* Washington, DC: VA/D.D.

Devilly, G. & Spence, S. (1999). The relative efficacy and treatment distress of EMDR and a cognitive behaviour treatment protocol in the amelioration of post traumatic stress disorder. *Journal of Anxiety Disorders, 13*(1–2), 131–157.

Edmond, T., Rubin, A. & Wambach, K (1999). The effectiveness of EMDR with adult female survivors of childhood sexual abuse. *Social Work Research, 23*, 103–116.

Edmond, T., Sloan, L., McCarty, D. (2004). Sexual abuse survivors' perceptions of the effectiveness of EMDR and eclectic therapy: A mixed-methods study. *Research on Social Work Practice, 14*, 259–272.

Fensterheim, H. (1996). Eye movement desensitization and reprocessing with complex personality pathology; an integrative therapy. *Journal of Psychotherapy Integration, 6*(1), 27–38.

Feske, U. (1998). Eye movement desensitization and reprocessing treatment for post traumatic stress disorder. *Clinical Psychology: Science and Practice, 5*, 171–181.

Figley, C. (1997). The active ingredients of the power therapies. Keynote presentation at The Power Therapies; a conference for the integrated and innovative use of EMDR, TFT, EFT, advanced NLP and TIR. Lakewood, Colorado.

Foa, E.B., Dancu, C.V. Hembree, E.A. *et al.* (1999). A comparison of exposure therapy, stress inoculation training, and their combination in reducing post traumatic stress disorder in female assault victims. *Journal of Consulting and Clinical Psychology, 67*, 194–200.

Foa, E.B. & Meadows, E.A. (1997). Psychological treatments for post traumatic stress disorders: A critical review. *Annual Review of Psychology, 48*, 449–480.

Foster, J. & Lendl, J. (1996). Eye movement desensitization and reprocessing – four case studies of a new tool for executive coaching and restoring employee performance after setbacks. *Consulting Psychiatry Journal: Practice and Research, 48*(3), 155–161.

Gerbode, F. (1989). *Beyond Psychology. An Introduction to Metapsychology.* Palo Alto, CA: IRM Press.

Goldstein, A. & Feske, U. (1994). Eye movement desensitization and reprocessing for panic disorder: A case series. *Journal of Anxiety Disorders, 8,* 351–362.

Hekmat, H, Groth, S. & Rogers, D. (1994). Pain ameliorating effects of eye movement desensitization. *Journal of Behaviour Therapy and Experimental Psychiatry, 25,* 121–129.

Henry, S.L. (1996). Pathological gambling: etiological considerations and treatment efficacy of eye movement desensitization/reprocessing. *Journal of Gambling Studies, 12*(4), 395–405.

Herbert, J.D., Lilienfeld, S.O., Lohr, J.M, *et al.* (2000). Science and pseudoscience in the development of eye movement desensitization and reprocessing: Implications for clerical psychology. *Clinical Psychology Review, 20,* 945–971.

Hyer, L. & Brandsma, J.M. (1997). EMDR minus eye movements equals good psychotherapy. *Journal of Traumatic Stress, 10*(3), 515–522.

Ironson, G., Freund, B., Strauss, J.L. & Williams, J. (2002). Comparison of two treatments for traumatic stress: A community based study of EMDR and prolonged exposure. *Journal of Clinical Psychology, 58*(1), 113–128.

Jaberghaderi, N., Greenwald, R., Rubin, A. *et al.* (2004). A comparison of CBT and EMDR for sexually abused Iranian girls. *Clinical Psychology and Psychotherapy, 11,* 358–368.

Jensen, J.A. (1994). An investigation of eye movement desensitization and reprocessing (EMDR) as a treatment of post traumatic stress disorder (PTSD) symptoms of Vietnam Combat Veterans. *Behaviour Therapy, 25,* 311–326.

Kavanagh, D., Freese, S., Andrade, J. & May, J. (2001). Effects of visuospatial tasks on desensitization to emotive memories. *British Journal of Clinical Psychology, 40,* 267–280.

Kuiken, D., Bears., M., Miall, D. & Smith, L., (2002). Eye movement desensitization reprocessing facilitates attentional orienting. *Imagination, Cognititon and Personality, 21*(1), 3–20.

Lang, P.J. (1979). A bioinformational theory of emotional imagery. *Psychophysiology, 16,* 495–512.

Lee, C., Gavriel, H., Drummond, P. *et al.* (2002). Treatment of post-traumatic stress disorder. A comparison of stress inoculation training with prolonged exposure and eye movement desensitisation and reprocessing. *Journal of Clinical Psychology, 58,* 1071–1089.

Lipke, M. (1996). A four activity model of psychotherapy and its relationship to eye movement desensitisation and reprocessing (EMDR) and other methods of psychotherapy. *International Electronic Journal of Innovations in the Study of the Traumatisation Process and Methods for Reducing or Eliminating Related Human Suffering.* www.fsu.edu/~trauma/art1v2i2.html.

Lohr, J., Klienknecht, R, Tolin, T. & Barrett, R. (1995). The empirical status of the clinical application of eye movement desensitization and reprocessing. *Journal of Behaviour Therapy and Experimental Psychiatry, 26*(4), 285–302.

Lohr, J.M., Lilienfeld, S.O., Tolin, D.F. & Herbert, J.D. (1999). Eye movement desensitization and reprocessing: An analysis of specific versus non-specific factors. *Journal of Anxiety Disorders, 13,* 185–207.

Lohr, J., Tolin, D. & Kleinknecht, R. (1996). An intensive design investigation of eye movement desensitization and reprocessing of claustrophobia. *Journal of Anxiety Disorders, 10,* 73–78.

Lohr, J.M., Tolin, D.F. & Lilienfeld, S.O. (1998). Efficacy of eye movement desensitization and reprocessing. Implications for behaviour therapy. *Behaviour Therapy, 29,* 123–156.

Manfield, P. (ed.). (1998). *Extending EMDR.* New York. Norton.

Marcus, S., Marquis, P. & Sakai, C. (1997). Controlled study of treatment of PTSD using EMDR in an HMO setting. *Psychotherapy, 34,* 307–315.

Marcus, S., Marquis, P. & Sakai, C. (2004). Three and six month follow up of EMDR treatment of PTSD in an HMO setting. *International Journal of Stress Management, 11,* 195–208.

Marks, I.M., Lovell, K., Noshirvani, H. *et al.* (1998). Treatment of post traumatic stress disorder by exposure and/or cognitive restructuring: A controlled study. *Archives of General Psychiatry, 55,* 317–325.

Maxfield, L. & Hyer, L. (2002). The relationship between efficacy and methodology in studies investigating EMDR treatment of PTSD. *Journal of Clinical Psychology, 58*(1), 23–42.

Maxfield, L. & Melnyk, W.T. (2000). Single session treatment of test anxiety with eye movement desensitization and reprocessing (EMDR). *International Journal of Stress Management, 7*, 87–101.

McCulloch, M. & Feldman, P. (1996). Eye movement desensitisation treatment utilises the positive visceral element of the investigatory reflex to inhibit the memories of post traumatic stress disorder. A theoretical analysis. *British Journal of Psychiatry, 169*, 571–579.

McNally, R.J. (1999). Research on eye movement desensitisation and reprocessing (EMDR) as a treatment for PTSD. *PTSD Research Quarterly, 10*(1), 1–7.

Montgomery, R. & Ayllon, T. (1994). Eye movement desensitization across subjects: Subjective and physiological measures of treatment efficacy. *Journal of Behaviour Therapy and Experimental Psychiatry, 25*, 217–230.

National Institute of Clinical Excellence (NICE) (2005). *Guidelines for the Management of PTSD*. London: NICE.

Perkins, B.R. & Rouanzoin, C.C. (2002). A critical evaluation of current views regarding eye movement desensitization and reprocessing (EMDR). Clarifying points of confusion. *Journal of Clinical Psychology, 58*, 77–97.

Pitman, R.K., Orr, S.P., Altman, B. *et al.* (1996). Emotional processing during eye movement desensitization and reprocessing therapy of Vietnam veterans with chronic post traumtic stress disorder. *Comprehensive Psychiatry, 25*, 231–239.

Poole, A.D., De Jongh, A. & Spector, J. (1999) Power therapies. Evidence versus emotion. A reply to Rosen, Lohr, McNally and Herbert. *Behavioural and Cognitive Psychotherapy, 27*, 3–8.

Power, K., McGoldrick, T., Brown, K. (2002). A controlled comparison of EMDR versus Exposure plus Cognitive Restructuring versus Wait List in the treatment of post traumatic stress disorder. *Clinical Psychology and Psychotherapy, 9*, 299–318.

Renfrey, G. & Spates, C.R. (1994). Eye movement desensitisation and reprocessing: A partial dismantling procedure. *Journal of Behaviour Therapy and Experimental Psychiatry, 25*, 231–239.

Rogers, S., Silver, S., Goss, J. *et al.* (1999). A single session group study of eye movement desensitization and reprocessing in treating post traumatic stress disorder among Vietnam War Veterans: preliminary data. *Journal of Anxiety Disorders, 13*(1–2), 119–130.

Rosen, G.M., Lohr, J.M., McNally, R.J. & Herbert, J.D. (1998). Power therapies, miraculous claims, and the cures that fail. *Behavioural and Cognitive Psychotherapy, 26*, 99–101.

Rosen, G.M., Lohr, J.M., McNally, R.J. & Herbert, J.D. (1999). Power therapies: Evidence versus miraculous claims. *Behavioural and Cognitive Psychotherapy, 27*, 9–12.

Rothbaum, B.O. (1997). A controlled study of eye movement desensitization and reprocessing in the treatment of post traumatic stress disordered sexual assault victims. *Bulletin of the Meninger Clinic, 61*(3), 317–334.

Rothbaum, B.O., Astin, M.C. & Marsteller, F. (2005). Prolonged exposure versus eye movement desensitization (EMDR) for PTSD rape victims. *Journal of Traumatic Stress, 18*, 607–617.

Scheck, M.M., Schaeffer, J. & Gillette, C. (1998). Brief psychological intervention with traumatised young women: The efficacy of EMDR. *Journal of Traumatic Stress, 11*, 25–44.

Shalev, A.Y., Friedman, M.J., Foa, E.B. & Keane, T.M. (2000). Integration and summary. In E.B. Foa, T.M. Keane, and M.J. Friedman (eds), *Effective Treatments for PTSD: Practice Guidelines from the International Society for Traumatic Stress Studies* (pp 359–379). New York: Guilford Press.

Shapiro, F. (1989). Eye movement desensitization: A new treatment for post traumatic stress disorder. *Journal of Behaviour Therapy and Experimental Psychiatry, 3*, 211–217.

Shapiro, F. (1991). Eye movement desenzitisation and reprocessing procedure. From EMD to EMDR: A new treatment model for anxiety and related traumata. *Behaviour Therapist, 14*, 133–135.

Shapiro, F, (1993). Eye movement desensitization and reprocessing (EMDR) in 1992. *Journal of Traumatic Stress, 6*, 417–421.

Shapiro, F. (1995). *Eye Movement Desensitization and Reprocessing: Basic Principles, Protocols and Procedures* (1st edn). New York: Guilford Press.

Shapiro, F. (1999). Eye movement desensitization and reprocessing (EMDR) and the anxiety disorders. Clinical and research implications of an integrated psychotherapy treatment. *Journal of Anxiety Disorders, 13*, 35–67.

Shapiro, F. (2001). EMDR 12 years after its introduction: Past and future research. *Journal of Clinical Psychology, 58*(1), 1–22.

Shapiro, F. (2002). *EMDR as an Integrative Psychotherapy Approach: Experts of Diverse Orientations Explore the Paradigm Prism.* Washington, DC. American Psychological Association Press.

Soberman, G., Greenwald, R. & Rule, D. (2002). A controlled study of eye movement desensitisation and reprocessing (EMDR) for boys with conduct problems. *Journal of Aggression, Maltreatment and Trauma, 6*, 217–236.

Solomon, S.D., Gerrity, E.T. & Muff, A.M. (1992). Efficacy of treatments for posttraumatic stress disorder. *Journal of American Medical Association, 268*, 633–638.

Spector, J. & Read, J. (1999). The current status of eye movement desensitization and reprocessing (EMDR). *Clinical Psychology and Psychotherapy, 6*, 165–174.

Sprang, G. (2001). The use of eye movement desensitisation and reprocessing (EMDR) in the treatment of traumatic stress and complicated mourning. Psychological and behavioural outcomes. *Research on Social Work Practice, 11*, 300–320.

Stickgold, R. (2002). EMDR: A putative neurobiological mechanism of action. *Journal of Clinical Psychology, 58*(1), 61–76.

Sweet, A. (1995). A theoretical perspective on the clinical use of EMDR. *The Behaviour Therapist 18*(1), 5–6.

Taylor, S., Thordarsen D.S., Maxfield L., Fedoroff, L.C., & Lovell, K. (2003). Comparative efficacy, speed and adverse effects of three PTSD treatments: Exposure therapy, EMDR, and relaxation training. *Journal of Consulting and Clinical Psychology, 71*, 330–338.

Teasdale, J.D. (1999). Emotional processing, three modes of mind and the prevention of relapse in depression. *Behaviour Research and Therapy, 37*, 53–77.

Van den Hout, M., Muris, P., Salemink, E. & Kindt, M. (2001). Autobiographical memories become less vivid and emotional after eye movements. *British Journal of Clinical Psychiatry, 40*, 121–130.

Van der Kolk, B., Burbridge, J. & Susuki, J. (1997). The psychobiology of traumatic memory: Clinical implications of neuroimagery studies. *Annals of the New York Academy of Sciences, 821*, 99–113.

Van Etten, M. & Taylor, S. (1998). Comparative efficacy of treatments for post traumatic stress disorder. *Clinical Psychology and Psychotherapy, 5*, 126–144.

Vaughan, K., Armstrong, M.F., Gold, R., *et al.* (1994). A trial of eye movement desensitization compared to image habituation training and applied muscle relaxation in post traumatic stress disorder. *Journal of Behaviour Therapy and Experimental Psychiatry, 25*, 283–291.

Welch, K.L. & Beere, D.B. (2002). Eye movement desensitization and reprocessing: a treatment efficacy model. *Clinical Psychology and Psychotherapy, 9*, 165–176.

Wilson, D.L., Silver, S.M., Covi, W.G. & Foster, S. (1996). Eye movement desensitization and reprocessing: Effectiveness and autonomic correlates. *Journal of Behaviour Therapy and Experimental Psychiatry, 27*(3), 219–229.

Wilson, S.A., Becker, L.A. & Tinker, R.H. (1995). Eye movement desisitization and reprocessing (EMDR) treatment for traumatized individuals. *Journal of Consulting and Clinical Psychology, 63*(6), 928–937.

Wolpe, J. (1958). *Psychotherapy by Reciprocal Inhibition.* Stanford, CA: Stanford University Press.

Wolpe, J. & Abrams, J. (1991). Post-traumatic stress disorder overcome by eye movement desensitization: A case report. *Journal of Behaviour Therapy and Experimental Psychiatry, 22*, 39–43.

Zabukovec, J., Lazrove, S. & Shapiro, F. (2000). Self healing aspects of EMDR: the therapeutic change process and perspectives of integrative psychotherapies. *Journal of Psychotherapy Integration, 10*, 189–206.

CHAPTER 7

The Effectiveness of Counselling

John McLeod

University of Abertay, UK

Counselling has become established as a widely available source of help for people who are troubled by a range of different problems in living. It is available from a variety of different agencies in the statutory, voluntary and private sectors. In addition, many doctors, nurses, social workers and teachers have been trained in the use of counselling skills. Counselling represents a form of help and support that is well received by members of the public, who generally recognise the wisdom of finding 'someone to talk to' when faced by challenging life issues. However, perhaps reflecting the diversity of counselling practice settings and populations and the substantial degree of overlap between interventions that might be described as 'psychotherapy' and those that might be viewed as 'counselling', there have been difficulties in defining the nature and characteristics of counselling as a distinctive form of psycho-social treatment. Roth & Fonagy (1996, p. 255) have commented that counselling 'is a term that is poorly defined both in clinical practice and in the research literature.' There has also been a lack of clarity over the evidence base for the effectiveness of counselling, reflected in a paucity of published reviews or meta-analyses.

The aim of the present chapter is to offer an overview of current knowledge regarding counselling. First, the distinctive features of counselling, as a form of psychotherapeutic practice, are identified. Second, issues in evaluating the effectiveness of counselling are discussed. The chapter then examines research evidence with respect to three key areas of counselling provision: counselling in primary care, student counselling, and workplace counselling. Finally, conclusions and recommendations are offered, with specific attention to the implications of the research evidence for professional and organisational issues related to the delivery of services in resource-limited situations.

WHAT IS COUNSELLING?

Historically, counselling and psychotherapy have been largely similar forms of practice in terms of the underlying theoretical rationale on which they are based, the training of

Handbook of Evidence-based Psychotherapies: A Guide for research and practice.
Edited by C. Freeman & M. Power. Copyright © 2007 John Wiley & Sons, Ltd.

therapists and the types of clients that are seen. Any approach to psychological therapy, whether labelled as counselling, as psychotherapy, or in other terms, relies on the development of a relationship between therapist and client/patient in which the latter becomes able to talk about problematic or painful aspects of their life, is offered a framework within which to understand these difficulties, and constructs personal strategies that enable learning, resolution and coping. However, despite the shared conceptual underpinnings of counselling and psychotherapy, there has been a growing divergence between these activities in terms of how these principles are applied in practice, leading to an increased recognition of counselling as a distinctive professional specialisation. The defining features of counselling can be described in the following terms:

- *A relational approach.* Counselling is built around a relationship of trust in which collaborative working is emphasised.
- *Contextualised knowledge/practice.* Counselling is almost always provided in specific settings or for specific social groups (infertility counselling, student counselling, marital/relationship counselling). As a result, psychotherapeutic theories and models are integrated with knowledge regarding the life situation of the person seeking help: the client is viewed as living within a social context, and struggling to resolve specific life issues.
- *Flexible approach, guided by the needs of the client.* Counsellors do not follow predefined treatment manuals, but work with the client to find strategies that are appropriate to individual circumstances.
- *Sensitivity to issues of power and control.* A central aim of counselling is that of facilitating the person's sense of being an agent, able to take action in the world. Interventions that might be perceived by the client as an imposition of external authority (for example, making a psychiatric diagnosis) are rarely used.
- *Resource-oriented approach.* Counselling gives no special priority to analysing the origins of problems unless the client decides that this would be helpful. Instead, counsellors aim to empower clients to make use of whatever personal and cultural resources that are available to them.
- *Negotiated outcomes.* The goals and outcomes of counselling, and criteria for success, are agreed between the client and practitioner on an individual basis.
- *Voluntary participation.* A person who enters counselling does so on the basis that he or she is taking personal responsibility for being there and for termination.

The implementation of these principles results in a psychotherapeutic service that is usually delivered on a one-to-one or couples basis. The importance of client empowerment within the counselling process means that, ideally, counselling will continue until client and counsellor negotiate a mutually acceptable ending. In practice, the majority of people who make use of counselling expect to receive, and attend, around six to eight sessions. There are some clients who appear to benefit from one or two sessions and a small group that require a long-term relationship with a counsellor. The community-based location of many counselling services means that some clients consult their counsellor intermittently, rather than for a sustained series of sessions in any one treatment episode. An understanding of counselling is not possible in the absence of an appreciation of the characteristics, training and working patterns of counsellors. It is important to note that the shape of counselling as a profession differs substantially across national boundaries – these observations refer primarily to the situation in the UK. Counselling training typically involves a three- or four-year part-time programme, encompassing counselling skills and theory, professional issues, personal development, research awareness and a practice placement, normally at postgraduate diploma or masters level. Professional accreditation, for example by the leading body in the UK, the British Association for Counselling and Psychotherapy, will normally require at least two years of post-qualification supervised practice and ongoing commitment to continuing professional development. The majority of counsellors enter training in their 30s or 40s, having previously worked in a profession such as nursing, social work, teaching or the clergy, or having engaged in voluntary work. Counsellors are a highly interdisciplinary workforce, with only perhaps 20 % having completed a psychology degree, whereas others bring into their work concepts and epistemologies derived from the arts, sciences, social sciences, humanities and professions. Regular clinical supervision, and ongoing personal development (often through participation in personal therapy) are mandatory for members of the counselling profession in the UK. These features are consistent with, and a necessary part of, an approach to practice that highlights the importance of the *relationship* between counsellor and client – counsellors tend to be people whose early career has given them experience of many different types and intensity of professional relationship. The requirement for supervision, consultation and personal therapy means that professional effectiveness is maintained through a network of relationships with colleagues.

In addition to a core professional cadre of around 20 000 fully qualified counsellors in the UK, there are also many other people who are trained to a paraprofessional level and offer counselling through voluntary agencies and helplines, as well as nurses, social workers and other human services personnel who have received training in counselling skills. It is important to note that the standard of training in many voluntary agencies matches or exceeds the accreditation criteria of BACP.

ISSUES IN EVALUATING THE EFFECTIVENESS OF COUNSELLING

Before moving to consideration of the research evidence for the effectiveness of counselling, it is necessary to take account of a number of issues and barriers associated with research in this area. It is clear that the level of control associated with randomised trials does not sit easily with everyday counselling practice. Formal assessment of clients, random non-negotiable allocation to treatment modalities, manualisation of therapist interventions, and fixed time lengths for therapy are all examples of essential features of well-run randomised trials that are in conflict with the values and conduct of counselling. One of the results of this conflict is that it has been difficult to achieve randomisation in controlled studies of counselling. For example, Fairhurst & Dowrick (1996) tried to set up a controlled study of counselling outcome in eight GP practices, comparing counselling with treatment as usual. They found that, five months after the start of the study, only one patient had been recruited. On conducting interviews with GPs on why this had happened, three main factors emerged: ethical dilemmas around refusing counselling to patients, patient refusal and a perception of counselling as a 'last resort', with the implication that referral to ongoing GP care was perceived as futile. Similar randomisation issues were reported in a major study of counselling in primary care carried out by Simpson et al. (2000).

In an attempt to be faithful to the nature of counselling practice, some researchers have sought to conduct naturalistic studies, in which clients receiving counselling complete questionnaires at the beginning and end of their treatment. Often, the results of these studies are difficult to interpret due to the proportion of missing data arising from unplanned endings of counselling and lack of adherence to research protocols. For example, in a large-scale naturalistic study of workplace counselling carried out by Highley-Marchington & Cooper (1998), 179 clients completed pre-counselling questionnaires, 103 completed post-counselling questionnaires, and 28 at follow-up.

Another limitation of current research into counselling arises from the contextual nature of much counselling practice. In many situations, the rationale for funding counselling services relies in part on the possibility that counselling will yield community or system benefits as well as helping individual clients. For example, the rationale for student counselling services includes the hope that the presence of a counselling service will reduce pressure on academic staff, by giving them a ready source of referral for 'difficult' students. However, systemic, organisational or societal outcomes of counselling are not easy to measure.

THE EFFECTIVENESS OF COUNSELLING

Three areas of counselling service delivery are discussed below – counselling in primary care, student counselling, and workplace counselling. These settings have been selected because they represent major areas of counselling practice and can be taken as exemplars for research into counselling outcomes as a whole.

Counselling in Primary Care

Counsellors have been employed in primary care settings in the UK since the 1980s, generally receiving referrals from GPs for patients reporting problems in such areas as relationship difficulties, moderate depression, anxiety and stress. Counselling is available in more than 50 % of GP practices in England (Mellor-Clark, 2000) and protocols have been developed which define the role and of counsellors in primary care (National Primary Care Research and Development Centre, 2001). A Scottish Office report conducted in the 1990s noted the potential value of counselling in primary care but called for further research to establish its effectiveness (National Medical Advisory Committee, 1998). A number of investigations of the effectiveness of counselling in primary care have been published, encompassing both controlled trials, and naturalistic studies.

Early randomised trials have compared the effectiveness of counselling with treatment as usual from the GP (Ashurst & Ward, 1983; Boot et al., 1994; Friedli et al., 1997; Harvey et al., 1998; Hemmings, 1997). More recently, randomised trials have compared counselling, cognitive-behaviour therapy (CBT) and treatment as usual (Ridsdale et al., 2001; Simpson et al., 2000, 2003; Ward et al., 2000), with patient preference conditions, and between counselling and drug treatment (Bedi et al., 2000). The patient groups taking part in these studies have included individuals assessed as suffering from moderate and chronic depression, anxiety and chronic fatigue. This set of studies has been systematically reviewed by Bower *et al.* (2002, 2003). The key findings to emerge from these reviews have been:

- significantly greater clinical effectiveness in the counselling group compared with 'usual care' in the short term but not the long term;
- similar levels of clinical effectiveness when counselling is compared to CBT or to drug treatment;
- higher levels of user satisfaction with counselling compared with other treatments;
- similar total costs associated with counselling and usual care over the long term;
- some evidence that counselling can reduce antidepressant use and number of GP visits.

These studies have all comprised pragmatic randomised trials, which have involved compromise between methodological rigour and the realities of routine service delivery in a primary-care setting (Scott & Sensky, 2003). Overall, the results of these studies suggest that counselling represents an intervention that is equivalent in effectiveness to any of the other forms of primary care intervention currently available for patients reporting moderate levels of mental health difficulty. The only distinctive advantage of counselling, against other interventions, is that patients prefer it and are more satisfied at the end of treatment.

Evidence from a number of naturalistic or uncontrolled studies allows a more comprehensive understanding of the role of counselling in primary care to emerge. In a major study conducted by Mellor-Clark *et al.* (2001), more than 2 800 clients receiving primary care counselling were invited to complete the CORE evaluation questionnaire (Evans *et al.*, 2000) at intake and end of counselling. Counsellors also completed questionnaires recording information about the type of therapy that was delivered. The findings of this study yield a unique picture of counselling in primary care practice. The average number of sessions received by clients was 4.3, with 32 % attending weekly, and 42 % fortnightly. The main approaches used by counsellors were person-centred, CBT and integrative. The mean age of client was 38 years, with women accounting for 70 % of the sample. The average waiting time was six weeks. At intake, 76 % of clients scored above clinical 'caseness' level on the CORE questionnaire, and 43 % were on medication to help with their psychological problems. Of those who completed questionnaires at termination, 75 % recorded clinically significant levels of change. The interpretation of these findings is problematic, however, due to the low (40 %) return rate for end-of-counselling client questionnaires in this study. Nettleton *et al.* (2000) collected evaluative data from a range of stakeholders involved with three GP practices in a rural area and reported that the counselling service was found to fill a gap by addressing the needs of a substantial group of patients for whom psychiatric care was seen to be inappropriate. Martinus *et al.* (2001) evaluated the effectiveness of a counselling service for alcohol problems, operated by a voluntary agency in a set of GP practices and found that 96 % of GPs regarded the service as very helpful and that the average alcohol use of clients had reduced substantially. Fletcher *et al.* (1995) examined the relationship between the provision of counselling and the prescribing of antidepressants, hypnotics and anxiolytics in general practice. They looked at differences between practices that directly employed a counsellor and those who had a visiting counsellor or who referred elsewhere. Highest levels of prescribing were in practices that employed a counsellor directly. Sibbald *et al.* (1996) analysed prescribing patterns for psychotropic drugs in practices with (n = 126) and without (n = 88) counsellors, drawn from a national survey. They found no appreciable differences for prescribing rates or drug costs.

In addition to studies that have evaluated the effectiveness of specialist counsellors in primary care, there has also been research into the use of counselling interventions by nursing staff in primary settings. Klerman *et al.* (1987) examined the efficacy of a brief psychosocial intervention for symptoms of stress and distress among patients in primary care delivered by nurse practitioners within minimal training (12 hours) in brief counselling. At follow-up, 83 % of counselling patients had returned to the non-clinical range of anxiety and depression scores, compared with 63 % of controls. There was some evidence that patients who had received counselling subsequently used more physician time. Holden, Sagovsky & Cox (1989) conducted a controlled study of health visitor intervention in the treatment of post-natal depression. Experienced health visitors trained for 6 hours in a Rogerian approach offered an average of nine weekly sessions of counselling to depressed women who had been randomly allocated to counselling or a treatment as usual condition. Patients who had received counselling showed significantly higher improvement on depression and psychiatric symptoms at follow-up (one month after the end of counselling).

In conclusion, the evidence as a whole suggests that counselling in primary care is highly acceptable to both patients and health professionals and produces short-term gains for patients compared to treatment as usual. Over the longer term, however, differential gains arising from counselling, as compared to treatment as usual, have not been observed. The effectiveness of counselling is equivalent to that achieved by other interventions that are available for primary-care treatment of moderate mental health problems, specifically CBT and drug treatment. The impact of counselling on health-care costs, such as drug bills and GP time, is unclear. It is possible that some patients who have benefited from counselling may require less assistance in future from the health-care system, whereas other may have been empowered to demand more care.

It seems clear that further research is needed in order to determine the effectiveness of counselling in primary care, in relation to a series of key factors. The quality of the collaborative relationship between GPs and counsellors employed in primary care practices would seem a crucial variable in terms of the appropriateness of referrals, and in containing difficult or complex cases. However, apart from a qualitative study by Hemmings (1997), this important contextual aspect of counselling in primary-care practice has not been examined. It would also be useful to evaluate the role of counselling from a stepped care perspective (Davison, 2000). In practice, as illustrated in the study by Mellor-Clark *et al.* (2001), many GPs seek to manage patients with moderate mental health problems within their own resources before referring them to counselling and may even regard counselling as a potential 'step' that in turn may lead to later referral to clinical psychology or a community mental health team. Finally, it is necessary to recognise that the outcome variables such as depression scores that have been used to evaluate the effectiveness of counselling in the majority of controlled studies are at best proxy measures for kind of learning and development, and capacity to use personal and social resources, that counsellors seek to facilitate in clients. It may be that a more sensitive evaluation of the longer term benefits of counselling in primary care will require the construction of appropriate methods for assessing these dimensions of change.

College and Student Counselling

Although counsellors have been employed in virtually all universities and in many colleges since the 1960s, there exists only a very limited evidence base regarding the effectiveness of counselling in this sector. Currently, there are no systematic reviews of the effectiveness of counselling in university and college settings available in the literature. Keilson, Dworkin & Gelso (1983) found that open-ended and time-limited counselling (eight sessions) were both more effective than a control condition for students seeking help for personal and social difficulties. In a study carried out at a UK university, Rickinson (1997) found that 79 % of undergraduate student clients reported symptom levels consistent with psychiatric 'caseness' at intake. Following counselling, clients recorded substantial improvement on a range of mental health dimensions. A comparison group of students who did not receive counselling exhibited minimal change over the same period of time. Turner *et al.* (1996) found that time-limited counselling had a modest impact on adjustment in a sample of student clients. Vonk & Thyer (1999), in a study of the effectiveness of short-term counselling (average 10 sessions), found that, compared to students in a waiting-list condition, those who received counselling recorded substantial levels of clinical improvement. In this study, 73 % of clients met the criteria for psychiatric 'caseness' at intake. Research has also examined the impact of counselling on the retention of students in higher education. Turner & Berry (2000) analysed the records of 2 365 student users of a university counselling service, seen over a six-year period, in terms of graduation and retention rates. Compared with students who had not used the counselling service, former clients were more likely to re-enrol in the year following counselling (85 % versus 74 %), and were equally likely to graduate. Wilson *et al.* (1997) examined the academic records, after a two-year period, of students who had made use of counselling, and found that counselled students were 14 % more likely than their non-counselled counterparts to remain enrolled. Rickinson (1998) followed up final-year students receiving counselling. While 95 % of these students reported that their academic performance had been affected by their problems prior to entering counselling, all of them graduated successfully.

Research into university and college counselling indicates that short-term counselling interventions are effective in addressing personal and social problems experienced by students, and in enabling students to remain within the educational system. Further research is required to establish the generalisability of these findings.

Workplace Counselling

Research into the outcomes of Employee Assistance Programme (EAP) and workplace counselling provision has largely focused on the impact of this type of intervention on three areas of psycho-social functioning:

- psychological, for example symptoms of stress and anxiety, and self-esteem;
- attitudes to work, for example job commitment and satisfaction
- work behaviour, for example sickness absence, job performance and accidents.

Several studies have also used client satisfaction as an indicator of the effectiveness of EAP/counselling programmes and some researchers have analysed the economic costs and benefits of workplace counselling provision. A scoping search conducted by McLeod (2001) identified 39 studies that examined the outcomes of workplace counselling. However, some of these studies were of poor methodological quality whereas others described interventions that comprised specific forms of psychotherapy, rather than counselling.

All of the studies that evaluated the effectiveness of specialist counsellors operating in workplace contexts used naturalistic designs, in which clients receiving counselling under routine circumstances were invited to complete questionnaires at the beginning of counselling, at the end, and at follow-up. Cheeseman (1996) carried out an investigation of two employee counselling services in the National Health Service. He reported that client levels of distress at the beginning of counselling were significantly higher than organisational norms and similar to psychotherapy out-patient clinical profiles. Substantial reductions in levels of distress and symptomatology were recorded between entering counselling and follow-up. Somewhat smaller, but also statistically significant, gains were found in relationship problems and use of positive coping strategies (particularly social support and the use of rational reflection). In an evaluation of a stress counselling service for Post Office workers, Allinson, Cooper & Reynolds (1989), Cooper *et al.* (1990) and Cooper & Sadri (1991) found that, at the beginning of counselling, clients had anxiety, depression and somatic scores that were significantly higher than those in a normative sample of UK workers. Post-counselling, clients showed significant improvement in anxiety, depression, somatic symptoms and self-esteem. There was no change in job satisfaction and a significant decrease in organisational commitment. Sickness absence events and days off both reduced significantly. Goss & Mearns (1997) evaluated the effectiveness of a local authority education department counselling service and found that 65 % of clients reported that counselling had improved their problems, and that sickness absence rates for a six-month period following counselling improved by 62 %. Guppy & Marsden (1997) analysed the outcomes of counselling provided for employees who had been referred to an alcohol misuse programme in a transportation company. Significant improvements were reported in mental health (35 % of clients showed clinically significant levels of gain), client and supervisor ratings of work performance and in absenteeism. There was no overall change in job commitment or satisfaction. Highley-Marchington & Cooper (1998) collected outcome data from nine different EAP/workplace counselling schemes, and found a high level of client satisfaction with services. Significant differences were found pre- and post-counselling on mental and physical health scales but no differences on job satisfaction measures. There was a significant improvement in sickness absence. Reynolds (1997) examined the effectiveness of counselling provided to local authority staff and found high levels of satisfaction with counselling, with 80 % of clients recording clinically significant change in depression. No effect on absenteeism or job satisfaction was found. Worrall (1999) evaluated the effectiveness of an external counselling scheme for public sector workers, and found high levels of client satisfaction and clinically significant levels of change in presenting problem ratings in 58 % of clients.

A limited amount of research into the economic costs and benefits of workplace counselling has been carried out. Blaze-Temple & Howat (1997) analysed the cost/benefit of an Australian EAP, and found that the service produced significant cost savings in absenteeism and turnover. Cost benefit ratio for counselling compared with no counselling was 1:1 (the EAP paid for itself). Bruhnsen (1989) conducted a cost-benefit analysis of university EAP and estimated a cost-benefit saving ratio of 1.5:1. The most significant savings were in alcoholism cases (21 % drop in sickness absence) and drug abuse cases (50 % drop). McClellan (1989) conducted a cost-benefit analysis of a local government EAP service in the US and concluded that the service did not produce a financial benefit to the employer because no plausible cost offsets could be identified in such areas as health insurance costs, paid sick leave, productivity improvements or employee turnover.

Although research into workplace counselling and EAP services consistently yields a generally positive view of the effectiveness of counselling in this setting, it is important to take account of the methodological limitations of the research base. While the studies that have been carried out on the impact of counselling on mental health, wellbeing and organisational commitment arrive at strong conclusions about the benefits of counselling, in almost all of these studies significant proportions of clients failed to complete end-of-counselling or follow-up questionnaires. Since it is likely that questionnaires are more often completed by satisfied service users, it is probable that the results of these somewhat over-estimate the effectiveness of counselling by an amount that is impossible to quantify. The findings of economic studies of workplace counselling are equivocal and it is clear that further research of this type needs to be carried out in this area.

CONCLUSIONS

Counselling is an activity that takes place within a wide range of settings. This review of re-search into the effectiveness of counselling has not attempted to encompass all of these areas but has instead focused on the evidence provided by key research studies into counselling in primary care, student counselling, and workplace counselling. There are some general conclusions that can be drawn from this body of research. There is evidence that counselling can claim levels of effectiveness that are broadly equivalent to those associated with other, more intensively researched mental health interventions such as CBT, psychotherapy and drug treatment. Counselling appears to have a particularly significant short-term impact, with long-term benefits in situations such as student counselling, where an individual may have good personal resources but need assistance in overcoming a specific crisis or diffi-culty. Counselling is well received by clients, who actively choose it as a form of help and are overwhelmingly satisfied with the service they receive. The majority of people who enter counselling report levels of distress and psychological disability that are similar to those found in psychiatric patients. Counselling seems to be able to make a difference to clients within six to 10 sessions. The contextual nature of counselling is reflected in re-search that demonstrates benefits in relation to organisational and systemic outcomes such as use of health resources, sickness absence, and student retention.

This largely positive picture of the effectiveness of counselling needs to be balanced against the methodological limitations of the research that has been carried out. Essentially, randomised controlled trials tend to create a research framework that diminishes the distinc-tive features of counselling whereas naturalistic studies tend to result in substantial levels of participant attrition, leading to difficulties in the interpretation of findings. It is essential for researchers within this field to develop pluralist methodologies that combine high standards of causal inference alongside greater sensitivity to the shape of routine practice.

What are the implications of research for anyone seeking to establish a counselling service within a community, organisational or health-care setting? There are three main recommendations that can be made. First, anyone setting up a counselling service can be reasonably confident that it will be well received by users, will be cost neutral and that between 50 % and 70 % of clients will report that counselling has had a significant impact on their presenting problems. Second, it is important that the design of the service takes into account the context within which counselling will take place. Ideally, counsellors should have personal experience of the organisational culture of the setting within which counselling is offered, or specific training in relation to the client group, so that they possess an informed awareness of the 'fit' between clients and their social context. Third, it should be recognised that effective counselling is not a matter of competence in delivering a standard intervention package but instead relies on building relationships within which clients can say whatever they need to say and explore different ways of approaching problems. In this respect, counselling practice reflects, in a basic way, the substantial body of research that demonstrates that client outcomes are influenced to a much greater extent by relationship factors than they are by therapeutic approach or mastery of technique (Norcross, 2002).

REFERENCES

Allison, T., Cooper C.L. & Reynolds, S. (1989). Stress counselling in the workplace. The Post Office experience. *The Psychologist, 12,* 384–388.

Ashurst, P.M. & Ward, D.F. (1983). *An Evaluation of Counselling in General Practice. Final Report of the Leverhulme Counselling Project.* London: Mental Health Foundation.

Bedi, N., Chilvers, C., Churchill, R. *et al.* (2000). Assessing effectiveness of treatment of depression in primary care. Partially randomised preference trial. *British Journal of Psychiatry, 177,* 312–318.

Blaze-Temple, D. & Howat, P. (1997). Cost benefit of an Australian EAP, *Employee Assistance Quarterly, 12*(3), 1–24.

Boot, D., Gillies, P., Fenelon, J. *et al.* (1994). Evaluation of the short-term impact of counseling in general practice. *Patient Education and Counseling, 24,* 79–89.

Bower, P., Byford, S., Sibbald, B. *et al.* (2000). Randomized controlled trial of non-directive counselling, cognitive-behavioural therapy and usual GP care for patients with depression. II: Cost effectiveness. *British Medical Journal, 321,* 1389–1392.

Bower, P., Rowland, N. & Hardy, R. (2003). The clinical effectiveness of counselling in primary care: A systematic review and meta-analysis. *Psychological Medicine, 33,* 203–216.

Bower, P., Rowland, N., Mellor Clark, J. *et al.* (2002). Effectiveness and cost effectiveness of counselling in primary care (Cochrane Review). In: *The Cochrane Library,* 1. Oxford: Update Software.

Bruhnsen, K. (1989). EAP evaluation and cost benefit savings: a case example. *Health Values, 13*(1), 39–42.

Cheeseman, M.J. (1996). *Is Staff Counselling an Effective Intervention into Employee Distress? An Investigation of Two Employee Counselling Services in the NHS.* Unpublished PhD thesis, Social and Applied Psychology Unit, University of Sheffield.

Cooper, C.L. & Sadri, G. (1991). The impact of stress counselling at work. In Perrewe, P.L. (ed.) Handbook on Job Stress (special issue). *Journal of Behavior and Personality, 6*(7), 411–423.

Cooper, C.L., Sadri, G., Allison, T. & Reynolds, P. (1990). Counselling in the Post Office. *Counselling Psychologist Quarterly, 3*(1), 3–11.

Davison, G.C. (2000). Stepped care: doing more with less? *Journal of Consulting and Clinical Psychology, 68,* 580–585.

Evans, C., Mellor-Clark, J., Margison, F. *et al.* (2000). CORE: Clinical outcomes in routine evaluation. *Journal of Mental Health, 9,* 247–255.

Fairhurst, K. & Dowrick, C. (1996). Problems with recruitment in a randomized controlled trial of counselling in general practice: Causes and implications, *Journal of Health Services Research and Policy, 1,* 77–80.

Fletcher, J., Fahey, T. & McWilliam, J. (1995). Relationship between the provision of counselling and the prescribing of antidepressants, hypnotics and anxiolytics in general practice, *British Journal of General Practice, 45,* 467–469.

Friedli, K., King, M.B., Lloyd, M. & Horder, J. (1997). Randomised controlled assessment of non-directive psychotherapy versus routine general-practitioner care. *Lancet, 350,* 1662–1665.

Gam, J., Sauser, W.I., Evans, K.L. & Lair, C.V. (1983). The evaluation of an employee assistance program, *Journal of Employment Consulting, 20,* 99–106.

Gammie, B. (1997). Employee assistance programs in the UK oil industry: An examination of current operational practice, *Personnel Review, 26*(1/2), 66–80.

Goss, S. & Mearns, D. (1997). Applied pluralism in the evaluation of employee counselling. *British Journal of Guidance and Counselling, 25*(3), 327–344.

Guppy, A. & Marsden, J. (1997). Assisting employees with drinking problems: Changes in mental health, job perceptions and work performance, *Work and Stress, 11*(4), 341–350.

Harvey, I., Nelson, S.J., Lyons, R.A. *et al.* (1998). A randomized controlled trial and economic evaluation of counselling in primary care. *British Journal of General Practice, 48*(428), 1043–1048.

Hemmings, A. (1997). Counselling in primary care: A randomised controlled trial. *Patient Education and Counselling, 32*, 219–30.

Highley-Marchington, J.C. & Cooper, C.L. (1998). *An Assessment of Employee Assistance and Workplace Counselling Programmes in British Organisations*. A *Report for the Health and Safety Executive*. Sudbury: HSE Books.

Holden, J.A., Sagovsky, R. & Cox, J.L. (1989). Counselling in a general practice setting: Controlled study of health visitor intervention in treatment of postnatal depression, *British Medical Journal, 298*, 223–226.

Keilson, M.V., Dworkin, F.H. & Gelso, C.J. (1983). The effectiveness of time-limited therapy in a university counselling center. In C.J. Gelso & D.H. Johnson (eds) *Explorations in Time-limited Counseling and Psychotherapy*. New York: Teacher's College.

Klerman, G.L., Budman, S., Berwick, D. *et al.* (1987). Efficacy of a brief psychosocial intervention for symptoms of stress and distress among patients in primary care. *Medical Care*, 25, 1078–1088.

Lambert, M.J. (ed.) (2003). *Bergin and Lambert's Handbook of Psychotherapy and Behavior Change* (5th edn). Chichester: Wiley.

Martinus, T., Anderson, B. & Carter, H. (2001). Counselling for alcohol problems in primary care in Forth Valley – an innovative approach? *Health Bulletin, 59*(3), 158–162.

McClellan, K. (1989). Cost-benefit analysis of the Ohio EAP. *Employee Assistance Quarterly, 5*(2), 67–85.

McLeod, J. (2001). *Counselling in the Workplace: The Facts. A Systematic Review of the Research Evidence*. Rugby: BACP.

Mellor-Clark, J. (2000).*Counselling in Primary Care in the Context of the NHS Quality Agenda: The Facts*. Rugby: BACP.

Mellor-Clark, J., Connell, J., Barkham, M. & Cummins, P. (2001). Counselling outcomes in primary health care: A CORE system data profile. *European Journal of Psychotherapy, Counselling and Health, 4*, 65–86.

National Medical Advisory Committee (1998) *Counselling in Primary Care.* Edinburgh: Scottish Office.

National Primary Care Research and Development Centre (2001). *Quality in Counselling in Primary Care: A Guide for Effective Commissioning and Clinical Governance*. http://www.npcrdc.man.ac.uk/Pages/Publications/PDF/cnsg-hbk.pdf.

Nettleton, B., Cooksey, E., Mordue, A. *et al.* (2000). Counselling: filling a gap in general practice. *Patient Education and Counseling, 41*(2), 197–207.

Norcross, J.C. (ed.) (2002). *Psychotherapy Relationships that Work. Therapist Contributions and Responsiveness to Patients*. New York: Oxford University Press.

Reynolds, S. (1997). Psychological well-being at work: Is prevention better than cure? *Journal for Psychosomatic Research, 43*(1), 93–102.

Rickinson, B. (1997). Evaluating the effectiveness of counselling intervention with final year undergraduates. *Counselling Psychology Quarterly, 10*, 271–285.

Rickinson, B. (1998). The relationship between undergraduate student counselling and successful degree completion. *Studies in Higher Education, 23*, 95–102.

Ridsdale, L., Godfrey, E., Chalder, T., *et al.* (2001). Chronic fatigue in general practice: Is counselling as good as cognitive behaviour therapy? A UK randomised trial. *British Journal of General Practice, 51*(462), 19–24.

Roth, A. & Fonagy, P. (1996). *What Works for Whom? A Critical Review of Psychotherapy Research*. New York: Guilford Press.

Sadu, G., Cooper, C. & Allison, T. (1989). A Post Office initiative to stamp out stress, *Personnel Management*, August, 40–45.

Scott, J. & Sensky, T. (2003). Methodological aspects of randomized controlled trials of psychotherapy in primary care. *Psychological Medicine, 33*, 191–196.

Sibbald, B., Addington-Hall, J., Brenneman, D. & Freeling, P. (1996). Investigation of whether on-site general practice counsellors have an impact on psychotropic drug prescribing rates and costs. *British Journal of General Practice, 46*, 63–67.

Simpson, S., Corney, R., Fitzgerald, P. & Beecham, J. (2000). A randomised controlled trial to evaluate the effectiveness and cost-effectiveness of counselling patients with chronic depression. *Health Technology Assessment, 4*(36), 1–83.

Simpson, S., Corney, R., Fitzgerald, P. & Beecham, J. (2003) A randomized controlled trial to evaluate the effectiveness and cost-effectiveness of psychodynamic counselling for general practice patients with chronic depression. *Psychological Medicine, 33*, 229–240.

Sprang, G. (1992). Utilizing a brief EAP-based intervention as an agent for change in the treatment of depression, *Employee Assistance Quarterly, 8*, 57–65.

Turner, A.L. & Berry, T.R. (2000). Counseling center contributions to student retention and graduation: a longtitudinal assessment. *Journal of College Student Development, 41*, 627–636.

Turner, P.R., Valtierra, M., Talken, T.R. *et al.* (1996). Effect of session length on treatment outcome for college students in brief therapy. *Journal of Counseling Psychology, 43*, 228–232.

Vonk, M.E., Thyer, B.E. (1999). Evaluating the effectiveness of short-term treatment at a university counseling center. *Journal of Clinical Psychology, 55*, 1096–1106.

Ward, E., King, M., Lloyd, M. *et al.* (2000). Randomized controlled trail of non-directive counselling, cognitive-behavioural therapy and usual GP care for patients with depression. I: Clinical effectiveness. *British Medical Journal, 321*, 1383–1388.

Wilson, S.B., Mason, T.W. & Ewing, M.J.M. (1997). Evaluating the impact of receiving university-based counseling services on student retention. *Journal of Counseling Psychology, 44*, 316–320.

Worrall, L. (1999) *Evaluation of the Effectiveness of an Employee Counselling Programme*. Unpublished PhD thesis, Department of Psychology, Keele University.

CHAPTER 8

Constructivist and Humanistic Therapies

David A. Winter
University of Hertfordshire and Barnet, Enfield and Haringey Mental Health NHS Trust, UK

The two broad approaches to psychotherapy that will be described in this chapter essentially arose in the middle of the twentieth century out of dissatisfaction with the reductionist, deterministic, and mechanistic assumptions evident in traditional psychodynamic and behavioural approaches and the need to develop a 'third force' (Bugental, 1964) in psychology. In contrast to such assumptions, constructivist and humanistic approaches share a holistic view of the person, consider the person to be self-directed and to make active choices and are concerned with the personal meaning of the individual's situation. However, there are also certain differences between these two approaches, each of which will now be considered separately.

CONSTRUCTIVIST THERAPIES

Theoretical Basis

There are several variants of constructivist therapy, many of them developed relatively recently, but all share the epistemological belief that individuals cannot directly experience reality and that instead they actively construct their worlds (Mahoney, 1988; Neimeyer, 1995; Neimeyer & Rood, 1997). The first such therapeutic approach to emerge, George Kelly's (1955) personal construct psychotherapy, was ahead of its time but is still the most well elaborated at the theoretical level. Its underlying philosophical assumption of 'constructive alternativism' asserts that 'all of our present interpretations of the universe are subject to revision or replacement' (Kelly, 1955, p. 15). The 'fundamental postulate' of personal construct theory essentially states that the anticipation of events is central to human functioning, with the person operating like a scientist. Eleven corollaries of this postulate indicate how this anticipation occurs. Each individual's anticipations, in Kelly's view, are derived from a hierarchically organised system of bipolar personal constructs. These constructs are not all verbal, nor is a person necessarily fully aware of how he or she construes the world.

Handbook of Evidence-based Psychotherapies: A Guide for research and practice.
Edited by C. Freeman & M. Power. Copyright © 2007 John Wiley & Sons, Ltd.

Although there may be certain similarities between the construct systems of different individuals, particularly within the same cultural group, each person's construct system is unique. It is in construing other people's construction processes, or trying to see the world through their eyes, that a social relationship develops. The individuality of construing may be reflected in the contrasting poles of some of a person's constructs and in the relationships between their constructs. For example, in the case of Nigel, who was referred for psychological assessment after behaving in such a way at university that he was likely not to be allowed to continue his course, one of his constructs contrasted being self-destructive with being egotistical. The positive implications of self-destructiveness for him were further indicated by the relationships of this construct with various others in his system: for example, 'aware – blinkered', 'free – conventional', and 'thoughtful – disinterested'.

Each construct presents the individual with a choice in that the self, or some other event, may be construed in terms of either of the construct's poles. From the personal construct theory perspective, the person will choose that option which appears to present greater possibilities for elaboration of his or her construct system and therefore for better anticipation of the world. For Nigel, self-destructiveness appeared to provide that option, just as for many of our clients their symptom provides them with a well elaborated 'way of life' (Fransella, 1970).

A person's anticipations may or may not be validated by his or her experiences of events. Optimally, if a particular anticipation is invalidated, reconstruing will occur. However, there is evidence that the more 'superordinate' constructs in an individual's system are particularly resistant to invalidation and this is especially likely to be the case if these are 'core' constructs, which are central to the person's identity. In Kelly's view, people are threatened by the awareness of an imminent comprehensive change in these core structures and feel guilty if they find themselves dislodged from their core role structure, their characteristic way of interacting with other people. Nigel, for example, would be likely to feel guilty if he behaved egotistically towards others, while a hardened criminal might experience guilt if interacting with another person in an honest, law-abiding fashion. From a personal construct theory perspective, a client's resistance to therapy may be explained in terms of therapy having provoked high levels of threat or guilt. Another emotion that is of considerable relevance to the therapeutic process is anxiety, which Kelly viewed as occurring when an individual's constructs do not enable him or her to anticipate events.

Instead of revising their construing in the face of invalidation, people occasionally try to change the world to make it fit with their construct systems. Thus, if Nigel were to meet someone whom he construed as neither self-destructive nor disinterested, he might behave in such an offensive manner that the other person would express disinterest in him, thus validating Nigel's original construction. This is hostility in Kelly's sense of the term. In psychological disorder, there is persistent use of a particular construction despite consistent invalidation. The disordered individual will generally use particular strategies to avoid invalidation and there is research evidence of the strategies of construing that characterise particular disorders (Winter, 1992, 2003a).

Although later personal construct theorists have elaborated these areas, Kelly did not give detailed attention to the development of construing or to social constructions. However, these have been central to some of the other variants of constructivist therapy. For example, Guidano's (1987) *developmental approach* views attachment processes, particularly in the parent-child relationship, as the basis for the development of an individual's 'personal meaning organisation', which gives some order to their experiences. In normal functioning, the personal meaning organisation is relatively flexible whereas in 'cognitive dysfunction' it adopts particular patterns of 'closure', related to certain developmental pathways and associated clinical problems. *Systemic constructivist* therapies (see, for example, Selvini-Palazzoli *et al.*, 1980; Efran *et al.*, 1990) consider meaning to have a basis in language and *social constructionist* approaches (McNamee & Gergen, 1992) regard it as being culturally determined. In several of these approaches (for example, White & Epston, 1990), as in the work of some post-Kellyan personal construct theorists (Mair, 1988; Neimeyer, 1994; Viney, 1993), people are viewed as structuring their experience in terms of stories.

Distinguishing Features of Therapy

An essential feature of the constructivist approach to therapy is that the therapist is not regarded as having privileged access to truth. He or she will take a 'credulous attitude' (Kelly, 1955) to the client's view of the world, although this does not preclude the use of 'diagnostic constructs' to understand clients' situations, to assess their available pathways of movement and to guide the therapeutic intervention. Although the aim of the intervention will be to facilitate reconstruing, it will not be to persuade the client to construe events in a particular way. In this respect, constructivist therapies stand in marked contrast to rationalist cognitive therapy, and there is some research evidence that the latter approach is more directive, and more negative in the attitude towards the client than is personal construct psychotherapy (Winter & Watson, 1999).

Therapeutic Practice

Constructivist therapies are 'technically eclectic' (Norcross, 1986) in that although they may use a range of techniques, some borrowed from other models, these are always selected on the basis of their likely effects on the client's construing. The various forms of constructivist therapy differ somewhat in the approach adopted, and the techniques likely to be employed, by the therapist.

In personal construct psychotherapy the initial focus will usually be on the elaboration of the client's construct system, often with the aid of various assessment techniques. The most familiar of these is the repertory grid (Beail, 1985; Fransella, Bell & Bannister, 2004; Kelly, 1955), in which a sample of the client's constructs is elicited by asking him or her to compare and contrast various elements or aspects of experience. These elements are usually significant people in the client's life and components of the self. In the final stage of the procedure, the client sorts all of the elements in terms of all of the constructs, generally by rating or ranking them. The grid is usually analysed by computer, and the measures thus derived provide indications of the personal meaning of the client's constructs, similarities and differences in the construing of particular elements, and the structural properties of the construct system (for example, its 'tightness' or degree of rigidity). Another technique, known as laddering (Hinkle, 1965), charts the hierarchical structure of the client's construct system by asking, for a particular construct, which pole he or she would prefer to be described by and why, and repeating the process for the next, and each succeeding, construct elicited. Each such construct is assumed to be superordinate to the last. A further assessment technique, originally proposed by Kelly (1955), is the self-characterisation, in which the client is asked to write an autobiographical sketch as if it were written by an intimate, sympathetic friend.

The personal construct psychotherapist may also use 'casual enactment', brief role-playing of situations in the client's life, to elaborate his or her construct system. In addition, this procedure may facilitate the client's experimentation with different ways of behaving and of construing events. Experimentation is the primary aim of a more formal enactment method devised by Kelly (1955), fixed-role therapy. This involves the therapist writing a sketch of a character who is orthogonal, rather than in marked contrast, to the client; and, if the client finds this character plausible, he or she being asked to 'become' the person in the sketch for two weeks. At the end of this period, the client's old self is invited to return, but the client will hopefully have discovered that there are alternative ways of construing the self and the world.

Numerous other issues may be addressed by the personal construct psychotherapist. For example, there may be a focus on loosening or tightening the client's construct system, therapeutic techniques being chosen accordingly. In 'experiential personal construct psychotherapy' (Leitner, 1988), the therapeutic relationship is of primary concern. As well as applications with individual clients, personal construct therapeutic methods have been developed for work with groups (for example, Landfield & Rivers, 1975; Neimeyer, 1988), couples (Neimeyer, 1985), and families (Feixas, 1992a; Procter, 1981). More detailed descriptions, and examples, of the approach may be found in Leitner & Dunnett (1993), Neimeyer & Neimeyer (1987), Winter (1992) and Winter and Viney (2005).

Guidano's (1987) *developmental approach* to therapy (which has also been referred to as process-oriented cognitive therapy) involves a stepwise process of self-observation using a 'moviola' technique in which clients are trained to 'zoom' in and out of particular scenes in their life. They are thereby encouraged to regard perceptions about the events concerned as hypotheses and to view emotional states as constructions associated with perceived imbalances in affective relationships. The therapist will offer a formulation of clients' problems in terms of the underlying personal meaning organisation, will consider clients' affective style in terms of their history of affective relationships, and in some cases may explore the development of their personal meaning organisation.

Other constructivist approaches to therapy (Neimeyer & Mahoney, 1995; Neimeyer & Rood, 1997) are too numerous to be described in any depth. Ivey's (1986) *developmental therapy* views therapy as a process analogous to the child's development through Piagetian stages, for which the therapist needs to ensure an equilibration between accommodation and assimilation. *Depth-oriented brief therapy* (Ecker & Hulley, 1996) regards the client as holding a conscious 'anti-symptom position', in which the symptom is viewed as problematic, and an unconscious 'pro-symptom position', in which the symptom is viewed as necessary. Therapy involves 'radical inquiry', in which the latter position is elaborated, and 'experiential shift', in which there is transformation of the constructs concerned. Therapeutic resolution entails change in either the anti- or the pro-symptom position. In *neurolinguistic psychotherapy* (O'Connor & Seymour, 1990), one of the therapist's concerns is to identify and then match interventions to clients' preferred systems (visual, auditory or kinesthetic) for representing their world. The interventions concerned involve a range of techniques and may be accompanied by the use of trance.

Systemic constructivist and *social constructionist* therapies tend to focus upon the 'languaging' about the problem, and co-construction of its meaning, by clients and therapists (Anderson & Goolishian, 1992). In the former approaches, a family's construing may be elucidated by such methods as 'circular questioning' (Selvini-Palazzoli *et al.*, 1980) in which the members are asked in turn how they view a particular issue. Social constructionist approaches are more concerned with how clients may 'reauthor' their lives to free themselves from oppressive cultural narratives. Techniques that may enable them to achieve this end include externalising their problems so that they are seen as alien (White & Epston, 1990).

Training

Kelly (1955) made it clear that training in psychotherapy should involve both the development of a system of professional constructs and the examination of the trainee's personal construct system. The former component of training is likely to include a focus on the role of the therapist as that of a 'professional scientist'. The latter component may involve identification of areas of hostility, in Kelly's sense of this term, and of aspects of the system in which some reconstruction may be considered necessary before the trainee embarks on therapeutic practice. A fundamental aim is that trainees develop a capacity for 'reflexivity', the ability to view their own processes in terms of constructivist concepts (Dunnett, 1988). This may well be facilitated by the trainee undergoing constructivist therapy but personal therapy is not generally a requirement of constructivist therapy training programmes. Instead, reflexivity may be developed by other means, such as keeping a personal journal written from a constructivist perspective.

In view of the personal aspects of constructivist therapy training, small group work is likely to figure prominently in such training. The overall focus of training, just as in constructivist therapy itself, is not on the transmission of information but on the trainee's development as a 'self-organised learner' (Kenny, 1988; Thomas & Harri-Augstein, 1983). The duration of training is generally at least three, and usually four, years.

Supervision

As with practitioners of other approaches, constructivist therapists are required to undergo regular supervision. As Feixas (1992b) indicates, the primary focus of such supervision is on the therapist's construing, and on the invalidation of this which is reflected in the problems which the therapist brings to supervision. In this respect, the relationship between supervisor and supervisee, like that between trainer and trainee, is equivalent to the therapist-client relationship. To quote Feixas (1992b, p. 197), 'the supervisor's task is similar to that of the therapist with the client, that is, to promote alternative, more viable constructions of both the client's problem and the therapy'.

Evidence of Effectiveness

The notion of an evidence base does not rest altogether easily with a constructivist approach in that it has been viewed as implying that there is a knowable reality (Botella, 2000). It is unsurprising, therefore, that there has been relatively little outcome research on some constructivist therapies. Nevertheless, there is a growing research literature on the effectiveness of personal construct psychotherapy (Metcalfe, Winter & Viney, 2006; Viney, Metcalfe &

Winter, 2005; Winter, 1992, 2003b) meta-analyses of which suggest effect sizes equivalent to those in cognitive-behavioural and psychodynamic therapies (Viney, 1998). One of the earliest studies of personal construct psychotherapy gave a 'not proven' verdict concerning its effects on thought disordered schizophrenics (Bannister *et al.*, 1975), but more positive outcomes have generally been demonstrated with other client groups. For example, some evidence has been provided of the effectiveness of variants of fixed-role therapy in the treatment of public speaking anxiety (Karst & Trexler, 1975), snake phobia (Lira *et al.*, 1975), and social anxiety (Beail & Parker, 1991; Nagae and Nedate, 2001). Agoraphobics have been demonstrated to show greater improvement in a treatment combining personal construct psychotherapy and exposure than while they were on the waiting list, although it was less clear whether the personal construct psychotherapy component was more effective than supportive therapy (Winter *et al.*, 2006). In a more heterogeneous group of clients referred to a clinical psychology service, Watson & Winter (2005) demonstrated significant improvement in those treated by personal construct psychotherapy, at a level comparable to that in cognitive-behavioural therapy. More complex levels of perceptual processing were observed during therapy in the personal construct psychotherapy clients in this study. Personal construct psychotherapy has also been found to be effective in the treatment of depression (Neimeyer *et al.*, 1985; Sheehan, 1985), as well as in that of clients presenting with deliberate self-harm (Winter *et al.*, 2006). Improvement in speech has been demonstrated in stutterers treated by personal construct psychotherapy (Fransella, 1972), who have been found to show a lower relapse rate than those solely treated by speech techniques (Evesham & Fransella, 1985). Changes in construing have been demonstrated during personal construct group psychotherapy for clients with eating disorders (Button, 1987) and for problem drinkers (Landfield, 1979), and this form of therapy has also been found to be effective with disturbed adolescents (Jackson, 1992; Sewell & Ovaert, 1997; Truneckova & Viney, 2005; Viney, Henry & Campbell, 1995), survivors of childhood sexual abuse (Alexander *et al.*, 1989) and people with problems involving poor anger control (Horley & Francouer, 2003; Pekkala & Dave, 2006). Older people have been found to benefit from a personal construct approach (Viney, 1986; Viney, Benjamin & Preston, 1989; Botella & Feixas, 1992–3), as have medical in-patients (Viney *et al.*, 1985a, 1985b, 1985c, 1985d), people with chronic pain (Haugli *et al.*, 2001; Steen & Haugli, 2001), breast cancer survivors (Lane & Viney, 2001), and AIDS caregivers (Viney, Walker & Crooks, 1995) and women attending menopause workshops (Foster and Viney, 2005).

Another constructivist approach that has received some research attention, although generally with less positive findings, is neuro-linguistic psychotherapy. Reviewing the literature, Sharpley (1987) concludes that 'the principles and procedures suggested by NLP have failed to be supported'. Although subsequent research has provided some evidence of improvement in clients treated by neuro-linguistic psychotherapy (Quaite & Winter, 2001) there is clearly a need for further investigation of the effectiveness of this and other constructivist approaches to psychotherapy.

HUMANISTIC THERAPIES

Theoretical Basis

As with constructivist therapies, humanistic therapies encompass a range of different approaches. However, as Elliott (2001, p. 38) indicates, they 'share a set of values, including grounding in immediate, lived human experiences; fostering of agency and self-determination; prizing of differences within and between people; relationships based on authentic presence; and pursuit of wholeness and growth throughout the life cycle.'

The first major humanistic therapies to be developed were Carl Rogers' (1961) *client-centred* (now usually referred to as *person-centred*) therapy and Fritz Perls' *Gestalt therapy* (Perls *et al.*, 1974). In the former approach, the person is seen as having an inherent tendency to actualise his or her potential. This tendency is manifested in the fully functioning person, who is characterised by openness to experience. However, the process is likely to be blocked, with consequent estrangement of the individual from his or her true self if the person is subjected to 'conditions of worth' from others who, for example, offer their love only if the person acts in a certain way. In such a case, the person may introject the attitudes of the other people concerned and develop a negative self-concept, which will be preserved by mechanisms of perceptual distortion and denial. His or her primary concern is likely to be with obtaining the approval of others.

Gestalt therapy shares with person-centred therapy a concern with awareness of the self, of the environment, and of the person's internal processes. Imbalances in or between these areas are experienced as needs, the person becoming aware of a 'Gestalt' in which their dominant need is differentiated as a figure against the ground of their total experiencing. The tension associated with the imbalance leads the person to satisfy the need, thereby destroying the Gestalt, which is replaced by another concerned with the person's next most dominant need. This ongoing, homeostatic process, involving the maintenance of the person's equilibrium, characterises healthy functioning. Psychological problems occur when this process is interrupted, perhaps by individuals being constantly prevented from expressing or meeting their needs with a consequent build-up of incomplete Gestalts, or unfinished business. This is likely to be associated with persistent disturbances at the 'contact boundary' between self and environment. Such disturbances include introjection of whole parts of the environment, such as attitudes of others; projection of disowned aspects of the self onto others or the environment; retroflection, in which energy is turned against the self; confluence, in which the self-environment boundary is unclear; and deflection of the person from contact with the environment. In general, there is an attempt to change the self or the environment to fit the person's image of them.

Transactional analysis (Berne, 1968) regards psychological disturbance as resulting from the person's autonomy having been interfered with by parents or other significant figures who have not adopted the respectful position of 'I'm OK – You're OK'. Decisions made by the person in childhood are viewed as determining the scripts that are followed, sometimes self-destructively, throughout life, essentially in an attempt to obtain love. A tripartite model of the person, consisting of Parent, Adult, and Child ego states, is employed, with pathology being reflected in one ego state being contaminated by another or there being insufficient energy to cathect, or invest in, one or more of the ego states. In general, therapy aims to enable the client to cathect their Adult ego state. Transactions between people are viewed in terms of the ego states that are involved, the patterns of 'strokes' that they exchange and the 'games' that they play.

Also within the broad humanistic tradition are *existential* approaches to therapy (Van Deurzen-Smith, 1988), which have their roots in existential philosophy and phenomenology. A primary concern in these approaches is the individual's confrontation with the 'givens of existence', namely the inevitability of death; the freedom that accompanies individuals' responsibility for their choices and actions; the existential isolation of each individual; and the essential meaninglessness of the universe (Yalom, 1980). The person who is able to face these givens can live an authentic existence (Heidegger, 1962), true to their experience of the world. However, attempts to avoid the angst, or existential anxiety, which accompanies the awareness of one's essential nothingness (Kierkegaard, 1954) can lead a person into a life of inauthenticity or bad faith (Sartre, 1951), in which, for example, their actions are determined by conformity with values other than their own. Another path to psychological disturbance, but in this case to a likely diagnostic label of psychosis, is an authenticity untrammelled by any acknowledgement of external reality.

Distinguishing Features of Therapy

Humanistic therapies aim to promote the client's self-awareness and in most cases also regard the facilitation of the client's personal growth as a therapeutic goal. They generally consider the therapeutic relationship to be of particular importance in this process. Although these features might appear to be shared with psychodynamic therapy, the focus in humanistic therapies is more on the here and now than on the past. The authenticity of the client-therapist relationship is considered of primary importance rather than its transferential aspects. This relationship is also more democratic than in many other forms of therapy. A further characteristic of some humanistic approaches, deriving from their holistic view of the person, is that, as well as more conventional areas of therapeutic focus, they may use body-oriented approaches or be concerned with transpersonal issues (Rowan, 1993).

Several studies have provided evidence of the distinctive features of humanistic therapies and of particular approaches within this tradition (Greenberg, Elliott & Lietaer, 1994).

Therapeutic Practice

The humanistic approaches that have placed greatest emphasis on the therapeutic relationship are *person-centred* and *existential therapy*. Rogers (1957), presenting the former approach, regarded as necessary and sufficient conditions for therapeutic change a relationship in which the therapist is perceived by the client as congruent (genuine), accepting, and empathic. In Rogers' view, the client who is provided with these 'core conditions', rather than the previously experienced conditions of worth, will naturally grow. The original non-directive Rogerian approach, in which the therapist acts as a reflective screen, has been replaced by a rather more task-oriented therapeutic style in some later variants of person-centred therapy. Wexler (1974), taking a cognitive perspective, views the therapist as a surrogate information processor whose accurate empathy allows an organisation of meaning which is more accurate than that of the client. Rice (1974) has developed, and manualised, a method of evocative unfolding of problematic reactions, in which an incident is re-evoked in therapy and more completely reprocessed. Gendlin (1996) uses a focusing method to allow the client to develop a 'felt sense' of experience, which is both psychic and bodily.

In *existential psychotherapy*, the focus is on the personal encounter, in an 'I-Thou' relationship (Buber, 1958), between therapist and client (Spinelli, 1994). In this relationship, the therapist helps the client to explore the meaning of his or her experiences by seeking clarification of, and occasionally challenging, the client's statements.

Various other humanistic therapies are characterised by a more active therapeutic style and a greater use of techniques. The first such approach was Moreno's (1964) *Psychodrama*, in which enactment is used to provide the client, or protagonist, with a cathartic re-experiencing of conflict situations. In the enactment, therapeutic aides or other members of a therapy group act as 'auxiliary egos' who play counter roles to the protagonist and may occasionally reverse roles with him or her; act as a 'double' by standing by, and perhaps speaking for and emphasising the feelings of, the protagonist; or 'mirror' the protagonist by re-enacting a scene that he or she has just enacted.

Gestalt therapy is also relatively active and directive, encouraging the client to engage in experiments to promote experiential learning. The Gestalt therapist may attempt to facilitate greater awareness by changing the client's use of language. This may, for example, involve the client being asked to make statements rather than to ask questions, to personalise these statements by using the first person pronoun when appropriate, and also to take greater responsibility by using 'won't' rather than 'can't'. The therapist will also attend to the client's non-verbal communication, helping the client to become more aware of its meaning by such means as asking him or her to exaggerate particular gestures. In 'two-chair dialogue' the client is asked to move backwards and forwards between chairs representing split and conflicting aspects of the self; while in 'empty chair dialogue' the client is encouraged to express feelings to an imagined significant other in an empty chair in an attempt to resolve unfinished business with this person. Chairs may also be used in *transactional analysis*, clients carrying out a dialogue between their three ego states by moving backwards and forwards between chairs representing these states.

The integration of Gestalt techniques and other active interventions into an essentially person-centred therapeutic approach has led to the development of *process-experiential therapy* (Elliott & Greenberg, 1995; Greenberg, Rice & Elliott, 1993). As well as its use with individual clients, this method has been adapted for work with couples (Johnson & Greenberg, 1985a). There has also been extensive use of all of the humanistic therapies in the group setting (Lietaer, Rombauts & Van Balen, 1990; Yalom, 1970).

Training

Consistently with their emphasis on the quality of the therapeutic relationship, humanistic therapies generally regard the personal development of the therapist as being at least as important as training in particular therapeutic approaches. The early training courses arising from the person-centred tradition included teaching in the provision of Rogerian therapeutic conditions (Truax & Carkhuff, 1967). As well as didactic components, training incorporated a quasi-group therapy experience in which the focus was on trainees' difficulties in their therapeutic role. Although a considerable amount of research was conducted on this training, the adequacy of the methods used in this research has been questioned (Matarazzo & Patterson, 1986).

Humanistic therapy courses now generally require their trainees to undergo therapy of the type that they are going to offer. They may also foster group interaction and support and an intense focus on subjective experience by such means as the inclusion of residential components. In addition, they may incorporate artistic, spiritual, and physical activities designed to promote all aspects of the personal growth of the therapist (Pierson & Sharp, 2001). The length of training is generally at least three to four years.

Supervision

Humanistic therapists are required to undergo regular supervision and, in most humanistic approaches, the supervisor-supervisee relationship, like that between therapist and client, is regarded as at least as important as more didactic aspects of the process. As Truax & Carkhuff (1967, p. 242) described, 'the supervisor himself provides high levels of therapeutic conditions'. Discussion of difficulties that have arisen in therapy will also focus at least as much on the therapist's role in these difficulties as on that of the client.

Evidence of Effectiveness

Many humanistic therapists, like several of those from the constructivist school, have been highly critical of published criteria for 'empirically validated treatments', considering that these may lead their therapies to be disenfranchised and 'empirically violated' (Bohart, O'Hara & Leitner, 1998). For example, the view has been taken that, to quote the Association of Humanistic Psychology Practitioners, 'Quantitative research methods are of doubtful value in relation to understanding people and their relationships.' Research on the humanistic therapies has therefore tended to rely heavily on the use of qualitative methods, and to give greater emphasis to investigation of the therapeutic process (Greenberg & Pinsof, 1986; Toukmanian & Rennie, 1992) than to that of outcome.

There is, however, a substantial research literature on the effectiveness of some humanistic therapies. Carl Rogers himself was very much involved in the earliest studies in this area, which provided evidence of the effectiveness of the person-centred approach in, for example, enhancing self-acceptance and adjustment (Cartwright, 1957; Rogers & Dymond, 1954). Several subsequent studies have used person-centred therapy as a placebo control in comparison with cognitive-behavioural and other therapies. Although these have found cognitive-behavioural therapies to be superior, there are indications that this difference between therapies disappears when allowance is made for researcher allegiance (Elliott, 2001). In addition, some more recent studies (Kay et al., 2000; Tarrier et al., 2000) have not supported the superiority of cognitive-behavioural over person-centered therapies. The effect of the therapeutic relationship on outcome in person-centred and other therapies has also received considerable research attention. These studies have supported the importance of the therapeutic alliance, and while evidence concerning the facilitative effect of Rogerian therapeutic conditions has been conflicting (Greenberg, Elliott & Lietaer, 1994), the therapist's empathic understanding and acceptance of the client have generally been related to favourable outcome, albeit to different degrees with different types of client (Bozarth, Zimring & Tausch, 2002; Sachse & Elliott, 2002). There has also been a certain amount of research on techniques that may be used in person-centred therapy, although in several cases these have been analogue studies. For example, successful evocative unfolding of problematic reactions has been related to reduction in anxiety (Lowenstein, 1985), and there is evidence that sessions in which this technique is used are of greater value than less task-oriented sessions (Rice & Saperia, 1984; Wiseman & Rice, 1989). Therapist 'processing proposals' in person-centred therapy have been found to be effective in influencing clients' information processing, whereas therapist facilitative conditions have not been found to be sufficient in this regard (Sachse, 1990; Sachse & Elliott, 2002). Greenberg, Elliott & Lietaer (1994) have reviewed studies of focusing that have found this to be associated with self-acceptance and reduction in internal disorganisation, with reduction in depression and improvement in body image in cancer patients and with greater improvement at follow-up in a weight-loss programme than in clients receiving cognitive-behavioural treatment.

Although the outcome of Gestalt therapy, at least in its pure form, has received rather less research attention, there is some evidence that this approach is as effective as behavioural and cognitive therapies (Beutler *et al.*, 1991; Cross, Sheehan & Khan, 1982; Strumpfel & Goldman, 2002). There has also been exploration of the effectiveness of particular techniques derived from Gestalt therapy. Two-chair dialogue for conflict splits has been found to be more effective in some respects than empathic reflection and focusing (Greenberg & Dompierre, 1981; Greenberg & Higgins, 1980; Greenberg & Rice, 1981) and to result in greater reduction in indecision in clients with decisional conflicts than did behavioural problem solving (Clarke & Greenberg, 1986). Further studies have investigated the mechanism of change produced by the two-chair technique (Greenberg, 1984). Empty-chair dialogue for unfinished business has also been examined by Paivio and Greenberg (1995), who found it to be more effective than a psycho-educational group both in terms of symptom reduction and resolution of unfinished business. More favourable treatment outcome occurred in those clients who expressed previously unmet needs and showed changes in their perception of the significant other (Greenberg & Malcolm, 2002). The use of this technique, particularly to facilitate expression of anger, in clients presenting with depression and chronic pain has also been found to lead to improvements in both these areas, although education groups were equally effective in reducing pain (Beutler *et al.*, 1988, 1991).

A related body of research has investigated the outcome of other forms of process-experiential therapy. This approach has been found to produce effects equivalent to those of cognitive and dynamic therapies with depressed clients (Elliott *et al.*, 1990; Greenberg & Watson, 1998), and there are indications of its effectiveness with survivors of abuse (Elliott & Greenberg, 2002). Marital process-experiential therapy has also been found to be very effective and more so than behavioural problem-solving treatment (Dandeneau & Johnson, 1994; Gordon Walker *et al.*, 1996; Johnson & Greenberg, 1985a, 1985b).

There has also been some outcome research on humanistic group therapy (Page *et al.*, 2002). For example, studies of psychodrama groups have demonstrated the value of 'doubling' in increasing group members' verbal output (Goldstein, 1967, 1971). An investigation of encounter groups by Lieberman *et al.* (1973) indicated that, although such groups can have powerful effects, these can result not only in positive change but also in 'casualties', therapeutic style appearing to be a major factor in determining outcome. Anderson (1978) found Rogerian and Gestalt groups to be effective in reducing depression and anxiety but no more so than a leaderless group. There have also been indications of the effectiveness of existentially oriented group therapy in populations ranging from drug users (Page, Weiss & Lietaer, 2002) to cancer patients (Van der Pompe *et al.*, 1997).

Although an early meta-analysis suggested less favourable outcomes for humanistic therapies (Smith, Glass & Miller, 1980), more recent meta-analyses have indicated large effect sizes for pre- to post-treatment change in these therapies, particularly with relationship problems, anxiety and depressive disorders and trauma, with treatment gains generally being maintained at follow-up (Elliott, 1996, 2001, 2002; Elliott, Greenberg & Lietaer, 2004; Greenberg, Elliott & Lietaer, 1994). There is also evidence of such therapies being 'possibly efficacious' for people diagnosed with anger-related problems, schizophrenia, severe personality disorders and physical health problems. In comparative outcome studies, these effect sizes are generally equivalent to those in the other therapies studied, but considerably greater than those in untreated controls. There are also indications of greater effect sizes for Gestalt and process-experiential than for non-directive humanistic therapies.

SUMMARY

For approximately half a century, constructivist and humanistic therapies have provided viable alternatives to the psychodynamic and cognitive-behavioural traditions. Although, with the exception of personal construct psychotherapy, humanistic approaches initially were the most prominent in this trend, constructivist approaches have flourished in the more recent climate of postmodernism. Some of these latter approaches, combining humanistic values with the use of diagnostic constructs and methods of assessment of the individual's view of the world, may be considered to provide what Rychlak (1977) has termed a 'rigorous humanism'. Within the humanistic therapies, there has been a trend to develop rather more focused approaches than some of the original, non-directive methods. Although there has been some resistance within both the constructivist and the humanistic school to empirical research, both approaches have developed research methods consistent with their particular models and there is now a growing evidence base indicating the effectiveness of some particular constructivist and humanistic approaches, notably personal construct psychotherapy and process-experiential therapy.

REFERENCES

Alexander, P.C., Neimeyer, R.A., Follette, V. *et al.* (1989). A comparison of group treatments of women sexually abused as children. *Journal of Consulting and Clinical Psychology, 57,* 479–483.

Anderson, H. & Goolishian, H. (1992). The client is the expert: A not-knowing approach to therapy. In S. McNamee & K.J. Gergen (eds), *Therapy as Social Construction* (pp. 25–39). London: Sage.

Anderson, J.D. (1978). Growth groups and alienation: A comparative study of Rogerian encounter, self-directed encounter, and Gestalt. *Group and Organization Studies, 3,* 85–107.

Bannister, D., Adams-Webber, J.R. *et al.* (1975). Reversing the process of thought disorder: A serial validation experiment. *British Journal of Social and Clinical Psychology, 14,* 169–180.

Beail, N. (ed.) (1985). *Repertory Grid Technique and Personal Constructs: Applications in Clinical and Educational Settings.* London: Croom Helm.

Beail, N. & Parker, C. (1991). Group fixed role therapy: A clinical application. *International Journal of Personal Construct Psychology, 4,* 85–96.

Berne, E. (1968). *Games People Play.* Harmondsworth: Penguin.

Beutler, L.E., Daldrup, R.J., Engle, D. *et al.* (1988). Family dynamics and emotional expression among patients with chronic pain and depression. *Pain, 32,* 65–72.

Beutler, L.E., Engle, D., Mohr, D., *et al.* (1991). Predictors of differential response to cognitive, experiential and self-directed psychotherapeutic procedures. *Journal of Consulting and Clinical Psychology, 59,* 333–340.

Bohart, A.C., O'Hara, M., and Leitner, L.M. (2000). Empirically violated treatments: Disenfranchisement of humanistic and other psychotherapies. *Psychotherapy Research, 8,* 141–157.

Botella, L. (2000). Personal Construct Psychology, constructivism, and psychotherapy research. In J.W. Scheer (ed.), *The Person in Society: Challenges to a Constructivist Theory* (pp. 362–372). Giessen: Psychosozial-Verlag.

Botella, L. & Feixas, G. (1992–3). The autobiographical group: A tool for the reconstruction of past life experience with the aged. *International Journal of Ageing and Human Development, 36,* 303–319.

Bozarth, J.D., Zimring, F.M. & Tausch, R. (2002). Client-centered therapy: The evolution of a revolution. In D.J. Cain & J. Semman (eds), *Humanistic Psychotherapies: Handbook of Research and Practice* (pp. 147–188). Washington, DC: American Psychological Association.

Buber, M. (1958). *I and Thou.* New York: Scribners.

Bugental, J. (1964). The third force in psychology. *Journal of Humanistic Psychology, 4,* 19–26.

Button, E. (1987). Construing people or weight? An eating disorders group. In R.A. Neimeyer & G.J. Neimeyer (eds), *Personal Construct Therapy Casebook* (pp. 230–244). New York: Springer.

Cartwright, D.S. (1957). Annotated bibliography of research and theory construction in client-centered therapy. *Journal of Counseling Psychology, 4*, 82–100.

Clarke, K.M. & Greenberg, L.S. (1986). Differential effects of the Gestalt two-chair intervention and problem solving in resolving decisional conflict. *Journal of Counseling Psychology, 33*, 11–15.

Cross, D.G., Sheehan, P.W. & Khan, J.A. (1982). Short- and long-term follow-up of clients receiving insight-oriented therapy and behavior therapy. *Journal of Consulting and Clinical Psychology, 50*, 103–112.

Dandeneau, M.L. & Johnson, S.M. (1994). Facilitating intimacy: Interventions and effects. *Journal of Marital and Family Therapy, 20*, 17–33.

Deurzen-Smith, E. van (1988). *Existential Counselling in Practice*. London: Sage.

Dunnett, G. (1988). Working with oneself. In G. Dunnett (ed.), *Working with People: Clinical Uses of Personal Construct Psychology* (pp. 17–23). London: Routledge.

Ecker, B. & Hulley, L. (1996). *Depth Oriented Brief Therapy*. San Francisco: Jossey Bass.

Efran, J.S., Lukens, M.D. & Lukens, R.J. (1990). *Language, Structure, and Change: Frameworks of Meaning in Psychotherapy*. New York: Norton.

Elliott, R. (1996). Are client-centered/experiential therapies effective? A meta-analysis of outcome research. In U. Esser, H. Pabst & G.-W. Speierer (eds), *The Power of the Person-Centered-Approach: New Challenges-Perspectives-Answers* (pp. 125–138). Cologne: GwG Verlag.

Elliott, R. (2001). Contemporary brief experiential psychotherapy. *Clinical Psychology: Science and Practice, 8*, 38–50.

Elliott, R. (2002). The effectiveness of humanistic therapies: a meta-analysis. In D.J. Cain & J. Seeman (eds), *Humanistic Psychotherapies: Handbook of Research and Practice* (pp. 57–81). Washington, DC: American Psychological Association.

Elliott, R., Clark, C., Wexler, M. *et al.* (1990). The impact of experiential therapy of depression: Initial results. In G. Lietaer, J. Rombauts & R. van Balen (eds), *Client-Centered and Experiential Psychotherapy in the Nineties* (pp. 549–577). Leuven: Leuven University Press.

Elliott, R. & Greenberg, L.S. (1995). Experiential therapy in practice: The process-experiential approach. In B. Bongar & L. Beutler (eds), *Foundations of Psychotherapy: Theory, Research, and Practice* (pp. 123–139). New York: Oxford University Press.

Elliott, R. & Greenberg, L.S. (2002). Process-experiential psychotherapy. In D.J. Cain & J. Seeman (eds), *Humanistic Psychotherapies: Handbook of Research and Practice* (pp. 279–306). Washington, DC: American Psychological Association.

Elliott, R., Greenberg, L.S. & Lietaer, G. (2004). Research on experiential psychotherapies. In M.J. Lambert (ed.), *Bergin and Garfield's Handbook of Psychotherapy and Behavior Change* (pp. 493–539). New York: Wiley.

Evesham, M. & Fransella, F. (1985). Stuttering relapse: the effects of a combined speech and psychological reconstruction programme. *British Journal of Disorders of Communication, 20*, 237–248.

Feixas, G. (1992a). Personal construct approaches to family therapy. In R.A. Neimeyer & G.J. Neimeyer (eds), *Advances in Personal Construct Psychology*, Vol. 2 (pp. 217–255). Greenwich, CT: JAI Press.

Feixas, G. (1992b). A constructivist approach to supervision: Some preliminary thoughts. *International Journal of Personal Construct Psychology, 5*, 183–200.

Foster, H. & Viney, L.L. (2005). Personal construct workshops for women experiencing menopause. In D.A. Winter & L.L. Viney (eds), *Personal Construct Psychotherapy: Advances in Theory, Practice and Research* (pp. 320–332). London: Whurr.

Fransella, F. (1970). Stuttering: not a symptom but a way of life. *British Journal of Communication Disorders, 5*, 22–29.

Fransella, F. (1972). *Personal Change and Reconstruction: Research on a Treatment of Stuttering*. London: Academic Press.

Fransella, F., Bell, R. & Bannister, D. (2004). *A Manual for Repertory Grid Technique*. Chichester: Wiley.

Gendlin, E.T. (1996). *Focusing-Oriented Psychotherapy*. New York: Guilford.

Goldstein, J. (1971). Investigation of doubling as a technique for involving severely withdrawn patients in group psychotherapy. *Journal of Consulting and Clinical Psychology, 37*, 155–162.

Goldstein, S. (1967). The effect of 'doubling' on involvement in group psychotherapy as measured by number and duration of patient utterances. *Psychotherapy: Theory, Research and Practice, 4*, 57–60.

Gordon-Walker, J., Johnson, S., Manion, I. & Cloutier, P. (1996). An emotionally focused marital intervention for couples with chronically ill children. *Journal of Consulting and Clinical Psychology, 64*, 1029–1036.

Greenberg, L.S. (1984). A task analysis of intrapersonal conflict resolution. In L. Rice and L. Greenberg (eds), *Patterns of Change*. New York: Guilford.

Greenberg, L.S. & Dompierre, L. (1981). The specific effects of Gestalt two-chair dialogue on intrapsychic conflict in counseling. *Journal of Counseling Psychology, 28*, 288–296.

Greenberg, L.S., Elliott, R.K. & Lietaer, G. (1994). Research on experiential psychotherapies. In A.E. Bergin & S.L. Garfield (eds), *Handbook of Psychotherapy and Behavior Change* (pp. 509–539). New York: Wiley.

Greenberg, L.S. & Higgins, H. (1980). The differential effects of two-chair dialogue and focusing on conflict resolution. *Journal of Counseling Psychology, 27*, 221–225.

Greenberg, L.S. & Malcolm, W. (2002). Resolving unfinished business: Relating process to outcome. *Journal of Consulting and Clinical Psychology, 70*, 406–416.

Greenberg, L.S. & Pinsof, W.M. (1986). *The Psychotherapeutic Process: A Research Handbook*. New York: Guilford.

Greenberg, L.S. & Rice, L.N. (1981). The specific effects of a Gestalt intervention. *Psychotherapy: Theory, Research and Practice, 18*, 31–37.

Greenberg, L.S., Rice, L.N. & Elliott, R. (1993). *Facilitating Emotional Change: The Moment-by-moment Process*. New York: Guilford.

Greenberg, L.S. & Watson, J. (1998). Experiential therapy of depression: Differential effects of client-centered relationship conditions and active experiential interventions. *Psychotherapy Research, 8*, 210–224.

Guidano, V.F. (1987). *Complexity of the Self: A Developmental Approach to Psychopathology and Therapy*. New York: Guilford.

Guidano, V.F. (1991). *The Self in Process: Towards a Post-Rationalist Cognitive Therapy*. New York: Guilford.

Haugli, L., Steen, E., Nygard, R. & Finset, A. (2001). Learning to have less pain – is it possible? A one-year follow-up study of the effects of a personal construct group learning programme on patients with chronic musculoskeletal pain. *Patient Education and Counseling, 45*, 111–118.

Heidegger, M. (1962). *Being and Time*. Blackwell: Oxford.

Hinkle, D. (1965). *The Change of Personal Constructs from the Viewpoint of a Theory of Construct Implications*. Unpublished PhD thesis, Ohio State University.

Horley, J. & Francoeur, A. (2003). Personal construct group therapy with domestic abusers: a program rationale and preliminary results. Paper presented at the Fifteenth International Congress of Personal Construct Psychology, Huddersfield.

Ivey, A.E. (1986). *Developmental Therapy*. San Francisco: Jossey Bass.

Jackson, S. (1992). A PCT therapy group for adolescents. In P. Maitland & D. Brennan (eds), *Personal Construct Theory Deviancy and Social Work* (pp. 163–174). London: Inner London Probation Service/Centre for Personal Construct Psychology.

Johnson, S.M. & Greenberg, L.S. (1985a). The differential effects of experiential and problem-solving interventions in resolving marital conflict. *Journal of Consulting and Clinical Psychology, 53*, 175–184.

Johnson, S.M. & Greenberg, L.S. (1985b). Emotionally focused marital therapy: An outcome study. *Journal of Marital and Family Therapy, 11*, 313–317.

Karst, T.O. & Trexler, L.D. (1970). Initial study using fixed role and rational-emotive therapy in treating speaking anxiety. *Journal of Consulting and Clinical Psychology, 34*, 360–366.

Kelly, G. (1955). *The Psychology of Personal Constructs*. New York: Norton (republished by Routledge, 1991).

Kenny, V. (1988). Changing conversations: a constructivist model of training for psychotherapists. In G. Dunnett (ed.), *Working with People: Clinical Uses of Personal Construct Psychology* (pp. 140–157). London: Routledge.

Kierkegaard, S. (1954). *Fear and Trembling and Sickness unto Death*. Princeton: Princeton University Press.

King, M., Sibbald, B., Ward, E. *et al.* (2000). Randomised controlled trial of non-directive counselling, cognitive behaviour therapy and usual general practitioner care in the management of depression as well as mixed anxiety and depression in primary care. *Health Technology Assessment, 4*, 1–84.

Landfield, A.W. (1979). Exploring socialisation through the Interpersonal Transaction Group. In P. Stringer & D. Bannister (eds), *Constructs of Sociality and Individuality* (pp. 133–151). London: Academic Press.

Landfield, A.W. & Rivers, P.C. (1975). An introduction to interpersonal transaction and rotating dyads. *Psychotherapy: Theory, Research, and Practice, 12*, 366–74.

Lane, L.G. & Viney, L.L. (2005). The effects of personal construct group therapy on breast cancer survivors. *Journal of Consulting and Clinical Psychology, 73*, 284–292.

Leitner, L.M. (1988). Terror, risk, and reverence: Experiential personal construct psychotherapy. *International Journal of Personal Construct Psychology, 1*, 251–261.

Leitner, L.M. & Dunnett, N.G.M. (1993). *Critical Issues in Personal Construct Psychotherapy*. Malabar: Krieger.

Lieberman, M.A., Yalom, I.D. & Miles, M.B. (1973). *Encounter Groups: First Facts*. New York: Basic Books.

Lietaer, G., Rombauts, J. & Van Balen, R. (eds), *Client-Centered and Experiential Psychotherapy in the Nineties*. Leuven: Leuven University Press.

Lira, F.T., Nay, W.R., McCullough, J.P. & Etkin, W. (1975). Relative effects of modeling and role playing in the treatment of avoidance behaviors. *Journal of Consulting and Clinical Psychology, 43*, 608–618.

Lowenstein, J. (1985). *A Test of a Performance Model of Problematic Reactions: An Examination of Differential Client Performances in Therapy*. Unpublished thesis. York University, Toronto.

Mahoney, M.J. (1988). Constructive metatheory I. Basic features and historical foundations. *International Journal of Personal Construct Psychology, 1*, 1–35.

Mair, M. (1988). Psychology as storytelling. *International Journal of Personal Construct Psychology, 1*, 125–137.

Matarazzo, R.G. & Patterson, D.R. (1986). Methods of teaching therapeutic skill. In S.L. Garfield & A.E. Bergin (eds), *Handbook of Psychotherapy and Behavior Change* (pp. 821–843). New York: Wiley.

McNamee, S. & Gergen, K.J. (1992). *Therapy as Social Construction*. London: Sage.

Metcalfe, C., Winter, D.A. & Viney, L.L. (2006). The effectiveness of personal construct psychotherapy in clinical practice: A systematic review and meta-analysis. *Psychotherapy Research*, in press.

Moreno, J.L. (1964). *Psychodrama*, Vol. 1. New York: Beacon.

Nagae, N. & Nedate, K. (2001). Comparison of constructivist cognitive and rational cognitive psychotherapies for students with social anxiety. *Constructivism in the Human Sciences, 6*, 41–49.

Neimeyer, G.J. (1985). Personal constructs in the counseling of couples. In F. Epting & A.W. Landfield (eds), *Anticipating Personal Construct Psychology* (pp. 201–215). Lincoln: University of Nebraska Press.

Neimeyer, G.J. & Rood, L. (1997). Contemporary expressions of constructivist psychotherapy. In G.J. Neimeyer & R.A. Neimeyer (eds), *Advances in Personal Construct Psychology*, Vol. 4 (pp. 185–205). Greenwich, CT: JAI Press.

Neimeyer, R.A. (1988). Clinical guidelines for conducting interpersonal transaction groups. *International Journal of Personal Construct Psychology, 1*, 181–190.

Neimeyer, R.A. (1994). The role of client-generated narratives in psychotherapy. *Journal of Constructivist Psychology, 7*, 229–242.

Neimeyer, R.A. (1995). Constructivist psychotherapies: features, foundations, and future directions. In R.A. Neimeyer & M.J. Mahoney (eds), *Constructivism in Psychotherapy* (pp. 11–38). Washington, DC: American Psychological Association.

Neimeyer, R.A., Heath, A.E. & Strauss, J. (1985). Personal reconstruction during group cognitive therapy for depression. In F. Epting & A.W. Landfield (eds), *Anticipating Personal Construct Psychology* (pp. 181–197). Lincoln: University of Nebraska Press.

Neimeyer, R.A. & Mahoney, M.J. (1995). *Constructivism in Psychotherapy*. Washington, DC: American Psychological Association.

Neimeyer, R.A. & Neimeyer, G.J. (eds) (1987). *Personal Construct Therapy Casebook*. New York: Springer.

Norcross, J.C. (1986). Eclectic psychotherapy: An introduction and overview. In J.C. Norcross (ed.) *Handbook of Eclectic Psychotherapy*. New York: Brunner/Mazel.

O'Connor, J. & Seymour, J. (1990). *Introducing Neuro-Linguistic Programming*. London: Aquarian.

Page, R.C., Weiss, J.F. & Lietaer, G. (2002). Humanistic group psychotherapy. In D.J. Cain & J. Seeman (eds), *Humanistic Psychotherapies: Handbook of Research and Practice* (pp. 339–368). Washington, DC: American Psychological Association.

Paivio, S.C. & Greenberg, L.S. (1995). Resolving 'unfinished business': Efficacy of experiential therapy using empty chair dialogue. *Journal of Consulting and Clinical Psychology, 63*, 419–425.

Pekkala, O. & Dave, B. (2006). Evaluation. In P. Cummins (ed.), *Working with Anger: A Constructivist Approach* (pp. 199–211). Chichester: Wiley.

Perls, F.S., Hefferline, R.F. & Goodman, P. (1974). *Gestalt Therapy*. Harmondsworth: Penguin.

Pierson, J.F. & Sharp, J. (2001). Cultivating psychotherapist artistry: A model existential-humanistic training program. In K.J. Schneider, J.F.T. Bugental & J.F. Pierson (eds), *The Handbook of Humanistic Psychology: Leading Edges in Theory, Research, and Practice*. Thousand Oaks, CA: Sage.

Procter, H.G. (1981). Family construct psychology: An approach to understanding and treating families. In S. Walrond-Skinner (ed.), *Developments in Family Therapy* (pp. 350–366). London: Routledge & Kegan Paul.

Quaite, A. & Winter, D. (2001). Evidence base for experiential constructivist psychotherapies research project: project update and summary report. Unpublished MS, Clinical Psychology Department, Barnet, Enfield and Haringey Mental Health Trust.

Rice, L.N. (1974). The evocative function of the therapist. In L.N. Rice & D.A. Wexler (eds), *Innovations in Client-Centered Therapy* (pp. 289–311). New York: Wiley.

Rice, L.N. & Saperia, E.P. (1984). Task analysis and the resolution of problematic reactions. In L.N. Rice & L.S. Greenberg (eds), *Patterns of Change*. New York: Guilford.

Rogers, C.R. (1957). The necessary and sufficient conditions of therapeutic personality change. *Journal of Consulting Psychology, 21*, 95–103.

Rogers, C.R. (1961). *On Becoming a Person*. Boston: Houghton Mifflin.

Rogers, C.R. & Dymond, R.F. (eds) (1954). *Psychotherapy and Personality Change*. Chicago: University of Chicago Press.

Rowan, J. (1993). *The Transpersonal in Psychotherapy and Counselling*. London: Routledge.

Rychlak, J.F. (1977). *The Psychology of Rigorous Humanism*. New York: Wiley-Interscience.

Sachse, R. (1990). The influence of therapist processing on the explication process of the client. *Person-Centered Review, 5*, 321–344.

Sachse, R. & Elliott, R. (2002). Process-outcome research on humanistic therapy variables. In D.J. Cain & J. Semman (eds), *Humanistic Psychotherapies: Handbook of Research and Practice* (pp. 83–115). Washington, DC: American Psychological Association.

Sartre, J.-P. (1951). *Being and Nothingness*. London: Methuen.

Selvini-Palazzoli, M., Boscolo, L., Cecchin, G. & Prata, G. (1980). Hypothesizing-Circularity-Neutralty: Three guidelines for the conductor of the session. *Family Process, 19*, 3–12.

Sewell, K.W. & Ovaert, L.B. (1997). Group treatments of posttraumatic stress in incarcerated adolescents: structural and narrative impacts on the permeability of self-construction. Paper presented at Twelfth International Congress of Personal Construct Psychology, Seattle.

Sharpley, C.F. (1987). Research findings on neuro-linguistic programming: Nonsupportive data or an untestable theory? *Journal of Counseling Psychology, 34*, 103–107.

Sheehan, M.J. (1985). A personal construct study of depression. *British Journal of Medical Psychology, 58*, 119–128.

Smith, M.L., Glass, G.V. & Miller, T.I. (1980). *The Benefits of Psychotherapy*. Baltimore: The Johns Hopkins University Press.

Spinelli, E. (1994). *Demystifying Therapy*. London: Constable.

Steen, E. & Haugli, L. (2001). From pain to self-awareness: a qualitative analysis of the significance of group participation for persons with chronic musculoskeletal pain. *Patient Education and Counseling, 42*, 35–46.

Strumpfel, U. & Goldman, R. (2002). Contacting Gestalt therapy. In D.J. Cain & J. Seaman (eds). *Humanistic Psychotherapies: Handbook of Research and Practice* (pp. 189–219). Washington, DC: American Psychological Association.

Tarrier, N., Kinney, C., McCarthy, E. *et al.* (2000). Two-year follow-up of cognitive – behavioral therapy and supportive counseling in the treatment of persistent symptoms in chronic schizophrenia. *Journal of Consulting and Clinical Psychology, 68,* 917–922.

Thomas, L. & Harri-Augstein, S. (1983). The self-organized learner as personal scientist: A conversational technology for reflecting on behavior and experience. In J. Adams-Webber & J.C. Mancuso (eds), *Applications of Personal Construct Theory* (pp. 331–363). Toronto: Academic Press.

Toukmanian, S.G. & Rennie, D.L. (1992). *Psychotherapy Process Research: Paradigmatic and Narrative Approaches.* London: Sage.

Truax, C.B. & Carkhuff, R. (1967). *Toward Effective Counseling and Psychotherapy: Training and Practice.* Chicago: Aldine.

Truneckova, D. & Viney, L.L. (2005). Personal construct group work with troubled adolescents. In D.A. Winter & L.L. Viney (eds) *Personal Construct Psychotherapy: Advances in Theory, Practice and Research* (pp. 271–286). London: Whurr.

Van der Pompe, G., Duivenvoorden, H.J., Antoni, M.H. *et al.* (1997). Effectiveness of a short-term group therapy program on endocrine and immune function in breast cancer patients: An exploratory study. *Journal of Psychosomatic Research, 42,* 453–466.

Viney, L.L. (1986). The development and evaluation of short-term psychotherapy programs for the elderly: Report to the Australian Institute of Health. Unpublished MS, University of Wollongong.

Viney, L.L. (1993). *Life Stories.* Chichester: Wiley.

Viney, L.L. (1998). Should we use personal construct therapy? A paradigm for outcomes evaluation. *Psychotherapy, 35,* 366–380.

Viney, L.L., Benjamin, Y.N. & Preston, C.A. (1989). An evaluation of personal construct therapy for the elderly. *British Journal of Medical Psychology, 62,* 35–42.

Viney, L.L., Clarke, A.M., Bunn, T.A. & Benjamin, Y.N. (1985a). Crisis-intervention counseling: an evaluation of long- and short-term effects. *Journal of Counseling Psychology, 32,* 29–39.

Viney, L.L., Clarke, A.M., Bunn, T.A. & Benjamin, Y.N. (1985b). An evaluation of three crisis intervention programmes for general hospital patients. *British Journal of Medical Psychology, 58,* 75–86.

Viney, L.L., Clarke, A.M., Bunn, T.A. & Benjamin, Y.N. (1985c). The effect of a hospital-based counseling service on the physical recovery of surgical and medical patients. *General Hospital Psychiatry, 7,* 294–301.

Viney, L.L., Clarke, A.M., Bunn, T.A. & Teoh, H.Y. (1985d). Crisis intervention counselling in a general hospital: Development and multi-faceted evaluation of a health service. *Australian Studies in Health Care Administration, 5.*

Viney, L.L., Henry, R.M. & Campbell, J. (1995a). An evaluation of personal construct and psychodynamic group work with centre-based juvenile offenders and school-based adolescents. Paper presented at Twelfth International Congress of Personal Construct Psychology, Seattle.

Viney, L.L., Metcalfe, C. & Winter, D.A. (2005). The effectiveness of personal construct psychotherapy: a meta-analysis. In D.A. Winter & L.L. Viney (eds.) *Personal Construct Psychotherapy: Advances in Theory Practice and Research* (pp. 347–364). London: Whurr.

Viney, L.L., Walker, B. & Crooks, L. (1995). Anxiety in community-based AIDS caregivers before and after counselling. *Journal of Clinical Psychology, 51,* 274–279.

Watson, S. & Winter, D.A. (2005). A process and outcome study of personal construct psychotherapy. In D.A. Winter & L.L. Viney (eds), *Personal Construct Psychotherapy: Advances in Theory, Practice and Research* (pp. 347–364). London: Whurr.

Wexler, D.A. (1974). A cognitive theory of experiencing self-actualization, and therapeutic process. In D.A. Wexler & L.N. Rice (eds), *Innovations in Client-Centered Therapy* (pp. 49–116). New York: Wiley.

White, M. & Epston, D. (1990). *Narrative Means to Therapeutic Ends.* New York: Norton.

Winter, D.A. (1992). *Personal Construct Psychology in Clinical Practice: Theory, Research and Applications.* London: Routledge.

Winter, D.A. (2003a). Psychological disorder as imbalance. In F. Fransella (ed.), *Personal Construct Psychology Handbook.* Chichester: Wiley.

Winter, D.A. (2003b). Personal construct psychotherapy: The evidence base. In F. Fransella (ed.), *Personal Construct Psychology Handbook*. Chichester: Wiley.

Winter, D.A., Gournay, K.J.M., Metcalfe, C., & Rossotti, N. (2006). Expanding agorophobics' horizons: an investigation of the effectiveness of a personal construct psychotherapy intervention. *Journal of Constructivist Psychology, 19*, 1–29.

Winter, D., Sireling L., Riley, T., Metcalfe C., Quaite, A. & Bhandari, S. (2006). A controlled trial of personal construct psychotherapy for deliberate self-harm. In *Psychology and Psychotherapy*, in press.

Winter, D.A. & Viney, L.L. (eds) (2005). *Personal Construct Psychotherapy: Advances in Theory. Practice and Research*. London: Whurr.

Winter, D.A. & Watson, S. (1999). Personal construct psychotherapy and the cognitive therapies: different in theory but can they be differentiated in practice? *Journal of Constructivist Psychology, 12*, 1–22.

Wiseman, H. & Rice, L.N. (1989). Sequential analysis of therapist-client interaction during change events: A task-focused approach. *Journal of Consulting and Clinical Psychology, 57*, 281–286.

Yalom, I.D. (1970). *The Theory and Practice of Group Psychotherapy*. New York: Basic Books.

Yalom, I.D. (1980). *Existential Psychotherapy*. New York: Basic Books.

PART II

Psychological Treatment of Disorder and Specific Client Groups

CHAPTER 9

Obsessive Compulsive Disorder

Katharine Logan

Royal Edinburgh Hospital, UK

INTRODUCTION

Obsessive compulsive disorder (OCD) involves the presence of obsessions or compulsions or both. Obsessions are defined as intrusive thoughts or images (for example, thoughts about harming others or becoming contaminated) and compulsions are defined as repetitive behaviours that are overt (for example, hand-washing), or mental acts which are covert (for example, silent counting). The obsessions cause distress and the compulsions are carried out to try to reduce the distress, or prevent a feared consequence of the obsession. The DSM-IV field trial found only two-thirds of OCD sufferers could identify consequences that they feared would follow from abstaining from rituals. The obsessions and compulsions must be repetitive, unpleasant and interfere with functioning. The person must also recognise that the obsessions or urge to perform a compulsive act originate within their own mind. Traditionally the person must acknowledge the obsessions and compulsions as excessive or unreasonable and must try to resist them. However DSM-IV includes a subtype of OCD 'with poor insight' recognising that in a minority of sufferers this is not the case. Lelliot *et al.* (1988) found 12 % of 49 OCD sufferers made no attempt to resist rituals and a third thought their obsessive thoughts were rational.

There are minor differences in the DSM-IV and ICD-10 criteria for OCD. DSM-IV requires symptoms to cause marked distress, be time consuming (take more than one hour per day) or significantly interfere with the person's normal functioning. ICD 10 requires symptoms to be present on most days for two weeks. However it is usual for symptoms to be present for much longer before presentation, as OCD sufferers are often secretive about their problems. Rasmussen & Tsuang (1986) found that sufferers first presented over seven years after the onset of significant symptoms. Sufferers of OCD may not report all their symptoms unless specifically asked. They may present in primary care (for instance with somatic obsessions) or to specialists (for example compulsive handwashers presenting to dermatologists) without OCD being identified as the underlying cause. Some sufferers are embarrassed about their symptoms (such as intrusive sexual thoughts) whereas others are unaware that their thought patterns or actions are outwith normal experience. General open questions about recent mood may pick up co-morbid conditions, such as depression. More specific questions should be asked if OCD is suspected, such as 'Have you had distressing thoughts or images that keep coming into your mind even though you try to stop them?' or 'Have you felt driven to repeat things or do things in a particular way?'

Manageable obsessions and compulsions do commonly occur in the general population and there is no clear dividing line between this occurrence and clinical OCD. In the sub-clinical form, although the content of obsessions and compulsions is similar, the symptoms are usually of shorter duration, less severe and ego-syntonic (Muris, Merckelbach & Clavan, 1997; Salkovskis & Harrison, 1984). The content of obsessions and rituals is affected by the prevailing concerns of the time or place (illness concerns have changed over time from plague or syphilis to cancer or AIDs) and usually involves themes that are particularly upsetting for the individual (such as blasphemous thoughts in a religious person).

Obsessive compulsive disorder commonly presents with co-morbid depression or anxiety disorders. Many disorders present with co-morbid obsessive-compulsive symptoms, including major depression, Tourette's disorder, schizophrenia and organic mental disorders. In these cases the obsessional and compulsive symptoms are probably secondary to the primary illness. There is also a related group of impulse control disorders and syndromes similar to OCD (including monosymptomatic hypochondriasis and body dysmorphic disorder), which sometimes respond to similar treatment approaches. Obsessive compulsive disorder is over-represented in Tourette's disorder and vice versa. The revised Obsessive-Compulsive Inventory is a reliable diagnostic screening tool (Foa *et al.*, 2002). The Yale-Brown Obsessive Compulsive Scale (observer-rated) and the Maudsley Obsessive Compulsive Inventory (self-rated) are validated assessment tools that measure symptom change (Taylor, 1995). Most clinical trials use the Yale-Brown Obsessive Compulsive Scale (Y-BOCS) and classify a reduction of 25 % from the baseline score as a measure of clinically significant improvement. The self-report version of the Compulsive Activity Checklist (CAC) (Steketee & Freund, 1993) has been found to be reliable, valid and sensitive to change in treatment. Salkovskis, Forrester & Richards (1998) highlighted difficulties with the Y-BOCS measuring change in obsessional thinking and made suggestions about changes.

EPIDEMIOLOGY

Studies in paediatric populations have found a peak in age of onset in the prepubertal years, with higher rates in males (Swedo *et al.*, 1989). Mean age at first onset in adults is generally mid-to-late twenties to early thirties (Weissman *et al.*, 1994), with earlier onset in males. The National Survey of Psychiatric Morbidity (Meltzer *et al.*, 1995; Jenkins *et al.*, 1997) used the Clinical Interview Scale, Revised (CIS-R) on a sample of approximately 10 000 adults randomly selected from the general population of the UK and showed an OCD prevalence of 1 % in males and 1.5 % in females. There was a peak at 20 to 24 years and no association with educational level. Cross-national, cross-cultural surveys confirmed that the prevalence was higher than previously thought (Weissman *et al.*, 1994). Data from seven international epidemiological surveys showed annual prevalence rates of OCD were remarkably consistent from 1.1 per 100 in Korea and New Zealand to 1.8 per 100 in Puerto Rico. The only exception was Taiwan at 0.4/100. Taiwan has the lowest prevalence for all psychiatric disorders. Lifetime prevalence rates fell between 1.9 per 100 and 2.5 per 100 (except for Taiwan).

AETIOLOGY

The aetiology of OCD has not been clearly established but genetic, neuroanatomical, neuro-chemical, behavioural and cognitive factors have been implicated. It is probably a syndrome that can develop through a number of pathways, including genetic, infectious and traumatic routes.

COURSE AND PROGNOSIS

Skoog & Skoog (1999) provide information about the natural course of OCD. In-patients with OCD (N = 144) were examined between 1954 and 1956, and then re-examined by the same doctor between 1989 and 1993. The mean length of follow-up from the onset of the illness was 47 years. Only a small number of patients received medication known to be effective as it became available towards the end of the study period. Four-fifths of the patients had improved but only half of all the patients had recovered, and three-fifths of these still had subclinical symptoms. Most improvements occurred early in the course of the disorder. A younger age of onset predicted a poorer outcome, especially in men. Often the illness initially ran an intermittent course and a chronic course was more common in the later follow-up period. Goodwin, Guze & Robins (1969) found three categories of course emerged from their review of follow up studies (before effective medication was available). About 10 % had an unremitting and chronic course; a further group had episodes of illness with periods of complete remission and the course for the majority was episodes of illness with incomplete remission. A further study in secondary care, which did not control for type of treatment offered, showed that over a two-year period, 12 % achieved full remission, 47 % achieved partial remission and there was a 48 % chance of relapse having achieved remission (Eisen *et al.*, 1999).

Koran *et al.* (1996) suggests that moderate to severe OCD is associated with a marked negative impact on quality of life. Data from the National Institute of Mental Health (NIMH) Epidemiologic Catchment Area survey (ECA) has shown an association between OCD and employment difficulties, especially chronic unemployment in men (Leon, Portera & Weissman, 1995) and another study found marital distress in about half of married people seeking treatment (Emmelkamp, De Haan & Hoogduin, 1990).

In summary, patients with OCD often delay many years before seeking treatment and the illness is often disabling and chronic. However there are effective treatments and studies have shown that patients can respond to treatment even after several decades of illness (Skoog & Skoog, 1999). Treatments aim to improve social functioning and quality of life by reducing symptoms and reducing the impact of symptoms.

THEORETICAL FORMULATIONS: BEHAVIOURAL AND COGNITIVE MODELS

In the behavioural model for OCD neutral internal stimuli, such as thoughts and images, become paired with an anxiety-provoking stimulus as the result of learning experiences. Because these previously neutral stimuli now cause anxiety, the patient develops avoidance behaviours, which result in an immediate reduction in anxiety. This encourages further use of the avoidance behaviours, which in time become more stereotyped and develop into a compulsive ritual. The ritual limits exposure to the initial stimulus and therefore there is no opportunity for the anxiety associated with it to be extinguished. The behavioural model is supported by evidence that obsessions cause anxiety and that compulsions reduce it (Hodgson & Rachman, 1972). Behavioural treatment involves exposure to the initial stimulus (which is now feared), while encouraging the patient not to carry out any behaviours to avoid this exposure and is known as exposure and response prevention (ERP).

Beck's (1976) cognitive model of emotion states that it is the meaning of events not the events themselves that trigger emotions. He describes the thoughts in OCD as related to an action that patients believe they either should or should not have taken. Compulsions are the patient's attempt to reduce excessive doubts. Therefore the anxiety is related to the consequences of being in a situation or thinking a thought, not to the initial thought or situation.

Salkovskis, Forrester & Richards (1998) suggests that intrusive thoughts are a universal experience but can develop into obsessions because of the way obsessional patients interpret the occurrence or content of the intrusions. Normal intrusions are interpreted as conferring responsibility for harm or preventing harm. Salkovskis (1985) describes five characteristic dysfunctional assumptions of OCD patients:

- 'Having a thought about an action is like performing the action.'
- 'Failing to prevent (or failing to try to prevent) harm to self or others is the same as having caused the harm in the first place.'
- 'Responsibility is not attenuated by other factors (e.g. low probability of occurrence).'
- 'Not neutralising when an intrusion has occurred is similar or equivalent to seeking or wanting the harm involved in the intrusion to happen.'
- 'One should (and can) exercise control over one's thoughts.'

Because of these assumptions the individual is distressed by normal intrusions and therefore overt or covert neutralising responses develop. Neutralising prevents disconfirmation of the individual's feared belief. An example is when a mother has a thought that she might harm her baby. If she responds by doing a ritual or giving her baby to someone else to look after, she interprets this as meaning that her baby is only alright because she did the ritual or let someone else look after the baby. Therefore the important factors are the negative automatic thoughts and responsibility appraisals accompanying intrusive thoughts. This model suggests that treatment should focus on identifying and modifying the dysfunctional assumptions and automatic thoughts, seeing the pathology in OCD in the content of thoughts.

Reed (1985) proposes that OCD is related to impairment in the organisation and integration of experiences, and pathology in the form of thinking. In this model OCD results from the individual's attempts to overstructure his life to compensate for this impairment. Foa & Kozak (1985) also suggest that there is an information-processing disturbance as well as a thought content abnormality. They suggest that OCD sufferers cannot make appropriate inferences from information about danger or the absence of danger.

THE EVIDENCE BASE FOR BEHAVIOUR THERAPY

The French neurologist Pierre Janet described exposure therapy for obsessions and compulsions more than a century ago. At the beginning of the twentieth century psychoanalytic theory proposed that obsessions and compulsions were the result of unconscious conflicts. However treatment using this principle was ineffective and until the late 1960s OCD was widely considered to be untreatable. Case reports demonstrated that OCD symptoms could be reduced by a combination of exposure and response prevention (Meyer, 1966). The treatment required the client to be exposed to the fear producing stimulus *and* to be prevented from carrying out the fear-reducing rituals. The first controlled studies of exposure for the treatment of OCD (Marks, Rachman, & Hodgson, 1975; Rachman, Marks, & Hodgson, 1971) would not be accepted as methodologically sound by today's standards. However they were an important part of the process of generating an evidence base.

Behaviour therapy has been shown to reduce symptoms compared with relaxation (Abramowitz, 1997) and anxiety management training (Lindsay, Crino & Andrews, 1997). Foa & Kozak (1996) reviewed 12 outcome studies and found 83 % of patients who completed exposure and response prevention treatment were post-treatment responders. Stanley & Turner (1995) concluded that about 75 % of OCD patients show substantial improvement after 12 to 15 sessions of behaviour therapy. O'Sullivan & Marks (1991) reviewed nine follow-up studies of OCD exposure and response prevention treatment completers. The follow-up duration was between one and six years with a mean follow up of three years. Seventy-nine per cent of patients had improved or were much improved and symptom improvement was maintained irrespective of the length of follow up. However, these results are for treatment completers. About 25 % of OCD patients offered ERP refuse it (Kozak, 1999) and others drop out or do not improve with ERP. Hiss, Foa & Kozak (1994) found using specific OCD relapse prevention techniques was effective in promoting gains at follow up.

Clinical trials often measure efficacy in particular sub-groups of the general OCD population, for example in-patients or patients with no co-morbid psychiatric diagnoses, but this cannot be directly extrapolated to typical clinical practice. Franklin *et al.* (2000) addressed this issue and found comparable outcome in 110 routine clinical patients receiving exposure and response prevention with the outcome reported in randomised controlled trials (RCTs). Abramowitz (1998) conducted a meta analysis to investigate the clinical significance of treatment gains following exposure therapy in OCD. This showed that after treatment the average patient's functioning was more similar to that of the general population than to individuals with untreated OCD. However the patients were not 'cured' by treatment as they did remain more symptomatic than members of the general population.

MODIFICATIONS AND VARIANTS OF BEHAVIOUR THERAPY

Foa *et al.* (1984) showed that concurrent exposure and response prevention had superior outcome to using either component alone. To be effective the exposure must continue until there is a reduction in anxiety *and* urge to ritualise. Studies have shown that this takes approximately 90 minutes (Foa & Chambless, 1978; Rachman, Desilva & Roper, 1976) which can act as a guide. There is no clear evidence about the necessary frequency of exposure sessions but, in general, patients with more severe symptoms and those who have more difficulty complying with the treatment and homework may need more intensive treatment. Abramowitz, Foa & Franklin (2003) compared 15 sessions over three weeks (daily treatment) or eight weeks (twice-weekly treatment), with 20 patients in each group. Both treatment programmes were effective, with a trend towards more improvement in the intensive group at post treatment but no differences at follow up.

A meta-analysis by Abramowitz (1996), found that therapist-supervised exposure was more effective than self-controlled exposure. However the individual studies produced conflicting results. If a patient can do effective self-controlled exposure by himself from the start it is likely to have a powerful effect. For those patients who are unable to do so, the therapist can provide support, coaching and supervision to ensure that exposure to the feared stimulus continues until the patient's anxiety decreases. The meta-analysis also found that a combination of *in vivo* (exposure in real life settings) and imaginal exposure gave similar reduction in OCD symptoms to *in vivo* exposure alone. However the combined treatment was significantly more effective in reducing post-treatment levels of general anxiety. Imaginal exposure is useful when *in vivo* exposure is not possible – for example, to expose an individual to a fear about a disastrous consequence of not doing rituals. Complete response prevention was superior to partial or no response prevention, and having more sessions of longer length was predictive of greater reductions in OCD and general anxiety symptoms.

PREDICTION OF OUTCOME WITH BEHAVIOUR THERAPY

Studies by Buchanan, Meng & Marks (1996), Castle *et al.* (1994), De Araujo, Ito & Marks (1996) and Keijsers, Hoogduin & Schaap (1994) have looked at variables predicting outcome. They found poor outcome was associated with depression, longer duration of illness, poorer motivation and dissatisfaction with the therapeutic relationship. De Araujo, Ito & Marks (1996) found that initial severity did not predict outcome, whereas the other studies found higher initial severity was associated with poorer outcome. The studies found that good outcome was associated with early adherence to exposure homework, employment, living with one's family, no previous treatment, having fear of contamination, overt ritualistic behaviour and the absence of depression. Castle *et al.* (1994) also found that having a co-therapist was positive for women.

Lelliot *et al.* (1998) found bizzarreness and rigidity of beliefs did not affect compliance with treatment or outcome following ERP. However Foa *et al.* (1999) found worse treatment outcome in those with fixed beliefs about the consequences of stopping compulsions and avoidance behaviours.

Beliefs that are part of an elaborate belief system, for example social or religious, can be resistant to change, and can be sanctioned and reinforced by others. Ciarrocchi (1998) presents some ideas about their treatment, including involving religious advisors to approve planned exposures. The aim may be to try to change the response to intrusions and learn to avoid sustained neutralising rather than to challenge the beliefs about obsessions.

THE EVIDENCE BASE FOR COGNITIVE THERAPY (CT) AND THE COMPARISON OF BEHAVIOUR THERAPY AND COGNITIVE THERAPY

James & Blackburn (1995) examined the evidence base for the use of CT in OCD. They found few controlled studies and that multiple forms of treatment were often used. They concluded that there was little evidence of improved outcome when CT was added to medication and behavioural techniques.

A systematic review by Abramowitz (1997) found no significant difference between behaviour therapy and cognitive therapy. In a further RCT Cottraux (2001) found a similar response rate following behavioural and cognitive therapy. Obsessive cognitions changed with BT and CT. Few studies have tried to investigate whether cognitive therapy and ERP share a psychological mechanism or achieve the same results through different mechanisms. Van Oppen *et al.* (1995) showed that there was no difference on the Irrational Beliefs Inventory or YBOCS obsessions or compulsions subscales between the groups treated with cognitive therapy or ERP. However they used cognitive therapy that included behavioural experiments and the reality is that treatments will rarely be purely behavioural or cognitive. Freeston *et al.* (1997) showed that cognitive-behavioural treatment was effective for patients with only obsessive thoughts who completed treatment. However there was a significant drop-out rate.

EVIDENCE FOR DRUG TREATMENTS

There is evidence that serotonin reuptake inhibitors (SRIs) are more effective than placebo (Abramowitz, 1997; Goodman *et al.*, 1990; Kobak *et al.*, 1998; Piccinelli *et al.*, 1995) and more effective than other kinds of antidepressants (Hoehn-Saric *et al.*, 2000; Picinelli *et al.*, 1995) in reducing OCD symptoms in clinical trials. The evidence suggests that different serotonin reuptake inhibitors have similar efficacy (Kobak *et al.*, 1998; Picinelli *et al.*, 1995) but clomipramine has a higher rate of adverse effects than selective serotonin reuptake inhibitors (Jenike, 1998). Unfortunately most drug studies assess response only over a short period. One prospective study showed that sertraline produced further significant improvement in a 40-week open label extension of a RCT (Rasmussen *et al.*, 1997). Over 50 % of patients respond to serotonin reuptake inhibitors (Erzegovesi *et al.*, 2001; Ravizza *et al.*, 1995) but there is evidence of a rapid return of symptoms in most treatment responders following discontinuation of medication (Pato *et al.*, 1988). Sixteen responders out of 18 had a substantial recurrence by the end of week seven following discontinuation.

Three small RCTs have demonstrated that adding an antipsychotic when people have failed to respond to an SRI improves the response rate compared to addition of placebo (Atmaca *et al.*, 2002; McDougle *et al.*, 1994, 2000).

PREDICTION OF OUTCOME IN DRUG STUDIES

Ackerman *et al.* (1994) found older age of onset and baseline depression predicted response to clomipramine. Ravizza *et al.* (1995) found a worse response to drug treatment (clomipramine or fluoxetine) was predicted by schizotypal personality disorder, presence of compulsions and longer length of illness. Ackerman *et al.* (1998) found greatest improvement for patients with a history of remissions, no previous drug treatment, more severe OCD and either high or low depression scores. Erzegovesi *et al.* (2001) found poor insight and a family history of OCD were the best predictors of poor and good drug treatment response respectively.

NEUROSURGERY

There are a small number of people with OCD who fail to respond to BT, CT or SRIs and remain severely incapacitated. Baer *et al.* (1995) found neurosurgery (cingulotomy) helped about a third of 18 such patients. At a mean follow up time of 26.8 months, five patients (28 %) were responders and three patients (17 %) were partial responders.

COMPARISON OF PSYCHOLOGICAL AND DRUG TREATMENTS AND COMBINATIONS OF TREATMENT

A meta-analysis by Cox *et al.* (1993) found that serotonin reuptake inhibitors and exposure-based behaviour therapy treatments were equally and significantly effective for reducing OCD symptoms. Another review found no significant difference between the effect sizes of serotonin reuptake inhibitors and behavioural therapy (Kobak *et al.* 1998).

One study showed a significantly greater improvement in obsessions with behavioural therapy plus the selective serotonin reuptake inhibitor drug fluvoxamine, compared to behavioural therapy plus placebo tablet (Hohagen *et al.*, 1998). O'Connor *et al.* (1999) found that a combination of cognitive behavioural therapy and medication seemed to potentiate treatment efficacy. However other studies have not shown any additional benefit of combining behavioural therapy or cognitive therapy with a serotonin reuptake inhibitor drug, compared to using any of the three treatments alone (De Haan *et al.*, 1997; Kobak *et al.*, 1998; Van Balkom *et al.*, 1998). De Haan *et al.* (1997) compared ERP, cognitive therapy, ERP plus fluvoxamine and cognitive therapy plus fluvoxamine and found no differences in efficacy between the four treatments. They found that a short-term positive response is a good predictor of long-term effect. However one-third of non-responders at post-treatment (16 weeks) had also become responders by follow-up (six months). Late responders had more severe complaints, had a history of previous treatment and a slower rate of change during treatment. They also noted that motivation was an important factor for successful outcome.

THE EFFECT OF CO-MORBID DEPRESSION ON RESPONSE TO BT, CBT AND SRI TREATMENT

Abramowitz *et al.* (2000) found that patients with severe depression showed significantly less improvement with CBT, yet even highly depressed patients showed moderate treatment gains. Cox *et al.* (1993) found that exposure was not significantly effective for depressed mood. Hoehn-Saric (2000) found an SRI (sertraline) was better for co-morbid OCD and major depressive disorder than a non-SRI (desipramine). Hohagen *et al.* (1998) showed that BT plus fluvoxamine had a significantly better reduction in YBOCS than BT plus placebo in severely depressed patients with OCD.

GROUP TREATMENT WITH BT AND CBT

One RCT found group and individual behaviour therapy were equally efficacious but with a faster response rate for individual therapy (Fals-Stewart *et al.*, 1993). However the individuals were not typical of the OCD population as they were OCD treatment naïve and did not have any co-morbid psychiatric conditions. McLean *et al.* (2001) compared CBT and ERP in a group treatment. Both treatments were superior to a waiting list control, with ERP being slightly more effective than CBT at the end of treatment and at three-month follow up.

Van Noppen *et al.* (1997) did an uncontrolled study on group and multifamily behavioural treatment for OCD. Patients were not randomised to treatment group and were not severely depressed. Both group treatments showed treatment effects similar to those reported for individual behaviour therapy at post-test and one-year follow-up, suggesting this cost-effective format is worthy of further study.

SELF-HELP BOOKS AND COMPUTER PROGRAMMES

There are many self-help books for OCD, such as *Living with Fear* (Marks, 1978) and *The OCD Workbook* (Hyman & Pedrick, 1999). An international group has developed and tested a computer-administrated system, called BT STEPS, for assessing and treating OCD via the telephone and computer. An initial trial (Bachofen *et al.*, 1999), of the computer programme treatment found an average 33 % improvement on Yale-Brown Obsessive Compulsive Scale (Y-BOCS), with significant change in YBOCS only in those who completed at least two exposure and response-prevention sessions. A recent trial of 218 patients compared the computer-guided behaviour treatment to clinician-guided behaviour treatment and relaxation (Griest *et al.*, 2002). The relaxation was ineffective, whereas both the behaviour therapy conditions were effective, with a significantly greater improvement in the clinician-guided group. Patients in the computer-guided treatment group improved more the longer they spent telephoning the computer and doing self-exposure. Benefits of this computer treatment include saving the time of the therapist for clients who do not benefit from self-administered treatments, enabling users from all locations to access as much therapy time as they want, and at the time they want it.

TREATMENT

The patient should first have a diagnostic interview to establish the diagnosis of OCD and any other co-morbid diagnoses. The symptom severity should be evaluated using the Y-BOCS and the CAC. Such scales also list a wide range of obsessional thoughts and compulsions, thus opening the way for patients to disclose thoughts and behaviours they find embarrassing. The history of the course of OCD symptoms, engagement with and response to previous treatments, patient's treatment goals, social functioning, mood, treatment preference and availability, will affect decision making about treatment. Severe depression may require drug treatment before ERP or concurrently. Sessions should probably take place at least weekly initially, to ensure exposure work is being carried out between sessions and to help the patient get the support and challenging he needs to build on success experiences.

Behavioural Treatment with ERP

Foa & Franklin (2001) provide a detailed description of their exposure and intensive response-prevention treatment programme.

Stage 1: Information Gathering

Throughout treatment the therapist tries to develop good rapport. The therapist must initially gather information about the current obsessions, avoidance patterns and the relationship between the two. This includes information about the external cues (for example, objects or situations) and internal cues (for example, thoughts or images) that provoke anxiety; the believed consequences of exposure to these cues and the strength of belief that these feared consequences will happen. It is important to access the patient's beliefs about thoughts (for example, 'if I tell someone my thoughts something bad will happen'), in order to access all thoughts. Avoidance can be passive (such as avoiding certain places) or can occur through rituals. Rituals can be overt observable behaviours or covert mental activities (for example, praying). Although treatment principles are the same, it is more difficult to monitor covert behaviours and ensure response prevention. In treatment it is essential the patient can distinguish between obsessions (involuntary thoughts that produce anxiety) and neutralising thoughts (voluntary thoughts that are intended to reduce anxiety). The patient should be advised to tell the therapist about any mental compulsions occurring during exposure.

The therapist should also gather information about interaction around the OCD by others, such as relatives, who may have accommodated their behaviour substantially because of the patient's OCD symptoms. Studies have found conflicting results about the outcome of using a family member as a co-therapist but it is generally useful to provide the family with information about OCD and advice about how to manage the patient's behaviour and requests for reassurance. Part of the exposure work may involve advising that other family members normalise their behaviours to ensure that the patient is not avoiding exposure at home – for example, family members may be advised to stop any excessive cleaning that they do at the insistence of the patient.

Stage 2: Devising and Explaining the Treatment Programme

It is very important to explain the treatment rationale and to instil hope by giving information about the evidence base for ERP. Unless patients understand this and agree to proceed they are unlikely to engage in treatment or continue to use the techniques outside the therapy sessions. Explain that the patient needs to maintain engagement with the feared stimulus rather than using distraction during exposure. Emphasise the importance of complete ritual prevention. Explain that patients who become actively involved in planning exposure tasks and those who face the items at the top of their hierarchy have most success. In the past patients were physically prevented from carrying out the rituals. However it is now recognised that this is both excessively coercive and will not promote generalisability to situations when the individual is alone. Therefore the individual is encouraged by being given support, education about the rationale, and suggestions about alternatives to carrying out rituals. Explain that the therapist will not use force or do anything without prior consent from the patient. Also explain that the therapist will not give reassurance. The therapist should be encouraging and understanding but also needs to be challenging and to make judgements about when the patient will tolerate and benefit from being pushed.

Introduce a subjective units of discomfort scale (SUDS) ranging from 0 (no distress) to 100 (maximum distress). Arrange exposure items in a hierarchy according to the SUDS. The programme should be adapted to include ERP for any substitute rituals appearing as treatment progresses. With time the patient should gradually take on responsibility for planning the exposure tasks.

Stage 3: Exposure and Response Prevention

After the initial session each session should start with a review of homework and ritual monitoring since the previous session. *In vivo* and imaginal exposure exercises are designed to gradually increase exposure to obsessional distress. Through prolonged and repeated exposure to the feared stimulus the individual accesses information disconfirming unhelpful evaluations and the exposure promotes habituation. Imaginal exposure can be used before *in vivo* exposure or in situations where it is impossible to do *in vivo* exposure.

Generally patients prefer to work through a hierarchy of increasingly difficult situations, rather than confront their greatest fear first. However it is important that therapists do not collude with the patient in avoiding exposure to the more distressing situations. Begin with an item around the middle of the hierarchy. Continue the ERP until the SUDS is reduced by half, then repeat that item until it provokes no more than minimal anxiety. Standardised information sheets (for example about washing or checking) with rules for ritual prevention during treatment and guidelines for 'normal behaviour' after treatment can be useful (Foa & Franklin, 2001). During treatment the individual is expected to learn to tolerate a greater degree of exposure than normal, e.g. compulsive washers afraid of contamination should be exposed to purposeful contamination and be encouraged to avoid 'normal' cleaning.

It is very important that exposure work is continued by the individual between sessions. Home visits can provide additional useful information and treatment at home is necessary if the symptoms are confined to home.

Difficulties

If patients are non-compliant the therapist should use motivational techniques and repeat the treatment rationale. If they still do not engage, give them the option to stop.

It is important to question the patient directly about the emergence of new rituals as treatment progresses and to add these to the hierarchy. Usually these will appear connected or have the same underlying theme.

Occasionally treatment has to be interrupted or postponed because of a personal crisis.

Cognitive Therapy

Three CT techniques have been described: challenging obsessional thoughts, thought stopping and challenging negative automatic thoughts. Patients can be taught to monitor the obsessional thoughts and then learn how to replace them with more helpful thoughts or learn to challenge the belief in the thoughts by employing rational counter claims. In thought stopping patients are taught to say a cue word, such as 'stop', to disrupt a chain of obsessional thoughts. The patients can also be instructed to picture a positive image after saying the cue word. The third technique uses Beckian principles to challenge the negative automatic thoughts that result from the obsessional intrusive thoughts, rather than targeting the obsessional thoughts. The patients are helped to consider alternative, less threatening explanations.

Cognitive Behavioural Therapy for Obsessions

Salkovskis, Forrester & Richards (1998) has devised a cognitive-behavioural treatment for obsessions. In assessment the therapist identifies the sequence of events in a recent episode, for example intrusion/interpretation/reactions, with emphasis on the interpretation of intrusions in terms of key responsibility assumptions and appraisals. Some patients show cognitive avoidance as they hold the belief that disclosing their thoughts will make the feared outcome more likely to happen. The impact of attempts to control intrusive thoughts is discussed. The occurrence of intrusive thoughts is normalised and the therapist helps the patient see their usefulness. The initial aims are to reach a shared understanding through formulation of an alternative and less threatening understanding of the patient's difficulties and to set the goals for therapy. If patients have understood the formulation they will agree that the therapy goals relate to dealing with the significance they attach to intrusions, not to getting rid of them completely. Patients therefore understand that they are individuals with worries about negative events, not individuals who are going to suffer negative events.

The next stage is engagement in treatment. A loop tape is used to record and play back the intrusions in the session. This allows the patient and therapist to deal with any difficulties with response prevention. The tape is repeated until the discomfort or urge to neutralise has reduced. Helping patients to challenge their appraisal of intrusions encourages them to do response prevention. They are encouraged to assess how new information fits with the two different formulations. Initially the therapist will play a major role in helping the patient plan behavioural experiments. In time patients should take on more of this planning, recording intrusions and the appraisals made during response prevention. Behavioural experiments should explicitly tests their beliefs and reinforce the alternative explanation. The belief that thoughts can influence events can be challenged by doing an experiment involving trying to cause a positive outcome by thinking. Behavioural experiments cannot falsify predicted negative outcomes that are vague or distant such as that something bad will happen to some relative at some time.

Through therapy the number of intrusions usually decreases as patients no longer seek to control their occurrence and as they lose their priority of processing as they are no longer considered important.

SUMMARY

Obsessive compulsive disorder is a disabling and often chronic disorder. Behavioural therapy is largely successful for treatment completers. Developing a therapeutic alliance and using motivational techniques are extremely important. Cognitive therapy has not shown clearly that it adds anything to behavioural therapy but may have a role in improving engagement in therapy and in improving outcome by treating co-morbid disorders. Medication is effective for many but symptoms commonly recur when medication is stopped.

REFERENCES

Abramowitz, J.S. (1996). Variants of exposure and response prevention in the treatment of obsessive-compulsive disorder: A meta-analysis. *Behavior Therapy, 27*, 583–600.

Abramowitz, J.S. (1997). Effectiveness of psychological and pharmacological treatments for obsessive-compulsive disorder: A quantitative review. *Journal Consulting Clinical Psychology, 65*, 44–52.

Abramowitz, J.S. (1998). Does cognitive-behavioral therapy cure obsessive-compulsive disorder? A meta-analytic evaluation of clinical significance. *Behavior Therapy, 29*, 339–355.

Abramowitz, J.S., Foa, E.B. & Franklin, M.E. (2003). Exposure and ritual prevention for obsessive-compulsive disorder: effects of intensive versus twice-weekly sessions. *Journal of Consulting and Clinical Psychology, 71*(2), 394–398.

Abramowitz, J.S., Franklin, M.E., Street, G.P. *et al.* (2000). Effects of comorbid depression on response to treatment for obsessive compulsive disorder. *Behavior Therapy, 31*, 517–528.

Ackerman, D.L., Greenland, S., Bystritsky, A. *et al.* (1994). Predictors of treatment response in obsessive-compulsive disorder: Multivariate analyses from a multicenter trial of clomipramine. *Journal of Clinical Psychopharmacology 14*(4), 247–254.

Ackerman, D.L., Greenland, S., & Bystritsky, A. (1998). Clinical characteristics of response to fluoxetine treatment of obsessive-compulsive disorder. *Journal of Clinical Psychopharmacology 18*(3), 185–192.

Atmaca, M., Kuloglu, M., Tezcan, E. & Gecici, O. (2002). Quetiapine augmentation in patients with treatment resistant obsessive-compulsive disorder: A single-blind, placebo-controlled study. *International Clinical Psychopharmacology, 17*, 115–119.

Bachofen, M., Nakagawa, A., Marks, I.M. *et al.* (1999). Home self-assessment and self-treatment of obsessive-compulsive disorder using a manual and a computer-conducted telephone interview: Replication of a UK-US study. *Journal of Clinical Psychiatry, 60*, 545–549.

Baer, L., Rauch, S.L., Ballantine, H.T. Jr. *et al.* (1995). Cingulotomy for intractable obsessive-compulsive disorder: Prospective long-term follow-up of 18 patients. *Archives of General Psychiatry, 52*, 384–392.

Beck, A.T. (1976). *Cognitive Therapy and the Emotional Disorders.* New York: International University Press.

Buchanan A.W., Meng, K.S. & Marks, I.M. (1996). What predicts improvement and compliance during the behavioural treatment of obsessive compulsive disorder? *Anxiety, 2*, 22–27.

Castle, D.J., Deale, A., Marks, I.M. *et al.* (1994). Obsessive-compulsive disorder: Prediction of outcome from behavioural psychotherapy. *Acta Psychiatrica Scandinavica, 89*, 393–398.

Ciarrocchi, J.W. (1998). Religion, scrupulosity, and obsessive-compulsive disorder. In M.A. Jenike, L. Baer & W.E. Minichiello (eds) *Obsessive-compulsive Disorders*. St Louis: Mosby.

Cottraux, J., Note, I., Yao, S.N. *et al.* (2001). A randomised controlled trial of cognitive therapy versus intensive behavior therapy in obsessive compulsive disorder. *Psychotherapy and Psychosomatics, 70*, 288–297.

Cox, B.J., Swinson, R.P., Morrison, B. & Lee, P.S. (1993). Clomipramine, fluoxetine, and behavior therapy in the treatment of obsessive-compulsive disorder: A meta-analysis. *Journal of Behaviour Therapy and Experimental Psychiatry, 24*(2), 149–153.

De Araujo, L.A., Ito, L.M. & Marks, I.M. (1996). Early compliance and other factors predicting outcome of exposure for obsessive-compulsive disorder. *British Journal of Psychiatry, 169*, 747–752.

De Haan, E., Van Oppen, P., Van Balkom, A. J. L. M. *et al.* (1997). Prediction of outcome and early vs late improvement in OCD patients treated with cognitive behaviour therapy and pharmacotherapy. *Acta Psychiatrica Scandinavica, 96*(5), 354–361.

Eisen, J.L., Goodman, W.K., Keller M.B. *et al.* (1999). Patterns of remission and relapse in obsessive-compulsive disorder: A 2-year prospective study, *Journal of Clinical Psychiatry, 60*, 346–351.

Emmelkamp, P.M.G., de Haan, E. & Hoogduin, C.A.L. (1990). Marital adjustment and obsessive-compulsive disorder. *British Journal of Psychiatry, 156*, 55–60.

Erzegovesi, S., Cavallini, M.C., Cavedinin, P. *et al.* (2001). Clinical predictors of drug response in obsessive-compulsive disorder. *Journal of Clinical Psychopharmacology, 21*(5), 488–492.

Fals-Stewart, W., Marks, A.P. & Schafer, B.A. (1993). A comparison of behavioral group therapy and individual therapy in treating obsessive-compulsive disorder. *Journal of Mental Disease, 181*, 189–193.

Foa, E.B., Abramowitz, J.S., Franklin, M.E. *et al.* (1999). Feared consequences, fixity of belief, and treatment outcome in patients with obsessive compulsive disorder. *Behavior Therapy, 30*, 717–724.

Foa, E.B. & Chambless, D.L. (1978). Habituation of subjective anxiety during flooding in imagery. *Behaviour Research and Therapy, 16*, 391–399.

Foa, E.B. & Franklin, M.E. (2001). Obsessive-compulsive disorder. In David H. Barlow (ed.) *Clinical Handbook of Psychological Disorders* (3rd edn). New York: Guilford.

Foa, E.B., Huppert, J.D., Leiberg, S. *et al.* (2002). The obsessive-compulsive inventory: Development and validation of a short version. *Psychological Assessment, 14*(4), 485–496.

Foa, E.B. & Kozak, M.J. (1985). Treatment of anxiety disorders: implications for psychopathology. In A.H. Tuma & J.D. Maser (eds), *Anxiety and the Anxiety Disorders* (pp. 421–452). Hillsdale, NJ: Erlbaum.

Foa, E.B. & Kozak, M.J. (1996). Psychological treatments for obsessive compulsive disorder. In M.R. Mavissakalian & R.P. Prien (eds), *Long-term Treatments of Anxiety Disorders* (pp. 285–309). Washington, DC: American Psychiatric Press.

Foa, E.B., Steketee, G., Grayson, J.B. *et al.* (1984). Deliberate exposure and blocking of obsessive-compulsive rituals: immediate and long-term effects. *Behavior Therapy, 15*, 450–472.

Franklin, M.E., Abramowitz, J.S., Kozak, M.J. *et al.* (2000). Effectiveness of exposure and ritual prevention for obsessive-compulsive disorder: randomized compared with nonrandomized samples. *Journal of Consulting and Clinical Psychology, 68*(4), 594–602.

Freeston, M.H., Ladouceur, R., Gagnon, F. *et al.* (1997). Cognitive-behavioral treatment of obsessive thoughts: a controlled study. *Journal of Consulting and Clinical Psychology, 65*(3), 405–413.

Goodman, W.K., Price, L.H., Delgado, P.L. *et al.* (1990). Specificity of serotonin reuptake inhibitors in the treatment of obsessive-compulsive disorder: comparison of fluvoxamine and desipramine. *Archives of General Psychiatry, 47*, 577–585.

Goodwin, D.W., Guze, S.B. & Robins, E. (1969). Followup studies in obsessional neurosis. *Archives of General Psychiatry 20*, 182–187.

Griest, J.H., Marks, I.M., Baer, L. *et al.* (2002). Behavior therapy for obsessive-compulsive disorder guided by a computer or by a clinician compared with relaxation as a control. *Journal of Clinical Psychiatry, 63*(2),138–145.

Hiss, H., Foa, E.B., & Kozak, M.J. (1994). A relapse prevention program for treatment of obsessive compulsive disorder. *Journal of Consulting and Clinical Psychology, 62*, 801–808.

Hodgson, R.J., & Rachman, S. (1972). The effects of contamination and washing in obsessional patients. *Behaviour Research and Therapy, 10*, 111–117.

Hoehn-Saric, R., Ninan, P., Black, D.W. *et al.* (2000). Multicenter double-blind comparison of sertraline and desipramine for concurrent obsessive-compulsive and major depressive disorders. *Archives of General Psychiatry, 57*, 76–82.

Hohagen, F., Winkelmann, G., Rashe-Ruchie, H. *et al.* (1998). Combination of behaviour therapy with fluvoxamine in comparison with behaviour therapy and placebo. Results of a multicentre study. *British Journal of Psychiatry, 35* (suppl): 71–78.

Hyman, B. & Pedrick, C. (1999). *The OCD Workbook*. Oakland, CA: New Harbinger Publications.

James, I.A. & Blackburn, I.-M. (1995). Cognitive therapy with obsessive-compulsive disorder. *British Journal of Psychiatry, 166*, 444–450.

Jenike, M.A. (1998). Drug treatment of obsessive-compulsive disorders. In M.A. Jenike, L. Baer & W.E. Minichiello (eds), *Obsessive-compulsive Disorders*. St Louis: Mosby.

Jenkins, R., Bebbington, P.E., Brugha, T., *et al.* (1997). The National Psychiatric Morbidity Surveys of Great Britain: 1. Strategy and methods. *Psychological Medicine, 27*, 765–774.

Keijsers, G.P., Hoogduin, C.A., Schaap, C.P. (1994). Predictors of treatment outcomes in the behavioural treatment of obsessive-compulsive disorder. *British Journal of Psychiatry, 165*, 781–786.

Kobak, K.A., Griest, J.H., Jefferson, J.W., *et al.* (1998). Behavioral versus pharmacological treatments of obsessive compulsive disorder: a meta-analysis. *Psychopharmacology, 136*, 205–216.

Koran, L. M., Thienemann, M.D. & Davenport, R. (1996). Quality of life for patients with obsessive-compulsive disorder. *American Journal of Psychiatry, 153*, 783–788.

Kozak, M.J. (1999). Evaluating treatment efficacy for obsessive-compulsive disorder: caveat practitioner. *Cognitive and Behavioral Practice, 6*, 422–426.

Lelliot, P.T., Noshirvani, H.F., Basoglu, M. *et al.* (1988). Obsessive-compulsive beliefs and treatment outcomes. *Psychological Medicine, 18*, 697–702.

Leon, A.C., Portera, L. & Weissman, M.M. (1995). The social costs of anxiety disorders. *British Journal of Psychiatry, 166*(suppl.), 19–22.

Lindsay, M., Crino, R. & Andrews, G. (1997). Controlled trial of exposure and response prevention in obsessive-compulsive disorder. *British Journal Psychiatry, 171*, 135–139.

Marks, I.M. (1978). *Living with Fear.* New York: McGraw-Hill.

Marks, I.M.., Rachman, S. & Hodgson, R. (1975). Treatment of chronic obsessive-compulsive neurosis by in vivo exposure. *British Journal of Psychiatry, 127*, 263–267.

McDougle, C.J., Epperson, C.N., Pelton, G.H. *et al.* (2000). A double-blind, placebo-controlled study of risperidone addition in serotonin reuptake inhibitor-refractory obsessive-compulsive disorder. *Archives of General Psychiatry, 57*, 794–801.

McDougle, C.J., Goodman, W.K., Leckman, J.F. *et al.* (1994). Haloperidol addition in fluvoxamine-refractory obsessive-compulsive disorder. A double-blind, placebo-controlled study in patients with and without tics. *Archives of General Psychiatry, 51*, 302–308.

McLean, P.D., Whittal, M.L., Thordarson, D.S. *et al.* (2001). Cognitive versus behavior therapy in the group treatment of obsessive-compulsive disorder. *Journal of Consulting and Clinical Psychology, 69*(2), 205–214.

Meltzer, H., Gill, B., Petticrew, M. & Hinds, K. (1995). *OPCS Surveys of psychiatric Morbidity in Great Britain. Report No. 1: The Prevalence of Psychiatric Morbidity Among Adults Aged 16–64 Living in Private Households in Great Britain.* London: Office of Population Censuses and Surveys.

Meyer, V. (1966). Modification of expectations in cases with obsessional rituals. *Behaviour Research and Therapy, 4*, 273–280.

Muris, P., Merckelbach, H. & Clavan, M. (1997). Abnormal and normal compulsions. *Behaviour Research and Therapy, 35*(3), 249–252.

O'Connor, K., Todorov, C., Robillard, S. *et al.* (1999). Cognitive-behaviour therapy and medication in the treatment of obsessive-compulsive disorder: A controlled study. *Canadian Journal of Psychiatry, 44*, 64–71.

O'Sullivan, G. & Marks, I. (1991). Follow-up studies of behavioral treatment of phobic and obsessive compulsive neuroses. *Psychiatric Annals, 21*, 6.

Pato, M.T., Zohar-Kadouch, R., Zohar, J. & Murphy, D.L. (1998). Return of symptoms after discontinuation of clomipramine in patients with obsessive-compulsive disorder. *American Journal of Psychiatry, 145*, 1521–1525.

Piccinelli M., Pini S., Bellantuono C., Wilkinson G. (1995). Efficacy of drug treatment in obsessive-compulsive disorder. A meta-analytic review *British Journal of Psychiatry, 166*, 424–440.

Rachman, S., DeSilva, P. & Roper, G. (1976). The spontaneous decay of compulsive urges. *Behaviour Research and Therapy, 14*(6), 445–453.

Rachman, S., Marks, I.M. & Hodgson, R. (1971). The treatment of chronic obsessive-compulsive neurosis. *Behaviour Research and Therapy, 9*, 237–247.

Rasmussen, S., Hackett, E., DuBoff, E. *et al.* (1997). A 2-year study of sertraline in the treatment of obsessive compulsive disorder. *International Clinical Psychopharmacology, 17*, 267–271.

Rasmussen, S.A. & Tsuang, M.T. (1986). Clinical characteristics and family history in DSM III obsessive-compulsive disorder. *American Journal of Psychiatry, 143*, 317–382.

Ravizza, L., Barzega, G., Bellino, S. *et al.* (1995). Predictors of drug treatment response in obsessive-compulsive disorder. *Journal of Clinical Psychiatry, 56*(8), 368–373.

Reed, G.E. (1985). *Obsessional Experience and Compulsive Behaviour: A Cognitive Structural Approach.* Orlando, FL: Academic Press.

Salkovskis, P.M. (1985). Obsessional-compulsive problems: A cognitive behavioural analysis. *Behaviour Research and Therapy, 23*, 571–583.

Salkovskis, P.M., Forrester, E. & Richards, C. (1998). Cognitive-behavioural approach to understanding obsessional thinking. *British Journal of Psychiatry, 173*(suppl.), 53–63.

Salkovskis, P.M. & Harrison, J. (1984). Abnormal and normal obsessions – a replication. *Behaviour Research and Therapy, 22*(5), 549–552.

Skoog, G. & Skoog, I. (1999). A 40-year follow-up of patients with obsessive-compulsive disorder. *Archives of General Psychiatry, 56*, 121–127.

Stanley, M.A. & Turner, S.M. (1995). Current status of pharmacological and behavioral treatment of obsessive-compulsive disorder. *Behavior Therapy, 26*, 163–186.

Steketee, G. & Freund, B. (1993). Compulsive Activity Checklist (CAC): Further psychometric analses and revision. *Behavioural Psychotherapy, 21*, 13–25.

Swedo, S., Rapoport, J., Leonard, H. *et al.* (1989). Obsessive-compulsive disorder in children and adolescents: Clinical phenomenology of 70 consecutive cases. *Archives of General Psychiatry, 46*, 335–341.

Taylor, S. (1995). Assessment of obsessions and compulsions: Reliability, validity, and sensitivity to treatment effects. *Clinical Psychology Review, 15*(4), 261–296.

Van Balkom, A.J., De Haan, E., Van Oppen, P. *et al.* (1998). Cognitive and behavioural therapies alone versus in combination with fluvoxamine in the treatment of obsessive compulsive disorder. *Journal of Nervous and Mental Disorders, 186*, 492–499.

Van Noppen, B., Steketee, G., McCorkle, B.H. & Pato, M. (1997). Group and multifamily behavioral treatment for obsessive compulsive disorder: A pilot study. *Journal of Anxiety Disorders, 11*(4), 431–446.

Van Oppen, P., De Haan, E., Van Balkom, A.J.L.M. *et al.* (1995). Cognitive therapy and exposure in vivo in the treatment of obsessive compulsive disorder. *Behaviour Research and Therapy, 33*(4), 379–390.

Weissman, M.M., Bland, R.C., Canino, G.J. *et al.* (1994). The cross national epidemiology of obsessive compulsive disorder: The Cross-National Collaborative Group. *Journal of Clinical Psychiatry, 55*(suppl. 3), 5–10.

CHAPTER 10

Eating Disorders

Jane Morris

Royal Edinburgh Hospital, Edinburgh, UK

INTRODUCTION

The world is polarised between the starving and the overfed. In the prosperous West, while obesity becomes a major public health concern, eating disorders (more accurately 'dieting disorders') are endemic. At the start of the twenty-first century, 4 % of young women meet criteria for bulimia nervosa (BN), 0.5 % have anorexia nervosa (AN) and many more have binge eating disorder (BED). See Figure 10.1.Ten per cent of patients with eating disorders are male. Children and even the elderly are presenting to clinics in greater numbers. The myth persists that this is the self-inflicted behaviour of spoilt middle-class teenage girls who read fashion magazines then go on silly diets, but eating disorders are often chronic, with high morbidity and – for anorexia nervosa – high mortality. Yet in contrast with other severe and enduring psychiatric disorders, complete recovery remains a possibility even after 20 years of illness. Another difference is that psychological therapies, rather than drugs, are acknowledged as the leading treatments. This chapter examines the evidence for psychotherapeutic effectiveness in the treatment of eating disorders.

Interpretation of the evidence base is complicated by changing diagnostic criteria (15 % rather than 25 % weight loss for AN), complex outcome measures (survival, weight gain, failure to meet diagnostic criteria, binge-purge frequency) and shifting epidemiology (increasing co-morbidity, fashions in patterns of diet and exercise). Diagnostic differentiation remains important. Bingeing and vomiting at low weight greatly increase mortality compared with purely restrictive starvation (Herzog *et al.*, 2000). On the other hand, bingeing and vomiting at normal weight are associated with little if any excess mortality (Keel & Mitchell, 1997). Co-morbidity is associated with bleaker prognosis. There is an important gap in the evidence base for treatment of eating disorders with co-morbid substance (including alcohol) abuse. Most clinical trials for bulimia concern out-patients, often American subjects who have responded to advertisements for free treatment. Research into management of severe, 'multi-impulsive' bulimia is more limited. In contrast, anorexia research favours severely affected tertiary referrals, reflecting the middle-class referral bias. Nearly all trial subjects are female.

Handbook of Evidence-based Psychotherapies: A Guide for research and practice.
Edited by C. Freeman & M. Power. Copyright © 2007 John Wiley & Sons, Ltd.

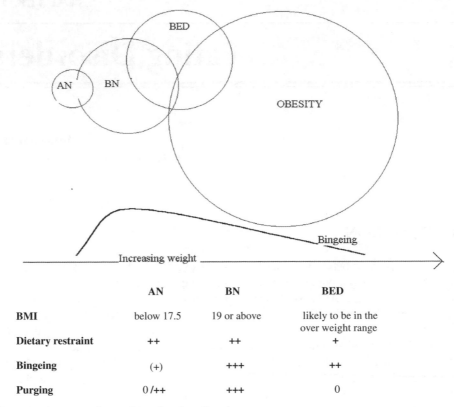

	AN	BN	BED
BMI	below 17.5	19 or above	likely to be in the over weight range
Dietary restraint	++	++	+
Bingeing	(+)	+++	++
Purging	0 /++	+++	0

Figure 10.1 Interrelationship of eating disorders.

Even manualised therapies lack the predictable consistency of a drug, and research into eating disorders must take into account setting, relationships with patients, families and other carers, and timing and sequencing of interventions. We need to address not just 'what works for whom' but also *by whom, with whom, where, when* and *for how long.*

BULIMIA NERVOSA

Bulimia nervosa appears to be a 'modern' disorder, reaching psychiatric awareness in the 1970s. It has been treated as a 'depressive equivalent' with antidepressant medication and therapies modified from antidepressant strategies. High-dose antidepressant medication (such as fluoxetine 60 mg daily) offers proven but often short-lived anti-bulimic benefit (Walsh *et al.*, 1991) and benefits are inferior to the best psychological therapies (Agras *et al.*, 1992). Extensive evidence supports cognitive behaviour therapy (CBT), in individual or group format, as the first-line treatment, with interpersonal therapy (IPT) a close second. Disappointingly, most individuals treated for BN do not receive evidence-based treatments (Crow *et al.*, 1999). This may partially explain the finding (Ben-Tovim *et al.*, 2001) that five-year outcome for BN (and other eating disorders) was independent of receiving treatment.

Whatever the therapy, lower BMI, greater frequency of binge-purge episodes, (Fairburn *et al.*, 1995) and poor self-esteem (Fairburn *et al.*, 1997) are associated with poorer prognosis. Those with co-morbid personality disorders, particularly the 'multi-impulsive' picture (Fichter, Quadlif & Rief, 1994) are hardest of all to treat successfully. Surprisingly, longer duration of symptoms is associated with better outcome (Turnbull *et al.*, 1996). In practice bulimia is a secret disorder with an average delay of six years from onset to presentation. Early intervention is rarely an option. This long delay also accounts for the belief that bulimia has a later onset than anorexia. Adolescents who are brought to help early may be harder to engage. At present little research addresses bulimia in the younger age group.

Subjects in research trials generally meet DSM or ICD criteria:

- by definition, subjects with BN are at least normal weight range, body mass index (BMI) 19 or over;
- the core symptom is of binges – rapid consumption of a large amount of food, substantially more than a normal meal, in a finite amount of time (not 'grazing');
- binges are followed by purging behaviour, such as vomiting, abuse of laxatives or diuretics and by renewed attempts to fast or restrain eating;
- there have been at least three binge-purge episodes a week for at least six months;
- abnormally high value is placed on body image and slimness.

Cognitive Behaviour Therapy (CBT-BN): The Evidence Base

In 1979, the same year that Russell alerted the world to BN as 'an ominous variant of anorexia nervosa', Beck and colleagues published the classic *Cognitive Therapy of Depression*. The convenient marriage between the worrying young disorder and hopeful new therapy has spawned more than 50 trials. Cognitive behaviour therapy remains the leading treatment for normal weight BN. About 50 % of subjects improve substantially, with an overall 50 % decline in bingeing and purging, for a disorder that shows minimal placebo response and continues chronically without treatment (Keller *et al.*, 1992). Cognitive behaviour therapy works faster than IPT and outcome can be predicted as early as the sixth session, when those who show no improvement are unlikely to respond.

Most trials use the modification of CBT manualised as 'CBT-BN' by Fairburn (1993) or similar adaptations, such as that of Cooper (1995). Manuals can be administered by minimally trained professionals or offered in workbook form as self-help. The model appears robust with regard to setting and therapist characteristics. Treatment is effective in individual or group format and even in self-help, or guided self-help format (Cooper, 1996). There have recently been pilot studies of telephone delivery (Hugo, 1999; Palmer *et al.*, 2002) and Internet delivery (Robinson, 2001).

Benefit from self-help is strongly correlated with outcome in formal CBT. Self-help approaches rely greatly on patients' capacity for self-monitoring and the mainstay of CBT-BN is the 'food diary', listing food intake, binge-purge episodes and associated feelings and thoughts. Therapists need tact and creativity to help patients who are disorganised or bored by the task, or show the common reluctance to detail embarrassing behaviour.

Use of CBT-BN in Clinical Practice

After the professional's usual assessment, patients complete baseline ratings such as the BITE (Henderson & Freeman, 1987) and measures of depression. These facilitate audit and research and are discussed collaboratively with the patient to monitor progress. Patients are encouraged to let the therapist take over weekly weighing. Full physical examination is rarely needed but blood tests may highlight low potassium, anaemia and (in drinkers) abnormal liver function.

Patients are offered CBT-BN as a course of about 20 one-hour sessions. Fairburn (1985) suggests two or three sessions a week early in treatment with later sessions spaced fortnightly. Mitchell *et al.* (1993) found high intensity approaches more effective. There are three main stages:

- a psychoeducational and monitoring phase, introducing regular eating;
- a more cognitive phase, teaching strategies to eliminate binge-purging and challenge obstacles to normal eating behaviour;
- final sessions to address relapse management, as this is common.

Case Illustration

> Belinda, a 22-year-old music student, had suffered from bulimia nervosa for six years. She binged and vomited most evenings, and took laxatives. She entered a research trial and was randomised to receive 19 weekly sessions of CBT.
>
> Belinda was given reading material and food diaries to complete. These were reviewed as part of the agenda of each session. She agreed to the therapist weighing her weekly instead of weighing herself several times a day. She borrowed books that discussed the health implications of bulimia and helped her to distinguish scientifically investigated information from her own assumptions about 'fattening foods'. She scheduled three mealtimes and three snacks each day and practised stimulus control techniques to structure these. At first distraction strategies failed to reduce binge-purge episodes. However, she stopped taking laxatives when she learned they did not get rid of any calories.
>
> By session eight, a planned review, Belinda's BITE score was lower, particularly on the severity subscale. Her depression inventory showed improvement too. She told the therapist she could now eat socially with friends.
>
> Therapy next focused on eliminating eating disordered behaviour and reintroducing 'forbidden' foods. Belinda used her diaries to monitor the automatic thoughts that occurred when she tried to eat normally or resist binge-purging. These included 'normal meals will make me fat' and 'I must fast today'. She learned techniques to challenge these thoughts and to generate and test out more helpful alternatives, such as 'eating regularly helps keep hunger under control'.
>
> The last three sessions were spaced fortnightly. Belinda feared she would slip up and go 'back to square one'. The therapist reminded her that lapses were common but need not be catastrophic. They prepared a written relapse management plan and arranged three- and six-month follow-up appointments. Belinda now binged less than once a month and ate a range of foods at normal mealtimes. She was spending time with a new boyfriend and their music group. Progress continued at six-month follow up.

Interpersonal Psychotherapy (IPT-BN): The Evidence Base

Klerman *et al.* (1984) drew on key skills of experienced therapists to design a set of techniques as a condition for inclusion in clinical trials of the management of depression. Their package developed into a versatile therapy in its own right. It was particularly attractive to Fairburn's group, as a structured, manualised, time-limited therapy against which to test out the specific effectiveness of CBT. At the end of active therapy CBT is consistently ahead of both behaviour therapy and of IPT. Remarkably, though, at one-year follow-up, IPT subjects catch up with the CBT cohort on all measures of functioning, including binge-purges (Fairburn *et al.*, 1995). Interpersonal psychotherapy when available, is a close second to CBT. Unfortunately there are no indicators of differential suitability.

Use of IPT-BN in Clinical Practice

The Fairburn model of IPT for bulimia nervosa differs in spirit from the original IPT model in that it does not 'prescribe the sick role' to the patient and does not begin each session with a review of the symptoms of bulimia. This was to avoid overlap with CBT in research trials. Including review of bulimic symptoms has not been evaluated.

Interpersonal psychotherapy is a three-part course of therapy.

* During the assessment phase (four sessions) the therapist formulates the onset and progression of the patient's eating disorder in relation to interpersonal events.
* The longest part of therapy is devoted to the patient's active work on the selected focus area – *interpersonal role transition, role dispute, grief (interpersonal loss)* or *interpersonal deficits*. No homework is formally set, but the patient improvises and practises new interpersonal skills between sessions.
* The final few sessions specifically address termination issues.

Case Illustration

Suppose that Belinda (described above) was allocated to the IPT arm of the research study:

> The therapist spent the early sessions mapping out the important people in Belinda's interpersonal network. He charted events, changes in her mood, and the onset and deterioration of her eating disorder, in a series of columns on a 'life chart'.
>
> Belinda's father had died eight years earlier and she became withdrawn, starving herself. Two years later, having lost so much weight that her periods stopped, she found exam revision interrupted by food binges. Her weight increased so she began to vomit. She took a year off and things improved. Her weight was normal, which reassured her mother. When she finally left home, though, Belinda's bingeing increased and she started to use laxatives. She made no friends at university, but spent weekends travelling home to her widowed mother.
>
> The therapist acknowledged the importance of grief in the onset of her symptoms and also a role dispute with her mother, which perpetuated the disorder. However, he proposed that they devote the middle part of therapy to the focus of the role transition from home to university life. (The other focus is *interpersonal deficits,* but Belinda's isolation was attributable to her move rather than to longstanding difficulties.)
>
> Belinda now worked hard to build a new network of friends and deal with personality clashes, rejections and overwhelming demands. The therapist used word for word 'replays' of incidents and role-play to examine and prepare for interpersonal problems. When Belinda spoke of bingeing or dieting, the therapist would refocus on interpersonal concerns.
>
> Late sessions were explicitly devoted to termination issues. Belinda recalled the guilt and homesickness she no longer felt. Her mother seemed more cheerful, although Belinda spent fewer weekends at home. Her bingeing and vomiting were somewhat reduced. She was busy with friends and music.
>
> At one year follow-up, symptoms continued to improve with less than monthly binge-purge episodes. She was playing in several bands and had a steady boyfriend. Her mother had remarried.

Other Options

Some centres practise a sequenced approach to therapy. At first referral patients might be offered guided self-help. Those who fail to improve would enter individual therapy using an evidence-based model. Fifty per cent of patients are not helped by CBT or IPT. If these were unsuccessful, different models of therapy might then be offered. Day-patient programmes or admission are a last resort.

In practice, few patients comply strenuously with further therapeutic efforts after 'failing,' unless there is a built-in expectation that therapy will occur in a series of blocks addressing different skills. Nevonen *et al.* (1999) have designed a group treatment for BN starting with CBT, then proceeding to group IPT. Preliminary evaluations are encouraging.

Other options, particularly where there is co-morbidity, include *cognitive analytic therapy* (CAT – Denman, 1995), *guided imagery* (Esplen *et al.*, 1998) and *dialectical behavioural therapy* (DBT) (Linehan, 1993; Safer *et al.*, 2000).

BINGE EATING DISORDER (BED)

The DSM IV provides research criteria for BED in Appendix B. The clinical picture is similar to BN, with the important absence of compensatory purging. CBT and IPT are at least as effective in treating BED as BN, and group treatment with either therapy is well accepted (Wilfley *et al.*, 1993). However, BED is extremely common and could easily overwhelm eating disorder services.

Many BED patients are overweight. Psychological approaches emphasise the benefits of stability, at whatever weight, and discourage dieting. However, medical services for obesity are more likely to urge dieting and weight reduction. Interdisciplinary dialogue is likely to be as important in the future management of obesity (with and without binge eating) as in the management of anorexia.

ANOREXIA NERVOSA

Historical and geographical studies suggest that anorexia nervosa has occurred wherever there are humans. The first formal medical account is in Richard Morton's *Phthisiologia* (1689). Anorexia nervosa responds to the same precipitants as bulimia but depends on a physiological capacity to tolerate extreme starvation, which may be genetic. The core psychopathology of anorexia nervosa is overwhelming concern about body shape and weight. Phobia of fatness increases as weight decreases. The controversial 'body image distortion' does not amount to a delusion (and is unresponsive to anti-psychotic drugs) but resembles an obsessive-compulsive conviction, attracting to itself all negative attributions generated in the course of everyday life.

Current diagnostic criteria for anorexia nervosa require that:

* Body weight is maintained at least 15 % below that expected (in adults, BMI 17.5 or less).
* This occurs either through sheer dietary restraint (restricting sub-type) or by restraint together with self-induced purging ('bulimic' subtype – although 'binges' are often simply episodes of unplanned eating). Both groups may compulsively over-exercise.

- In women menstruation ceases (or never starts). Men have atrophied genitalia and loss of erections.

Diagnostic criteria have changed over time, to include less emaciated individuals. Earlier criteria demanded weight 25 % below expected. Some women apparently in the 'normal' weight range have starved from a high weight that is their own norm and experience similar symptoms – so-called 'cryptic' anorexia. It has been suggested that amenorrhoea should not be obligatory (and is often masked by the contraceptive pill). Some women menstruate and give birth at unhealthily low weight.

The widening of the diagnosis is problematic when considering epidemiological data – prevalence increases overnight! – and for prognostic studies. For instance, Theander's (1985) classic outcome studies are no longer directly applicable to all who are diagnosed with anorexia nervosa today.

Anorexia Nervosa: The Evidence Base

It is ironic that the most lethal of all psychiatric disorders should be the Cinderella of research – there are few randomised controlled trials of treatment for anorexia nervosa. However, psychotherapies have a unique role in anorexia – drug treatments have repeatedly been found ineffective, as well as potentially dangerous to starved patients, except in the reduction of relapse (Kaye *et al.*, 1991).

It is hard to engage subjects with anorexia for treatment, let alone research. Early in the disorder symptoms are ego-syntonic; later on anorexia takes over the patient's whole identity – the prospect of relinquishing it is terrifying. Serfaty (1999) recruited 35 subjects to compare CBT with dietary advice in anorexia. Two of the CBT group and all of the dietary group dropped out of treatment!

We cannot assume that subjects who drop out of treatment are worse off. Victims of rigid behavioural refeeding programmes who 'eat their way out of hospital' and then starve again may be at greater physical risk than before and certainly 'immunised' psychologically against further treatment. A recent Australian survey found that overall prognosis for patients with anorexia (and other eating disorders) is independent of whether treatment is received or not (Ben-Tovim *et al.*, 2001). Therapy may be an expensive irrelevance, or perhaps some treatment does help while some is downright harmful.

Coercive approaches, which march roughshod over the anorexic demand for control and self-respect, make patients more likely to identify with and cling on to the anorexia. Gowers *et al.* (2000) found that hospital admission was strongly correlated with poor outcome. Ramsay *et al.* (1999) have shown that long-term prognosis is worse for patients compulsorily detained in an in-patient facility than for those treated voluntarily in the same unit, with more deaths in the former group. However, the use of brief hospital admissions to acute medical wards at times of life-threatening crisis or following overdose may be associated with lower mortality (De Filippo, Signorini & Bracale, 2000).

The weight of the patient is a deceptively clear outcome measure in AN. Certainly a healthy weight is necessary but it should reflect the patient's psychological and hence physical recovery. Unless patients are responsible for their own food intake, weight is merely the transient result of the efforts of staff. Short-term weight restoration is a very poor predictor of long-term outcome.

Follow-up times must be very long indeed to measure real benefits in anorexia. Theander (1985) and colleagues, who have followed cohorts over several decades, find that a substantial proportion of cases take six to 12 years to resolve, and a few take longer still. Lowe *et al.* (2001) have recently shown that full recovery is possible even after 21 years of chronic severe AN. Late relapse also occurs.

Anorexia Nervosa: Components of Treatment

Anorexia nervosa is precipitated as a psychological coping mechanism against, for instance, developmental challenges, transitions, family conflicts and academic pressures. However, the ensuing sequelae of self-starvation may involve a constellation of medical professionals as well as psychotherapists – not just a treatment but a co-ordinated campaign.

Manuals, such as those for BN, cannot address the chronic and complex nature of AN. Integrated care pathways (ICPs) are designed to standardise and guide management of whole episodes of medical illness (Coffey *et al.*, 1992). Detailed guides to formulating optimal sequencing and collaborative multi-disciplinary efforts for people with AN are starting to appear. Lock (1999) has described the development and first three years of implementation of an ICP for adolescents with AN.

Evidence at present favours longer term, more wide-ranging, complex therapies, using psychodynamic understanding and, often, systemic principles. Whatever the therapist's core model, or chosen medley of techniques, three main strands must be juggled throughout therapy of anorexia nervosa:

1. Motivational Issues, and Building a Collaborative Relationship

Early on, especially with younger patients, motivation for treatment tends to lie with parents, school teachers or medical professionals. The guiding principle of motivational enhancement is to acknowledge and explore rather than fight the patient's ambivalence about recovery. The therapist discovers the benefits of the anorexia to the patient and explores other ways to achieve or renounce these. Therapy is more effective when the therapist collaborates *with* the patient *against* the anorexia. Such a relationship may allow necessary hospital admissions or other essential treatments without the need to invoke the Mental Health Act – or at least permit the survival of a working relationship even after 'sectioning'. Motivation is not an all-or-nothing battle to be won before therapy can start but an active strand throughout treatment.

2. Medical Monitoring and Attainment of a Healthy Stable Weight

There are two contrasting approaches to weight gain. In countries where all treatment is given in hospital, refeeding is an early intervention. Subsequent therapy helps patients tolerate, maintain or regain normal weight. This may be the preferred approach for children and young adolescents, where long periods at low weight are detrimental to growth and development. Hospital refeeding requires physiological fine-tuning and may expose the patient to iatrogenic complications such as infections and the sequelae of passing tubes. There may also be a risk of 'learning' anorexic behaviours or becoming unhealthily immersed in pathological cultures on wards. It may be possible to avoid both Scylla and Charybdis if the family is able to accept the task of gradual refeeding.

A second approach temporarily accepts low weight, if stable and subject to medical monitoring, while patients take responsibility for their own refeeding. It is helpful to provide dietetic expertise separately from the psychotherapy. Weight gain is slower but more likely to be maintained. This approach avoids many iatrogenic risks. However, clinicians still need access to medical wards for physical emergencies. Medical safety requires weight stability. There is no magic safe cutoff weight or BMI. Some outpatients maintain BMIs below those specified in old medical textbooks to be incompatible with life. Analyses of survival show that death is unusual where low weight is maintained purely by starvation (Herzog *et al.*, 2000; Lowe *et al.*, 2001). Deaths are more likely at BMIs of 13 or 14 if there is rapid weight fluctuation, frequent purging or co-morbid substance abuse, than at stable BMI even below 12.

Adolescents, especially, find it difficult to appreciate links between starvation and other symptoms and it is counterproductive to try to frighten the patient into getting better. There is no good evidence that psychoeducational strategies are effective either preventatively or as treatment for AN. However, results shared with the patient in a concerned and constructive way provide an extra perspective on the advantages and disadvantages of remaining anorexic. The classic Minnesota Starvation Study of Keys *et al.* (1950) is available in accessible digests (for example, Garner & Garfinkel, 1997: Ch 8; Treasure, 1997: Ch. 11) both for therapists and their patients.

Someone needs to monitor and communicate the patient's weight on a regular basis (at least weekly), both for physical safety and so that links can be made within therapy. Patients who 'work' calmly and cheerfully in therapy often turn out to have lost rather than gained weight.

3. Interpersonal and Life Skills

Patients need a new repertoire of coping strategies if they are to renounce anorexic responses. Many patients become 'stuck' just under a normal weight range until they gain the confidence to face the social and sexual jungle of adult life. Assertiveness training, DBT skills groups, relaxation, mindfulness and IPT are offered but still lack formal evaluation. Family work is the only well-researched intervention to show favourable impact.

Family Therapy

The Maudsley Hospital family therapy studies are an honourable exception to the general lack of research in AN. They represent the work of the same group, so it is hard to tease out differential effects of therapeutic techniques from the personal qualities of the highly trained and experienced individuals concerned. Early studies showed that family therapy gave better results than individual therapy for teenage girls with relatively recent onset anorexia. (Russell *et al.*, 1987) Further studies showed that while conjoint family therapy – if tolerated – gave the best results in terms of family psychological adjustment, weight gain was greater when families were seen separately from the affected patient (Eisler *et al.*, 2000). Both family interventions were more effective than individual work.

The 'separated family therapy' model involved straightforward supportive psychoeducational counselling, and proved particularly useful where there were high levels of expressed emotion in the families. (These families were unable to benefit from traditional family therapy.) More recently, Maudsley professionals have piloted 'multi-family groups' in the treatment of resistant eating disorders (Dare & Eisler, 2000). Work from Toronto (Geist *et al.*, 2000) supports the effectiveness of both family therapy and 'family group psychoeducation' for adolescents with newly diagnosed eating disorders, and highlights the economic benefits of the latter.

Individual Dynamic Therapy and Cognitive Analytic Therapy

The Maudsley group have compared individual focused dynamic therapy with dynamically informed family therapy and with individual cognitive analytic therapy (CAT) in a sample of low-weight outpatients over the course of a year (Dare *et al.*, 2001). 'Controls' were seen weekly by psychiatric trainees supervised by a senior therapist. Best results were achieved by the dynamically informed therapies, both family and individual. However, the same highly experienced therapists who carried out the family studies described above gave both treatments. Cognitive analytic therapy was administered by a group of fairly experienced, trained therapists and gave intermediate results. The study faced the challenge of studying severely ill anorexic patients managed as outpatients and demonstrated the benefits of continuity of therapist and of therapist expertise. Nothing can be concluded about the specific model of therapy provided.

Anorexia Nervosa: Clinical Practice

The majority of teenagers who develop AN make a good recovery in the relatively short term.

Case Illustration

Annette, a 15-year-old schoolgirl, was brought to the clinic by her worried parents. Her weight was falling again after a precipitous weight loss two years earlier, when her grandmother died. She menstruated for only six months before her periods stopped. She failed to grow as tall as expected. She performed brilliantly in examinations, though, and said she felt 'fine'. Teachers expressed concern and she was taken out of sports. They now suggested that she seek help before returning to school to take higher exams. BMI was 15.2. DEXA scan showed bone density considerably lower than expected.

Her father declined to take time out of work but her mother met with the therapist with Annette's permission. Annette worked on a series of motivational exercises, writing about her anorexia as if it were a friend and then as an enemy. Her therapist left the service but she continued to meet with a dietitian who helped design meal plans. She managed to stabilise her weight but became terrified if the scales showed the slightest increase. Her parents discovered that she was vomiting to offset extra calories.

It was agreed that Annette should start cognitive analytical therapy with a new nurse therapist. She was fascinated by the diagrams and carried her therapist's reformulation letter, like a talisman. Her weight remained low, though, and she became depressed as former classmates moved on. Her father was now more concerned and pushed for intensive treatment.

Annette reluctantly agreed to attend a full-time day-patient programme with staff-supported meals and regular family sessions. Before discharge the family was encouraged to reinstitute family meals – these had not been possible for several years, and were even now difficult. Throughout the programme and after discharge Annette continued to work with the same individual CAT therapist. Therapy was stormy and Annette became 'stuck' for a while around the weight at which menstruation returned. Finally she managed to achieve a healthy weight and returned to school.

Sometimes a 'course' of therapy for anorexia nervosa will need to be conceived in terms of years rather than weeks or months, and goals may shift over time. It is more realistic for some patients to aim for stability and damage limitation rather than full physical and psychological cure. Staff need skills of containment, patience and support rather than the more challenging techniques characteristic of structured psychotherapies.

Case Illustration

Anna, a 39-year-old woman, suffered from severe anorexia nervosa since the age of 13. She had menstruated for less than a year when she reduced her weight to 28 kg (BMI 13) with no obvious precipitant. She was a much-loved only child, born to elderly parents after a series of miscarriages.

For most of Anna's teens she was subjected to assertive behavioural regimes in a paediatric ward. She reached 'target weights' only transiently and once discharged would quickly lose weight. On one admission she 'learned' purging behaviours from another patient and it was finally agreed that admission was detrimental. She was discharged back to the care of her GP and things stabilised sufficiently for her to complete a history degree. Then her father died. She was admitted – voluntarily – to a medical ward as an emergency, dangerously emaciated and dehydrated, although no longer purging. For the first time, she asked for therapy.

She agreed to transfer to a specialist unit where she was obliged to take prescribed meals, but was not tube fed. She attended motivational and self-image groups as well as drama therapy and volunteered for trials of treatments for her now severe osteoporosis. She formed a close attachment to her individual CAT therapist and became anxious about relapse when she returned home, hundreds of miles away. She decided to enrol for a higher degree in the university nearest her clinic.

She moved into a hostel for a year with fellow patients, continuing to attend the unit as an out-patient. She initially lost weight but then stabilised. She remained amenorrhoeic and had lost height as a result of vertebral collapse from osteoporosis. She lived an austere but fairly contented life, coping well with the death of her mother. She remained in touch with the specialist unit, transferring her attachment to new therapists when staff moved away.

Behavioural, Cognitive and Interpersonal Therapies for AN

Discredited behavioural regimes for anorexia involved incarceration in hospital with removal of all 'privileges' – such as visiting, TV, independent use of bathroom – and their return as reinforcement for weight gain. There is no evidence for lasting benefit. Behavioural principles are implicit, though, when realistic concerns are used to limit anorexic behaviour. For instance, ballet schools and athletic associations refuse to allow individuals below a certain BMI to participate. School trips and holiday plans, too, may depend on stable weight.

There are convincing cognitive models for the development and maintenance of AN (Garner & Bemis, 1985) but CBT for anorexia requires a therapist experienced in the field of eating disorders as well as in CBT to adapt the model and sidestep pitfalls. The controlled trial of Channon *et al.* (1989) showed no difference in outcome between behaviour therapy and cognitive therapy. A study in New Zealand has given disappointing preliminary results for both CBT and IPT in comparison with treatment as usual (McIntosh & Jordan, 2005). It is certainly time to design and test out sophisticated twenty-first century models of CBT for AN, and to re-examine the components of integrated packages of care so that we can mobilise more powerful treatments.

REFERENCES

Agras, W.S., Rossiter, E.M., Arnow, B. *et al.* (1992). Pharmacologic and cognitive-behavioural treatment for bulimia nervosa: A controlled comparison. *American Journal of Psychiatry,* 149, 82–87.

Agras, W.S., Walsh, B.T., Fairburn, C.G., *et al.* (2000). A multicentre comparison of cognitive-behavioural therapy and interpersonal psychotherapy for bulimia nervosa. *Archives of General Psychiatry, 57,* 459–466.

Beck, A.T., Rush, J.A., Shaw, B.F. & Emery, G. (1979). *Cognitive Therapy of Depression.* New York: Guilford Press.

Ben-Tovim, D.I., Walker, K., Gilchrist, P. *et al.* (2001). Outcome in patients with eating disorders: A 5-year study. *Lancet, 357,* 1254–1257.

Channon, S., De Silva, W.P., Hemsley, D. *et al.* (1989). A controlled trial of cognitive-behavioural and behavioural treatment of anorexia nervosa. *Behaviour Research and Therapy, 27,* 529–534.

Coffey, R.J., Richards, J.S., Remmert, C.S. *et al.* (1992). An introduction to critical paths. *Quality Management in Health Care, 1,* 45–54.

Cooper, P.J. (1995). *Bulimia and Binge Eating: A Guide to Recovery.* London: Robinson.

Cooper, P.J., Coker, S. & Fleming, C. (1996). An evaluation of the efficacy of cognitive behavioural self-help for bulimia nervosa. *Journal of Psychosomatic Research, 28,* 493–499.

Crisp, A.H., Norton, K., Gowers, S., *et al.* (1991). A controlled study of the effect of therapies aimed at adolescent and family psychopathology in anorexia nervosa. *British Journal of Psychiatry, 159,* 325–333.

Crow, S., Mussell, M.P., Peterson, C. *et al.* (1999). Prior treatment received by patients with bulimia nervosa. *International Journal of Eating Disorders, 25,* 39–44.

Dare, C. (1995). The place of psychotherapy in the management of anorexia nervosa. In G.O. Gabbard (ed.), *Psychotherapy in Psychiatric Practice* (pp. 2129–2151). Washington DC: American Psychiatric Press.

Dare, C. & Crowther, C. (1995). Living dangerously: Psychoanalytic psychotherapy of anorexia nervosa. In G. Smukler, C. Dare & J. Treasure (eds). *Eating Disorders: Handbook of Theory, Treatment and Research.* Chichester: John Wiley & Sons.

Dare, C. & Eisler, I. (2000). A multi-family group day treatment programme for adolescent eating disorder. *European Eating Disorders Review, 8,* 4–18.

Dare, C., Eisler, I., Russell, G.F.M. *et al.* (2001). Psychological therapies for adults with anorexia nervosa: Randomised controlled trial of out-patient treatments. *British Journal of Psychiatry, 178,* 216–221.

De Filippo, E., Signorini, A. & Bracale, R. (2000). Hospital admission and mortality rates in anorexia nervosa: Experience from an integrated medical-psychiatric outpatient treatment. *Journal of Eating and Weight Disorders, 5,* 211–216.

Denman, F. (1995). Treating eating disorders using CAT: Two case examples. In A. Ryle (ed.), *Cognitive Analytic Therapy: Developments in Theory and Practice.* Chichester: John Wiley & Sons.

Eisler, I., Dare, C., Hodes, M. *et al.* (2000). Family therapy for anorexia nervosa in adolescents: The results of a controlled comparison of two family interventions. *Journal of Child Psychology and Psychiatry, 41,* 727–736.

Eisler, I., Dare, C., Russell, G.F.M. *et al.* (1997). Family and individual therapy in anorexia nervosa. *Archives of General Psychiatry, 54,* 1025–1030.

Esplen, M.J., Garfinkel, P.E., Olmsted, M. *et al.* (1998). A randomized controlled trial of guided imagery in bulimia nervosa. *Psychological Medicine, 28,* 1347–1357.

Fairburn, C.G. (1985). Cognitive-behavioral treatment for bulimia. In D. M. Garner, & P. E. Garfinkel (eds), *Handbook of Psychotherapy for Anorexia Nervosa and Bulimia* (pp. 160–192). New York: Guilford Press.

Fairburn, C.G., Kirk, J., O'Connor, M. *et al.* (1987). Prognostic factors in bulimia nervosa. *British Journal of Clinical Psychology, 26,* 223–224.

Fairburn, C.G., Marcus, M.D. & Wilson, G.T. (1993). Cognitive behaviour therapy for binge eating and bulimia nervosa: A treatment manual. In C.G. Fairburn & G.T. Wilson (eds), *Binge Eating: Nature, Assessment and Treatment.* New York: Guilford Press.

Fairburn, C.G., Norman, P.A., Welch, S.L., *et al.* (1995). A prospective study of outcome in bulimia nervosa and the long-term effects of three psychological treatments. *Archives of General Psychiatry, 52,* 304–312.

Fichter, M.M., Quadflig, N., & Rief, W. (1994). Course of multi-impulsive bulimia. *Psychological Medicine, 24,* 591–604.

Garner, D.M. & Bemis, K.M. (1985). Cognitive therapy for anorexia nervosa. In D.M. Garner & P.E. Garfinkel (eds), *Handbook of Psychotherapy for Eating Disorders.* New York: Guilford.

Garner, D.M. & Garfinkel, P.E (eds) (1997). *Handbook of Treatment for Eating Disorders.* New York: Guilford.

Geist, R., Heinmaa, M., Stephens, D. *et al.* (2000). Comparison of family therapy and family group psychoeducation in adolescents with anorexia nervosa. *Canadian Journal of Psychiatry, 45,* 173–178.

Gowers, S.G., Weetman, J., Shore, S. *et al.* (2000). Impact of hospitalization on the outcome of anorexia nervosa. *British Journal of Psychiatry, 176,* 138–141.

Hamburg, P. (1996). How long is long-term therapy for anorexia nervosa? In J. Werne (ed.), *Treating Eating Disorders* (pp. 71–99). San Fransisco, CA: Jossey-Bass.

Hay, P.J. & Bacaltchuk, J. (2001). Psychotherapy for bulimia nervosa and bingeing (Cochrane Review). In *The Cochrane Library Issue 1.* Chichester: John Wiley & Sons.

Henderson, M. & Freeman, C.P.L. (1987). A self-rating scale for bulimia. The BITE. *British Journal of Psychiatry, 150,* 18–24.

Herzog, D.B., Greenwood, D.N., Dorer, D.J. *et al.* (2000). Mortality in eating disorders: A descriptive study. *International Journal of Eating Disorders, 28,* 20–26.

Hugo, P., Segwick, P., Black, A. & Lacey, H. (1999). Telephone counselling   the EDA approach. *European Eating Disorders Review, 7,* 300–309.

Johnson, C. (ed). (1991). *Psychodynamic Treatment of Anorexia Nervosa and Bulimia.* New York: Guilford.

Kaye, W.H., Weltzin, T.E., Hsu, L.K. *et al.* (1991) An open trial of fluoxetine in patients with anorexia nervosa. *Journal of Clinical Psychiatry,* 52 (11): 464–471.

Keel, P.K. & Mitchell, J.E. (1997). Outcome in bulimia nervosa. *American Journal of Psychiatry, 154,* 313–321.

Keller, M.B., Herzog, D.B., Lavori, P.W. *et al.* (1992). The naturalistic history of bulimia nervosa: Extraordinarily high rates of chronicity, relapse, recurrence and psychosocial morbidity. *International Journal of Eating Disorders, 12,* 1–10.

Keys, A., Brozek, J., Henschel, A. *et al.* (1950). *The Biology of Human Starvation,* 2 vols. Minneapolis: University of Minnesota Press.

Klerman, G.L. , Weissman, M.M., Rounsaville, B.J. & Chevron, E.S. (1984). *Interpersonal Psychotherapy of Depression.* Northvale, NJ: Jason Aronson.

Linehan, M.M. (1993). *Cognitive Behavioral Therapy of Borderline Personality Disorder.* New York: Guilford Press.

Lock, J. (1999). How clinical pathways can be useful: An example of a clinical pathway for the treatment of anorexia nervosa in adults. *Clinical Child Psychology and Psychiatry, 4,* 331–340.

Lowe, B., Zipfel, S., Buchholz, C. *et al.* (2001). Long-term outcome of anorexia nervosa in a prospective 21-year follow-up study. *Psychological Medicine, 31,* 881–890.

McIntosh, V.V.W. & Jordan, J. (2005). Three psychotherapies for anorexia nervosa. *American Journal of Psychiatry, 162,* 741–747.

Mitchell, J.E., Pyle, R.L., Pomery, C. *et al.* (1993). Cognitive-behavioural group psychotherapy of bulimia nervosa: Importance of logistical variables. *International Journal of Eating Disorders, 14*, 277–287.

Morgan, H.G. & Hayward, A.E. (1988). Clinical assessment of anorexia nervosa. The Morgan-Russell outcome assessment schedule. *British Journal of Psychiatry, 152*, 367–372.

Morton, R. (1689). *Phthisiologia, seu exercitations de phthisi.* London: S. Smith.

Nevonen, L., Broberg, A.G., Lindstrom, M. & Levin, B. (1999). A sequenced group psychotherapy model for bulimia nervosa patients: a pilot study. *European Eating Disorders Review, 7*, 17–27.

Palmer, L.R., Birchall, H., McGrain, L. & Sullivan, V. (2002). Self-help for bulimic disorders: A randomised controlled trial comparing minimal guidance with face-to-face or telephone guidance. *British Journal of Psychiatry, 181*, 230–238.

Ramsay, R.R, Ward, A., Treasure, J. *et al.* (1999) Compulsory treatment in anorexia: short-term benefits and long-term mortality. *British Journal of Psychiatry, 175*, 147–153

Robinson, P.H., & Serfaty, M.A. (2001). The use of e-mail in the identification of bulimia nervosa and its treatment. *European Eating Disorders Review, 9*, 182–193.

Russell, G.F.M. (1979). Bulimia nervosa: An ominous variant of anorexia nervosa. *Psychological Medicine, 9*, 429.

Russell, G.F.M., Szmukler, G., Dare, C. *et al.* (1987). An evaluation of family therapy in anorexia nervosa and bulimia nervosa. *Archives of General Psychiatry, 44*, 1047–1056.

Safer, D.L., Telch, C.F. & Agras, W.S. (2001). Dialectical behaviour therapy for bulimia nervosa. *American Journal of Psychiatry, 158*, 632–634.

Schmidt, U. & Marks, I. M. (1989). Exposure plus prevention of bingeing versus exposure plus prevention of vomiting in bulimia nervosa: A crossover study. *Journal of Nervous and Mental Disease, 177*, 259–266.

Serfaty, M.A. (1999). Cognitive therapy versus dietary counselling in the outpatient treatment of anorexia nervosa: Effects of the treatment phase. *European Eating Disorders Review, 7*, 334–350.

Sharp, C.W. & Freeman, C.P.L. (1993). The medical complications of anorexia nervosa. *British Journal of Psychiatry, 162*, 452–462.

Theander, S. (1985). Outcome and prognosis in anorexia nervosa and bulimia. Some results of previous investigations compared with those of a Swedish long-term study. *Journal of Psychiatric Research, 19*, 493–508.

Treasure, J. (1997). *Anorexia Nervosa: A Survival Guide for Families, Friends and Sufferers.* Hove: Psychology Press.

Treasure, J., Todd, G., Brolly, M. *et al.* (1995). A pilot study of a randomized trial of cognitive analytic therapy versus educational behavioural therapy for adults with anorexia nervosa. *Behaviour Research and Therapy, 33*, 363–367.

Turnbull, S., Ward, A., Treasure, J. *et al.* (1996) The demand for eating disorder care. An epidemiological study using the general practice research database *British Journal of Psychiatry, 169*, 705–712.

Walsh, B.T., Hadigan, C.M., Devlin, M.J. *et al.* (1991). Longterm outcome of antidepressant treatment for bulimia nervosa. *American Journal of Psychiatry, 148*, 1206–1212.

Weissman, M.M, Markowitz, J.C., & Klerman, G.L. (2000). *A Comprehensive Guide to Interpersonal Psychotherapy.* New York: Basic Books.

Wilfley, D.E., Agras, W.S., Telch, C.F. *et al.* (1993). Group cognitive-behavioral therapy and group interpersonal therapy for the non-purging bulimic: A controlled comparison. *Journal of Consulting and Clinical Psychology, 61*, 296–305.

World Health Organization (1992). *The ICD10 Classification of Mental and Behavioural Disorders: Clinical Descriptions and Diagnostic Guidelines.* Geneva: World Health Organization.

CHAPTER 11

Personality Disorders

Katherine Cheshire
Lynebank Hospital, Fife, UK

Health professionals are likely to agree that personality disorder is common and difficult to treat but beyond this generalisation there is limited consensus. Despite the controversies and ambiguities that characterise work in this field, there has been increasing interest in developing psychological therapies for treatment of personality disorder. This chapter presents the evidence base for these therapies, which is modest but encouraging and justifies the growing optimism among those working in this area.

DEFINITIONS

Most fundamentally, there is continuing controversy about how to define personality disorder. The International Classification of Mental and Behavioural Disorders (ICD-10) (World Health Organisation, 1992) defines personality disorder as: 'a severe disturbance in the characterological condition and behavioural tendencies of the individual, usually involving several areas of the personality, and nearly always associated with considerable personal and social disruption.'

ICD-10 lists eight specific personality disorders: paranoid, schizoid, dissocial, emotionally unstable (with two sub-types – impulsive and borderline), histrionic, anankastic, anxious (avoidant) and dependent.

The definition of personality disorder offered by the Diagnostic and Statistical Manual of Mental Disorders (DSM-IV) (American Psychiatric Association, 1994) is similar: 'an enduring pattern of inner experience and behaviour that deviates markedly from the expectations of the individual's culture, is pervasive and inflexible, has an onset in adolescence or early adulthood, is stable over time, and leads to distress or impairment.'

DSM-IV identifies ten specific personality disorders, but organises them into three clusters based on descriptive similarities:

Cluster A (odd; eccentric):

Paranoid Personality Disorder is a pattern of distrust and suspiciousness such that others' motives are interpreted as malevolent.

Schizoid Personality Disorder is a pattern of detachment from social relationships and a restricted range of emotional expression.

Schizotypal Personality Disorder is a pattern of acute discomfort in close relationships, cognitive or perceptual distortions, and eccentricities of behaviour.

Cluster B (dramatic; emotional; erratic):

Antisocial Personality Disorder is a pattern of disregard for, and violation of, the rights of others.

Borderline Personality Disorder is a pattern of instability in interpersonal relationships, self-image, and affects, and marked impulsivity.

Histrionic Personality Disorder is a pattern of excessive emotionality and attention seeking.

Narcissistic Personality Disorder is a pattern of grandiosity, need for admiration, and lack of empathy.

Cluster C (anxious; fearful):

Avoidant Personality Disorder is a pattern of social inhibition, feelings of inadequacy, and hypersensitivity to negative evaluation.

Dependent Personality Disorder is a pattern of submissive and clinging behaviour related to an excessive need to be taken care of.

Obsessive-Compulsive Personality Disorder is a pattern of preoccupation with orderliness, perfectionism and control.

Both classificatory systems agree that personality disorder can be distinguished by its persistence (usually beginning in late adolescence and continuing throughout most of adult life), the impairment it produces in social and occupational functioning, and the degree of distress it causes. However, whereas the DSM system locates personality disorder within a separate diagnostic dimension, or axis (Axis II), from that containing clinical syndromes such as major depression, anxiety disorders and schizophrenia (Axis I), no such distinction is made in the ICD classification.

Although the ICD and DSM classificatory systems are categorical, many researchers and clinicians argue that personality disorder (and other manifestations of psychological distress) may be understood more accurately using a dimensional approach (for example, Cloninger, 1987; Widiger, 1992, 1993). This approach assumes that normal and abnormal personality types form a continuum and recognises the artificiality of divisions between categories – an observation that rings true with clinicians who routinely assess individuals meeting criteria for more than one ICD/DSM personality disorder. While a dimensional approach may have heuristic value, it does not solve the problems of case identification that bedevil the literature on personality disorder (see below).

Current classifications of personality disorder have not only been criticised on theoretical grounds but also appear to have limited value as a basis for treatment. A large study by Tyrer *et al.* (1990) assessed 210 patients with diagnoses of anxiety disorder, panic disorder and dysthymia using the Personality Assessment Schedule (PAS) (Tyrer & Alexander 1979) and found that 36 % of the cohort were comorbid for personality disorder and had more severe psychopathology than the rest of the sample. The PAS ratings were converted into 14 personality types corresponding to draft ICD-10 and DSM-III categories. The category of personality disorder had no predictive value regarding outcome of pharmacological/psychological treatments, suggesting that the classificatory systems were over-determined. Rutter (1987) proposed the pragmatic solution of abandoning trait-based categories and simply identifying those individuals who are unable to form and maintain satisfactory relationships. More recently, Tyrer and colleagues have proposed the clinically useful approach of distinguishing treatment-seeking and treatment-resistant personality disorders (Tyrer *et al.*, 2003).

PREVALENCE

Epidemiological surveys using a variety of diagnostic criteria estimate a prevalence of 10 % to 15 % of at least one personality disorder within the general population (Mattia & Zimmerman, 2001). The diagnosis is more commonly made in younger people (25 to 44 years). The sex ratio varies according to the specific disorder: for example, women are more likely to be diagnosed with borderline personality disorder (BPD) whereas most individuals diagnosed with antisocial personality disorder are men. Unsurprisingly, both prisons and psychiatric hospitals have a particularly high prevalence of personality disorder. Within the former this has been estimated to be as high as 78 % Singleton, Meltzer & Gatward (1998), while figures for the latter range from one-third to two-thirds. The role of personality disorder in psychological morbidity is also significant in general practice. In a one-year prevalence study of 'conspicuous psychiatric morbidity' in patients attending two general practices in Nottinghamshire, Casey & Tyrer (1990) found that 28 % of identified cases also had personality disorders.

IMPACT ON HEALTH SERVICES

In the health service, individuals with difficulties encompassed by the DSM-IV Cluster B categories make the heaviest demands on services – often presenting in crisis. A few recent studies have attempted to quantify these demands (Seivewright *et al.*, 1991; Saarento *et al.*, 1997). Smith *et al.* (1995) calculated that the cost to the NHS of treating individuals with personality disorders was £61.3 million in 1986. Much of the discussion about the cost of treating personality disorder has focussed, quite reasonably, on secondary and tertiary services. However Rendu and colleagues recently investigated the economic impact of personality disorders in UK primary care attenders in a prospective study that recruited from four general practices in London (Rendu *et al.*, 2002). Personality disorders were not independently associated with increased health or non-health costs (lost productivity costs due to illness or unemployment) in this sample but non-health service costs were significantly associated with an interaction between personality disorder and psychological morbidity assessed by the General Health Questionnaire (Goldberg, 1972). This finding highlights the importance of considering the economic impact of personality disorder in the broadest terms (encompassing primary, secondary and tertiary care in the health service and both health service and non-health service costs) and underlines the contribution of comorbid conditions to the impairment of those with personality disorders (see below).

AETIOLOGY

A growing body of research supports a multifactorial model of personality disorder, incorporating both biological and environmental factors. A recent review found that about half the variance in personality trait scores is attributable to the genetic differences between individuals (Bouchard, 1997), but investigators have not yet managed to identify the genes responsible for specific personality traits or disorders. Lang & Vernon (2001) observe that the controversies about definitions and classifications of personality disorder have hampered progress in the field because the clearly defined phenotypes required by genetic methodologies are not yet available to provide a suitable starting point. Meanwhile, research continues into neurophysiological, cognitive and structural correlates of personality disorder. Among the neurotransmitters, serotonin has been most extensively investigated and has been consistently linked with aggression and impulsivity. A smaller number of studies into the role of the catecholamines in personality disorder have so far yielded conflicting results but suggest that dopamine function may be positively correlated with positive symptoms in schizotypal patients and negatively correlated with deficit symptoms in those individuals. Neuroimaging and neuropsychological studies have mainly focussed on individuals with schizotypal personality disorder and show that these subjects, particularly those with deficit symptoms, are likely to demonstrate impairment on attentional tasks and tests of executive function, which seems to be associated with increased ventricular size and reduced dopamine function (Coccaro, 2001).

Psychosocial perspectives on personality disorder identify the main risk factors for development of these disorders as dysfunctional families (family breakdown, parental psychopathology and inadequate/abusive parenting); trauma (particularly childhood abuse or neglect) and social stressors such as the reduced availability of extrafamilial social supports in modern society (Millon, 1993; Paris 1992, 1996). Attachment theory has received renewed attention in understanding the genesis of the interpersonal difficulties that identify personality disorders (Bartholomew, Kwong & Hart, 2001). Reviewing the literature, Paris (2001) concludes:

- the psychosocial risk factors for many types of psychological disorder are similar;
- many (perhaps most) children exposed to any of these risk factors will not develop a psychological disorder; and
- multiple adversities have a cumulative effect, eventually overwhelming children's natural resilience.

The current consensus is that childhood adversities interact with biological vulnerabilities expressed as personality traits to produce personality disorders; these traits may also increase the individual's exposure to adverse events (Rutter & Rutter, 1993).

NATURAL HISTORY AND LONG-TERM OUTCOME IN PERSONALITY DISORDER

Data on the natural history of personality disorders are skewed towards the most severe cases and most of these have been identified in psychiatric hospitals and forensic settings. Furthermore, most of the follow-up studies in this area are not really accounts of the natural history of these disorders, but are reports of long-term outcome after variable degrees of widely divergent interventions. Borderline and antisocial personality disorders have attracted particular attention because the impulsive and destructive behaviour of these individuals causes such concern among both carers and society in general. As noted above, borderline patients often make heavy demands on the health service. In contrast, individuals with antisocial personality disorder are unlikely to seek treatment voluntarily and are more likely to be seen by psychiatrists in prison than in hospital. Meanwhile, personality disordered individuals who are functioning reasonably well may never seek treatment; if they do, it may be for an Axis I disorder and the personality disorder may never be identified.

Stone (2001) reviews the available data on the natural history and long-term outcome of personality disorders, noting that individuals within the 'antisocial realm' historically constituted a diverse group incorporating those meeting criteria for DSM antisocial personality disorder; psychopaths, as defined by Hare *et al.* (1990); and individuals with sadistic personality disorder (Appendix, DSM-III). The Hare Psychopathy Checklist-Revised (PCL-R) (Hare *et al.*, 1990) allows for the differentiation of psychopaths from individuals who are antisocial without scoring high on psychopathy. Recent studies suggest that the prognosis is considerably better for those in the latter group than it is for the former, who score high on the extreme narcissistic traits subsumed in Hare's Factor-I. While Dinwiddie & Daw (1998) found that antisocial personality disorder was largely stable over an eight-year follow-up, other studies have shown a tendency for criminality to decrease over time (Arboleda-Florez & Holley, 1991; Robins, Tipp & Przybeck, 1991; Stone, 1990). Sadistic personality is common among serial killers and there is no evidence that it burns out over time (Stone, 2001).

Large studies during the 1980s followed up individuals diagnosed with BPD over an average of 15 years – the 'Chestnut Lodge' study (McGlashan, 1985, 1986a, 1986b; Paris, Brown & Nowlis, 1987; Plakun, Burckhardt & Muller, 1985) and the 'PI-500' study (Stone, 1990; Stone, Hurt & Stone, 1987). All these subjects had previously been hospitalised. At trace time two-thirds were functioning within the GAS (Global Assessment Scale) (Endicott *et al.*, 1976) range 61-70, or above: they were therefore functioning within the normal range. Among the third who fared less well, some had died from suicide (3 % in McGlashan's study and 9 % in the studies of Paris and Stone). Age was a significant risk factor for suicide: the late 20s were a high-risk period for this group. Both the Chestnut Lodge and PI-500 studies showed that these cohorts typically experienced their greatest difficulties during their twenties and were likely to improve thereafter if they survived, although individuals who remained chronically angry often encountered renewed difficulties when they reached middle age because they had alienated carers and companions. Factors associated with poor outcome for BPD are a history of sexual abuse (particularly incest occurring pre-puberty and involving penile penetration – Paris, 1994; Van der Kolk, 1996); parental brutality; antisocial traits and chaotic impulsivity. Stone (2001) cautions that available data on prognosis for BPD may well be overly optimistic because individuals with BPD who have also experienced significant socioeconomic disadvantages are underrepresented in existing studies. However, Fonagy & Bateman (2006) suggest that the natural course of BPD may be more benign than previously thought. Citing recent prospective studies (Shea *et al.*, 2004; Zanarini *et al.*, 2003) they note remission in 75 % of patients diagnosed with BPD over a 6-year period.

There are fewer data on natural history and long-term outcome in other personality disorders. Existing findings suggest that the prognosis for schizotypal personality disorder may be limited (Aarkrog, 1981, 1993; McGlashan, 1986a; Stone, 1993). McGlashan found that these patients fared only slightly better than those with schizophrenia and a Scandinavian study providing a 20-year follow-up of 50 schizotypal individuals showed poor social and occupational functioning (Aarkrog, 1993). Schizoid personality disorder, infrequently seen in psychiatric settings in the absence of comorbidity, also appears stable over time (Wolff &

Chick, 1981). Long-term outcome for narcissistic personality disorder was similar to that of BPD in both the Chestnut Lodge and PI-500 studies.

DIFFICULTIES IN ASSESSING OUTCOME RESEARCH

The following section summarises the main obstacles to assessing the outcome data in this field identified by Bateman & Fonagy (2000).

Assessment and Identification of Cases

Since the late 1980s a number of semi-structured interviews and self-report measures have been developed (see, for example, Clark 1993; Hyler, 1994; Hyler *et al.*, 1988; Loranger *et al.*, 1987; Millon *et al.*, 1994; Spitzer *et al.* 1990; Tyrer *et al.*, 1988) but there is little agreement between measures and not all of them are comprehensive. Some of the usual problems – such as respondents supplying socially desirable answers – arise with these standardised measures and reliability also depends on respondents having adequate insight into their longstanding difficulties. Another problem, linked to the question of comorbidity discussed below, is that the behaviours indicative of personality disorder may fluctuate in the presence/absence of Axis I disorders, obscuring the contribution of the personality traits (Klein, 1993). Accurate diagnosis is therefore assisted by assessing or re-assessing individuals once the Axis I disorder has been adequately treated. Zimmerman (1994) has reviewed the issues that arise in identifying personality disorder and suggests that reliability of diagnosis can be increased by using informants in addition to self-report/interview.

Compounding the difficulty of assessment is the dilemma of classification. Within the literature, subjects are most frequently designated by the ICD or DSM categories yet there is poor cross-classificatory reliability (Sara, Raven & Mann, 1996) and a lack of empirical evidence to support the clustering of categories used in DSM-IV (Mulder & Joyce, 1997). Some studies have instead grouped subjects according to a theoretical approach to personality disorder – for example, Beck, Freeman & Davis (2004) (cognitive) and Kernberg (1984) (psychoanalytic), but this prevents meaningful comparison of results across models. Dimensional approaches have so far been equally problematic in outcome research because investigators disagree about which traits to measure and whether or not these are on a continuum with normal personality characteristics.

Comorbidity

In clinical practice it is rare to meet an individual who only meets ICD-10/DSM-IV criteria for a single personality disorder. As noted above, many individuals meet criteria for more than one personality disorder and others meet criteria for both Axis I and Axis II disorders (Oldham *et al.*, 1995). This makes it difficult to decipher improvements observed clinically or reported in the literature. For example, a person with BPD and major depression may become more impulsive and destructive as the depression lifts (appearing to become more 'borderline') or this behaviour may diminish with the anergia of depression, creating the impression of improved impulse control. Despite the confounding effect of comorbidity when measuring outcome, published studies have generally failed to report this clearly.

Outcome Measures

Measurement of outcome is inherently problematic without reliable case identification. Most recent studies of personality disorder do not attempt to measure change in the syndrome itself but instead measure change in symptoms, behaviour and social adjustment. Studies of personality disordered offenders usually rely on reconviction rates as a measure of outcome although researchers in this field identify obvious problems with this approach (Dolan & Coid, 1993). A few investigators have attempted to measure change in the syndromes more directly by assessing whether or not individuals meet fewer diagnostic criteria over time (Dolan et al., 1997; Monsen, Odland & Eilertsen, 1995; Stevenson & Meares, 1992) but this approach does not prevent the confounding of personality change and symptomatic improvement in coexisting Axis I disorders. Bateman & Tyrer (2002) go so far as to argue that 'any measured change in personality should be regarded in the first instance as an artefact related to improvement or deterioration in mental state.' These authors observe that there is no standardised method for recording global outcome measures in long-term follow-up studies and note that some individuals may appear to improve over time purely as a consequence of changing their circumstances so that their personality disorder no longer generates interpersonal conflict. Finally, it is worth considering that categorical diagnoses of personality disorder permit individuals to change status from cases to non-cases without any greater personality change than those who remain cases throughout a study because their personality disturbance is more significant at baseline assessment (Tyrer et al., 1997).

Other Research Issues

In addition to the usual challenges of conducting randomised controlled trials to assess treatment efficacy (Roth & Fonagy, 2005), the main difficulty facing researchers who are interested in personality disorder is the length of time required to conduct an adequate treatment trial, with the associated problems of cost, increased risk of drop-outs and confounding effects of other treatment received during the study period. Dialectical-behaviour therapy, for example, was developed for treatment of BPD and 'Stage 1' was designed to be delivered intensively over a one-year period. Bateman & Fonagy (1999) evaluated a psychoanalytically informed day hospital programme for treatment of BPD that ran for 18 months. These study periods are considerably longer than the norm of three to four months in most drug trials or RCTs comparing psychological therapies for Axis I disorders. Furthermore, long-term follow-up beyond the active treatment phase is particularly important for adequate evaluation of efficacy in personality disorder (Høglend, 1993).

   With these caveats in mind we will proceed to examine the evidence base for psychological therapies in the treatment of personality disorder. Recent systematic reviews (Bateman & Fonagy, 2000; Bateman & Tyrer, 2002; Binks et al., 2006; Perry, Banon & Ianni, 1999; Roth & Fonagy, 2005; Roy & Tyrer, 2001; Shea, 1993) have varied in their inclusiveness. For reasons of space the following section is limited to consideration of large-cohort and controlled studies in which patients were selected on the basis of Axis II disorders, treatments were clearly described and adequate measures were used. The approaches considered are dynamic psychotherapy, cognitive therapy, interpersonal group psychotherapy, behaviour therapy and dialectical behaviour therapy delivered through outpatient, day hospital or inpatient programmes. Therapeutic communities will be briefly considered at the end, together with treatment programmes for personality disordered offenders.

DYNAMIC PSYCHOTHERAPY

To date, this is the most extensively investigated psychotherapeutic approach to personality disorder.

Day Hospital Programmes

Karterud *et al.* (1992) completed a prospective study of 97 patients in a psychodynamically orientated day hospital in Oslo; 76 % had an Axis II disorder. The treatment programme in the unit consisted of two daily community meetings, plus group and individual psychotherapy sessions. After a mean stay of six months treatment results were very good for patients with Axis I disorders only, good for Cluster C personality disorders, modest for patients with BPD and very modest for those with schizotypal personality disorder. The dropout rate for patients with BPD and SPD was 38 %. There were no suicides during the treatment period and only two suicide attempts; medication levels were moderate. The authors concluded that the programme adequately contained these patients; that a unit of this type needs backup from an acute ward; that the length of treatment was too short; and that post-discharge psychotherapy should be offered to those who complete the programme. Patients with BPD and SPD are now offered 12 to 18 months of treatment.

Piper *et al.* (1993) evaluated a dynamically orientated, intensive, group-focussed, 18-week day-treatment programme for individuals with affective and personality disorders. Sixty per cent of the total sample (N = 120) had personality disorders, with borderline and dependent types being most common. Patients were randomised to treatment or control (delayed treatment) conditions and assessed at baseline, end of treatment and eight months later. Outcome for the active treatment group was significantly better than for controls regarding social and family dysfunction, interpersonal behaviour, mood, life satisfaction, self-esteem and severity of disturbance relating to individual treatment goals. Benefits were maintained at follow-up in the 50 patients available for assessment.

More recently, a British RCT compared TAU with treatment in a psychoanalytically informed day-hospital programme that included both individual and group therapy (Bateman & Fonagy, 1999). Thirty-eight individuals with BPD were included in the 18-month trial. The day hospital programme included individual and group psychotherapy, weekly expressive therapy using psychodrama techniques and weekly community meetings. All the therapy was delivered by psychiatric nurses with no formal psychotherapy qualifications. Patients in the day hospital programme showed a statistically significant improvement on all measures compared with the control group. The day hospital attenders engaged in less parasuicide/self-harm and required fewer admissions during the study period. They also reported more improvement in mood, interpersonal function and social adjustment relative to the TAU group, beginning at six months into treatment and continuing over the next 12 months. The dropout rate was low (12 %) and improvements were maintained or increased at three-year follow-up, although further treatment was received by many of these individuals during the follow-up period (Bateman & Fonagy, 2001).

Outpatient Treatment

Winston *et al.* (1991) compared short-term dynamic psychotherapy (STDP: N = 15) with brief adaptational psychotherapy (BAP: N = 17) over 40 weeks, against a waiting-list control condition. The authors describe STDP, based on the work of Davanloo, as more active and confrontational than BAP. The study included patients who met DSM-III criteria for compulsive, avoidant, dependent, or histrionic personality disorder, or more than one of these. The authors found no difference between therapies but patients in both groups were significantly improved compared with the waiting list condition on their primary complaint (Battle *et al.*, 1966), the SCL-90 (Derogatis & Cleary, 1977) and the Social Adjustment Scale (Weissman & Bothwell, 1976). The original study by this group excluded patients with borderline and narcissistic features but a later study by the same group (Winston *et al.*, 1994) incorporated some patients with Cluster B disorders and obtained similar results.

Stevenson & Meares (1992, 1999) reported on 48 outpatients with BPD treated with psychoanalytic therapy delivered by closely supervised trainee therapists twice weekly for one year. Thirty patients completed the course and showed significant reductions in self-harm, violent behaviour and impulsivity and time spent as inpatients in addition to other improvements. At the end of treatment, one-third of the sample no longer met criteria for BPD. Improvement was maintained over one year post-treatment and persisted over a five-year follow-up.

Monsen *et al.* (1995) conducted a prospective study of 25 outpatients in a unit specialising in personality and psychosis: 23 patients met DSM-III criteria for personality disorder at the outset. Treatment consisted of intensive psychodynamic psychotherapy, based on self-psychology and object relations, delivered over an average of 25.4 months. At the end of therapy 72 % of patients no longer met criteria for personality disorder and showed significant change in affect consciousness, characterological defences and symptoms as measured by the clinical scales of the Minnesota Multiphasic Personality Inventory and the Welsh Anxiety and Repression scales. At follow-up (mean period of 5.2 years) these changes remained generally stable.

Combined Inpatient and Outpatient Treatment

Chiesa & Fonagy (2000) report on a non-randomised prospective study conducted at the Cassel Hospital in collaboration with the psychoanalysis unit, University College London. The study compared a 'one-stage programme' of inpatient treatment (11 to 16 months) with no arranged follow-up and a 'two-stage programme' that offered a briefer inpatient stay (six months) plus 12 to 18 months' outpatient group psychotherapy with six months of concurrent community outreach nursing. The inpatient treatment included twice-weekly individual psychoanalytic psychotherapy. Ninety patients with DSM-III-R diagnoses of personality disorder were recruited over a five-year period: 70 % met criteria for BPD, 17 % for avoidant, 12 % for paranoid and 11 % for self-defeating personality disorder. Twelve months after admission patients in both samples had improved significantly on the Symptom Check List (SCL-90) (Derogatis, 1983), the Global Assessment Scale (GAS) (Endicott *et al.*, 1976) and the Social Adjustment Scale (SAS) (Weissman & Bothwell, 1976). However, the two-stage sample fared significantly better than those in the one-stage programme according to the GAS and the SAS.

COGNITIVE THERAPY

Giesen-Bloo *et al.* (2006) report on a multicentre randomised treatment study comparing the effectiveness of schema-focussed cognitive therapy (SFT) and psychodynamically based transference-focussed psychotherapy (TFP) in 88 patients with BPD. The intervention con-sisted of three years of SFT or TFP, with twice-weekly 50-minute sessions. Schema-focussed therapy employs a range of cognitive, behavioural and experiential techniques focussing on the therapeutic relationship, as well as past and present experiences. Recovery is predicted to occur when dysfunctional schema no longer control the individual's behaviour. In TFP, recovery is achieved through interpretation of the transference relationship, with a focus on present circumstances.

The primary outcome measure in this study was the BPD Severity Index-IV (Arntz *et al.*, 2003); a secondary outcome measure was quality of life assessed by the EuroQol thermometer (The EuroQol Group, 1990) and the World Health Organization quality of life assessment (The WHOQOL Group, 1998). A range of additional clinical measures was also used. Intention-to-treat analysis showed statistically and clinically significant improvements for both interventions on all measures at one- two-, and three-year intervals. However, SFT was more effective than TFP on all measures and was associate with a lower drop-out rate. The authors urge caution in comparing their results with trials of dialectical behaviour therapy (DBT) and 'psychoanalytically oriented mentalization-based treatments' (MBT – for example, Bateman & Fonagy 1999; 2001). They identify differences in the primary objectives of these approaches – arguing that SFT and TFP aim for overall personality change while DBT and MBT prioritise reduction in self-destructive behaviour.

INTERPERSONAL GROUP PSYCHOTHERAPY

Monroe-Blum & Marziali (1995) compared time-limited (35 weeks) group therapy fo-cussing on interpersonal transactions with open-ended individual psychodynamic therapy for treatment of BPD. Participants were recruited from inpatient and outpatient psychiatric units linked with the University of Toronto; 79 of the 110 patients who were randomly allocated to the two conditions accepted treatment. The investigators found that both approaches produced significant improvement and were equally effective at 12 and 24 months on all major outcome variables measuring social dysfunction, global symptoms and depression. However, the group therapists (typically two therapists worked with groups of seven patients) reported less anxiety and increased empathic connections with their patients compared with the individual therapists. This study therefore suggests that the model of interpersonal group therapy investigated here may be cost-effective in terms of staff burnout as well as service delivery.

MacKenzie (2001) summarises other models of group psychotherapy for BPD including experiential group psychotherapy based on principles described by Yalom (1995); this approach yielded modest results in a small cohort with various personality disorders (Budman *et al.*, 1996).

BEHAVIOUR THERAPY

In their review of the evidence base for treatment of personality disorder, Roth & Fonagy (2005) include several controlled studies that employed behavioural approaches. Most of these studies focussed on the difficulties with social interaction experienced by individuals with avoidant personality disorder. Argyle *et al.* (1974) found that these patients benefited from both social skills training and psychodynamic therapy; Stravynski *et al.* (1994) compared social skills training conducted in the clinic with training in the clinic plus *in vivo* and found both equally effective, although dropout rates were much higher when *in vivo* work was included. Alden (1989) Cappe & Alden (1986) and Marzillier *et al.* (1976) evaluated social skills training, exposure and systematic desensitisation and found that patients with APD made modest gains with all three relative to a waiting-list control. Alden & Capreol (1993) concluded from a trial of 76 patients with APD that individuals presenting as angry and distrustful benefited more from exposure therapy while those whose primary problem was lack of assertiveness responded better to social skills training. Results suggest that patients with APD are likely to demonstrate only modest improvements in social functioning following these interventions.

Liberman & Eckman (1981) compared brief insight-oriented therapy with a behavioural intervention that was predominantly social skills training in a group of inpatients with a history of parasuicide. At nine months post-treatment, patients who had received social skills training reported less suicidal ideation than the other cohort though the two groups did not differ significantly in number of suicide attempts.

Dialectical Behaviour Therapy

The first published study to suggest the usefulness of this approach (Linehan *et al.*, 1991) compared weekly outpatient dialectical behavior therapy (DBT) treatment (individual plus group sessions) with treatment as usual (TAU) for female BPD patients with histories of parasuicide (N = 46). The DBT group showed significantly more improvement in para-suicidal behaviour and spent less time as inpatients than controls during the year of active treatment. The DBT group also had a lower dropout rate (17 % versus 58 %). The groups did not differ on other measures such as depression and hopelessness. A naturalistic follow-up assessed the two groups at one year post-treatment and found no significant difference between them except in terms of hospitalisation, with the DBT group requiring fewer admissions (Linehan, Heard & Armstrong, 1993).

Most recently, Linehan's group has extended its earlier findings with a two-year randomised controlled trial and follow-up of DBT versus community treatment by experts (CTBE) for 101 women with BPD and recent suicidal/self-harming behaviour (Linehan *et al.* 2006). This dismantling study demonstrated that, compared with the CTBE cohort, patients receiving DBT were half as likely to make a suicide attempt; required less hospitalisation for suicidal ideation; had lower medical risk following parasuicidal/self-harming behaviour and had a lower drop-out rate (19.2 % DBT versus 42.9 % CTBE).

In a study from the Netherlands (Verheul *et al.*, 2003) describes a one-year randomised controlled trial of DBT versus TAU (treatment in the community) for 58 women with BPD who were referred from either addiction/psychiatric services. The DBT group again demonstrated a lower dropout rate (37 % versus 77 %) and a significantly greater reduction in both self-mutilating and self-damaging impulsive behaviour, particularly among participants with a history of frequent self-harm. At six month follow-up the benefits of DBT over TAU were sustained in terms of parasuicidal and impulsive behaviours, as well as alcohol use. There was no difference between the treatment conditions for drug abuse (Van den Bosch *et al.*, 2005).

Other studies have adapted the Linehan model of DBT delivery in different ways. Evans *et al.* (1999) conducted an RCT (N = 34) to assess the efficacy of manualised DBT and cognitive therapy (MACT) for treatment of outpatients who met criteria for Cluster B personality disorders and had made a parasuicide attempt in the past 12 months. Individuals were assigned to MACT or TAU and assessed at six months. The rate of parasuicide was significantly lower in the MACT group, and self-ratings of depression also showed significantly more improvement in this cohort.

Inpatient Treatment

Inpatient versions of DBT have also been investigated but have not yet been adequately evaluated. Barley *et al.* (1993) compared inpatient DBT with standard inpatient psychiatric care for treatment of BPD and found a significant drop in parasuicide in the DBT group compared with their rate of self-harm before the intervention and compared with the TAU group. However, patients were not randomised in this study and the comparability of the groups is unclear. A group of researchers from the Netherlands (Bohus *et al.*, 2000) assessed the benefit of inpatient DBT over a three-month period prior to long-term outpatient therapy as a means of accelerating and enhancing the course of therapy. The results of a small pilot study were encouraging but this model requires further investigation.

THERAPEUTIC COMMUNITY TREATMENT

Bateman & Tyrer (2002) define a therapeutic community as 'an intensive form of treatment in which the environmental setting becomes the core therapy in which behaviour can be challenged and modified, essentially through peer pressure'. Dolan, Warren & Norton (1997) compared 70 patients admitted to the Henderson Hospital, a national specialist inpatient unit for severe personality disorder, with 67 non-admitted patients at assessment and then 12 months later. On average subjects met criteria for seven of the eleven DSM-III-R personality disorder categories, with borderline and paranoid types being most common (80 %). The admitted sample showed significantly greater reduction on the Borderline Syndrome Index (Conte *et al.*, 1980); baseline BSI scores correlated positively and significantly with initial severity of personality disorder as assessed by the Personality Diagnostic Questionnaire (PDQ-R) (Hyler & Reider, 1987).

A New Zealand study reports on 31 patients (81 % with Cluster C and 19 % with Cluster B personality disorders) who were treated in a day and semi-residential psychotherapy setting informed by feminist values (Krawitz, 1997). Patients were offered 'psychodynamically informed' therapy in group and individual sessions combined with cognitive-behavioural skills training. Therapy also included gender role analysis and exploration of social factors contributing to individuals' distress. Mean duration of treatment was four months. The authors report significant gains on the SCL90, the Global Assessment Scale and the Goal Attainment Scale lasting up to two years post-treatment. The study is notable for its emphasis on social factors influencing patient's difficulties, its unusual structure and its minimal resources. One full-time psychotherapist and one half-time psychiatrist treated up to eight patients at a time in an open group that accepted new members as vacancies arose. Individuals attended as day patients or lived in for half a week at a time – returning home in the interim to maintain community links and assist generalisation of skills.

Lees, Manning & Rawlings (1999) published a systematic review of the studies that have attempted to evaluate the effectiveness of therapeutic communities. They identified 29 studies for analysis, of which 22 were conducted in secure settings. The authors concluded that existing evidence does support the effectiveness of therapeutic community treatment in both secure and non-secure settings, with the strongest evidence for programmes aimed at substance misuse in secure settings.

TREATMENT OF PERSONALITY DISORDERED OFFENDERS

Craissati *et al.* (2002) reviewed effective treatment models for this group. The authors selected from standardised treatment programmes in England and Wales and identified the key treatment models as

* cognitive-behavioural approaches incorporating social skills training, problem-solving and social perspective taking (including programmes that specifically target aggressive/challenging behaviour or sex offenders);
* dialectical behaviour therapy;
* forensic psychoanalytic therapy and
* therapeutic communities.

They conclude that the evidence base is currently strongest for the first of these categories, which covers programmes used in prisons and the community. Friendship *et al.* (2002) compared 670 male offenders with custodial sentences of at least two years who had voluntarily participated in a cognitive skills programme offered by the prison service with 1 801 matched offenders who had not. They found that individuals who had taken part in the programmes experienced lower reconviction rates than the others, with those considered at medium risk of recidivism demonstrating the largest reduction (14 %). The literature suggests that most studies of cognitive-behaviour therapy-based programmes show reductions in reconviction rates of 10 % to 15 % among participants (see also Vennard, Hedderman & Sugg, 1997).

Craissati and colleagues conclude that dialectical behaviour therapy and psychoanalytic psychotherapy have yet to demonstrate efficacy with offenders, although the former is currently being evaluated in several UK prisons including Rampton High Security Hospital. Results for the therapeutic community approach seem encouraging but this is not widely available. The only remaining therapeutic community for offenders is HMP Grendon Underwood, which accepts males with personality disorders on a voluntary basis from the general prison system. Two large studies show lower reconviction rates for offenders who stayed at Grendon for at least 18 months than for matched inmates who remained within the general prison system (Marshall, 1997; Taylor, 2000).

CONCLUSION

The existing evidence base most strongly supports the use of dynamic psychotherapy, variants of cognitive-behaviour therapy (particularly dialectical behaviour therapy) and therapeutic communities in the treatment of personality disorders, with the usefulness of the latter being limited by its inaccessibility. Quite how much change occurs in the core features of personality disorders in response to psychotherapy remains a moot point since completed research has often failed to differentiate this from amelioration of comorbid conditions. However, we have enough evidence to support the conclusion that psychological therapies can effect sufficient change in individuals with a range of personality disorders, generally coexisting with other difficulties, to improve their quality of life.

Bateman & Tyrer (2002) identify the core features of psychological therapies that have demonstrated efficacy with personality disorders. They:

- are well structured;
- emphasise the facilitation of compliance;
- have a clear focus;
- are theoretically coherent for both therapist and patient;
- are relatively long term;
- encourage strong attachment between therapist and patient; and
- are integrated with other services available to the patient.

We would expect all effective therapy to fulfil the first four criteria, but the remaining three are also essential if we are to assist people who, as Rutter suggests, struggle most fundamentally with the challenge of forming and maintaining healthy relationships.

REFERENCES

Aarkrog, T. (1981). The borderline concept in childhood, adolescence and adulthood. *Acta Psychiatrica Scandinavica, 64*(suppl.), 243.

Aarkrog, T. (1993). *Borderline Personality Disorder Adolescents 20 Years Later.* Paper presented at the third international conference of the International Society for the Study of Personality Disorders, Cambridge, MA.

Alden, L.E. (1989). Short-term structured treatment for avoidant personality disorder. *Journal of Consulting and Clinical Psychology, 56,* 756–764.

Alden, L.E. & Capreol, M.J. (1993). Avoidant personality disorder: Interpersonal problems as predictors of treatment response. *Behaviour Therapy, 24,* 357–376.

American Psychiatric Association (1994). *Diagnostic and Statistical Manual of Mental Disorders: Fourth Edition.* Washington, DC: American Psychiatric Association.

Arboleda-Florez, J. & Holley, H.L. (1991). Antisocial burnout: An exploratory study. *Bulletin of the American Academy of Psychiatry and the Law, 19,* 173–183.

Argyle, M., Bryant, B.M. & Trower, P. (1974). Social skills training and psychotherapy: A comparative study. *Psychological Medicine, 4,* 435–443.

Barley, W.D., Buie, S.E., Peterson, E.W. *et al.* (1993). Development of an in-patient cognitive-behavioural treatment program for borderline personality disorder. *Journal of Personality Disorders, 7,* 232–240.

Bartholomew, K., Kwong, M.J. & Hart, S.D. (2001). Attachment. In W.J. Livesley (ed.), *Handbook of Personality Disorders: Theory, Research and Treatment* (pp 196–230). New York: Guilford Press.

Bateman, A. & Fonagy, P. (1999). Effectiveness of partial hospitalisation in the treatment of borderline personality disorder: A randomised controlled trial. *American Journal of Psychiatry, 156,* 1563–1569.

Bateman, A.W. & Fonagy, P. (2000). Effectiveness of psychotherapeutic treatment of personality disorder. *British Journal of Psychiatry, 177,* 138–143.

Bateman, A. & Fonagy, P. (2001). Treatment of borderline personality disorder with psychoanalytically oriented partial hospitalisation: An 18-month follow-up. *American Journal of Psychiatry, 158,* 36–42.

Bateman, A. & Tyrer, P. (2002). Effective management of personality disorder.

Battle, C., Imber, S., Hoehn-Saric, R. *et al.* (1966). Target complaints as a criteria of improvement. *American Journal of Psychotherapy, 20*, 184–192.

Beck, A.T., Freeman, A. & Davis, D. (2004). *Cognitive Therapy of Personality Disorders,* 2nd edn. New York: Guilford Press.

Binks, C.A., Fenton, M., McCarthy, L. *et al.* (2006). *Psychological Therapies for People with Borderline Personality Disorder (Review).* Chichester: Cochrane Collaboration. John Wiley & Sons.

Bohus, M., Haaf, B., Stiglmayr, C. *et al.* (2000). Evaluation of inpatient dialectical-behavioural therapy for borderline personality disorder – a prospective study. *Behaviour Research and Therapy, 38*, 875–887.

Bouchard, T.J., Jnr. (1997). The genetics of personality. In K. Blum & E.P. Noble (eds) *Handbook of Psychiatric Genetics* (pp. 273–296). Boca Raton, FL: CRC Press.

Budman, S.H., Demby, A., Soldz, S. & Merry, J. (1996). Time-limited group psychotherapy for patients with personality disorders: Outcomes and dropouts. *International Journal of Group Psychotherapy, 46*, 357–377.

Cappe, R.F. & Alden, L.E. (1986). A comparison of treatment strategies for clients functionally impaired by extreme shyness and social avoidance. *Journal of Consulting and Clinical Psychology, 54*, 796–801.

Casey, P.R. & Tyrer, P. (1990). Personality disorder and psychiatric illness in general practice. *British Journal of Psychiatry, 156*, 261–265.

Chiesa, M. & Fonagy, P. (2000). Cassel personality disorder study: Methodology and treatment effects. *British Journal of Psychiatry, 176*, 485-491.

Clark, L.A. (1993). *Manual for the Schedule for Nonadaptive and Adaptive Personality.* Minneapolis, MN: University of Minnesota Press.

Cloniger, C.R. (1987). A systematic method for clinical description and classification of personality variants: A proposal. *Archives of General Psychiatry, 44*, 576–588.

Coccaro, E.F. (2001). Biological and treatment correlates. In W.J. Livesley (ed.) *Handbook of Personality Disorders: Theory, Research and Treatment* (pp. 124–135). New York: Guilford Press.

Conte, H.R., Plutchik, R., Karasu, T.B. *et al.* (1980). A self-report borderline scale: Discriminant validity and preliminary norms. *Journal of Nervous and Mental Disease, 168*, 428–435.

Craissati, J., Horne, L. & Taylor, R. (2002). *Effective Treatment Models for Personality Disordered Offenders.* London: National Institute for Mental Health.

Davidson, K.M. & Tyrer, P. (1996). Cognitive therapy for antisocial and borderline personality disorders: Single case series. *British Journal of Clinical Psychology, 35*, 413–429.

Derogatis, L.R. (1983). SCL-90-R. *Administration, Scoring and Procedures.* Towson, MD: Clinical Psychometric Research.

Derogatis, L.R. & Cleary, P. (1977). Factorial invariance across gender for the primary symptom dimensions of the SCL-90. *British Journal of Social and Clinical Psychology, 16*, 347–356.

Dinwiddie, S.H. & Daw, E.W. (1998). Temporal stability of antisocial personality disorder: Blind follow-up study at 8 years. *Comprehensive Psychiatry, 39*, 28–34.

Dolan, B. & Coid, J. (1993). *Psychopathic and Antisocial Personality Disorders: Treatment and Research Issues.* London: Gaskell.

Dolan, B., Warren, F.M. & Norton, K. (1997). Change in borderline symptoms one year after therapeutic community treatment for severe personality disorder. *British Journal of Psychiatry, 171*, 274–279.

Endicott, J., Spitzer, R.L. Fleiss, J.L. *et al.* (1976). The Global Assessment Scale. *Archives of General Psychiatry, 33*, 766–771.

Evans, K., Tyrer, P., Catalan, J. *et al.* (1999). Manual-assisted cognitive-behaviour therapy (MACT): A randomised controlled trial of a brief intervention with bibliotherapy in the treatment of recurrent deliberate self-harm. *Psychological Medicine, 29*, 19–25.

Fonagy, P. & Bateman, A. (2006). Progress in the treatment of borderline personality disorder. *Lancet, 188*(1), 1–3.

Friendship, C., Blud, L., Erikson, M. & Travers, R. (2002). *An Evaluation of Cognitive Behavioural Treatment for Prisoners.* Home Office Research Findings No. 161. London: HMSO.

Giesen-Bloo, J., Van Dyck, R., Spinhoven, P. *et al.* (2006). Outpatient psychotherapy for borderline personality disorder: Randomized trial of schema-focused therapy vs transference-focused psychotherapy. *Archives of General Psychiatry, 63*(6), 649–658.

Goldberg, D. (1972). *The Detection of Psychiatric Illness by Questionnaire*, vol. 21. Oxford: Oxford University Press.

Hare, R.D., Harpur, T.J., Hakstian, A.R. *et al.* (1990). The revised Psychopathy Checklist: Reliability and factor structure. *Psychological Assessment, 2*, 338–341.

Hoglend, P. (1993). Personality disorders and long-term outcome after brief psychodynamic psychotherapy. *Journal of Personality Disorders, 7*, 168–181.

Hyler, S. (1994). *Personality Diagnostic Questionnaire PDQ-4*. New York State Psychiatric Institute.

Hyler, S. & Reider, R.O. (1987). *Personality Diagnostic Questionnaire Revised (PDQ-R)*. New York: New York State Psychiatric Institute.

Hyler, S., Reider, R. & Williams, J.B.W. *et al.* (1988). Personality diagnostic questionnaire: development and preliminary results. *Journal of Personality Disorders, 2*, 229–237.

Karterud, S., Vaglum, S., Friis, S. *et al.* (1992). Day hospital therapeutic community treatment for patients with personality disorders: An empirical evaluation of the containment function. *Journal of Nervous and Mental Disease, 180*, 238–243.

Kernberg, O.F. (1984). *Severe Personality Disorders: Psychotherapeutic Strategies*. New Haven, CT: Yale University Press.

Klein, M.H. (1993). Issues in the assessment of personality disorders. *Journal of Personality Disorders*, (Suppl) *1*, 18–33.

Krawitz, R. (1997). A prospective psychotherapy outcome study. *Australian and New Zealand Journal of Psychiatry, 31*, 465–473.

Lang, K.L. & Vernon, P.A. (2001). Genetics. In W.J. Livesley (ed.) *Handbook of Personality Disorders: Theory, Research and Treatment* (pp 177–195). New York: Guilford Press.

Lees, J., Manning, N. & Rawlings, B. (1999). *Therapeutic Community Effectiveness: A Systematic International Review of Therapeutic Community Treatment for People with Personality Disorders and Mentally Disordered Offenders*. Report 17. York: University of York, NHS Centre for Reviews and Dissemination.

Liberman, R.P. & Eckman, T. (1981). Behaviour therapy versus insight-oriented therapy for repeated suicide attempters. *Archives of General Psychiatry, 38*, 1126–1130.

Linehan, M.M., Armstrong, H.E., Suarez, A. *et al.* (1991). Cognitive-behavioural treatment for chronically parasuicidal borderline patients. *Archives of General Psychiatry, 48*, 1060–1064.

Linehan, M.M., Heard, H.L. & Armstrong, H.E. (1993). Naturalistic follow-up of a behavioural treatment for chronically parasuicidal borderline patients. *Archives of General Psychiatry, 50*, 971–974.

Linehan, M.M., Comtois, K.A., Murray, M. *et al.* (2006). Two-year randomized controlled trial and follow-up of dialectical behaviour therapy vs therapy by experts for suicidal behaviours and Borderline Personality Disorder. *Archives of General Psychiatry, 63*(7), 757–766.

Loranger, A.W., Susman, V.L., Oldham, J.M. & Russakoff, L.M. (1987). The Personality Disorder Examination: A preliminary report. *Journal of Personality Disorders, 1*, 1–13.

MacKenzie, K.R. (2001). Group Psychotherapy. In W.J. Livesley (ed.) *Handbook of Personality Disorders: Theory, Research and Treatment* (pp. 497–526). New York: Guilford Press.

Marshall, P. (1997). *A Reconviction Study of HMP Grendon Therapeutic Community*. Home Office Research Findings No. 53. London: HMSO.

Marzillier, J.S., Lambert, C. & Kellett, J. (1976). A controlled evaluation of systematic desensitization and social skills training for socially inadequate psychiatric patients. *Behaviour Research and Therapy, 14*, 225–238.

Mattia, J.I. & Zimmerman, M. (2001). Epidemiology. In W.J. Livesley (ed.), *Handbook of Personality Disorders: Theory, Research, and Treatment* (pp. 107–123). New York: Guilford Press.

McGlashan, T.H. (1985). The prediction of outcome in borderline personality disorder: Part V of the Chestnut Lodge follow-up study. In T.H. McGlashan (ed.) *The Borderline: Current Empirical Research* (pp. 63–98). Washington, DC: American Psychiatric Press.

McGlashan, T.H. (1986a). The Chestnut Lodge follow-up study: III. Long-term outcome of borderline personalities. *Archives of General Psychiatry, 43*, 20–30.

McGlashan, T.H. (1986b). Chestnut Lodge follow-up study: VI. Long-term follow-up perspectives. *Archives of General Psychiatry, 43*, 329–334.

Millon, T. (1993). Borderline personality disorder: A psychosocial epidemic. In J.Paris (ed.), *Borderline Personality Disorder: Etiology and Treatment* (pp. 197–210). Washington DC: American Psychiatric Press.

Millon, T., Millon, C. & Davis, R.D. (1994). *Millon Clinical Multiaxial Inventory-III*. Minneapolis: National Computer Systems.

Monroe-Blum, H. & Marziali, E. (1995). A controlled trial of short-term group treatment of borderline personality disorder. *Journal of Personality Disorders, 9*, 190–198.

Monsen, J.T., Odland, T. & Eilertsen, D.E. (1995). Personality disorders: Changes and stability after intensive psychotherapy focusing on affect consciousness. *Psychotherapy Research, 5*, 33–48.

Mulder, R.T. & Joyce, P.R. (1997). Temperament and the structure of personality disorder symptoms. *Psychological Medicine, 27*, 91–106.

Oldham, J.M., Skodol, A.E., Kellman, H.D. *et al.* (1995). Comorbidity of Axis I and Axis II disorders. *American Journal of Psychiatry, 152*(4), 571–578.

Paris, J. (1992). Social risk factors in borderline personality disorder: A review and a hypothesis. *Canadian Journal of Psychiatry, 37*, 510–515.

Paris, J. (1994). *Effects of Incest in Borderline Patients*. Paper presented at a symposium in honour of Otto Kernberg, New York Hospital/Westchester Division, 8 June.

Paris, J. (1996). *Social Factors in the Personality Disorders*. New York: Cambridge University Press.

Paris, J. (2001). Psychosocial Adversity. In W.J. Livesley (ed.) *Handbook of Personality Disorders: Theory, Research and Treatment* (pp 231–241). New York: Guilford Press.

Paris, J., Brown, R. & Nowlis, D. (1987). Long-term follow-up of borderline patients in a general hospital. *Comprehensive Psychiatry, 28*, 530–535.

Perry, J.C., Banon, E. & Ianni, F. (1999). Effectiveness of psychotherapy for personality disorders. *American Journal of Psychiatry, 156* (9), 1312–1321.

Piper, W.E., Rosie, J.S., Azim, H.F.A. & Joyce, A.S. (1993). A randomized trial of psychiatric day treatment for patients with affective and personality disorders. *Hospital and Community Psychiatry, 44*(8), 757–763.

Plakun, E.M., Burckhardt, P.E. & Muller, J.P. (1985). Fourteen-year follow-up of borderline and schizotypal personality disorders. *Comprehensive Psychiatry, 26*, 448–455.

Rendu, A., Moran, P., Patel, A. *et al.* (2002). Economic impact of personality disorders in UK primary care attenders. *British Journal of Psychiatry, 181*, 62–66.

Robins, L.N., Tipp, J. & Przybeck, T. (1991). Antisocial personality. In L.N. Robins & D. Regier (eds) *Psychiatric Disorders in America* (pp. 258–290). New York: Macmillan.

Roth, A. & Fonagy, P. (2005). *What Works for Whom? A Critical Review of Psychotherapy Research*, 2nd edn. New York: Guilford Press.

Roy, S. & Tyrer, P. (2001). Treatment of personality disorders. *Current Opinion in Psychiatry, 14*(6), 555–558.

Rutter, M. (1987). Temperament, personality and personality disorder. *British Journal of Psychiatry, 150*, 443–458.

Rutter, M. & Rutter, M. (1993). *Developing Minds: Challenge and Continuity Across the Life Span*. New York: Basic Books.

Ryle, A. & Golynkina, K. (2000). Effectiveness of time-limited cognitive analytic therapy of borderline personality disorder: Factors associated with this outcome. *British Journal of Medical Psychology, 73*(2), 197–210.

Saarento, O., Nieminten, P., Hakko, H. *et al.* (1997). Utilization of psychiatric in-patient care among new patients in a comprehensive community-care system: a 3 year follow-up study. *Acta Psychiatrica Scandinavica, 95*, 132–139.

Sara,G., Raven, P. & Mann, A. (1996). A comparison of DSM-III-R and ICD-10 personality disorder criteria in an outpatient population. *Psychological Medicine, 26*, 151–160.

Seivewright, H., Tyrer, P., Casey, P. *et al.* (1991). A three-year follow-up of psychiatric morbidity in urban and rural primary care. *Psychological Medicine, 21*, 495–503.

Shea, M.T. (1993). Psychosocial treatment of personality disorder. *Journal of Personality Disorder, 7*(suppl.), 167–180.

Shea, M.T., Stout, R.L., Yen, S. *et al.* (2004). Associations in the course of personality disorders and axis I disorders over time. *Journal of Abnormal Psychology, 113*, 499–508.

Singleton, N., Meltzer, H. & Gatward, R. (1998). *Psychiatric Morbidity among Prisoners in England and Wales*. London: Stationery office.

Smith, K., Shah, A., Wright, K. *et al.* (1995). The prevalence and costs of psychiatric disorders and learning disabilities. *British Journal of Psychiatry, 166*, 9–18.

Spitzer, R.L., Williams, J.B.W., Gibbon, M. & First, M. (1990). *User's Guide for the Structured Clinical Interview for DSM-III-R*. Arlington, VA: American Psychiatric Association.

Stevenson, J. & Meares, R. (1992). An outcome study of psychotherapy for patients with borderline personality disorder. *American Journal of Psychiatry, 149*, 358–362.

Stevenson, J. & Meares, R. (1999). Psychotherapy with borderline patients: II. A preliminary cost benefit study. *Australian and New Zealand Journal of Psychiatry, 33*, 473-477.

Stone, M.H. (1990). *The Fate of Borderline Patients: Successful Outcome and Psychiatric Practice*. New York: Guilford Press.

Stone, M. (1993). Long-term outcome in personality disorders. *British Journal of Psychiatry, 162*, 299–313.

Stone, M.H. (2001). Natural history and long-term outcome. In W.J. Livesley (ed.) *Handbook of Personality Disorders: Theory, Research and Treatment* (pp. 259–276). New York: Guilford Press.

Stone, M.H., Hurt, S.W. & Stone, D.K. (1987). The P.I.-500: Long-term follow-up of borderline inpatients meeting DSM-III criteria. I: Global outcome. *Journal of Personality Disorders, 1*, 291–298.

Stravynski, A., Belisle, M., Marcouiller *et al.* (1994). The treatment of avoidant personality disorder by social skills training in the clinic or in real-life settings. *Canadian Journal of Psychiatry, 39*, 377–383.

Taylor, R. (2000). *A Seven-Year Reconviction Study of HMP Grendon Therapeutic Community*. Home Office Research Findings No. 115. London: HMSO.

Tyrer, P. & Alexander, J. (1979). Classification of personality disorder. *British Journal of Psychiatry, 135*, 163–67.

Tyrer, P., Alexander, J. & Ferguson, B. (1988). Personality Assessment Schedule (PAS). In P. Tyrer (ed.), *Personality Disorders: Diagnosis, Management and Course* (pp. 140–167). London: Wright.

Tyrer, P., Gunderson, J., Lyons, M. & Tohen, M. (1997). Special feature: Extent of comorbidity between mental state and personality disorders. *Journal of Personality Disorders, 11*, 242–259.

Tyrer, P., Mitchard, S., Methuen, C. & Ranger, M. (2003). Treatment-rejecting and treatment-seeking personality disorders: Type R and Type S. *Journal of Personality Disorders, 17*(3), 263–268.

Tyrer, P., Seivewright, N., Ferguson, B. *et al.* (1990). The Nottingham study of neurotic disorder: relationship between personality status and symptoms. *Psychological Medicine, 20*, 423–431.

The EuroQol Group (1990). EuroQol: A new facility for the measurement of health-related quality of life. *Health Policy, 16*, 199–208.

The WHOQOL Group (1998). The World Health Organization Quality of Life Assessment (WHOQOL): Development and general psychometric qualities. *Social Science Medicine, 46*, 1569–1585.

Van den Bosch, L.M.C., Koeter, M.W.J., Stijnen, T. *et al.* (2005). Sustained efficacy of dialectical behaviour therapy for borderline personality disorder. *Behaviour Research and Therapy, 43*(9), 1231–1241.

Van der Kolk, B.A. (1996). The complexity of adaptation to trauma: Self-regulation, stimulus discrimination, and characterological development. In B.A. van der Kolk, A.C. McFarlane & L. Weisaeth (eds) *Traumatic Stress: The Effects of Overwhelming Experience on Mind, Body, and Society* (pp. 182–213). New York: Guilford Press.

Vennard, J., Hedderman, C. & Sugg, D. (1997). *Changing Offenders' Attitudes and Behaviour: What Works?* Home Office Research Findings No 61. London: HMSO.

Verheul, R., Van den Bosch, L.M.C., Koeter, M.W.J. *et al.* (2003). Dialectical behaviour therapy for women with borderline personality disorder. *British Journal of Psychiatry, 182*, 135–140.

Weissman, M.M. & Bothwell, S. (1976). Assessment of social adjustment by patient self-report. *Archives of General Psychiatry, 33*, 111–115.

Widiger, T.A. (1992). Categorical versus dimensional classification: Implications from and for research. *Journal of Personality Disorder, 6*, 287–300.

Widiger, T.A. (1993). The DSM-III-R categorical personality disorder diagnoses: A critique and alternatives. *Psychological Inquiry, 4*, 75–90.

Winston, A., Laikin, M., Pollack, J. *et al.* (1994). Short-term dynamic psychotherapy of personality disorders. *American Journal of Psychiatry, 150*, 190–194.

Winston, A., Pollack, J., McCullough, L. *et al.* (1991). Brief psychotherapy of personality disorders. *Journal of Nervous and Mental Disease, 179*, 188–193.

Wolff, S. & Chick, J. (1981). Schizoid personality in childhood: A controlled follow-up study. *Annual Progress in Child Psychiatry and Child Development,* 550–580.

World Health Organization (1992). *The ICD-10 Classification of Mental and Behavioural Disorders: Clinical Descriptions and Diagnostic Guidelines.* Geneva: World Health Organization.

Yalom, I.D. (1995). *The Theory and Practice of Group Psychotherapy,* 4th edn. New York: Basic Books.

Zanarini, M.C., Frankenburg, F.R., Hennen, J. *et al.* (2003). The longitudinal course of borderline psychopathology: 6-year prospective follow-up of the phenomenology of borderline personality disorder. *American Journal of Psychiatry, 160,* 274–283.

Zimmerman, M. (1994). Diagnosing personality disorders: a review of issues and research methods. *Archives of General Psychiatry, 51,* 225–245.

CHAPTER 12

Intellectual Disabilities

William R. Lindsay
University of Abertay, Dundee, UK
and
Peter Sturmey
City University of New York, USA

INTRODUCTION

When one is asked to complete an exercise such as this, acceptance is always accompanied by a sense of the ridiculous, even arrogance. To write about the whole field of intellectual disabilities and the evidence base for its treatments in one chapter by two individuals cries for better judgement. Treatments for the range of problems associated with any generic client group such as autistic spectrum disorders, behavioural difficulties, anxiety, depression, substance abuse, aggression, sexual problems, relationship and social difficulties, should all be addressed. Specific treatment approaches such as pharmacological, the cognitive therapies, psychotherapy, social skills training, social problem solving, educational approaches, the vast range of behavioural therapies and the newer alternative therapies are all subsumed within the generic topic of intellectual disabilities. Intellectual disability is not equivalent to anxiety or depression nor is it equivalent even to schizophrenia in that no one is kidding anyone that they can find 'a cure'. Therefore no one is trying – the notion is ridiculous. Clinicians are directed to concomitant difficulties some of which might have an increased incidence in intellectual disabilities, others that occur in the same way as they would in other generic populations. One always wonders whether it would be seen as transparently ridiculous if one were to write a chapter on the evidence base for treatments developed for members of MENSA, the society for those with superior intellect. (Do we detect one or two of you raising an eyebrow at the possibility of a new research field?) Similarly, no one is looking for a cure for giftedness. One is left with two options – either refuse in a fit of pique, in which case intellectual disabilities is not represented in the volume, or accept, distinguished by the accompanying feelings of arrogance and grandiosity. Needless to say, we have taken the latter course.

When the notion of evidence-based practice was first introduced it was treated with a very cynical eye by the authors. As aspiring clinical psychologists in the late 1960s and 1970s, the notion of linking treatment approaches to experimental methods was axiomatic. Therefore, we felt that the whole essence of clinical practice within psychology was fundamentally based upon experimentally validated approaches and the notion of evidence-based practice was both latter day and irrelevant. The first issues of essential therapeutic journals contained evidence-based work on intellectual disabilities. Wolf, Risley & Mees (1964) used operant conditioning treatments to improve sleep problems, temper tantrums and other behaviour problems in an autistic child. The improvements were still evident at a six-month follow-up assessment. Berkowitz, Sherry & Davis (1972) taught self-feeding skills to 14 profoundly disabled boys aged between nine and 17 years. Using reinforcement and fading procedures they successfully taught the boys, who were still feeding themselves independently 41 months later. Miller, Patton & Henton (1972) used behaviour modification techniques to improve independent standing and self-feeding in a profoundly retarded child. Behaviour therapies have always insisted on establishing the effectiveness of procedures using a variety of increasingly ingenious experimental designs. In this study, Miller *et al.* used a simple reversal design to demonstrate that the procedures employed made the personal differences to the child since, when the behavioural procedures were removed, the improvements disappeared. Therefore the therapeutic procedures promoted his feeding and standing. As we shall see later, behavioural therapies have increased exponentially in scope and complexity but the science underpinning them has remained as good as that in any therapeutic field and better than most.

Were the behavioural therapies not able to validate themselves with a sound scientific base, then they would have been (rightly) dismissed. The evidence base is essential to its therapeutic investigation. However, looking across therapies for this client group, one quickly realises that this view is smug. Therapies spring up right left and centre and can be carried forward more effectively by evangelical zeal than they can by scientific rigour. Indeed, when dealing with a class of individuals who are generally devalued, as the current chapter does, one becomes aware that they may be vulnerable to anyone who takes a genuine interest, however idiosyncratic. It has therefore become extremely important to review the evidence base for the range of mainstream and alternative therapies that are currently used in the field of intellectual disabilities.

Evidence-Based Practice (EBP)

There is a tension between EBP and tailored psychological treatment, which is at the heart of many psychological therapies including the most scientifically validated group of therapies – the behaviour therapies. Good psychological treatment is tailored to individual requirements. Individual assessments and a functional analysis unique to that person will produce hypotheses about the personal, environmental and societal influences, which both cause and maintain the problem. Therefore, ideally, it should be impossible to group individuals into a generic class suffering from, say, anxiety or aggression. Behavioural therapies and some cognitive therapies in intellectual disabilities have developed on the basis of individual case studies. On the other hand, EBP requires a formatted protocol for treatment that can be used across a group of individuals randomly selected from the population of individuals who have that problem. This formatted approach can then be tested against a control group of similarly randomly selected individuals. Clearly this is the antithesis of idiomatic formulation and treatment and is an essential contradiction in much of the scientific literature on treatment effectiveness.

Deductive and Inductive Science

Most psychologists are brought up on one kind of scientific method: hypothetico-deductive science. This approach is characterised by development of null and alternative hypotheses, which are used to predict future results. Hence, hypothetico-deductive science begins with theory and then proceeds to data. For example, in the case of outcome studies we usually hypothesise that there will be a difference between the treatment and other groups on some measure and then go to look at the data after it has been collected to verify our theory. This approach to science is drilled into psychologists from the first year of undergraduate study and is the dominant approach to science. Indeed the double-blind cross-over placebo trial is viewed by many as the *sine qua non* of experimental approaches to treatment evaluation. But it is not the only approach. Several sciences are not experimental: the sciences of astronomy and palaeontology have a hard time manipulating independent variables.

An alternative approach is inductive science. Inductive science is characterised by beginning close to the data. Inductive science makes observations – many observations – and then manipulates independent variables that might influence the phenomenon of interest. It repeatedly asks the question, 'I wonder what would happen if . . . ' (Chiesa, 1994, p. 153). Induction also refers to making statement of generalities based on many specific instances. For example, observations of the effects of withdrawing a reinforcer from a previously reinforced behaviour in a pigeon, a rat, a marmoset and a human, and withdrawing a reinforcer from previously reinforced human play, writing, talking and crying, might all permit one to induce some generalisation about the nature of extinction. This might constitute a general law of science (Chiesa, 1994).

Group and Small *N* Designs

The commonly used methods associated with hypothetico-deductive science are group experiments and analyses of variance. Great weight is placed on statistical significance as the arbiter of which observations are importance. These approaches were originally developed for use in agricultural research but are they good for research with people? Increasing the weight of an average potato is an important outcome for a farmer and someone selling fertiliser but who is interested in the average person?

Group designs have important limitations. First, the logic of group designs requires that samples are drawn randomly from a population. The results of the sample are then generalised to the population of interest. However, most group research neither defines the population of interest nor draws randomly from that population and hence is unable to generalise the results to the undefined population. Instead, evaluating psychological treatment by group designs is hobbled by sequences of studies drawn from many different samples of convenience that are representative of no population of interest. When effects are not replicated between experiments, it is unclear if the results reflect differences in samples, variable outcome of treatment or interactions between treatment and sample characteristics.

Group designs are limited in a more serious way. Enslaved to statistical significance and the mythical average subject – a client none of us have worked with – group designs often ignore the clinical or practical significance of the treatment outcome. Statistical significance is relatively easy to achieve with large groups; indeed trivial and unimportant differences can easily reach statistical significance if the group size is large enough and the measures reliable. Yet, within the differences between average subjects are large individual differences in treatment outcome, and interactions between individual differences and treatment effects. Hence, although the scores of majority of subjects may increase, others may not change and indeed others may decrease. Hence, a statistically significant F test is of little comfort to either the client or therapist if the person seeking help responds minimally, not at all, or adversely to the best available treatment. Clients and therapists alike are not truly interested in statistically significant changes in average subjects; they are interested in large and meaningful changes in multiple outcome measures in the client sitting in the office today!

Single-subject research designs involve a different approach to science. Rather than pursuing statistical significance, single-subject research pursues demonstrating a replicable and consistent functional relationship between an independent variable and client behaviour. If a therapist or experimenter can turn a behaviour on and off by systematically applying and withdrawing an independent variable and observe a systematic change in the client's behaviour, then we can say that we have truly identified an independent variable (Baer, Wolf & Risley, 1968). Hence, reversal, multiple baseline and other single-subject designs can show causal relationships between independent and dependent variables. Single-subject experimental designs can be clearly differentiated from case studies, including case studies with data. Single-subject designs demonstrate a functional relationship between treatment and outcome, whereas case studies do not.

Single-subject experimental designs by themselves do not directly address the social significance of behaviour change: it would be possible to have experimental control over an effect of trivial magnitude. Single subject designs do address social significance by a variety of methods known as *social validity* (Wolf, 1978). Social validity can be demonstrated using ratings of the importance of behaviour change from the client, and significant others in the environment. Sometimes comparative data from the behaviour of other typically functioning people can be used to evaluate the social significance of change. For example, if one wanted to increase the time on task of children with mild intellectual disabilities then one might observe the on-task behaviour of typical children in the classroom and use their data to indicate the range of typical performance in that environment. If the intervention results in children with intellectual disabilities spending less or more time on task than typical children, then one would not be satisfied with treatment outcome.

Summary

Given the caveats noted above – and with apologies to the host of outstanding researchers and therapists in intellectual disabilities who would have done it differently or better – we will proceed with our review of EBP in intellectual disabilities. This chapter first reviews the results of consensus panels on therapies with people with intellectual disabilities. The next section reviews the results of several generic meta-analysis. The subsequent three sections review the evidence base for four commonly used psychological therapies for people with intellectual disabilities: behaviour therapy, cognitive therapy, counselling and sensory therapies.

CONSENSUS PANELS

Rush & Frances (2000) developed the expert consensus guidelines for psychiatric and behavioural problems. Fifty-six behavioural and 51 pharmacological experts were invited to participate; 86 % and 88 % replied respectively. They asked the raters to rate a series of statements concerning a variety of psychosocial treatments.

When asked to rate appropriate assessment methods, direct observation and functional assessment were identified as first-line choices in the assessment of psychiatric and behavioural problems. When asked to identify the most appropriate methods of psychosocial interventions there were large and significant differences between different treatment methods. Applied behaviour analysis (ABA), managing the environment and client and family education all received average ratings of 8 on a 9-point scale. All identified as first-rank treatments and significantly more effective then other treatment methods. Cognitive behaviour therapy, classical behaviour therapy and supportive counselling were identified as second-rank treatments and received average ratings of approximately 5. Psychotherapy was identified as the least effective treatment and received an average rating of only 3. These results were broadly replicated for ratings of treatment of aggression and self-injury, psychiatric disorders and across individuals with mild or moderate and severe or profound intellectual disabilities. Thus, the results of the expert consensus guidelines provided strong support for differentiation between the effectiveness of different treatment methods and strong and uniform support for the effectiveness of behavioural methods over counselling and psychotherapy.

The New York Department of Health (1999a, 1999b, 1999c) conducted an expert panel review of the effectiveness of intervention for pre-school children with autism and pervasive developmental disorders. The guidelines were based on a systematic review of the scientific literature, involved operationalised criteria for including and excluding studies in the review and involved a panel of expert readers to identify and review the papers. A wide range of behavioural and non-behavioural interventions was identified. The review provided a rating of the status of their conclusions; for example some were identified as panel consensus and others were identified as evidence based. They gave their conclusions in unequivocal terms by stating that certain therapies were recommended or not recommended.

The panel concluded that early behavioural intervention for children was strongly recommended and should include at least 20 hours per week. Applied behaviour analysis was also identified as an effective method for young children with autism. The panel made recommendations concerning clear operational definitions of target behaviours, use of reinforcer assessments, functional assessments, planning for generalisation, parents and peer training and so on. They also recommended that ABA was an effective intervention to reduce maladaptive behaviours, to teach social interactions and promote language skills. The strength of the evidence for specific conclusions varied widely from a strong evidence base – at least to well-designed studies – to panel consensus. This is perhaps unsurprising given the very narrow age range that the panel reviewed.

The panel was also clear on the effectiveness of other interventions. Floor time, sensory integration therapy, music therapy, touch therapy, auditory integration therapy, facilitated communication, hormone therapies, immunological therapies, anti-yeast therapies, vitamin therapies and dietary therapies were all specifically not recommended for use with children with autism and pervasive developmental disorders (PDD) aged 0 to 3 years! There was no evidence base to support their use.

GENERAL META-ANALYSES

There have been several general meta-analyses of different kinds of treatment outcome for people with intellectual disabilities. (Three meta-analyses that focused exclusively on behavioural approaches are discussed later in this chapter.) They have necessarily focused on behavioural interventions because of the large number of treatment studies and extensive history of empirical research in this area. However, they have permitted direct comparison of behavioural with other treatment methods.

Scotti *et al.* (1991) reviewed 403 studies published from 1976 to 1987. The main behaviours of concern were stereotyped behaviour and self-injurious behaviour. Interestingly, they found that medication had the poorest impact on these problems and that interventions conducted in natural, integrated settings were more effective than those conducted when the individual was in a segregated setting. The strongest influence on outcome was whether or not the investigators had performed a functional analysis on the problem behaviour. They concluded that 'the use of functional analysis of multiple responses is perhaps a necessity for adequate treatment design' (Scotti *et al.*, 1991, p. 252).

Didden, Duker & Korzilius (1997) reported a meta-analysis of 482 empirical studies involving 1 451 comparisons of treatment with baseline. This meta-analysis included a larger range of years than that reported by Scotti *et al.* The most common problem behaviours were again stereotyped, self-injury, disruption and aggressive behaviour. The dependent variable for the meta-analysis was the percentage of intervention data points not overlapping with baseline data points. They found that externally directed problems, such as destructiveness and aggression towards others, were more difficult to treat than internally directed and socially disruptive problems. They found that response contingent procedures were more effective than antecedent control procedures; pharmacology; and response non-contingent procedures. Level of disability did not seem to influence either the type of intervention or the effectiveness of the intervention.

Response non-contingent procedures were superior to pharmacology. Combined behavioural treatments were superior to single behavioural treatment procedures. Finally, interventions based on functional assessment and especially functional analysis were associated with the largest effect sizes. The more precise the method used to assess the function of the target behaviour, the larger the effect sizes. Thus, larger effect sizes were associated with experimental functional analyses than with informal, descriptive functional assessment such as ABC charts, interviews and questionnaires. Therefore, the more technically sophisticated the treatment, the greater the therapeutic impact.

These two meta-analyses both reached similar conclusions: there is stronger evidence for the effectiveness of behavioural interventions than other forms of therapies, including pharmacotherapy. It is important to note that many other commonly used therapies, such as counselling, psychotherapy, sensory and dietary treatments receive little mention in these studies. This presumably reflects the absence or very small quantity of good quality evaluations of these interventions.

BEHAVIOUR THERAPIES

The behaviour therapies have relied on sophisticated individual experimental case designs applied to therapies for intractable personal problems. The literature is replete with outstanding examples although, as an extensive and successful series of treatment approaches, they have not been without criticism. The main criticisms have been that many behavioural treatments tend to focus on reducing single-target problems whereas, in reality, clients are likely to have multiple difficulties related to lack of communicative skill, a range of problem behaviours and so on. The second trenchant criticism has been that successful case examples are often derived from highly staffed, specialist units whereas most individuals with intellectual disabilities are cared for, managed and treated within generic community facilities. More recently, there have been a number of reports that are larger in scale both for individuals and groups. Graff, Green & Libby (1998) reported on the intensive behavioural treatment of a severely disabled, destructive and autistic four-year-old boy who had no functional or communicative skill. Treatment was comprehensive employing the full range of behavioural methods to reduce problem behaviours and increase pro-social and communicative skills. Following treatment, he was able to take instruction reliably, showed no aberrant behaviour, generalised his skills and developed some non-verbal communication. As independent validation, his medication was discontinued after treatment. Given the level of disability and destructiveness described by Graff *et al.*, these changes and improvements are impressive indeed.

One of the most influential behavioural therapies has been based on a seminal study by Carr & Durand (1985) in which they developed the methods of functional communications training. In this study they hypothesised that problem/challenging behaviour, rather than being viewed as an aberrant condition, intrinsic to the individual, should be construed as a means of communicating the needs of the individual to others. Carr and Durand developed functional communication training, whereby the individual was taught alternative ways of communicating his or her needs. This was a very attractive hypothesis and generated a considerable research and treatment literature. However, studies have tended to find that functional communications training on its own may be of limited effectiveness without concurrent extinction of the target behaviour. Therefore, in addition to developing new ways of communicating, researchers have found it necessary to implement procedures to reduce the problem behaviour (Drasgow, Halle & Ostrosky, 1998; Fisher *et al.*, 1998). Thompson *et al.* (1998) employed functional communications training with extinction for a range of problem behaviours in a six-year-old child. They found that the combined procedures reduced all forms of aggression except the one that their functional analysis indicated was maintained independent of contingencies. Following their functional analysis, they hypothesised that the remaining behaviour (chin grinding) was automatically reinforced. Following the provision of an alternative source of reinforcement, this problem was also eliminated. Hagopian *et al.* (1998) reported a series of 21 case studies of participants who had a range of intellectual disabilities and behavioural problems. Using carefully balanced research designs they found that functional communications training on its own was of limited value. When combined with extinction (not delivering a consequence for a problem behaviour) or punishment (for example, time out in a room or a chair) directed at the target behaviour, there were massive (90 %) reductions in target behaviour for 50 % of clients in the extinction condition and 100 % of clients in the punishment condition. It should be noted that extinction on its own as a treatment has been shown to produce increases in aggression and destruction and the importance of matching extinction procedures to target behaviours has been demonstrated frequently (Horner *et al.*, 2002).

Positive Behavioural Programming

Positive behavioural programming is a behaviour therapy based on the influential writings and teachings of a number of behaviour analysts including LaVigna & Donellan (1986) and Carr & Durand (1985). These procedures were developed to concentrate solely on interventions designed to increase desired behaviours with the theoretical argument that these would then replace problem behaviours. Put simply, if someone persistently bangs their head with their right hand, they should be taught to engage in an adaptive, constructive act with their right hand that would then replace the maladaptive behaviour. Functional communications training is clearly an example of positive behavioural programming. While there have been many encouraging reports and case studies concerning positive behavioural programming, research has suggested that methods for promoting prosocial, constructive abilities are more successful when they are employed in combination with methods directed at reducing antisocial, maladaptive behaviours. Time and again it has been shown that functional assessment increases the likelihood that treatment intervention will be successful (Horner & Carr, 1997).

Iwata *et al.* (1994) instigated the most influential system of functional analysis for the assessment of problem behaviours and subsequent research has developed and refined these methods. These authors set up analogue systems to identify the reinforcement contingencies that maintain certain challenging behaviours. In a series of experimental trials, the assessor introduces a variety of reinforcing conditions such as social reinforcement, tangible reinforcement, automatic (intrinsic) reinforcement, escape from demands (negative reinforcement) and so on, in order to assess their effect on the target behaviour in question. When the assessor ascertains which kind of reinforcement is controlling the behaviour, treatment is based on these findings. Clearly this work is of a highly individual nature and, as a result, most of the studies in the field are small *N* experimental designs). Recent research has focused on variables, setting conditions and events that can predict or maintain the occurrence of problem behaviour. Functional assessment has developed beyond analogue assessments into considering the same variables in natural settings, thus addressing one of the criticisms mentioned above.

Meta-analyses of Behavioural Interventions

Several meta-analyses have been conducted exclusively on outcome studies of behaviour therapy. For example, Carr *et al.* (1999) published a meta-analysis on interventions using specific types of behavioural interventions – those using positive behavioural support (PBS). This is a specific development of ABA. Like typical ABA it emphasises skills training and intervention based on functional assessment. However, PBS eschews punishment procedures and other procedures such as differential reinforcement of other behaviours because of their potentially aversive nature. Positive behavioural support also places at least equal weight on antecedent control and environmental redesign procedures as do contingency-based procedures. It is also concerned not merely with changing specific behaviours but to improve the quality of a person's life. Hence, it is interested in the broader ecology, social validity and systems issues related to positive client outcomes.

Carr *et al.* (1999) identified 216 articles from 36 journals using multiple methods including online and hand searches and contacting leading researchers in the field. Positive behavioural support articles included at least one intervention using stimulus intervention methods such as interspersed training, expansion of choice or curriculum modification, or reinforcement based interventions including functional communication training, self-management and differential reinforcement of alternative behaviours. Articles using non-PBS methods included differential reinforcement of other behaviour, extinction and time out were excluded. All of these methods were included in the Scotti *et al.* (1991) and Didden *et al.* (1997) meta-analyses. Other exclusion criteria were articles that had no data, used AB designs, group studies with no individual data, group design with no control group and *n* designs with fewer than three baseline data points. The dependent variable used in this meta-analysis was the percentage reduction over baseline calculated using the last three intervention data points. Of the 216 articles identified by Carr *et al.*, 107 were excluded using the above criteria. The remaining 109 yielded 366 outcomes, because some studies used more than one dependent variable.

Changes in positive behaviours were reported in only 45 % of papers. They found that positive behaviours often increased substantially during PBS interventions. However, they noted that there were wide variations in this outcome measure. They found that 68 % of PBS interventions were associated with an 80 % or greater reduction in the target behaviour. This was true for interventions that used both stimulus-based and reinforcement-based interventions. Fifty-two per cent of studies achieved 90 % or greater reduction in the target behaviour. The outcome literature was limited in that response and stimulus generalisation was rarely addressed in the PBS literature and maintenance data were generally absent and few studies reported maintenance data beyond 12 months. Data on lifestyle change was taken in only 3.5 % of the papers reviewed and social validity data were taken in only approximately 10 % of papers. Input from clients, family members and staff on evaluations was rarely included in papers on PBS.

The effectiveness of PBS was mediated by several salient variables. Interventions that included significant others as change agents, which used environmental re-organisation and used typical agents of change were associated with larger effect sizes. Paradoxically, interventions in atypical settings were associated with larger effect sizes when compared with interventions in typical settings. This is particularly problematic because it suggests that interventions in experimental situations were more effective than interventions in naturalistic situations. However, it is the latter that are crucially important in any treatment intervention.

Carr *et al.* (2000) were modestly optimistic that interventions often have a large impact on a wide range of target behaviours. However, they were more cautious about the broader social validity, generalisation and maintenance of PBS interventions.

Although there are relatively few randomised controlled studies within the field of behaviour modification and the behaviour therapies, as we have argued, the scientific integrity of the field is beyond reproach. Where there are problems, they are in the generalisability of the treatment methods from experimental situations where those implementing the programmes are highly trained, to realistic situations where it is likely that individuals who are supporting clients are relatively untrained and not sophisticated in relation to behavioural methods. The Carr *et al.* (1999) meta-analysis has identified this weakness. However it is being addressed increasingly by those involved with applied behaviour analysis and behaviour modification. Corrigan (1991) conducted a meta-analysis of 73 social skills training studies conducted with people with intellectual disabilities, psychotic disorders, other psychiatric disorders and offenders. They found that studies of social skills training with people with intellectual disabilities were associated with the largest effect sizes. Hence, social skills training seems to be especially effective with people with intellectual disabilities.

Campbell (2003) conducted a meta-analysis of behavioural interventions of behavioural interventions for persons with autism using single subject designs. He identified 117 articles involving 181 individuals from 15 journals. Campbell again found strong evidence that behavioural interventions could reduce maladaptive behaviours in people with autism. Horner *et al.* (2002) review the existing literature on problem behaviour interventions for young children with autism. Reviewing peer reviewed research from 1996 to 2000, they used the following criteria for studies: subjects with autism less than 97 months old; problem behaviour as a dependent variable; an experimental design that allowed identification of a causal relationship between reduction and problem behaviour and intervention; data for individual subjects and at least three data points for pre-intervention and three data points for post-intervention phases. Nine articles were identified fulfilling these criteria with a total of 24 participants and 37 comparisons evaluated. The most frequent problem behaviour identified was tantrums (76 %) followed by aggression (59 %), stereotyped behaviour (14 %), and self-injury (11 %). Some functional assessment was conducted in 68 % of comparisons with a full functional analysis in 14 %. Interventions were stimulus based (43 %), instruction based (81 %), extinction (51 %), reinforcement of appropriate behaviour (30 %), punishment (32 %) and systems change (27 %). Multiple intervention components were included in 62 % of the comparisons and none included pharmacological procedures. In 62 %, intervention agent and context were typical and most likely to occur in the home or at school with the agent a parent or teacher. Of the 37 comparisons, the mean reduction in problem behaviour was 85 % with a median of 93.2 % and a mode of 100 %. Fifty-nine per cent of the comparisons recorded behaviour reductions of greater than 90 % and 68 % recorded reductions of 80 % or greater. Fifty-seven per cent of comparisons recorded maintenance data at an average of 12 weeks (longest one year) and in all cases, the level of improvement remained within 15 % of initial improvements during the intervention phase. There was no pattern for generalisation data. In this very careful review, the authors noted several limitations to their very positive conclusions. The two most important of these were that only nine studies were identified and that 'both single-subject and group design studies are more likely to be published if important effects are demonstrated than if no effects are found. This logical standard for publication means that the pattern of effects (or effect size) experienced in clinical contexts may not match that observed in published research' (Horner *et al.*, 2002, p. 436).

Early Intervention Studies on Autism

Autism is a pervasive developmental disorder that has many incapacitating behavioural and cognitive features including an association with low IQ, chronic disruption of social function, severe behavioural problems and several features of developmental delay. Intervention research on individuals with autism is both extensive and far reaching and clearly illustrates the challenges for EBP at every level – scientific, political, legal, emotional and personal. By far the most comprehensive and detailed intervention is the early intervention project (EIP) developed by Lovaas (1987). EIP itself is designed to run for 40 hours or more per week, 365 days a year over a period of three years. Treatment during the first year is directed at reducing behavioural problems such as aggressive behaviours and self-stimulatory behaviours and also begins to promote prosocial behaviours such as appropriate play with toys and imitation responses. During the first year the family is also involved in treatment. Social deficits are addressed during the second year with programmes to encourage peer interaction and individual approaches to teaching both abstract and expressive language. In the third year, while continuing to maintain gains made during the previous part of the programme, pre-academic skills such as attending, concentration and basic reading, writing and arithmetic skills are taught. In addition, emotional recognition and expression are taught through the final year of the programme. Outcome claims by Lovaas (1987) and McEachin, Smith & Lovaas (1993) indicated that there were massive benefits in an EIP experimental group when compared to a control group. By using two outcome measures, IQ and educational placement, they found that 47 % of the experimental group achieved normal IQ and these improvements were maintained at 13 years of age (mean IQ = 84.5) compared to a mean IQ for the control subjects of 54.9.

Gresham & MacMillan (1998) review the Lovaas studies and the political and legal sequelae. They note a large number of internal and external validity threats to the experimental designs. Subjects were not randomly assigned to treatments but rather were matched in pairs. The measures should have been more targeted and discreet, giving information on individual adaptive function rather than the very global measures that were used. According to Smith & Lovaas (1997), those who deliver the programme require extensive, detailed training. Therefore the fidelity of replications or the fidelity of service developments far removed from the Lovaas Centre is very difficult to achieve. More recent developments in the field differentiate clinical subtypes. Although these developments were not available to the original authors, they have not modified their claims in light of these advances. Consideration of these subtypes might allow a better understanding of those individuals who might and might not achieve benefit from an EIP. As Gresham & MacMillan (1998, p. 11) note

> the stakes are high as these exchanges are not mere academic exercises; rather, families with the children with autism deserve critical analysis as do taxpayers who will be asked to finance the estimated $60 000 per child per year and . . . limited financial resources are frequently diverted into attorney's fees and high cost programmes such as EIP.

They note ruefully 'if anything positive has accrued from these disputes, it only may be the gainful employment of attorneys who appear more than willing to take these cases to fair hearings and/or the courts' (Gresham & MacMillan, 1998, p. 12). This clearly illustrates the challenges facing EBP on several fronts.

Subsequent research has supported the positive outcomes for EIP but, because of the length of treatment and the obvious nature of the programme, blind comparisons with a control group are not possible. Sheinkopf & Siegel (1998) addressed some of the criticisms by extending the work to home-based programmes implemented by parents and community based clinicians. The programme was less intensive with 27 hours being delivered over 11 weeks and post-treatment assessments were conducted between 18 and 20 months' follow-up. Therefore the researchers addressed the limitation that treatment had only been tested in specialist centres delivered by highly trained staff. Eleven children in the experimental treatment group were matched to 11 children in a control group who received conventional school-based and individual interventions. Strong cognitive gains were made by children receiving treatment despite the fact that it was far less intensive than in the Lovaas studies and much smaller, but statistically significant, effects were recorded on symptom severity. After treatment all experimental subjects still met the diagnostic criteria for autism. On this occasion, the authors note several study limitations including the low intensity school-based nature of the control group, the confounding of treatment intensity and treatment type in the experimental group and difficulties in establishing treatment fidelity.

Other programmes based on behavioural principles have also been assessed with promising results, but similar limitations. Ozomoff & Cathcart (1998) evaluated the effectiveness of a well-established home-based intervention. In this case, parents were taught the principles and methods in the programme typically lasting 10 weeks with around 10 hours intervention per week. Eleven children were assigned to the treatment group and 11 matched children received their normal programme (nine attended specific programmes for children with autism and two attended non-categorical programmes). Progress in the treatment group was three to four times greater than in the control group on a range of outcome tests including abilities on imitation, perception, fine motor skills, gross motor skills, eye hand integration and cognitive performance. Follow up was only four months. Jocelyn *et al.* (1998) reported a randomised treatment study comparing an experimental treatment group of 16 children and a control group of 19 children. Treatment consisted of a 12-week programme of educational seminars and support with consultations to parents and childcare workers who also worked with the children. Results indicated that the experimental group improved over the control group on language skills and that their parents felt more in control of their children. Follow-up was only 12 weeks.

McConnell (2002) has similarly reviewed interventions designed to facilitate social interaction for young children with autism. As with other reviewers in these areas, he notes that studies are predominantly single-case designs but also records that the studies typically maintain the highest standards of internal validity and scientific integrity. He reviews five general categories of methodology: ecological variations, collateral skills interventions, child-specific interventions, peer behavioural interventions and comprehensive interventions. The 11 studies identified under the category of ecological variations suggest that simply locating children with autism with more competent peers does not increase social interaction. However some weak-to-moderate effects were noted in initiations received. The nine studies identified in collateral skills interventions again suggested some effects on increasing social interaction by activating natural processes for social development. However, again the effects were modest. Fifteen studies were identified under the category child-specific interventions, most frequently social skills training, and the author concluded that child-specific interventions increased social interaction and promoted generalisation in maintenance of improvements. However, since they focus more on social initiations, these interventions may be constrained regarding long-term effectiveness. Thirty studies were identified in the category of peer mediated interventions and treatment effects were consistently substantial and robust. Treatment effects generalised to untrained peers and novel situations and maintenance of improvements was extensive. Seven studies employed comprehensive interventions (two or more of the previous categories) and the evidence, though small, suggested significant effects with some evidence of generalisation to other settings. One study (Odom *et al.*, 1999) randomly assigned 98 pre-school children with a variety of disabilities including autism to five intervention conditions: ecological variation, child specific intervention, peer mediated intervention, comprehensive intervention and a control condition (pre-existing arrangements). At one-year follow-up only the peer-mediated condition demonstrated an effect in comparison to the control condition in terms of increased interaction. The authors considered that the comprehensive intervention may have been overly complex for a field trial with subsequent challenges on fidelity.

The work on treatment for children with autism is extensive and robust. There have been several reviews grading evidence, evaluating the best studies, making recommendations for future experimental and field trials and setting the work in a cultural, political and legal context. As has been pointed out, work has then been conducted addressing these criticisms. The available evidence suggests that interventions are effective although the criticisms of Gresham & MacMillan (1998) remain relevant. Indeed, because of the transparent and intensive nature of interventions, blind trials are impossible. However, efforts have been made to add randomised, controlled trials to the research literature. All of this work continues to attest to the effectiveness of interventions but the caution of Horner *et al.* (2002) regarding the publication of results, should be borne in mind.

COGNITIVE THERAPIES

Adapted versions of the cognitive therapies are being used increasingly with people with ID. It had been considered by earlier writers that methods for cognitive therapy would have to be adapted considerably in order to be understood clearly by individuals with mild ID (Kroese, 1997). However, more recent research suggests that with minor adaptations, simplification and so on, assessment and treatment are extremely similar to those seen in mainstream therapy. Dagnan & Sandhu (1999) used an adapted version of the Rosenberg Self-esteem Scale (Rosenberg, Schooler & Scoenbach, 1989) and the Gilbert & Allen (1994) Social Comparison Scale in a study of the impact of social comparison and self-esteem on depression in people with mild intellectual disabilities. Psychometric analysis of these scales indicated a factor structure that is consistent with the factor structure of the original scales when used in the mainstream population and a good level of internal and test/re-test reliability. Kellett *et al.* (2004) conducted a similar investigation using the Brief Symptom Inventory with 335 participants. Again they found a factor structure with a high degree of overlap with the original factor solution presented by the developers of the scale. Powell (2003) demonstrated a similar finding with the Beck Depression Inventory and the Zung Self-Rating Depression Scale. Given that these assessments show similar internal consistency, factor structure and so on when used with participants with ID, it suggests that assessment and treatment methods may not have to change substantially when used with this client group. Lindsay (1999) reviewed the existing published clinical material and noted that the essential structure of cognitive therapy remained the same with some simplification and adaptation. Therefore the major characteristics of assessment and form of cognitive therapy structures remain very similar with this client group.

At the outset it should be noted that people with intellectual disabilities form approximately the lowest 1 % of the population in terms of measured IQ. Below an IQ of approximately 65, represents less than the lowest 1 % of the population. Even within this relatively small group, there is an heterogeneity of ability ranging from individuals who can function normally in the community, perhaps with a little support, to profoundly handicapped individuals who will have no expressive language, have difficulty in feeding or dressing themselves and may be doubly incontinent. Cognitive therapies rely on verbal skills, ability to accurately report thoughts and feelings to weigh evidence and to engage in a variety of quite abstract verbal skills, such as Socratic reasoning. People with ID are specifically handicapped in these areas. Problems that require combinations of memory and verbal skills are likely to be specifically impaired. Sturmey (2004) has identified deficits in a range of cognitive, problem-solving, planning and memory strategies that may present difficulties for the implementation of cognitive therapy in this client group. He also notes that interviewing people with ID presents problems in relation to the reliability and validity of information obtained. Finlay & Lyons (2001) and Dagnan & Lindsay (2004) have elucidated a range of difficulties in interviewing including how interviewers ask questions, how they deal with acquiescence and nay saying, item content, response media and formats all of which may affect the information obtained from interviews. However, these authors also suggest simple modifications and solutions to overcome any difficulties.

Using these frameworks, Dagnan, Chadwick & Proudlove (2000) evaluated the cognitive/emotional skills of 19 men and 21 women with mild ID. They used cognitive emotional skills tests of recognising emotions from pictures with faces, describing the emotional state of participants and stories and identifying the emotional antecedents, beliefs and the subsequent behavioural consequences. They found that 75 % of participants could link beliefs, emotions and behaviours. However, only 10 % could do better than chance on choosing an emotion to match a situation and belief and only 25 % scored better than chance when choosing a belief given an emotion and a situation. The authors concluded that although people with mild ID have some prerequisite skills to engage in cognitive therapy, they would require preparatory training to learn many skills needed to participate, including understanding the idea of cognitive mediation. Sturmey (2004) notes that 'At this time we do not know what degree of competency of skill is needed in such tasks in order to achieve levels of competence that would permit effective participation in cognitive therapy.' This statement seems as true for mainstream populations as for populations with ID. In his review, Sturmey (2004) also notes that therapies based on applied behaviour analysis have been evaluated in the hundreds of big data based studies and three significant meta analyses (already mentioned) have endorsed their effectiveness.

The field in general suffers from a paucity of controlled investigations and there are few randomised controlled trials. In general, the field is developed with a large number of uncontrolled case investigations with weak experimental designs (for example, Lindsay et al., 1998). Therefore there are a significant number of case series reports on anxiety and depression. None of these achieve scientific respectability in relation to the Cochrane collaboration or EBP.

The one area that does now contain five controlled studies is that of anger and aggression. The cognitive therapy tested is that based on Novaco's analysis of anger and aggression, which emphasises the misinterpretation of internal and external cues, which leads to the individual perceiving threat in a situation which may be ambiguous or neutral. Novaco's (1975) model of anger expression and anger management has led to a three-phase anger treatment consisting of education about anger and understanding the relationship between anger and other emotions (phase one), perception of situations and emotional arousal in order to manage anger in general anger-provoking situations (phase two), and treatment involving specific, individual anger-provoking situations (phase three). An early controlled trial (Benson, Johnson Rice & Miranti, 1986) compared anger management treatment with other relaxation-based procedures both separately and in co-ordination. They found that four different treatment groups all improved in terms of anger management but that there was no differences between the groups. This study suffered for lack of a control group.

More recently there have been five further controlled studies all employing waiting list controls and all demonstrating the superiority of anger treatment (Lindsay et al., 2004; Rose, West & Clifford, 2000; Taylor et al., 2002; Taylor, Novaco, Guinan & Street, 2004; Willner et al., 2002). The Lindsay et al. study in particular has larger numbers with 33 participants receiving anger treatment and 14 waiting list controls and, in addition, subjects are followed up for up to four years both in terms of proximal measures of anger such as an anger provocation inventory and in terms of aggressive incidents both prosecuted and reported to the authors. Therefore, in the one area where there is more scientifically sound evidence, there are clear indications for the effectiveness of the cognitive treatment.

However, even in this area with the greatest scientific integrity, Sturmey (2004) has pointed out several serious shortcomings. Anger programmes include a number of non-cognitive procedures such as relaxation training, staff education and skill rehearsal. There are problems with treatment integrity, reliable independent variables, the design of case series, and social validity. He notes that there is a promising series of case studies using cognitive therapy for sex offenders but that included in their treatment are multi-component packages of relaxation, social, vocational and staff training alongside cognitive therapy (for example, Lindsay *et al.*, 2002). Therefore the cognitive therapies are confounded with other interventions. In terms of EBP, the work on cognitive therapy can only form a basis for future systematic better designed evaluations.

COUNSELLING

There is along tradition of the use of counselling with people with intellectual disabilities, especially with adults with mild and moderate intellectual disabilities. Prout & Novak-Drabik (2003) conducted a meta-analysis of counselling outcome studies with people with intellectual disabilities. They cast their net broadly and reviewed articles published between 1968 and 1998 from multiple databases, used a variety of synonyms and re-lated terms for intellectual disabilities and counselling and an operational definition of counselling. They identified an initial pool of 103 articles, which was reduced to a final group of 92 studies because of removal of studies that did not meet the criteria for the meta-analysis. They rated the studies' outcomes using a five-point Likert scale, which ranged from 1 for minimal change to 5 for marked change. They also calculated effect sizes. The average rating was approximately 3 indicating 'significant change'. The average effect size was 1.01 (range 0.06 to 1.85) but was only based on nine studies using suffi-cient subjects and group designs. They found that behavioural treatments were associated with significantly larger ratings of effectiveness than other forms of counselling. Prout & Noval-Drabik (2003, p. 87) concluded that 'psychotherapy with individuals who have mental retardation yields a moderate amount of change and is moderately effective or beneficial.'

This conclusion can be challenged. The authors include a list of the 92 papers included in their meta-analysis of counselling. A quick review of these references shows that the studies in the meta-analysis included the following counselling techniques: anger management, assertiveness training, social skills training, exposure treatment for obsessive compulsive disorder, desensitisation, relaxation training, cognitive therapy, group cognitive behaviour therapy, shaping, reinforcement of non-depressed behaviours and implosion. Hence, the possibility that the apparent effectiveness of counselling was due largely to the inclusion of traditional behaviour therapy cannot be excluded. At this time we must conclude that there are very limited data to support the use of counselling with people with intellectual disabilities.

SENSORY THERAPIES

Sensory therapies with people with severe and profound intellectual disabilities in popularity have increased since the mid-1990s. There are two main reasons for the increase. First, these individuals have relatively little language and sensory therapies do not require speech. Second, advocates of sensory therapy have noted that people with developmental disabilities are at greater risk for sensory and proprioceptive disorders and handicaps than the general population. There are a variety of sensory therapies that have been developed. They include sensory integration therapy (SIT), auditory integration therapy (AIT) and Snoezelen.

Sensory Integration Therapy

Sensory integration therapy is based on the hypothesis that some people with intellectual disabilities have a sensory deprivation and that maladaptive behaviours provide that missing stimulation. For example, self-injury might provide self-stimulation to the skin, muscles and joints. Sensory integration therapy is needed to provide this missing stimulation through massage, stimulation of the skin with brushing exercises and stimulation of the joints through deep massage and manipulation.

This approach has been extensively evaluated. Indeed, Vargas & Camilla (1999) conducted a meta-analysis of 16 SIT outcome studies. The overall effect size (ES) was small (ES = 0.290). Earlier, less well controlled studies reported larger ESs of 0.6. However, more recent, better controlled studies had effect sizes of essentially zero (0.09). Vargas and Camilla's meta-analysis appears to be a replication of the old phenomenon that novel poorly evaluated treatments appear to be promising, but often these promising effects disappear upon careful evaluation and appropriate control conditions.

Mason & Iwata (1990) evaluated the effects of SIT on three persons who displayed self-injurious behaviour (SIB). Analogue baselines indicated that in one subject SIB was maintained by attention. The rate of SIB depended upon the attention being either withheld or provided non-contingently during SIT. The second subject, whose SIB was maintained by automatic reinforcement, showed a systematic *increase* in the SIB during SIT. The third subject's SIB function to escape task demands. There was no difference in SIB during baselines with no demands and SIT sessions when there was also no demands. Mason & Iwata (1990) went on to compare SIT with differential reinforcement, which presumably did not provide additional sensory stimulation. For all three participants SIB was effectively reduced by reinforcement methods.

Lindsay *et al.* (1997, 2001) conducted a comparison of hand massage, physical therapy, Snoezelen and relaxation therapy with eight subjects using a counter balanced, crossover design. They found that hand massage and active therapy either produced no improvements in a range of measures or were mildly aversive.

These studies demonstrate that there is no evidence that SIT is an effective treatment. The last author has commonly observed the practice of providing SIT activities *contingent* upon maladaptive behaviours, rather than on a time-based schedule as SIT. Hence, it is possible that inappropriate application of SIT might inadvertently promote maladaptive behaviours in some persons with intellectual disabilities. At this time there are no data on this phenomenon, and hence it is unclear how commonly this occurs.

Auditory Integration Training

Auditory integration therapy (AIT) was based on the theory that behaviour problems in some people were due to supersensitivity to certain tones. Behaviour problems can be alleviated by dampening down these supersensitivities. In AIT, participants listen to 10 hours of modified music via headphones. Specific frequencies that the person is sensitive to are filtered out in order to reduce these hypothesised super-sensitivities.

Mudford *et al.* (2000) reported a double blind, crossover trial of AIT in 16 children with autism. Measures included parent and teacher ratings of behaviour, direct observational recordings, IQ, language and social/adaptive tests. The control condition was superior to AIT on parent behavioural measures. No significant differences were found on teacher measures. Parents could not detect when their children started on the AIT. There is no evidence that AIT reduces challenging behaviour and there are no reports of AIT causing harm to participants. However, the first author recalls that, during his training in the early 1970s, an outside expert attended a ward to review a multiply handicapped blind deaf young woman. During the course of the review he played excessively loud music through headphones in order to ascertain her sensitivity to sound and vibration. The woman became extremely excited by this procedure, which pleased the assessor because he had found some responsiveness and sensitivity in the woman. That evening, she bit through her bottom lip, permanently disfiguring her face. It seemed to the author at the time that it may have been a result of the stimulation that afternoon.

Music Therapy

Auditory integration therapy should not be confused with music therapy, for which there are some indications of modest individual benefits. Hooper & Lindsay (1990) and Hooper, Lindsay & Richardson (1991), using experimental designs borrowed from applied behaviour analysis, have shown improvements in interactional skills and reduction in behaviour problems during and after individual and group music therapy sessions. These changes were modest, but were not evident in a non-directive control condition, drinking tea with the therapist. However the experimental designs were not sufficiently robust and one cannot conclude that music therapy had any specific impact on behaviour.

Snoezelen

By far the most multi-sensory intervention is Snoezelen. The rationale is that it provides pleasant sensory experiences to promote relaxing leisure activities for individuals. It has been suggested that maladaptive behaviours, motivated by sensory consequences might decrease by the provision of sensory stimulation provided by Snoezelen. The multi-sensory environment (MSE) is designed with apparently pleasant sounds, lights and smells provided by special equipment such as fibre optic curtains, bubble tubes, the sound of water and birds and so on. The enabler (staff person) interacts with each participant in turn so that each participant receives equal time interacting with the enabler. The enabler assists the clients to have pleasant, enjoyable experiences with the MSE by interacting with the clients frequently. It has been hypothesised that Snoezelen might reduce maladaptive behaviours such as aggression and stereotypies and might improve mood and attention (Hulsegge & Verheul, 1987).

Several uncontrolled studies have suggested that persons with mental retardation might benefit from Snoezelen in some of the ways described above (Ashby *et al.*, 1995; DeBunsen,

1994; Hagger & Hutchinson, 1991). However, all of these studies lacked control conditions, and used non-blind measurement or retrospective data collection. Lindsay *et al.* (1997, 2001) in the study already described above found that although there were improvements in rated enjoyment and relaxation in the Snoezelen condition, they were no greater than those in the relaxation condition which was considerably less expensive to implement. Meijs-Roos (1990) in a study of six individuals found no effects from Snoezelen exposure on affective behaviour, stereotypies and other challenging behaviours. The best controlled study is that of Martin, Gaffan & Williams (1998) in which 27 adults with severe or profound intellectual disability participated. The two conditions evaluated were Snoezelen and a control condition. The control condition consisted of a similar shaped and sized room without the equipment, but with the enabler present interacting with the client non-contingently for an equal time. Observational data were collected on challenging behaviours outside the MSE and control conditions. No effects of MSE over the control condition was found on any measure. There was no evidence that challenging behaviours motivated by access to sensory stimulation reduced more than any other kinds of challenging behaviour.

Hogg *et al.* (2001) reviewed 16 publications on Snoezelen (there were 18 papers but two reported on data already published in other reports). Only seven studies adhered to recognisable research designs presenting their data in a clear fashion. They concluded that reports of positive effects of Snoezelen settings tended to occur in less formal studies and in more carefully designed studies the effects of Snoezelen were no greater than other sensory experiences. There was no substantive demonstration that the effects either generalised across situations or maintained over time. Hogg *et al.* (2001) are understanding in the difficulties experienced by those who wished to evaluate the effects of Snoezelen but still conclude that 'on the present balance of evidence, the use of Snoezelen as a first choice for dealing with challenging behaviours must be viewed as highly questionable' (Hogg *et al.*, 2001, p. 370). In the light of evidence reviewed previously for the robust effects of other psychological therapies, this conclusion can only be judged as benign.

Summary

The evidence demonstrates that sensory interventions are ineffective and sometimes causes increases in behavioural problems. It is possible that, depending on the function of SIB, the extra sensory input might inadvertently increase SIB or other challenging behaviours for some participants. Providing additional stimulation for persons who are already over aroused may be aversive and set the occasion for escape from that stimulation. Sensory interventions may also set the occasion for high rates of interaction or demands, or be an occasion when there are high rates of interaction. All of these mechanisms might increase escape motivation or attention maintained behaviour. We therefore urge caution because sensory input might sometimes cause harm to some participants. It may be that there are indeed groups of participants who benefit from extra sensory input but at this time we have no reliable method for evaluating who these participants might be.

CONCLUSIONS

Although extensive in its scope, this review has not addressed all prominent interventions in the field of ID. We have confined ourselves to therapeutic interventions rather than macro-environmental interventions. There is no doubt that the most influential political development in the field has been that of deinstitutionalisation. This has led to massive programmes of relocation of individuals from large institutions to community settings. This 'practice' has been extensively evaluated and has a comprehensive, scientific evidence base (Cummins & Lau, 2003; Emerson *et al.*, 2000; Felce, Lowe & Jones, 2002). As we outlined at the beginning, to review the whole field of ID and the evidence for the extensive range of practice is beyond the scope of a single chapter.

We have provided robust arguments that scientific integrity is not limited to randomised controlled trials but extends to well-controlled case studies. We have given several examples of such experimental rigour in individual case illustrations. As a result we have demonstrated that there is an extensive evidence base to evaluate psychological treatment for people with intellectual disabilities. The position that therapies have not been evaluated and no guidance is available is untrue.

The evidence base to support the use of behaviour therapy is massive, comprehensive and superior to the evidence base supporting any other kind of therapy. Behavioural approaches have also addressed a very wide range of problems. There is also convergence from numerous sources that behavioural interventions based on functional assessment and that involve manipulation of contingencies are associated with larger effect sizes. Although there is evidence for the effectiveness of PBS, that evidence base is somewhat weaker because of the more modest size of the available database. Future work on behavioural interventions should vigorously pursue topics such as mental health needs, generalisation, maintenance, social validity, and dissemination of effective technologies.

Although there is the beginning of an evidence base for cognitive therapy with people with intellectual disabilities, especially for anger management, it is much more limited. The possibility that the effects of cognitive therapy merely reflect the behavioural procedures contained in most treatment packages labelled 'cognitive therapy' has yet to be addressed (Sturmey, 2004). There is currently no convincing evidence base to support the use of counselling or sensory therapies with people with intellectual disabilities.

REFERENCES

Ashby, M., Lindsay, W.R., Pitcaithly, D., *et al.* (1995). Snoezelen: its effects on concentration and responsiveness in people with profound multiple handicaps. *British Journal of Occupational Therapy, 58,* 303–307.

Baer, D.M., Wolf, M.M. & Risley, T.R. (1968). Some current dimensions of applied behaviour analysis. *Journal of Applied Behaviour Analysis, 1,* 91–97.

Benson, B.A., Johnson Rice, C. & Miranti, S.V. (1986). Effects of anger management training with mentally retarded adults in group treatment. *Journal of Consulting in Clinical Psychology, 54,* 728–729.

Berkowitz, S., Sherry, P.J. & Davis, B.A. (1972). Teaching self feeding skills to profound retardates using reinforcement and fading procedures. *Behaviour Therapy, 2,* 62–71.

Campbell, J.M. (2003). Efficacy of behavioral interventions for reducing problem behavior in persons with autism. *Research in Departmental Diabities, 24,* 120–138.

Carr, E.G. & Durand, V.M. (1985). Reducing behaviour problems through functional communication training. *Journal of Applied Behaviour Analysis, 18,* 111–126.

Carr, E.G., Horner, R.H., Turnbell, A.P. *et al.* (1999). *Positive Behavior Support for People with Developmental Disabilities: A Research Synthesis.* Washington, DC: American Association on Mental Retardation.

Carr, J.E., Coriaty, S., Wilder, D.A. *et al.* (2000). A review of 'noncontingent' reinforcement as treatment for the aberrant behaviour of individuals with development disabilities. *Research in Development Disabilities, 21,* 377–391.

Chiesa, M. (1994). *Radical Behaviourism: The Philosophy and the Science.* Boston: Authors Co-operative Inc., Publishers.

Corrigan, P.W. (1991). Social skills training in adult psychiatric populations: A meta-analysis. *Journal of Behaviour Therapy and Experimental Psychiatry, 22,* 203–210.

Cummins, R.A. & Lau, A.L.D. (2003). Community integration or community exposure? A review and discussion in relation to people with an intellectual disability. *Journal of Applied Research in Intellectual Disabilities, 16,* 145–157.

Dagnan, D., Chadwick, P. & Proudlove, J. (2000). Towards an assessment of suitability of people with mental retardation for cognitive therapy. *Cognitive Therapy and Research, 24,* 627–636.

Dagnan, D. & Lindsay, W.R. (2004). Research paradigms in cognitive therapy. In E. Emerson, C. Hatton, T. Thompson & T. Parmenter. *International Handbook of Applied Research in Intellectual Disabilities.* Chichester: Wiley & Sons.

Dagnan, D. & Sandhu, S. (1999). Social comparison, self-esteem and depression in people with learning disabilities. *Journal of Intellectual Disability Research, 43,* 372–379.

DeBunsen, A. (1994). A study in the implication of the Snoezelen resource at Limington House School. *Sensations and Disability: Sensory Environments for Leisure, Snoezelen, Education and Therapy* (pp. 128–162). Chesterfield: Rompa.

Didden, R., Duker, P.C. & Korzilius, H. (1997). Meta-analytic study on treatment effectiveness for problem behaviours with individuals who have mental retardation. *American Journal of Mental Retardation, 101,* 387–399.

Drasgow, E., Halle, J.W. & Ostrosky, M.M. (1998). Effects of differential reinforcement on the generalisation of a replacement in three children with severe language delays. *Journal of Applied Behaviour Analysis, 31,* 357–374.

Emerson, E., Robertson, J., Gregory, N. *et al.* (2000). The quality and costs of community bases residential supports and residential campuses for people with severe and complex disabilities. *Journal of Intellectual and Developmental Disability, 25,* 263–279.

Felce, D., Lowe, K. & Jones, E. (2002). Association between the provision characteristics and operation of supported housing services and resident outcomes. *Journal of Applied Research in Intellectual Disabilities, 15,* 404–418.

Finlay, W.M. & Lyons, E. (2001). Methodological issues in interviewing and using self-report questionnaires with people with mental retardation. *Psychological Assessment, 13,* 319–335.

Fisher, W.W., Adelinis, J.D., Thompson, R.H. *et al.* (1998). Functional analysis and treatment of destructive behaviour maintained by termination of 'don't' (and symmetrical 'do') requests. *Journal of Applied Behaviour Analysis, 31,* 339–356.

Gilbert, P. & Allen, S. (1994). Assertiveness, submissive behaviour and social comparison. *British Journal of Clinical Psychology, 33,* 295–306.

Graff, R.B., Green, G. & Libby, M. (1998). The effects of two levels of treatment intensity on a young child with severe disabilities. *Behavioural Intervention, 13,* 21–41.

Gresham, F.M. & MacMillan, D.L. (1998). Early intervention project: can its claims be substantiated and its effects replicated? *Journal of Autism and Developmental Disorders, 28,* 5–13.

Hagger, L.E. & Hutchinson, R.B. (1991). Snoezelen: an approach to the provision of a leisure resource for people with profound and multiple handicaps. *Mental Handicap, 19,* 51–55.

Hagopian, L.P., Fisher, W.W., Sullivan, M.T. *et al.* (1998). Effectiveness of functional communication training with and without extinction and punishment: a summary of 21 in-patient cases. *Journal of Applied Behaviour Analysis, 31,* 211–235.

Hogg, J, Cavet, J., Lambe, L. & Smeddle, M. (2001). The use of Snoezelen as multisensory stimulation with people with intellectual disabilities: A review of the research. *Research in Developmental Disabilities, 22,* 353–372.

Hooper, J. & Lindsay, W.R. (1990). Music and the mentally handicapped: the effect of music on anxiety. *Journal of British Music Therapy, 4,* 18–26.

Hooper, J., Lindsay, W.R. & Richardson, I. (1991). Recreation and music therapy: An experimental study. *Journal of British Music Therapy, 5,* 10–13.

Horner, R.H. & Carr, E.G. (1997). Behavioural support for students with severe disabilities: Functional assessment and comprehensive intervention. *Journal of Special Education, 31,* 84–104.

Horner, R.H., Carr, E.G., Strain, P.S. *et al.* (2002). Problem behaviour interventions for young children with autism: A research synthesis. *Journal of Autism and Developmental Disorders, 32,* 423–446.

Hulsegge, J. & Verheul, A. (1987). *Snoezelen: Another World.* Chesterfield: Rompa.

Iwata, B.A., Dorsey, M.F., Slifer, K.J. *et al.* (1994). Towards a functional analysis of self-injury. *Journal of Applied Behaviour Analysis, 27,* 197–209. (Reprinted from Iwata, B.A., Dorsey, M.F., Slifer, K.J. *et al.* (1983). Towards a functional analysis of self-injury. *Analysis and Interventions in Developmental Disabilities, 2,* 3–20.)

Jocelyn, L.J., Casiro, O.G., Beattie, D. *et al.* (1998). Treatment of children with autism: A randomised controlled trial to evaluate a care giver based intervention programme in community day care centres. *Developmental & Behavioural Paediatrics, 19,* 326–334.

Kellett, S., Beail, N., Newman, D.W. & Hawes, A. (2004). The factor structure of the brief symptom inventory: intellectual disability evidence. *Clinical Psychology and Psychotherapy, 11,* 275–281.

Kroese, B.S. (1997). Cognitive behaviour therapy for people with learning disabilities: Conceptual and contextual issues. In B.S. Kroese, D. Dagnan & Loumidis, K. (eds), *Cognitive Behaviour Therapy for People with Learning Disabilities* (pp. 1–15). London: Routledge.

Kroese, B.S., Dagnan, D. & Loumidis, K. (1997). *Cognitive Behaviour Therapy for People with Learning Disabilities.* London: Routledge.

LaVigna, G.W. & Donnellan, A.M. (1986). *Alternatives to Punishment: Solving Behaviour Problems with Non-aversive Strategies.* New York: Irvington.

Lindsay, W.R. (1999). Cognitive therapy. *The Psychologist, 12,* 238–241.

Lindsay, W.R., Allan, R., Parry, C. *et al.* (2004). Anger and aggression in people with intellectual disabilities: Treatment and follow-up of consecutive referrals and a waiting list comparison. *Clinical Psychology and Psychotherapy, 11,* 255–264.

Lindsay, W.R., Black, E., Pitcaithly, D. *et al.* (2001). The effects of four therapy procedures on communication in people with profound intellectual disabilities. *Journal of Applied Research in Intellectual Disabilities, 14,* 111–119.

Lindsay, W.R., Olley, S., Jack, C. *et al.* (1998). The treatment of two stalkers with intellectual disabilities using a cognitive approach. *Journal of Applied Research in Intellectual Disabilities, 11,* 333–344.

Lindsay, W.R., Pitcaithly, D., Geelan, N. *et al.* (1997). A comparison of the effects of four therapy procedures on concentration and responsiveness in people with profound learning disabilities. *Journal of Intellectual Disability Research, 41,* 201–207.

Lindsay, W.R., Smith, A.H.W., Law, J. *et al.* (2002). A treatment service for sex offenders and abusers with intellectual disability: Characteristics of referrals and evaluation. *Journal of Applied Research in Intellectual Disability, 15,* 166–174.

Lovaas, O.I. (1987). Behavioural treatment and normal educational and intellectual functioning in young autistic children. *Journal of Consulting in Clinical Psychology, 55,* 3–9.

Martin, N.T., Gaffan, E.A. & Williams, T. (1998). Behavioural effects of long term multisensory stimulation. *British Journal of Clinical Psychology, 37,* 69–82.

Mason, S.A. & Iwata, B.A. (1990). Artifactual effects of sensory-integrative therapy on self-injurious behavior. *Journal of Applied Behavior Analysis, 23,* 361–370.

McConnell, S.R. (2002). Interventions to facilitate social interaction for young children with autism: review of available research and recommendations for educational intervention and future research. *Journal of Autism and Developmental Disorders, 32,* 351–372.

McEachin, J.J., Smith, T. & Lovaas, O.I. (1993). Long term outcome for children with autism who received early intensive behavioural treatment. *American Journal on Mental Retardation, 97,* 359–372.

Meijs-Roos, K. (1990). Effect van Snoezelen op het gedrag en kennelijk welbevinden van diepzwakzinnigen. *Nederlands Tijdschrift Voor Zwakzinnigenzorg, 7,* 144–150.

Miller, H.R., Patton, M.F. & Henton, K.R. (1972). Behaviour modification in a profoundly retarded child. *Behaviour Therapy, 2,* 275–284.

Mudford, B.A., Breen, S., Cullen, C. *et al.* (2000). Auditory integration training for children with autism: no behavioural benefits detected. *American Journal on Mental Retardation, 105,* 118–129.

New York Department of Health (1999a). *Clinical Practice Guidelines: Report of the Recommendations. Autism/Pervasive Developmental Disorders. Assessment and Intervention for Young Children (Age 0–3 Year).* Publication number 4215. Albany: New York Department of Health.

New York Department of Health (1999b). *Clinical Practice Guidelines: Quick Reference Guide. Autism/Pervasive Developmental Disorders. Assessment and Intervention for Young Children (Age 0–3 Year)*. Publication number 4216. Albany: New York Department of Health.

New York Department of Health (1999c). *Clinical Practice Guidelines: The Guideline Technical Report. Autism/Pervasive Developmental Disorders. Assessment and Intervention for Young Children (Age 0–3 Year)*. Publication number 4217. Albany: New York Department of Health.

Novaco, R.W. (1975). *Anger Control: The Development and Evaluation of An Experimental Treatment*. Lexington, MA: Heath.

Odom, S.L., McConnell, S.R., McEvoy, M.A. *et al.* (1999). Relative effects of interventions supporting the social competence of young children with disabilities. *Topics in Early Childhood Special Education, 19,* 75–91.

Ozomoff, S. & Cathcart, K. (1998). Effectiveness of a home programme intervention for young children with autism. *Journal of Autism and Developmental Disorders, 28,* 25–32.

Powell, R. (2003). Psychometric properties of the Beck Depression Inventory and the Self Report Scale on adults with mental retardation. *Mental Retardation, 41,* 88–95.

Prout, H.T. & Novak-Drabik, K.M. (2003). Psychotherapy with persons who have mental retardation: An evaluation of effectiveness. *American Journal on Mental Retardation, 108,* 82–93.

Rose, J., West, C. & Clifford, D. (2000). Group interventions for anger and people with intellectual disabilities. *Research in Developmental Disabilities, 21,* 171–181.

Rosenberg, M., Schooler, S. & Scoenbach, C. (1989). Self-esteem and adolescent problems: Modelling reciprocal effects. *American Sociological Review, 54,* 1004–1016.

Rush, A.J. & Frances, A. (eds) (2000). Expert consensus guideline series. treatment of psychiatric and behavioural problems in mental retardation. *American Journal on Mental Retardation, 105,* 159–228.

Scotti, J.R., Evans, I.M., Meyer, L.H. & Walker, P. (1991). A meta-analysis of intervention research with problem behaviour: treatment validity and standards of practice. *American Journal on Mental Retardation, 96,* 233–256.

Sheinkopf, S.J. & Siegel, B. (1998). Home based behavioural treatment of young children with autism. *Journal of Autism and Developmental Disorders, 28,* 15–23.

Smith, T. & Lovaas, O.I. (1997). The UCLA young autism project: A reply to Gresham and MacMillan. *Behavioural Disorders, 22,* 202–218.

Smith, T., McEachin, J. & Lovaas, O.I. (1993). Comments on replication and evaluation of outcome. *American Journal on Mental Retardation, 97,* 385–391.

Sturmey, P. (2004). Cognitive therapy with people with intellectual disabilities: A selective review and critique. *Clinical Psychology & Psychotherapy, 11,* 223–232.

Taylor, J.L., Novaco, R.W., Gillmer, B. & Thorne, I. (2002). Cognitive behavioural treatment of anger intensity among offenders with intellectual disabilities. *Journal of Applied Research in Intellectual Disabilities, 15,* 151–165.

Taylor, J.L., Novaco, R.W., Guinan, C. & Street, N. (2004). Development of an imaginal provocation test to evaluate treatment for anger problems in people with intellectual disabilities. *Clinical Psychology and Psychotherapy, 11,* 233–246.

Thompson, R.H., Fisher, W.W., Piazza, C.C. & Kuhn, D.E. (1998). The evaluation and treatment of aggression maintained by attention and automatic reinforcement. *Journal of Applied Behaviour Analysis, 31,* 103–116.

Towell, R. (2003). Psychometric properties of the Beck Depression Inventory and the Zung Self Rating Depression Scale in adults with mental retardation. *Mental Retardation, 41,* 88–95.

Vargas, S. & Camilla, G. (1999). A meta-analysis of research on sensory integration treatment. *American Journal of Occupational Therapy, 53,* 189–198.

Willner, P., Jones, J., Tams, R. & Green, G. (2002). A randomised controlled trial of the efficacy of a cognitive behavioural anger management group for clients with learning disabilities. *Journal of Applied Research in Intellectual Disabilities, 15,* 244–253.

Wolf, M. (1978). Social validity: the case for subjective measurement or how applied behaviour analysis is finding its heart. *Journal of Applied Behaviour Analysis, 11,* 203–214.

Wolf, M., Risley, T. & Mees, H. (1964). Application of operant conditioning procedures to the behaviour problems of an autistic child. *Behaviour Research in Therapy, 1,* 305–312.

CHAPTER 13

Anger and Forensic Problems

Mark C. Ramm

The Orchard Clinic, Edinburgh, UK

and

Stanley J. Renwick

Care Principles, York, UK

GENERAL CONSIDERATIONS

It is commonly asserted that, as a subject of academic interest and clinical consideration, anger has not enjoyed the attention that it manifestly deserves (Siegman & Smith, 1994). This is apparent not only within the psychological literature but also psycho-biological literature (Anderson & Silver, 1998). This despite the fact that, experienced as a transient emotion (Novaco, 1975), it is woven into the fabric of our daily circumstances in just the same fashion as any of the other primary emotions. Why this should be so has been the subject of much conjecture. It has, for example, been proposed that it reflects the duality of functional consequences that arise from anger, involving both positive and negative characteristics. Hence, anger is associated with a host of problematic consequences such as loss of personal controls, compromise of critical reasoning faculties, negative health effects and relationship problems. Such an array of difficulties perhaps helps explain the antiquarian view of anger as a base emotion (Novaco, 1994b). In contrast to other domains of emotional difficulty, however, anger has counterbalancing positive characteristics such as the capacity to energise, mobilise, signal emotional state and restore perceived control in situations of threat or challenge.

In this context, we consider it likely that our tendency to ambivalence regarding this emotion is reflective of this complexity, and the problems in disentangling the positive and negative components of the presentation. Specifically, we postulate that people have an understandable tendency to suspect some wilful intent on the part of an angry person or patient, even in the face of protestations about loss of control!

This characterisation of dyscontrol lies without question at the heart of the perceived significance of specialist interventions/treatments for anger. The critical assumption is that persistent failures to control anger arousal and reactivity and/or exaggerated reactivity in the face of (direct or indirect) provocation, characterise people who experience an anger problem. Any view of such behaviour as wilful therefore implies presence, not absence, of control. This, and similar attributional processes become apparent in the clinical arena, where such patients are often viewed as ambivalent, unmotivated, resentful, unhelpful, and ungrateful (Novaco, Ramm & Black, 2001; Renwick *et al.*, 1997). This may occur even when there is a clinical awareness of just how threatening and challenging our interventions are likely to be viewed by our clients!

Such difficulties are all the more surprising given the significant contribution that anger makes across the spectrum of psychiatric/psychological disorders. Hence, anger is acknowledged to contribute to a range of disorders across the Axis I and II domains. It is indicated in such diverse populations as those suffering from depression (Novaco, 1977), post-traumatic stress disorder (PTSD) (Novaco & Chemtob, 1998), psychotic disorders (Haddock *et al.*, 2004), individuals with learning difficulties (Taylor *et al.*, 2002, 2005), disorders of personality (Dahlen & Deffenbacher, 2001; Jones & Hollin, 2004; Linehan, 1993; McMurran *et al.*, 2001), eating disorders (Fassino *et al.*, 2003) and childhood disorders such as attention deficit hyperactivity disorder (ADHD) (Sukhodolsky, Kassinove & Gorman, 2004).

Similarly, difficulties can be seen to emerge across the age spectrum, from children (Sukhodolsky, Kassinove & Gorman, 2004) and adolescents (Feindler & Ecton, 1986) through to elderly populations (Renwick, Fox & Edwards, 2002).

Despite the above, the status of anger as a clinical problem has been derived from its association in forensic contexts with aggressive behaviour (Novaco, 1994a) – that is, as a causal determinant of aggression and violence. Indeed, in many respects, the nature and extent of this causal relationship is critical to any review or consideration of practice analyses for it is generally acknowledged that anger and aggression are neither synonymous nor unidirectionally or unerringly related. This places considerable challenges on the shoulders of those implementing anger programmes as a means of achieving reductions in violent offences. Given this, it is perhaps surprising that so little attention appears to have been paid within the forensic literature to substantiating the nature and extent of this association. Of particular salience therefore, has arguably been the work on anger as part of the MacArthur (Violence) Risk Assessment Programme (Grisso *et al.*, 2000; Monahan & Steadman, 1994; Novaco, 1994a) as well as our own work with mentally disordered populations (Novaco & Renwick, 1998, 2002). Such work retrospectively, concurrently and prospectively has supported the salience of anger as a potentiator of violence and violence risk in these forensic populations (cf. McNeil, Eisner & Binder, 2003).

Consideration of pertinent literature within the anger domain highlights the degree to which surprisingly little attention has been paid, thus far, to matters of nosology. This is despite the fact that clinical and personal experiences accord with the view that anger, both in terms of expression and exposure, is in fact a matter of much complexity and heterogeneity. That is, the circumstances that provoke us, the cognitive attributional processes that mediate our reactions, our emotional and behavioural responses, all can range in form and content in a most dynamic fashion and often as a result of powerful contextual drivers. This is clearly evident in client reports of the circumstances where problems of dyscontrol have (or indeed have not) been manifest. And yet, this diversity of process and presentation is arguably not well represented in current clinical and academic analyses. Some efforts have been made in this regard (as we will argue later) but it must be cautioned that developments in assessment, therapeutic intervention and subsequent outcome evaluation have often either implicitly or indeed explicitly made an assumption of homogeneity. That is, that everyone presenting as having an anger problem is roughly equivalent in respect of such problems and can be broadly treated in the same manner.

This is most graphically highlighted in the apparent failure within the literature to agree appropriate criteria for a pathognomic state of anger. As previously stated, this perhaps arises as a consequence of anger's absence from the main diagnostic systems (DSM and ICD). This clearly constitutes less of a difficulty for those therapists and therapies that construe anger as an embedded feature of broader primary disorders. For those whose conceptualisation and interventions are based upon a 'discrete-entity' perspective, this is a major challenge. This uncertainty permeates the assessment, intervention and outcome literature, with the attendant consequence of making critical comparison and evaluation problematic. Practitioners new to the field therefore have to be mindful of the possibility that study populations may or may not reach clinical 'caseness' criteria (even if this is just defined in terms of the judgement of a reasonable practitioner). If sample populations do not, then we would argue that the potential contribution of such work to the clinical literature is likely to be severely limited. Sadly, we caution that much of the current US-based work, being predominantly undergraduate student based, may fall into this category (for example, Deffenbacher, Demm & Brandon, 1986; Del Veccio & O'Leary, 2004; Rimm et al., 1971).

Efforts to address this concern can be seen to fall into two categories. The first is the establishment of normative-derived standardised assessment measures. A comprehensive review of such material is clearly beyond the scope of the present analysis but it is indisputable that the two major contributions to the field are the Spielberger State-Trait Anger Expression Inventory (STAXI) (Spielberger, 1996) and the Novaco Anger Scale-Provocation Inventory (NAS-PI) (Novaco, 1994a, 2003). Within the limitations of self-reporting, both measures confer the benefits of being able to quantify global degrees of anger difficulty and also provide the opportunity to consider different constituent aspects of an individual's anger problem. The STAXI offers a number of potentially salient aspects of anger (for example, Anger-in, Anger-out or Anger Expression), which can be seen (at least in part) as an attempt to address the nosological challenges raised previously. In contrast, the NAS-PI has been structured to mirror the constituent treatment components underpinning Novaco's (1975, 1977) treatment approach (described below).

Sadly, as we will see, the feedthrough of such assets to treatment development and implementation and, indeed, outcome evaluation, appears somewhat restricted. Even when the utility of such measures is recognised, their use appears to have been predominantly focussed upon relatively crude indication of global change, with the implicit assumption that broadly similar degrees of change across individuals represents the same thing for everyone (i.e. the homogeneity assumption). Ironically the principles obviously driving the development of these measures clearly reflect the converse! There is much need for further conceptual development in this area.

The alternative approach to the 'pathology' problem that has been apparent is the call to current psychiatric diagnostic systems to embrace the anger construct directly and hence to provide agreed diagnostic criteria in line with mainstream psychological disorders/syndromes. Although such a move would signal a fairly radical departure from current convention, the development and adoption of PTSD into the psychiatric lexicon reflects how this can be achieved. Such is the enthusiasm of some advocates that 'shadow' criteria have already been proposed outlining how such a diagnostic array might be configured (Eckhart & Deffenbacher, 1995). Though commendable, current proposals appear to reflect a relatively crude adaptation of other Axis I models rather than the process of consensual decision making favoured by, for example, the DSM committees. Certainly, there is little evidence that researchers and practitioners are starting to adopt these criteria in their practice. Nonetheless we commend continuing work on the development of such ideas.

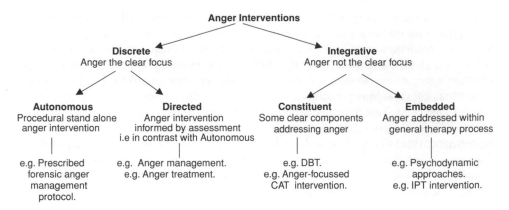

Figure 13.1   A classification system for anger interventions.

Where, then, is one left in addressing the critical questions of when is an anger problem actually an anger problem and how should it best be treated? We believe that, given the areas of uncertainty described above, the most practical solution is to progress an individualised formulation-based approach to intervention. Such an approach could realistically be underpinned by standardised assessments and, indeed, shadow diagnostic criteria but would also make use of detailed aetiological and behavioural evidence to provide a bespoke profile of difficulties in respect of individual clients. This would include consideration of problem intensity, duration, chronicity and severity. We consider this the gold standard in current (individual and group) practice in anger interventions and, as such, published analyses should be evaluated against this yardstick.

This is particularly so given that we believe that the typology problem is best resolved by considering anger disorder as a broad-spectrum disorder, ranging from 'normal' expression and experience of anger, through varying co-morbid contributions to psychopathological states, and finally to more discrete and enduring predominant anger problems. Such a proposal carries the double-edged implication that, although it is arguably more ecologically valid (according with clinical experience) and makes accessible a broader range of clinical activity for consideration, it raises the requirement to offer sufficiently sophisticated mechanisms of assessment of complex anger (as indicated above) and also systems to categorise the diversity of (current) relevant treatment interventions. As described previously, as yet no such agreed categorisation has been generated. We therefore argue that one parsimonious solution is provided by the framework described in Figure 13.1. We believe that classifying therapies within a general continuum (from discrete to integrative) offers a means of capturing and evaluating the rich array of clinical work brought to bear on this most complex of clinical phenomena.

APPROACHES TO THERAPY

Discrete Anger Therapy

In Discrete approaches anger is identified as the clear focus of the therapy and it is broadly separated from other clinical issues or problems in intervention. This is so even when it is adjunctive to a wider programme of therapy. Discrete approaches are sub-classified as Discrete/Directed if the nature and scope of intervention is guided by assessment, or as Discrete/Autonomous if assessment is minimal and the intervention is delivered on an inflexible and stand alone basis. The latter includes several large scale programmes delivered within criminal justice systems targeting offenders with a history of aggression and violence, but with little or no assessment of anger variables.

Most of the literature in this domain refers to a wide spectrum of therapies comprising a mix of approaches and components. Broadly, most follow a cognitive-behavioural orientation. Although much of this has remained true to the cognitive framework classically advanced by Beck (Deffenbacher *et al.*, 2000), without question the most influential intervention system in this area has been provided by Novaco (1975, 1977, 1994b).

Novaco proposes that the anger experience is a function of four dimensions that interact over time:

- External events;
- Cognitive appraisals;
- Physiological arousal; and
- Behavioural reactions.

The time-line analysis is helpful for seeing how provocations may result in anger-mediated responses and identifies points in this sequence at which interventions might be appropriate.

Consistent with this model, Novaco's (1975, 1977) early cognitive-behavioural 'anger management' therapy consisted of a multi-component therapy package seeking to target each of the four identified dimensions. The therapy components were organised within Michenbaum's (1975, 1985) stress inoculation phases of treatment (Michenbaum & Novaco, 1978; Novaco, 1977):

1. The 'cognitive preparation phase' is predominantly educational in that the client learns about the nature of anger and the therapeutic rationale. More is also learned about client's anger patterns, by both the client and the therapist, through active monitoring and reflection. This involves the use of anger diaries and the constructing of personal hierarchies of provoking situations or triggers for anger.
2. The 'skills acquisition phase' involves the client learning new ways of coping, which may help anger to be managed more effectively. These skills include utilising arousal control techniques, cognitive restructuring, problem solving, self-instruction techniques and alternative behavioural responses. In general it involves the modelling and rehearsal of these cognitive, affective and behavioural techniques.
3. The 'application training phase' encourages clients to use their new understanding and skills. This can be done through imaginal visualisation, scenario role-play, and *in vivo* implementation of acquired skills.

Generally, prototypic 'anger management' packages can be characterised as discrete, time-limited, protocol-driven interventions that are essentially psycho-educational in nature. As they are tailored more to problem areas than the specific needs of individual clients, they can often be implemented with a minimal degree of participant assessment. Equally, participation can require a lower level of personal investment and disclosure than other interventions. The therapy provides information concerning the nature of anger and attempts to instil new skills and solutions for critical incident management. The methods typically involve explicit step-by-step instruction of new skills, modelling, role-playing, feedback to help shape new behaviours and skills, and personal assignments to practice these skills. The aim of all such therapy is to develop preventative, regulatory and response focussed anger-control skills.

Although much work in the literature is subsumed under the heading of anger management the exact nature and content of these approaches often varies widely in practice. The basic format has understandably been adapted considerably to meet the needs of populations with distinctive issues and/or the constraints or demands of the clinical setting or practitioner preference. Apart from being delivered in either individual or group formats, one of the most evident differences has been in terms of therapy length. The length of a session can vary widely and so can the number of sessions. The number of sessions typically range between six (Dangel, Deschner & Rasp, 1989; Stermac, 1986) and 24 or 25 (Dowden, 1999; Winogron, 1997) with an average of about 12 sessions (DiGiuseppe & Tafrate, 2003). However, even two-session interventions have been explored (McDougall *et al.*, 1990; Munro & McPherson, 2001) and the presence or absence of additional booster or relapse prevention sessions is also relevant (Dowden, Antonowicz & Andrews, 2003). Now self-administered computerised anger programmes are also beginning to appear in the literature (Bosworth, Espelage & DuBay, 1998) although these have not yet been applied to clinical populations. Such differences make simple comparison problematic.

It is of note that even in the face of increasing recognition that 50 to 100^+ hours of therapy may be necessary to make significant gains with individuals who have complex clinical and forensic anger problems (Howells *et al.*, 2005), some authors continue to argue that interventions in excess of eight sessions may be inefficient or even counterproductive (Glancy & Saini, 2005). Determination of such matters has yet to be achieved.

Across such approaches, however, there does appear to be a consensus that the cognitive, arousal and behavioural domains are all systemically important to the instigation and expression of anger, and hence they use variations of the Novaco-style multi-component intervention. Again, however, they may differ in terms of the emphasis given to a particular domain or strategy. Some may be almost entirely educational or insight-based in nature, with the presumption that new information will lead to positive change. Others place predominant focus on cognition and cognitive restructuring or arousal control or exposure-based techniques to weaken the bond between stimulus and response. Some may emphasise behavioural skills enhancement. Thus, although most practitioners have tended to follow a Novaco-esque multi-modal CBT approach, it should be cautioned that no two programmes are likely to comprise the same elements in equivalent fashion. This can be viewed as problematic but it is at least consistent with models of emotional regulation that recognise the existence of multiple pathways towards the experience and expression of emotion (Power & Dalgleish, 1999; Teasdale, 1999). For some individuals anger seems predominantly shaped by their appraisals and attributions; for others it may be more automatic. Alternatively, pathways of activation may be situationally triggered. However, rarely are clients assessed, or offered one therapy as opposed to another, with such issues in mind.

In noting that not all cognitive behaviour therapy (CBT)-based interventions are the same, we have argued (Ramm, 1998) that this is not just about chosen constituents but also reflects differing levels of complexity, modalities of delivery and degree of tailoring to individual client need. In this regard, Novaco, Ramm & Black (2001) make a critical distinction between 'anger management' and 'anger treatment', the latter reflecting this more idiographic approach to assessment and content.

'Anger treatment' therefore describes those interventions that are substantially informed and directed by assessment and therefore result in a much more bespoke and intensive approach to therapy. This includes the integration of assessment and treatment activities; investment in the therapeutic relationship and motivational processes; a greater focus on formative experiences; targeting enduring change in cognitive, arousal and behavioural systems; and addressing distressed emotions (anxiety, sadness, anger) in the therapeutic arena. As we have previously discussed, this necessitates a more formulation-driven, interactive and more intensive therapy, clearly requiring more client contact. Although many of the methods found in 'anger management' may be used, these may involve more intensive application and augmentation. This may follow an identified protocol and be delivered in individual or group format but requires a relatively high degree of psychological sophistication by therapists in order to tailor treatment to individual patient need. This requires specialist therapist training and appropriate ongoing supervision.

In contrast to CBT, there are few reports of psycho-dynamic or analytic interventions being used as Discrete interventions for anger problems (Lanza *et al.*, 2002; Quayle & Moore, 1998).

Integrative Anger Therapy

Integrative anger approaches do not identify anger as the focus of therapy. They are sub classified as Integrative/Embedded if addressing anger is in fact subsumed within a larger therapy process, or as Integrative/Constituent if addressing anger can still be seen a clear component of a larger, more general therapy.

The predominant 'Integrative' approaches are various forms of psychoanalytic therapy. These are of particular interest because anger features as an important factor in many complex psychodynamic formulations of human functioning and distress (Fairburn, 1978; Freud, 1912; Kernberg, 1992; Klein, 1957; Kohut, 1978, 1984 and Winnicott, 1958) and is explored in relation to key constructs such as 'transference', 'attachment', 'repression', and 'projection' issues.

Despite this, anger rarely enjoys specific consideration in psychoanalytic literature, perhaps because it is often understood as being an undifferentiated process rather than isolated for particular attention. Because addressing anger is usually 'Embedded' in the therapy process, it is not considered in the focussed fashion that is common in other approaches (such as CBT). Secondly, angry-aggressive individuals are likely to find engagement in most forms of psychodynamic psychotherapy difficult, as the therapeutic style and content may serve to magnify perceptions of being challenged or judged and lead quickly to deep resentment towards the therapist. Despite this, it is our view that either directly or (more likely) indirectly, these orientations may have much more to contribute to this area than is conventionally recognised. This is especially so in the conceptualisation and operationalisation of key process elements (such as the therapeutic relationship) in therapy, and the treatment of anger problems that do not manifest themselves in overt aggression towards others (for example, passive aggression; unacknowledged anger; anger towards the self).

Other forms of Integrative interventions that address anger also exist. One example is interpersonal therapy (IPT) (Klerman *et al.*, 1984), which is now acknowledged as being directly applicable to various forms of emotional distress (Stuart & Robertson, 2003; Weissman *et al.*, 2000). In this context, it can be described as an Integrative/Embedded therapy because, although anger may be acknowledged within the therapy, rather than focussing on it directly, it is addressed through broader therapeutic processes. In the case of IPT, this process is a collaborative attempt to reduce psychological symptoms by targeting relationship difficulties. This focus on the interpersonal dimension is arguably salient to anger (since anger is generally an interpersonal emotion) but IPT, like other integrative therapies, can hardly be described as an 'anger treatment'.

When constituent components for addressing anger can still be identified within a broader integrative intervention, these can be termed 'Integrative/Constituent' anger interventions. It is argued that the application of CBT elements to address anger within a broader CBT intervention, or the targeting of specific anger-related 'procedures' within a Cognitive Analytic Therapy (Ryle & Kerr, 2002), or modules to develop specific anger coping skills within Dialectical Behaviour Therapy (DBT) (Linehan, 1993), all potentially constitute 'Integrative/Constituent' anger interventions.

REVIEW OF ANGER TREATMENT OUTCOMES

The challenge in making sense of the array of relevant outcome studies has been made much easier due to the increasing number of pertinent meta-analyses that are now published (for example, Beck & Fernandez, 1998; Del Vecchio & O'Leary, 2004; DiGiuseppe & Tafrate, 2003; Edmonson & Conger, 1996; Tafrate, 1995). Perhaps it is no surprise that such work has reviewed the field from a predominantly CBT standpoint with outcome research focussing particularly on group therapy interventions for anger and aggression. Whereas the consistent findings appear to be moderate to strong effect sizes for CBT-based procedures, consideration of inclusion criteria and other procedural characteristics render direct comparison between the different analyses highly problematic. Hence, for example, whilst acknowledging the contribution of the previous reviewers, Del Vecchio & O'Leary (2004) are critical of this earlier work for a number of reasons. These reflect concerns regarding the 'caseness' of sample populations, selection of only published studies, conceptual confusion about the anger construct itself and finally the homogeneity of the study populations covered by the analysis. In order to address some of these concerns in their own study, they focussed exclusively on adult outpatients whose 'caseness' rested on scores on standardised measures. As a result of such restrictions almost three-quarters of the papers included involved (routinely self-selecting) undergraduate students. Strangely, this powerful bias did not appear to concern the authors, although they at least acknowledged that these papers were almost exclusively drawn from the same laboratory!

In order to make sense of this confusing picture, we earlier proposed a classification of approaches into four distinct classes: 'Discrete/Autonomous'; 'Discrete/Directed'; 'Integrative/Constituent'; 'Integrative/Embedded' (Figure 13.1). The remainder of our consideration of outcome evidence will use these in the hope of assisting comparison.

Discrete Anger Therapy Outcome

The bulk of the programmatic approaches to anger management and treatment appear to fall into this class of activities and the evidence presented in a number of the meta-analyses (Beck & Fernandez, 1998; Edmonson & Conger, 1996; Tafrate, 1995) generally support the broad efficacy of Directed anger treatment approaches. The strongest evidence relates to Discrete/Directed applications where there has been some clinical assessment/diagnosis of (various offender or non-offender populations) and an informed application of anger techniques (particularly 'anger management' and 'anger treatment').

Additional, evidence has been presented regarding mentally ill (Haddock *et al.*, 2004) and mentally disordered offender populations (Renwick *et al.*, 1997) which attests to the potential utility of anger treatment with patients diagnosed with serious mental illness. Indeed with respect to the latter, material in preparation from work at the State Hospital in Scotland (Ramm & Novaco, 2003) confirms substantial treatment gains and behavioural change with such patients following anger treatment interventions. Although clearly an area of significance to both practitioners and legislators (Novaco, 1996), as yet there appears to have been insufficient work to justify specific meta-analytical review. Certainly, this is an area requiring further development.

Equally pertinent to this Directed application of anger techniques is activity undertaken in respect of child and adolescent populations (Dangel, Deschner & Rasp, 1989; Lochman, Barry & Pardini, 2003; Sharry & Owens, 2000). Much of the outcome analyses in this domain has been subject to recent meta-analytic review (Sukhodolsky, Kassinove & Gorman, 2004). Evidence found the mean effect size was in the 'medium' range and broadly consistent with other psychotherapeutic interventions with this population. Their analysis of both component and multi-modal approaches, concluded that the latter produced greater treatment gains in respect of aggressive behaviour and interpersonal functioning.

Work falling under the Discrete/Autonomous descriptor has predominantly consisted of procedural programatic anger management packages with general inclusion criteria. In the US this has almost exclusively involved outpatient student samples; by contrast, elsewhere (especially the UK and Australia), the majority of the activity has been centred around mainstream offender populations (Ireland, 2004; Law, 1997; Munro & MacPherson, 2001; Towl, 1995; Towl & Dexter, 1994). In respect of the latter, the body of published material covering this field is certainly heterogeneous in respect of a number of critical issues, including client characteristics, programme content and outcome evidence. Overall, therefore, we would wish to sound a fairly cautious note regarding any conclusions that can be drawn, other than self-evidently anger management cannot be applied as a universal remedy for violent offending. It has been concluded that the routine allocation of violent offenders to a common anger intervention package may be counter-productive and wasteful of resources (Howells *et al.*, 1997; Travis, 2006). Therefore, some criminal justice models of intervention may benefit from incorporating elements of the Discrete/Directed approach found more readily in mental health, which emphasises individual assessment, formulation and treatment planning (Howells, Day & Thomas-Peter, 2004). Again, much systematic work requires to be undertaken to provide clarity in a clearly critical area.

Integrative Anger Therapy Outcome

This class of activities was sub-divided into Embedded and Constituent. Integrative Embedded describes those (often unreported) circumstances where anger issues emerge during the course of more general psychotherapeutic intervention, and are construed as an aspect of the case formulation. In this context, it is commonly the case that the anger aspect of formulation and treatment remains unreported, minimised or undifferentiated. As a result of this (and for other reasons), adherents of such approaches have abstained from conducting empirical examination in this area. We have argued above that this can be seen to typify more traditional psychodynamic psychoanalytic orientations but this is by no means exclusive to this approach. Thus for example, conventional CBT-based approaches towards the assessment and treatment of PTSD (for example, Foa, Steketee & Olasov-Rothbaum, 1989) continue to underestimate the significance of anger, despite compelling evidence regarding its salience (Gerlock, 1994; Novaco & Chemtob, 1998).

By contrast, the term Integrative/Constituent was used to describe those circumstances where addressing anger, although remaining integrated within broader therapeutic activity, is more clearly delineated. Examples of such an approach can be found within both the psychoanalytic and cognitive behavioural literatures but, as yet, the only systematic outcome evidence that falls into this category comprises 'component' CBT procedures for addressing client anger difficulties. In this regard evidence has been accrued indicating the utility of relaxation procedures (O'Donnell & Worell, 1973), exposure-based procedures (Brondolo, DiGuiseppe & Tafrate, 1997; Grodnitzky & Tafrate, 2000); systematic desensitisation (Rimm *et al.*, 1971) and cognitive-based techniques (Dahlen & Deffenbacher, 2000; Tafrate & Kassinove, 1998). It is to be noted that this work has, again, predominantly involved student samples, hence its application to more serious clinical populations cannot be assured.

IMPLICATIONS AND FUTURE DIRECTIONS

It would appear that anger interventions have a general tendency to benefit the client but it is not at all clear what else can be confidently asserted! It is our contention that much of the work in the field at present is predicated upon simplistic assumptions that do not survive contact with the client. Alternatively, it is our experience that anger constitutes a complex problem, which requires a similar complexity of response. As such there would appear to be a number of critical issues that the practitioner can and should address when considering the needs of an angry client:

- *Selection.* It is clear from the above that attempts to treat anger may not be appropriate and efforts to evaluate outcome will be limited, unless valid methods are used to establish the presence of a clinically significant anger dyscontrol problem. Further, it must be acknowledged in the provision of anger interventions that no two individuals are likely to be equivalent in respect of their anger problems. At present, however, one might assume the opposite, given that most intervention programmes following rigid collective goals and activities. Equally, the manner in which intervention is often rigidly structured assumes that all anger problems are optimally resolvable in equivalent fashion. Clinical experience tells a different story. This is why we have previously advocated a formulation-based approach to selection for (either individual or group) intervention and determining the appropriate balance of therapeutic elements required to achieve progress. Furthermore, it permits due consideration (where relevant) of wider process considerations such as the effects different participants may have on each other in group settings. In our view, this is the assessment gold standard and it is chastening to realise how many programmes have either cursory or no assessment process at all.
- *Intervention.* What is clear from the preceding review is that insufficient attention is often paid to the detailed elements of therapy and appropriate contrast and comparison with other approaches. Hence, it is very difficult to confidently compare two different programmes even when they may both be classed as CBT. In this regard we consider, for example, that the distinction proposed (Novaco, Ramm & Black, 2001) between anger

management and anger treatment offers a clear delineation of very different intervention styles and should be generally adopted. Furthermore there should be much clearer exposition of what the key elements in the therapy programme actually entail, as this can often lead to misunderstanding and confusion. This can be graphically highlighted by the manner in which stress inoculation can be used very specifically to describe specific clinical activities, as opposed to being used as a blanket description of the global process of intervention. Additionally, thus far, there has been little examination of the influence of 'preparatory work' or the effects of 'follow-up' sessions with regard to outcome. Indeed, it seems practitioners have made little comment on the inherent differences between providing group versus individual interventions and there is clearly a need to gain greater clarity as to the relative costs and benefits of each modality, and when indicated. Ramm & Novaco (2003) describe an intermediate approach that may capitalise on the benefits of both within a single intervention. Once again, much remains to be accomplished.

- *Outcome.* Appropriate evaluation of intervention effects is crucial in any therapeutic activity and anger is no different. It is commonly most straightforward to rely on patient self-report (for example, Hacker-Hughes & Renwick, 2004) but this is often compromised by the medico-legal context in which the angry client is operating (Howells & Day, 2003). Practitioners (especially in the forensic domain) are therefore required to give thought to concurrent multi-modal measures that may supplement self reports. Our own efforts in this domain have involved the development of instruments such as the Ward Anger Rating Scale (WARS) (Novaco & Renwick, 2002) and the Managing Anger and Resolving Conflict Scale (MARCS) (Ramm & Novaco, 2003) for staff-rated anger assessment but other mechanisms for critical behaviour sampling desperately require to be developed and routinely used.

- *Motivation and engagement.* Arguably more than any other clinical problem, people with serious anger difficulties are often highly ambivalent or indeed hostile to participation in therapy. This is particularly so in the forensic domain (Howells & Day, 2003) but it is also the case in more general outpatient settings (Siddle, Jones & Awenat, 2003). This does not only arise when clients feel justified in respect of their problems. Even when acknowledging and remorseful, such clients can find therapeutic work threatening and undermining (Novaco, 1996, 2000). The usefulness of strategies for addressing such challenges like 'motivational interviewing' are now acknowledged (McMurran, 2002) but it is to be cautioned that motivational processes are multifaceted and both intrinsic and extrinsic to the individual (Hodge & Renwick, 2002). Again, much requires to be understood about these critical factors.

New Directions

It is clear from the above that much work still requires to be done in order to aid our clinical understanding of anger and direct our clinical activities. Developments in respect of these matters, we believe, may well involve the integration of current CBT and psychodynamic approaches. One such approach that offers much promise is cognitive analytic therapy (CAT) (Pollock, Gopffert & Stowell-Smith, 2006; Ryle & Kerr, 2002) although as yet there is little substantive evidence regarding the utility of this approach. In parallel, moves to conceptualise the contribution of constructs such as shame, guilt, acceptance and forgiveness may well drive the development of therapy content.

What is very clear is that, to date, work concerning these matters has followed a very intrapsychic approach, with insufficient consideration of the powerful social and contextual forces around which individuals' difficulties are played out (Hodge & Renwick, 2002; Novaco, 1993; Ramm, 1998; Robbins & Novaco, 1999). It is to be hoped that future developments will see progress in our understanding of these key issues.

REFERENCES

Anderson, K. & Silver, J.M. (1998). Modulation of anger and aggression. *Seminars in Clinical Neuropsychiatry, Psychiatric Ambulatory Services, 3*(3), 232–242.

Beck, R., & Fernandez, E. (1998). Cognitive-behavioral therapy in the treatment of anger: A meta-analysis. *Cognitive Therapy and Research, 22,* 63–74.

Bosworth, K., Espelage, D. & DuBay, T. (1998). A computer-based violence prevention intervention for young adolescents: pilot study. *Adolescence, 3*(132), 785–795.

Brondolo, E., DiGuiseppe, R. & Tafrate, R.C. (1997). Exposure-based treatment for anger problems: Focus on the feeling. *Cognitive and Behaviour Practice, 4*(1), 75–98.

Dahlen, E.R. & Deffenbacher, J.L. (2000). A partial component analysis of Beck's cognitive therapy for the treatment of general anger. *Journal of Cognitive Psychotherapy, 14*(1), 77–95.

Dahlen, E.R. & Deffenbacher, J.L. (2001). Anger management. In W.J. Lydon (ed.), *Empirically Supported Cognitive Therapies: Current and Future Applications* (pp. 163–181). New York: Springer.

Dangel, R.F., Deschner, J.P. & Rasp, R.R. (1989). Anger control training for adolescents in residential treatment. *Behaviour Modification, 13*(4), 447–458.

Deffenbacher, J.L., Dahlen, E.R., Lynch, R.S. *et al.* (2000). An application of Beck's cognitive behaviour therapy to general anger reduction. *Cognitive Therapy and Research, 24*(6), 689–697.

Deffenbacher, J.L., Demm, A., Brandon, A.D. (1986). High general anger: Correlates and treatment. *Behaviour Research and Therapy, 24,* 481–489.

Del Vecchio, T. & O'Leary, K.D. (2004). Effectiveness of anger treatments for specific anger problems: A meta-analytic review. *Clinical Psychology Review, 24*(1), 15–34.

DiGuiseppe, R. & Tafrate, R.C. (2003). Anger treatment for adults: A meta-analytic review. *Clinical Psychology: Science and Practice, 10*(1), 70–84.

Dowden, C., Antonowicz, D. & Andrews, D.A. (2003). The effectiveness of relapse prevention with offenders: A meta-analysis. *International Journal of Offender Therapy and Comparative Criminology, 47,* 516–528.

Dowden, C., Blanchette, K. & Serin, R. (1999). *Anger Management Programming for Federal Male Inmates: An Effective Intervention.* Research Report R82e. Ottawa: Correctional Service.

Eckhart, C.I. & Deffenbacher, J.L. (1995). Diagnosis of anger disorders. In H. Kassinove (ed.), *Anger Disorders: Definition, Diagnosis and Treatment* (pp. 27–48). Washington DC: Taylor & Francis.

Edmondson, C.B. & Conger, J.C. (1996). A review of treatment efficacy for individual with anger problems: Conceptual, assessment, and methodological issues. *Clinical Psychology Review, 16*(3), 251–275.

Fairburn, W.R.D. (1978). *Psychoanalytic Studies of the Personality.* London: Routledge.

Fassino, S., Leombruni, P., Piero, A. *et al.* (2003). Mood eating attitudes and anger in obese women with and without binge eating disorder. *Journal of Psychosomatic Research, 54*(6), 559–566.

Feindler, E.L. & Ecton, R.B. (1986). *Adolescent Anger Control: Cognitive Behavioral Techniques.* New York: Pergamon Press.

Foa, E.B., Steketee, G. & Olasov-Rothbaum, B. (1989). Behavioral/cognitive conceptualization of post-traumatic stress disorder. *Behavior Therapy, 20,* 155–176.

Freud, S. (1912). *The Dynamics of Transference,* Standard Edition XII. London: Hogarth Press.

Gerlock, A.A. (1994). Veterans' responses to anger management intervention. *Issues in Mental Health Nursing, 15,* 393–408.

Glancy, G. & Saini, M. (2005). An evidence-based review of psychological treatments of anger and aggression. *Brief Treatment and Crisis Intervention, 5*(2), 229–248.

Grisso, T., Davis, J., Vesselinov, R. *et al.* (2000). Violent thoughts and violent behavior following hospitalization for mental disorder. *Journal of Consulting and Clinical Psychology, 68,* 388–398.

Grodnitzky, G.R. & Tafrate, R.C. (2000). Imaginal exposure for anger reduction in adult outpatients: A pilot study. *Journal of Behaviour Therapy and Experimental Psychiatry, 31*(3–4), 259–279.

Hacker-Hughes, J. & Renwick, S.J. (2004). *Issues in the Group Treatment of Anger Problems in Military Populations.* Unpublished manuscript.

Haddock, G., Lowens, I., Brosnan, N. *et al.* (2004). Cognitive-behaviour therapy for inpatients with psychosis and anger problems within a low secure environment. *Behavioural and Cognitive Psychotherapy, 32,* 77–98.

Hodge, J.E. & Renwick, S.J. (2002). Motivating mentally disordered offenders. In M. McMurran (ed.) *Motivating Offenders to Change: A Guide to Enhancing Engagement in Therapy.* Chichester: Wiley.

Howells, K. & Day, A. (2003). Readiness for anger management: clinical and theoretical issues. *Clinical Psychology Review, 23,* 319–337.

Howells, K., Watt, B., Hall, G. & Baldwin, S. (1997). Developing programmes for violent offenders. *Legal and Criminological Psychology, 2,* 117–128.

Howells, K., Day, A. & Thomas-Peter, T. (2004). Changing violent behaviour: forensic mental health and criminological models compared. *The Journal of Forensic Psychiatry and Psychology, 15*(3), 391–406.

Howells, K., Day, A., Williamson, P. *et al.* (2005). Brief anger management programmes with offenders: Outcomes and predictors of change. *Journal of Forensic Psychiatry and Psychology, 16*(2), 296 311.

Ireland, J.L. (2004). Anger management therapy with young male offenders: An evaluation of treatment outcome. *Aggressive Behaviour, 30*(2), 174–185.

Jones, D. & Hollin, C.R. (2004). Managing problematic anger: The development of a treatment programme for personality disordered patients in high security. *International Journal of Mental Health, 2,* 197–210.

Kernberg, O.F. (1992). *Aggression in Personality Disorders and Perversions.* New Haven: Yale University Press.

Klein, M. (1957). *Envy and Gratitude.* London: Hogarth Press.

Klerman, G.L., Weissman, M.M., Rounsaville, B.J. & Chevron, E.S. (1984). *Interpersonal Psychotherapy of Depression.* New York: Basic Books.

Kohut, H. (1978). Thoughts on narcissism and narcissistic rage. In P.H. Ornstein (ed.), *The Search of the Self* Vol. 2. (pp. 615–658). New York: International Universities Press.

Kohut, H. (1984). *How Does Analysis Cure?* Chicago: University Chicago Press.

Lanza, M., Anderson, J., Bosvert, C. *et al.* (2002). Assaultive behaviour intervention in the Veterans Administration: Psychodynamic group psychotherapy compared to cognitive behaviour therapy. *Perspectives in Psychiatric Care, 38,* 89–97.

Law, K. (1997). Further evaluation of anger management courses at HMP Wakefield: An examination of behavioural change. *Inside Psychology, 3*(1), 91–95.

Linehan, M.M. (1993). *Cognitive-behavioural Treatment of Borderline Personality Disorder.* New York: Guilford Press.

Lochman, J.E., Barry T.D. & Pardini D.A. (2003). Anger control training for aggressive youth. In: A.E. Kazdin (ed.), *Evidence-based Psychotherapies for Children and Adolescents* (pp. 263–281). New York: Guilford Press.

McDougall, C., Boddis, S., Dawson, K. & Hayes, R. (1990). Developments in anger control training. *Issues in Criminological and Legal Psychology, 15,* 39–44.

McMurran, M. (2002). *Motivating Offenders to Change: A Guide to Enhancing Engagement in Therapy.* Chichester: Wiley.

McMurran, M., Charlesworth, P., Duggan, C. & McCarthy, L. (2001). Controlling angry aggression: A pilot group intervention with personality disordered offenders. *Behavioural and Cognitive Psychotherapy, 29,* 473–483.

McNeil, D.E., Eisner, J.P. & Binder, R.L. (2003). The relationship between aggressive attributional style and violence by psychiatric patients. *Journal of Consulting and Clinical Psychology, 71,* 399–403.

Meichenbaum, D. (1975). A self-instructional approach to stress management: a proposal for stress inoculation. In C. Spielberger & I. Sarason (eds), *Stress and Anxiety* Vol. 2. New York: Wiley.

Meichenbaum, D. (1985). *Stress Inoculation Training*. Oxford: Pergamon Press.

Meichenbaum, D. & Novaco, R.W. (1978). Stress inoculation: A preventative approach. In C. Spielberger & I. Sarason (eds), *Stress and Anxiety* Vol 5. (pp. 419–435). New York: Halstead Press.

Monahan, J. & Steadman, H. (1994). *Violence and Mental Disorder*. Chicago: University of Chicago Press.

Munro, F. & MacPherson, G. (2001). Anger management fast-track: A waiting list initiative utilizing a large group format. *Clinical Psychology Forum, 147*, 30–34.

Novaco, R.W. (1975). *Anger Control: The Development and Evaluation of an Experimental Treatment*. Lexington, MA: DC Health.

Novaco, R.W. (1977). Stress inoculation: A cognitive therapy for anger and its application to a case of depression. *Journal of Consulting and Clinical Psychology, 5*, 327–346.

Novaco, R.W. (1993). Clinicians ought to view anger contextually. *Behaviour Change, 10*, 208–218.

Novaco, R.W. (1994a). Anger as a risk factor for violence among the mentally disordered. In, J. Monahan & H. Steadman (eds), *Violence and Mental Disorder: Developments in Risk Assessment* (pp. 21–59). Chicago: University of Chicago Press.

Novaco, R.W. (1994b). Clinical problems of anger and its assessment and regulation through a stress coping skills approach. In W. O'Donohue & L. Krasner (eds), *Handbook of Psychological Skills Training: Clinical Techniques & Applications* (pp. 320–338). Boston: Allyn & Bacon.

Novaco, R.W. (1996). Anger treatment and its special challenges. *NCP Clinical Quarterly, 6*(3), 58–60.

Novaco, R.W. (1997). Remediating anger and aggression with violent offenders. *Legal and Criminological Psychology, 2*, 77–88.

Novaco, R.W. (2000). *Anger Encyclopaedia of Stress* Vol 1 (pp. 188–195). New York: Academic Press.

Novaco, R.W. (2003). *The Novaco Anger Scale and Provocation Inventory (NAS-PI)*. Los Angeles: Western Psychological Services.

Novaco, R.W. & Chemtob, C.M. (1998). Anger and trauma: Conceptualization, assessment and treatment. In V. Follette, J.I. Ruzek & F.R. Abueg (eds), *Cognitive-behavioural Therapies for Trauma* (pp. 162–190). New York, Guilford Press.

Novaco, R.W., Ramm, M. & Black, L. (2001). Anger treatment with offenders. In Hollin, C. (ed.), *Handbook of Offender Assessment and Treatment* (pp. 281–296). London: Wiley.

Novaco, R.W. & Renwick, S. (1998). Anger predictors of the assaultiveness of forensic hospital patients. In E. Sanario (ed.), *Behaviour and Cognitive Therapy Today: Essays in Honour of Hans J. Eysenck* (pp. 199–208). Amsterdam: Elsevier Science.

Novaco, R.W. & Renwick, S. (2002). Anger predictors and the validation of a ward behaviour scale for anger and aggression. Manuscript submitted for publication.

O'Donnell, C.R. & Worrell, L. (1973). Motor and cognitive relaxation in the desensitization of anger. *Behaviour Research and Therapy, 11*(4), 473–481.

Pollock, P.H., Gopffert, M. & Stowell-Smith, M. (eds) (2006). *Cognitive Analytic Therapy for Offenders*. London: Routledge.

Power, M. & Dalgleish, T. (1999). Muti-level theories of emotion. *Behavioural and Cognitive Psychotherapy, 27*, 129–141.

Quayle, M. & Moore, E. (1998). Evaluating the impact of structured groupwork with men in a high security hospital. *Criminal Behavior and Mental Health, 8*, 77–92.

Ramm, M.C. (1998). *An Anger Strategy for the State Hospital: Revised*. Unpublished manuscript. The State Hospital, Lanarkshire. UK.

Ramm, M.C. & Novaco, R.W. (2003). *An Evaluation of Anger Management Groupwork with Continuing Care Psychiatric Patients at the State Hospital*. Unpublished manuscript. The State Hospital, Lanarkshire. UK.

Renwick, S., Black, L., Ramm M. & Novaco, R. W. (1997). Anger treatment with forensic hospital patients. *Journal of Legal and Criminological Psychology, 2*(1), 103–116.

Renwick S.J., Fox, G.C. & Edwards, C. (2002). Operationalising anger and aggression in mental health settings: The application of validated theories of anger to interventions with people with dementia. *Neurobiology of Aging, 23*, 545.

Rimm, D.C., DeGroot, J.C., Boord, P. *et al.* (1971). Systematic desensitization of an anger response. *Behaviour Research and Therapy, 9*, 273–280.

Robins S., & Novaco R.W. (1999). Systems conceptualisations and treatment of anger. *Journal of Clinical Psychology, 55*, 325–337.

Ryle, A. & Kerr, I.B. (2002). *Introducing Cognitive Analytic Therapy: Principles and Practice.* Chichester: Wiley.

Siddle, R., Jones, F. & Awenat, F. (2003). Group cognitive behaviour therapy for anger: A pilot study. *Behavioural and Cognitive Psychotherapy, 31*, 69–83.

Siegman, A.W. & Smith, T.W. (1994). *Anger; Hostility, and the Heart.* Hillsdale, NJ: Erlbaum.

Sharry, J. & Owens, C. (2000). 'The rules of engagement': a case study of a group with 'angry' adolescents. *Clinical Child Psychology and Psychiatry, 5*, 53–62.

Spielberger, C.D. (1996). *State-Trait Anger Expression Inventory Professional Manual.* Florida: Psychological Assessment Resources.

Stermac, L. (1986). Anger control treatment for forensic patients. *Journal of Interpersonal Violence, 1*, 446–457.

Stuart, S. & Robertson, M. (2003). *Interpersonal Psychotherapy: A Clinician's Guide.* Oxford: Oxford University Press.

Sukhodolsky, D.G., Kassinove, H. & Gorman, B.S. (2004). Cognitive-behavioural therapy for anger in children and adolescents: A meta-analysis. *Aggression and Violent Behaviour, 9*(3), 247–269.

Tafrate, R.C. (1995). Evaluation of treatment strategies for adult anger disorders. In H. Kassinove, *Anger Disorders.* Washington, DC: Taylor & Francis.

Tafrate, R.C. & Kassinove, H. (1998). Anger control in men: barb exposure with rational, irrational, and irrelevant self-statements. *Journal of Cognitive Psychotherapy, 12*(3), 187–211.

Taylor, J.L., Novaco, R.W., Gillmer, B.T. *et al.* (2005). Individual cognitive-behavioural anger treatment for people with mild-borderline intellectual disabilities and histories of aggression: A controlled trial. *British Journal of Clinical Psychology, 144*, 367–382.

Taylor, J.L., Novaco, R.W., Gillmer, B. & Thorne, I. (2002). Cognitive-behavioural treatment of anger intensity among offenders with intellectual disabilities. *Journal of Applied Research on Intellectual Disabilities, 15*(2), 151–165.

Teasdale, J.D. (1999). Multi-level theories of cognition-emotion relations. In T. Dalgleish & M. Power (eds), *Handbook of Cognition and Emotion.* Chichester: Wiley.

Towl, G. (1995). Anger management groupwork. *Issues in Criminological Psychology, 23*, 31–35.

Towl, G. & Dexter, P. (1994). Anger management groupwork with prisoners: an empirical evaluation. *Groupwork, 7*, 256–269.

Travis, A. (2006). Offenders' anger control classes help make some more dangerous. *Guardian*, Monday 24 April.

Watt, B.D. & Howells, K. (1999). Skills training for aggression control: evaluation of an anger management programme for violent offenders. *Legal and Criminological Psychology, 4*, 285–300.

Weissman, M.M., Markowitz, J.W. & Klerman, G.L. (2000). *Comprehensive Guide to Interpersonal Psychotherapy.* New York: Basic Books.

Winnicott, D.W. (1958). *Collected Papers: Hate in the Counter-transference.* New York: Basic Books.

Winogron, W., Van Dieten, M. & Gauzas, L. (1997). *CALM: Controlling Anger and Learning to Manage it Program.* New York: Multi-Health Systems.

CHAPTER 14

Psychological Therapy for Depression and Anxiety in Older Adults

Ken Laidlaw
University of Edinburgh, UK

INTRODUCTION

This chapter considers the empirical evidence base for psychotherapy with older adults. The main focus will be on psychotherapy interventions for late-life anxiety and late-life depression. This chapter will mainly consider cognitive-behaviour therapy, interpersonal therapy and psychodynamic psychotherapy when discussing psychotherapeutic interventions with older people as these approaches are the most commonly used in the clinical setting. As the aim is to provide an accessible and useable guide to psychotherapeutic interventions with older people, consideration will also be given to practice elements of therapy with these people and in particular whether adaptations are beneficial when working psychologically with them.

DEMOGRAPHIC CHANGES: OLDER PEOPLE IN SOCIETY

When working with older people, knowledge about normal ageing and the experience of ageing is useful in order to understand the realities of growing older in society today. A fuller account for therapists is beyond the scope of this chapter but interested readers should see Laidlaw *et al.* (2003). It is important to take time to understand the individual's own experience and attitude towards ageing (Knight, 2004). Chronological age is, at best, a poor guide especially as attitudes appear to be important in predicting how people respond to the ageing process (Levy, Slade & Kasl, 2002). Older people are *the least* homogenous of all age groups especially as there are a minimum of two generations contained within this age grouping and, with the increase in longevity, there may well be four decades separating the youngest old from the oldest old (Zeiss & Steffen, 1996).

Handbook of Evidence-based Psychotherapies: A Guide for research and practice.
Edited by C. Freeman & M. Power. Copyright © 2007 John Wiley & Sons, Ltd.

A combination of low fertility rates and increased life expectancy has resulted in the relative ageing of societies worldwide (Kinsella & Velkoff, 2001). The world's older adult population is estimated to show a threefold increase over the next 50 years, from 606 million people in 2000 to 1.9 billion in 2050. In the developed countries, the proportion of the population aged 60 years and over was 19 % in 2000 rising to 32 % by 2050 (United Nations, 2003). The most dramatic increases in proportions of older people are evident in the oldest old section of society (people aged 80 years plus) with an almost fivefold increase from 69 million in 2000 to 377 million in 2050 (source: United Nations, 2003).

Life expectancy at birth in the UK in 1901 was 45 years for men and 49 years for women, whereas by 2000 life expectancy had increased to 75 years for men and 80 years for women (Matheson & Babb, 2002). In 2000, at age 65 years men have an estimated 15 years of life expectancy and women have an estimated 19 years (Kinsella & Velkoff, 2001). In the UK, by 2014 it is expected that the number of people aged 65 years and over will outnumber those aged 16 years and under. The average age of the population is estimated to increase from 38.8 years in 2000 to 42.6 years in 2025 (Matheson & Babb, 2002). In the UK currently, 4 % of the population is aged 80 years and over (United Nations, 2003). Compared to 1971, in 2000 there were over three times as many people over the age of 90 and 78 % of this group were female (Matheson & Babb, 2002). It is evident that there will be a greater likelihood of psychotherapists coming in contact with older people and a consequent increase in knowledge about prevalence and efficacy of treatment for late-life anxiety and depression.

PREVALENCE OF LATE-LIFE DEPRESSION AND ANXIETY

The Epidemiological Catchment Area Study (ECA) (Regier *et al.*, 1988) was a major study investigating rates of depression and anxiety in the community carried out across five sites in the US. The ECA prevalence rates of major depressive disorder amongst older adults were lower than for younger adults (for review see Powers *et al.*, 2002). In the UK, Lindesay, Brigs & Murphy (1989) reported prevalence rates of 4.3 % for severe depression and 13.5 % for mild/moderate depression in a community dwelling urban sample. Beekman, Copeland & Prince (1999) carried out a systematic review of community-based studies examining prevalence of depression in older adults. Overall, Beekman, Copeland & Prince (1999) calculated prevalence rates of 13.5 % for clinically relevant depression but concluded that major depression is relatively rare in later life (1.8 %) whereas minor depression is relatively more common (9.8 %). Similar figures reported by Copeland *et al.* (1987) and Livingston *et al.* (1990) have led to a number of authors suggesting that minor rather than major depressive disorder may be more common in older people (Beekman *et al.*, 2002; Blazer, 2002). Minor depression (Blazer, 2002) may still have a major impact on a person's quality of life (Alexopoulos, 2001; Zarit & Zarit, 1998).

Depression is often thought of as the common cold of geriatric mental health but Blazer (1997) states that anxiety is more common than major depression in later life. Using data from the ECA, Regier *et al.* (1988) reported one-month prevalence rates of 5.5 % for older adults. As with depression, anxiety was less common in later life as the prevalence rate was 7.3 % for younger adults (for review see Powers *et al.*, 2002). Lindesay, Brigs & Murphy (1989) reported prevalence rates of 10 % overall for anxiety disorders in their older adults sample. In older people, generalized anxiety disorder (GAD) and the phobias (agoraphobia, social phobia, simple phobia) are considered more common than other anxiety disorders such as panic disorder, obsessive-compulsive disorder and post-traumatic disorder (Stanley & Beck, 2000). Although phobias are the most common form of anxiety disorder among older people, social anxiety is much less prevalent in older people when compared to younger people (Gretarsdottir et al., 2004). As with depression, there is a suggestion that sub-syndromal levels of anxiety, particularly GAD, are common in older people and that minor GAD symptoms may cause enough problems to merit attention from clinicians (Carter et al., 2001; Diefenbach et al., 2003; Wetherell, LeRoux & Gatz, 2003).

Generally rates of depression and anxiety change depending on the characteristics of the sample with higher rates of anxiety and depression reported for non-community dwelling samples (Katz et al., 1989; Kogan et al., 2000). Prevalence rates increase when physical health conditions are taken account of, although it is a mistake to assume that lack of physical health automatically results in psychological distress (Zeiss et al., 1996). Many older people do not consider themselves ill even if they are prescribed multiple medications and in the eyes of their physicians are seen as chronically ill (Valliant & Mukamal, 2001) as older people generally accommodate to chronic illness over very many years (Laidlaw et al., 2003). The physical decline that may be seen in old age is, according to Valliant & Mukamal (2001), confined to the last few years of life.

There is a general consensus that depression and anxiety in older people have a poor prognosis with low rates of spontaneous remission (Beckman et al. 2002; Cole, Bellavance & Mansour, 1999; Livingston et al., 1997). Depression and anxiety in later life, are often under-detected and under-treated. Treatments primarily are medication-based and this may be considered problematic in terms of their side-effects profile (Blazer, 1997). Fears about tolerability of medication in older people often result in the prescription of medications at sub-therapeutic levels thus diluting their potential effectiveness (Alexoponlos, 2001; Blazer, 1997; Isometsa et al., 1998; Laidlaw, 2003; Nelson 2001; Orrell et al., 1995; Small, 1997). The foregoing provides the rationale for examining whether psychological treatments for depression and anxiety are efficacious for older people.

PSYCHOTHERAPY WITH OLDER PEOPLE: BASIC ISSUES

The following outlines some basic issues to be considered when working with older adults. For a fuller consideration of the basic issues in psychotherapy with older adults, there are a number of alternative resources to consult – see Knight, 2004; Laidlaw et al., 2003, 2004; Miller, et al., 1998; Nordhus & Neilson, 1999; Steuer & Hammen, 1983; Zeiss & Steffen, 1996). It is important to make sure that these are thought out in advance – for instance, is there a specific room set aside for the purposes of psychotherapy? Is it well ventilated and light? Is it soundproofed and free from external noise sources or other distractions. As many older adults have sensory deficits in hearing and or vision these basic aspects to a consultation cannot be ignored. As older patients may have concerns about the functioning of their memory, they can be encouraged to use notebooks in therapy to remember important details (Thompson, 1996). Using an audiocassette recorder to provide a patient with a tape of the session to listen to for homework can also be helpful. It is recommended that the therapist repeat important points throughout therapy and encourage patients to provide feedback to the therapist about their understanding of what has been said (Dick et al., 1996). In working with older people, the pace and length of treatment may be slower than with younger adults, although the coverage of topics may be the same. Sessions may be shorter and therefore more treatment sessions may have to be planned (Zeiss & Steffen, 1996). The age of the therapist may be an issue, as may be the therapist's credibility. The age difference can be discussed early in session if this is considered a barrier to developing a collaborative working relationship (Knight, 2004).

Older people are often unused to psychotherapy and so may need encouragement to talk about personal issues outside of family and friends. Encouragement to talk may take the form of simply saying to the patient their problems are not trivial and that depression is an illness, not a defect of character. It is common for older people to 'wander' off topics. In many cases therapists, mindful of being respectful to elders, will allow their patients to talk without interruption, often losing the focus entirely. This can result in a frustrating and confusing experience for both therapist and patient, leaving both feeling uncertain about the value of future sessions. In working with older people the therapist should be active and directive and it can be helpful to have a discussion with the patient in order to seek their permission to interrupt stories, if necessary, in order to keep the focus on the clinical problem. This should be done with some humour to avoid interruptions seeming to be too rude. At the end of therapy it is important to consider some summarizing sessions to develop a relapse-prevention set of strategies. In some circumstance the issue of ending therapy may need to be discussed well in advance (if possible) with patients, especially if they live alone. The fears of the patient and the therapist may need to be explored prior to completion of therapy. Therapists need to bear in mind that older people are remarkably resilient. The nature of the therapeutic relationship between client and therapist is very important in this setting.

EVIDENCE-BASED PSYCHOTHERAPY WITH OLDER PEOPLE

The following section reviews the empirical evidence for psychological treatments for depression and anxiety, including cognitive behaviour therapy, interpersonal therapy, and psychodynamic psychotherapy. Powers *et al.* (2002) and Blazer (2002) have provided comprehensive reviews of both psychological and physical treatments for late-life depression. Perhaps the most noteworthy feature of research in this area is that there is simply not enough of it to draw firm conclusions about the differential effectiveness of various psychosocial and pharmacotherapy treatments when used alone. In the sections that follow, meta-analytical evidence for the efficacy of psychotherapy with older adults is considered prior to a further examination using systematic outcome studies. Where possible, evidence for the different psychotherapeutic approaches are outlined.

Psychological Therapy for Anxiety in Older Adults

Despite an increasing awareness of the importance of anxiety disorders in older people there still remains a limited number of systematic studies examining psychotherapy for anxiety in later life (Gatz *et al.*, 1998; Nordhus & Pallesen, 2003; Stanley & Beck, 2000; Woods & Roth, 1996). This paucity of systematic studies is all the more surprising given the evidence supporting cognitive therapy as a treatment of choice for panic disorder and phobic disorders (Laidlaw *et al.*, 2003). There are many more papers published that comment on process issues in the treatment of late-life anxiety than those reporting on the outcome of clinical trials (Gorenstein, Papp & Kleber, 1999; Sheikh & Cassidy, 2000; Stanley & Averill, 1999; Stanley & Beck, 2000; Stanley & Novy, 2000). The systematic studies that are published investigating psychological therapy as a treatment for late-life anxiety have all evaluated cognitive behaviour therapy (CBT). This finding should come as no real surprise as interpersonal psychotherapy (IPT) was developed as a treatment for depression and has only recently started to be considered for use with other affective disorders (see Weissman, Markowitz & Klerman, 2000 for review). Psychodynamic psychotherapy has a very poor outcome for anxiety disorders. Life review is another type of psychological intervention that is unlikely to be considered as a treatment for anxiety disorders in later life.

Meta-Analytic Review of Psychological Treatment for Late-life Anxiety

To date the only meta-analytic review of the nonpharmacological treatment of anxiety disorders has been carried out by Nordhus & Pallesen (2003). For this meta-analysis, the authors identified 15 psychosocial studies looking at the treatment of anxiety disorders in older people. The selection criteria used were quite flexible in order to include enough studies to permit an adequate meta-analysis. The studies varied in quality and many used relaxation as a primary treatment approach for anxiety reduction. Some of the studies were pilot studies and some were published as proceedings of a conference. Overall, Nordhus & Pallesen (2003) calculated a mean effect size for psychosocial treatments of 0.55. Using the classification adopted for the behavioural sciences (Cohen, 1977) 0.2 is considered a small effect size, 0.5 is considered a moderate effect size and 0.8 is considered a large effect size. It was noted that effect sizes are reduced when considering psychosocial treatments with active control conditions, thus suggesting that active control conditions are probably variants on active treatment conditions (Nordhus & Pallesen, 2003). It may also reflect the type of studies included in this meta-analysis. It is useful to include as many studies as possible but broad inclusion criteria probably lead to more confusion than clarity in determining the true effectiveness of structured psychosocial treatments evaluated in systematic controlled research trials. To that end the next section of this chapter reviews four systematic psychosocial outcome studies for the treatment of anxiety disorders in older people.

Cognitive Behaviour Therapy for Late-life Anxiety

King & Barrowclough (1991) developed a series of individual case studies to evaluate CBT's effectiveness as a treatment for late-life anxiety. The study was a naturalistic one as reflects the pilot nature of interventions being evaluated. Many of the participants were prescribed medication at a stable dose during their participation in the study. Outcome was impressive as seven out of 10 patients benefited from CBT. King & Barrowclough (1991) used standard procedures for treating panic disorder such as those that would be routinely applied with younger adults; no modifications to treatment procedures were deemed necessary to accommodate the needs of older people with anxiety. King & Barrowclough (1991) note that those patients who improved after receiving cognitive therapy had previously not benefited from pharmacotherapy.

Stanley, Beck & Glassco (1996) compared cognitive behaviour therapy with non-directive supportive therapy in 48 older adults aged 55 years and over diagnosed (using DSM-IIIR Criteria) with GAD. Stanley, Beck & Glassco (1996) used *group* treatment approaches over a 14-week treatment period, with each session lasting 90 minutes. Cognitive behaviour therapy followed standard procedures and included homework tasks. Supportive psychotherapy (SP) consisted of non-directive group discussions of anxiety symptoms and personal experiences of anxiety. Outcome was evaluated at the end of treatment and at six-months follow-up. The mean age of the sample was 68 years and 70 % were female with a mean duration of GAD of 35.5 years. All participants were medication free during the treatment phase. Both groups reported benefiting from the psychosocial interventions. There were no statistical significant differences between the groups on standardized measures of anxiety and worry. At the end of treatment, 28 % of CBT participants compared to 54 % of SP participants were classified as treatment responders. At the six-month follow-up, 50 % of the CBT participants and 77 % of the SP participants were classified as treatment responders (figures based upon complete sample). Given the small size of this study and given some methodological issues in this study there is still need for more treatment trials of anxiety in later life.

Barrowclough *et al.* (2001) produced the first systematic randomized controlled trial of the effectiveness of *individual* cognitive-behaviour therapy (CBT) for anxiety symptoms in older adults. Cognitive-behaviour therapy was compared to supportive counselling (SC). In this study all participants were aged 55 years and over with the mean age of the sample 72 years (77 % of the sample was female). All participants met DSM-IV criteria for anxiety disorders. Overall, 225 patients were referred with only 55 satisfying eligibility criteria, all participants were prescribed medication at a stable dose, with the majority being prescribed benzodiazepines In this study, there was a six-week baseline period with no evident change in treatment scores during this period. Out of the 55 participants who entered treatment, 43 completed treatment (CBT 19; SC 24), with 39 available for three-month follow-up (CBT 16; SC 23) and 40 were available for six-month follow-up (CBT 17, SC 23). At the end of treatment, the CBT group reported lower scores on the Beck Anxiety Inventory and Geriatric Depression Scale (GDS). There were also significant differences between the treatment conditions on the Beck Depression Inventory, GDS, Hamilton Rating Scale for Anxiety (HRSA) and the State-Trait Anxiety Inventory over the course of treatment. Barrowclough *et al.* (2001) also reported that 71 % of CBT and 39 % of SC participants met treatment responder status for anxiety at 12 month follow-up. Responder status was defined as a 20 % reduction on two anxiety measures: BAI & HRSA. Barrowclough *et al.* (2001) also assessed outcome in terms of the number of participants in each group who met high endstate functioning (defined as scores less than 10 on both the BAI and the HRSA) with 41 % of CBT and 26 % of SC participants meeting high endstate function for anxiety at 12 month follow-up. Overall Barrowclough *et al.* (2001) concluded that CBT was superior to SC at follow-up although SC did prove its usefulness.

Stanley *et al.* (2003) compared the efficacy of group-based CBT with a minimal contact control condition (MCC). The MCC group received weekly telephone contact with no active intervention and both interventions lasted 15 weeks. All participants (n = 85) were aged 60 years and above and were diagnosed with GAD. The CBT participants reported significant improvements in worry, anxiety, depression and quality of life in comparison to the MCC group. At the end of treatment 45 % of the CBT group in comparison to 8 % of the MCC group met classification as treatment responders. While those participants who made gains maintained these at one-year follow-up Stanley *et al.* (2003) note that post-treatment anxiety scores failed to return to normative levels. Currently work by this group of researchers is still in progress.

Overall, there are insufficient evaluations to reach a conclusion on the merits of psychological treatments for anxiety disorders in late life. Nonetheless, the data presented so far would suggest some optimism about the applicability of psychological treatments, essentially cognitive-behavioural interventions, for late-life anxiety, especially if one takes account of case reports (for review see Stanley & Beck, 2000). The development of efficacious psychological approaches for late-life anxiety is particularly welcomed because anxiety is a significant cause of emotional distress for a substantial minority of older people (Kogan *et al.*, 2000; Stanley & Averill, 1999). While there is much still to be evaluated, there are enough indications to suggest that with more high quality studies, cognitive behaviour therapy is likely to become a welcome addition to the treatment options available for late-life anxiety disorders. This is especially important as Nordhus & Pallesen (2003) comment that pharmacotherapy treatments for anxiety are traditionally seen as less desirable for use with older people.

Psychological Therapy for Late-life Depression

Psychological treatments for depression have been more systematically evaluated than the anxiety disorders (Gatz *et al.*, 1998; Powers *et al.*, 2002; Woods & Roth, 1996). In recognition of the larger amount of systematic research carried out for late-life depression, this section separately evaluates the evidence for cognitive-behaviour therapy, interpersonal therapy and psychodynamic psychotherapy. Meta-analytical data are considered in the evaluation of psychotherapy for late-life depression prior to an in-depth analysis of individual and group evaluations of psychosocial treatments for late-life depression.

Meta-Analytic Review of Psychological Treatment for Late-life Depression

Scogin & McElreath (1994) produced the first meta-analysis of the efficacy for psychosocial treatments in late-life depression. Scogin & McElreath (1994) included 17 studies published from 1975 to 1990. In their analyses they reported mean effect sizes for treatment versus no treatment or placebo of 0.78, similar to effect sizes of 0.73 reported by Robinson *et al.* (1990) in their review of psychotherapy for depression across all age ranges. Scogin & McElreath (1994) also carried out separate analyses using a subset of studies satisfying diagnostic criteria for major depressive disorder and reported an effect size of 0.76. They also calculated a mean effect size of 0.3 when comparing cognitive and behavioural therapies with other psychosocial treatments. They investigated treatment delivery methods and reported a mean effect size of 0.74 for group treatments and a mean effect size of 0.77 for individual treatments. Despite the clear superiority of psychological treatments versus no treatment, there was no evidence to support the superiority of any single treatment modality or method of treatment delivery.

Scogin & McElreath (1994) note that in their meta-analyses they used a relatively small number of studies with small sample sizes to determine their effect sizes but nonetheless state that their effect size calculations are consistent with other published studies. Laidlaw (2001, 2003) considered Scogin & McElreath (1994) to have included too broad a definition of psychosocial treatments and considered this overly inclusive. In addition it is questionable whether combining markedly different treatments (psychodynamic psychotherapy and behaviour therapy) together to derive a single composite measure of effect is justifiable. Nonetheless, Scogin & McElreath (1994) produced a timely and comprehensive analysis demonstrating the efficacy of psychosocial treatments for older adults at a time when this was being questioned (Zeiss & Breckenridge, 1996).

A more focused meta-analysis was published by Koder, Brodaty & Anstey (1996) evaluating cognitive therapy for the treatment of depression in older adults. They identified seven treatment comparison studies published from 1981 to 1994. There were marked methodological differences between these studies with different recruitment sources, and different methods of treatment delivery (three out of the seven used individual rather than group treatment). Three of these seven studies favoured CT over other treatment modalities, three failed to find significant treatment differences between modalities and one study was positive for some aspects of cognitive treatment. Out of the seven studies included in the Koder, Brodaty & Anstey (1996) analyses, only four provided sufficient BDI information to permit effect size comparisons across treatment modality. Koder, Brodaty & Anstey (1996) report mean effect sizes of 0.41 in favour of cognitive therapy compared to psychodynamic psychotherapy in four studies. A mean effect size of 1.22 in favour of cognitive therapy compared to a waiting-list control group was reported in two studies. Obviously this meta-analysis merely provides indications given that such a small number of studies were included in their calculations. Koder, Brodaty & Anstey (1996) correctly concluded that although there were too few studies of sufficient scientific and methodological merit upon which a definitive conclusion could be reached over the relative efficacy of cognitive therapy over other treatment modalities, cognitive therapy is nevertheless an effective treatment procedure for late-life depression.

Engels & Verney (1997) reviewed 17 psychological outcome studies for late-life depression published from 1974 to 1992. Like the studies used by Scogin & McElreath (1994), treatments were broadly psychosocial and including cognitive therapy, behaviour therapy, psychodynamic therapy, bibliotherapy, reminiscence/life review, music therapy, physical training and anger expression. The calculation of a combined mean effect size for the range of therapies used by Engels & Verney (1997) in their analyses meets with the same objections raised in relation to the Scogin & McElreath (1994) study. The mean effect size calculated in this meta-analysis was moderate at 0.63, although lower than other reported effect sizes. On average older adults receiving psychosocial treatment for depression are better off than 74 % of older people not receiving treatment. Not all of the studies included in the analysis by Engels & Verney (1997) had control conditions but, of the 13 studies that did include a control, a mean effect size of 0.52 was reported in favour of the psychosocial treatments. Cognitive therapy and behavioural therapy were the most effective treatments with mean effect sizes of 0.78 and 0.85 respectively. A surprising result showing that combined cognitive and behavioural therapy (CBT) was less effective than either cognitive treatment or behavioural therapy alone may be explained by an idiosyncratic definition for CBT. Engels & Verney (1997) characterized studies as purely cognitive when they are probably more accurately described as cognitive-behavioural. For example, studies published by Gallagher-Thompson, Thompson and colleagues are considered to be cognitive therapy by Engels & Verney (1997) when in fact they would certainly consider their approach to be more accurately labelled CBT as they generally stress the behavioural components of treatment within a framework of cognitive strategies (Thompson and Gallagher-Thompson, personal communication).

An interesting finding by Engels & Verney (1997) is that individual therapy is more efficacious than group therapy for late-life depression with older adults. This would appear to be particularly so for cognitive and behavioural treatments. Overall in this meta-analysis, psychotherapy with older adults appears to be most efficacious when the diagnosis is major depression or depression rather than multiple complaints. Psychosocial treatments appeared equally efficacious regardless of the severity of depression. Overall, Engels & Verney (1997) report a meta-analysis that produces interesting results on variables of high importance to practising psychotherapists (for example, type of therapy, mode of delivery, severity, diagnosis, age, gender, and so forth) but the inclusion of markedly different treatments combined to produce a mean effect size is likely to confuse rather than clarify issues of differential effectiveness of psychological treatments for late-life depression.

While meta-analyses reported thus far have considered psychosocial treatments, Gerson *et al.* (1999) investigated the effectiveness of pharmacological and psychological treatments for depression in older people. Gerson *et al.* (1999) reviewed 45 studies published from 1974 to 1998. Four of these used non-drug (psychological) methods of treatment for depression in later life. All patients were diagnosed with major depressive disorder and to be included in the analyses had to report outcomes using observer-rated data as well as self-report. Gerson *et al.* (1999) also used stricter inclusion criteria for their analyses, such as a minimum of 15 patients in each treatment group, description of dose regime in both treatment and control groups, documentation of side-effects by self-report or questionnaire, specification of attrition rates and, lastly, statistical evaluation. Using the stricter criteria reduced the number of studies entered into the meta-analysis to 28, two of which used psychological methods of treatment.

The results of Gerson *et al.*'s meta-analyses were identical using either criteria (inclusive versus strict) in that pharmacological and psychological treatments for major depressive disorder in late life were equally efficacious. There were no significant differences in the relative reduction on quantitative measures of mood between treatments with a 54 % reduction in pre-post treatment scores for the drug studies and a 51 % reduction in pre-post treatment scores for the psychotherapy studies. Analyses also revealed no significant difference in attrition rates between pharmacological and psychological treatments (29.2 % and 29.4 % respectively). Gerson *et al.* (1999) noted that both pharmacotherapy and psychotherapy were superior to placebo. In a very well written and thoughtful conclusion Gerson *et al.* (1999) state

> Effective psychological interventions constitute a much-needed addition to antidepressant medication for depressed older patients, particularly in light of these patients' high prevalence of medical problems, their use of multiple medications, their increased sensitivity to adverse drug effects, and the many psychological stresses to which they are exposed.

Cognitive Behaviour Therapy for Late-life Depression

Cognitive-behaviour therapy (CBT) is an active, directive time-limited and structured treatment approach whose primary aim is symptom reduction (Laidlaw *et al.*, 2003). It can be differentiated from other forms of psychotherapy by its emphasis on the empirical investigation of the patient's thoughts, appraisals, inferences and assumptions. The most basic premise of CBT is that the way in which people feel and behave determines the way that they think and make sense of their experiences. This premise has historical roots in the writings of Greek philosophers such as Epictetus who wrote 'Men are disturbed not by things, but by the views which they take of them.'

Cognitive behavioural therapy works best when clear goals are set. An important element is the use of problem-focussed strategies for helping older people deal with their current concerns. The problem-focus orientation is important as this makes CBT particularly appropriate for use with older people dealing with current concerns (Laidlaw *et al.*, 2004). In many instances CBT techniques are used to assist an older adult in rediscovering old tricks rather than learning new ones (Thompson, 1996).

Since 1982 there have been nine systematic outcome studies looking at CBT as a treatment for late-life depression; four of these studies use individual CBT and are the product of one research group based at Stanford University in California (Gallagher & Thompson, 1983; Gallagher-Thompson, Hanley-Peterson & Thompson, 1990; Thompson *et al.*, 2001; Thompson, Gallagher & Breckenridge, 1987). Five other systematic evaluations have also been carried out into the efficacy of group based CBT for depression (Arean *et al.*, 1993; Beutler *et al.*, 1987; Kemp, Corgiat & Gill, 1991/2; Rokke, Tomhave & Jocic, 2000; Steuer *et al.*, 1984).

Individual CBT for Late-life Depression

Gallagher & Thompson (1983) produced the first systematic evaluation of CBT for late-life depression, and assigned 30 participants to one of three possible treatment conditions: behavioural, cognitive or psychodynamic (insight-oriented) psychotherapy. Treatment consisted of 16 sessions delivered over 12 weeks. The cognitive treatment followed the approach of Beck *et al.* (1979) whereas the behavioural treatment component used the approach of Lewinsohn *et al.* (1978) and emphasized activity scheduling of pleasant activities. The insight-oriented approach was heavily influenced by traditional psychodynamic theories and emphasized the use of the therapeutic relationship as a vehicle for change (Gallagher & Thompson, 1983). All three treatment approaches were equally efficacious, despite apparent differences in treatment content and style. Gallagher & Thompson (1983) noted that participants considered to have an 'endogenous' type of depression achieved a poorer outcome at the end of therapy.

In a later study that adopted the design used in their previous study, Thompson, Gallagher & Breckenridge (1987) randomized 91 out-patients diagnosed with major depressive disorder to one of the three treatment conditions; cognitive, behavioural and insight-oriented psychotherapy. Each treatment condition was identical to that described in Gallagher & Thompson (1983). As before, participants acted as their own treatment controls by the use of a six-week delayed treatment waiting-list control condition, with time treatment consisting of 16 to 20 sessions of therapy over 16 weeks. Overall the three treatment modalities produced a significant treatment effect compared with the waiting-list control condition, with 52 % of the sample overall achieving remission of symptoms at the end of treatment. A further 12 % of participants reported substantial improvements by the end of treatment, resulting in a positive treatment response overall for 70 % of participants overall. There were no significant differences noticeable between the three treatment modalities with positive treatment responses for cognitive, behavioural and insight-oriented interventions of 62 %, 80 % and 70 % respectively.

Regarding two-year follow-up, Gallagher-Thompson, Hanley-Peterson & Thompson (1990) reported that gains made initially by patients were maintained at one year follow-up with 52 %, 58 % and 72 % of patients who received cognitive, behavioural and psychodynamic treatments respectively remaining depression free. Of the initial 52 % who had achieved remission in the Thompson, Gallagher & Breckenridge (1987) study, 83 % were depression free at one-year follow-up, with 53 % of these participants remaining in remission for the whole year. At two-year follow-up, 77 % of participants were still depression free. Gallagher-Thompson et al. (1990) note that gains were maintained in a population that is likely to experience an increased frequency of life events and thus the effectiveness of psychotherapy is that participants learn specific skills that are useful later in dealing with depressogenic stressors. The prognosis at two-year follow-up for those participants who did not respond to treatment was poor.

Thompson et al. (2001) randomized 100 out-patients diagnosed with major depressive disorder to one of the three treatment conditions: CBT alone, Desipramine (an antidepressant) medication (ADM) alone and combined CBT/ADM. In each case treatment lasted three to four months and in the CBT condition participants received 16 to 20 sessions. All participants in the three treatment conditions showed substantial improvements, with the combined CBT/ADM group reporting the greatest improvement. When the sample was split into high and low levels of depression severity, the CBT/ADM combined condition proved to be a superior treatment for depression in comparison to ADM alone but was equivalent to CBT alone (i.e CBT/ADM = CBT alone > ADM alone). However this finding was inconsistent as those participants who were on higher levels of medication and considered to be more severely depressed appeared to do best with CBT/ADM combined overall.

In summary, there are strong grounds to recommend individual CBT as an efficacious treatment for late-life depression. Cognitive-behaviour therapy alone is a good treatment alternative for those patients who cannot tolerate medication, or for those older adults who do not wish to be prescribed antidepressants. For more severe levels of depression, there is evidence that CBT in combination with adequate dosages of medication constitutes an appropriate treatment regime (Gerson et al., 1999; Thompson et al., 2001). The main criticism is that the evaluations of individual CBT have mainly been carried out on healthy, community-dwelling older adults who are mainly young-old rather than old-old. Another major criticism of CBT for late-life depression is that research has largely focused on outcome, while generally ignoring the importance of process issues (see Laidlaw et al., 2004, for a fuller discussion of this issue).

Group-based CBT for Late-life Depression

Steuer et al. (1984) reported on a treatment comparison between CBT and psychodynamic psychotherapy for late-life depression. Thirty-three participants were enrolled into the research with 20 completing treatment. Seventy-six per cent of participants were female. Steuer et al. (1984) had a nine-month treatment period and on average participants attended 37.5 sessions. Of those who completed treatment, 80 % reported improvement, with 40 % in remission of depression. Overall 27 % of those participants entering treatment achieved remission of symptoms. Give that at the end of treatment there were only 10 participants in each treatment group, Steuer et al. (1984) rightly urge caution when considering the differential effectiveness of each treatment. Cognitive-behaviour therapy was more effective than the psychodynamic treatment when using the BDI as the main criterion for measuring change. However, Steuer *et al.* (1984) state that for each treatment condition there were comparable numbers who achieved remission.

Beutler *et al.* (1987) investigated the effectiveness of alprazolam compared with group cognitive therapy. Fifty-six participants were randomly assigned to one of four treatment conditions: alprazolam and support only, CBT and alprazolam and support, placebo and support only, CBT and support and placebo. Cognitive-behaviour therapy plus alprazolam and placebo produced the largest effect sizes of all treatment combinations using BDI self-report scores of participants. Cognitive therapy plus support and placebo appeared more efficacious in comparison to cognitive therapy in combination with medication in this study. It is interesting that this study had very high attrition rates for medication groups – double that of non-medication treatment groups. This result perhaps indicates that the side effects of medication proved intolerable to patients in this trial or that this medication was not appropriate for this study. As Woods & Roth (1996) state, this study is very difficult to evaluate, especially as Alprazolam is not widely used as an antidepressant.

Kemp, Corgiat & Gill (1991/2) carried out a 12-week group cognitive therapy intervention and compared individuals with and without disabling illnesses. Fifty-one participants started treatment with 41 completing treatment. Of those completing treatment, 18 had chronic disabling illnesses that limited activities of daily living. The remaining 23 participants did not have a disabling illness although some did have chronic non-limiting medical conditions. All participants met diagnostic criteria for major depressive disorder. Both groups benefited from the intervention but the non-disabled group continued to improve at six months' follow-up whereas the disabled group maintained gains but did not improve further. As Kemp *et al.* (1991/2) note, these results are very encouraging as they counter the belief that older people with disabling conditions who are depressed are unlikely to benefit from psychotherapy.

Arean *et al.* (1993) randomized 75 participants diagnosed with major depressive disorder to one of three treatment conditions: cognitive behavioural problem-solving therapy, life review/reminiscence and a waiting-list control condition. Treatment took place over 12 weeks and each session lasted for 90 minutes. Waiting list controls received treatment after 12 weeks. Both active treatment conditions proved efficacious although problem solving appears to result in better outcome than life review/reminiscence when comparing scores on the Hamilton Rating Scale for Depression and the Geriatric Depression rating scale but not on the BDI. The waiting-list control group showed no evidence of spontaneous improvement. Arean *et al.* (1993) note that significantly fewer participants in the problem-solving group remained depressed (11 %) in comparison to those in the life review/reminiscence group (60 %). Notably this is one of the few psychological comparison studies to show differential effectiveness between active treatments.

Rokke, Tomhave & Jocic (2000) randomized 34 participants diagnosed with major depressive disorder to one of three treatment conditions: self-management therapy and education and support and a waiting-list control condition. Self-management therapy required participants to monitor mood and activities on a daily basis. The education and support group was provided with information about depression and therapy procedures; participants were also encouraged to talk about their problems and to offer constructive support to one another. Each treatment session lasted for 90 minutes and took place over a 10-week course. Overall, 89 % of participants registered an improvement in depression diagnostic status at the end of treatment. Rokke, Tomhave & Jocic (2000) state that 71 % of the self-management group and 62 % of the education/support group achieved clinically significant reductions in depressive symptoms. The education/support group as originally conceived by Rokke, Tomhave & Jocic (2000) was to be a psychological placebo in that it provided an attention control and expectancy for outcome control comparison to the self-management group. Rokke, Tomhave & Jocic (2000) noted that psychoeducation delivered in a supportive environment can constitute a useful and helpful treatment.

In summary, group-based CBT can take many forms and in some circumstances could be considered to constitute a different type of CBT (see Malik *et al.*, 2003). Although there have been some suggestions that group treatments would provide a superior therapeutic supportive environment for older people, especially those living alone, this is not supported by the empirical evidence for group-based CBT (see Engels & Verney, 1997). As Karel & Hinrichsen (2000) note, some older people may feel more uncomfortable with the process of group therapy and it may not be flexible enough to meet the cognitive and emotional needs of all older participants. Despite this, Arean *et al.* (1993) manage to produce the only evidence of differential effectiveness between psychological treatments. This is a rare finding and suggests that older people especially respond to the common-sense approach evident in problem-solving therapy.

Interpersonal Psychotherapy for Late-life Depression

Interpersonal psychotherapy (IPT) is a short-term focussed treatment programme for depression (Weissman, Markowitz & Klerman, 2000). It recognizes that many of the stressors that may predispose an individual to develop depression are interpersonal in nature (Karel & Hinrichsen, 2000). Frank *et al.* (1993) developed it as a treatment for late-life depression. Sholomskas *et al.* (1993) state that although IPT is easily applicable with older people, there are three main considerations to take into account. The IPT therapist needs to adopt an active non-neutral stance in therapy. The IPT therapist may need to take the lead in finding solutions for the patient. And in some circumstances, the problems facing the older adults may not be amenable to resolution and a process of acceptance may be appropriate (see also Frank *et al.*, 1993, for a fuller review).

Interpersonal psychotherapy focusses on four main problem areas in its treatment approach to depression, these are:

- grief;
- interpersonal disputes (conflict with significant others);
- role transitions (changes in a significant life situation); and
- interpersonal deficits (problems with an individual initiating, maintaining or sustaining relationships).

A number of authors have argued that IPT is a form of psychotherapy particularly well suited to use with older adults (Frank *et al.*, 1993; Hinrichsen, 1999; Karel & Hinrichsen, 2000; Miller *et al.*, 1998; Miller & Silberman, 1996). Hinrichsen (1999) notes that as late life is a time of change and adjustment, many older people will be dealing with the loss of a spouse, many will be negotiating changes in the nature of their relationships with friends, spouses and adult children and many will be dealing with role transitions due to retirement or adjustments to functional health status, these are stressors that are very interpersonal in nature. Miller & Silberman (1996) state that IPT is relevant to late-life depression because it is a time-limited, practical and goal-oriented therapy with a focus on the 'here and now'. As described by Miller & Silberman (1996) IPT and CBT share many features in terms of their relevance as treatments for late-life depression and indeed the characterization of IPT as an appropriate treatment procedure for older adults is very similar to that specified by Morris & Morris (1991).

The main empirical evidence for IPT's efficacy as a treatment for late-life depression comes from the Maintenance in Late-Life Depression Study (MTLLD) (Frank et al., 1993; Miller et al., 1998; Reynolds et al., 1999a, 1999b). This study was designed to reduce high rates of depression relapse in late-life depression. Interpersonal psychotherapy and nortriptyline (NT) in combination are evaluated as maintenance treatments for older adults with a high risk of recurrent major depressive disorder. The basic design (see Miller et al., 1998) is that in the acute phase of treatment participants receive combined IPT and NT, and once remission has been achieved they are randomized for a three-year follow-up of NT or placebo in combination with either IPT or medication check contact. Miller et al. (1998) report limited interim results on 127 participants and state that 81 % showed a full response to combined treatment in the acute phase of the study.

Reynolds et al. (1999a) report on the use of nortriptyline (NT) and IPT alone and in combination as a treatment for bereavement-related depression. Eighty participants were randomly assigned to one of four treatments: NT plus IPT, NT alone, placebo plus IPT, and placebo alone. The use of IPT plus NT was associated with lowest attrition rate and highest remission rate. The rate of remission for IPT plus NT was 69 %; for NT alone it was 56 %; for placebo alone it was 45 % and for IPT plus placebo the remission rate was 29 %. Although the numbers were small in this study when broken down into four groups, IPT was not superior to placebo whereas NT was.

Reynolds et al. (1999b) investigated the efficacy of maintenance nortriptyline (NT) and IPT for the prevention of recurrence of depression. Over a seven-year period, 187 participants were recruited. As with the design outlined by Miller et al. (1998), all participants received combined IPT and NT during the acute phase of depression until remission was achieved. Reynolds et al. (1999b) note that 18 % of participants failed to achieve remission and a small number of participants relapsed prior to the maintenance phase of treatment, leaving 107 participants in total who began the second phase of treatment. Participants who achieved remission were the randomly assigned to one of four treatment conditions: NT plus IPT, NT alone, placebo plus IPT, and placebo alone. The best outcome was achieved in the NT/IPT combination treatment as 80 % of participants remained depression-free. Recurrence rates of depression over three years are reported by Reynolds et al. (1999b) and are as follows: rate of recurrence for IPT plus NT was 20 %, for NT alone it was 43 %, for IPT plus placebo it was 64 %, and for placebo alone it was 90 %.

In summary, the Maintenance in Late-Life Depression Study (MTLLD) is potentially very important in evaluating the efficacy of a psychosocial treatment as a maintenance treatment for late-life depression. Although the number of studies that evaluate IPT alone is severely limited the evidence suggesting that combined medication and IPT is efficacious is potentially very exciting. The questions remain as to the efficacy of IPT in comparison with the placebo condition in the MTLLD is disappointing. Overall there are not enough studies completed at this time to properly evaluate the efficacy of IPT as a treatment for late-life depression.

Psychodynamic Psychotherapy for Late-life Depression

There is no one single form of psychodynamic psychotherapy with older people (Gatz et al., 1998; Karel & Hinrichsen, 2000; Knight, 1996) and the term can be interpreted very broadly, although any psychodynamic approach tends to focus on the therapeutic relationship and uses of transference and counter-transference (Knight, 2004). Freud's view that people over the age of 50 were uneducable has in many ways prevented psychodynamic approaches being applied for the treatment of depression in older adults. As Steuer (1982) points out, not all the early pioneers of psychodynamic theory held such ageist attitudes. In fact, the work of Eriksson recognized that there was a lot of potential for psychological growth and development in later life. Jung saw the purpose of later life as individuation or integrating previously unacknowledged or unconscious aspects of the psyche (Steuer, 1982). There are a number of commonalities amongst the various forms of psychodynamic psychotherapy, such as an emphasis on the role of unresolved developmental issues for the later developmental of psychopathology or difficulties in coping and an emphasis on the curative aspects of a corrective emotional relationship between patient and therapist (Nordhus & Neilson, 1999). In many descriptions of psychodynamic psychotherapy with older people, transference and countertransference are considered to be important (Gallagher & Thompson, 1983; Gatz et al., 1998; Karel & Hinrichsen, 2000; Nordhus & Neilson, 1999; Steuer, 1982).

A lot of the empirical support for psychodynamic psychotherapy with older people comes, surprisingly, from research carried out in CBT treatment trials as noted above (Beutler et al., 1987; Gallagher & Thompson, 1983; Steuer et al., 1984; Thompson, Gallagher & Breckenridge, 1987). In the research trials carried out by the Thompson group, the form of psychodynamic psychotherapy used in their treatment trials was broadly as effective as cognitive or behavioural treatments. Steuer et al. (1984) concluded that psychodynamic and cognitive treatments were equally efficacious for the treatment of depression in older adults. In general, the meta-analysis literature provides empirical support for the use of psychodynamic approaches for the treatment of depression in older adults as results suggest equivalence in outcome between different forms of psychological treatments (Engels & Verney, 1997; Scogin & McElreath, 1994). Of course Koder et al. (1996) did note that CBT produced small to medium effect sizes in comparison to psychodynamic psychotherapy, this analysis was based upon very small numbers of studies.

CONCLUSIONS AND SUMMARY

Psychological treatments constitute a much-needed effective treatment alternative to physical treatments for late-life anxiety and depression because many older adults are unable to tolerate antidepressants or there may contra-indications to their use with older people with cardiac problems (Orrell et al., 1995) and in the case of anxiety disorders there may be a number of concerns about the prescription of benzodiazepines (Gerson et al., 1999). Future research is required into the effectiveness of psychological treatment for depression and anxiety in common medical conditions such as dementia, post-stroke depression and Parkinson's disease. A number of studies are currently at early stages of evaluation of efficacy in terms of psychological and physical treatments for depression and anxiety. At present a lot remains unknown about the potential for psychological therapies in a range of settings such as in nursing homes.

There is simply not enough psychological research into late-life depression or anxiety to draw firm conclusions about the differential effectiveness of various psychosocial treatments. One may also concur with Karel & Hinrichsen (2000) and Nordhus & Pallesen (2003) that the majority of research has so far been conducted on healthy, community-residing older adults and, for many clinicians, this brings into question the generalizability of research findings with the population with whom they may find themselves working. With these previous two points in mind one can draw a cautious conclusion that psychological treatments for anxiety and depression are efficacious and provide older people, service providers and clinicians with a treatment choice. The evidence base is strongest with regard to cognitive-behaviour therapy for depression and anxiety and interpersonal psychotherapy for depression. The evidence that exists to support psychodynamic psychotherapy as a treatment for late-life depression primarily comes from the CBT research literature. A more robust test of psychodynamic psychotherapy would be research carried out primarily by psychodynamic researchers. With the recent developments of cognitive analytical therapy being modified for use with older people (see Hepple & Sutton, 2004), there may be the promise of future empirical evaluation of this approach. Research in life review as a treatment for late-life depression is inconclusive and much more empirical evaluation is required. Given the increase in the numbers of older people living longer, the psychological needs of this important section of society are likely to increase rather than decrease, with the need for more high quality research also likely to increase.

REFERENCES

Alexopoulos, G.S. (2001). Interventions for depressed elderly primary care patients. *International Journal of Geriatric Psychiatry, 16*, 553–555.

Arean, P.A., Perri, M.G., Nezu, A.M. *et al.* (1993). Comparative effectiveness of social problem-solving therapy and reminiscence therapy as treatments for depression in older adults, *Journal of Consulting and Clinical Psychology, 61*, 1003–1010.

Barrowclough, C., King, P., Colville, J. *et al.* (2001). A randomized trial of the effectiveness of cognitive-behavioral therapy and supportive counselling for anxiety symptoms in older adults. *Journal of Consulting and Clinical Psychology, 69*, 756–762.

Beck, A.T., Rush, A.J., Shaw, B. F. & Emery, G. (1979). *Cognitive Therapy of Depression.* New York: Guilford Press.

Beekman, A.T., Copeland, J.R.M. & Prince, M.J. (1999). Review of community prevalence of depression in later life. *British Journal of Psychiatry, 174*, 307–311.

Beekman, A.T., Geerlings, S.W., Deeg, D.J.H. *et al.* (2002). The natural history of late-life depression: A 6 year prospective study in the community. *Archives of General Psychiatry, 59*, 605–611.

Beutler, L.E., Scogin, F, Kirkish, P. *et al.* (1987). Group cognitive therapy and alprazolam in the treatment of depression in older adults. *Journal of Consulting and Clinical Psychology, 55*, 550–556.

Blazer, D. (1997). Generalized anxiety disorder and panic disorder in the elderly: A review. *Harvard Review of Psychiatry, 5*, 18–27.

Blazer, D. (2002). The prevalence of depressive symptoms. *Journal of Gerontology – A. Biological Sciences and Medical Sciences, 57*, 155–161.

Carter, R.M., Wittchen, H.U., Pfister, H., & Kessler, R.C. (2001). One-year prevalence of subthreshold and threshold DSM IV generalized anxiety disorder in a nationally representative sample. *Depression and Anxiety, 13*, 78–88.

Cohen, J. (1977). *Statistical Power Analysis for the Behavioral Sciences.* New York: Academic Press.

Cole, M.G. Bellavance, F. & Mansour, A. (1999). Prognosis of depression in elderly community and primary care populations: A systematic review and meta-analysis. *American Journal of Psychiatry, 156*, 1182–1189.

Copeland, J.R.M., Gurland, B.J., Dewey, M.E. *et al.* (1987). Distribution of dementia, depression, and neurosis in elderly men and women in an urban community: Assessed using the GMS-AGECAT package. *International Journal of Geriatric Psychiatry, 2*, 177–184.

Dick, L.P., Gallagher-Thompson, D. & Thompson, L.W. (1996). Cognitive-Behavioural Therapy. In R.T. Woods (ed.), *Handbook of the Clinical Psychology of Ageing*. Chichester: John Wiley & Sons.

Diefenbach, G. J., Hopko, D.R., Feigon, S. *et al.* (2003). *Behaviour, Research and Therapy, 41*: 481–487.

Engels, G.I. & Verney, M. (1997). Efficacy of nonmedical treatments of depression in elders: A quantative analysis. *Journal of Clinical Geropsychology, 3*, 17–35.

Frank, E, Frank, N., Cornes, C. *et al.* (1993). Interpersonal psychotherapy in the treatment of late-life depression. In G.L. Klerman & M.M. Weissmna (eds), *New Applications of Interpersonal Psychotherapy*. Washington, DC: American Psychiatric Press.

Gallagher, D.E. & Thompson, L.W. (1983). Effectiveness of psychotherapy for both endogenous and nonendogenous depression in older adult outpatients. *Journal of Gerontology, 38*, 707–712.

Gallagher-Thompson, D., Hanley-Peterson, P. & Thompson, L.W. (1990). Maintenance of gains versus relapse following brief psychotherapy for depression. *Journal of Consulting and Clinical Psychology, 58*, 371–374.

Gatz, M., Fiske, A., Fox, L.S. *et al.* (1998). Empirically validated psychological treatments for older adults. *Journal of Mental Health and Aging, 4*, 9–46.

Gerson, S., Belin, T.R., Kaufman, M.S. *et al.* (1999). Pharmacological and psychological treatments for depressed older patients: A meta-analysis and overview of recent findings. *Harvard Review of Psychiatry, 7*, 1–28.

Gorenstein, E.E., Papp, L.A. & Kleber, M.S. (1999). Cognitive behavioral treatment of anxiety in late life. *Cognitive and Behavioral Practice, 6*, 305–320.

Gretarsdottir, E., Woodruff-Borden, J., Meeks, S. & Depp, C. (2004). Social anxiety in older adults: Phenomenology, prevalence, and measurement. *Behaviour, Research and Therapy, 42*, 459–475.

Hepple, J. & Sutton, L. (2004). Cognitive analytical therapy and later life: A new perspective on old age. London: Brunner-Routledge.

Hinrichsen, G.A. (1999). Treating older adults with interpersonal psychotherapy for depression. *JCLP/In Session: Psychotherapy in Practice, 55*, 949–960.

Isometsa, E., Seppala, I., Henriksson, M. *et al.* (1998). Inadequate dosaging in general practice of tricyclic versus other antidepressants for depression. *Acta Psychiatrica Scandinvica, 98*(6), 429–431.

Karel, M.J. & Hinrichsen, G. (2000). Treatment of depression in late-life: Psychotherapeutic interventions. *Clinical Psychology Review, 20* (6), 707–729.

Katz, I.R., Lesher, E., Kleban, M. *et al.* (1989). Clinical features of depression in the nursing home. *International Psychogeriatrics. 1*, 5–15.

Kemp, B.J., Corgiat, M. & Gill, C. (1991/2). Effects of brief cognitive-behavioral group psychotherapy on older persons with and without disabling illness. *Behavior, Health and Aging, 2*, 21–28.

King, P. & Barrowclough, C. (1991). A clinical pilot study of cognitive-behavioural therapy for anxiety disorders in the elderly. *Behavioral Psychotherapy, 19*, 337–345.

Kinsella, K. & Velkoff, V.A. (2001). *An Aging World: 2001*. US Census Bureau, Series P95/01-1. Washington, DC: US Government Printing Office.

Knight, B. (1996). Psychodynamic therapy with older adults: Lessons from scientific gerontology. In R.T. Woods (ed.), *Handbook of the Clinical Psychology of Ageing*. Chichester: John Wiley & Sons.

Knight, B. (1999). The scientific basis for psychotherapeutic interventions with older adults: An overview. *Journal of Clinical Psychology, 55*, 927–934.

Knight, B. (2004). *Psychotherapy with Older Adults*. 3rd edn. Thousand Oaks: Sage Publications.

Koder, D.A., Brodaty, H. & Anstey, K.J. (1996). Cognitive therapy for depression in the elderly. *International Journal of Geriatric Psychiatry, 11*: 97–107.

Kogan, J.N., Edelstein, B.A., & McKee, D.R. (2000). Anxiety in older adults: Current status. *Journal of Anxiety Disorders, 14*, 109–132.

Laidlaw, K. (2001). An empirical review of cognitive therapy for late-life depression: Does research evidence suggest adaptations are necessary for cognitive therapy with older adults? *Clinical Psychology & Psychotherapy, 8*, 1–14.

Laidlaw, K. (2003). Depression in older adults. In M.J. Power (ed.), *Mood Disorders: A Handbook of Science and Practice*. Chichester: John Wiley & Sons Ltd.

Laidlaw, K., Thompson, L.W., Dick-Siskin, L. & Gallagher-Thompson, D. (2003). *Cognitive Behaviour Therapy with Older People.* Chichester: John Wiley & Sons.

Laidlaw, K. Thompson, L.W., & Gallagher-Thompson, D. (2004). Comprehensive conceptualization of cognitive behaviour therapy for late-life depression. *Behavioural and Cognitive Psychotherapy, 32*, 389–399.

Levy, B.R., Slade, M.D. & Kasl, S.V. (2002). Increased longevity by positive self-perceptions of aging. *Journal of Personality and Social Psychology, 83*, 261–270.

Lindesay, J., Brigs, K. & Murphy, E. (1989). The Guys/Age Concern survey: Prevalence rates of cognitive impairment, depression and anxiety in an urban elderly community. *British Journal of Psychiatry, 155*, 317–329.

Livingston, G., Hawkins, A., Graham, N. *et al.* (1990). The Gospel Oak study: Prevalence rates of dementia, depression and activity limitation among elderly residents in inner London. *Psychological Medicine, 20*, 137–146.

Livingston, G., Watkin, V., Milne, B. *et al.* (1997). The natural history of depression and the anxiety disorders in older people: The Islington study. *Journal of Affective Disorders, 46*, 255–262.

Malik, M.L., Beutler, L.E., Alimohamed, S. *et al.* (2003). Are all cognitive therapies alike? A comparison of cognitive and noncognitive therapy process and implications for the application of empirically supported treatments. *Journal of Consulting and Clinical Psychology, 71*, 150–158.

Matheson, J. & Babb, P. (2002). *National Statistics: Social Trends, No. 32.* London: The Stationery Office.

Miller, M.D. & Silberman, R.L. (1996). Using interpersonal psychotherapy with elders. In S.H. Zarit & B.G. Knight (eds), *A Guide to Psychotherapy and Aging: Effective Clinical Interventions in a Life-stage Context.* Washington, DC: American Psychological Association.

Miller, M.D., Wolfson, L., Frank, E. *et al.* (1998). Using interpersonal psychotherapy (IPT). in a combined psychotherapy/medication research protocol with depressed elders. *Journal of Psychotherapy Practice and Research, 7*, 47–55

Morris, R.G. & Morris, L.W. (1991). Cognitive and behavioural approaches with the depressed elderly. *International Journal of Geriatric Psychiatry, 6*, 407–413.

Nelson, J.C. (2001). Diagnosing and treating depression in the elderly. *Journal of Clinical Psychiatry, 62*(suppl. 24), 18–22.

Nordhus, I.H. & Nielson, G.H. (1999). Brief dynamic psychotherapy with older adults. *Journal of Clinical Psychology, 55*, 935–947.

Nordhus, I.H., & Pallesen, S. (2003). Psychological treatment for late life anxiety: An empirical review. *Journal of Consulting & Clinical Psychology, 71*, 643–654.

Orrell, M., Collins, E., Shergill, S., & Katona, C. (1995). Management of depression in the elderly by general practitioners: use of antidepressants. *Family Practice, 12*, 5–11.

Powers, D.V., Thompson, L.W., Futterman, A. & Gallagher-Thompson, D. (2002). Depression in later life: epidemiology, assessment, impact and treatment. In I.H. Gotlib & C.L. Hammen (eds), *Handbook of Depression* (pp. 560–580). New York: Guilford Press.

Regier, D.A., Boyd, J.H., Burke, J.D. & Rae, D.S. (1988). One-month prevalence of mental disorders of in the United States: Based on five Epidemiological Catchment Area sites. *Archives of General Psychiatry, 45*, 977–986.

Reynolds, C.F., Frank, E., Perel, J.M. *et al.* (1999b). Nortriptyline and interpersonal psychotherapy as maintenance therapies for recurrent major depression: A randomized controlled trial in patients older than 59 years, *Journal of the American Medical Association, 281*, 39–45.

Reynolds, C.F., Miller, M.D., Pasternak, R.E. *et al.* (1999a). Treatment of bereavement-related major depressive episodes in later life: A controlled study of acute and continuation treatment with nortriptyline and interpersonal psychotherapy. *American Journal of Psychiatry, 156*, 202–208.

Robinson, L.A., Berman, J.S. & Neimeyer, R.A. (1990). Psychotherapy for the treatment of depression: a comprehensive review of controlled outcome research. *Psychological Bulletin, 108*, 30–49.

Rokke, P.D., Tomhave, J.A. & Jocic, Z. (2000). Self-management therapy and educational group therapy for depressed elders. *Cognitive Therapy and Research, 24*, 99–119.

Scogin, F. & McElreath, L. (1994). Efficacy of psychosocial treatments for geriatric depression: A quantitative review. *Journal of Consulting and Clinical Psychology, 62*, 69–74.

Sheikh, J., & Cassidy, E. (2000). Treatment of anxiety disorders in the elderly: issues and strategies. *Journal of Anxiety Disorders, 14*, 173–190.

Sholomskas, A.J., Chevron, E.S., Prusoff, B.A., *et al.* (1993). Short-term interpersonal therapy (IPT). with the depressed elderly: Case reports and discussion. *American Journal of Psychotherapy, 37,* 552–566.

Small, G. W. (1997). Recognizing and treating anxiety in the elderly. *Journal of Clinical Psychiatry, 58* (suppl. 3), 41–50.

Stanley, M.A. & Averill, P.M. (1999). Strategies for treating generalized anxiety disorder in the elderly. In M. Duffy (ed.), *Handbook of Counseling and Psychotherapy with Older Adults.* New York: John Wiley & Sons.

Stanley, M.A. & Beck, J.G. (2000). Anxiety disorders. *Clinical Psychology Review, 20,* 731–754.

Stanley, M.A., Beck, J.G. & Glassco, J.D. (1996). Treatment of generalized anxiety in older adults: A preliminary comparison of cognitive behavioral and supportive approaches. *Behavior Therapy, 27,* 565–581.

Stanley, M.A., Beck, J.G., Novy, D.M. *et al.* (2003). Cognitive-behavioral treatment of late-life generalized anxiety disorder. *Journal of Consulting and Clinical Psychology, 71,* 309–319.

Stanley, M.A. & Novy, D.M. (2000). Cognitive-behavior therapy for generalized anxiety in late life: An evaluative overview. *Journal of Anxiety Disorders, 14,* 191–207.

Steuer, J.L. (1982). Psychotherapy with the elderly. *Psychiatric Clinics of North America, 5,* 199–213.

Steuer, J.L. & Hammen, C.L. (1983). Cognitive-behavioral group therapy for the depressed elderly: Issues and adaptations. *Cognitive Therapy & Research, 7,* 285–296.

Steuer, J.L., Mintz, J., Hammen, C.L. *et al.* (1984). Cognitive-behavioral and psychodynamic group psychotherapy in the treatment of geriatric depression. *Journal of Consulting and Clinical Psychology, 52,* 180–189.

Thompson, L.W. (1996). Cognitive-behavioral therapy and treatment for late-life depression. *Journal of Clinical Psychiatry, 57* (suppl. 5), 29–37.

Thompson, L.W., Coon, D.W., Gallagher-Thompson, D.G. *et al.* (2001). Comparison of desipramine and cognitive behavioral therapy in the treatment of elderly outpatients with mild-to-moderate depression. *American Journal of Geriatric Psychiatry, 9,* 225–240.

Thompson, L.W., Gallagher, D. & Breckenridge, J.S. (1987). Comparative effectiveness of psychotherapies for depressed elders. *Journal of Consulting and Clinical Psychology, 55,* 385–390.

United Nations (2003). *World Population Prospects: The 2002 Revision.* New York: United Nations Population Division.

Vaillant, G.E. & Mukamal, K. (2001). Successful aging. *American Journal of Psychiatry, 158,* 839–847.

Weissman, M., Markowitz, J.C. & Klerman, G.L. (2000). *Comprehensive Guide to Interpersonal Psychotherapy.* New York: Guilford Press.

Wetherell, J.L., Le Roux, H. & Gatz, M. (2003). DSM-IV criteria for generalized anxiety disorder in older adults: Distinguishing the worried from the well. *Psychology and Aging, 18,* 622–627.

Woods, R. & Roth, A. (1996). Effectiveness of psychological interventions with older people. In A. Roth & P. Fonagy (1996). *What Works for Whom: A Critical Review of Psychotherapy Research.* London: Guilford Press.

Zarit, S. & Zarit, J. (1998). *Mental Disorders in Older Adults: Fundamentals of Assessment and Treatment.* New York: Guilford Press.

Zeiss, A. & Breckenridge, J. (1997). Treatment of late life depression: a response to the NIH consensus conference. *Behavior Therapy, 28,* 3–21.

Zeiss, A., Lewinsohn, P.M., Rohde, P., & Seeley, J.R. (1996). Relationship of physical disease and functional impairment to depression in older people. *Psychology & Aging, 11,* 572–581.

Zeiss, A. & Steffen, A. (1996). Treatment issues with elderly clients. *Cognitive and Behavioral Practice, 3,* 371–389.

CHAPTER 15

Alcohol Problems

Nick Heather

Northumbria University, UK

Although there has been much recent interest in various forms of pharmacotherapy for alcohol problems, treatment in this field has traditionally consisted of 'talk therapy' and this remains true today. Beginning in the 1930s, medical interest in treating alcohol problems lagged behind the efforts of 'recovering alcoholics' to help each other in the classic mutual-aid group, Alcoholics Anonymous (AA). Following a growing recognition of the individual and social harm caused by alcohol dependence during the 1950s, the medical response continued to be based on the model of recovery pioneered by AA. Subsequently, the influence of more professionally based forms of psychotherapy began to appear, including during the 1960s and 1970s treatment modalities based on theories of learning developed by psychologists. This last has been the dominant general influence on professional treatment up to the present day.

The most important recent development in the way alcohol problems are conceptualised has been a shift from an exclusive preoccupation with 'alcoholism' (severe alcohol dependence) to a 'broadening of the base' of treatment (Institute of Medicine, 1990) to include the very large number of people in society who damage their own or others' health and welfare, or risk doing so, because of their excessive consumption of alcohol. This has resulted in great interest in the potential benefits of 'brief interventions' for hazardous and harmful drinking delivered by generalist workers to individuals who are not seeking help for alcohol problems and whose problems, even if they have become manifest, are typically early and mild (Heather, 2003; Heather & Kaner, 2003). Thus these brief interventions are offered mainly in the interests of early intercession and secondary prevention. Since brief interventions of this sort can be as short as 5 to 10 minutes in duration, it might seem odd to include them in a chapter concerned with psychotherapy for alcohol problems. However, to omit brief interventions would fail to give a true picture of the current response to alcohol-related harm. Moreover, as we shall see, some of the principles that have influenced the content and style of brief interventions would be familiar to practitioners of psychotherapy proper.

For these reasons, this chapter will include attention to brief interventions. Also included will be modern approaches to treatment that rely to a varying extent on the client's social network to bring about change. In more general terms, the rough definition of psychotherapy used in this chapter is any form of interaction between helper and helped in which language

Handbook of Evidence-based Psychotherapies: A Guide for research and practice.
Edited by C. Freeman & M. Power. Copyright © 2007 John Wiley & Sons, Ltd.

is the predominant means of bringing about a change in behaviour, including modalities that are primarily seen as 'performance based'. As an illustration, this definition excludes aversion therapy, electrical or chemical, but includes 'covert sensitisation therapy' (Rimmele, Howard & Hilfrink, 1995) in which aversive conditioning is thought to proceed in imagination, prompted by the therapist's verbal suggestions. For obvious reasons, detoxification will not be considered beyond the observation that by itself it has little or no long-term effect on alcohol problems.

THE EVIDENCE BASE

It has not proved possible to carry out formal meta-analysis successfully (i.e., with pooling of data from a range of similar studies and estimations of effect sizes) for alcohol problems treatment as a whole. This is because the science of treatment in this field has not matured sufficiently to have arrived at standard forms of treatment modalities and control conditions, common use of outcome measures, consensually agreed reporting of client characteristics and other features necessary for formal meta-analysis to proceed. Instead, it is necessary to rely on the 'box-score' method in which individual studies are rated for the degree to which they either support or do not support a specific modality and an aggregate effectiveness score is arrived at by summing these ratings. This method of data synthesis has been criticised (for example, by Finney, 2000) but it is probably the best source of information available at present.

The leading and most recent box-score synthesis is an update on the so-called *Mesa Grande* ('large table' in Spanish) by Miller, Wilbourne & Hettema (2003) from the University of New Mexico. This included 381 controlled trials, mainly randomised controlled trials (RCTs), of different types or intensities of treatment or the same type of treatment with and without the addition of a special therapeutic component. Two independent raters judged the methodological quality of all studies included in the *Mesa Grande* on 12 dimensions, resulting in a methodological quality score (MQS) for each study. Outcome logic scores (OLS), reflecting the degree to which inferences about the effectiveness of the treatment could properly be derived from the study design, were arrived at by a similar rating process and resulted in a classification of each study as providing strong positive evidence (+2), positive evidence (+1), negative evidence (–1) or strong negative evidence (–2) for a particular treatment modality. The MQS and OLS were then multiplied to arrive at a weighting of the study's contribution to the evidence on treatment outcome by its methodological quality. These products were then summed across all studies bearing on the effectiveness of a specific treatment modality, resulting in the cumulative evidence score (CES) for each modality. Some interventions might be effective among problem drinkers identified in community samples but not in clinical samples, so separate ratings were calculated among those studies confined to clinical samples (see Table 15.1).

Table 15.1 shows a selection of treatment modalities from the *Mesa Grande*, with their respective CESs and other data. The selection is based on the 10 highest rated modalities and the five lowest but also includes other modalities for illustrative purposes. Two modalities from a separate section of the *Mesa Grande* devoted to treatments with only one or two investigations have been inserted in Table 15.1. The *Mesa Grande* will be the main source of evidence on treatment outcome in this chapter. The complete table and fuller details, including a listing of all studies comprising the *Mesa Grande,* will be found in Miller, Wilbourne & Hettema (2003).

Table 15.1 A selection of treatment modalities from the *Mesa Grande*

Treatment modality	Rank	CES	N	%+	Mean MQS	Mean severity	% Excellent
Brief intervention	1	390	34	74	13.29	2.47	53
Motivational enhancement	2	189	18	72	12.83	2.72	50
GABA agonist (Acamprosate)	3	116	5	100	11.60	3.80	20
Community reinforcement	4.5	110	7	86	14.00	3.43	71
Self-change manual (bibliotherapy)	4.5	110	17	59	12.65	2.59	53
Opiate antagonist (e.g., Naltrexone)	6	100	6	83	11.33	3.17	0
Behavioural self-control training	7	85	31	52	12.77	2.91	52
Behaviour contracting	8	64	5	80	10.40	3.60	0
Social skills training	9	57	20	55	10.90	3.80	25
Marital therapy – behavioural	10	44	9	56	12.33	3.44	44
Cognitive therapy	13	21	10	40	10.00	3.70	10
Aversion therapy, covert sensitisation	14.5	18	8	38	10.88	3.50	0
Client-centred counselling	18	5	8	50	11.13	3.38	13
Therapeutic community	—	−4	1	0	4.00	3.00	0
Antidipsotropic – Disulfiram	22	−6	27	44	11.07	3.69	26
Minnesota Model	—	−11	1	0	11.00	4.00	100
Antidepresssant – SSRI	23	−16	15	53	8.60	2.67	0
Problem solving	24	−26	4	25	12.25	3.75	50
Lithium	25	−32	7	43	11.43	3.71	29
Marital therapy – non-behavioral	26	−33	8	38	12.25	3.63	25
Group process psychotherapy	27	−34	3	0	8.00	2.67	0
Functional analysis	28	−36	3	0	12.00	2.67	33
Relapse prevention	29	−38	22	36	11.73	3.23	31
Self-monitoring	30	−39	6	33	12.00	3.17	50
Twelve-step facilitation	37	−82	6	17	15.00	3.67	83
Alcoholics Anonymous	38	−94	7	14	10.71	3.14	29
Anxiolytic medication	39	−98	15	27	8.13	3.40	0
Milieu therapy	40	−102	14	21	10.86	3.64	29
Antidepressant medication (non-SSRI)	42	−104	6	0	8.67	3.17	0
Relaxation training	44	−152	18	17	10.56	3.06	17
Confrontational counselling	45	−183	12	0	10.25	3.00	33
Psychotherapy	46	−207	19	16	10.89	3.26	21
General alcoholism counselling	47	−284	23	9	11.26	3.22	22
Education (tapes, lectures or films)	48	−443	39	13	9.77	2.44	15

CES = Cumulative Evidence Score.
N = Total number of studies evaluating modality.
% + = Percent of studies with positive finding for modality.
Mean MQS = Average methodological quality (0–17) score of studies.
Mean Severity = Average severity rating (1–4) of treated populations.
% Excellent = Percentage of studies with MQS > 13.
Source: Adapted from Miller, Wilbourne & Hettema (2003).

One of the main advantages of conducting a meta-analysis of treatment for a particular disorder is that pooling of data from numerous studies allows a large sample of clients to be considered and reduces the risk of Type 2 error – of accepting the null hypothesis of no effect for a treatment when that hypothesis is false and the treatment is in fact effective. However, the alcohol problems field is remarkable for existence of the largest multi-centre trial of psychosocial treatment ever conducted, not only of treatment for alcohol problems but for any kind of behavioural disorder.

This was Project MATCH (Matching Alcoholism Treatment to Client Heterogeneity) (Project MATCH Research Group, 1997a,b; 1998a), which included 1 726 individuals seeking treatment for alcohol problems, divided into two parallel but independent clinical trials – an outpatient arm (n = 952) and an aftercare arm (n = 774). Project MATCH was a rigorously designed and executed study and, in view particularly of its size, is guaranteed a special place in the evidence base on treatment for alcohol problems. Its findings will be used here to supplement those of the *Mesa Grande*.

As its name suggests, the project was designed to test the 'matching hypothesis' that appropriate allocation of clients to the form of treatment best suited to them would produce an overall improvement in outcome of treatment. Three types of psychosocial (i.e. non-drug) treatments were compared:

- cognitive-behavioural therapy (CBT);
- motivational enhancement therapy (MET); and
- twelve-step facilitation therapy (TSF) based on the philosophy and methods of AA and its famous '12-step' recovery programme.

The main conclusion of Project MATCH was that, whereas some clinically valuable client-treatment matches were found, the general matching hypothesis referred to above was not confirmed: matching on *a priori* grounds did not increase overall treatment effectiveness. The large sample size used in Project MATCH was necessary to provide sufficient statistical power to test interactions in the data between client characteristics and treatment modalities but it also provided very high power for the detection of main effects of treatment and these will be discussed below.

More recently, there has been a multi-centre RCT of alcohol problems treatment in the UK, with a sample size (n = 742) approaching that of Project MATCH or, at least, one of its arms. This is the United Kingdom Alcohol Treatment Trial (UKATT) (UKATT Research Team, 2001), which compared the effects of Social Behaviour and Network Therapy (SBNT) (Copello *et al.*, 2002), a new form of treatment integrating a range of successful or promising social/ interpersonal approaches reported in the treatment literature, with MET (Miller *et al.*, 1992), one of the modalities investigated in Project MATCH. Findings from UKATT will also be discussed in this chapter.

INEFFECTIVE TREATMENT MODALITIES

We shall consider first treatment modalities that have been shown by research to be ineffective (as shown by a negative CES in the *Mesa Grande*) and those for which there is little or no evidence either for or against effectiveness (a CES close to zero in the *Mesa Grande*). The intention is not to list all treatment modalities fitting this description but to focus on a few prominent examples of modalities that continue to be widely implemented despite the absence of good evidence to support them.

Group Therapy

The traditional model of treatment in the alcohol problems field is group therapy. It was the principal type of intervention in the residential *alcoholism treatment units* that dominated the response to alcohol problems in the UK and in other countries from the pioneering work of Dr Max Glatt in the 1950s to the 1980s (Ettore, 1984, 1988). The conduct of group therapy in this tradition was heavily influenced by the teachings of AA and group therapy of this kind is still widely practised today.

Unfortunately, there is no evidence that group therapy for alcohol problems is effective. This is shown by the low negative CES for 'group process psychotherapy' in Table 15.1, based on three studies. The involvement of groups of people in the treatment process may be an important principle but there is little justification without further research for continued use of group therapy in the traditional way it has been used in the alcohol field.

Alcoholics Anonymous and Twelve-step Facilitation

The inclusion of AA in a section on ineffective treatments needs special justification. This is firstly because AA affiliates would deny that AA is a 'treatment' of any kind but rather a self-help or mutual-aid group outside the formal treatment system. Secondly, because of the anonymity of its affiliates and for other reasons, it has proved extremely difficult to conduct research on the effectiveness of AA. However, the Fellowship does make claims for its own effectiveness, sometimes startling ones, and this issue is therefore one for serious scientific consideration. Thirdly, there can be no doubt that, over the years, AA has helped a huge number of people with alcohol problems and saved many thousands of lives. Nevertheless, the professional in the field has to decide whether a particular client should or should not be encouraged to attend AA, a decision that must be based at least partly on research evidence.

The *Mesa Grande* in Table 15.1 shows a negative CES for AA. However, this is unfair on AA in one important sense. Because of the difficulties referred to above, it has not been possible to carry out randomised controlled trials of AA's effects among the anonymous, voluntary members it is primarily intended for; the only controlled studies to date have been conducted with individuals mandated by the courts to attend AA or some alternative and there are obvious grounds for suspecting that such individuals might have poorer outcomes in AA than voluntary affiliates. Thus the evidence in the *Mesa Grande* should be interpreted a providing no support for *compulsory* attendance at AA as part of court orders or employee assistance programmes.

While on the topic of AA, we may also note the negative CES in Table 15.1 for 'Twelve-step facilitation'. This refers to a one-to-one approach in which the Twelve Steps, the body of principles in which the spiritual message of AA is conveyed, are explained to and discussed with the clients, with attendance at the Fellowship itself the immediate objective (Emrick, 2003). Despite the negative CES, results of Project MATCH were that TSF was as effective as CBT and MET, a finding that supporters of the latter two approaches must have found surprising. Indeed, in the aftercare arm of the project, TSF was slightly but significantly superior to the other two therapies in terms of frequency of abstinence following treatment. In addition, there were three 'matches' favouring TSF:

- in the outpatient arm, clients low in psychiatric severity (those with low psychiatric comorbidity) reported more days abstinence after TSF than after CBT, an effect present at the one-year follow-up but not at the three-year follow-up;
- in the aftercare arm, clients with high alcohol dependence reported more abstinent days with TSF than with CBT at one-year follow-up;
- in the outpatient arm, those individuals with a social network supportive of drinking (those with a lot of heavy drinking friends) did better with TSF than MET, an effect that did not emerge until the three-year follow-up, but the largest matching effect identified in the trial when it did emerge. This last finding is especially interesting in view of accumulating evidence (Beattie, 2001; Kaskutas, Bond & Keith, 2002; Weisner, Matzger & Kasklutas, 2003; Zywiak, Longabaugh & Wirtz, 2002) that clients with heavy drinking social networks tend to show poor treatment outcomes and that intervening in the social network may be an effective component of therapy (Copello *et al.*, 2002).

All the above effects are clearly predicated on attendance at AA meetings and, on a cautionary note, might be affected by the specific cultural context of the US in which AA attendance is popular and AA's influence in the field of alcohol problems very strong. If replicated in other countries, however, the indications are that clients without accompanying psychiatric disorder, with high levels of alcohol dependence or with social networks supportive of drinking, are best suited for referral to AA. Since it is a purely mutual aid organisation AA is also likely to be highly cost-effective.

Insight-oriented Psychotherapy

As is well known, Freud and other early psychoanalysts largely ignored treatment of alcohol dependence and other addictions (Forrest, 1985). Later research suggests that this neglect was justified. The 'psychotherapy' category in Table 15.1 embraces psychotherapeutic methods designed to bring about change by increasing insight into motivations for drinking and revealing underlying psychodynamic processes. It will be seen that this category obtains one of the lowest CESs in the *Mesa Grande*.

Counselling

A national census of UK alcohol treatment agencies carried out in 1996 showed that two-thirds of clients being treated for alcohol problems on a particular day were seen in the non-statutory sector (Luce *et al.*,2000). Depending on the way treatment services are organised, a similar conclusion may apply to other countries. The main approach to helping clients in the non-statutory sector, in the UK at any rate, comes under the heading of 'counselling'. Unfortunately, so little is know about what precisely is covered by counselling in this general sense that it is difficult to arrive at any firm conclusions regarding its effectiveness.

As far as research evidence goes, Table 15.1 reflects the fact that counselling covers a range of different activities. 'General alcoholism counselling', an ill-defined category that presumably includes atheoretical information giving and exhortation, obtains a very low CES, exceeded only by 'educational lectures and films' given in a group format. Unfortunately, both these categories are staples of treatment programmes throughout the world. So too, 'confrontational counselling', based on a misinterpretation of AA principles (Miller & Rollnick, 1991, p. 7) and aimed at breaking down the client's 'denial' and 'resistance', fares badly in the *Mesa Grande* but, again, is commonly practised, particularly in the US. Against this, 'client-centred counselling' based on the work of Carl Rogers (1951) appears as an effective modality, although not as effective as other approaches in the table to which we now turn.

EFFECTIVE TREATMENT MODALITIES

In this section, we shall consider some of the modalities that can be considered effective, as shown by high CESs in the *Mesa Grande*. Again, the idea is not to describe every single effective treatment for alcohol problems but merely to focus on a few general approaches that are supported by research evidence and can easily be implemented in practice.

Brief Interventions

The highest CES in Table 15.1 is for brief interventions; however, there are a number of important considerations to bear in mind here. First, the category of brief interventions contains two different kinds of activity: very brief interventions given by generalist workers (for example, general medical practitioners) in community settings to excessive drinkers not complaining of an alcohol-related problem and longer brief interventions, better called 'brief treatment', given by alcohol or addiction workers in specialist treatment centres to those who do complain, or have been persuaded to complain, of an alcohol-related problem (Heather, 2003). The existence of the second class of brief interventions makes especially relevant the inclusion of figures for 'clinical populations only' in Table 15.1. It will be seen that nearly half the studies of brief interventions are of this type and that it retains its first-place ranking for cumulative effectiveness. What is not made clear in the *Mesa Grande* is that, even though it is directed at a clinical population, this sort of brief treatment would normally be offered to clients with less severe problems among those attending specialist treatment centres. Since the brief interventions in the generalist subcategory are by definition aimed at individuals with less severe problems, the direct comparison of brief interventions with other modalities in the *Mesa Grande* is in a sense misleading because it does not compare like with like.

The above distinction between subcategories of brief intervention was accepted by Moyer *et al.* (2002) who carried out separate meta-analyses for each. For studies of generalist brief interventions, in which the comparison was with control conditions in non-treatment-seeking samples, small to medium effect sizes were found in favour of brief interventions. At earlier follow-up points, the effect size was increased when individuals with more severe problems were excluded. For studies of specialist brief interventions, where the comparison was with more extended intervention in treatment-seeking samples, there was no evidence that the briefer interventions were less effective. Thus, provided they are used in the right circumstances with the appropriate types of client, the effectiveness of brief interventions is supported by a very large amount of research evidence.

Brief interventions are certainly suitable for those with mild alcohol dependence and/or problems but we do not yet know with any confidence the upper limit of seriousness for the application of brief interventions and therefore which clients should be excluded from brief interventions and offered more intensive treatment. In the meantime it is better to be cautious and restrict brief interventions mainly to those with mild to moderate alcohol problems.

The behaviour change methods used in brief interventions vary considerably. Brief interventions in specialist settings, and sometimes in generalist settings when more time is available (Israel *et al.*, 1996), often represent a condensed version of cognitive-behavioural treatment (see below). Many generalist brief interventions, however, consist of little more than advice, albeit given in sympathetic and constructive terms and preferably tailored to the circumstances of the individual client. Even here, though, practitioners are advised to adhere as far as possible to the six ingredients of effective brief interventions identified by Bien, Miller & Tonigan (1993) and summarised by the acronym FRAMES (see Box 15.1).

Box 15.1 Ingredients of effective brief interventions (from Bien, Miller & Tonigan, 1993)

- *F*eedback of personal risk or impairment.
- emphasis on personal *r*esponsibility for change.
- clear *a*dvice to change.
- a *m*enu of alternative change options.
- therapeutic *e*mpathy as a counselling style.
- enhancement of *s*elf-efficacy or optimism.

Motivational Enhancement

The treatment modality known as 'motivational interviewing' was developed by W.R. Miller (1983) and has been described at greater length by Miller & Rollnick (1991, 2002). The somewhat more general heading in the *Mesa Grande* of 'motivational enhancement' includes more structured forms of intervention, such as the Drinker's Check-up (Miller, Sovereign & Krege, 1988) and Motivational Enhancement Therapy (MET) as used in Project MATCH (Miller *et al.*, 1992), in which results of assessments are fed back to the client and discussed in a motivational interviewing style. The basic objective of motivational interviewing in all its forms is to elicit from clients an increase in motivation to change behaviour without attempting to impose such an increase on them. The motivational interviewing style owes much to Rogers' (1951) non-directive, client-centred counselling but has been described by its authors as client-centred and *directive* (Rollnick & Miller, 1995). Motivational interviewing has become extremely popular among practitioners in the alcohol problems field, the addictions field more generally and increasingly in other areas of behaviour change such as exercise, diet and forms of sexual behaviour, where clients experience an ambivalence about giving the behaviour up. Several accounts of the principles and techniques of motivational interviewing are available, including Miller & Rollnick (1991, 2002), Miller *et al.* (1992) and Rollnick & Allison (2003).

Many of the brief interventions that have been subject to research trials are based on brief forms of motivational interviewing (for example, Bennett, Edwards & Bailey, 2002; Gentilello *et al.*, 1999; Hulse & Tait, 2002; Longabaugh *et al.*, 2001; Marlatt *et al.*, 1998; Monti *et al.*, 1999; Smith *et al.*, 2003; Stein *et al.*, 2002) and this is an increasing tendency. However, these studies are included under the motivational enhancement category in the *Mesa Grande* rather than under brief interventions. The CES in Table 15.1 is highly positive, both in the clinical population and for alcohol problems of all severities. This occurs despite the fact that few studies of motivational interviewing include quality control of treatment fidelity and it is often not clear whether what was offered to clients conformed to the method as described by its originators (Rollnick & Miller, 1995). A specific use of motivational interviewing is as a preparation for more extended treatment and two randomised studies in the alcohol problems field have shown this application to improve treatment outcome (Bien, Miller & Boroughs, 1993; Brown & Miller, 1993). Motivational interviewing has also been subject to systematic review and formal meta-analysis by Noonan & Moyers (1997) and Dunn, Deroo & Rivara (2001), with positive conclusions.

In findings from Project MATCH (Project MATCH Research Group, 1997b), in the outpatient arm of the trial, clients who were initially high in anger reported more days of abstinence and fewer drinks per drinking day if they had received MET than if they had received CBT. This effect persisted from the one-year to the three-year follow-up point (Project MATCH Research Group, 1998a). This presumably reflects the deliberately non-confrontational nature of MET and high client anger at initial assessment is clearly a positive indicator for the offer of MET, at least as a first step in treatment.

A study in New Zealand (Sellman *et al.*, 2001) showed that four sessions of MET were more effective than four sessions of 'non-directive reflective listening' and to a non-intervention control group, suggesting that it is the specific ingredients of MET rather than any non-specific effects that are responsible for its success.

Community Reinforcement Approach and Related Treatments

Among problem drinkers with severe problems and high dependence – those traditionally labelled 'chronic alcoholics' – one of the most effective treatment modalities is the community reinforcement approach (CRA) and this is reflected in the *Mesa Grande* where it occupies fourth position. The full CRA consists of a broad range of treatment components, which all have the aim of engineering the client's social environment (including the family and vocational environment) so that sobriety is rewarded and intoxication un-rewarded. Although based firmly in the traditional Skinnerian principles of instrumental learning (Bigelow, 2001), the modern form of CRA includes methods to change clients' beliefs and expectations (Smith & Myers, 1995) and several ingredients of the standard cognitive-behavioural approach to treatment (see below).

It is often claimed that the CRA is too expensive to implement in routine practice. This conclusion is challenged by Myers & Miller (2001) who point out that better outcomes from the CRA relative to traditional approaches have been based on treatments of between five and eight sessions, comfortably within the range of intensity of treatments usually offered in the UK and other countries. Even if this is not accepted, however, the *principles* of the approach (those designed to change the social environment so that sobriety is reinforced and heavy drinking unreinforced) can be applied to the individual case. The CRA has proved especially impressive with socially unstable and isolated clients with a poor prognosis for traditional forms of treatment, including those who have failed in treatment several times in the past.

The CRA was one of the influences on the development of SBNT, the treatment modality that was compared with MET in the UKATT. Other influences were social skills training (Oei & Jackson, 1980), behavioural marital therapy (McCrady *et al.*, 1991) and network therapy (Galanter, 1993). The first two of these obtain high ratings in the *Mesa Grande*, whereas the third remains unevaluated. More generally, leaving aside the two highest ratings (brief interventions and motivational enhancement), which may apply to modalities more suitable for clients with less severe problems, it is striking that many of the best supported treatments in the *Mesa Grande* contain a social or at least interpersonal component. This is consistent with evidence mentioned above on the importance of the client's social networks in the response to treatment (Beattie, 2001) and with the way that AA is thought to exert its beneficial effects (by demanding a change in lifestyle and modes of social interaction) (Kaskutas *et al.*, 2002). However, UKATT failed to reveal any overall superiority of SBNT, scheduled for 8 50-minute sessions, over MET of three sessions (UKATT Research Team 2005a). These two forms of treatment showed no differences in their effectiveness in reducing alcohol problems.

Cognitive-behavioural Therapy

There is no single category for CBT in Table 15.1 but several treatment methods usually classified under this more general heading obtain a high CES (behavioural self-control training, behaviour contracting, social skills training and behavioural marital therapy). On the whole, therefore, CBT is strongly supported by the *Mesa Grande* (see also Parks, Marlatt & Anderson, 2003).

Behavioural self-control training (Hester, 1995) is usually aimed at a goal of moderate use of alcohol rather than total abstinence and, as such, is normally offered to problem drinkers with lower levels of dependence and problems. It is also the approach to treatment that most often forms the basis for the written guidance on how to change drinking behaviour in self-change manuals, another modality well supported by the *Mesa Grande*. Behavioural contracting (Keane *et al.*, 1984) is a common ingredient of the CBT approach to alcohol problems and aims to ensure that the client's relationships with significant others are helpful to the treatment process rather than unhelpful; it also forms part of the CRA (see above). Social skills training (Monti *et al.*, 1995) focuses on a particular behavioural deficit that is commonly found in problem drinkers but is only one approach to enabling the client to cope with stressful situations without recourse to heavy drinking. Lastly, it should be noted that behavioural marital therapy (O'Farrell, 1993) obtains a high positive CES whereas non-behavioural marital therapy does not. Considered as single entities, a range of other methods commonly associated with the CBT approach, such as 'problem solving', 'functional analysis', 'self-monitoring' and 'relaxation training' are not supported by the *Mesa Grande*.

In the alcohol problems field, 'cognitive therapy' is regarded as somewhat different from CBT. The former derives from the work of Beck and his colleagues in the substance-abuse field (Beck *et al.*, 1993) and entails an attempt to modify maladaptive cognitions that are thought to underlie the drinking problem, as contrasted with the more performance-based methods of CBT. This distinction is not entirely clear because cognitive therapy often includes role-play, homework assignments and so forth, whereas CBT often includes attention to modifying automatic thoughts and the cognitive restructuring of unhelpful beliefs, but the 10 studies that have explicitly evaluated cognitive therapy resulted in only a modest positive CES in Table 15.1.

'Relapse prevention' is another category needing clarification in the *Mesa Grande*. In an important sense, relapse prevention is a goal of treatment, one that is an inherent part of the CBT approach in this area, rather than a specific treatment method (Parks, Anderson & Marlatt, 2003). The studies subsumed under the relapse prevention category in Table 15.1, where it has a negative CES, were focussed on various methods for helping clients anticipate and cope with high-risk situations for heavy drinking. Again, in isolation, relapse prevention in this sense appears ineffective. However, as we have seen, the CBT methods with which the relapse prevention goal forms an integral part are heavily endorsed by the *Mesa Grande*.

Pharmacotherapy

Table 15.1 shows first that several medications that have been successful in the treatment of other disorders (for example, antidepressants – both SSRIs and non-SSRIs, lithium, anxiolytic drugs in general) have not been found to be effective in the alcohol problems field. However, two relatively recently developed drugs, acamprosate (purportedly a GABA agonist) and naltrexone (an opiate antagonist) score in third and sixth place respectively in Table 15.1. The effects of these newer drugs are more specific to alcohol and they are thought to work by reducing craving for alcohol and/or its rewarding properties (Chick, 2003). Even here, however, psychosocial treatment may have an important role to play. Volpicelli *et al.* (1992) found that a combination of naltrexone and psychotherapy produced better outcome than either alone and O'Malley (1996) reported a similar findings for naltrexone and coping skills therapy. The effects of combining pharmacotherapies and psychosocial treatments for alcohol problems is currently the subject of a large, multi-centred trial (Project COMBINE) in the US. However, an internationally recognised authority on pharmacotherapies in the alcohol field has written: 'At best, these treatments are only an aid to establishing a change in lifestyle' (Chick, 2003, p. 64), thereby endorsing the view that pharmacotherapy remains adjunctive in the treatment of alcohol problems.

A common ingredient of the CRA is the deterrent drug disulfiram, which produces a very unpleasant physiological reaction if alcohol is taken and whose effects can also be understood in terms of operant conditioning principles. Myers & Miller's (2001) conclusion was that disulfiram is not necessary to the effectiveness of the CRA. On the other hand, disulfiram does increase the effectiveness of traditional treatment. The evidence strongly suggests that disulfiram is only effective if compliance with taking medication is based on supervision by a professional or relative in a behavioural contract (Brewer, 1993). If consideration were confined to studies where this 'compliance assurance' method was used, the CES for disulfiram would probably be higher than shown in Table 15.1 and would suggest that drug treatment for alcohol problems must be understood and implemented in a social psychological context.

INTENSITY, SETTING AND COST-EFFECTIVENESS OF TREATMENT

With the advent of brief interventions, treatment for alcohol problems has become more variable in length (duration) and intensity (amount of therapist contact). There is little doubt that, for heavy drinkers not seeking treatment and identified by screening in generalist settings, brief interventions of one or two sessions are all that is necessary in most cases; for those in the treatment-seeking population with more serious problems the optimal intensity of treatment is unknown. Project MATCH (1997a) found that four sessions of MET were generally as effective as eight sessions of CBT or TSF although, as we have seen, certain types of client benefited more from the more intensive treatments. Nevertheless, the Project MATCH findings suggest that, on the whole, less intensive treatment by MET is more cost-effective than more intensive alternatives (Cisler et al., 1998). Against this, in a reanalysis of the MATCH economic data, Holder et al. (2000) reported that, for certain types of client with typically poor prognoses, CBT or TSF was more cost-effective than MET. In the UKATT results, three sessions of MET were significantly cheaper to implement than eight sessions of SBNT and, as has already been stated, no less effective in reducing alcohol problems. Surprisingly perhaps, MET and SBNT did not differ in cost-effectiveness (UKATT Research Team, 2005b). The economic evaluation here was done from a societal perspective, taking into account costs and benefits in the health, social services and criminal justice sectors. However, from the perspective of the individual service provider, MET would be clearly more cost-effective, if only because more clients could be treated within a given time period and waiting lists proportionately reduced. Irrespective of treatment modality, it was found that treatment resulted in savings in costs averted in the one-year follow-up period of roughly five times what treatment cost to implement (UKATT Research Team, 2005b).

An interesting response to the problem of the optimal intensity of treatment is the development of the stepped-care model (Breslin et al., 1997; Sobell & Sobell, 2000) in which clients enter a treatment system at the lowest appropriate level, are followed up and then receive successively more intensive treatment if they have not shown improvement. Humphreys (2004) has suggested that the lowest rung on this ladder might be mutual aid organisations in the community, with obvious advantages for cost savings. Next levels might be brief interventions in generalist settings, brief treatment in specialist settings and more intensive treatment in specialist settings. Despite its interesting possibilities for the provision of effective and cost-effective treatment services, the stepped-care model remains to be properly evaluated.

There has been much attention in the alcohol problems treatment literature to the comparison of outpatient and inpatient services in terms of effectiveness and cost-effectiveness. An early conclusion (Miller, 1986) was that outpatient treatment was no less effective than inpatient treatment but that, since the latter was up to 10 times more expensive, outpatient treatment should generally be preferred. Finney, Haan & Moos (1996) carried out a systematic review of this area and concluded that residential treatment may be indicated for clients who have shown themselves to be unresponsive to treatment in the past, who have meagre financial resources and whose home environments are inimical to recovery.

In terms of cost-effectiveness, while inpatient or residential programmes lasting more than four weeks do not produce better outcomes than very brief hospitalisation, partial hospitalisation programmes are equal to or superior in effectiveness to inpatient programmes. Clients with relative greater social resources, in terms of employment and relationships, were better suited to outpatient treatment.

Certainly, there is little evidence for the cost-effectiveness of expensive, profit-making treatment programmes found under the headings of 'the Minnesota Model' or 'milieu therapy' (see Table 15.1). People with alcohol problems have a right, of course, to spend their own money how they wish but there is no justification for the expenditure of *public* funds on these residential facilities.

THERAPIST FACTORS

This chapter has focussed on research into the effectiveness of different treatment modalities in the response to alcohol-related problems, with some attention to issues of intensity, setting and implications for cost-effectiveness. What has not yet been covered is research on the non-specific features of treatment that are common to all modalities and delivery settings – chiefly characteristics of therapists and their interactions with clients that are associated with the variance in treatment outcome. There are grounds for believing that these therapist and interactional factors are nearly as important to treatment success as differences between treatment modalities based on psychological or therapeutic theories – some would say more important (Luborsky *et al.*, 1986).

The factor of this kind that has received most attention in the alcohol field is therapist *empathy*. Miller, Taylor & West (1980) reported that behavioural self-control training on a one-to-one basis was no more effective than a self-help manual without therapist contact. However, when the authors examined differences between therapists more closely, they found that clients of therapists rated as most empathic fared better than those given a self-help manual, whereas clients of those rated least empathic did worse. Therapist empathy accounted for two-thirds of the variance in outcome of treatment at various follow-up points. Valle (1981) reported similar findings from a study of client-centred counselling for alcohol problems. A further remarkable finding was reported by Miller, Benefield & Tonigan (1993) who showed that half the variance in treatment outcome could be predicted by the degree to which the therapist had confronted the client, in many ways the opposite of empathy, during treatment sessions.

The issue of therapist factors was explored in Project MATCH (1998b) but this analysis was limited by the fact that therapists were selected by their preferences for each of the three modalities studied. This may be the reason why no clear picture emerged of therapist characteristics or skills associated with better outcome. However, in all three of the treatments under study, at least one 'outlier' therapist produced results much worse that the remainder.

One other feature of Project MATCH findings deserves comment in this section on non-specific factors. Whatever method of accounting is used, this project produced highly successful outcomes of treatment and these outcomes were associated with highly trained therapists delivering standardised treatment manuals written by some of the best clinicians and researchers in the field in the US (Kadden *et al.*, 1992; Miller *et al.*, 1992; Nowinski, Baker & Carroll, 1992). Thus the issue of professional training for alcohol therapists, and the degree to which the success of treatment as a whole can be improved by better training and greater quality control, is an important one for any treatment system. With regard to manualised treatments, it is not known whether this produces better treatment than allowing therapists more flexibility in the conduct of treatment but this is an issue clearly in need of research attention.

CONCLUSIONS

We need to learn more about the influence of therapist and interactional variables on the outcome of treatment for alcohol problems but this chapter has shown that there exists a range of effective treatment approaches, each backed by a body of consistent findings from acceptably rigorous research, with which to help people recover. Project MATCH has provided some indication of what works best for which type of client. In the majority of cases, however, client-treatment matching must rest, for the time being, on the preferences of both client and therapist, the expertise and resources available to treatment providers and the particular needs and unique characteristics of the individual problem drinker.

The chapter has also shown that there is a range of widely practised treatments, which have either been shown conclusively to be ineffective by research or for which no evidence of effectiveness currently exists. Miller & Hester (1986) complained of an almost perfect inverse relationship between effective and practised treatments in the treatment system in the US with which they were familiar: those treatments that were supported by research were not practised and those that were practised were not supported by research. This state of affairs was relevant in varying degrees to all national treatment systems. It is difficult to be certain whether and how far this situation has improved because there is a dearth of reliable data on what actually takes place in day-to-day treatment provision. What can be asserted with some confidence, however, is that there remains some way to go before practice in the alcohol problems treatment field can meaningfully be said to be evidence-based.

ACKNOWLEDGEMENTS

I thank Delilah Yao for secretarial assistance in the preparation of this chapter. Thanks also to Griffith Edwards, John Finney and William R. Miller for advice on specific points.

REFERENCES

Beattie, M.C. (2001). Meta-analysis of social relationships and post-treatment drinking outcomes: comparison of relationship structure, function and quality. *Journal of Studies on Alcohol, 62*, 518–527.

Beck, A.T., Wright, A.T., Newman, C.F. & Liese, B.S. (1993). *Cognitive Therapy of Substance Abuse*. New York NY: Guilford.

Bennett, G. A., Edwards, S. & Bailey, J. (2002). Helping methadone patients who drink excessively to drink less: short-term outcomes of a pilot motivational intervention. *Journal of Substance Use, 7*, 191–197.

Bien, T.H., Miller, W.R. & Boroughs, J. (1993). Motivational interviewing with alcohol outpatients. *Behavioural and Cognitive Psychotherapy, 21*, 347–356.

Bien, T. H., Miller, W. R., & Tonigan, J. S. (1993). Brief interventions for alcohol problems: A review. *Addiction, 88*, 315–335.

Bigelow, G. (2001). An operant behavioural perspective on alcohol abuse and dependence. In N. Heather, T.J. Peters & T. Stockwell (eds), *International Handbook of Alcohol Dependence and Problems* (pp. 299–316). Chichester: John Wiley.

Breslin, F.C., Sobell, M.B., Sobell, L.C. *et al.* (1997). Toward a stepped care approach to treating problem drinkers: The predictive utility of within-treatment variables and therapist prognostic ratings. *Addiction, 92,* 1479–1489.

Brewer, C. (ed.) (1993). *Treatment Options in Addiction: Medical Management of Alcohol and Opiate Abuse.* London: Gaskell.

Brown, J. M. & Miller, W. R. (1993). Impact of motivational interviewing on participation and outcome in residential alcoholism treatment. *Psychology of Addictive Behaviors, 7,* 211–218.

Chick, J. (2003). Pharmacological treatments. In N. Heather & T. Stockwell (eds), *Essential Handbook of Treatment and Prevention of Alcohol Problems* (pp. 53–68). Chichester: John Wiley.

Cisler, R., Holder, H.D., Longabaugh, R. *et al.* (1998). Actual and estimated replication costs for alcohol treatment modalities: case study from Project MATCH. *Journal of Studies on Alcohol, 50,* 503–512.

Copello, A., Orford, J., Hodgson, R. *et al.* (2002). Social behaviour and network therapy: Basic principles and early experiences. *Addictive Behaviors, 27,* 354–366.

Dunn, C., Deroo, L. & Rivara, F.P. (2001). The use of brief interventions adapted from motivational interviewing across behavioural domains: a systematic review. *Addiction, 96,* 1725–1742.

Emrick, C.D. (2003). Alcoholics Anonymous and other mutual aid groups. In N. Heather & T. Stockwell (eds), *Essential Handbook of Treatment and Prevention of Alcohol Problems.* Chichester: John Wiley.

Ettore, E.M. (1984). A study of alcoholism treatment units: Treatment activities and the institutional response. *Alcohol and Alcoholism, 19,* 243–255.

Ettore, E.M. (1988). A follow-up study of alcoholism treatment units: Exploring consolidation and change. *British Journal of Addiction, 83,* 57–65.

Finney, J.W. (2000). Limitations in using existing alcohol treatment trials to develop practice guidelines. *Addiction, 95,* 1491–1500.

Finney, J.W., Hahn, A.C. & Moos, R.H. (1996). The effectiveness of inpatient and outpatient treatment for alcohol abuse: The need to focus on mediators and moderators of setting effects. *Addiction, 91,* 1773–1796.

Forrest, G.G. (1985). Psychodynamically-oriented treatment of alcoholism and substance abuse. In T.E. Bratter & G.G. Forrest (eds), *Alcoholism and Substance Abuse: Strategies for Clinical Intervention* (pp. 307–336). New York: Free Press.

Galanter, M. (1993). *Network Therapy for Alcohol and Drug Abuse: A New Approach in Practice.* New York: Basic Books.

Gentilello, L.M., Rivara, F.P., Donovan, D.M. *et al.* (1999). Alcohol interventions in a trauma center as a means of reducing the risk of injury recurrence. *Annals of Surgery, 230,* 473–480.

Heather, N. (2003). Brief interventions. In N. Heather & T. Stockwell (eds), *Essential Handbook Treatment and Prevention of Alcohol Problems* (pp. 117–138). Chichester: John Wiley.

Heather, N. & Kaner, E. (2003). Brief interventions against excessive alcohol consumption. In D.A. Warrell, T.M. Cox, J.D. Firth with E.J. Benz Jr. (eds), *Oxford Textbook of Medicine,* Vol. 3 (4th edn) (pp. 1334–1337). Oxford: Oxford Medical Publications.

Hester, R.K. (1995). Behavioral self-control training. In R.K. Hester & W.R. Miller (eds), *Handbook of Alcoholism Treatment Approaches: Effective Alternatives* (2nd edn) (pp. 148–159). Boston MA: Allyn & Bacon.

Holder, H. D., Cisler, R. A., Longabaugh, R. *et al.* (2000). Alcoholism treatment and medical care costs from Project MATCH. *Addiction, 95,* 999–1013.

Hulse, G.K. & Tait, R.J. (2002). Six-month outcomes associated with a brief alcohol intervention for adult in-patients with psychiatric disorders. *Drug and Alcohol Review, 21,* 105–112.

Humphreys, K. (2004). *Circles of Recovery: Self-help Organisations for Addictions.* Cambridge: Cambridge University Press.

Institute of Medicine (1990). *Broadening the Base of Treatment for Alcohol Problems.* Washington, DC: National Academy Press.

Israel, Y., Hollander, O., Sanchez-Craig, M. *et al.* (1996). Screening for problem drinking and counseling by the primary care physician-nurse team. *Alcoholism: Clinical and Experimental Research, 20*, 1443–1450.

Kadden, R.P., Carroll, K., Donovan, D. *et al.* (1992). *Cognitive-behavioral Coping Skills Therapy: A Clinical Research Guide for Therapists Treating Individuals with Alcohol Abuse and Dependence,* Project MATCH Monograph Series, vol. 3, DHHS Pub. No. (ADM) 92–1895. Washington DC: Department of Health & Human Services.

Kaskutas, L.A., Bond, J. & Keith, H. (2002). Social networks as mediators of the effect of Alcoholics Anonymous. *Addiction, 97*, 891–900.

Keane, T.M., Foy, D.W., Nunn, B. & Rychtarik, R.G. (1984). Spouse contracting to increase antabuse compliance in alcoholic veterans. *Journal of Clinical Psychology, 40*, 340–344.

Longabaugh, R., Woolard, R.F., Nirenberg, T.D. *et al.* (2001). Evaluating the effects of a brief motivational intervention for injured drinkers in the emergency department. *Journal of Studies on Alcohol, 62*, 806–816.

Luborksy, L., Crits-Cristoph, P., McLellan, A.T. *et al.* (1986). Do therapists vary much in their success? Findings from four outcome studies. *American Journal of Orthopsychiatry, 56*, 501–512.

Luce, A., Heather, N. & McCarthy, S. (2000). National census of UK alcohol treatment agencies: I. Characteristics of clients, treatment and treatment providers. *Journal of Substance Use, 5*, 112–121.

Marlatt, G.A., Baer, J.S., Kivlahan, D.R. *et al.* (1998). Screening and brief intervention for high-risk college student drinkers: results from a 2-year follow-up assessment. *Journal of Consulting and Clinical Psychology, 66*, 604–615.

McCrady, B.S., Stout, R.L., Noel, N.E. *et al.* (1991). Comparative effectiveness of three types of spouse-involved behavioural alcoholism treatment: Outcomes 18 months after treatment. *British Journal of Addiction, 86*, 1415–1424.

Miller, W., Benefield, R. & Tonigan, S. (1993). Enhancing motivation for change in problem drinking: a controlled comparison of two therapeutic styles. *Journal of Consulting and Clinical Psychology, 61*, 455–461.

Miller, W.R. (1983). Motivational interviewing with problem drinkers. *Behavioural Psychotherapy, 11*, 147–172.

Miller, W.R. (1986). The effectiveness of alcoholism treatment: What research reveals. In W.R. Miller & N. Heather (eds), *Treating Addictive Behaviours: Processes of Change* (pp. 121–174). New York: Plenum Press.

Miller, W.R. & Hester, R.K. (1986). Inpatient alcoholism treatment: Who benefits? *American Psychologist, 41*, 794–805.

Miller, W.R. & Rollnick, S. (1991). *Motivational Interviewing: Preparing People to Change Addictive Behavior.* New York: Guilford.

Miller, W.R., & Rollnick, S. (2002). *Motivational Interviewing: Preparing People for Change* (2nd edn). New York: Guilford.

Miller, W.R., Sovereign, R.G. & Krege, B. (1988). Motivational interviewing with problem drinkers: II the drinkers check-up as a preventive intervention. *Behavioural Psychotherapy, 16*, 251–268.

Miller, W.R., Taylor, C.A. & West, J.C. (1980). Focused versus broad spectrum behavior therapy for problem drinkers. *Journal of Consulting and Clinical Psychology, 48*, 590–601.

Miller, W.R., Wilbourne, P.L. & Hettema, J.E. (2003). What works? A summary of alcohol treatment outcome research. In R.K. Hester & W.R. Miller (eds), *Handbook of Alcoholism Treatment Approaches: Effective Alternatives* (3rd edn) (pp. 13–63). Boston, MA: Allyn & Bacon.

Miller, W.R., Zweben, A., DiClemente, C. & Rychtarik, R. (1992). *Motivational Enhancement Therapy: A Clinical Research Guide for Therapists Treating Individuals with Alcohol Abuse and Dependence.* Project MATCH Monograph Series, vol. 2, DHHS Pub. No. (ADM) 92–1894. Washington DC: Department of Health & Human Services.

Monti, P.M., Colby, S.M., Barnett, N.P. *et al.* (1999). Brief intervention for harm reduction with alcohol-positive older adolescents in a hospital emergency department. *Journal of Consulting and Clinical Psychology, 67*, 989–994.

Monti, P.M., Rohsenow, D.J., Colby, S.M. & Abrams, D.BV. (1995). Coping and social skills training. In R.K. Hester & W.R. Miller (eds), *Handbook of Alcoholism Treatment Approaches: Effective Alternatives* (2nd edn) (pp. 221–241). Boston, MA: Allyn & Bacon.

Moyer, A., Finney, J., Swearingen, C. & Vergun, P. (2002). Brief interventions for alcohol problems: A meta-analytic review of controlled investigations in treatment-seeking and non-treatment seeking populations. *Addiction, 97,* 279–292.

Myers, R.J. & Miller, W.R. (eds) (2001). *A Community Reinforcement Approach to Addiction Treatment.* Cambridge: Cambridge University Press.

Noonan, W.C. & Moyers, T.B. (1997). Motivational interviewing. *Journal of Substance Misuse, 2,* 8–16.

Nowinski, J., Baker, S. & Carroll, K. (1992). *Twelve Step Facilitation Therapy: A Clinical Research Guide for Therapists Treating Individuals with Alcohol Abuse and Dependence,* Project MATCH Monograph Series, vol. 1, DHHS Pub. No. (ADM) 92-1893. Washington DC: Department of Health and Human Services.

Oei, T.P.S. & Jackson, P. (1980). Long term effects of group and individual social skills training with alcoholics. *Addictive Behaviors, 5,* 129–136.

O'Farrell, T.J. (ed.) (1993). *Treating Alcohol Problems: Marital and Family Interventions.* New York: Guilford.

O'Malley, S.S. (1996). Six month follow-up of naltrexone and psychotherapy for alcohol dependence. *Archives of General Psychiatry, 53,* 217–224.

Parks, G.A., Anderson, B.K. & Marlatt, G.A. (2003). Relapse prevention therapy. In N. Heather & T. Stockwell (eds), *Essential Handbook of Treatment and Prevention of Alcohol Problems* (pp. 87–104). Chichester: John Wiley.

Parks, G.A., Marlatt, G.A. & Anderson, B.K. (2003). Cognitive-behavioural alcohol treatment. In N. Heather & T. Stockwell (eds), *Essential Handbook of Treatment and Prevention of Alcohol Problems* (pp. 69–86). Chichester: John Wiley.

Project MATCH Research Group (1997a). Matching alcoholism treatment to client heterogeneity: Project MATCH posttreatment drinking outcomes. *Journal of Studies on Alcohol, 58,* 7–29.

Project MATCH Research Group (1997b). Project MATCH secondary a priori hypotheses. *Addiction, 92,* 1671–1698.

Project MATCH Research Group (1998a). Matching alcoholism treatments to client heterogeneity: project MATCH three-year drinking outcomes. *Alcoholism: Experimental and Clinical Research, 22,* 1300–1311.

Project MATCH Research Group, P. M. R. (1998b). Therapist effects in three treatments for alcohol problems. *Psychotherapy Research, 8,* 455–474.

Rimmele, C.T., Howard, M.O. & Hilfrink, M.L. (1995). Aversion therapies. In R.K. Hester & W.R. Miller (eds), *Handbook of Alcoholism Treatment Approaches: Effective Alternatives* (2nd edn) (pp. 134–147). Boston, MA: Allyn & Bacon.

Rogers, C.R. (1951). *Client-centred Therapy.* Boston, MA: Houghton Mifflin.

Rollnick, S. & Allison, J. (2003). Motivational interviewing. In N. Heather & T. Stockwell (eds), *Essential Handbook of Treatment and Prevention of Alcohol Problems* (pp. 105–115). Chichester: John Wiley.

Rollnick, S. & Miller, W.R. (1995). What is motivational interviewing? *Behavioural and Cognitive Psychotherapy, 23,* 325–334.

Sellman, J.D., Sullivan, P.F., Dore, G.M., *et al.* (2001). A randomised controlled trial of Motivational Enhancement Therapy (MET) for mild to moderate alcohol dependence. *Journal of Studies on Alcohol, 62,* 389–396.

Smith, A. J., Hodgson, R. J., Bridgeman K. & Shepherd, J.P. (2003). A randomised controlled trial of a brief intervention after alcohol-related facial injury. *Addiction, 98,* 43–52.

Smith, J.E. & Myers, R.J. (1995). The community reinforcement approach. In R.K. Hester & W.R. Miller (eds), *Handbook of Alcoholism Treatment Approaches: Effective Alternatives* (2nd edn) (pp. 251–266). Boston, MA: Allyn & Bacon.

Sobell, M.B. & Sobell, L.C. (2000). Stepped care as a heuristic approach to the treatment of alcohol problems. *Journal of Consulting and Clinical Psychology, 68,* 573–579.

Stein, M.D., Charuvastra, A., Maksad, J. & Anderson, B.J. (2002). A randomised trial of a brief alcohol intervention for needle exchangers (BRAINE). *Addiction, 97,* 691–700.

UKATT Research Team (2001). United Kingdom Alcohol Treatment Trial: hypotheses, design and methods. *Alcohol and Alcoholism, 36,* 11–21.

UKATT Research Team (2005a). Effectiveness of treatment for alcohal problems: findings of the randomised UK Alcohol Treatment Trial (UKATT). *British Medical Journal, 351*, 541–544.

UKATT Research Team (2005b). Cost-effectiveness of treatment for alcohol problems: findings of the randomised UK Alcohol Treatment Trial (UKATT). *British Medical Journal, 351*, 544–548.

Valle, S.K. (1981). Interpersonal functioning of alcoholism counsellors and treatment outcome. *Journal of Studies on Alcohol, 42*, 783–790.

Volpicelli, J.R., Alterman, A.I., Hayashida, M. & O'Brien, C.P. (1992). Naltrexone in the treatment of alcohol dependence. *Archives of General Psychiatry, 49*, 876–880.

Weisner, C., Matzger, H. & Kaskutas, L.A. (2003). How important is treatment? One-year outcomes of treated and untreated alcohol-dependent individuals. *Addiction, 98*, 901–911.

Zywiak, W.H., Longabaugh, R. & Wirtz, P.W. (2002). Decomposing the relationships between pre-treatment social network characteristics and alcohol treatment outcome. *Journal of Studies on Alcohol, 63*, 114–121.

CHAPTER 16

Bereavement

Fiona Cathcart

St Columba's Hospice, Edinburgh, UK

INTRODUCTION

Death poses a challenge for society. The findings of archaeology and of sociology indicate that social groups have developed many different ways of dealing with the loss of their members. It is only relatively recently that the variability across cultures as well as the variation of the individuals within them has been acknowledged. There is continuing debate as to what might be considered 'normal' grief and what components characterise what was termed 'pathological' grief and now is described as 'complicated' grief (Stroebe, Stroebe & Hansson, 1993). This debate is relevant when considering at what point, if any, there should be a psychological intervention. The debate is not new. Claudius chides Hamlet for his continuing display of grief for his father. The audience is unaware at this point in the drama that Cladius has his own reasons for wanting few public reminders of the death. Hamlet's friends commiserate at the rapid remarriage of his mother. 'Indeed, my lord. It followed hard upon.' These interactions are meaningless unless Shakespeare's audience share the debate of what is timely in grief and how one should behave in bereavement.

This chapter explores current practice with reference to a historical context. Major models of bereavement are described and specific issues are discussed.

DEFINITIONS OF BEREAVEMENT, GRIEF, MOURNING

The term 'bereavement' is derived from the Anglo-Saxon word berēafian, which means to be robbed. The sense of a love and life taken resonate through literature and the narratives of bereaved people. The sense of emptiness is a common experience. A study day on perinatal loss was entitled 'The Aching Void'. The term 'grief' is often used to describe the emotional experience of loss but it is understood more widely as being not only the affective experience but also the cognitive, physical and behavioural changes that accompany it. C.S. Lewis (1966) describes the autonomic experience: 'No-one told me that grief felt so much like fear . . .' The type of emotional reaction may be unexpected but bereaved people do expect to feel upset. Fewer anticipate the temporary loss of concentration and memory and this can add to loss of confidence and the sense of life being out of control. The emotional, cognitive and behavioural responses do not take place within a social vacuum but will be shaped by it.

'Mourning' was used by Freud to mean what is now understood as 'grief' but the term 'mourning' has come to mean the rituals associated with the expression of grief and is socially determined (Gorer, 1965). There is social pressure to conform to the rituals of the time and place but mourning rituals change and there may be resistance to this by those who have a vested commercial interest in existing practice. In 1686 the Scots Parliament passed the *Act anent burying in Scots Linen* to promote the local linen trade. It had to be certificated by witnesses that the corpse was buried in Scots linen or severe financial penalties were imposed. In 1707 this was changed to woollen material because of lobbying by the Edinburgh merchants (Gordon, 1984). In the following century Yorkshire manufacturers of the black cloth used in making mourning clothes wrote to Queen Victoria lamenting that the custom of wearing mourning was becoming less common and they were in danger of losing their livelihoods.

METHODOLOGICAL ISSUES

Many studies have been published since the mid-1970s on the effectiveness of bereavement intervention but there are major methodological flaws with most of them (Allumbaugh & Hoyt, 1999; Dowdney, 2000; Kato & Mann, 1999). Stroebe, Stroebe & Schut (2003) argue it is unethical to carry out poorly designed bereavement research given the sensitivity of the subject. The following aspects have been criticised frequently in study design.

Recruitment and Attrition

Recruiting and maintaining subjects in large studies is problematic. Bereavement research is no exception. Parkes & Weiss (1983) reported that of 274 potential subjects 'nearly three-fifths agreed to be interviewed' and Schut et al. (1997) report that only just over one fifth (22%) of 358 eligible subjects agreed to participate in their study of gender differences and counselling programmes. Gallagher-Thompson et al. (1993) mailed 2450 bereaved individuals of whom 735 (30%) replied and only 212 met the criteria for age and proximity for domiciliary interviews. Large numbers of potential subjects need to be identified before adequate numbers of suitable subjects can be found to evaluate the effect of different variables.

It is tempting to speculate on the mental health of those who decline to participate in research. Some would argue that these individuals have coped well and are reluctant to invest time and energy into something for which they feel no need. Others would argue an opposing view and suggest these individuals are not coping well and feel too distressed. The situation is further complicated by the suggestion that the decision whether or not to participate in bereavement research may be gender related (Stroebe & Stroebe, 1989). A different rate of recruitment or attrition between groups adds to the dilemma in identifying the effects of different interventions. A third of participants in one study dropped out after finding out to which one of four groups they had been allocated (Barrett, 1978, cited in Kato & Mann, 1999). People may choose the intervention with which they feel most comfortable rather the one that is more effective for their needs (Parkes, 2000) but it is arguable that the client's perception of the credibility of an intervention may enhance its effectiveness.

The social context of the recruitment invitation can influence uptake. Couples who had experienced perinatal loss were more likely to accept the offer of counselling support if the therapist was present with the clinician at the time of the interview (Lilford *et al.*, 1994).

Bereaved children can be difficult to access because carers are protective and concerned that questioning would distress their children further. If adequate numbers of children are recruited, assessing the effectiveness of a programme continues to present challenges (Stokes, Wyer & Crossley, 1997)

Gender

Most participants in bereavement research are widows. A meta-analysis of 35 studies reported that 84 % of the participants were female with the modal person being a widow of 52 years (Allumbaugh & Hoyt, 1999). It has been suggested by Stroebe (1998) that within Western culture men and women respond differently to bereavement and this effect may confound results in studies in which gender has not been controlled. Earlier work by Stroebe & Stroebe (1989) found that widowers who agreed to participate in research were less depressed than those who declined whereas widows who agreed to participate were more depressed than those who declined. Bereaved women are more likely than bereaved men to be members of support groups and this is relevant if a sample is recruited in this way. In addition, it is arguable that there are differences between joiners and non-joiners of social groups regardless of their gender.

Nature of the Death

Some deaths are sudden but even where there has been a period of forewarning it may be seen as sudden by those bereaved. Anticipatory grief was described by Lindemann (1944) and the concept was refined by Rando (1988). The term originated to describe the experience of grieving so fully before an expected death that emotional ties are relinquished – the missing soldier returns but finds no welcome. A different view is that attachment strengthens in the face of loss and anticipatory grief is not the same as the grief felt subsequently. A preparatory period can offer advantages but if the final illness is of a protracted and uncertain duration then this brings different stressors. A study of 73 caregivers bereaved by the death of an elderly relative identified that quality of support prior to the death was more important in adjustment to bereavement than subsequent support (Bass, Bowman & Noelke, 1991).

Sudden, unexpected death is considered more problematic for the bereaved person and the research of Parkes & Weiss (1983) supports this, but there are confounding variables. Sudden death is more likely to be the cause of death in a younger population and so those bereaved may be younger and possible have dependent children. The death is more likely to be violent, whether this is caused by an industrial accident or major incident, and in these circumstances the death will involve lengthy legal processes and publicity. These issues are discussed later.

The Type and Nature of the Relationship

For a parent there is an untimeliness about the death of a child whether that child is in its early years or has become an adult. A source of practical and emotional support may be lost with the death of an adult child. If the dead person was not valued by their community then the bereaved survivor will feel isolated in grief as can happen with the bereaved parents of children with learning disabilities (Cathcart, 1996).

Parkes (1972) suggested that an ambivalent relationship is more complicated to grieve as unresolved tensions are left with the survivor. Pincus (1974) explored how the psychodynamics of marital relationships influence living with subsequent bereavement. The apparently stronger partner may have gained self-esteem by caring for the apparently less confident but this need is unmet by the death of the latter.

Age

Researchers have varied in their definition of 'elderly'. Gallagher-Thompson *et al.* (1993) set the limit at 55 years and over whereas Strobe & Stroebe (1993) used a sample with a mean age of 53 years in a study of younger widows. Lund, Caserta & Dimond (1993) examined bereavement in 'later life' and surveyed a bereaved population over the age of 50 years. This lack of agreement adds to the difficulty in drawing conclusions about the impact of bereavement on an elderly population. The participants in the Lund, Caserta & Dimond (1993) study ranged from 50 years to 93 years but the authors note with surprise that age was not an important predictor of outcome in spousal bereavement but personal resources such as flexibility and a sense of self-competence were more significant.

Culture and Ethnicity

Rosenblatt has been exploring the universality of grief for nearly three decades (Rosenblatt, 1996; Rosenblatt, Walsh & Jackson, 1976) and reflects how his own perception has shifted from believing that social scientists can understand another culture by careful observation and recording to an acknowledgement that these observations are shaped by the culture which is an integral part of the observer. Practices that may seem callous to one observer such as a certain way of disposing of a body may be seen as commendable by another because this preserves the future wellbeing of the whole community.

There will be individual variation within a culture and there can be conflict within a family over the 'proper' way to show respect for the dead when practice is changing within a society. Two separate traditions may come together. Viking graves have been found in Scotland carved with Christian symbols as well as containing the material goods associated with pagan burial.

Social Desirability

This factor may be relevant if answering questionnaires or being interviewed in bereavement when there are strong expectations from the social group. It may be acceptable that there is a sense of relief at a death that follows a lengthy period of poor quality of life but it may be less easy to acknowledge a sense of relief if the relationship had private tensions. Bereaved relatives or families in the public eye will find their reactions scrutinised and be offered sympathy or criticism depending on whether their behaviour is considered 'appropriate'.

Length of Follow-up

Some studies report a follow-up period of a few months only, whereas others report a year or more. Yet during the first year of bereavement there are many 'firsts', such as the first holiday, birthday or anniversary, significant events that bereaved people may use as milestones. Lake *et al.* could trace only half their 78 participants at six months. Parkes & Weiss (1983) were unusual in tracking some participants for two to four years. The authors of one major meta-analysis criticised the lack of long-term follow-up in many of the studies they surveyed (Allumbaugh & Hoyt, 1999).

ASSESSMENT AND INTERVENTION

There have been many attempts to categorise grief but little consensus beyond a general view that for most people there is a reduction and change in the nature of distress over time. What is an appropriate time interval or the nature of the distress is less easy to determine. Many studies have used general assessment measures such as the Beck Depression Inventory or the General Health Questionnaire, which were not designed to measure the changes specific to the distress of bereavement. Efforts continue to distinguish 'typical' from 'atypical' grief. The Texas Revised Inventory of Grief (Faschingbauer, 1981) is the best known but it has been criticised for a lack of sensitivity to variation in some items and retrospective judgements. For a comparison for the strengths and limitations of instruments used in the assessment of grief see Neimeyer & Hogan (2001).

Many UK hospices use simple assessment questionnaires to assess which relatives should be offered additional bereavement support. These are based on Parkes' early work yet the measures are of uncertain validity (Payne & Relf, 1994).

An assessment scale that attempts to categorise grief will reflect the model of grief and mourning practices that are dominant in that culture, for example, how often the bereaved person should visit the grave or when and at what level social activity should be resumed. These measures are unlikely to be useful in working with someone from a different culture. Visiting the grave less frequently might be seen as beneficial for one person but as avoidance by another. Rosenblatt (1997) suggests there may be an indigenous sense of normality but the definition of pathology will vary across cultures. Some cultures rewrap bodily remains over time but a request by a British twentieth-century widow to do this would be seen as morbid. Also, there can be rapid change of practice within a generation, and within a subculture; for example, it has become more acceptable for women of the Western Isles of Scotland to attend the graveside following the funeral service. What is seen as 'normal' is not constant. The validity of the concept of a universal model of grief is challenged by those who argue there is no place for this in the postmodern world (Small, 2001). However it is the hypothetical models that generate the interventions used to work with those who seek help in their bereavement. Influential models are described below.

Psychoanalytic Model

Freud (1917) acknowledged that mourning is painful but cautioned 'although mourning involves grave departures from the normal attitude to life, it never occurs to us to regard it as a pathological condition and to refer it to medical treatment. We rely on it being overcome after a certain lapse of time and we look upon any interference with it as useless or even harmful.'

He states that reality demands that all libidinal energy is withdrawn from the lost object and this process will happen gradually as all emotional investment and hopes are gradually relinquished. 'When the work of mourning is completed the ego becomes free and uninhibited again . . . The ego severs its attachment to the object that has been abolished.'

Freud regards melancholia as very similar to mourning but with an important exception 'the disturbance of self-regard is absent in mourning'. He makes the distinction by stating 'In mourning it is the world which has become poor and empty; in melancholia it is the ego itself.'

Small (1999) argues that Freud has been misunderstood in suggesting the relationship with the deceased is abandoned and suggests that mourning is better understood as the withdrawal of projective identification by which the reality of what is lost is acknowledged and the separate boundaries of the self are rediscovered and developed. Klein had postulated that the infant learns that it is separate from its carer and this is a terrifying realisation but with a loving carer the infant gains security through internalising the object. Vaillant (1988) asserts that it is not the loss of the loved object in itself but the failure to create an adequate internal model that causes psychological harm.

Volkan (1972) describes the way in which some bereaved people maintain their relationship with the dead person by 'linking objects'. These objects are not the comfortable mementoes that many keep or can wear with comfort such as a watch or a brooch. These linking objects are invested with great emotional significance and cause great distress rather than sadness if lost because of their significance. Linking objects are used by Ramsay (1977) working from a behavioural model of phobic avoidance of grief, which is discussed later.

The Freudian model is cathartic and postulates that by ventilating emotional distress the person can withdraw libidinal energy and reinvest it in other object relations. Freud terms this 'grief work' and this concept of 'work' has been developed by therapists such as Worden (1983, 2003). Worden's delineation of the tasks of grief has been extremely influential in bereavement counselling. He proposes four key tasks:

1. *To accept the reality of the loss.* There may be particular difficulties in accepting that this separation is permanent if the relationship had frequent separations because of work abroad or military duty. The reality of the death is hard to accept for different reasons if the body is absent – for example, if it has been destroyed in a major incident or is missing. This is explored further in the section on sudden/unexpected death. Religious faiths that believe in personal reunion after death or contact through a spiritualist would be viewed as denial by those who do not share their beliefs.
2. *To experience the pain associated with it.* Some would argue that grief work cannot be avoided: 'it is also likely that grief work cannot be put off indefinitely, that an avoidance of certain reminders of a loss makes it likely that one will grieve later on . . . as one encounters still other reminders that set off the process of dealing with emotionally charged memories and hopes' (Rosenblatt, 1996). A high level of manifest grief is not necessarily an

indication of a cathartic process that will inevitably resolve with time. People who obtain high scores on posttraumatic stress disorder (PTSD) scales after a major incident are often those individuals whose scores remain elevated a year later. A chronic sense of personal distress, which is exacerbated by bereavement, may be mistaken for expressed grief precipitated by bereavement. Alarcon (1984) suggests that an individual with a personality disorder will have difficulties that reflect ongoing problems in establishing interpersonal relationships rather than grief for a lost relationship. Rosenblatt (1997) cautions that talking about the loss is seen as healthy expression of grief in Euro-American counselling now but may not be seen as appropriate bereavement behaviour in another culture. There is some evidence that those who avoided intense feelings of grief did not have a worse outcome at 14 months than those who experienced emotional distress Bonnano *et al.* (1995). A study of 253 bereaved adults found that those who engaged in ruminative thinking were more depressed at six months even after controlling for initial levels of depression, social support, gender and other factors (Nolen-Hoeksema, Parker & Larson, 1994).

3. *Adjust to an environment in which the deceased is missing.* The sense of the presence of the dead person is common and usually felt as comforting rather than unpleasant. One widow recounted the strong sense of her husband lying close to her in bed but on being questioned said she had never stretched out her arm to touch him because she knew he could not be there and did not want to confront the emptiness. Most of the widows interviewed by Conant (1996) had sensed their husband's presence vividly and unexpectedly at times. During sleep there may be dreams in which the fact of the death is acknowledged openly between the bereaved and the deceased (Cathcart, 1984).

4. *Emotionally relocate the deceased and move on with life.* Sometimes the final task has been described as 'resolution' but this term is problematic for the reasons described earlier. Originally Worden (1983) listed the need to withdraw emotional energy and reinvest it in another relationship but he later modified this to an understanding that the bereaved will maintain a different kind of relationship with the deceased and acknowledged the work of Klass, Silverman & Nickman (1996).

Attachment Model

Bowlby was influenced by the research of animal ethologists, which described the critical period during which the offspring attach to the parent. This attachment provides security as well as food and warmth. Ethology and other animal research indicated the importance of early social relationships on the development of later relationships and maturation.

Disruption of the bond was observed to cause pining and searching to recover the lost object. The Robertson's recordings of young children separated by hospitalisation supported his argument that this research was relevant for human behaviour. Bowlby (1980) developed his theories of attachment and loss over decades and influenced the early work of Parkes, which described a phase model of grief with initial protest and disbelief followed by disorganisation manifest by searching and pining then resignation.

The formation of secure attachments in early life enables one to face future challenges and losses. On hearing the news of her elderly husband's death Ursula Bowlby (1991) wrote:

> Instead of being shattered I felt suddenly comforted. He seemed secure in my heart and I knew I would carry him about with me for the rest of my life. I have this sense of continuous

companionship . . . I didn't expect it, I recognise it . . . the same thing happened . . . (when my mother died). I had spent my life dreading losing her, yet when she died I felt her safe in my heart, and free, free from the disabilities of old age.

Behavioural Model

The similarities between phobias and the avoidance of grief by some bereaved people led Ramsay (1977) to suggest that those who avoid their grief yet remain distressed could be helped by confrontation with the feared cues that trigger painful emotions. Systematic desensitisation to stimuli such as favourite music, photos and 'linking objects' without the possibility of distraction or escape should facilitate anxiety reduction. He argued that avoidance maintained the person in a state of grief and also learned helplessness develops at the loss of social reinforcement (Seligman, 1975). The grieving person no longer engages with the world and therefore does not find alternative sources of gratification. Ramsay asserts that linking objects can be used effectively as cues in the desensitisation hierarchy without psychodynamic interpretation or awareness of unconscious psychological processes and disagrees strongly with Volkan on this point. He states that a 'limited number' of people were helped by prolonged exposure and flooding but no more information is given about the sample.

Lieberman (1978) selected 19 bereaved patients whom he identified as having morbid grief and intervened using what he termed 'a forced mourning' procedure using behavioural principles of systematic desensitisation and implosion and involving family members where possible to facilitate generalisation. Sixteen were reported to have benefited, one was un-changed and two deteriorated. Closer examination of those who had improved led him to suggest that this strategy is most helpful to those with family support and, in addition, different grief patterns may require different emphasis. Some individuals may be helped by an initial opportunity to ventilate displaced anger and then receive forced mourning and others required a combination of behavioural strategy and interpretative psychotherapy with attention directed to their nightmares.

A small controlled study of guided mourning by Mawson *et al.* (1981) randomly allocated 12 people to either a guided mourning treatment in which they were encouraged to confront painful or avoided stimuli in the manner described by Ramsay or to a control treatment in which they were advised to avoid any distressing thoughts and to conceal painful reminders such as photos and possessions. Those who received guided mourning demonstrated greater improvement than the control group on a number of measures, which was maintained at 10- and 28-week follow-up. The authors acknowledge that the intervention had not been as effective as earlier studies had hoped and quote Parkes' comment that this type of intervention may not be useful for people who can readily express themselves but in a self-punitive way or if grief is used as a reason to avoid new challenges.

Cognitive-behavioural Intervention

Further criticism of the limits of a narrow behavioural model is made by Kavanagh (1990) who agrees that 'searching' to recover the lost object is more prominent than avoidance of reminders and chronic preoccupation with grief is more common than phobic avoidance of the distress. He notes that this approach can help alleviate anxiety but he concurs with Parkes that there are more effective ways of managing depressive symptoms such as a goal-oriented approach. This is supported by an earlier paper by Sireling *et al.* (1988), which used a guided mourning intervention. One group was told to focus on bereavement cues and the second group to avoid them but both groups were encouraged to engage in enjoyable activities and advised about resuming social relationships. Both groups experienced similar levels of improvement in depressive mood.

Kavanagh argues that the Lazarus & Folkman (1984) model of stress and coping skills offers a constructive way forward for people experiencing problems in their bereavement. A situation is perceived to be stressful if the repertoire of coping strategies is judged to be inadequate to the challenge. If support is given to develop and extend coping skills, depending on individual need, then the situation will be perceived as less stressful. Learning cognitive strategies to detect and challenge negative cognitions is part of this. He summarises that a balance between exploring the loss and managing the depressive symptoms will be the most effective intervention.

The Dual-process Model

The two processes described in this model are that of loss orientation and restoration orientation. Stroebe & Schut (2001) suggest that effective mourning requires a balance of both and people oscillate between the two processes. They suggest that these processes are similar but not identical to emotion-focused and problem-focused coping. An activity that is restoration oriented could involve both confronting emotion and managing a practical task.

There is some indication that gender differences are relevant. In Western culture women express emotional distress more readily and men tend to focus on the practical tasks. A small study by Schut *et al.* (1997) compared two interventions and found that each gender benefited most by being directed towards its less familiar strategy. There is some support for this in an unpublished study (Duran, 1987) cited by Kato & Mann (1999). When interventions were analysed by gender it was revealed that a social support intervention, which was unhelpful to the women, was beneficial to the male participants. A social activities group had no effect for the women but was harmful to the male participants. Parkes (2000) comments that if given choice, people may choose the intervention that is easier for them but this might not be the most effective for them.

Existential Model

Existential philosophy states that existence precedes essence. The perspective that grief is an active process of construction is closer to the existential writers such as Neimeyer *et al.* (2002) who consider bereavement a challenge to our sense of identity and meaning.

Bereaved people need to develop a changed sense of self and the world around them, a process that is variously described as revising the assumptive world or a need to 'incorporate the experience into their ongoing life-narrative' (Neimeyer, Prigerson & Davies, 2002). This may be particularly difficult for some people because of their maladaptive inner models of the world but it is difficulty in assimilating change that causes grief to become complicated.

Klatt (1991) states 'It is not illness or death which are a challenge but the failure to find meaning in life.' Bereavement may provoke an existential crisis only if it challenges the sense of meaning and a new sense of meaning is not developed. Some become more aware of life's transience and can identify positive change (Landsman and Spear, 1995). This perspective reminds us that a crisis is also an opportunity for growth. One young woman bereaved traumatically by the death of a partner for the second time acknowledged this had changed and deepened her personal philosophy of life but was able to smile and remark ruefully 'If this is being wise, I'd rather be foolish.' A study of 30 caregivers whose partners had died of AIDS reported that those who found meaning in their caring were less depressed and were more likely to demonstrate positive wellbeing at bereavement and better recovery at 12 months (Stein *et al.*, 1997).

THE EFFECTIVENESS OF INTERVENTIONS

Reviews of the effectiveness of bereavement intervention do not indicate a strong evidence base for much current clinical practice. The methodological flaws described at the start of the chapter have resulted in few studies that meet the criteria set by reviewers. Schneiderman *et al.* (1994) found only four articles out of 53 published that satisfied their criteria. These four studies had conflicting results and the authors concluded there was little sound evidence for or against bereavement programmes. Both a qualitative and quantitative approach was used by Kato & Mann (1999) in an analysis of 13 adult studies that met their criteria, including random allocation to intervention and control groups. They concluded that there was little strong evidence that intervention was effective. Small effect sizes only were found and theory and practice were not clearly linked in the research. The relevance of bereavement research to clinical practice is questioned by Allumbaugh & Hoyt (1999) who argue that the findings of their own meta-analysis reveal more about the limited nature of the research studies than answering any questions about the effectiveness of grief interventions. They found so few studies reporting long-term follow-up that they restricted their analysis to those studies reporting immediate post-treatment results. They concluded tentatively that recently bereaved clients who request help are more likely to benefit than those selected for research studies who have been bereaved longer. Also the studies surveyed in this meta-analysis did not support the common view that high-risk individuals benefit more from intervention than low-risk ones but the authors acknowledge definitions of 'high risk' varied so much across studies that this question remains open.

A later review of bereavement efficacy concurred with Allumbaugh and Hoyt's suggestion that self-selected clients are more likely to gain from bereavement intervention (Schut, Stroebe, Van den Bout & Terheggen, 2001). Schut *et al.* disagree with Allumbaugh and Hoyt's finding that early intervention is optimal. They divided preventive studies into primary interventions, secondary intervention for high-risk groups and tertiary intervention for complicated grief. They found little evidence of any lasting positive effects in primary prevention for adults and some indication of possible harm in some studies. The results for children seemed more promising. Secondary prevention studies gave mixed results with effects suggesting limited and temporary benefit. Tertiary intervention for people experiencing complicated grief gave more lasting and positive benefit but even with this type of intervention the gains were modest and studies were flawed.

Jordan & Neimeyer (2003) suggest explanations for the limited evidence base that is reported in these reviews and meta-analyses. Most bereaved people will recover over time with the support of their family and community. The nature of the intervention may not be appropriate for the bereaved minority who could benefit because of its timing, its length or its narrow theoretical model. Individuals selected for bereavement groups may be selected simply on the basis of bereavement status rather than screened for a number of variables as is usual with group therapy. This could affect the dynamics of the group and therefore its effectiveness. Outcome is assessed in simplistic ways by a reduction in pathological symptoms rather than by changed values or revised priorities, which may reveal that sadness is accompanied by increased personal growth. Gains for some individuals may be masked by losses for others so the overall effect is cancelled out rather than revealing subtleties between subsets of individuals. They conclude with recommendations for both researchers and clinicians, which reiterate the need for more rigorous methodology and closer integration between research and practice.

DISCUSSION

It is apparent that there is no strong evidence base as yet to decide which interventions would be most beneficial to individuals who request help. The factors that have been assumed to increase risk of complicated grief are also questioned by Stroebe & Schut (2001) who argue that these factors are subject to mediating variables such as social support and are complicated further because some risk factors are not static, for example, self-care. It is beyond the scope of this chapter to examine all aspects of bereavement therefore specific areas of bereavement have been selected to illustrate the changing practice and debates.

Research evidence can follow clinical practice rather than lead it. In the UK the management of perinatal loss was changed by Bourne's observations that medical staff struggled with the emotional impact of stillbirth (Bourne, 1968). This work was developed by Lewis (1976) in a classic paper that changed the management of mothers who had experienced stillbirth. The customary practice had been to remove the baby promptly and not to encourage parents to view or hold their dead child. Lewis argued that stillbirth leaves a painful void, which is better overcome by facilitating memories and participation in funeral rituals rather than avoidance. There is some evidence for this practice from a later Swedish study of 380 women using a postal questionnaire (Radestad et al., 1996). This study reported that mothers who had tokens of remembrance and felt they had been able to spend as much time as they had wished with the child's body experienced fewer anxiety and depression-related symptoms.

Perinatal practice changed rapidly and extensively which resulted in Bourne & Lewis (1991) cautioning that there were iatrogenic dangers in extrapolating their comments on the management of stillbirth to early miscarriage This does not imply that sensitive communication and support is not desirable following miscarriage. A survey of 100 mothers using questionnaires, interviews and focus groups indicated that the balance of normalising the relatively common experience of early miscarriage and acknowledging the personal impact for an individual is not easy to achieve (Wong et al., 2003).

Rutter (1981) reviewed the effects of maternal deprivation on children and argued that other variables such as the quality of substitute parenting were not taken into account. Dowdney (2000) reviewed studies of childhood bereavement following parental death and noted the varying outcomes caused by methodological differences, for example, whether children were recruited from community samples or from referrals to mental health services. She concluded that mild depression was common and one in five children was likely to express non-specific disturbance with emotional and behavioural symptoms to such a degree that there should be referral to specialist services but only a very few would experience psychiatric disorder.

The view that most children are resilient is shared by Harrington & Harrison (1999) who caution that unnecessary professional counselling can do harm by fostering dependency. They acknowledge that some children such as those with multiple deprivations may require bereavement support but agree with Dowdney's view that bereavement is rarely a cause of major mental health problems. They argue that there is little systematic evidence that the majority of children benefit on any observable measures and that for most bereaved children the mental health and accessibility of the surviving parent is the key factor. Black's earlier research also indicates the mental health of the surviving parent was predictor of outcome in children one year after bereavement (Black, 1996).

There is increasing awareness of other problems that may co-exist with bereavement, such as PTSD, and this may be caused by witnessing a violent death or viewing a disfigured body. Societies had developed rituals to minimise the intrusive imagery of dead bodies many years before PTSD was described. It was a recent Scottish custom to touch the dead body on the forehead to avoid having nightmares (Bennett, 1992). The cause of the death may have destroyed the body or if it is damaged then statutory services are protective of bereaved relatives who may be advised not to view. There may be little opportunity for discussion to help make a choice but retrospective interviews indicate that very few of those who choose to view the body regret this subsequently whereas many of those who do not view the body do regret this. It is not possible to carry out a controlled study for ethical reasons. Singh & Raphael (1981) interviewed those bereaved by an Australian rail disaster and found one of the eight people who had viewed the body regretted this whereas 22 of the 36 who had not viewed now regretted this. A British study of over 100 bereaved parents by Finlay & Dallimore (1991) reported only one parent of 81 regretted viewing but 17 of the 28 who had not viewed regretted the lost opportunity deeply. This trend is supported by a study into the needs of the families of murder victims in the UK (Brown, Christie & Morris, 1990). It cannot be assumed that all of those who did not view would have been satisfied if they had done so and it should be remembered that some chose not to view and never regretted their decision.

The search for meaning is marked after traumatic death. Relatives endeavour to change systems so that their wider society can gain something from their personal tragedy and they can feel their loved one did not die in vain. Security systems are challenged in airports and safety mechanisms are modified on car ferries. Professional carers review procedures to identify lessons that might be learned.

One type of sudden death that is assumed to cause problems for those bereaved is suicide. It can be a respected social act in specific and carefully defined circumstances – for example, *hara-kiri*. The Christian Church forbade it and those who died by suicide were forbidden burial within consecrated ground and buried at crossroads or lonely places such as headlands. Their bodies could be used for dissection as were those of murderers. The tools used to make the coffin would be destroyed or buried with it. Suicide was a crime in England and Wales until 1959 and in Scotland until 1961.

The recent social disapproval and fear of suicide can cause increased isolation for those bereaved by it (Wertheimer, 1991). Death notification is a familiar task for police officers but dealing with a suicide remains challenging. A suicidal man telephoned his daughter at her work to inform her where his body could be found. The officer dealing with this suicide found it difficult to understand how a parent could do this (personal communication). There may be additional difficulties for a child if death was by murder or suicide in that the truth can be concealed or distorted by relatives or carers who may have different perspectives from the legal system (Hendriks, Black & Kaplan, 1993).

Jordan (2001) argues that bereavement after suicide is sufficiently distinct from those bereaved by other forms of sudden death to require specialist clinical services. He asserts there are qualitative differences with themes of loss of meaning, guilt and self-reproach for not preventing the death as well as a sense of abandonment and anger towards the dead.

The needs of bereaved spouses and bereaved children have been addressed in the bereavement literature, albeit inadequately, but the needs of people with learning disabilities were neglected until relatively recently. Oswin (1981, 1991) pioneered this work in the UK and during the 1990s there was increased awareness of the gaps in service provision and more resources have been developed to aid comprehension and discussion about death and bereavement (Blackman, 2003; Cathcart 1991, 1994, 1995; Harper and Wadsworth, 1993; Hollins and Sireling, 1991). A systematic study of 50 parent-bereaved people with learning disabilities compared them with a matched control group using a semistructured bereavement questionnaire, the Aberrant Behaviour Checklist, the Psychopathology Instrument for Mentally Retarded Adults and the Life Event Checklist. Highly significant differences between the groups were found but carers did not attribute behaviour problems or psychopathology to the bereavement (Hollins & Esterhuyzen, 1997). The authors concluded the impact of bereavement with its concomitant life events was underestimated. The cohort was followed-up for two years and it was found that there was a small increase in aberrant behaviour but an improvement on measures of psychopathology with a decrease in anxiety. Participants had adapted more easily when emotional needs were met but only a quarter of the group had received informal or formal bereavement support such as opportunities to talk about the death, attend the funeral or visit the grave (Bonnell-Pascual et al., 1999).

SUMMARY

- Since the early 1980s there has been a change in theoretical framework from one in which grieving was seen as a finite process in which grief was resolved when emotional investment in the deceased was withdrawn (decathexis) to one in which the bereaved person has a continuing but different kind of relationship with the dead person. 'The inner representation of who died changes as mourners move through the life cycle and their sense of self and other continues to evolve' (Klass, Silverman & Nickman, 1996).
- The search for meaning may take place at several levels. An official inquiry may explain the specific cause of death for an individual but cannot answer the question 'why did the individual I love die?'
- Changing social patterns in Western society such as increased family mobility and the growth of a more secular society have contributed to the development of bereavement services such as self-help groups, counsellors and new social rituals around death.
- There is little unequivocal research evidence that proactive bereavement intervention is effective and there is evidence that it can do harm to some individuals. It may be beneficial for bereaved people who request help. Despite this there is both a social and professional

expectation that bereavement services should be provided (National Institute for Clinical Excellence (2004) Scottish Executive: NHSQIS, 2002).

- Recent meta-analyses and reviews of bereavement studies have identified ways of developing the evidence base to identify who might be helped by which intervention, at what point and by whom. The assumption that grief counselling should be available more widely should be treated cautiously until such evidence is available.

REFERENCES

Alarcon, R.D. (1984). Personality disorder as a pathogenic factor in bereavement. *Journal of Nervous and Mental Disease, 172*, 45–47.

Allumbaugh, L. & Hoyt, W. (1999). Effectiveness of grief therapy: A meta-analysis. *Journal of Counseling Psychology, 46*, 370–380.

Barrett, C.J. (1978). Effectiveness of widows' support groups in facilitating change. *Journal of Consulting and Clinical Psychology, 46*, 20–31.

Bass, D.M., Bowman, K. & Noelke, L.S. (1991). The influence of care-giving and support on adjusting to an older relative's death. *The Gerontologist, 31*(1), 32–42.

Bennett, M. (1992). *Scottish Customs from the Cradle to the Grave.* Edinburgh: Polygon.

Black, D. (1996). Childhood bereavement: distress and long-term sequelae can be lessened by early intervention. *British Medical Journal, 312*, 1496.

Blackman, N. (2003). *Loss and Learning Disability.* London: Worth.

Bonnano, G.A., Keltner, D. Holen, A. & Horowitz, M.J. (1995). When avoiding unpleasant emotion might not be such a bad thing: Verbal-autonomic response dissociation and, midlife conjugal bereavement. *Journal of Personality and Social Psychology, 69*(5), 975–989.

Bonnell-Pascual, E., Huline-Dickens, S., Hollins, S. *et al.* (1999). Bereavement and grief in adults with learning disabilities. *British Journal of Psychiatry, 175*, 348–350.

Bourne, S. (1968). The psychological effects of stillbirths on women and their doctors. *Journal of the Royal College of General Practitioners, 16*, 103.

Bourne, S. & Lewis, E. (1991). Perinatal bereavement. *British Medical Journal 302*, May 18, 1167–1168.

Bowlby, J. (1980). *Attachment and Loss,* vol. 3. Loss, Separation and Death. London: Hogarth.

Bowlby, U. (1991). Reactions to the death of my husband. *Bereavement Care, 10*, 5.

Brown, L., Christie, R. & Morris D (1990). *Families of Murder Victim Project.* Final Report. London: Victim Support.

Caserta, M. & Lund, D. (1993). Intrapersonal resources and the effectiveness of self-help groups for bereaved older adults. *Gerontologist, 33*(5), 619–629.

Cathcart, F. (1984). Bereavement. In Doyle, D. (ed.), *Palliative Care; The Management of Far Advanced Illness.* (pp. 391–413). Beckenham: Croom Helm.

Cathcart, F. (1991). Bereavement and mental handicap. *Bereavement Care, 10*, 9–11.

Cathcart, F. (1994). *Understanding Death and Dying.* Kidderminster: British Institute of Learning Disabilities.

Cathcart, F. (1995). Death and people with learning disabilities: interventions to support clients and carers. *British Journal of Clinical Psychology, 34*, 165–175.

Cathcart, F. (1996). The death of a child with learning disabilities. *The Compassionate Friends Newsletter, 108*, 29.

Christ, G.H. (1998). Outcomes of childhood bereavement. *Psycho-Oncology, 4* (supplement), 187.

Conant, R.D. (1996). Memories of the death and life of a spouse: the role of image and sense of presence in grief. In D. Klass, P. Silverman & S. Nickman (eds), *Continuing Bonds: New Understandings of Grief* (pp. 179–196). Philadelphia, PA: Taylor & Francis.

Dowdney, L. (2000). Childhood bereavement following parental death. *Journal of Child Psychology and Psychiatry, 7*(41), 819–930.

Duran, A.C. (1987). A grief intervention for adults experiencing conjugal bereavement. Unpublished doctoral dissertation, University of Utah.

Faschingbauer, T.R. (1981). *Texas Revised Inventory of Grief.* Houston, TX: Honeycomb.

Field, D., Hockey, J. & Small, N. (eds) (1997). *Death, Gender and Ethnicity.* London: Routledge.

Finlay, I. & Dallimore, D. (1991). Your child is dead. *British Medical Journal, 302,* 1524–1525.

Freud S. (1917). Mourning and melancholia. *The Standard Edition of the Complete Psychological works of Sigmund Freud,* volume XIV (pp. 243–259). Edited by J. Strachey. London: Hogarth Press.

Gallagher-Thompson, D.E., Futterman A., Farberow, N. *et al.* (1993). The impact of spousal bereavement on older widows and widowers. In M. Stroebe, W. Stroebe & R. Hansson (eds). *Handbook of Bereavement: Theory, Research and Intervention* (pp. 227–239). Cambridge: Cambridge University Press.

Gordon, A. (1984). *Death is for the Living.* Edinburgh: Paul Harris.

Gorer, G. (1965). *Death, Grief and Mourning.* London:Cresset Press.

Harper, D.C. & Wadsworth, J.S. (1993). Grief in adults with mental retardation: Preliminary findings *Research in Developmental Disabilities, 14,* 313–330.

Harrington, R. & Harrison, L. (1999). Unproven assumptions about the impact of bereavement on children. *Journal of the Royal Society of Medicine, 92,* 230–233.

Hendriks, J., Black, D. & Kaplan, T. (1993). *When Father Kills Mother.* London: Routledge, London.

Hockey, J., Katz, J. & Small, N. (2001). *Grief Mourning and Death Ritual.* Buckingham: Open University.

Hollins, S. & Esterhuyzen, A. (1997). Bereavement in grief in adults with learning disabilities. *British Journal of Psychiatry, 170,* 497–501.

Hollins, S. & Sireling, L. (1991). *When Dad died; Working through loss with People who have Learning Disabilities or with Children.* Berkshire: NFER – Nelson Publishing.

Jordan, J.R. (2001). Is suicide bereavement different? A reassessment of the literature. *Suicide and Life-threatening Behaviour, 31,* 91–102.

Jordan, J.R. & Neimeyer, R.A. (2003). Does grief counselling work? *Death Studies, 27,* 765–786.

Kato, P. & Mann, T. (1999). A synthesis of psychological interventions for the bereaved. *Clinical Psychology Review, 19,* 275–296.

Kavanagh, D.J. (1990). Towards a cognitive-behavioural intervention for adult grief reactions. *British Journal of Psychiatry, 157,* 373–383.

Klass, D., Silverman, P. & Nickman, S. (1996) (eds). *Continuing Bonds: New Understandings of Grief.* Philadelphia, PA: Taylor & Francis.

Klatt, H.J. (1991). In search of a mature concept of death. *Death Studies, 15,* 177–187.

Lake, M.F., Johnson, T.M., Murphy, J. & Knuppel, R.A. (1987). Evaluation of a grief support team. *American Journal of Obstetrics and Gynaecology, 157,* 1203–1206.

Landsman, I.S. & Spear, E. (1995). Meaning in the wake of trauma. Paper presented at the Fourth European Conference on Traumatic Stress Studies. May 10, Paris, France.

Lazarus, R.S. & Folkman, S. (1984). *Stress, Appraisal and Coping.* New York: Springer.

Lewis, C.S. (1966). *A Grief Observed.* London: Faber & Faber.

Lewis, E. (1976). The management of stillbirth: Coping with an unreality. *Lancet, 2,* 619–612.

Lieberman, S. (1978). Nineteen cases of morbid grief. *British Journal of Psychiatry, 132,* 159–163.

Lilford, R.J., Stratton, P., Godsil, S. & Prasad, A. (1994). A randomised trial of routine versus selective counselling in perinatal bereavement from congenital disease. *British Journal of Obstetrics and, Gynaecology, 191,* 291–296.

Lindemann, E. (1944). Symptomatology and management of acute grief. *American Journal of Psychiatry, 101,* 141–148.

Lund, D.A., Caserta, M. & Dimond, M. (1993). The course of spousal bereavement in later life. In Stroebe, M., Stroebe, W. & Hansson, R.O. (eds) *Handbook of Bereavement: Theory, Research and Intervention* (pp. 240–254). Cambridge: Cambridge University Press.

Mawson, D., Marks, I., Ramm, L. & Stern, R.S. (1981). Guided mourning for morbid grief: A controlled study. *British Journal of Psychiatry, 138,* 185–193.

National Institute for Clinical Excellence (2004). *Improving Supportive & Palliative Care for Adults with Cancer.* London: NICE.

Neimeyer, R. (2002). *Meaning Reconstruction and the Experience of Loss.* Washington, DC: American Psychological Association.

Neimeyer, R. & Hogan, N. (2001). Quantitative or qualitative: measurement issues in the study of grief. In Stroebe, M., Hansson, R.O., Stroebe, W. & Schut, H. (eds). *Handbook of Bereavement Research.* Washington, DC: American Psychological Association.

Neimeyer, R., Prigerson, H. & Davies, B. (2002). Mourning and meaning. *American Behavioural Scientist, 46,* 235–251.

Nolen-Hoeksema, S., McBride, A. & Larson, J. (1997). Rumination and psychological distress among bereaved partners. *Journal of Personality and Social Psychology, 72*(4), 885–862.

Nolen-Hoeksema, S., Parker, L. & Larson, J. (1994). Ruminative coping with depressed mood following loss. *Journal of Personality and Social Psychology, 67*(1), 92–104.

Oswin, M. (1981). *Bereavement and Mentally Handicapped People.* London: King's Fund Centre.

Oswin, M. (1991). *Am I Allowed to Cry?* London: Souvenir Press.

Parkes, C. (1972). *Bereavement; Studies of Grief in Adult Life* (2nd edn). London Routledge.

Parkes, C. (1980). Bereavement counselling; does it work? *British Medical Journal 281,* 3–6.

Parkes, C. (2000). Counselling bereaved people; help or harm? *Bereavement Care, 19,* 19–20.

Parkes, C. & Weiss, R.W. (1983). *Recovery from Bereavement.* New York: Basic Books.

Payne, S., Horn, S. & Relf, M. (1999). *Loss and Bereavement.* Maidenhead: Open University Press.

Payne, S. & Relf, M. (1994). Assessment of need for bereavement follow-up in hospice and palliative care. *Palliative Medicine, 8,* 291–297.

Pincus, L. (1974). *Death in the Family.* New York: Pantheon.

Radestad, I., Steineck, G., Nordin, C. & Sjogren, B. (1996). Psychological complications after stillbirth. *British Medical Journal, 312,* 1505–1508.

Ramsay, R.A. (1977). Behavioural approaches to bereavement. *Behaviour Research and Therapy, 15,* 131–135.

Rando, T. (1988). Anticipatory grief: the term is a misnomer but the phenomenon exists. *Journal of Palliative Care, 4,* 70–73.

Riches, G. & Dawson, P. (2000). *An Intimate Loneliness: Supporting Bereaved Parents and Siblings.* Buckingham: Open University Press.

Rosenblatt, P. (1996). Grief that does not end. In D. Klass, P. Silverman & S. Nickman (eds), *Continuing Bonds: New Understandings of Grief.* Philadelphia, PA: Taylor & Francis.

Rosenblatt, P. (1997). Grief in small-scale societies. In C.M. Parkes, P. Laungani, & B. Young (eds), *Death and Bereavement across Cultures.* London: Routledge.

Rosenblatt, P., Walsh, R.P. & Jackson, D.A. (1976). *Grief and Mourning in Cross-cultural Perspective.* New Haven, CT: Human Relations Area Files Press. Washington, DC: HRAF Press.

Rutter, M. (1981). *Maternal deprivation Reassessed.* Harmondsworth: Penguin.

Schneiderman, G., Winders, P., Tallet, S. & Feldman, W. (1994). Do child and/or parent bereavement programmes work? *Canadian Journal of Psychiatry, 39,* 215–218.

Schut, H., Stroebe, M.S., Van den Bout, J. & De Keijser J. (1997). Intervention for the bereaved: Gender differences in the efficacy of two counselling programmes. *British Journal of Clinical Psychology, 36,* 63–72.

Schut, H., Stroebe, M., Van den Bout, J. & Terheggen, M. (2001). The efficacy of bereavement interventions; determining who benefits. In M. Stroebe, R. Hansson, W. Stroebe & H. Schut. *Handbook of Bereavement Research; Consequences, Coping and Care* (pp. 705–737). Washington, DC. American Psychological Association.

Scottish Executive: NHSQIS (2002). *Standards for Specialist Palliative Care Services.* Edinburgh: HMSO.

Seligman, M.S.P. (1975). *Helplessness.* San Francisco: Freeman.

Singh, B.S. & Raphael, B. (1981). Post-disaster morbidity of the bereaved. *Journal of Nervous and Mental Disease, 169,* 203–212.

Sireling, L., Cohen, D. & Marks, I. (1988). Guided mourning for morbid grief; a controlled replication. *Behavior Therapy, 19,* 121–132.

Small, N. (2001). Theories of grief: A critical review. In J. Hockey, J. Katz & N. Small (eds) *Grief, Mourning and Death Ritual* (pp. 19–48). Buckingham: Open University Press.

Stein, N., Folkman, S., Trabasso T. & Richards, T.A. (1997). Appraisal and goal-processes as predictors of social wellbeing in bereaved care-givers. *Journal of Personality and Social Psychology, 72*(4), 872–884.

Stokes, J., Wyer, S. & Crossley, D. (1997). The challenge of evaluating a child bereavement programme. *Palliative Medicine, 11,* 179–190.

Stroebe, M. (1998). New directions in bereavement research; exploration of gender differences. *Palliative Medicine, 12*(1), 5–12.

Stroebe, M., Hansson, R.O., Stroebe, W. & Schut, H. (eds) (2001). *Handbook of Bereavement Research: Consequences, Coping and Care.* Washington, DC: American Psychological Association.

Stroebe, M. & Schut, H. (2001). Meaning making in the dual process model of coping with bereavement. In R.A. Neimeyer (ed.), *Meaning Reconstruction and the Experience of Loss.* Washington, DC: American Psychological Association.

Stroebe, M. and Stroebe W (1989). Who participates in bereavement research? A review and empirical study. *Omega; Journal of Death and Dying, 20,* 1–29.

Stroebe, M., Stroebe, W. & Hansson, R.O. (1993). *Handbook of Bereavement: Theory, Research and Intervention.* Cambridge: Cambridge University Press.

Stroebe, M., Stroebe, W. & Schut, H. (2003). Bereavement research: methodological issues and ethical concerns, *Palliative Medicine, 17,* 235–240.

Vaillant, G.E. (1988). Attachment, loss and recovery. *Hillside Journal of Psychiatry, 10,* 148–169.

Volkan, V. (1972). The linking objects of pathological mourners. *Archives of General Psychiatry, 27,* 215–221.

Wertheimer, A. (1991). *A Special Scar. The Experience of People Bereaved by Suicide.* London: Routledge.

Wong, M.K.Y., Crawford, T.J., Gask, L. & Grinyer, A. (2003). A qualitative investigation into women's experiences after a miscarriage. *British Journal of General Practice,* (September), 697–702.

Worden, W. (1991). *Grief Counselling and Grief Therapy* (3rd edn). New York: Brunner Routledge.

Wortman, C.B. & Silver, R.C. (2001). The myths of coping with loss.revisited. In Stroebe, M., Hansson, R., Stroebe, W. & Schut, H. (eds) (2001). *Handbook of Bereavement Research: Consequences, Coping and Care* (pp. 405–430). Washington, DC: American Psychological Association.

CHAPTER 17

Evidence-based Psychological Interventions in Psychosis

N. Sanjay Kumar Rao
The County Hospital, Durham
and
Douglas Turkington
Royal Victoria Infirmary, Newcastle Upon Tyne

INTRODUCTION

Psychological conceptualisation of psychosis was first attempted by the founding father of psychotherapy: Sigmund Freud (1911). He considered psychosis to be a narcissistic process resulting from withdrawal of libidinal energy from the external world (decathexis) to the sufferer's ego (Freeman, 1977). In such cases he considered psychological work impossible as no transference could be established between the therapist and the patient.

Eugene Bleuler invented the hallmark term schizophrenia and conceptualised psychosis as splitting of thinking and feeling (Bleuler, 1911). His psychological explanation for psychosis was influenced by Freudian theory. His son Manfred Bleuler, in a follow up study of 208 patients, first demonstrated that a proportion of patients with schizophrenia recovered or improved over time (Bleuler, 1978). However, Kraeplin's observational study on schizophrenia (Kraeplin, 1919) was much more powerful in shaping the view of schizophrenia as a deteriorating illness where improvement was a relative rarity. Jaspers, the existential phenomenologist, placed a great emphasis on the form of symptoms rather than the actual content (Jaspers, 1963). Delusions and hallucinations became characteristic symptoms of psychosis, albeit with scant regard to the actual content or meaning behind the symptoms. Later theorists like Laing (1960) and Szasz (1960) tried to enlarge upon a postulated meaning behind the symptoms of psychosis but the approach was lost in the rhetoric of the antipsychiatry movement, with little formulation of any therapeutic approach.

Harry Stack Sullivan saw schizophrenia as a problem of human connectedness and espoused an active role of the therapist as a participant observer (Sullivan, 1962). Varied attempts by different thinkers led to fashionable theories of different times like the stigmatising 'schizophrenogenic mothers' theory (Fromm-Reichmann, 1950), marital schism (Lidz,

Fleck & Cornelison, 1965) and double-bind communications (Bateson, 1962) in families with individuals affected by schizophrenia. All of these studies had severe methodological drawbacks and are now consigned to the history section of chapters on schizophrenia.

The biological origins of schizophrenia were not in doubt when the serendipitous discovery of chlorpromazine led to a reasonably effective short-term treatment of positive symptoms of schizophrenia (Meyer & Simpson, 1997). Twin studies, brain imaging and neurotransmitter studies established the biological model for understanding the schizophrenic process. This was largely an expansion of Jasper's form-based classification of symptoms and Kraeplin's hypothesis of schizophrenia as a 'brain disease'. Yet, in the same period, evidence had accumulated that schizophrenia had a significant psychological component, as apparent by an increase in negative symptoms in impoverished environments (Wing & Brown, 1961) and by the successful application of behaviour modification (Bellack, 1986) in case studies of behavioural disturbances in schizophrenia. The IPPS study (WHO, 1973) distinctly proved that the incidence of 'process schizophrenia', as defined by first-rank symptoms was similar across the countries but the outcome of schizophrenia was better in developing countries. This finding was confirmed in a 10-year follow up study (Jablensky et al., 1992). One could argue that there were more psychosocial rather than biological differences between citizens of different countries, and therefore the outcome of schizophrenia could be influenced powerfully by psychological factors. However, the spate of exclusive biological hypothesisation continued in the face of evidence for psychosocial factors influencing the course of schizophrenia. The success of antipsychotic therapy lead to mass de-institutionalisation programmes (Thornicroft & Bebbington, 1989) across the world. This paradoxically led to a closer psychological encounter between society and the sufferer with schizophrenia. However, despite the efficacy of drug therapies, a proportion of patients continued to be unwell and several underwent periodic relapses (Lehman et al., 2004). This highlighted the problem of mental illness in communities and families. The success and failure of drug therapies paradoxically reignited psychological thinking about schizophrenia.

Before the reader delves further into this chapter, it would be pertinent to point out that psychological therapies for psychosis are not stand-alone interventions. There is ample evidence that antipsychotic treatment is the mainstay of therapy in schizophrenia (Lehman et al., 2004; NICE, 2002). Psychosocial interventions are added to enhance the management of schizophrenia and reduce the burden of the condition on the individual sufferer and the family. The rest of this chapter will examine the development of an evidence base in psychological interventions in schizophrenia.

FAMILY INTERVENTIONS

As mentioned earlier in the chapter, several ineffectual family theories of schizophrenia were postulated, but led to very little in terms of actual therapy. The hegemony of psychological therapies arising out of the private therapist's couch was poorly adapted for the everyday reality of families of individuals with schizophrenia.

The goals of family approaches to schizophrenia are to reduce relapse, improve functioning and contain the burden on the family.

The earliest evidence in this area relates to the effect of expressed emotions (EE) on outcome of schizophrenia (Leff & Vaughn, 1985). Expressed emotions are reactions of the family members to the person with psychosis. Initially five areas of EE were identified.

However only three (criticality, hostility and overinvolvement) were found to be clinically meaningful and are elicited through a two to two-and-a-half hour standardised Camberwell Family interview (Vaughn & Leff, 1976a). Brown & Birley (1968) showed that relapse in schizophrenia was preceded by both pleasant and unpleasant events in the weeks before the episode. Subsequently, Vaughn and Leff found that patients with more than 35 hours per week of face-to-face contact with relatives with high expressed emotion were highly likely to relapse over a nine-month period – even if they were on drug therapy – compared with those who were exposed to less than 35 hours per week of the same or to relatives with low expressed emotions (Vaughn & Leff, 1976b). In this study high EE-exposed patients were more likely to relapse compared to low EE patients who were not on medications. An aggregate analysis of 25 studies (Bebbington & Kuipers, 1994) confirmed the role of EE in schizophrenia outcome across different cultures. Butzlaff & Hooley (1998) performed a meta-analysis, which corroborated this and showed that the magnitude of relapse-producing effect of EE varied from highest in Eastern Europe to lowest in Australia. Interestingly, although EE is a robust indicator of outcome in schizophrenia, the Butzlaff analysis found that EE was even more strongly predictive of relapse in depression and eating disorders.

However, expressed emotion intervention requires a specialised interview (Leff & Vaughn, 1985) and work, which may not be always possible in routine clinical care. Might there be a way of providing good-quality family intervention without having to focus directly on structured assessment of EE? It would seem so. A systematic review of psychoeducation of family or individual patients showed a clear effect on relapse (NNT 9, CI 6-22) (Pekkala, 2002). Some studies have addressed psychoeducation as an intervention for the individual and others have delivered it as a family intervention. The evidence as an aggregate is positive. There are over 20 controlled studies on family psychoeducation.

The intervention is delivered in a structured manner through a multidisciplinary team and should last at least nine months although some programmes last up to three years.

It is possible to deliver family interventions to single or multiple families although the latter is likely to be more effective (McFarlane, 1994). The effectiveness may be mediated through the element of support derived from facing a common problem or through having a wider catch of experiences in dealing with something as complex as schizophrenia in the family. The intensity of the intervention itself does not seem to be important (Lehman et al., 2004).

Behavioural methods of change and problem solving are both common ingredients of family intervention. Family treatment of schizophrenia can decrease the relapse rate by almost 50 % (Mari & Streiner, 1994; Pilling et al., 2002b). Studies show that there is an additional advantage of decreasing the family burden (Cuijpers, 1999). Family therapy has also been successfully applied in non-Western settings (Wang & Phillips, 1994; Xiong et al., 1994; Zhang et al., 1993).

In summary, family interventions need to be structured, with adequate duration. They appear to have a specific effect in reducing relapse rates. Family interventions have the advantage that they can be delivered at a time when the family is in crisis either in the first episode of schizophrenia or during a relapse phase.

BEHAVIOUR THERAPY

With Freud's conceptualisation of psychosis as a narcissistic process, there was very little effort at developing face-to-face interventions in sufferers of schizophrenia. Behaviour therapy, with its origins in empirical psychology, took up the challenge and used principles of differential reinforcement with problem behaviours in schizophrenia. As medication treatment brought promise to the treatment of positive symptoms, behaviour therapy found its applications mainly in the deficit symptoms of schizophrenia. Early behaviour therapy used case series and small trials and focused on behaviours resulting from symptoms of schizophrenia (Haddock *et al.*, 1998).

Social Skills Training

Social skills training became a hallmark psychosocial intervention and empirical science found support through results of clinical trials (Benton & Schroeder, 1990; Dilk & Bond, 1996). Not only did behavioural techniques improve social skills, there is also some evidence that this was retained in longer term follow-ups (Eckman *et al.*, 1992; Wallace *et al.*, 1992). Social skills training is a highly structured approach to learning very specific skills like making conversations, asking for help and living in the community. Role playing, rehearsal and modelling are used. The training can be delivered to individuals and groups. Although there are studies showing retention of skills up to one year after training (Eckman *et al.*, 1992; Holmes, Hansen & St Lawrence, 1984; Mueser, Wallace & Liberman, 1995; Wallace *et al.*, 1992), a recent meta-analysis focusing only on randomised controlled trials reported no benefits from social skills training (Pilling *et al.*, 2002a). This may mean several things: smaller trials with variable results are unable to show a clear effect with meta-analysis or, as the authors note, social skills training may not provide the same benefits in all settings. Huxley *et al.* (2000) suggested that the remit of skills training should be expanded to extend over wider areas of functioning.

Life Skills Training

Life skills training is a related concept. It applies to developing day-to-day skills required for functioning in an increasingly complex society, like shopping, paying bills or making enquiries. Behavioural principles of learning are used to break down the tasks and acquire them through modelling and repetition. There is initial evidence that this may be effective (Robertson, 1998).

Token Economy

To improve the functioning of patients with negative symptoms, the token economy was introduced in psychiatric practice in the 1970s. It involved reward of tokens for 'desirable' behaviours. The tokens could be exchanged for items that were important to the patient, like cigarettes or items of food.

Despite the issues of political correctness and freedom of choice, the token economy emerged as the only evaluated psychological method of producing concrete improvements in negative symptoms (McMonagle, 2000). Unfortunately the total number of subjects in controlled studies is not more than 100 and the treatment has virtually disappeared from mainstream psychiatry in the West.

Conclusion

Behavioural management today finds a place in rehabilitation units in psychiatry. Interventions are adapted for both individual and group work. There are concerns about whether behavioural improvements generalise to patients' own settings (Haddock *et al.*, 1998).

Behaviour therapy did conceptualise the direct management of positive symptoms of schizophrenia, but possibly the time was not ripe for large-scale studies of psychological interventions for such symptoms in face of the pharmaceutical persuasion for the use of antipsychotics. Many of the techniques are found in the repertoire of cognitive behaviour therapy and will be addressed in that section of this article.

COGNITIVE BEHAVIOUR THERAPY

Although the school of behaviour therapy evolved empirical treatments for the management of schizophrenia, it chiefly focused on social skills and behavioural disturbances (Meichenbaum, 1969). Moreover the behavioural work was dominated by operant reward systems through external reinforcers, both positive and negative. This was an acceptable option in the 1970s. In the postmodern era this began to be seen as mechanistic with no reference to the patient's own attitudes and inner experiences. As management of schizophrenia shifted to the community, there were serious concerns whether the reinforcement-based improvement would generalise to the community settings. Unfortunately studies were not devised to answer this issue.

The cognitive behavioural approach, with its success in the management of depression and anxiety disorders (Department of Health, 2001), soon turned its focus to schizophrenia. It had the advantage of collaborative relationship and shared formulation of the patient's problem based on common sense. Most importantly, it de-stigmatised psychosis by giving due importance to the patient's perspective (Kingdon & Turkington, 1994) on the experience of psychosis – the sufferer now had a say. Cognitive behavioural and family work could all be woven into the work with the individual (Kuipers, 2000).

The first account of use of a cognitive approach to delusions was described by Beck (1952) in the treatment of a patient with a seven-year history of a paranoid delusional system. Beck used a Socratic approach to reality test his delusional belief. Since then, and particularly after the late 1980s, several trials have confirmed the efficacy of CBT in treatment of psychotic symptoms (Pilling *et al.*, 2002b). There are specific effects on reduction in the intensity and frequency of positive symptoms, reduced drop out rates and reduced distress associated with symptoms.

Cognitive behaviour therapy for schizophrenia uses a wide variety of approaches. Turkington *et al.* tested the patient's attitudes and reactions to their psychotic experiences and used a normalising rationale (Turkington & Kingdon, 1991). This led to an improved working alliance and reduced stigma. Evidence to support or refute psychotic experiences was examined by peripheral questioning and reality testing leading to the development of less dysfunctional explanations. Underlying assumptions are then examined through a process of Socratic enquiry and homework tasks. The normalising strategy also uses inputs from members of staff and family. They demonstrated that with a 10-day training in CBT for psychosis, community psychiatric nurses were able to deliver this package, under supervision, in community settings (Turkington *et al.*, 2002). This approach makes therapy feasible in general psychiatric settings. Specific cognitive work on delusions using engagement, Socratic enquiry, reality testing, reducing emotional and behavioural investment have been described (Turkington & Kingdon, 1999). Hallucinations are dealt with by exploring and testing out beliefs about hallucinatory experiences (Kingdon & Turkington, 2002). A wide variety of behavioural techniques like distraction, monoaural occlusion, coping skill enhancement and relapse prevention strategies (Haddock *et al.*, 1998) are also used in CBT for schizophrenia. The CBT therapist establishes an empathic, non-threatening relationship with an investigative attitude towards symptoms. Symptoms are not seen as abnormal per se, but linked with distress and beliefs about them. The therapy then moves to the examination of beliefs, reattribution and behavioural experiments.

There is evidence that the gains made through cognitive therapy are durable at least in the medium term (Sensky *et al.*, 2000). However, adequate evidence does not exist to support the view that CBT can reduce relapse rates in schizophrenia except when a specific focus is taken on relapse prevention (Gumley *et al.*, 2003). This can be explained by the fact that patients enrolled in the majority of CBT trials have chronic or treatment-resistant symptoms and relapse rates are not meaningful measurements or outcomes. A reduction in re-hospitalisation is a possible benefit of CBT (Bach & Hayes, 2002) as patients have often learned techniques to aid quicker discharge. Cognitive behaviour therapy may also hasten recovery from acute psychotic episodes (Drury *et al.*, 1996; Lewis *et al.*, 2002), although one study (Haddock *et al.*, 1999) did not show any benefit. More research is needed in this area.

Cognitive behaviour therapy is emerging as a useful mode of therapy in treatment-resistant populations. Recent evidence shows that CBT and family approaches may target both symptom reduction and relapse prevention (Sellwood *et al.*, 2001). There is initial evidence that CBT could be formulated to work on negative symptoms of schizophrenia (Sensky *et al.*, 2000). Duration of therapy has not been defined clearly but it would appear that CBT for psychosis may require more sessions than that for anxiety and depression (Turkington & McKenna, 2003). The outcomes appear to improve with longer duration of therapy (Pilling *et al.*, 2002b). Kemp *et al.* (1998) demonstrated the role of CBT in improving medication compliance but the evidence in this area is not definitive (O'Donnell *et al.*, 2003).

Cognitive behaviour therapy is the latest entrant in the arena of evidence-based treatments for schizophrenia. Most of the trials have small sample sizes, which prevents definitive conclusions as a recent systematic review (Jones, 2004) noted. However the strengths of CBT trials are that they have focused on the chronically unwell patients and provided a longer period of follow up compared to drug therapy trials. More work needs to be done to verify the utility of different techniques of CBT in different populations of patients, such as those with negative symptoms. Turkington & Kingdon (2000) showed that it is possible for psychiatrists to deliver CBT for schizophrenia within their practice settings; however, the study psychiatrist was also an experienced therapist. For service development, CBT is an attractive health economic option: the therapist trained in CBT will be able to deliver interventions in a wide variety of other mental health problems where this particular therapy has been recommended (Department of Health, 2001). The challenge is to make therapy available in community mental health teams rather than confine it to specialist centres.

Relapse Prevention

Studies have shown that episodes of psychosis are preceded by prodromal symptoms (Lehman *et al.*, 2004) but these symptoms do not always lead to relapse (Herz & Lamberti, 1995). The rationale of relapse prevention is to intervene in the prodromal stage to prevent progression into a full-blown psychosis. The typical approach is to construct a relapse signature, which is specific to the particular patient (Birchwood *et al.*, 1989). A plan of early detection of relapse signatures along with intervention constitutes the full programme of relapse prevention approaches. Controlled trials have shown effectiveness of this approach (Lehman *et al.*, 2004), but this area begs well-designed, randomised controlled and pragmatic trials to advise on the applicability of this intervention in the comprehensive management of psychosis.

Early Intervention Programmes

As the onset of schizophrenia is often marked by prodromal symptoms (Yung & McGorry, 1996), proponents of early intervention state the case for treatment in the pre-psychotic phase. Early intervention also offers the premise that such a treatment would alter the natural course of psychosis. However prodromal symptoms do not necessarily progress to psychosis (Miller *et al.*, 2002; Yung *et al.*, 1998) and there is the immense complexity of carrying an epidemiological study to show advantage of such an approach at a population level. By targeting high-risk individuals with a family history of psychosis, researchers (McGorry *et al.*, 2002) did a randomised open label study to show reduced incidence of schizophrenia. The package involved medication and CBT. This study did not inform whether combined treatment has an additive effect. It did highlight the potency of the combined treatment in delaying transition to psychosis. McGlashan *et al.* (2003) showed positive effects with use of second-generation antipsychotics in a study with random assignment to treatment and control group. Very recently Morrison *et al.* (2004) performed a controlled study using CBT in high-risk individuals. The findings are positive and this area needs further study. However, the current level of evidence is not sufficient to advise treatment of prodromal symptoms in routine clinical practice (Marshall, 2003).

PERSONAL THERAPY

Hogarty's 'personal therapy' (Hogarty *et al.*, 1997a, 1997b) deserves a mention, as it is an effort to combine various approaches to devise an individually tailored integrated treatment for patients with schizophrenia. Personal therapy is a multimodal approach, which includes pharmacotherapy, family work, individual work and any other required support. This can be delivered over months to years and is paced according to the patient's needs. Relapse rates decreased with personal therapy but only in patients who lived with their family whereas those living without family experienced increased relapse rates. Social adjustment continued to improve with personal therapy in the second year and third year as compared to supportive therapy where improvement reached a plateau after the first year.

Personal therapy requires long-term commitment and that may be one of the reasons for the absence of replication studies.

COGNITIVE REMEDIATION

Cognitive remediation is much more popular in the US than the UK (Turkington, Dudley & Warman, 2004). It is a rehabilitative approach, which has traditionally been applied to cognitive deficits in stroke and traumatic head injuries, with good evidence (Cicerone *et al.*, 2000). Therapists using this approach hope to correct the cognitive deficits of schizophrenia, which affect neuropsychological functioning in the affected individuals. Studies show improvement in the laboratory environment, but do not appear to generalise to patients' own environment (Lehman *et al.*, 2004). Trials of cognitive remediation have focussed on attention, verbal memory, visual memory and executive functioning. Although there are few positive results, a meta-analysis of pooled data did not show clear differences between cognitive remediation and controls (Pilling *et al.*, 2002a). Moreover, trials are small in size and not adequately controlled for medication effects. Perhaps the mechanisms of cognitive deficits in schizophrenia are different from that induced by lesions. The disturbed functioning of an individual with schizophrenia cannot all be explained by cognitive dysfunction, therefore it makes sense to use remediation strategies in combination with other therapeutic inputs.

PSYCHODYNAMIC THERAPY

Psychodynamic therapy has had a historical role in emphasising a psychological perspective of psychosis. Concepts of psychodynamic therapy may inform understanding of psychotic experiences. Clinicians working with psychosis will frequently sense the avoidant defensive attitude some patients have when confronted with reality. Moreover a sense of dissolution of ego boundaries is distinct in acute psychotic episodes. However, psychodynamic therapy for schizophrenia is not a viable approach (Mueser & Berenbaum, 1990) as there is little evidence to suggest that psychodynamic techniques are effective in the management of symptoms of psychosis (Malmberg, 2001).

CONCLUSION

Researching psychological interventions is difficult due to the complexity of the treatment package and difficulty in standardisation of interventions. There is no 'placebo' intervention for psychotherapy and all control interventions will have some 'active' components, particularly in schizophrenia where psychosocial inputs are part and parcel of standard care. There is evidence from the literature that such active placebos reduce the effect size of the control intervention (Quitkin, 1999).

Despite the above disadvantages, it is clear that psychological interventions in schizophrenia have evidence of effectiveness in clinical practice. Of note is that different therapies target patients in different phases of the illness. Family therapy and psychoeducational approaches appear to reduce relapse and offer good engagement points during crisis. Pure behavioural approaches seem to have more evidence in the area of deficit symptoms. Cognitive behaviour therapy appears to be useful in the presence of residual positive and negative symptoms, poor compliance and lack of insight. Most therapies have arisen from work done in specialist therapy settings or by specialist therapists. However, the recent trend, at least with cognitive behaviour therapy, is to provide this through therapists based in the community mental health teams.

We may be heading towards a unified approach to psychosis. There is early evidence supporting the pragmatic combination of therapy approaches in a well-formulated manner. Cognitive behaviour therapy and family therapy combination certainly have value (Sellwood *et al.*, 2001). Moreover, family therapy in schizophrenia has several behavioural coping strategies and problem-solving components, which are also a part of the CBT approach (Tarrier & Wykes, 2004). Similarly psychoeducation can be a part of several types of intervention.

Substance misuse is a rising cause of co-morbidity in severe mental illness (Crome & Myton, 2004) with not enough evidence for effective approaches to treatment (Jeffery, 2004). Research is needed in this area as also in helping patients with other co-morbidities including personality disorder, and posttraumatic stress disorder. With the high incidence of depression and completed suicide in psychosis the future direction in psychological therapies needs to address these issues as a part of comprehensive and balanced management of psychosis. Furthermore research on matching psychological intervention to clients' clinical and social needs is appropriate and timely.

The current treatment of psychosis is based on the case management model. However, there is no evidence that increasing the intensity of care will provide better outcomes (Burns *et al.*, 2002). A more therapeutic or recovery-based model is appropriate (Roberts & Wolfson, 2004).

Current mental health training programmes do not offer sufficient skills training to provide psychological interventions in psychosis. Considering the fact that management of psychosis is core business of mental health teams, it is important to address this lacuna. Apart from research, more lobbying is needed to include skills early in the training (Turkington & McKenna, 2003) rather than provide it as an optional follow-on specialised training model.

REFERENCES

Bach, P. & Hayes, S.C. (2002). The use of acceptance and commitment therapy to prevent rehospitalisation of psychotic patients: a randomised controlled trial. *Journal of Consulting and Clinical Psychology, 70*, 1129–1139.

Bateson, G. (1962). A note on double bind. In D. Jackson (ed.), *Communication, Family and Marriage* (pp. 55–62). Palo Alto, CA: Science and Behaviour Books.

Bebbington, P. & Kuipers, L. (1994). The predictive utility of expressed emotion in schizophrenia: An aggregate analysis. *Psychological Medicine, 24*, 707–718.

Beck, A.T. (1952). Successful outpatient psychotherapy of a chronic schizophrenic with a delusion based on borrowed guilt. *Psychiatry, 15*, 305–312.

Bellack A.S. (1986). Schizophrenia: behavior therapy's forgotten child. *Behavior Therapy, 17*, 199–214.

Benton, M.K. & Schroeder, H.E. (1990). Social skills training with schizophrenics: A meta-analytic evaluation. *Journal of Consulting and Clinical Psychology, 58*, 741–747.

Birchwood, M., Smith, J., MacMillan, F. *et al.* (1989). Predicting relapse in schizophrenia: the development and implementation of an early signs monitoring system using patients and families as observers. *Psychological Medicine 19*, 649–656.

Bleuler, E. (1911). *Dementia Praecox or the Group of Schizophenias.* New York: International University Press.

Bleuler, M. (1978). *The Schizophrenic Disorders: Long-Term Patient and Family Studies.* London: Yale University Press.

Brown, G.W. & Birley, J.L. (1968). Crises and life changes and the onset of schizophrenia. *Journal of Health and Social Behaviour, 9*, 203–214.

Burns, T., White, I., Byford, S. *et al.* (2002). Exposure to case management: relationships to patient characteristics and outcome: report from the UK700 trial. *British Journal of Psychiatry, 181*, 236–241.

Butzlaff, R.L. & Hooley, J.M. (1998). Expressed emotion and psychiatric relapse: A meta-analysis. *Archives of General Psychiatry, 55,* 547–552.

Cicerone, K.D., Dahlberg, C., Kalmar, K., *et al.* (2000). Evidence-based cognitive rehabilitation: recommendations for clinical practice. *Archives of Physical Medicine and Rehabilitation, 81*, 1596–1615.

Crome, I.B. & Myton, T. (2004). Pharmacotherapy in dual diagnosis. *Advances in Psychiatric Treatment, 10*, 413–424.

Cuijpers P (1999). The effect of family interventions on relative's burden: a meta-analysis. *Journal of Mental Health, 24*, 565–578.

Department of Health (2001). *Treatment Choice in Psychological Therapies and Counselling.* London: Department of Health.

Dilk, M.N. & Bond, G.R. (1996). Meta-analytic evaluation of skills training research for individuals with severe mental illness. *Journal of Consulting and Clinical Psychology, 64*, 1337–1346.

Drury, V., Birchwood, M., Cochrane, R. & Macmillan, F. (1996). Cognitive therapy and recovery from acute psychosis: a controlled trial. II. Impact on recovery time. *British Journal of Psychiatry, 169*, 602–607.

Eckman, T.A., Wirshing, W.C., Marder, S.R., *et al.* (1992). Technique for training schizophrenic patients in illness self-management: a controlled trial. *American Journal of Psychiatry, 149*, 1549–1555.

Freeman, T. (1977). On Freud's theory of schizophrenia. *International Journal of Psychoanalysis, 58*, 383–388.

Freud, S. (1911). *Psycho-analytical Notes on an Auto-biographical Account of a Case of Paranoia.* London: Hogarth Press.

Fromm-Reichmann, F. (1950). *Principles of Intensive Psychotherapy.* Chicago: University of Chicago Press.

Gumley, A., O'Grady, M., McNay, L. *et al.* (2003). Early intervention for relapse in schizophrenia: results of a 12-month randomized controlled trial of cognitive behavioural therapy. *Psychological Medicine, 33,* 419–431.

Haddock, G., Tarrier, N., Morrison, A.P. *et al.* (1999). A pilot study evaluating the effectiveness of individual inpatient cognitive-behavioural therapy in early psychosis. *Social Psychiatry and Psychiatric Epidemiology, 34*, 254–258.

Haddock, G., Tarrier, N., Spaulding, W. *et al.* (1998). Individual cognitive-behavior therapy in the treatment of hallucinations and delusions: A review. *Clinical Psychology Review, 18*, 821–838.

Herz, M.I. & Lamberti, J.S. (1995). Prodromal symptoms and relapse prevention in schizophrenia. *Schizophrenia Bulletin, 21*, 541–551.

Hogarty, G.E., Greenwald, D., Ulrich, R.F., *et al.* (1997a). Three-year trials of personal therapy among schizophrenic patients living with or independent of family, II: effects on adjustment of patients. *American Journal of Psychiatry, 154*, 1514–1524.

Hogarty, G.E., Kornblith, S.J., Greenwald, D. *et al.* (1997b). Three-year trials of personal therapy among schizophrenic patients living with or independent of family, I: description of study and effects on relapse rates. *American Journal of Psychiatry, 154*, 1504–1513.

Holmes, M.R., Hansen, D.J. & St Lawrence, J.S. (1984). Conversational skills training with aftercare patients in the community: Social validation and generalization. *Behavior Therapy, 15*, 84–100.

Huxley, N.A., Rendall, M. & Sederer, L. (2000). Psychosocial treatments in schizophrenia: A review of the past 20 years. *Journal of Nervous and Mental Disorders, 188*, 187–201.

Jablensky A, Sartorius N, Ernberg G, *et al.* (1992). Schizophrenia: manifestations, incidence and course in different cultures. a World Health Organization ten-country study. *Psychological Medicine – Monograph Supplement, 20*, 1–97.

Jaspers, K. (1963). *General Psychopathology.* Manchester: Manchester University Press.

Jeffery, D.P., Ley, A., McLaren, S. & Siegfried, N. (2000). Psychosocial treatment programmes for people with both severe mental illness and substance misuse. *The Cochrane Database of Systematic Reviews*, Issue 2. Art. No.: CD001088. DOI: 10.1002/14651858.CD001088.

Jones, C., Cormac, I., Silveira da Mota Neto, J.I. & Campbell, C. (2004). Cognitive behaviour therapy for schizophrenia. *The Cochrane Database of Systematic Reviews.* Issue 4. Art. No.: CD000524. pub2. DOI: 10.1002/14651858.CD000524.pub2.

Kemp, R. & David, A. (1996). Compliance therapy: An intervention targeting insight and treatment adherence in psychotic patients. *Behavioural and Cognitive Psychotherapy, 24*, 331–350.

Kemp, R., Kirov, G., Everitt, B. *et al.* (1998). Randomised controlled trial of compliance therapy. 18-months follow-up. *British Journal of Psychiatry, 172*, 413–419.

Kingdon, D.G. & Turkington, D. (1994). *Cognitive Behavioural Therapy of Schizophrenia.* Oxford: Psychology Press.

Kingdon, D.G. & Turkington, D. (2002). *Cognitive-behavioural Therapy of Schizophrenia.* New York: Guilford Press.

Kraepelin, E. (1919). *Dementia Praecox and Paraphrenia.* Edinburgh: Churchill Livingstone.

Kuipers, E. (2000). Psychological treatments for psychosis: Evidence based but unavailable. In Corrigan, P. (ed.) *Psychiatric Rehabilitation Skills,* Vol. 4. Chicago: Recovery Press.

Laing, R.D. (1960). *The Divided Self: An Existential Study in Sanity and Madness.* London: Tavistock.

Leff, J. & Vaughn, C. (1985). *Expressed Emotions in Families.* New York: Guilford Press.

Lehman, A.F., Lieberman, J.A., Dixon, L.B., *et al.* (2004). Practice guideline for the treatment of patients with schizophrenia, second edition. *American Journal of Psychiatry, 161*, 1–56.

Lewis, S., Tarrier, N., Haddock, G. *et al.* (2002). Randomised controlled trial of cognitive-behavioural therapy in early schizophrenia: Acute-phase outcomes. *British Journal of Psychiatry Supplement, 43*, 91–97.

Lidz, T., Fleck, S. & Cornelison, A.R. (1965). *Schizophrenia and The Family.* New York: New York International University Press.

Malmberg, L.F.M. (2001). Individual psychodynamic psychotherapy and psychoanalysis for schizophrenia and severe mental illness. Malmberg, L. & Fenton, M. Individual psychodynamic psychotherapy and psychoanalysis for schizophrenia and severe mental illness. *The Cochrane Database of Systematic Reviews*, Issue 3. Art. No.: CD001360.DOI: 10.1002/14651858. CD001360.

Mari, J.J. & Streiner, D.L. (1994). An overview of family interventions and relapse on schizophrenia: Meta-analysis of research findings. *Psychological Medicine, 24*, 565–578.

Marshall, M.L.A. (2003). Early Intervention for psychosis. M. Marshall & A. Lockwood. Early intervention for psychosis. *The Cochrane Database of Systematic Reviews*, Issue 2. Art. No.: CD004718. DOI: 10.1002/14651858.CD004718.

McFarlane, W.R. (1994). Multiple-family groups and psychoeducation in the treatment of schizophrenia. *New Directions for Mental Health Services*, 13–22.

McGlashan, T.H., Zipursky, R.B., Perkins, D. *et al.* (2003). The PRIME North America randomized double-blind clinical trial of olanzapine versus placebo in patients at risk of being prodromally symptomatic for psychosis. I. Study rationale and design. *Schizophrenia Research, 61*, 7–18.

McGorry, P.D., Yung, A.R., Phillips, L.J. *et al.* (2002). Randomized controlled trial of interventions designed to reduce the risk of progression to first-episode psychosis in a clinical sample with subthreshold symptoms. *Archives of General Psychiatry, 59*, 921–928.

McMonagle, T.S.A. (2000). Token economy for schizophrenia. T. McMonagle & A. Sultana. Token economy for schizophrenia. *The Cochrane Database of Systematic Reviews*, Issue 3. Art. No.: CD001473. DOI: 10.1002/14651858.CD001473.

Meichenbaum, D. (1969). The effects of instructions and reinforcement on thinking and language behavior of schizophrenics. *Behavior Research and Therapy, 7*, 101–114.

Meyer, J.M. & Simpson, G.M. (1997). From chlorpromazine to olanzapine: A brief history of antipsychotics. *Psychiatric Services, 48*, 1137–1139.

Miller, T.J., McGlashan, T.H., Rosen, J.L. *et al.* (2002). Prospective diagnosis of the initial prodrome for schizophrenia based on the Structured Interview for Prodromal Syndromes: Preliminary evidence of interrater reliability and predictive validity. *American Journal of Psychiatry, 159*, 863–865.

Morrison, A.P., French, P., Walford, L. *et al.* (2004). Cognitive therapy for the prevention of psychosis in people at ultra-high risk: randomised controlled trial. *British Journal of Psychiatry, 185*, 291–297.

Mueser, K.T. & Berenbaum, H. (1990). Psychodynamic treatment of schizophrenia: Is there a future? *Psychological Medicine, 20*, 253–262.

Mueser, K.T., Wallace, C.J. & Liberman, R.P. (1995). New developments in social skills training. *Behaviour Change 12*, 31–40.

NICE (2002). *Schizophrenia: Core Interventions in the Treatment and Management of Schizophrenia in Primary and Secondary Care.* London: National Institute for Clinical Excellence.

O'Donnell C., Donohoe G., Sharkey L. *et al.* (2003). Compliance therapy: A randomised controlled trial in schizophrenia. *British Medical Journal, 27*(7419): 834–837.

Pekkala, E.M.L. (2002). Psychoeducation for schizophrenia. E. Pekkala & L. Merinder. Psychoeducation for schizophrenia. *The Cochrane Database of Systematic Reviews*, Issue 2. Art. No.: CD002831. DOI: 10.1002/14651858.CD002831.

Pilling, S., Bebbington, P., Kuipers, E. *et al.* (2002a). Psychological treatments in schizophrenia: II. Meta-analyses of randomized controlled trials of social skills training and cognitive remediation. *Psychological Medicine, 32*, 783–791.

Pilling, S., Bebbington, P., Kuipers, E. *et al.* (2002b). Psychological treatments in schizophrenia: I. Meta-analysis of family intervention and cognitive behaviour therapy. *Psychological Medicine, 32*, 763–782.

Quitkin, F.M. (1999). Placebos, drug effects, and study design: A clinician's guide. *American Journal Psychiatry, 156*, 829–836.

Roberts, G. & Wolfson, P. (2004). The rediscovery of recovery: open to all. *Advances in Psychiatric Treatment, 10*, 37–48.

Robertson L. (1998). Life skills programmes for chronic mental illnesses. L. Robertson, J. Connaughton & M. Nicol. Life skills programmes for chronic mental illnesses. *The Cochrane Database of Systematic Reviews*, Issue 3. Art. No.: CD000381. DOI: 10.1002/14651858. CD000381.

Sellwood, W., Barrowclough, C., Tarrier, N. *et al.* (2001). Needs-based cognitive-behavioural family intervention for carers of patients suffering from schizophrenia: 12-month follow-up. *Acta Psychiatrica Scandinavica, 104*, 346–355.

Sensky, T., Turkington, D., Kingdon, D. *et al.* (2000). A randomised controlled trial of cognitive-behavioural therapy for persistent symptoms in schizophrenia resistant to medication. *Archives of General Psychiatry, 57*, 165–172.

Sullivan, H.S. (1962). *Schizophrenia as a Human Process.* New York: W.W. Norton.

Szasz, T. (1960). The myth of mental illness. *American Psychologist, 15*, 113–118.

Tarrier, N. & Wykes, T. (2004). Is there evidence that cognitive behaviour therapy is an effective treatment for schizophrenia? A cautious or cautionary tale? *Behaviour Research and Therapy, 42*, 1377–401.

Thornicroft, G. & Bebbington, P. (1989). Deinstitutionalisation – from hospital closure to service development. *British Journal of Psychiatry, 155*, 739–753.

Turkington, D., Dudley, R., Warman, D.M. & Beck, A.T. (2004). Cognitive-behavioral therapy for schizophrenia: a review. *Journal of Psychiatric Practice, 10*, 5–16.

Turkington, D. & Kingdon, D. (1991). Ordering thoughts in thought disorder. *British Journal of Psychiatry, 158*, 160–161.

Turkington, D. & Kingdon, D. (2000). Cognitive-behavioural techniques for general psychiatrists in the management of patients with psychoses. *British Journal of Psychiatry, 177*, 101–106.

Turkington, D., Kingdon, D. & Turner, T. (2002). Effectiveness of a brief cognitive-behavioural therapy intervention in the treatment of schizophrenia. *British Journal of Psychiatry, 180*, 523–527.

Turkington, D. & McKenna, P.J. (2003). Is cognitive-behavioural therapy a worthwhile treatment for psychosis? *British Journal of Psychiatry, 182,* 477–479.

Vaughn, C. & Leff, J. (1976a). The measurement of expressed emotion in the families of psychiatric patients. *British Journal of Social and Clinical Psychology, 15,* 157–165.

Vaughn C. & Leff, J. (1976b). The influence of family and social factors on the course of psychiatric illness. A comparison of schizophrenic and depressed neurotic patients. *British Journal of Psychiatry, 129,* 125–137.

Wallace, C.J., Liberman, R.P., MacKain, S.J. *et al.* (1992). Effectiveness and replicability of modules for teaching social and instrumental skills to the severely mentally ill. *American Journal of Psychiatry, 149,* 654–658.

WHO (1973). *International Pilot Study of Schizophrenia*, vol. 1. Geneva: World Health Organization.

Wing, J.K. & Brown, G.W. (1961). Social treatment of chronic schizophrenia: A comparative study of three mental hospitals. *Journal of Mental Science, 107,* 847–869.

Xiong, W., Phillips, M., Hu, X. *et al.* (1994). Family based intervention for schizophrenic patients in China: A randomised controlled trial. *British Journal of Psychiatry, 165,* 239–247.

Yung, A.R. & McGorry, P.D. (1996). The initial prodrome in psychosis: Descriptive and qualitative aspects. *Australian and New Zealand Journal of Psychiatry, 30,* 587–599.

Yung, A.R., Phillips, L.J., McGorry, P.D. *et al.* (1998). Prediction of psychosis. A step towards indicated prevention of schizophrenia. *British Journal of Psychiatry Supplement, 172,* 14–20.

Zhang, M., Wang, M., Li, J. & Phillips, M.R. (1994). Randomised-control trial of family intervention for 78 first-episode male schizophrenic patients. An 18-month study in Suzhou, Jiangsu. *British Journal of Psychiatry Supplement, 24,* 96–102.

Zhang, M., Yan, H. & Yao, C. *et al.* (1993). Effectiveness of psychoeducation of relatives of schizophrenic patients; a prospective cohort study in five cities of China. *International Journal of Mental Health, 22,* 47–59.

CHAPTER 18

Bipolar Disorders

Jan Scott
Institute of Psychiatry, London, UK

INTRODUCTION

The basic aims of therapy in bipolar disorder (BP) are to alleviate acute symptoms, restore psychosocial functioning, and prevent relapse and recurrence. The mainstay of treatment has been and currently remains pharmacotherapy. However, the use of anti manic drugs can be accompanied by significant side effects (particularly if used in conjunction with mood stabilizers) and the treatment of acute depressive episodes with antidepressant medications carries a small but significant risk of 'switching' from depression into hypomania. Prophylactic treatment also has problems and there is a significant 'efficacy-effectiveness' gap in the reported response rates to all mood stabilizers (Guscott & Taylor, 1994; Scott, 2001; Scott & Pope, 2001). Even under optimal clinical conditions, prophylaxis protects fewer than 50 % of individuals with BP against further episodes (Dickson & Kendell, 1994). Given this scenario, the development of specific psychological therapies for BP appears a necessary and welcome advance. However, until recently, progress in this area was slow.

Historically, individuals with BP were not offered psychological therapies for three main reasons (Scott, 1995). First, aetiological models highlighting genetic and biological factors in BP dominated the research agenda and medication was not just the primary treatment but the only treatment considered appropriate. Second, there was a misconception that virtually all clients with BP made a full inter-episode recovery and returned to their pre-morbid level of functioning. Third, psychotherapists historically expressed greater ambivalence about the suitability for psychotherapy of individuals with BP than those with other severe mental disorders. Fromm-Reichman (1949) suggested that in comparison to individuals with schizophrenia, clients with BP were poor candidates for psychotherapy because they lacked introspection, were too dependent and were likely to discover and then play on the therapist's 'Achilles' heel'. Although clients with BP and their significant others argued strongly in favour of the use of psychological treatments (Goodwin & Jamison, 1990), these voices went unheard. Furthermore, the relative lack of empirical support (few randomized controlled trials have ever been published) meant that clinicians who believed adjunctive

Handbook of Evidence-based Psychotherapies: A Guide for research and practice.
Edited by C. Freeman & M. Power. Copyright © 2007 John Wiley & Sons, Ltd.

therapy might be beneficial had few clear indicators of when or how to incorporate such approaches into day-to-day practice.

Over the last 20 years, two key aspects have changed. First, there is increasing acceptance of stress-vulnerability models that highlight the interplay between psychological, social and biological factors in the maintenance or frequency of recurrence of episodes of severe mental disorders (Goodwin & Jamison, 1990). Second, evidence has accumulated from randomized controlled treatment trials regarding the benefits of psychological therapies as an adjunct to medication in other severe mental disorders, particularly treatment-resistant schizophrenia and severe and chronic depressive disorders (Falloon *et al.*, 1985; Paykel *et al.*, 1999; Sensky *et al.*, 2000; Thase, Greenhouse & Frank, 1997). Although research on the use of similar interventions in BP is still limited, there are encouraging reports from research groups exploring the role of 'manualized' therapies in this population (American Psychiatric Association, 1994).

This chapter briefly outlines the rationale for using psychological therapies in combination with medication in the treatment of adult clients with BP. Outcome data from randomized controlled trials is reviewed and the characteristics of therapies that are likely to be effective in BP are highlighted.

THE RATIONALE FOR ADJUNCTIVE PSYCHOLOGICAL TREATMENTS

Bipolar disorder has a median age of onset in the mid-20s, but most individuals report that they experienced symptoms or problems up to 10 years before diagnosis. Thus, the early evolution of BP may impair the process of normal personality development or may mean that the person starts to employ maladaptive behaviours from adolescence onwards. Co-morbid anxiety disorders, including panic and post-traumatic stress disorder (PTSD) and other mental health problems are common accompaniments of BP and as many as 40 % of subjects may have inter-episode sub-syndromal depression (Judd *et al.*, 2002). Although many individuals manage to complete tertiary education and establish a career path, they may then experience loss of status or employment after repeated relapses. One year after an episode of BP, only 30 % of individuals have returned to their previous level of social and vocational functioning. Interpersonal relationships may be damaged or lost as a consequence of behaviours during a manic episode and/or the individual may struggle to overcome guilt or shame related to such acts. Thirty per cent to 50 % of individuals with BP also meet criteria for substance misuse or personality disorders, which usually predict poorer response to medication alone. Recent studies of clinical populations of BP identify that (like persons with chronic medical disorders such as diabetes, hypertension and epilepsy), 30 % to 50 % of individuals with BP do not adhere with prescribed prophylactic treatments. Furthermore, attitudes and beliefs about BP and its treatment explain a greater proportion of the variance in adherence behaviour than medication side-effects or practical problems with the treatment regime (Scott & Pope, 2002).

The above problems identify a need for general psychological support for an individual with BP. However, there is a difference between the general non-specific benefits of combined pharmacotherapy and psychotherapy and the unique indications for psychological interventions. For a specific psychological therapy to be *indicated* as an adjunct to medication in BP it is necessary to identify a psychological model of relapse that:

• Describes how psychological and social factors may be associated with episode onset. For example, social rhythm disrupting life events may precipitate BP relapse and so stabilizing social rhythms is a key additional element in interpersonal therapy as applied in BP.
• Provides a clear rationale for which interventions should be used in what particular set of circumstances. For example, the use of family focused therapy (FFT) is supported by research demonstrating that a negative affective style of interaction and high levels of expressed emotion in a family are associated with an increased risk of relapse in an individual with BP.

Systematic research is currently under way, exploring cognitive, behavioural, emotional and interpersonal aspects of BP. These psychological models can be integrated with the 'instability model of BP relapse' as proposed by Ehlers and colleagues (Ehlers, Frank & Kupfer, 1988) and promoted by Goodwin & Jamison (1990). Briefly stated, the instability model identifies that in individuals with biological vulnerability to BP, there are four basic mechanisms of relapse and each mechanism is associated with biological dysregulation (neurotransmitter or neuroendocrine disturbances), and each mechanism is hypothesized to act through the final common pathway of sleep disruption. As shown in Figure 18.1 (working from left to right) an individual may experience internal change in biological functioning that leads to the development of the early 'prodromal' symptoms of relapse. Second, medication non-adherence may destabilize their physical state. Third, disruption to regular social routines (alterations to meal times, erratic weekly schedules, changes to the sleep-wake cycle) may produce circadian rhythm dysregulation, leading to relapse. Fourth, life events with specific personal meaning for that individual (as described in Beck's cognitive model) may lead to stress that ultimately leads to biological dysregulation. Obviously,

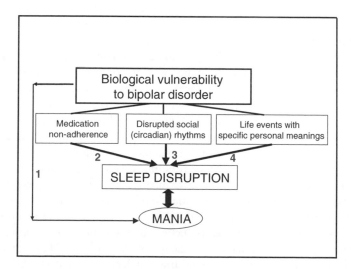

Figure 18.1   The instability model of bipolar relapse.

family attitudes and interactions can 'stress' the individual's biological system via any of the last three pathways described. Likewise, an individual may engage in substance misuse as a consequence of specific beliefs and attitudes (pathway 4), or its impact may be directly via the third pathway.

Although this brief description is an oversimplification, the instability model is helpful when considering the potential use of psychological treatments. For example, where no external stressor is identified it may still be possible to teach the individual to recognize the key early warning signs (such as sleep disruption) of episode onset and instigate a cognitive-behavioural relapse prevention package (Perry *et al.*, 1999). Psychoeducation and adherence therapy can be used to target the second pathway (Colom *et al.*, 2003; Scott & Tacchi, 2002), interpersonal social rhythms therapy (IPSRT) can be used to stabilize circadian rhythms (Frank *et al.*, 1994) whereas cognitive therapy (CT) mainly focuses on the fourth pathway (Lam, Bright, Jones *et al.*, 2000; Scott, Garland & Moorhead, 2001). However, this is not to suggest that each therapy 'maps' exclusively onto one particular pathway; the boundaries between therapies are flexible and there are several common elements. For example, CT also addresses attitudes toward medication adherence and employs self-regulation techniques. Likewise, IPSRT explores an individual's understanding of BP and his or her beliefs about relationships or personal roles that may otherwise impair their functioning. Family therapy may also target a number of pathways simultaneously (Miklowitz *et al.*, 2000), including malevolent interpretations and attributions.

STUDIES OF PSYCHOLOGICAL TREATMENTS IN BIPOLAR DISORDERS

Early Treatment Studies

There is a large literature of individual case studies on the use of a variety of psychological therapies in BP. The benefits to individuals with BP described in these papers led to a number of open studies and case series. Between 1960 and 1998 there were 32 published papers describing the combined use of psychological and pharmacological treatments in BP. However, the majority were small-scale studies, with an average sample size of about 25. The combined sample size for all studies was just over 1 000 participants, of which about 75 % received the experimental or novel psychological treatment. The majority of the papers addressed group (n = 14) or family approaches (n = 13), with only 15 % of papers reporting on individual therapy. Most importantly, less than half of all studies (only 13) were randomized controlled trials. The studies also had many methodological limitations. However, it was clear in many of these studies that those receiving adjunctive psychological treatments had better subjective and objective clinical and social outcomes than those receiving usual treatments (comprising mainly of mood stabilizers and outpatient support) and that many of these differences reached statistical significance (for a review see Scott, 1995). These encouraging results facilitated the development of randomized controlled trials of more targeted interventions that primarily focused on the issue of BP relapse.

In the last five years, interest in psychological interventions in BP has increased dramatically with about 20 randomized controlled trials under way in the US, UK and Europe. Given the current emphasis on the use of brief evidence-based therapies in clinical guidelines for the treatment of unipolar disorders, it is not surprising that the new treatment trials for BP have focussed on psychoeducational models, the three most well-researched manu-alized psychological approaches – interpersonal social rhythms therapy (IPSRT), cognitive therapy (CT) and family focused therapy (FFT) – or techniques derived directly from these manualized therapies. The latter are used primarily to improve medication adherence or to teach recognition of prodromes and relapse prevention techniques.

Key Randomized Treatment Trials

Brief Technique-driven Interventions

There are two randomized controlled trials of brief six- to 12-session interventions delivered on an individual basis to persons with BP. Each study compared the experimental inter-vention with a treatment-as-usual condition (usually medication plus outpatient support) and each study followed up participants for at least 12 months. Cochran (1984) undertook a small trial that compared 28 clients who were randomly assigned to standard clinical care alone or standard clinical care plus a six-session intervention that used cognitive and behavioural techniques to improve medication adherence. Following treatment, en-hanced lithium adherence was reported in the intervention group with only three patients (21 %) discontinuing medication as compared with eight patients (57 %) in the group re-ceiving standard clinical care alone. There were also fewer hospitalizations in the group receiving CT (two versus eight). Unfortunately no information was available on the nature of any affective relapses.

Perry *et al.* (1999) recruited 69 participants at high risk of further relapse of BP who were in regular contact with mental health services in the UK. Individuals were randomly assigned to usual treatment or to usual treatment plus six to 12 sessions of cognitive and behavioural techniques that helped individuals to identify and manage early warning signs of relapse. The problem-solving strategies included identification of high-risk situations as well as prodromal symptoms (the relapse signature) and taught clients to self-medicate and to access mental health professionals at the earliest possible time to try to avert the development of full-blown episodes. Over 18 months, the results demonstrated that, in comparison to the control group, the intervention group had significantly fewer manic relapses (27 % versus 57 %), significantly fewer days in hospital, significantly longer time to first manic relapse (65 weeks versus 17 weeks) and higher levels of social functioning and better work performance. However, there was no effect of the adjunctive therapy on rates of depressive relapse.

Group Psychoeducation

Van Gent and colleagues (Van Gent, Vida & Zwart, 1988; Van Gent & Zwart, 1991, 1993) undertook two small-scale trials using a group therapy format for individuals with BP and one trial of psychoeducation for the partners of individuals with BP. The trials were carried out in a clinical setting and would not today meet the rigorous criteria required for random-ized trials. Nevertheless, they provide important and useful information that is worthy of review. The first study (Van Gent, Vida & Zwart, 1988) allocated 20 participants with BP to four sessions of 90 minutes of group psychoeducation and 14 other participants to a waiting list control condition (usual treatment). Each group was followed for 15 months. More individuals in the intervention group (75 %) than the control group (29 %) reported significant subjective improvements in self-confidence and those receiving psychoeducation also demonstrated significant improvements in behaviour and social functioning. However, these between-group differences did not extend to mood, anxiety or general symptom ratings. In their second study, Van Gent & Zwart (1991) randomly assigned 15 participants to five sessions of psychoeducation and 20 other participants to 10 sessions of psychoeducation plus psychotherapy. At 15-month follow-up both groups showed improved psychosocial functioning but the only between-group difference was that those receiving the extended intervention demonstrated a greater improvement in their thinking and behaviour as measured on a general symptom checklist. The last study by this group (Van Gent & Zwart, 1993) explored the benefits of providing five structured group sessions for 14 partners of individuals with BP and compared their knowledge of BP, its treatment and psychosocial management strategies over six months with 12 partners who were randomly allocated to a control condition. The study demonstrated that 'partner-only' education sessions led the experimental group to gain and sustain a significantly greater understanding of BP than those allocated to the control group. However, perhaps the most significant finding was that the individuals with BP became significantly more anxious after their partner attended the experimental group without them. This suggests that individuals with BP may benefit from attendance at group psychoeducation sessions but it may be more appropriate to use family sessions if the goal is for both partners and the individual with BP to benefit.

Colom et al. (2003) have undertaken the largest group therapy study so far. It involved randomly assigning 120 participants with BP who were euthymic and receiving medication and standard outpatient follow-up to either 20 sessions of group psychoeducation (approximately eight to 12 individuals per group) or to an unstructured support group. Sessions were 90 minutes in duration and were run by two experienced clinical psychologists. Overall, when the mean number of relapses per subject, the total relapses per group, time to first relapse, length of hospitalization and serum lithium levels were evaluated, there were clear and statistically significant advantages to psychoeducation as compared with the non-directive group. Reductions in depressive relapses were particularly noticeable, and were significantly lower in both the treatment phase (psychoeducation 12 % versus control 31 %) and the follow-up phase (31 % versus 71 %). Furthermore, there was a similar significant reduction in relapse rates into hypomania, and the same trend that sometimes reached significance for manic and mixed states.

Family or Couples Therapy

Four small randomized trials all identified that family therapy may be an important adjunct to pharmacotherapy in BP. Honig et al. (1997) demonstrated that six sessions of a multi-family psychoeducational intervention (n = 23) produced a non-significantly greater reduction in expressed emotion in the experimental as compared to the waiting-list control group (n = 23). Van Gent, Vogtlander & Vrendendaal (1998) compared 'couples psycho-education' (n = 14) with usual treatment (n = 12) and found that those couples receiving the active intervention showed greater knowledge of BP and its treatment and improved coping skills at the end of the psychoeducation sessions and at six month follow-up. Glick et al.

(1994) studied 50 inpatients of whom 19 had been admitted following a BP relapse. They demonstrated that those randomly allocated to additional family therapy (n = 12) showed significant improvements in social and work functioning and family attitudes compared with those who received usual inpatient care alone (n = 7). These gains were particularly noticeable in females with BP and many of the immediate benefits associated with family therapy were maintained at 18-month follow-up (Haas, Glick & Clarkin, 1988). Clarkin *et al.* (1990) randomly assigned 42 outpatients to 11 months of standard treatment (n = 23) or standard treatment plus 25 sessions of 'couples therapy' (n = 19). Unfortunately the analysis was restricted to 33 treatment completers (couples therapy 18; control treatment 15). Receipt of a course of 'couples therapy' was associated with significantly higher levels of social adjustment and medication adherence compared with the control group, although there were no differences in overall symptom levels in the groups.

Miklowitz *et al.* (2000) undertook the largest trial of family therapy using their 20-session FFT model. They randomly allocated 101 participants with BP who were receiving usual treatment to FFT (n = 31) or to case management (n = 70), which comprised two sessions of family psychoeducation and crisis intervention as required. Over a 12-month period, individuals receiving FFT plus usual treatment as compared to case management plus usual treatment survived significantly longer in the community without relapsing (71 % versus 47 %) and showed significantly greater reductions in symptom levels. However, further analysis demonstrated that these benefits were limited to depression and there was no specific reduction in manic relapses or symptoms. Overall, the benefits of FFT were most striking in individuals living in a high expressed-emotion environment.

Rea *et al.* (2003) randomly allocated 53 persons with a recent admission with mania to 21 sessions of FFT (n = 28) or 21 sessions of individual support and problem-solving treatment. The active treatment phase was nine months and individuals were followed up for a further 15 months post-therapy. The groups did not differ significantly in likelihood of a first relapse, and in the first year 52 % of those receiving individual treatment and 46 % of those receiving FFT experienced a BD episode. However, the respective relapse rates during the second year were 60 % and 28 % and those receiving FFT were also significantly less likely to be re-hospitalized during the follow-up period.

Interpersonal Social Rhythms Therapy (IPSRT)

The IPSRT intervention was one of the first systematic psychological therapies developed specifically for individuals with BP. A randomized treatment trial with a two-year follow-up is under way. Interim reports are available on 82 participants initially allocated to IPSRT or intensive clinical management. The trial has two phases – an acute treatment phase and a maintenance phase – and 50 % of participants in each group remain in the same treatment arm throughout the study while the remaining participants cross over to the other treatment arm (Frank *et al.*, 1999). The key findings so far are that IPSRT does induce more stable social rhythms (Frank *et al.*, 1994). There were no statistically significant between-treatment differences in time to remission but those entering the trial in a major depressive episode showed a significantly shorter time to recovery with IPSRT compared to intensive clinical management (21 weeks versus 40 weeks) (Hlastala *et al.*, 1997). Interestingly, those receiving the same treatment throughout the acute and maintenance phases of the study showed greater reductions in symptoms, suicide attempts and total number of relapses than those who were assigned to the cross-over condition. This suggested that consistency in treatment was more important than type of treatment alone.

Cognitive Therapy

A study by Scott, Garland & Moorhead (2001) examined the effect of 20 sessions of CT in 42 clients with BP. Participants could enter the study during any phase of BP. Clients were initially randomly allocated to the intervention group or to a 'waiting-list' control group who then received CT after a six-month delay. The randomized phase (six months) allowed assessment of the effects of CT plus usual treatment as compared with usual treatment alone. Individuals from both groups who received CT were then monitored for a further 12 months post-CT. At initial assessment, 30 % of participants met criteria for an affective episode: 11 participants met diagnostic criteria for depressive disorder, three for rapid cycling disorder, two for hypomania, and one for a mixed state. As is typical of this client population, 12 participants also met criteria for drug and/or alcohol problems or dependence, two met criteria for other Axis I disorders and about 60 % of the sample met criteria for personality disorder. The results of the randomized controlled phase demonstrated that, compared with participants receiving treatment as usual, those who received additional CT experienced statistically significant improvements in symptom levels, global functioning and work and social adjustment. Data were available from 29 participants who received CT and were followed up for 12 months post-CT. These demonstrated a 60 % reduction in relapse rates in the 18 months after commencing CT as compared with the 18 months prior to receiving CT. Hospitalization rates showed parallel reductions. Scott *et al.* concluded that CT plus treatment as usual may offer some benefit and is a highly acceptable treatment intervention to about 70 % of clients with BP. This study was the forerunner of a large five-centre trial of treatment as usual versus CT plus treatment as usual. The sample (n = 250) is the largest for a psychological therapy in BP and results will be available in the near future.

Lam *et al.* (2000) followed up their pilot study (25 participants randomized to CT or to usual treatment) of 12 to 20 sessions of outpatient CT for BP with a large-scale randomized controlled trial (Lam *et al.*, 2003). They randomly allocated 103 participants with BP who were currently euthymic to 'individual CT as an adjunct to mood stabilizing medication' or to 'usual treatment alone' (mood stabilizers plus outpatient support). After controlling for gender and illness history, the intervention group had significantly fewer BP relapses (CT group = 43 %; control group = 75 %), psychiatric admissions (15 % versus 33 %) or total days in episode (about 27 days versus 88 days) over 12 months than the control group. The reduction in total number of episodes comprised significant reductions in major depressive (21 % versus 52 %) and manic episodes (17 % versus 31 %) but not mixed episodes. The intervention group also showed significantly greater improvements in social adjustment and better coping strategies for managing prodromal symptoms of mania.

Similarities and Differences in Therapy Outcomes

As shown in Table 18.1, the use of adjunctive therapy leads to significant reductions in relapse rates and symptom levels and significant improvements in social functioning. A number of studies reported improvements in medication adherence in those receiving

Table 18.1 Key randomized controlled trials of psychological therapies for bipolar disorders

Key study	Sample size	Experimental intervention	Main differences in outcome between experimental and control treatments
Perry *et al.* (1999)	N = 69	Relapse prevention using cognitive and behavioural strategies	Reduced lengths of hospitalization. Increased time between episodes. More effective in preventing relapses into MANIA. No effect on depression.
Frank *et al.* (1999)	N = 82	Inter-personal social rhythms therapy (IPSRT)	Increased stability of social rhythms. IPSRT more effect on DEPRESSION, with trend towards shorter time to recovery from a major depressive episode. No effect on manic relapse.
Miklowitz et al. (2000)	N = 101	Family focussed therapy	Significantly fewer relapses but FFT more effective in reducing DEPRESSION than mania. FFT particularly helpful in families with high levels of expressed emotion.
Lam *et al.*, (2003)	N = 103	Cognitive therapy	Significantly fewer episodes of MANIA and DEPRESSION. Improved social functioning. Greater awareness and better coping with manic prodromes.
Colom *et al.*, (2003)	N = 120	Group psycho-education	Significantly fewer BP episodes (manic, depressive and mixed), greatest effect on DEPRESSION but also HYPOMANIA.

psychological therapy. However, this alone did not account for the improved outcomes of participants in the intervention group. Some studies also improved the understanding and attitudes of family members toward the individual with BP and the treatment of the disorder.

It is noticeable that therapies sometimes differed in their relative effectiveness in reducing depressive or manic relapses. The reasons for this are not entirely clear but at least two hypotheses can be put forward. First, there may be different active ingredients in the therapy that more successfully tackle the syndrome of depression or mania. Alternatively, it should be noted that the symptoms of manic relapse are qualitatively different from day-to-day experiences whereas depressive prodromes often represent quantitative variations from normal experience; mania also has a longer prodrome than depression (median time approximately three weeks as compared to two weeks) (Jackson, Cavanagh & Scott, 2003). This means that interventions that focus primarily on teaching individuals to recognize early warning symptoms and to make effective interventions (behaviour change or increases in medication) may prevent isolated manic symptoms cascading into a full-blown maniac relapse but may be less effective at identifying and intervening in a timely manner with a depressive prodrome (see Jackson, Cavanagh & Scott, 2003). Interventions that tackle subsyndromal or acute BP depression often require complex multifaceted approaches such as those included in CBT and IPT and already known to be effective in the treatment of unipolar depression.

In summary, although the randomized trials reviewed here are relatively small by comparison to medication trials, there is encouraging evidence for the clinical effectiveness of each key approach. In addition, randomized trials of group therapies targeting comorbid BP and substance misuse (Weiss *et al.*, 2000) or using Bauer *et al.*'s (1997) 'life goals' programme are nearing completion. Importantly, large-scale studies are now under way on both sides of the Atlantic (the Medical Research Council study in the UK and the STEP-BD project in the US). These trials are likely to answer basic questions about the benefits and limitations of psychological therapies in the acute and maintenance treatment of BP.

WHICH THERAPY SHOULD BE OFFERED?

There is no definitive evidence about which therapy a clinician might preferentially recommend in BP. However, there are a number of shared characteristics in the therapies reported to be effective. Scott & Gutierrez (2004) identify that the 12- to 20-session courses of therapy all include four key interventions: psychoeducation, medication adherence, lifestyle regularity (including reduction in substance misuse) and relapse prevention. Furthermore, each of these interventions assumes that cognitive, behavioural, emotional and interpersonal domains are inter-related and, in interaction with biological factors, are associated with the persistence or recurrence of affective symptoms (Scott, 2001a). The therapies all regard these five domains as the key targets for change, although the relative emphasis of each approach varies, giving clinicians some opportunity to select between approaches. For example if the individual lives in an environment with high levels of expressed emotion it may be beneficial to use FFT.

Not only do the psychological interventions overlap in their objectives but, as noted previously by Teasdale (1985), the brief psychotherapies of proven effectiveness demonstrate similarities in their core clinical characteristics (see Box 18.1). The therapies identify unique aspects of people's reactions or adaptations to their illness and develop an individualized plan for treatment. By taking a collaborative and educational approach, the therapy allows individuals (and their significant others if appropriate) to be engaged as equal partners in the treatment process. There is also an emphasis on the development and independent maintenance of new coping skills and strategies.

The above characteristics are critical to the approach required for BP. For example, many individuals with BP would resist and challenge a more didactic approach to treatment (Scott, 1995). Individuals with BP, and sometimes significant others in their lives, play an active role in developing the formulation of the problems, so the interventions used appear rational and logical, giving therapy for BP a sense of coherence. The structured approach to each session with agenda setting, prioritization of problems for discussion and joint development of 'homework' (*in vivo*) tasks, enables clients to retain their focus on the session even when hypomania leads to greater distractibility. The approaches also offer individuals respect, information and choice. These features help increase their sense of self-efficacy as they begin to learn to gain control over what they can realistically control and accept or acknowledge what they cannot. This may be particularly helpful to individuals who experience low self-esteem and perceive a loss of identity following repeated episodes of BP.

Box 18.1   Shared characteristics of effective brief therapies

1. The therapy offers a specific formulation that can be applied to the individual's problems.
2. The model of therapy is shared openly with the client.
3. There is a clear rationale for the techniques used and the techniques are applied in a logical sequence.
4. There is an emphasis on skill development and transfer of learning outside of therapy sessions.
5. Change is attributed to the clients' rather than the therapists' efforts.
6. The client maintains the use of the techniques beyond the termination of therapy, increasing the prospects that the benefits will be durable.

CONCLUSIONS

This chapter highlights the fact that psychological factors may be associated with the onset and the outcome of BP episodes and that the instability model of relapse allows clinicians to recognize the potential mechanisms by which psychological therapies may improve the prognosis of those at risk of persistent symptoms or frequent relapse. The three core brief manualized therapies (IPSRT, CT and FFT) have all developed specific models for use in BP. As such, the choice between the three specific individual approaches is more likely to be dictated by client choice or the availability of a trained therapist. The group psychoeducation model (Colom *et al.*, 2003) appears to be a hybrid therapy incorporating a number of key elements from each of the specific individual approaches but it has the additional advantage of allowing individuals to share their views of BP with others and to learn adaptive coping strategies from other group members. Individuals who need help with more circumscribed problems such as adapting to the disorder, adhering to medication or identifying and self-managing early warning signs and symptoms of relapse may benefit from more targeted interventions. Adherence therapy, relapse prevention training or brief group psycho-education may be helpful in these circumstances. The fundamental difference between these technique-driven interventions and the specific models is that the former are briefer than the specific therapies (about six to nine sessions compared to about 20 sessions) and usually offer a generic, fixed treatment package rather than an individualized, more flexible formulation-based approach. However, these simpler and briefer interventions appear to be potentially very useful in day-to-day clinical practice in general adult psychiatry settings and so further randomized trials should be encouraged (Scott & Tacchi, 2002).

The use of psychological therapy as an adjunct to medication is likely to be clinically effective and cost effective as well as contributing to a significant improvement in the quality of life of individuals with BP and, indirectly, their significant others. As such, brief evidence-based therapies represent an important component of good clinical practice in the management of BP. Studies of a comprehensive 'whole-system' approach to the collaborative psychobiosocial management of BP (described in Bauer *et al.*, 1997) are also being undertaken in the US. If these improve the quality and continuity of care for individuals with BP it will have implications for the future organization of health services. The number and variety of trials of psychological interventions is exciting for researchers and clinicians interested in BP. However, for individuals with BP and their significant others, this work is long overdue (Jamison, Gardner & Goodwin, 1979).

REFERENCES

American Psychiatric Association (1994). Practice guideline for the treatment of patients with bipolar disorders. *American Journal of Psychiatry, 151* (supplement), 1–36.

Bauer, M., McBride, L., Chase, C. *et al.* (1998). Manual-based group psychotherapy for bipolar disorder: a feasibility study. *Journal of Clinical Psychiatry, 59*, 449–445.

Bauer, M., McBride, L., Shea, N. *et al.* (1997). Impact of easy access clinic based program for bipolar disorder: Quantitative analysis of a demonstration project. *Psychiatric Services, 44*, 159–168.

Clarkin, J., Carpenter, D. & Hull, J. (1998). Effects of psychoeducation for married patients with bipolar disorder and their spouses. *Psychiatric Services, 49*, 531–533.

Cochran, S. (1984). Preventing medication non-compliance in the outpatient treatment of bipolar affective disorders. *Journal of Consulting and Clinical Psychology, 52*, 873–878.

Colom, F., Martinez-Aran, A. & Reinares, M. (2001). Psychoeducation and prevention of relapse in bipolar disorders: Preliminary results. *Bipolar Disorders, 3* (supplement), 32.

Colom, F., Vieta, E., Martinez-Aran, A. *et al.* (2003). A randomized trial of group psychoeducation in bipolar disorder. *Archives of General Psychiatry, 60*, 402–406.

Dickson, W.E. & Kendell, R.E. (1994). Does maintenance lithium therapy prevent recurrences of mania under ordinary clinical conditions? *Psychological Medicine, 16*, 521–530.

Ehlers, C., Frank, E. & Kupfer, D. Social zeitgebers and biological rhythms: A unified approach to understanding the etiology of depression. *Archives of General Psychiatry, 45*, 948–952.

Falloon, I., Boyd, J., McGill, C., Fadden, G. (1985). Family management in prevention of morbidity in schizophrenia: Clinical outcome of a two-year longitudinal study. *Archives of General Psychiatry, 42*, 887–896.

Frank, E., Hlastala, S., Ritenour, A. *et al.* (1994). Inducing lifestyle regularity in recovering bipolar patients: results from the maintenance therapies in bipolar disorder protocol. *Biological Psychiatry, 41*, 1165–1173.

Frank, E., Swartz, H., Mallinger, A. *et al.* (1999). Adjunctive psychotherapy for bipolar disorder: effect of changing treatment modality. *Journal of Abnormal Psychology, 108*, 579–587.

Fromm-Reichman, F. (1949). Intensive psychotherapy of manic-depressives: a preliminary report. *Confina Neurologica, 9*, 158–165.

Glick, I., Berti, L., Okonogi, K. & Sacks, M. (1994). Effectiveness in psychiatric care: psychoeducation and outcome for patients with major affective disorder and their families. *British Journal of Psychiatry, 164*, 104–106.

Goodwin, F. & Jamison, K. (1990). *Manic Depressive Illness* (pp. 530–592). Oxford: Oxford University Press.

Guscott, R. & Taylor, L. (1994). Lithium prophylaxis in recurrent affective illness: efficacy, effectiveness and efficiency. *British Journal of Psychiatry, 164*, 741–746.

Haas, G., Glick, I. & Clarkin, J. (1988). Inpatient family intervention: a randomized clinical trial. Results at hospital discharge. *Archives of General Psychiatry, 45*, 217–224.

Hlastata, S., Frank, E. & Mallinger, A. (1997). Bipolar depression: an underestimated treatment challenge. *Depression and Anxiety, 5*, 73–83.

Honig, A., Hofman, A., Rozendaal, N. & Dingemans, P. (1997). Psychoeducation in bipolar disorder: effect on expressed emotion. *Psychiatry Research, 72*, 17–22.

Jackson, A., Cavanagh, J. & Scott, J. (2003). A systematic review of prodromal symptoms of mania and depression. *Journal of Affective Disorders, 74*, 209–217.

Jamison, K.R., Garner, R.H. & Goodwin, F.K. (1979). Patient and physician attitudes toward lithium. *Archives of General Psychiatry, 36*, 866–869.

Judd, L.L., Akiskal, H.S. & Schlettler, P.J. *et al.* (2002). The long-term natural history of the weekly symptomatic status of bipolar 1 disorder. *Archives of General Psychiatry, 59*, 530–537.

Lam, D., Bright, J., Jones, S. *et al.* (2000). Cognitive therapy for bipolar illness – a pilot study of relapse prevention. *Cognitive Therapy and Research, 24*, 503–520.

Lam, D., Bright, J., Jones, S. *et al.* (2003). A randomized controlled trial of cognitive therapy for relapse prevention in bipolar disorders. *Archives of General Psychiatry, 60*, 145–152.

Miklowitz, D., Simoneau, T., George, E. *et al.* (2000). Family focused treatment of bipolar disorder: one-year effects of a psychoeducational program in conjunction with pharmacotherapy. *Biological Psychiatry, 48*, 582–592.

Paykel, E., Scott, J., Teasdale, J. *et al.* (1999). Prevention of relapse in residual depression by cognitive therapy: A controlled trial. *Archives of General Psychiatry, 56*, 829–835.

Perry, A., Tarrier, N., Morriss, R. *et al.* (1999). Randomized controlled trial of efficacy of teaching patients with bipolar disorder to identify early symptoms of relapse and obtain treatment. *British Medical Journal, 318*, 149–153.

Rea, M., Tompson, M., Miklowitz, D. *et al.* (2003). Family-focused treatment versus individual treatment for bipolar disorder: Results of a randomized clinical trial. *Journal of Consulting and Clinical Psychology, 71*, 482–492.

Scott, J. (1995). Psychotherapy for bipolar disorder: An unmet need? *British Journal of Psychiatry, 167*, 581–588.

Scott, J. (2001a). Cognitive therapy for depression. *British Medical Bulletin, 57*, 101–113.

Scott, J. (2001b). Cognitive therapy as an adjunct to medication in bipolar disorders. *British Journal of Psychiatry Supplement, 178*, s164–168.

Scott, J., Garland, A., Moorhead, S. (2001). A pilot study of cognitive therapy in bipolar disorder. *Psychological Medicine, 31*, 459–467.

Scott, J. & Gutierrez, M. (2004). The current status of psychological therapies in bipolar disorders: A systematic review. *Journal of Bipolar Disorders*, in press.

Scott, J. & Pope, M. (2002). Non-adherence with mood-stabilizers: prevalence and predictors. *Journal of Clinical Psychiatry, 65*, 384–390.

Scott, J. & Tacchi, M.J. (2002). A pilot study of concordance therapy for individuals with bipolar disorders who are non-adherent with lithium prophylaxis. *Bipolar Disorders, 4*, 386 392.

Sensky, T., Turkington, D., Kingdon, D. *et al.* (2000). A randomised controlled trial of cognitive behavioural therapy for persistent symptoms in schizophrenia resistant to medication. *Archives of General Psychiatry, 57*, 165–172.

Teasdale, J. (1985). Psychological treatments for depression: How do they work? *Behaviour Research and Therapy, 23*, 157–165.

Thase, M.E., Greenhouse, J.B. & Frank, E. (1997). Treatment of major depression with psychotherapy or psychotherapy-pharmacotherapy combinations. *Archives of General Psychiatry, 54*, 1009–1015.

Van Gent, E., Vida, S. & Zwart, F. (1988). Group therapy in addition to lithium in patients with bipolar disorders. *Acta Psychiatrica Belgica, 88*, 405–418.

Van Gent, E., Vogtlander, L., Vrendendaal, J. (1998). Two group psychoeducation programs compared. APA, Toronto, Abstract 177.

Van Gent, E. & Zwart, F. (1991). Psychoeducation of partners of bipolar manic patients. *Journal of Affective Disorders, 21*, 15–18.

Van Gent, E., Zwart, F. (1993). Ultra-short versus short group therapy in addition to lithium. *Patient Education and Counseling, 21*, 135–141.

Weiss, R., Kolodziej, M., Najavits, L. *et al.* (2000). Utilization of psychosocial treatments by patients diagnosed with bipolar disorder and substance misuse. *American Journal of Addictions, 9*, 314–320.

CHAPTER 19

Depression

Roslyn Law
Royal Edinburgh Hospital, UK

INTRODUCTION

Low mood is a universal experience. It is most often a temporary emotional response to losses, disappointments or conflicts, which are an inevitable part of human experience. Fortunately for most of us the transitory nature of ordinary mood changes means that periods of lower mood impose only a passing additional burden. With time or a change of fortune the emotional temperature changes and so mood adapts. The point at which low mood becomes characterised as clinically depressed mood is difficult to determine and rests somewhere along a spectrum of emotional experiences from sadness to desolate emptiness. The overlap with associated emotional states such as hopelessness and grief further add to difficulties of clear definition.

It has been argued that depressed mood can be a functional response, preventing dangerous or futile actions in unfavourable circumstances (Nesse, 2000) or facilitating mourning necessary to accommodate loss (Freud, 1917). Depression, however, is also used to refer to a persistent and intense alteration in mood, associated with concomitant cognitive, behavioural and physiological changes resulting in functional impairment. In such cases depression is no longer a relatively isolated, contained and transitory emotional state but describes a more pervasive change in status. It demands a high cost from those living with it both directly and indirectly. In such cases depression is a collective term used to refer to a clinical disorder and may be anticipated to have further implications both personally and interpersonally.

Both DSM-IV and ICD-10 describe a cluster of physical, cognitive and emotional symptoms that, when presented together over a period of at least two weeks, are regarded as consistent with a diagnosis of major depression. DSM-IV presents a threshold of five out of nine symptoms, including low mood, loss of interest, weight loss or gain, sleep difficulties, agitation or slowing down, feelings of worthlessness or inappropriate guilt, difficulty thinking and concentrating and thoughts of death or self-harm. Both diagnostic systems agreeing that persistent low mood and loss of interest are core and necessary for diagnosis. ICD-10 additionally specifies reduced self-esteem and self-confidence and a bleak and pessimistic view of the future with an increasing number of the additional symptoms anticipated as the

Handbook of Evidence-based Psychotherapies: A Guide for research and practice.
Edited by C. Freeman & M. Power. Copyright © 2007 John Wiley & Sons, Ltd.

severity of the episode increases. Although not included in either diagnostic system, indicators of social dysfunction including social withdrawal and isolation and sexual dysfunction are common features of a depressive state.

Current classification systems focus on the commonality of experience between depressed individuals, drawing lines of demarcation along subtypes, severity, patterns of recurrence and, to a limited extent, co-morbidity. However such systems do not similarly accommodate the differences between depressed individuals, which may be of significant bearing on their response to treatment and interaction with different treatment formats, such as personality, gender and the impact of historical and current relationship and socio-economic factors. Such factors continue to rely on the skill and wisdom of the clinician to integrate and accommodate into any treatment plan.

Depression is a very common disorder, most commonly emerging in early adult life, but potentially having onset from childhood to late life. Large-scale community prevalence studies have shown lifetime prevalence rates of approximately 17 %, and 6 % to 10 % in the last year (Kessler *et al.*, 1994; Kessler *et al.*, 2003). Rates show significant interactions with social and economic status (Brown & Harris, 1978; NICE, 2004) especially for women who are at greater risk during early and mid-adult life but less so in later life when the gender pattern reverses. The majority of identified community cases are rated as moderate severity or above, with almost 13 % having very severe symptoms (Kessler *et al.*, 2003) although it is uncertain how valid a symptom count definition of severity is in practical terms. The impact of moderate to severe depression is reflected in over 59 % of individuals who have suffered from depression in the last year reporting severely or very severely impaired role functioning, with particular difficulties noted in the social domain (Kessler *et al.*, 2003). The fortune of those suffering with depression is further hampered by the fact that depression rarely presents in isolation. Co-morbidity has been identified in 72 % of those with a lifetime diagnosis and in 78 % with a diagnosis in the last 12 months. The most common presentation is co-morbidity with an anxiety disorder (Kessler *et al.*, 1998, 2003). The impact of this diagnosis is reflected in it being one of the major causes of social, physical and occupational impairment, and associated with increased mortality risk, with two-thirds of suicides completed in the midst of an episode of depression (Sartorius, 2001).

Depression is often described as an episodic disorder, with widely varying estimates of mean duration, ranging from 3–12 months, while 10–30 % experience more than 12 months of symptoms (Keller *et al.*, 1982, 1992; Spijker *et al.*, 2002). Thus the delineation among and between episodes is not always clear and, for many, the disorder can run on for months or years in a chronic or repeatedly relapsing course. The World Health Organisation found that one year after diagnosis with depression 66 % continue to meet criteria for a mental health disorder, 50 % of those being depressed (NICE, 2004). It is also known that once depressed the risk of becoming depressed again increases. This is important in understanding what it means to someone's life to become depressed – whether it is a temporary difficulty or lifelong challenge. Kupfer (1991) reports a 50 % risk of recurrence following first episode, higher if onset is before 20 (Giles *et al.*, 1989). The odds of future episodes further increase with each subsequent episode, rising to 70 % and 90 % after second and third episodes (Kupfer, 1991).

A persuasive body of theoretical argument and evidence has developed since the 1960s supporting the use of psychological interventions in the treatment of this disorder. This is further promoted by the demonstration of patient preference for such talking therapy as treatment approach of choice (Ward *et al.*, 2000). The goals of psychotherapy reflect those of pharmacotherapy in reducing depressive symptoms, improving social and occupational functioning and preventing a recurrence of the symptomatic and functional difficulties in the future. In addition psychotherapies provide a framework for understanding, addressing and correcting cognitive, behavioural, social and interpersonal factors hypothesised to play a precipitating, exacerbating or maintaining role in the spectrum of depressive symptoms.

A number of models of therapy have been examined in relation to relieving the symptoms of depression, and these have undergone varying degrees of evaluation with respect to their clinical value. Numerous meta-analyses have been conducted and clinical guidelines produced to review the wealth of research that has been published on psychological interventions for depression (De Rubeis & Crits-Christoph, 1998; Frank *et al.*, 1993; Jorgensen, Dam & Bolwig, 1998; NICE, 2004; Robinson *et al.*, 1990) and to help clinicians and researchers alike to determine whether all that shines is in fact gold. Empirical evidence points to cognitive behavioural therapy (CBT), interpersonal psychotherapy (IPT) and problem solving therapy (PST) as primary treatment options for depression, with more limited evidence supporting the use of behaviour therapy, couples therapy, and forms of brief psychodynamic therapy.

INTERPERSONAL PSYCHOTHERAPY

Rationale

Interpersonal therapy provides a pragmatic, time-limited and interpersonally focused approach to the treatment of major depression. It is modest in its use of psychotherapy jargon and promotes attention to the relationship-based issues that are central to the experience of many depressed patients. The treatment does not become entangled in questions of causation, acknowledging the capacity for depression to both precipitate and reflect interpersonal change, difficulty and loss. Instead it attends to difficulties arising in the daily experience of maintaining relationships and resolving difficulties while depressed. The fundamental clinical task of IPT is to help patients to learn to understand their depressive symptoms in an interpersonal context, and to work towards resolution of interpersonal difficulties such that they will no longer precipitate or sustain the depressive state and so facilitate more effective symptom management.

Evidence Base

Interpersonal psychotherapy (Klerman *et al.*, 1984, Weissman, Markowitz & Klerman, 2000) was originally devised in a research context and has been developed and evaluated in a wide range of clinical trials, with both depressed and non-depressed populations and as both an acute intervention (Elkin *et al.*, 1989) and as a maintenance therapy (Frank *et al.*, 1991; Klerman *et al.*, 1974). It has also been adapted for use with different age groups including depressed adolescents (Mufson *et al.*, 1999) and older adults (Reynolds *et al.*, 1999a, b), as well as depressed medically ill patients (Markowitz, 1998) and anti-partum and post-partum mothers (O'Hara *et al.*, 2000; Spinelli, 1997). Interpersonal psychotherapy was originally designed as an individual therapy but it has been modified for use in a group setting (Wilfley *et al.*, 1993) and as a conjoint therapy for couples with marital disputes (Foley *et al.*, 1989).

Research evaluations comparing IPT to established treatments for depression, both medical and psychological, have repeatedly demonstrated its equivalence and in some instances superiority (DiMascio *et al.*, 1979; Elkin *et al.*, 1989). In the earliest study of IPT with an acutely depressed population, IPT and Amitriptyline were compared as individual and combined treatments and compared to a minimal contact control condition (DiMascio *et al.*, 1979). Both active treatments were found to be superior to the control condition and the combined treatment was found to have a significantly superior additive effect. Medication was found to have a quicker initial effect on symptoms but this balanced out by the end of the treatment period. This study also revealed the slow release effect of IPT on social functioning, with significantly greater improvement being demonstrated for IPT subjects, whether receiving IPT alone or in combination than for the other conditions.

The National Institute of Mental Health (NIMH) Treatment of Depression Collaborative Research Program (TDCRP) provided a major evaluation of psychological treatments for depression (IPT and CBT) and comparison with a primarily medical approach (Elkin *et al.*, 1989). Primary analyses revealed a pattern of significant symptomatic improvement but few significant differences between the active treatments and interestingly between the active and control conditions. When the initial severity of the depressive symptoms was used to define the sample, treatment with Imipramine primarily but in some instances IPT, demonstrated superiority over the placebo/clinical management in the more severely depressed sample. Cognitive-behavioural therapy failed to demonstrate significance over placebo under these conditions. Significantly, however, only 26 % of IPT subjects who recovered remained well over the 18-month follow-up period and one-third of those who had recovered at end of treatment relapsed during this period (Shea *et al.*, 1992). Relapse was reported to come late in this period (mean 67 weeks) but it came nonetheless. This was very similar to the rates recorded for CBT and superior to the rates for Imipramine and placebo, although the latter figures may be attributable to the clinically unsound withdrawal of medication at the end of treatment. Numerous statistical reworkings of this landmark study have done little to change the outcome pattern (Gibbons *et al.*, 1993; Klein & Ross, 1993). Schulberg *et al.* (1996, 1998) also reported a more rapid and effective outcome for IPT compared with GP treatment as usual in primary care patients with depression but found that initial severity of depression and functional ability were unrelated to clinical course.

Three further randomized control trials have been conducted to evaluate the prophylactic effect of IPT as a continuation or maintenance therapy (IPT-M) for successfully treated patients with recurrent depression. The original research evaluation of IPT (Klerman *et al.*, 1974) revealed the superiority of IPT and Amitriptyline over placebo and a similar non-significant trend for IPT alone. The IPT subjects also demonstrated superior social functioning gains over the one-year follow up period than either placebo or medication subjects (Weissman *et al.*, 1974). Frank *et al.*'s (1991) work has specifically evaluated the additional effect of monthly IPT either alone or in combination with active or placebo medication following successful acute combination IPT and Imipramine. Unlike the originators, Frank's group argue for the importance of treating depression to recovery rather than a standard time-limited protocol, consequently the acute and consolidation period may be longer than the standard 16 sessions. This study revealed that those who received IPT over the follow up period remained well for significantly longer than those who did not, with those who received combined treatment remaining symptom free for longest. Subsequent work (Thase *et al.*, 1997) demonstrated that the treatment combination necessary to achieve recovery was also necessary to keep patients well after treatment: effective combined therapy could not be reduced to monotherapy and produce similar effects. Frank *et al.* (1991) also revealed that those patients whose therapy was rated as more consistently and specifically interpersonal had a significantly greater survival time than those with lower IPT conformity. Reynolds *et al.* (1999a) reported that IPT-M and Nortriptyline combined and as monotherapy were superior to placebo in preventing relapse in older adults with recurrent depression. Combined therapy was significantly superior to IPT alone and had a trend towards superiority over medication alone. Comparison of effect for older adults and general adult population revealed a comparable but slower effect for the older population from combined treatment (Reynolds *et al.* 1996) and a higher and more rapid relapse rate in the older adults, although this was reported to respond well to brief periods of more intense therapy (Reynolds, 1994). Lenze *et al.* (2002) in an IPT maintenance study with older adults, found that social functioning was maintained in those receiving combined therapy (IPT and Nortriptyline) while it declined in those receiving monotherapy (pharmacotherapy or psychotherapy). The specific needs of older adults with bereavement-related depression did not appear to be best served by IPT alone. While combined treatment produced the highest remission rate IPT with placebo produced the lowest (Reynolds *et al.* 1999b).

Various prognostic factors have been examined in relation to IPT. Marital adjustment in the NIMH study was reported to show significant improvement with treatment but no specific interaction with treatment type and was mediated by change in depression (Kung & Elkin, 2000). Poorer pre-treatment adjustment was revealed as an indicator of poor prognosis at the end of treatment and poorer end-of-treatment marital functioning was a negative indicator for follow up. Imber *et al.* (1990), reporting on the same sample, revealed the importance of tailoring therapy to patients' strengths as IPT produced better outcome in those patients with lowest social dysfunction at the start of treatment. Repeated studies have examined the impact of co-morbid anxiety symptoms and while GAD symptoms have been found to slow response to treatment they have not been associated with poorer outcome (Brown *et al.*, 1996). Panic/agoraphobic symptoms however have been associated with higher early termination rates and poorer clinical outcome and delayed treatment response (Brown *et al.*, 1996; Feske *et al.*, 1998; Frank *et al.*, 2000). Thase *et al.*'s (1997) meta-analysis examined the impact of initial symptom severity and found that outcome for IPT alone was not significantly different from combined therapy with milder depressions but it fared significantly less well in more severely depressed individuals.

Given the clear interpersonal perspective of IPT it is not surprising that it has also been tested for couples caught in a pattern of disputes. Foley *et al.* (1989) compared outcome for depressed outpatients randomised to the individual or couples version of the therapy. Both groups demonstrated significant reduction in depressive symptoms and improved general interpersonal functioning by the end of treatment, with neither showing an advantage over the other. When outcome was defined specifically in terms of marital satisfaction the conjoint worked fared better than the individual format, suggesting a limited advantage for couples work with this subgroup.

Clinical Practice

The major goals of IPT, namely to reduce depressive symptoms and improve inter-personal and social functioning, are achieved through the resolution of the primary interpersonal problem area. In IPT interpersonal problems are conceptualized under four principal headings: interpersonal role dispute, interpersonal role transition, unresolved grief and interpersonal deficits or sensitivity. At first this may appear to limit the application of this interpersonal model but in practice the challenge is more often to decide with clients which of the competing options generated by this framework will best contribute to their recovery and improved function. By proposing that a single focus be selected IPT does not assume that depressed individuals only experience one difficulty at a time. Rather it provides a framework whereby difficulties may be prioritized for attention based on their relevance to the current depressive symptoms and potential to respond to efforts to achieve change over the time-limited contract. Often presenting difficulties may overlap, such as marital disputes that emerge in the context of the stress generated by job loss – a dispute in the context of a transition. Interpersonal therapy helps to tell the patient's story in a manner that acknowledges the process through which difficulties emerge and offers sign posts and strategies to assist work towards change and resolution.

Interpersonal therapy emphasises the interpersonal environment through assessment, problem resolution and termination. Depressive symptoms are understood not simply in terms of presence or absence but within a particular timeframe, which promotes attention to particular life events and interactions that triggered or arose from depressive symptoms. The interpersonal implications of depressive symptoms are similarly given marked attention – for example, does excessive guilt lead to a pattern or subservience, withdrawal or demands for reassurance? Effective management of depressive symptoms is held as a primary goal and the optimal utilisation of interpersonal resources is a recurrent theme to support efforts in this direction: the question is not simply 'what can you do to help yourself feel better?' but 'who can help you to do that?' In order to facilitate this IPT therapists conduct a thorough review of the person's interpersonal world, the interpersonal inventory, considering availability, utilisation, reciprocity, satisfaction and importantly connection to the current depressive symptoms. The selection of a focus for treatment, derived from the assessment process, has an additional benefit in modelling an effective problem solving strategy and relieving the person of the burden of simultaneously trying to resolve all the difficulties with which he or she is faced. Conjoint IPT, in which both partners in a relationship are present throughout, follows a similar course but additionally takes both parties history of the depression and their relationship.

Middle Sessions

During the middle sessions the therapist helps the patient to link the weekly onset of symptoms to the interpersonal context or vice versa, clarify the issues and themes which emerge, and attends to the associated emotional experience. Sessions focus on here and now concerns and events, and strategies are selected and implemented as appropriate to the stage of therapy and the experiences of the week. Patients are helped to understand their experiences within the focus framework and to consider and ultimately attempt alternative responses, which may disentangle their relationships and role performance from their depressive symptoms.

Role transition is the most commonly selected focus area, reflecting the multitude and diversity of roles held by each individual. The IPT model identifies three interrelated phases of the intervention, during which the patient is assisted in moving away from the old role through realistic evaluation and mourning, reflecting on the process of change and its impact on successful transition, and finally re-evaluating the possibilities and opportunities in the new role and clarifying and mastering the current demands to restore self-esteem.

The disputes focus attention on a significant relationship that is the primary area of difficulty in relation to this episode of depression. This may be a recent conflict or the exacerbation of a longer standing dispute. The objective is then to understand the mechanisms by which the dispute is perpetuated through detailed replaying of affect-laden exchanges. Attention is then directed to modifying those aspects that are amenable to change, facilitating more effective and productive communication patterns to allow resolution. In conjoint work IPT assumes that disputes are the focus and unlike some other couples therapies continues to focus primary attention on the problems of the depressed individual rather than equal attention to both parties.

The grief focus attends to the difficulties experienced when the patient maintains a significant attachment to a person who has died such that it interferes with current functioning, through the onset and maintenance of depressive symptoms. Interpersonal therapy helps the patient to review the relationship that has been lost, considering all its dimensions, and helps the patient to become more engaged with the current social environment by realigning expectations with the members of the patient's current network.

The patients for whom interpersonal sensitivity is the primary focus often have a history of interpersonal difficulties or isolation extending far beyond the period of the most recent episode of depression. This distinguishes them from many of the other IPT patients, as they may not have experienced a higher level of social functioning prior to the onset of depressive symptoms. Given the more pervasive nature of the interpersonal difficulties these patients experience, it is important to tailor the expectations of therapy accordingly. The authors of IPT recommend that if a reasonable alternative to sensitivity is available this should be negotiated as the primary focus. While this is certainly one of the more difficult areas to work with in IPT, interpersonal deficits is not one to be avoided at all costs. As a secondary focus in particular interpersonal deficits can provide a very helpful framework with which to understand the recurrent and pervasive difficulties these patients experience with other people.

Termination

As with any time-limited therapy, the end of treatment is in focus from the start of the contract, which by definition draws attention to the ending, as is monitored with a weekly countdown of sessions to keep therapist and patient oriented in treatment. The IPT model makes more explicit and direct reference to the end of treatment during the last four sessions, although this issue may be broached earlier if this is appropriate to the patient's needs, history and response. Patients are actively invited to reflect on their experience and response to the end of treatment and to look back over the experience to review progress and evaluate the impact. It is important that progress in terms of depressive symptoms and interpersonal functioning is reviewed at this stage. Patients are encouraged to reflect on their own contribution to their recovery but the facilitative impact of engaging interpersonal support within and beyond the therapy relationship is also highlighted. Plans are made in terms of management of anticipated life events, which may increase the risk of depressive symptoms returning, and also to address needs that have emerged through the course of therapy but may have been beyond the limit of the specific focus. The recurrent nature of depressive illness is directly addressed in the final stages of treatment to ensure that more active use of personal resources and links to more formal support are thought through to facilitate their use at a subsequent stage.

COGNITIVE BEHAVIOURAL THERAPY

Rationale

Cognitive behavioural therapy for depression, rather than referring to a single system of therapy, now more accurately describes a range of practices derived from the original work by Aaron Beck (Beck *et al.* 1979), focusing on the thinking patterns and associated emotional, behavioural and physiological systems operating within the depressed individual. Problematic schema, acquired in and reflecting the course of development are retained into later life and can be triggered by thematically congruent events. Such triggering events are argued to lead to characteristic negative automatic thoughts, thinking errors and erroneous or negatively biased (Power & Dalgleish, 1997) information processing and associated behavioural, emotional and physiological responses. The first goal of CBT is the identification of any such systematic errors and the second is the modification of thinking and reasoning patterns to replace them with evidence-based and rationale alternatives, thus facilitating behavioural, emotional and physiological change through the same interconnected systems.

Evidence Base

Cognitive behavioural therapy for depression is the most commonly used and researched of the psychological therapies in the NHS. It is also commonly thought to be the psychological therapy with the most clearly established evidence base (NICE, 2004). It has been repeatedly shown to offer equivalent benefit to established anti-depressant medication for the treatment of depression (Hollon *et al.*, 1992; Murphy *et al.*, 1984; Rush *et al.*, 1977) and superior outcome to no treatment or wait-list control. However its relative efficacy in relation to other psychological therapies is not yet as clearly established, perhaps confusing quantity for quality. Dobson's (1989) meta-analysis found CBT to be more effective than no treatment, behavioural treatment alone and anti-depressants but Robinson *et al.* (1990) revised this to report equivalent efficacy to anti-depressant medication when controlling for therapist allegiance. Gloaguen *et al.* (1998) in a meta analysis of almost 3 000 patients, concluded that CBT was superior to no treatment and all other treatment methods, with the exception of behaviour therapy, although this is challenged by Parker, Roy & Eyers (2003) who cite evidence that contradicts the conclusions drawn. De Rubeis & Crits-Christoph (1998) cite three large-scale studies in which CBT was shown to be equivalent but not superior to other forms of psychotherapy – namely IPT (Elkin *et al.*, 1989), psychodynamic interpersonal psychotherapy (Shapiro *et al.*, 1994) and behaviour therapy (Jacobson & Hollon, 1996), findings that are at odds with the predominance of CBT in clinical practice. In smaller studies a similar pattern has been found. Ward *et al.* (2000) found CBT to be superior to TAU in general practice but showed no significant difference to non-directive counselling at the end of treatment and no significant difference to TAU after one year. Gloaguen *et al.*'s (1998) meta-analysis of patients with mild to moderate depressions concluded that cognitive therapy (CT) patients had 29 % greater improvement than placebo/waiting list subjects, 15 % greater improvement than patients receiving anti-depressant medication and 10 % more improvement than patients receiving other therapies, with the exception of behaviour therapy where no difference in outcome was found. It was also of note that there was between trial heterogeneity in the comparison with other therapies creating difficulty in generalising the overall finding to each of the individual therapies included.

Such findings do not argue against CBT as a treatment for depression. On the contrary they demonstrate its consistently robust performance in the face of many comparative evaluations. However they highlight the relative absence of studies with depressed patients in which CBT was found to be superior to an alternative psychological treatment, a superiority tacit in the predominance of this model of practice. Cognitive behavioural therapy has demonstrated equivalence in good quality pharmacology studies (De Rubeis *et al.*, 1999; Hollon *et al.*, 1992; McKnight, Nelson-Gray & Barnhill, 1992). Hollon *et al.* (1992) also found no difference in CBT outcome with more severely depressed patients, in contrast to the findings of the TDCRP (Elkin *et al.* 1995). De Rubeis *et al.* (1999) also conducted a meta-analysis of four studies comparing CBT and medication for patients with severe depression. Direct comparisons between the two lines of intervention showed no significant differences but overall effect sizes favoured CBT. Deckersbach, Gershuny & Otto (2000) argue that although there is scant evidence beyond trend level for the additive effect of CBT and anti-depressant medication with mild to moderate depression, more evidence exists with the chronically and more severely depressed, perhaps offering combined independent effects rather than a synergistic mode of action. Keller *et al.* (2000) conducted a multi-site trial (n = 681) in which the CBT focused primarily on interpersonal issues, including interactions with the therapist. A significantly higher proportion of patients receiving combined treatment rather than those receiving CBT or medication alone met responder and remission criteria.

In addition to the benefits of CBT as an acute intervention, follow-up data from a number of studies suggest that CBT offers longer term relapse prevention effects (Evans *et al.*, 1992; Kovacs *et al.*, 1981; McLean & Hakstian, 1990; Simons *et al.*, 1986), resulting in two to three times as many CBT patients remaining well as medication patients. Parker, Roy & Eyers (2003), however, note that naturalistic follow-up confuses the prophylactic effects of acute CT and the impact of maintenance treatment in sustaining initial gains. Fava *et al.* (1996) concluded that CBT for residual symptoms reduces the risk of relapse in depressed patients compared to clinical management and, although the overall effect faded after four years, CBT patients experienced fewer relapses than the control group (Fava, 1998a, b). Paykel *et al.* (1999) also found that CBT for residual depressive symptoms resulted in 38 % lower rates of relapse and symptoms persistence than clinical management alone over 68 weeks follow up. Blackburn & Moore (1997) found no difference between groups who received either CBT or medication for 2 years following a 16-week acute intervention. Interestingly Gortner *et al.* (1998) found no difference in relapse prevention rates for full CBT and its component parts in a two-years follow up to the dismantling study previously cited.

Clinical Practice

Cognitive behavioural therapy offers a present focused, collaborative and problem oriented approach to the treatment of depression, targeting characteristic patterns of thinking, behaviour and emotional regulation. Specific emphasis is given to returning the individual to productive and pleasurable activities and the more successful management of any skills deficits and thinking patterns that create a barrier to this. Such deficits may be longstanding or more directly reflective of the current depressed state. This intervention of collaboratively set programmes of activity scheduling encourages individuals to do what they planned rather than what they feel in the midst of a depression episode. The specific skills training provided, for example social or problem-solving skills, will reflect the presenting difficulties for the individual and their contribution to the depressed state. In parallel with this and informed by it is consistent attention to maladaptive thinking and reasoning style, with a view to developing and reinforcing a more adaptive and evidence-based cognitive style. This integrated approach acknowledges the interconnections between emotions, cognition, behaviour and physical state and capitalises on this by approaching the system from a number of different angles in order to intervene where change is possible. This integrated approach is contained within the case formulation, which guides the choice of intervention and provides a framework from which to understand the presenting difficulties.

The assessment phase of CBT, as with any psychotherapy, aims to foster a safe and collaborative relationship. Details are gathered about the nature and extent of the current depressive difficulties and these are placed in context with a history of depression to date as well as recent precipitating events and losses consequent to the depression, both of which are more common in depressed populations. Systematic assessment is completed with standardised forms, such as the CBT-compatible Beck Depression Inventory (BDI) (Beck *et al.*, 1961) and clinical interviews. Given the prominence of formative experiences in the CBT formulation, care is taken to listen for the character of and meaning given to these early experiences. Cognitive behavioural therapy provides the individual with a strong component of psychoeducation, immediately promoting an evidence-based approach to presenting problems. The cognitive model of depression with negative cycles of interacting thoughts, depressed affect, decreased activity and withdrawal is offered as framework within which to understand current experience. Written material outlining the cognitive model and basic information about depression is provided early in the therapy relationship to be reviewed as a between-session task. This provides a means of both understanding current activation of the depressive cycle and the developmental origins of depressive thinking and behavioural patterns. The level of intervention varies across different CBT models, with some restricting attention to the surface level negative automatic thoughts and associated responses, whereas others (Young, Weinberger & Beck, 2001) direct attention to the systems of belief or schema that underlie the current manifestations. The provision of this framework of understanding is a powerful intervention for some individuals, helping them to step outside of the automatic patterns and take up a more objective perspective.

Psychoeducation also provides guidance on the individual's role within the therapy. CBT is a collaborative exercise and as such promotes active participation on the part of the patient. The patient has the role of co-therapist rather than passive recipient of treatment and as such is required to make active use of the information provided. Preparing the patient for this role is an important early task of CBT.

The collaborative nature of CBT is illustrated at the start of each of the treatment sessions, when a shared agenda is negotiated to serve as the basis for the session to follow. This should reflect a review of the important or salient points from the previous meeting, difficulties that may have emerged and a detailed examination of progress with the negotiated homework tasks to be completed between each of the sessions. The specific nature of the homework task will reflect the stage of therapy and the nature of the presenting difficulty and consequently may shift across and between behavioural and cognitive themes. The issues addressed will consistently be examined in the light of the case formulation and with reference to the agreed treatment goals.

Monitoring the completion of these negotiated tasks forms the largest part of the treatment sessions of CBT. The detailed examination of the homework tasks provides the material to be used for cognitive restructuring exercises or behavioural experiments. The systematic nature of this examination provides an opportunity to model an adaptive problem solving approach and the individual is encouraged to arrive at his or her own conclusions by means of Socratic questioning and guided discovery, which support the investigation but does not impose conclusions or judgements.

Examination of the individual's thought processes in relevant situations – those associated with depressed mood – is facilitated by systematic recording of thoughts in daily record sheets, which prompt consideration of supportive and contradictory evidence, vulnerability to characteristic reasoning errors, alternative explanations and connection to emotional response. The patient is supported in examining these incidents in more detail during the session, approaching them as testable hypotheses rather than automatically accepted facts. At the most basic level Socratic questioning helps the individual to re-examine the recorded examples in order to derive an evidence based conclusion. However the supportive relationship between the co-therapists can also be a valuable resource through the use of shared meaning and metaphor and role plays which bring the scenario to life emotionally for the individual and facilitate the exploration of different perspectives, potentially highlighting the limitations of the initial formulation. Such work will assist the exploration of the underlying beliefs about self and others, which provide the backdrop for recurrent automatic thought and feeling responses. Drawing individual examples together to identify recurrent themes can help broaden the impact of interventions.

Examining previous experience also provides the basis for behavioural experiments and activity scheduling in anticipation of the next session. In this way the guided discovery continues outside of the sessions as the patient explores the possibilities raised by the previous discussion and works to address identified areas of overactivity or underactivity. The therapist also has an important role to support the patient in maintaining attention on the depression specific incidents and avoided or diminished pleasurable activity. In this way activity remains goal directed and weekly recordings become a valuable resource charting the impact of the previous activities and the connection to depressed mood and thinking.

Just as CBT sessions start with a collaboratively agreed agenda so they end with a mutually acceptable summary. This provides an opportunity to review important material, monitor the patients retention and understanding, highlights misconceptions and as the sessions continue provides an opportunity for the transfer of responsibility from the therapist to the patient. This process is mirrored in the approach to ending therapy as a whole, which should be maintained in focus from an early stage. Cognitive behavioural therapy offers a particular strength in directing attention to relapse prevention in the latter sessions, anticipating potential areas of difficulty and rehearsing constructive responses. Given the recurrent nature of depression this is another opportunity to model the application of evidence based information in practice.

PROBLEM-SOLVING THERAPY

Rationale

Problem-solving therapy is a time-limited, structured intervention, which helps patients use their own skills and resources to cope with specific current problems and which is in keeping with cognitive- behavioural approaches. The connection between psychological symptoms and impaired capacity to resolve psychosocial problems is a basic assumption of this approach and the primary aim is to develop more effective problem-solving skills leading to symptom improvement. Problem solving capacity is conceptualised as a moderator in the problem-distress interaction such that improved capacity should ameliorate symptomatic distress. The causal factors leading to symptomatic distress are argued to be multiple and variable, interacting directly and distally (Nezu *et al.*, 1997). Problem-solving aims to adapt beliefs that inhibit problem solving, to promote functional attention to emotions as a signal of a problem and reduce the tendency to reactive responses rather than systematic problem solving. Training assists in identification and clarification of problems, prioritisation of areas to be addressed, breaking the problems down into manageable tasks with achievable goals, generating a range of alternative solutions, selecting and implementing preferred solutions and evaluation of outcome.

Empirical Evidence

Research evaluations of problem-solving therapy have been exclusively conducted in primary care and community samples, with patients with mild depressive symptoms. Dowrick *et al.* (2000), Nezu *et al.* (1986), and Nezu, Nezu & Perri (1989) have shown problem-solving therapy to achieve greater symptom reduction than no-treatment control conditions for depressed patients at the end of treatment. Nezu's studies reported better outcome for full problem-solving therapy over components of the therapy and this was maintained over a six-month follow up. Dowrick's community sample did not maintain the initial gains over a naturalistic 12-month follow up.

Mynors-Wallis *et al.* (2000) conducted a randomised controlled trial of PST, antidepressant medication and combined treatment in depressed primary care patients and found no difference between individual and combined treatment.

Clinical Practice

Problem-solving treatment has three main steps: patients' symptoms are linked with their problems, problems are defined and clarified, and an attempt is made to solve the problems in a structured way. The treatment involves approximately six to 10 individual sessions.

The first treatment session lasts one hour, with subsequent sessions lasting 30 minutes and emphasis placed on between-session activity to implement the solutions generated. Problems are selected to be highly relevant to the patient's life situation rather than teaching abstract skills. Each stage of the problem-solving process is distilled to a series of steps to assist patients in acquiring a reasoned and deliberate approach to problem resolution.

The first three sessions provide an introduction to the approach and primarily address problem-orientation – addressing interfering beliefs and promoting a constructive problem-solving approach. The experience of difficulties is normalised and the potential to aggravate symptoms is made clear. An active coping stance is encouraged to empower the depressed individual to achieve change and symptom relief. The extent to which cognitive strategies are employed varies between individuals from minimal to the primary techniques. Subsequent sessions revolve around ongoing training and practice of rational problem-solving skills. Progress with problem definition, generating solutions, evaluating potential consequences to aid selection and monitoring outcomes is repeatedly revisited and solutions refined in the light of each attempt.

Problem definition is collaboratively encouraged to help individuals to develop a measure of what troubles them and to determine the direction in which to target their energies. If this is not already loosely defined in the patient's mind a period of self-monitoring may help to specify the difficulty. Problems are listed rather than narrowed down to a single example, and efforts to resolve are prioritised, based on the relative contribution to the depression. It is important to try to generate an optimally comprehensive list of difficulties to prevent misdirecting the process or failing to uncover the connection between problems. Assessment should cover the individual and the environment, examining cognitive, affective, behavioural and biological components of the individual's experience and the physical and social environment (Nezu *et al.*, 1997). Current and past experience may inform problem definition – significant changes in perspective may clarify deficits or excesses. The extent of the symptomatic problem is also clarified with use of standardized measures in conjunction with clinical assessment, both to give an indication of the work likely to be involved and as a means of monitoring progress. The sequence and reciprocity of interactions – triggers and consequences – is made clear rather than a generic statement of association between the identified components.

Creativity is encouraged in generating possible solutions, looking both internally and externally for exits. The expansive nature of brainstorming helps to combat the filtering and self-criticism, which can undermine and halt problem solving and loop back into depression. As problem solving focuses on the skill of the patient to bring about change, this stage also involves an assessment of patients' resources, actively directing attention to what they have and can do rather than what they cannot. Action is encouraged and supported in choosing a potential solution and testing out its effect. Targets are selected based on their potential to achieve the ultimate goal of treatment or to an intermediary step towards this. The basic assumption that more than one solution might be implemented and run through the same process to test the limits and responsiveness of the problem can also help to counteract the disappointment and frustration that can arise if success is not immediately forthcoming. Whenever possible the goals identified in relation to the target problem should be described in behavioural terms, offering a clear and realistic guide for the patient. Regularly monitoring progress helps to ensure that energy is not unduly wasted on ineffective strategies and supports a self-correcting approach. Progress is reviewed both through repeated administration of standardized measures and through the session-by-session review of the patient's diary of activities. Obstacles that emerge through this process, such as negative expectations, can be worked on more directly to increase the chances of subsequent success. As with all time-limited therapies patients should be prepared for the ending from the outset, with a clear expectation of treatment duration. Care should be taken not to extend therapy unnecessarily to work through all the identified problems once the patient has demonstrated an independent capacity to use problem-solving skills.

BEHAVIOUR THERAPY

Rationale

Behaviour therapies for depression are underpinned by learning theory as a means of explaining the decline into and resolution of the depressive state and are primarily aimed at engaging or re-engaging the patient in pleasurable and consequently positively reinforcing behaviours. Relative to psychotherapy, behaviour therapy concentrates more on behaviour itself and less on a presumed underlying cause. The basic premise of behavioural treatments is that depression is a learned response in light of low rates of positively reinforcing behaviours and insufficient positive reward from routine behaviour. The aim therefore is to increase the reward experience through behavioural activation. Interventions combine skills based learning such as relaxation skills and problems solving with distress tolerance for negative emotions.

Evidence Base

Behaviour therapy approaches generally follow the framework developed by Lewinsohn (1975), with no trials evaluating behavioural interventions based on classical conditioning. Despite the emphasis on empirical evidence there are very few studies supporting the preferential use of behaviour therapy as a treatment for depression. National Institute for Clinical Excellence (NICE) guidelines accepted only two (Gallagher, 1983 and McLean & Hakstian, 1979) and concluded that there was insufficient evidence to support clinically significant differences in outcome between behaviour therapy and other psychotherapies.

Two studies have shown this approach to outperformed control conditions. Shaw (1977) found that although behaviour therapy patients did not outperform those in CT, they did improve more than a waiting-list condition. Treatment gains were maintained at one month but failure to follow up the waiting-list group prevented comparison. McLean & Hakstian (1979) reported a relatively short-lived advantage for behaviour therapy in a comparative study with psychotherapy, relaxation therapy and amitriptyline. The clearest finding was for behaviour therapy over psychotherapy, with some advantage recorded over Amitriptyline at the end of treatment. At the three-month follow-up, the mean difference in depression scores was no longer significant.

Jacobson & Hollon (1996) conducted a dismantling study with 152 depressed subjects, in which behavioural activation (BA) alone was compared with BA plus cognitive coping skills and full CT. No significant differences were found between the three treatment formats on a range of outcome measures at the end of treatment or over a two-year follow up (Gortner et al., 1998), with all treatments producing significant (58 % to 68 %) and sustained improvement.

As with other models of therapy for depression, behaviour therapy has also been employed as a couples therapy. When compared with individual CBT (Jacobson *et al.*, 1991) found no difference in capacity to reduce depressive symptoms and reported that only those receiving behavioural marital therapy (BMT) demonstrated a significant improvement in marital adjustment. Similarly, Beach & O'Leary (1992) found BMT and CT to be equally effective in reducing depression and superior to waiting list controls but only BMT improved the marital relationship. Both studies found that depressive symptoms were mediated by marital adjustment, suggesting a specific mechanism of change whereby depression reduces with increase marital satisfaction.

Clinical Practice

Behaviour therapy concentrates on the present and sets specific, clearly defined treatment goals within a time-limited and structured intervention. Given the emphasis on engaging patients in rewarding behaviours and reducing punishing behaviours, one of the initial tasks is collaboratively identifying the impact of behaviour on depressive symptoms. Specific interventions are then scheduled to elucidate patterns of reinforcement, for example through monitoring daily activities and rating the associated mastery and pleasure. Tasks are then assigned to gradually increase mastery and pleasure and decrease negatively reinforcing patterns. Progress may be made through imaginal or *in vivo* exposure to problematic situations with the ultimate aim of identifying and implementing behavioural techniques for managing identified difficulties. Specific areas of difficulty are addressed through appropriate skills training, for example assertiveness or social skill training.

Behavioural marital therapy progresses through three stages, employing social learning, behavioural change and cognitive techniques. The initial phase concentrates on the patterns of reinforcement that exist within the couple and aims to eliminate the stressors and re-establish or introduce positive interactions through agreed homework tasks that promote mutually satisfying activity. The potential for mood elevation through successful completion of these tasks is used as a foundation for the second phase, which focuses more closely on the mechanics of the relationship, tackling communication patterns, problem-solving strategies and day-to-day interactions. These tasks further aim to tip the balance of reinforcement in favour of patterns through more effective problem resolution. This is achieved by supporting the couple to make expression of emotion safe and acceptable and enhancing perceived capacity to cope, mutual trust, dependability and closeness. Negotiating tasks in advance is used to make responses more predictable and to increase the opportunity for a positively reinforcing cycle. By default the reduction in uncontrolled conflict will also diminish the potential for negatively reinforcing patterns to be repeated. From this stronger position the couple then prepares for termination in the final stage. This concentrates on relapse prevention, tolerating transitory return of conflict or symptoms and promoting early response to high-risk situations.

PSYCHODYNAMIC PSYCHOTHERAPY

Rationale

Psychodynamic psychotherapy, like CBT, is more accurately understood as a range of approaches with a common origin, namely psychoanalytic psychotherapy, with specific prominence given to object relations theory. The specific focus of attention varies between models but each explores internal conflicts, the early developmental origins of conscious and unconscious defences – particularly those developed to protect against loss, hostility or powerlessness – and their current depressive manifestations. All include explicit reference to and use of the therapeutic relationship, working repeatedly in the transference. The psychodynamic approach aims to promote new experience and to develop new insight into intra-psychic conflicts and enduring maladaptive patterns through empathic listening, emotional catharsis and therapeutic interpretation, to potentially aid resolution. Treatment targets are characterological rather than explicitly symptomatic, ascribing to the idea of depressive personality, rejected by other models of psychotherapy, and interventions are non-directive and not skills based. Psychodynamic interpersonal psychotherapy (PIP) (Shapiro *et al.*, 1994) is based on Hobson's conversational model (Hobson, 1985) and offers a bridge between psychodynamic psychotherapy and IPT. It relies more heavily on interpretations of the therapeutic relationship than the latter, while working in a time limited and focused way.

Evidence Base

Psychodynamic psychotherapy has been widely criticised for failing to produce empirical evidence to support this form of intervention. Few quality comparative studies exist despite this form of treatment having the longest history of those discussed. The general trend in those studies that have been produced is for better outcome for alternative treatments. Burnand *et al.* (2002) did, however, report an additive effect for combined therapy over pharmacotherapy with supportive care in symptom reduction, reduced service use and improved cost-effectiveness. However the degree to which the intervention described could be accurately conceptualised as formal psychodynamic psychotherapy is questionable, limiting the support offered by this study. The NICE guidelines (NICE, 2004) failed to find any conclusive empirical data favouring a psychodynamic approach for the treatment of depression.

Shapiro & Firth (1987) and Shapiro & Firth-Cozens (1990) reported on two studies comparing PIP and CBT for professional/ managerial subjects with depression and/or anxiety. The trend across all outcome measures in the first Sheffield study was modestly in favour of prescriptive (CBT) treatment over exploratory (PIP). These differences were, however, noted to be of little clinical significance, with the exception of the SCL-90, where CBT produced twice as much improvement and were also largely attributable to the performance of one therapist (Shaprio, Firth-Cozens & Stiles, 1989). These differences, however, remained stable over a two-year follow-up (Shapiro & Firth-Cozens, 1990). In the second Sheffield study the same treatments were examined but were delivered over different time periods – eight or 16 sessions for CBT and PIP – and to a larger sample. There was little evidence of either treatment performing more effectively or efficiently, although both produced substantial clinical improvement.

Clinical Practice

Psychodynamic interpersonal psychotherapy uses a number of psychodynamic and interpersonal concepts to aid use of the therapeutic relationship as a means of exploring, clarifying and resolving interpersonal problems, which are conceptualised as being at the root of depressive difficulties. The assumption of the interpersonal origins of depressive difficulties aligns this model closely with IPT. The explicit use of the therapy relationship and the dialogue between participants as the vehicle through which understanding and change is achieved testifies to the psychodynamic foundations. The method encourages exploration and is non-directive in character to the extent that questions are avoided in preference to statements and hypotheses to be accepted, revised or rejected. Hypotheses potentially aim to develop understanding, to link different aspects of experience or to provide an explanation for behaviour or experience. In other psychodynamic models such links would be clarified through interpretation. The treatment has a strongly collaborative feel with an extended assessment at the start of treatment and an emphasis on shared language. The treatment focuses on here and now concerns within the session and will examine interpersonal interactions in considerable detail, encouraging and supporting the full experience of affect in the moment, through the use of metaphor. Other forms of psychodynamic therapy would be expected to give more explicit attention to early, formative experiences, through which current interaction could be understood as re-enactments of internalised interpersonal templates. Evidence of transference enactments would be examined in detail to develop insight into conscious and unconscious conflicts and work these through to a more satisfactory resolution. Language and experience take precedence over skills training and problem solving in PIP and other psychodynamic models. Although considerable attention is given to the therapeutic relationship the aim is also to extrapolate from this to other relationships outside of therapy where similar interactions may be enacted. As previously noted the time-limited nature of these interventions maintains attention on the issues on ending throughout the intervention, with more specific attention given to the end of the therapeutic relationship in these transference-based models.

REFERENCES

Beach, S.R.H. & O'Leary, K.D. (1992). Treating depression in the context of marital discord. Outcome and predictors of response for marital therapy vs cognitive therapy. *Behavior Therapy, 19*, 355–368.

Beck, A.T., Rush, A.J., Shaw, B.F. & Emery, G. (1979). *Cognitve Therapy for Depression*. New York: John Wiley & Sons.

Blackburn, I.M. & Moore R.G. (1997). Controlled acute and follow up trial of cognitive therapy and pharmacotherapy in out-patients with recurrent depression. *British Journal of Psychiatry, 171*, 328–334.

Brown, G. & Harris, T. (1978). *The Social Origins of Depression*. London: Tavistock.

Brown, C., Schulberg, H.C., Madonia, M.J. *et al.* (1996). Treatment outcomes for primary care patients with major depression and lifetime anxiety disorders. *American Journal of Psychiatry, 153*(10), 1293–1300.

Burnand, Y., Andreoli, A., Kolatte, E. *et al.* (2002). Psychodynamic psychotherapy and clomipramine in the treatment of depression. *Psychiatric Services, 53*(5), 585–590.

Deckersbach, T., Gershuny, B.S. & Otto, M.W. (2000). Cognitive therapy for depression: Applications and outcome. *Psychiatric Clinics of North America, 23*(4), 795–809.

De Rubeis, R.J. & Crits-Christoph, P. (1998). Empirically supported individual and group psychological treatments for adults. *Journal of Consulting and Clinical Psychology, 66*(1), 37–52.

De Rubeis, R., Gelfand, L.A., Tang, T. & Simons, A.D. (1999). Medications versus cognitive behavior therapy for severely depressed outpatients: mega-analysis of four randomized comparisons. *American Journal of Psychiatry, 156*(7), 1007–1013.

Di Mascio, A., Weissman, M.M, Prusoff, B.A. *et al.* (1979). Differential symptoms reduction by drugs and psychotherapy in acute depression. *Archives of General Psychiatry, 36,* 1450–1456.

Dobson, K.S. (1989). A met-analysis of the efficacy of cognitive therapy for depression. *Journal of Consulting and Clinical Psychology, 57,* 414–419.

Dowrick, C., Dunn, G., Ayuso-Mateos, J.L. *et al.* (2000). Problem solving treatment and group psychoeducation for depression. Multi-centre randomized controlled trial. *British Medical Journal, 321,* 1450–1454.

Elkin I., Shea, M.T., Watkins, J.T. *et al.* (1989). NIMH Treatment of Depression Collaborative Research Program: 1. General effectiveness of treatments. *Archives of General Psychiatry, 46,* 971–982.

Elkin, I., Gibbons, R.D., Shea, M.T. *et al.* (1995). Initial severity and differential treatment outcome in the National Institute of Mental Health Treatment of Depression Collaborative Research Program. *Journal of Consulting and Clinical Psychology, 63*(5), 841–847.

Evans, M.D., Hollon, S.D., De Rubeis, R.J. *et al.* (1992). Differential relapse following cognitive therapy, pharmacotherapy, and combined cognitive-pharmacotherapy for depression. *Archives of General Psychiatry, 49,* 802–808.

Fava, G.A., Grandi, S., Zielezny, M. *et al.* (1996). Four-year outcome for cognitive behavioral treatment of residual symptoms in major depression. *American Journal of Psychiatry, 153*(7), 945–947.

Fava, G.A., Ottolini, F., Ruini, C. (1999). The role of cognitive behavioural therapy in the treatment of unipolar depression [letters to the editor]. *Acta Psychiatrica Scandinavica, 99*(5), 394–395.

Fava, G.A., Rafanelli, C., Grandi, S. *et al.* (1998a). Prevention of recurrent depression with cognitive behavioral therapy: preliminary findings. *Archives of General Psychiatry, 55*(9), 816–820.

Fava, G.A., Rafanelli, C., Grandi, S. *et al.* (1998b). Six-year outcome for cognitive behavioral treatment of residual symptoms in major depression. *American Journal of Psychiatry, 155*(10), 1443–1445.

Feske, U., Frank, E., Mallinger, A.G. *et al.* (1998). Anxiety as a predictor of response to interpersonal psychotherapy for recurrent major depression: an exploratory investigation. *Depression and Anxiety, 8*(4), 135–141.

Foley, S.H.S., Rounsaville, B.J., Weissman, M.M. *et al.* (1989). Individual versus conjoint interpersonal psychotherapy for depressed patients with marital disputes. *International Journal of Family Psychiatry, 10,* 29–42.

Frank, E., Karp, J.F., & Rush, A.J. (1993). Efficacy of treatments for major depression. *Psychopharmacology Bulletin, 29*(4), 457–475.

Frank, E., Kupfer, D.J., Wagner, E.F. *et al.* (1991). Efficacy of interpersonal psychotherapy as a maintenance treatment of recurrent depression. *Archives of General Psychiatry, 48,* 1053–1059.

Frank, E., Shear, M.K., Rucci, P.D. *et al.* (2000). Influence of panic-agoraphobic spectrum symptoms on treatment response in patients with recurrent major depression. *American Journal of Psychiatry, 157*(7), 1101–1107.

Frank, E. & Spanier, C. (1995). Interpersonal psychotherapy for depression: Overview, clinical efficacy, and future directions. *Clinical Psychology Scientist Practitioner, 2,* 349–369.

Freud, S. (1917). Mourning and melancholia. *Standard Edition of the Complete Works of Sigmund Freud,* vol. 14 (pp. 243–258). London: Hogarth Press.

Gallagher, D.E. (1983). Effectiveness of psychotherapy for both endogenous and nonendogenous depression in older adult outpatients. *Journal of Gerontology, 38,* 707–712.

Gibbons R.D, Hedecker, D., Elkin,, I. *et al.* (1993) Some conceptual and statistical issues in analysis of longitudinal psychiatric data. Application to the NIMH treatment of depression Collaborative Research Program dataset. *Archives of General Psychiatry, 50*(9), 739–750.

Giles, D. Jarrett, R., Biggs, M. *et al.* (1989). Clinical predictors of reoccurrence in depression. *American Journal of Psychiatry, 146,* 764–767.

Gloaguen, V., Cottraux, J., Cucherat, M. & Blackburn, I.M. (1998). A meta-analysis of the effects of cognitive therapy in depressed patients. *Journal of Affect Disorders, 49,* 59–72.

Gortner, E.T., Gollan, J.K., Dobson, K.S. & Jacobson, N.S. (1998). Cognitive-behavioral treatment for depression: Relapse prevention. *Journal of Consulting and Clinical Psychology, 66*(2) 377–384.

Hawton, K. Salkovskis, P.M., Kirk, J. & Clark, D.M. (eds) (1989). *Cognitive Behaviour Therapy for Psychiatric Problems: A Practical Guide.* Oxford: Oxford University Press.

Hobson, R.F. (1985). *Forms of Feeling the Heart of Psychotherapy.* New York: Basic Books.

Hollon, S. D., De Rubeis, R. J., Evans, M.D. *et al.* (1992). Cognitive therapy and pharmacotherapy for depression: singly and in combination. *Archives of General Psychiatry, 49*, 774–781.

Imber, S.D, Pilkonis, P.A., Sotsky, S.M. *et al.* (1990). Mode-specific effects among three treatments for depression. *Journal of Consulting and Clinical Psychology, 58*(3), 352–359.

Jacobson, N.S., Dobson, K., Fruzzetti, A.E. *et al.* (1991). Marital therapy as a treatment for depression. *Journal of Consulting and Clinical Psychology, 59,* 547–557.

Jacobson, N.S. & Hollon, S. (1996). Prospects for future comparisons between drugs and psychotherapy: lessons from the CBT-versus-pharmacotherapy exchange. *Journal of Consulting and Clinical Psychology, 64*(1), 104–108.

Jorgensen, M.B., Dam, H. & Bolwig, T.G. (1998). The efficacy of psychotherapy in non-bipolar depression: A review. *Acta Psychiatrica Scandinavica, 98*(1), 1–13.

Keller, M.B., Lavori, P.W., Mueller, T.I. *et al.* (1992). Time to recover, chronicity and levels of psychopathology in major depression. *Archives of General Psychiatry, 49*, 809–816.

Keller, M.B., McCullough, J.P., Kelin D.N. *et al.* (2000). A comparison of nefazodone, the cognitive behavioural analysis system of psychotherapy, and their combination for the treatment of chronic depression. *New England Journal of Medicine, 342*, 1462–1470.

Keller, M.B., Shapire, R.W., Lavori, P.W. *et al.* (1982). Recovery in major depression. Analysis with life tables and regression models. *Archives of General Psychiatry, 39*, 905–910.

Kessler, R.C., Berglund, P., Demler, O. *et al.* (2003). The epidemiology of depressive disorder: results from the National Comorbidity Survey Replication (NCS-R). *Journal of the American Medical Association, 289*(23), 3095–3105.

Kessler, R.C, McGonagle, K.A, Zhao, S. *et al.* (1994). Lifetime and 12 month Prevalence of DSM-III-R psychiatric disorders in the United States: results form the National Comorbidity Survey. *Archives of General Psychiatry, 51*(1), 8–19.

Kessler, R.C., Stang, P.E., Wittchen, H. *et al.* (1998). Lifetime panic-depression comorbidity in the National Comorbidity Survey. *Archives of General Psychiatry, 55*(9), 801–808.

Klein, D.F & Ross, D.C (1993). Reanalysis of the National Institute of Mental Health Treatment of Depression Collaborative Research Program General Effectiveness Report. *Neuropsychpharmacology*, 8(3), 241–251.

Klerman, G.L., DiMascio, A., Weissman, M. *et al.* (1974). Treatment of depression by drugs and psychotherapy. *American Journal of Psychiatry, 131,* 186–191.

Klerman, G.L., Weissman, M.M., Rounsaville, B.J. & Chevron, R.S. (1984). *Interpersonal Psychotherapy of Depression.* New York: Basic Books.

Kovacs, M., Rush, A.T., Beck, A.T. & Hollon, S.D. (1981). Depressed outpatients treated with cognitive therapy or pharmacotherapy: a one-year follow-up. *Archives of General Psychiatry, 38*, 33–39.

Kung, W.W & Elkin, I.E (2000). Marital adjustment as a predictor of outcome in individual treatment of depression. *Psychoterapy Research, 10*(3), 267–278.

Kupfer, D.J. (1991). Long-term treatment of depression. *Journal of Clinical Psychiatry, 52*, 28–34 (suppl).

Lave, J.R., Frank, R.G., Schulberg, H.C. & Kamlet, M.S. (1998). Cost-effectiveness of treatments for major depression in primary care practice. *Archives of General Psychiatry, 55*(7), 645–651.

Lenze, E.J., Dew, M.A., Mazumdar, S. *et al.* (2002). Combined pharmacotherapy and psychotherapy as maintenance treatment for late-life depression: effects on social adjustment. *American Journal of Psychiatry, 159*(3), 466–468.

Lewinsohn, P.M. (1975). The behavioral study and treatment of depression. In M. Hersen, R.M. Eisler & P.M. Miller (eds) *Progress in Behavior Modification*, vol. 1. New York: Academic Press.

Markowitz, J.C., Kocsis, J.H., Fishman, B., Speilman, L.A., Jacobsberg, L.B., Frances, A.J., Klerman, G.L., & Perry, S.W. (1998). Treatment of HIV-positive patients with depressive symptoms. *Journal of Affective Disorder, 24*, 63–71.

McKnight, D.L., Nelson-Gray, R.O. & Barnhill, J. (1992). Dexamethasone suppression test and response to cognitive therapy and antidepressant medication. *Behaviour Therapy, 23*, 99–111.

McLean, P.D. & Hakstian, A.R. (1979). Clinical depression: comparative efficacy of outpatient treatments. *Journal of Consulting and Clinical Psychology, 47*, 818–836.

McLean, P.D. & Hakstian, A.R. (1990). Relative endurance of unipolar depression treatment effects: longitudinal follow up. *Journal of Consulting and Clinical Psychology, 58*, 482–488.

Mufson, L., Weissman, M.M., Moreau, D. & Garfinkel, R. (1999). Efficacy of interpersonal psychotherapy for depressed adolescents. *Archives of General Psychiatry, 56*(6), 573–579.

Murphy,G.E., Simons, A.D., Wetzel, R.D. & Lustman, P.J. (1984). Cognitive therapy and pharmacotherapy: singly and together in the treatment of depression. *Archives of General Psychiatry, 41*, 33–41.

Mynors-Wallis, L., Gath, D., Day, A. & Baker, F. (2000). Randomised controlled trial of problem solving treatment, antidepressant medication, and combined treatment for major depression in primary care. *British Medical Journal, 320*, 26–30.

Mynors-Wallis, L., Gath, D., Lloyd-Thomas, A., Tomlinson, D. (1995). Randomised controlled trial comparing problem solving treatment with amitriptyline and placebo for major depression in primary care. *British Medical Journal, 310*, 441–445.

Nesse, R.M. (2000). Is depression an adaptation? *Archives of General Psychiatry, 57*, 14–20.

Nezu, A.M., Nezu, C.M., Friedman, S.H. & Haynes, S.N. (1997). Case formulation in behavior therapy: Problem solving and functional analytic strategies. In T.D. Eells (ed.), *Handbook of Psychotherapy Case Formulation*. New York: Guilford Press.

Nezu, A.M., Nezu, C.M. & Perri, M.G. (1989). *Problem Solving Therapy for Depression: Theory, Research and Clinical Guidelines*. New York: Wiley.

Nezu, A.M., Nezu, C.M., Saraydarian, L. *et al.* (1986). Social problem solving as a moderating variable between negative life stress and depression. *Cognitive Therapy and Research, 10*, 489–498.

NICE (2004). *Depression: Management of Depression in Primary and Secondary Care. Clinical Guideline 23*. London: National Institute for Clinical Excellence.

O'Hara, M.W. Stuart, S., Gorman, L.L. & Wenzel, A. (2000). Efficacy of interpersonal psychotherapy for postpartum depression. *Archives of General Psychiatry, 57*(11), 1039–1045.

Parker, G., Roy, K. & Eyers, K. (2003). Cognitive behaviour therapy for depression? Choose horses for courses. *American Journal of Psychiatry, 160*(5), 825–834.

Paykel, E.S., Scott, J., Teasdale, J.D. *et al.* (1999). Prevention of relapse in residual depression by cognitive therapy. A controlled trial. *Archives of General Psychiatry, 56*, 829–835.

Power, M.J. & Dalgleish, T. (1996). *Cognition and Emotion: From Order to Disorder*. Hove: Erlbaum.

Reynolds, C.F., Frank, E., Kupfer, D. *et al.* (1996). Treatment outcome in recurrent major depression: a post hoc comparison of elderly ("young old") and midlife patients. *American Journal of Psychiatry, 153*(10), 1288–1292.

Reynolds, C.F., Frank, E., Perel, J.M. *et al.* (1994). Treatment of consecutive episodes of major depression in the elderly. *American Journal of Psychiatry, 151*(12), 1740–1743.

Reynolds, C.F., Frank, E., Perel, J.M. *et al.* (1999a). Nortriptyline and interpersonal psychotherapy as maintenance therapies for recurrent major depression: a randomized controlled trial in patients older than 59 years. *Journal of the American Medical Association, 281*(1), 39–45.

Reynolds, C.F., Miller, M.D., Pasternak, R.E. *et al.* (1999b). Treatment of bereavement-related major depressive episodes in later life: a controlled study of acute and continuation treatment with nortriptyline and interpersonal psychotherapy. *American Journal of Psychiatry, 156*(2), 202–208.

Robinson, L.A., Berman, J.S., Neimeyer, R.A (1990). Psychotherapy for the treatment of depression: a comprehensive review of controlled outcome research. *Psychological Bulletin, 108*(1), 30–49.

Rush, A.J., Beck, A.T., Kovacs, M., & Hollon, S. (1977). Comparative efficacy of cognitive therapy and pharmacotherapy in the treatment of depressed outpatients. *Cognitive Therapy and Research, 1*, 17–37.

Sartorius, N.(2001). The economic and social burden of depression. *Journal of Clinical Psychiatry, 62* (supplement 15), 8–11.

Schulberg, H.C., Block, M.R., Madonia, M.J. *et al.* (1996). Treating major depression in primary care practice: Eight-month clinical outcomes. *Archives of General Psychiatry, 53*(10), 913–919.

Schulberg, H.C., Pilkonis, P.A. & Houck, P. (1998). The severity of major depression and choice of treatment in primary care practice. *Journal of Consulting and Clinical Psychology, 66*(6), 932–938.

Scott, J. (1998). Where there's a will . . . cognitive therapy for people with chronic depressive disorders. In N. Tarrier, A.Wells & G. Haddock (eds), *Treating Complex Cases: The Cognitive Behavioural Therapy Approach*. Chichester: John Wiley & Sons.

Shapiro, D.A., Barkman, M., Rees, A. *et al.* (1994) Effects of treatment duration and severity of depression on the effectiveness of cognitive-behavioural and psychodynamic-interpersonal psychotherapy. *Journal of Consulting and Clinical Psychology, 62*(3), 522–534.

Shapiro, D.A. & Firth, J. (1987). Prescriptive vs exploratory psychotherapy. outcomes of the sheffield psychotherapy project. *British Journal of Psychiatry, 151*, 790–799.

Shapiro, D.A. & Firth-Cozens, J. (1990). Two-year follow up of the Sheffield Psychotherapy Project. *British Journal of Psychiatry, 157*, 389–391.

Shapiro, D.A., Firth-Cozens, J. & Stiles, W.B. (1989). The question of therapist's differential effectiveness. A Sheffield Psychotherapy Project addendum. *British Journal of Psychiatry, 154*, 383–385.

Shaw, B.F. (1977). Comparison of cognitive therapy and behavior therapy in the treatment of depression. *Journal of Consulting and Clinical Psychology, 45*, 543–551.

Shea M.T, Elkin, I., Imber, S. *et al.* (1992). Course of depressive symptoms over follow-up: findings from the National Institute of Mental Health Treatment of Depression Collaborative Research Program. *Archives of General Psychiatry, 49*, 782–789.

Simons, A.D., Murphy, G.E., Levine, J.L. & Wetzel, R.D. (1986). Cognitive therapy and pharmacotherapy for depression: sustained improvement over one year. *Archives of General Psychiatry, 43*, 43–48.

Spijker, J., DeGraaf, R., Bijl, R.V. *et al.* (2002). Duration of major depresive episodes in the general population: results from the Netherlands Mental Health Survey and Incidence Survey (NEMESIS). *British Journal of Psychiatry, 181*, 208–213.

Spinelli, M.G. (1997). Interpersonal psychotherapy for depressed antepartum women: a pilot study. *American Journal of Psychiatry, 154*(7), 1028–1030.

Thase, M.E., Greenhouse, J.B., Frank, E. *et al.* (1997). Treatment of major depression with psychotherapy or psychotherapy-pharmacotherapy combinations. *Archives of General Psychiatry, 54*(11) 1009–1015.

Ward, E., King, M., Lloyd, M. *et al.* (2000). Randomised controlled trial of non-directive counselling, cognitive-behaviour therapy, and usual general practitioner care for patients with depression. I: Clinical effectiveness. *British Medical Journal, 321*(7273) 2, 1383–1388.

Weissman, M.M, Klerman, G.L., Paykel, E.S. *et al.* (1974). Treatment effects on the social adjustment of depressed patients. *Archives of General Psychiatry, 30*, 771–778.

Weissman, M.M., Klerman, G.L., Prusoff, B.A. *et al.* (1981). Depressed outpatients one year after treatment with drugs and/or interpersonal psychotherapy (IPT). *Archives of General Psychiatry, 38*, 51–55.

Weissman, M.M., Markowitz, J.C. & Klerman, G.L. (2000). *Comprehensive Guide to Interpersonal Psychotherapy.* New York: Basic Books.

Whisman, M.A. (2001). Marital adjustment and outcome following treatments for depression. *Journal of Consulting and Clinical Psychology*, 69(1), 125–129.

WHO (1996). *WHO Guide to Mental Health in Primary Care. A Guide to Mental Ill Health in Adults.* London: Royal Society of Medicine Press.

Wilfley, D.E., Agras, W.S., Telch, C.F. *et al.* (1993). Group cognitive-behavioural therapy and group interpersonal psychotherapy for nonpurging bulimic individuals: a controlled comparison. *Journal of Consulting and Clinical Psychology, 61*, 296–305.

Young, J.E., Weinberger, A.D. & Beck, A.T. (2001). Cognitive therapy for depression. In D.H. Barlow (ed.) *Clinical Handbook of Psychological Disorders* (pp. 264–308). New York: Guilford.

CHAPTER 20

Specific Phobias

Stan Lindsay
Institute of Psychiatry, London, UK

INTRODUCTION

The fourth Diagnostic and Statistical Manual (DSM IV) (American Psychiatric Association, 2000, p. 443) describes 'specific phobias', hitherto 'simple phobias', as 'marked and persistent fear of clearly discernible, circumscribed objects or associations.' The subject's response to such objects can include panic attacks and avoidance if possible. The phobia causes significant interference with the subject's 'daily routine, occupational functioning or social life' and even serious ill health such as cardiovascular disease (Bowen *et al.*, 2000). Theories of causation are reviewed by Merckelbach *et al.* (1996) and Ollendick *et al.* (2002) for adults and children respectively.

The attention given to specific phobias has varied over the years. Compare early surveys (such as Marks, 1975), where many studies were of spider phobias, with later reviews (such as Davey, 1997) in which agoraphobia, panic disorder and social phobia receive more attention. Furthermore, the emphasis has shifted from specific phobias, providing opportunities to test hypotheses about treatment of phobia (Kazdin, 1978) almost regardless of its nature, to studies specific to each different fear, such as social phobia. In addition, the emphasis in reviews has shifted from studies of theoretical interest to phobias that can have a major clinical impact on subjects. These include phobias of medical and dental treatment. Uncommon fears, for example of buttons, owls and choking, continue to be documented in case studies.

Nevertheless, specific phobias are still exploited for interests that could be common to all fears such as the return of fear after being diminished by treatment (Rose & McGlynn, 1997), the correspondence among different measures of anxiety (Forsyth & Eifert, 1996), new methods of treatment such as eye-movement desensitisation (Muris *et al.*, 1998) or delivery of treatment by computer (Dewis *et al.*, 2001) or more veridical ways of presenting fear-provoking objects (Maltby *et al.*, 2002). Any scientific study of hypnosis (Kirsch *et al.*, 1995), which has a long history as a treatment for the specific phobia of dentistry, could be innovative because of the scarcity of such studies.

RELATIONSHIPS AMONG SPECIFIC FEARS
AND OTHER PROBLEMS

Factor analyses of subjects' responses to inventories of fear-provoking situations have confirmed, in part, the classifications listed by DSM-IV. For example, Hallam & Haffner (1978) classified fears as agoraphobia, social fears, and the specific fears, of small animals, of hospitals, death and blood. A general fear, which could be associated with others, was characterised by anxiety about dizziness and shortness of breath. Similar analyses in children have identified fears of failure, the unknown, and the specific fears of minor surgery, small animals, danger, death and medical situations (Ollendick *et al.*, 1989).

Such surveys could have advantages for studies of treatment in showing that certain fears can have causal relationships with one another (Rachman, 1992). Agoraphobic patients often complain of claustrophobia, being nervous of confinement in small spaces such as lifts (Hallam & Haffner, 1978). Thus the use of claustrophobia-provoking situations might promote an understanding of agoraphobia (Rachman, 1992). It is not surprising, therefore, that, although subjects can be classified according to such inventories as DSM-IV, accurate discrimination among subjects, according to their fears, is not high (Beck *et al.*, 1998).

Furthermore, certain resemblances among fears have long been of interest and have contributed to the study of specific fears as models for the treatment of other fears. Most notable are subjects' responses in anticipation of frightening situations: verbal expression of fear, physiological arousal and escape from, or avoidance of, those situations (Marks, 1987). The ease with which the approach to some specific phobic stimuli, such as spiders in jars, has contributed to the study of approach-avoidance is of relevance to other phobias. The occurrence of panic attacks in most fears has suggested that the treatment of panic disorder might benefit from an examination of specific fears where the production of a panic may be more easily stimulated and controlled (Craske, 1991). In agreement with Barlow *et al.* (1985) who examined very small samples of subjects, Starcevic & Bogojevic (1997) estimated that, of their group with specific fears, over 65 % experienced panic attacks. Craske (1991) argues further that specific fear, provoked by discernible cues, could illuminate the occurrence of panic attacks in panic disorder where they occur in response to cues that are not readily apparent.

However, as such resemblances have been noted, the cognitions and emotions of subjects with some specific fears have been shown to differ from others where panics occur. Several doctoral theses and empirical studies have shown that subjects experience disgust in some fears but not others (Sawchuk *et al.*, 2002) and can be characterised by a degree of disgust sensitivity (De Jongh & Merckelbach, 1998; Muris *et al.*, 1999).

Large epidemiological surveys have shown that specific phobias are very common and this has encouraged their examination as examples of fear. Curtis *et al.* (1998) reported that 49 % of their respondents had experienced at least one of eight specific fears in their lifetime. Nearly 12 % had experienced an intense fear of closed spaces; 22 % had been highly nervous of some animal.

Subjects with other anxiety disorders, such as agoraphobia or panic disorder, often have several specific phobias: comorbidity (Hofman *et al.*, 1997). Moreover, Magee *et al.* (1996) found that major depression occurred in 42 % of their subjects who experienced simple phobias and nearly a quarter of that group had been dependent on alcohol. Over 48 % of people with schizophrenia had at least one specific fear according to a standard interview of over 18 000 subjects by Boyd et al.(1990). High levels of comorbidity have also been observed in children (Ollendick, King & Frary, 2002).

In addition, subjects who have specific fears report that they interfere with their lives and produce other impairments such as the need to seek professional help. Of those adults with four or five fears, 41 % reported significant interference with daily living (Magee et al., 1996). Therefore, comorbidity and impairment of daily living are very common in subjects with specific fears. Furthermore, people with several fears and other disorders and whose daily activities are much impaired, are probably more likely than others to see help (Kazdin, 1999; Ollendick, King & Muris, 2002).

Rachman (1992) noted the need to explain the co-occurrence of fears and other afflictions and thus described the association of claustrophobia and agoraphobia. The treatment of the fear of internal sensations that can occur in each may benefit both. Roth & Fonagy (2005) have claimed that comorbidity can impede treatment. However, they note that it is difficult to predict outcome of treatment in the presence of comorbid disorders. They and Nathan & Gorman (2002) pay less attention to the effect of treatment as it might affect, or be affected by, the impairment in daily living produced by psychological troubles. The present review, therefore, has sought to determine, among other things, the effect of comorbidity and impairment on the treatment of specific fears and the effect of such treatment on disability and the quality of life.

THE CLINICAL SIGNIFICANCE OF TREATMENT OUTCOME

The argument has long been put forward that rejection of a null hypothesis in a statistical test, such as an analysis of variance, does not provide sufficient evidence that the treatment is of benefit to the subjects. Therefore, additional criteria (Jacobson, Folette & Ravensdorff, 1984; Jacobson & Truax, 1991; Kazdin, 1999) have been proposed to test the clinical significance, to the subjects, of the outcome of such treatment.

After treatment, the subjects, according to the outcome measures, should fall within the range found in the non-dysfunctional population and outside the range for pathological subjects. Statistical guidelines are provided (Jacobson, Folette & Ravensdorff, 1984; Jacobson & Truax, 1991). Other criteria include impairment of daily functioning and 'quality of life', an overlapping construct for which there is a plethora of measures for the effects of serious mental illness (Gladis, Gosch & Dishuk, 1999; Holloway & Carson, 2002). These have received little attention in the treatment of specific fears (Gladis et al., 1999; Mogotsi, Kamineer & Stein, 2000).

CRITERIA FOR EVALUATING THE OUTCOME OF TREATMENT

Comprehensive surveys of treatment (Nathan & Gorman, 2002; Roth & Fonagy, 2005) have outlined the minimum criteria against which the efficacy of psychological treatment should be judged. As outlined by Nathan & Gorman (2002) these are as follows. Treatments should be tested by studies that examine groups of patients; the treatment must be more effective than a pharmacological or psychological placebo or similar in effect to an established treatment. Many single cases may suffice. Studies should use good experimental designs and treatment must be capable of being replicated by therapists elsewhere. Instruction manuals may help that.

Kazdin (1994) and Lambert &Hill (1994) emphasise that measures of outcome should be of proven reliability and validity and should be sensitive to change. Kazdin (1994) and Roth & Fonagy (1996) note that several measures are probably necessary to represent all aspects of patients' wellbeing. However, it is then necessary to make sure that change in only a few of several measures is not the result of chance variation. Subjects should be assigned at random to treatments and procedures should be conducted for comparison. Their characteristics, including diagnoses and demographic measures, should be reliably recorded to ensure that the groups are comparable, especially if the samples are small. A sufficiently large number of subjects should be recruited to ensure that the design has sufficient power to reject the null hypothesis if it is false. Studies that meet all these standards are very rare. The outstanding example has been the multicentre trial of cognitive therapy for depression (Elkin, 1994).

Such research should be published in articles which are subject to review by critical experts. However, the editors of prestigious journals receive far too many articles to be able to publish more than a small proportion. Studies are more likely to be published, it is often suggested, if they have a positive outcome, confirming the research hypothesis. Consistent with this, Stern & Jones (1997) found that of 748 proposals for studies that had been passed by an ethical committee at the University of Sydney, those with a positive outcome were most likely to be published. Roth & Fonagy (1996) noted the possibility of such a bias in the treatment studies that they reviewed but there have been few attempts to identify and correct this in psychotherapy research.

THE OUTCOME OF PSYCHOLOGICAL TREATMENT FOR SPECIFIC PHOBIAS

The following review discusses the treatment of: claustrophobia, fear of flying, routine dental treatment, injections and blood injury and of spiders because, according to a Medline search from 1984, they have probably received the most attention in psychological studies. In addition, however, these phobias probably differ in the impairment of daily functioning and quality of life that they produce in afflicted people. Spider phobia probably has least impact on subjects but others, most notably injection phobia, can be life threatening. On the other hand, the treatment of spider phobia has probably been investigated for theoretical interest more than other fears. Reviews have claimed that the most successful treatment of specific phobias has required the exposure of subjects to the situations that have provoked their fear (Marks, 1987). The present review discusses subsequent studies that have examined different approaches and new ways of implementing exposure, as suggested by technological innovation or theoretical conceptions of fear (Cameron, 1997). All the studies in Tables 20.1 to 20.4 used repeated outcome measures, before and after treatment. Other specific phobias, which have received attention in case studies, are reviewed in Davey (1997).

DENTAL PHOBIA

Of the phobias in this review, fear of routine dentistry has probably received the greatest attention from theories of cognitive processing. Many people are unable to tolerate routine treatment that might save them from ill-health requiring even more alarming treatment such as extractions. Around a third of adults in an early survey were so afraid of dental treatment they would prefer to have it conducted while they were in a state of oblivion (Lindsay, Humphris & Barnby, 1987). It is possible to conduct dental treatment for patients under sedation or general anaesthesia, which would have that effect, but evidence suggests that those interventions, unlike successful psychological preparation, would not enable patients to accept dentistry while fully conscious (Thom, Sartory & Joehren, 2000).

Around 40 % of people with dental phobia have other clinically significant psychological problems such as depression or anxiety (Roy-Byrne *et al.*, 1994). Furthermore, those people have a higher degree of impairment than those with no comorbidity. This is not surprising because more than a third of patients, unselected for dental phobia, are in continual pain when they decide to visit dentists (Green *et al.*, 1997). Those with a phobia of treatment would probably be in more pain because of greater dental disease (Berggren, 1993). Most patients who are too fearful to tolerate dentistry are afraid of experiencing pain that they believe can occur without warning during treatment and they are afraid that they lack control over this (DeJongh *et al.*, 1995; Lindsay & Jackson, 1993). Cognitive interventions would have to address those expectations.

A clinically significant outcome to psychological treatment must enable patients to accept routine dental care without exceptional measures such as sedation. Furthermore, because patients would have to undergo regular dental inspections and treatment, if necessary, for the rest of their lives, it would be desirable for psychological treatment to promote acceptance of dentistry for several visits. Evidence would have to be dentists' records of treatment because patients' reports of this are probably highly inaccurate (Eddie, 1984).

The studies of phobic patients in Table 20.1 show that exposure to video displays of patients receiving dentistry can reduce anxiety under test conditions. That has enabled subjects to accept one invasive dental procedure according to verifiable records in three studies (Bernstein & Kleinknecht, 1982; Harrison, Berggren & Carlsson, 1989; Jerremalm, Jansson & Oest, 1986). The studies that have tested cognitive therapy (De Jongh *et al.*, 1995; Ning & Liddell, 1991) provide no evidence that the patients were more able to accept dental treatment even though improvements in anxiety on standard measures were recorded. Hypnosis, which is popular among dentists, has been examined in very few controlled studies. Moore *et al.* (1996) compared hypnotherapy plus graded exposure to dentistry, systematic desensitisation, group therapy and a waiting-list control group. The subjects in all treatments showed a greater reduction in anxiety than the control group but half those who received hypnosis failed to complete the study. Significantly fewer in the desensitisation group, around 8 %, failed to seek dental treatment.

No study has identified subjects with the comorbid disorders or pain that have been recorded in dental phobics. Impairment in daily living is also overlooked in all studies even though quality of life has been noted in dental phobics who avoid treatment and who have poor dental health (Berggren, 1993).

BLOOD-INJURY AND INJECTION PHOBIA

People who require frequent administration of medication by injection, such as diabetics or those with chronic psychosis, are in danger if they are not able to tolerate injections. In a sample of over 1 200 people with insulin-dependent diabetes (Mollema *et al.*, 2001) around

Table 20.1 Outcome studies for treatment of dental phobia

Study	Comorbidity	Design (including repeated measures)	Outcome measures	Statistical outcome	Clinical significance
Bernstein & Kleinknecht (1982)	Not addressed	Five Groups: graded video-aided exposure, video-presented models, participant modelling (in vivo exposure), attention-placebo, 'positive-dental experience' in vivo	Included Fear. Survey Schedule (FSS), Dental Fear Survey (DFS). Health Locus of Control and personality measures; palmar sweat index etc. Records of attendance for dental exam or treatment	Only on state anxiety and expected pain was there an improvement. No group better than any other. No difference in dental appointment-making/attending	Not addressed but attendance for dental care recorded
De Jongh et al. (1995)	Not addressed	Three Groups: one session of cognitive therapy, or dental information, waiting list	State/Trait Anxiety (STAI); Dental Anxiety Scale (DAS), Frequency and credibility of cognitions (Dental Cognitions Q(DCQ))	Negative cognitions decreased in credibility and frequency in all groups. Cognitive therapy showed greatest change but was not superior in frequency of cognitions on follow-up. Dental Anxiety declined most rapidly with cognitive therapy	Not addressed. Not clear if all Ss tolerated the dental inspection. No reports of dental treatment undergone

Study	Comorbidity	Design (including repeated measures)	Outcome measures	Statistical outcome	Clinical significance
Getka & Glass (1992)	Not addressed	Four groups: stress inoculation, six sessions training or semi-automated behaviour therapy (modelling, relaxation, video-exposure); Waiting-list; 'positive dental experience' from dentist	Twenty measures: Dental Anxiety Scale (DAS); Dental Fear Survey (DFS); two analogue scales of fear; Dental Self Efficacy Scale (OSES); rating; expectations of pain; Palmar Sweat Index	Anxiety less in stress inoculation and behaviour therapy groups than in others. Not clear if this represents an improvement from pre- to post-therapy	Not addressed but all subjects had a cavity restoration after psychological treatment. No comparison in dentistry acceptance between groups
Hammarstrand et al. (1995)	Not addressed	Two groups: eight sessions of hypnotherapy (relaxation reinforced with suggestions) or behaviour therapy (relaxation, exposure to anxiety provoking hierarchy, biofeedback)	Dental Anxiety Scale (DAS), Mood Adjective Checklist (MACL); Geer Fear Scale (GFS); Dental Situation Reactions (DSR); dentist rating of co-operation	Hypnotherapy showed no improvement on any measure. Behaviour therapy showed improvement on four of five measures reported by Ss	Not addressed. All but one Ss 'could be referred to dentist to conclude treatment' but no record of such treatment
Harrison et al. (1989)	Not addressed	Two groups: systematic desensitisation (SD) (to graded video scenes, relaxation, EMG biofeedback) alone or SD and 'cognitive coping' SDCC, challenging negative self-statements)	Dental Anxiety Scale (DAS); Dental Treatment (cavity restoration with local anaesthesia) completed	More patients in SD group than the SDCC Ss completed two assigned dental treatments. Both groups improved on DAS	Fifteen of 16 SD Ss completed dental treatment; 12 of 16 SDCC Ss completed. No other aspect of clinical significance addressed

(continued)

Table 20.1 (*continued*)

Study	Comorbidity	Design (including repeated measures)	Outcome measures	Statistical outcome	Clinical significance
Jerremalm *et al.* (1986)	Not addressed	Four groups allocated to self-instruction training or applied relaxation; 'cognitive or physiological reactors'	Fear Survey Schedule (FSS), Dental Anxiety Scale (DAS), Dental Fear Survey (DFS); Behavioural Test: no of steps tolerated in dental exam; dentist's rating of Ss anxiety; pulse rate Autonomic Perception Q (APQ)	No change in behavioural measure; pulse rate declined in physiological reactors in both treatments but no change in cognitive reactors. Inconsistent improvement on Dental Fear and Dental Anxiety	Not addressed but 96 % of Ss had undergone invasive dental treatment – probably a significant improvement
Makkes *et al.* (1987)	Not addressed	Single group, various anxiety management procedures including nitrous oxide sedation	Dental Anxiety Scale (DAS) and other unattributed measures	Reduction in DAS anxiety but impossible to tell if this was due to anxiety management or because dentistry had been finished	Not addressed
Mathews & Rezin (1976)	Excluded	Five groups: all combinations of high/low arousal and coping/no coping instruction cf. relaxation control group	The Dental Anxiety Q; Semantic Differentials; Behavioural Test	Anxiety during behavioural tests improved more for low arousal than for high arousal. No comparisons with control groups	No difference between groups in dental attendance

Study	Comorbidity	Design (including repeated measures)	Outcome measures	Statistical outcome	Clinical significance
Miller, Murphy & Miller (1978)	Not addressed. Ss receiving treatment from other health professionals were excluded	Three groups: 10 sessions: EMG feedback, progressive relaxation; control group (self-relaxation)	Included EMG, Dental Anxiety Scale (DAS); State-Trait Anxiety Inventory (STAi)	DAS and state anxiety reduced in all groups but more in 2 treatment groups than in the control group	Not addressed
Moore et al. (1991)	Dental phobic Ss high and low in general anxiety	Two groups: given imaginal exposure with video stimuli or untreated Ss from waiting-list given 'attention placebo'	Dental Anxiety Scale (DAS), State-Trait Anxiety Inventory (STAI); Fear Survey Schedule	Treated group improved on all measures including trait anxiety and non-dental fears and more than the control group	Not addressed
Ning & Liddell (1991)	General anxiety (by Symptom Q): Ss 'not unduly anxious'	Two groups: massed/spaced cognitive therapy and relaxation	Ss making dental appointment; attending dentist; Dental Anxiety Scale (DAS). Ss' reports of anxiety, behaviour and physiology ('Discanf')	All Ss made appointment and attended. DAS and Discan scores reduced in both groups	Not addressed. No reports of dental treatment completed
Shaw & Thoresen (1974)	Not addressed	Four groups: systematic desensitisation (audio presented hierarchy), video modelling and relaxation and imaginal desensitisation relaxation placebo. Waiting-list	Visits to dentist and completion of treatment; six ad hoc measures of anxiety and attitudes to dentistry; Fear Survey Schedule (FSS); IPAT Anxiety Scale	Considered together, the two treatment groups had more successful visits to dentist, and showed significant reductions in seven of eight anxiety measures. The comparison groups showed significant irbprovements on three measures only (the placebo group)	Not addressed but dental treatment completion recorded

120 expressed extreme fear of injections. There is a danger, therefore, that they would miss or postpone insulin injections with serious consequences, including death. However, there appear to be no other studies of injection fear in such groups.

Research has shown that many of those who are afraid of injections are prone to fainting during the procedure and during operations, such as blood sampling, a requirement for some of the recent neuroleptic medications. They present a diphasic response in heart rate to the sight of blood – acceleration and then deceleration and bradycardia. Blood pressure changes in a similar fashion, the extreme drop in pressure accompanying fainting (Ost et al., 1984; Page, 1994).

Treatment studies, which have concentrated on subjects who are prone to fainting at the sight of blood, have distinguished the fall in blood pressure and the fear experienced in anticipation of the procedure. Page (1994) has proposed that the experience of the former causes the anticipatory fear. However, studies have depended on the subjects being able to practise the tension exercises that can be used at every blood exposure to control blood pressure. It may not be necessary, therefore, to demonstrate that this has a carry-over effect: that, after practice of the tension exercises, blood pressure is increased without the use of the exercises. The few studies of cognitions in blood-injury and injection phobia have shown that thoughts of disgust are less common than in other phobias, notably of spiders (DeJong & Merckelbach, 1998). A clinically significant outcome to treatment could nevertheless include, for some people, the acceptance of injections and a reduction in disgust as well as fear.

Only three studies using groups of subjects have been recorded (Ost, Fellenius & Sterner, 1991; Ost, Hellstrom & Kaver, 1992; Ost, Sterner & Fellenius, 1989), all by the same group. They have addressed both the fear of anticipated procedures and fall in blood pressure on exposure to blood. Applied tension enabled the subjects to raise their blood pressure. That, and in vivo exposure, reduced most measures of fear but was not successful in maintaining blood pressure on testing without applied tension. Subjects with comorbid disorders were excluded in all reports. However, impairment was partially addressed in all studies, most notably by Ost, Hellstrom and Kaver (1992) in whose study eight of 35 women allowed themselves to become pregnant and so endure venupunctures because they had overcome their fear of injections. However, the number of subjects who came to accept injections is not clear. This is disappointing given the need to enable some subjects, such as diabetics, to receive injections repeatedly.

CLAUSTROPHOBIA

There have been only a few studies, most by Rachman and his colleagues (Rachman, 1997) who found that the responses to the items in a claustrophobia questionnaire could be characterised by two factors describing fears of restriction or of suffocation. The former was most evident, for example, in response to the situation 'lying in a tight sleeping bag enclosing legs and arms, tied at the neck'. The latter was apparent in answers to 'swimming with a nose plug'. Rachman (1997) notes the resemblance to fears of suffocation in panic attacks. Claustrophobic patients, compared with others, anticipate more events that provoke such fears (Ost & Csatlos, 2000). If subjects acknowledge that they anticipate a catastrophe as the result of suffocation or restriction and this is a main influence on their claustrophobia, modification of these beliefs should occur with treatment. Furthermore, treatment that addressed those cognitions explicitly should be effective.

No study summarises the clinical significance of claustrophobia but instances of life-threatening incapacity are described: fear and intolerance of radiological examination in an MRI scanner (McIsaac *et al.*, 1998), of an airway mask for sleep apnoea (Edinger & Rodney, 1993), of gas masks in military personnel (Ritchie, 2002) and hyperbaric delivery of oxygen (Hillard, 1990).

All but one of the studies in Table 20.2 (Botella *et al.*, 2000) examined groups of subjects and all showed consistent improvement with exposure treatment on measures of fear. One study showed that, among subjects designated as physiological factors, those on a waiting list were as successful as the treatment groups on behavioural measures. (Ost, Johansson & Jerremalm, 1982). Only one study (Booth & Rachman, 1992) found no advantage over exposure of explicitly addressing the cognitions experienced in claustrophobia. However, no predictions were made about the power of the statistical design: perhaps too few subjects were selected to test the null hypothesis.

It is not possible to determine the effect of comorbid disorders because subjects with such disorders were excluded in all studies. Furthermore, the impact of, or on, impairment was also ignored in all studies.

FLYING PHOBIA

Although fear of flying is very common, affecting up to 40 % of airline passengers, so that many airlines offer treatment programmes (Van Gerwen, Lucas & Diekstra, 2000), there are few studies of the experience of flying phobia. These include lists of preoccupations associated with the fear: for example fear of the aircraft crashing and of losing control of one's reactions (Van Gerwen *et al.*, 1997; Wilhelm & Roth, 1997). It is not difficult, therefore, to imagine catastrophic predictions that people might make: the confusion and disorder prior to a crash, being crushed and torn apart by the impact and being identified by one's dental records. The triggers for these fears and elaborations probably occur most often and most intensely during takeoff, landing and turbulence (Girodo & Roehl, 1978; Van Gerwen *et al.*, 1997) and this may be seen in the interoceptive feedback from one's body during these phases. However, studies have paid no attention to cognitive processing that might be influenced by sensational reports of flying disasters. Instead they have concentrated on diagnostic issues (Aitken *et al.*, 1981; Van Gerwen *et al.*, 1997; Wilhelm & Roth, 1997).

Nevertheless, studies of comorbid disorders in people with flying phobia, claustrophobia, agoraphobia with panic and social phobia, suggest imaginings (McNally & Louro, 1992; Van Gerwen *et al.*, 1997; Wilhelm, 1997) such as suffocating and dying of a heart attack during a panic or causing a visible commotion and provoking ridicule. Those who report agoraphobia express little concern about the occurrence and consequences of the aircraft crashing (McNally & Louro, 1992). Although there have been descriptions of passengers using alcohol to excess and losing control, so that airlines now enforce prosecution, there appear to be no surveys of alcohol use and fear of flying. In civilians, quality of life may be impaired by flying phobia. For example, it might prevent them from flying when it is essential in their employment. In military personnel, whose training entails great expense, the phobia may require aircrew to be retrained or taken off flying duties.

All but two studies of treatment have exposed subjects to some experience of flying (Table 20.3). Many airlines have treatment programmes (Van Gerwen *et al.*, 1997). These could use flight simulators, which reproduce aircraft movement in flight, such as roll, for training aircrew. Computer-driven virtual reality displays, although very expensive, are

Table 20.2 Outcome studies for treatment of claustrophobia

	Comorbidity	Design (including repeated measures)	Outcome measures	Statistical outcome	Clinical significance
Booth & Rachman (1992)	Excluded	Four groups: all had three sessions: exposure to external stimuli, exposure to anxiety symptoms, cognitive therapy, control group	Anxiety Sensitivity Index (ASI), Behavioural Test (BAT), pulse rate in BAT, ad hoc rating scales of predicted and experienced fear, checking of negative cognitions and physical symptoms	Exposure group better than control group on 6 of 7 measures (+ tests) but a multivariate analysis of variance showed no significant differences among the treatment groups	Not clearly addressed
Botella et al. (2000)	Not clearly addressed but two Ss were asked to discontinue psychotropic medication. One S had fear of storms	Four Ss in controlled multiple-baseline design: baseline then virtual reality	Behavioural Avoidance Test, four self-report measures	Improvement in all measures but no statistical tests	Not clearly addressed
Craske et al. (1995)	Excluded	Four groups: claustrophobics and spider/snake phobics given in vivo exposure and relaxation (ER) or in vivo exposure and disconfirmation of misappraisals of bodily sensation (ESF)	Behavioural Tests (BATS), anxiety rating in BATS Anxiety Sensitivity Index (ASI), Self Analysis Q (SAQ). Fear Generalisation Q (FGQ); Heart rate before BATS	Twenty-six per cent of Ss failed to complete treatment. ESF reduced four measures of fear to greater extent than ER. ASI reduced by both	Not addressed

	Comorbidity	Design (including repeated measures)	Outcome measures	Statistical outcome	Clinical significance
Ost et al. (1982)	Excluded	Five groups: Ss assessed as 'behavioural' or 'physiological' reactors; both groups divided to receive exposure or applied relaxation over eight sessions. Waiting-list control	Fear Survey Schedule (FSS); Automatic Perception Q (APQ); Claustrophobia Scale (CS); Behavioural Avoidance Test (BAT)	All groups improved on all measures but greater improvement on all measures in 'behavioural reactors' given exposure and in 'physiological reactors' given relaxation	These results confirmed by statistical criteria of clinical significance
Ost et al. (2001)	Excluded but anxiety, agoraphobia and depression measured	Four groups: one session exposure, five sessions exposure, five sessions cognitive therapy, waiting list	Behavioural tests (BATS); blood pressure, heart rate; Claustrophobia Scale (CS); Agoraphobia Scale (AS), Fear Survey Schedule (FSS); Anxiety Sensitivity Index (ASP) etc.	Four Ss dropped out; the three treatment groups combined were better than the waiting-list Ss on almost all measures but differences among treatment groups not consistent	No clinically significant difference among treatment groups according to statistical criteria

Table 20.3 Outcome studies for treatment of flying phobia

Study	Comorbidity	Design (including repeated measures)	Outcome measures	Statistical outcome	Clinical significance
Denholtz & Mann (1975) and Denholtz et al. (1978)	Excluded according to MMPI but undisclosed number reported improvement in claustrophobic symptoms	Four groups: systematic desensitisation to film; similar procedure without grading of exposure, similar without relaxation, relaxation only and placebo	Subsequent flight, according to self-report; Taylor Manifest Anxiety Scale (TMAS)	Seventy-eight per cent of Ss flew on free flight. Number of Ss flying being greater in Ss given full systematic desensitisation (SD) than in others. However Ss were transferred into SD from others	Not clearly addressed. Numbers of Ss unable to fly pre-treatment not given. Therefore, extent of improvement is unclear. 23 of 26 Ss reported having flown in 3–5 years subsequently
Girodo & Roehl (1978)	Not addressed	Eight groups: preparatory information, self-statement training, those combined, pseudo treatment. These divided into flying with cockpit door open/closed	SR Anxiety Inventory, ad hoc Treatment Effectiveness Questionnaire	Self-talk Ss less anxious than pseudo treatment. Differences among other groups not clear	Not addressed. All Ss were able to fly as part of treatment
Haug et al. (1987)	Not addressed	10 Ss in four groups: stress inoculation, applied relaxation. 'Cognitive' and 'physiological' responders	Fear Survey Schedule (FSS), Fear of Flying Scale (ad hoc for present study) rating scales for expected anxiety, negative thoughts rating scale, Behavioural Test (BT), heart rate	Both groups improved on all measures but inconsistent differences between groups	All Ss took part in arranged flight post-treatment but pre-treatment behavioural assessment not clear

Study	Comorbidity	Design (including repeated measures)	Outcome measures	Statistical outcome	Clinical significance
Howard et al. (1983)	Excluded	Five groups: eight sessions imaginal desensitisation, flooding, implosion, relaxation and no treatment	Fear Survey Schedule (FSS) and ad hoc Q on Attitudes to Flying (QAF) self-report rating scales, pulse rate, observer check list	All groups improved on QAF comparing pre-treatment and follow-up after a flight. Improvement pre- to post-treatment only in four treatment groups	Most Ss flew on test flight after intervention, including no treatment group. In subsequent three months. No treatment and systematic desensitisation Ss both flew less than others
Maltby et al. (2002)	Some Ss had agoraphobia or panic disorder with agoraphobia	Two groups Virtual Reality (VR) exposure of 'attention-placebo' group treatment	Flight Anxiety Situations Q (FAS); Flight Anxiety, Modality Q (FAM); Flight History; Subjective Units of Discomfort (SUDS)	On four of six measures, VR showed greater improvement immediately post-treatment; on only one measure at six months was VR superior	Assessed by standard statistical test: improvement mean cf 2 SDs above population. No in vivo test of outcome
Muhlberger et al. (2001)	Self-medication by alcohol etc. recorded but impact not assessed	Two groups: extensive virtual reality (VR) and relaxation	Fear of Flying Scale (FFS); General Fear of Flying Scale (CFFS); Danger Expectancy Scale (DES), Anxiety Expectance Scale (AES), Anxiety Sensitivity Index (ASI); heart rate (HR); skin conductance level (SCL)	No significant differences between groups for FFS, GFPS, DES, AES or ASI. 'Avoidance of flying rating' favoured VR only group, but both groups improved on all measures	None mentioned. No record of subsequent in vivo flying

(continued)

Table 20.3 (continued)

Study	Comorbidity	Design (including repeated measures)	Outcome measures	Statistical outcome	Clinical significance
Ost et al. (1997)	Depression and anxiety both minimal, assessed by questionnaire	Two groups: one session or five sessions of exposure and 'cognitive restructuring' and information	Fear of Flying Scale (FFS); Fear Survey Schedule (FSS), State–Trait Anxiety Inventory (STAI); Beck Depression Inventory (BDI; Beck Anxiety Inventory (BAI); Credibility and Expected Success Scales: Behavioural Test (in vivo flight-extent accomplished)	Both groups improved on all measures but there was a deterioration on the Behavioural Test one year later	Not addressed but 93 % and 79 % had flown once after treatment
Rothbaum et al. (2000)	Included Ss with agoraphobia with/ without panic disorder. Ss with psychosis or drug/alcohol abuse excluded	Three groups: virtual reality exposure (VRE), in vivo exposure up to sitting in stationary aircraft all for eight sessions, waiting-list	Attitudes to Flying Q (QAF), Fear of Flying Inventory, (FFI), Clinical Global Improvement (CGI)	VRE superior to waiting-list control on all measures after treatment and on two of three measures at six months. VRE no better than Exposure	VRE Ss (11 of 14) and Exposure Ss (14 of 15) groups more likely than waiting-list Ss to complete a flight arranged by the Experimenter after treatment
Walder et al. (1987)	Excluded? But includes Ss described as 'claustrophobic'	Two groups: information, graded exposure in vivo in groups and no treatment	State Anxiety Inventory, Self rating anxiety scales. Self-report of flying experience	Improvement on ratings of anxiety in treatment group. Flying experience post-treatment unclear. Differences between treatment and control groups unclear	Unclear

now being exploited. No study has addressed catastrophic imaginings explicitly. One study (Girodo & Roehl, 1978) instructed subjects to recite encouragement to themselves but they had selected subjects who were not too afraid to fly.

Two studies included subjects who had other anxiety disorders that could have contributed to their fear of flying (Maltby *et al.*, 2002; Rothbaum *et al.*, 2000) but these were not addressed directly. No study determined if subjects flew more than once after treatment although most showed improvement on measures of fear greater than baseline and in comparison with control groups. Two studies examined military aircrew but they used no valid or reliable measures or experimental design (Aitken *et al.*, 1971; McCarthy & Craig, 1995).

In conclusion, relaxation training or exposure to the experience of simulated flying can reduce the fear of flying. However, the effect of these interventions on the capacity of subjects to undertake flights is not clear. Moreover, there has been no test of the effect of comorbid anxiety disorders, common in flying phobia, or the effect of treatment on the quality of life.

SPIDER PHOBIA

Studies of recall and perceptual bias in spider phobia have been contradictory (Cameron, 1997). Disgust and fear evoked by spiders are largely independent of one another (Smits, Telch & Randall, 2002; Thorpe & Salkovskis, 1995) even though both decline with brief exposure (Smits, Telch & Randall, 2002; Thorpe & Salkovskis, 1997). Disgust as well as fear is, therefore, probably worthy of attention. Many people with spider phobia are also afraid, in the presence of spiders, of being unable to move, of making a fool of themselves, screaming and feeling faint (Thorpe & Salkovskis, 1995). Responses on measures that address these beliefs improve with brief exposure coupled with cognitive therapy, a change that is correlated with a reduction in fear (Thorpe & Salkovskis, 1997). However, it is not clear if cognitive therapy was necessary for that.

Trials in adults and children (Table 20.4) show, without exception, that exposure to live spiders, usually in a graded manner, produces improvement in measures of anxiety and behavioural tolerance. Simulated exposure by virtual reality (VR) or computer-aided presentation of somebody else being confronted by spiders (vicarious exposure), exposure with distraction, focussed or elaborated attention or with counter-conditioning (reciprocal inhibition) or exposure plus cognitive therapy or self-instruction manuals all reduce anxiety and improve tolerance. One session, an hour or more, can be sufficient. In one study (Smith *et al.*, 1997), however, exposure to irrelevant stimuli, elevators, by computer display was as effective as similar exposure to spiders but it is not clear if sufficient subjects were tested to examine differences between the treatments. No study has included subjects with additional psychological problems. In only five is impairment of functioning addressed, all by Work Adjustment Ratings; more extensive measures of quality of life are examined in none. However, there is no consistent improvement among studies in work adjustment but several show statistical evidence of clinically significant improvement. There are few differences to suggest that any treatment is better than an other. However, very few studies predict the numbers of subjects necessary to confirm differences among treatments. Among the most controversial approaches for specific phobias, eye movement desensitisation (EMDR) has been tested most often for spider phobia. The one study that consistently supported EMDR,

Table 20.4 Outcome studies for treatment of spider phobia

Study	Comorbidity	Design (including repeated measures)	Outcome measures	Statistical outcome	Clinical significance
Anthony *et al.* (2001)	Not addressed	Two groups and two conditions: Single session exposure and modelling under distraction or attention focussed conditions; Ss identified as 'blunters' or 'monitors'	Spider Q (SPQ), Behavioural Approach Test (BAT), Diagnostic Symptom Q (DSQ), Heart Rate (HR) during BAT	All groups improved on all measures but differences among conditions and groups were not consistent across measures	Not addressed
Arntz and Lavy (1993)	Excluded	Two groups: Ss' Elaboration of spider stimuli in exposure; Ss prevented from elaborating	Spider Phobia Q (SPQ), self-rating of fear and avoidance, Spider Belief Q(SBQ). Behavioural Approach Test (BAT)	Ss improved on all measures but no difference between groups	Not addressed
Arntz *et al.* (1993)	Not addressed but spider phobia was 'the main psychopathological problem'	Three groups: 2 hours exposure with a placebo or low dose opioid antagonist or high dose naltrexone	Spider Phobia Q (SPQ); Fear Questionnaire (FQ); Spider Belief Q (SBQ); Behavioural Avoidance Test (BAT); heart rate and skin conductance in BAT	Both groups improved on all measures except skin conductance and heart rate. These improvements had diminished one week later especially in the high dose naltrexone Ss	Not addressed
Bates *et al.* (1996)		Two groups: EMDR; control group	Heart rate, skin conductance, fear ratings; Behavioural Approach Test (BAT)	Improvement in fear ratings and BAT in both groups but no group consistently better than other	Not addressed

Study	Comorbidity	Design (including repeated measures)	Outcome measures	Statistical outcome	Clinical significance
De Jong et al. (2000)	Not addressed	Two groups: one session in vivo exposure with or without counter conditioning (music or food to counteract disgust)	Fear rating (SPQ) Behavioural Avoidance Test (BAT); valence ratings; Spider-disgust Q (SDQ); Cookie Preference Behavioural Test	Both groups improved on SPQ, BAT and Disgust but no difference between groups	Sixty-seven percent (SPQ), 76 % (BAT), 47 % (Disgust) and 77 % (Valence) met statistical criteria for clinically significant improvement
De Jong et al. (1997)	Not addressed	One group of children: one session of eye-movement desensitisation (EMDR) followed by in vivo exposure	Spider Phobia Q for Children (SPQ-C); Disgust Sensitivity (DQ), Disgust (two items added to DQ)	SPQ improved with treatment; results for disgust are unclear. No change in DQ	Not addressed
Dewis et al. (2001)	Excluded. WAIS and WISC cognitive 'screening' but use not clear	3 Groups of children: computer-aided vicarious exposure (CAVE), live graded exposure, or waiting list	Behavioural Avoidance Test (BAT). Other measures included self-report of fear. Data collectors blind to treatment groups	Improvement on most measures for both groups but live exposure showed greatest improvement. The CAVE group showed no greater improvement man the waiting list Ss	'Large' statistical effect size for live exposure. Results of Work Adjustment Rating not fully reported but did not differ between treatments
Fraser et al. (2001)	Excluded	Two groups: three or six sessions of computer-aided vicarious exposure	Behavioural Assessment Test (BAT) and Subjective Units of Distress (SUD) Spider Phobia Q (SPQ), Fear Q, Phobic Targets, Work Adjustment Rating Scale (WARS), Cognitive Functioning (NART) as statistical correction	Both groups improved on all measures but no differences between groups. Use of NART not reported	'Large effect' size on some measures for both groups. Both improved on Work Adjustment but clinical significance unclear

(continued)

Table 20.4 *(continued)*

Study	Comorbidity	Design (including repeated measures)	Outcome measures	Statistical outcome	Clinical significance
Garcia-Palacios et al. (2002)	'No other psychiatric problems…alcohol or drug dependence'	Two groups: virtual reality (VR) exposure versus waiting list	Anxiety Diagnostic Interview (ADIS); Fear of Spiders Q (FSQ); Behavioural Avoidance Test (BAT; Clinician rating	Improvement greater for VR group than for others on all measures	Eighty-three per cent improved to be within range of normal and non-phobic Ss (cf Jacobson et al., 1984). No other criteria addressed
Gilroy et al. (2000)	Excluded. IQ assessed by National Adult Rading Test but use not clear	Three groups: live graded exposure (LGE), computer-aided vicarious exposure (CAVE); relaxation	Behavioural Avoidance Test (BAT), self-report ratings of fear, Spider Q (SQ), Fear Q (FQ). Work Adjustment Rating Scales (WARS) etc.	On all measures except VARS there was a greater improvement for the two treatment groups than for the relaxation group but no consistent differences between the treatment groups	No effect on Work Adjustment (WARS)
Heading et al. (2001)	Excluded	Three groups: one session of computer-aided vicarious exposure (CAVE) or therapist-aided live graded exposure	Similar to Fraser et al. (2001)	Both groups improved on all measures except Work Adjustment but greater improvement for live graded exposure. No report of effect of cognitive functioning (NART)	Both groups showed 'large' effect size on all measures (except for one in the CAVE Ss
Hellstroem & Ost (1995)	Not addressed but anxiety and depression measured	Five groups: one session of therapist-directed exposure, manual-based specific treatment at home or clinic, general manual based at home, or clinic	Similar to Ost (1996)	Improvement on most measures in all groups but therapist directed treatment better than most manual based treatments	Results similar to Ost et al. (1997)

Study	Comorbidity	Design (including repeated measures)	Outcome measures	Statistical outcome	Clinical significance
Muris & De Jong (1995)	Not addressed	Within Ss before and after exposure treatment	Spider Phobia Questionnaire (SPQ); Behavioural Avoidance Test (BAT)	Improvement on both measures	Not addressed
Muris et al. (1997)	Not addressed	Two groups of children in crossover: one session EMDR then in vivo exposure or vice versa	Muris et al. (1998)	Anxiety and Approach behaviour improved after first treatment; further behavioural improvement only in Ss given exposure second	Not addressed
Muris & Merckelbach (1997)	Not addressed	Three groups of adults: EMDR, imaginal exposure, control group. Then all underwent in vivo exposure	Heart-rate, skin conductance, fear ratings; Behavioural Approach Test (BAT)	Improvement in fear ratings and BAT in both groups but no group consistently better than other	Not addressed
Muris et al. (1993)	Not addressed	Two groups: 'Monitors' and 'Blunters' both received one session of in vivo exposure and modeling	Spider Phobia Q (SPQ); Spider Belief Q (SBQ), Behavioural Approach Test (BAT); heart rate, skin conductance level	Both groups improved on all measures, sustained at one week. Monitors improved to a lesser degree than blunters on SPQ and BAT but this appears to have been contradicted by the physiological measures	Not addressed

(continued)

Table 20.4 (*continued*)

Study	Comorbidity	Design (including repeated measures)	Outcome measures	Statistical outcome	Clinical significance
Muris *et al.* (1998)	Excluded	Three groups of children: EMDR; exposure *in vivo*, computerised exposure. All Ss then received *in vivo* exposure	Spider Phobia Q (SPQ–C); Self Assessment Manikin (SAM) in presence of spider. Behavioural Avoidance Test (BAT). Rating of treatment affectiveness	Improvement with *in vivo* exposure in all four measures. EMDR showed improvement on only one measure, (SAM); computer exposure on none	Not addressed
Ost (1996)	'No other psychiatric problems' but depression and anxiety measured	Two groups: one session of exposure in large or small groups of Ss	Spider Phobia Q (SPQ), spider Q (SQ), fear and avoidance and handicap ratings, Fear Survey Schedule, State-Trait Anxiety. Assessor rating, Behavioural Avoidance Test (BAT), etc.	Both groups improved on most measures	Seventy-six per cent showed clinically significant improvement by statistical criteria. This increased to 85 % at one year. Both groups improved in anxiety, depression and degree of handicap imposed by phobia
Ost *et al.* (1998)	Not addressed but depression and anxiety measured	Four conditions within Ss: self-help manual, video, group and individual exposure	Behavioural Approach Test (BAT); Assessor's rating. Self-rating of anxiety; dropping out of treatment; Spider Phobia Q (SPQ); Spider Q; fear and avoidance ratings, Fear Survey Schedule (FSS), Self-efficacy, etc.	Forty-three per cent of Ss dropped out, most Ss reporting clinically significant improvement during group treatment but measures confounded with sequence effects. All treatments showed improvements on most measures but very few differences between treatments	The best condition (group treatment) showed clinically significant improvement for 44 %. Ss by statistical criteria

Study	Comorbidity	Design (including repeated measures)	Outcome measures	Statistical outcome	Clinical significance
Ost et al. (1997)	Not addressed but anxiety and depression measured	Three groups: exposure and individual participation in group (direct), observation of group member participating in exposure (direct observation). Group watches video of S being exposed (indirect observation)	Similar to Ost (1996)	Improvement on all measures for all groups. Inconsistent differences among groups in this improvement	By statistical criteria, more Ss in Direct treatment compared with other groups showed clinically significant improvement. Improvement in degree of handicap imposed by phobia: improvement greatest in Direct treatment. Both groups unproved on anxiety and depression
Ost et al. (1991)	Excluded	Two groups: one session therapist directed exposure or self-directed exposure with instruction manual	Spider Q1 (SQP1) Spider Q2 (SPQ2) – by different authors, clinician rating, Behavioural Approach Test (BAT), a self-rating of anxiety	Eighty-two per cent in therapist group but only 12 % of self-exposure group allowed spider to crawl over their hands. On ratings and Spider Questionnaires there was greater improvement for the therapist-directed treatment	By statistical criteria, 71 % of the therapist-directed Ss but only 6 % of the manual-guided Ss showed a clinical improvement

(continued)

Table 20.4 (continued)

Study	Comorbidity	Design (including repeated measures)	Outcome measures	Statistical outcome	Clinical significance
Smith et al. (1997)	Not addressed but 'none was taking anxiolytic medication'	Three groups, computerised: Relevant exposure (RE) and feedback; RE no feedback; irrelevant exposure with feedback	Spider Q I; Spider Q II; Behaviour Targets; Work Adjustment Rating Scales	All groups improved on SQ I and II, Work Adjustment and Performance targets	Not addressed but Work Adjustment improved (qv)
Smits et al. (2002)	Not addressed	Within Ss before and after exposure treatment	Fear of Spider Q (FSQ); Spider Fear Q (SFQ), Spider Belief Q (SBQ); Disgust Sensitivity and Contamination (DSQ); Armfield et al. Disgust Q. (AMDQ); Behavioural Avoidance Tests (BATs)	Improvement on all subjective measures except Disgust Sensitivity and on one of the BATs. Decline in spider-specific disgust not sufficient to explain change in fear	Not addressed
Thorpe & Salkovskis (1997)	Not addressed but depression, state and trait anxiety were assessed	Two groups: one session of exposure and modelling and information, untreated Ss	Two Spider Phobia Spider Qs (SPQs). Phobic Beliefs Q, modified from a published Agoraphobia Q; Beck Depression Inventory (BDI), State-Trait Anxiety Q (STAI) and ad hoc rating scales, Stroop Test of spider and disgust-related words	Improvement on all measures except Stroop test	Not addressed

in children, showed an improvement in only one of two measures of anxiety and it is not clear if that is a Type I statistical error (Muris *et al.*, 1998). Of the other studies (Table 20.4), Muris & Merckelbach (1997) showed that improvement occurred only after *in vivo* exposure, which followed all treatments, including EMDR. It is not clear if enough subjects were tested in any of the quoted studies of EMDR to detect the effects of treatments. However, most reviews have dismissed claims for the effectiveness of EMDR (see, for example, Davidson & Parker, 2001).

CONCLUSIONS

Studies continue to show that exposure is effective in the treatment of specific phobias and now this can be successfully delivered by computer and Virtual Reality Displays. However, the effect on behaviour, notably the capacity to accept injections and to fly in aircraft following the corresponding treatment programmes, has not been well demonstrated. Innovations based on information-processing theories of fear have been tested only in a handful of studies, most notably for claustrophobia and the fear of dental treatment. However, studies of the latter also have sought no evidence that patients would accept dentistry more readily, an indispensable outcome for patients who have avoided dentistry so risking detriment to their health.

Of particular note, however, is the fact that most studies have excluded or failed to describe subjects with comorbid disorders or impairment in daily functioning that could be attributed directly or indirectly to their specific fears. This is disappointing in view of the fact that people seek help when they have widespread difficulties. This neglect is puzzling in light of the definition of specific fears quoted at the beginning of this review, which emphasises impairment in functioning. The question, therefore, remains to be answered: how effective are psychological treatments for people with specific phobias and associated psychological difficulties whose quality of life is impaired as a result?

REFERENCES

Aitken, R.C.B. (1981). Identification of features associated with flying phobia in aircrew. *British Journal of Psychiatry, 139*, 38–42.

Aitken, R.C.B., Daly, R., Lister, J.A. & O'Connor, P.J. (1971). Treatment of flying phobia in aircrew. *American Journal of Psychotherapy, 25*, 530–542.

American Psychiatric Association. (2000). *Diagnostic and Statistical Manual – IV* (text revision). Washington: American Psychiatric Association.

Anthony, M.M., McCabe, R.E, Leuw, I. *et al.* (2001). Effect of distraction and coping style on in vivo exposure for specific phobia of spiders. *Behaviour Research and Therapy, 39*, 1137–1150.

Arntz, A. & Lavy, E. (1993). Does stimulus elaboration potentiate exposure *in vivo* treatment? Two forms of one-session treatment of spider phobia. *Behavioural Psychotherapy, 21*, 1–12.

Arntz, A., Merckelbach, H. & De Jong, P.J. (1993). Opioid antagonist affects behavioral effects of exposure in vivo. *Journal of Consulting and Clinical Psychology, 61*, 865–870.

Barlow, D.H, Vermilyea, J., Blanchard, E.B. *et al.* (1985). The phenomenon of panic. *Journal of Abnormal Psychology, 94*, 320–328.

Bates, L.K, McGlynn, F.D, Montgomery, R.W. & Mattke, T. (1996). Effects of eye-movement desensitisation versus no treatment on repeated measures of fear of spiders. *Journal of Anxiety Disorders, 10*, 555–569.

Beck, J.G, Carmin, C.N. & Henninger, N.J. (1998). The utility of the Fear Survey Schedule – III: an extended replication. *Journal of Anxiety Disorders, 12*, 177–182.

Berggren, U. (1993). Psychosocial effects associated with dental fear in adult dental patients. *Psychology and Health, 8,* 185–196.

Bernstein, D.A. & Kleinknecht, R.A. (1982). Multiple approaches to the reduction of dental fear. *Journal of Behaviour Therapy and Experimental Psychiatry, 13*, 287–292.

Booth, R. & Rachman, S. (1992). The reduction of claustrophobia: I. *Behaviour Research and Therapy, 30*(3), 207–221.

Botella, C., Banos, R.M., Villa, A. *et al.* (2000). Virtual reality in the treatment of claustrophobic fear: a controlled, multiple-baseline design. *Behavior Therapy, 31*, 583–595.

Bowen, R.C., Senthilselvan, A. & Barale, A. (2000). Physical illness as an outcome of chronic anxiety disorders. *Canadian Journal of Psychiatry, 45*, 459–464.

Boyd, J. H., Rae, D. S, Thompson, J. W. *et al.* (1990). Phobia: prevalence and risk factors. *Social Psychiatry and Psychiatric Epidemiology, 25*, 314–323.

Cameron, C.M. (1997). Information – processing approaches to phobias. In G. Davey (ed.) *Phobias. A Handbook of Theory, Research and Treatment.* Chichester: Wiley.

Craske, M.G. (1991). Phobic fear and panic attacks: the same emotional states triggered by different cues? *Clinical Psychology Review, 11*, 599–620.

Craske, M.G., Mohlman, J., Yi, J. *et al.* (1995). Treatment of claustrophobias and snake/spider phobias: Fear of arousal and fear of context. *Behaviour Research and Therapy, 33*(2), 197–203.

Curtis, G.C., Magee, W.J., Eaton, W.W. *et al.* (1998). Specific fears and phobias: Epidemiology and classification. *British Journal of Psychiatry, 173*, 212–217.

Davey, G. (ed.) (1997). *Phobias: A Handbook of Theory, Research and Treatment.* Chichester: Wiley.

Davidson, P.R. & Parker, K.C.H. (2001). Eye-movement desensitisation and reprocessing (EMDR): A meta analysis. *Journal of Consulting and Clinical Psychology, 69*, 305–316.

De Jongh, A., Muris, P., Schoenmakers, N. & Ter Horst, G. (1995). Negative cognitions of dental phobics: Reliability and validity of the Dental Cognitions Questionnaire. *Behaviour Research and Therapy, 33*(5), 507–515.

De Jong, P.J., Andrea, H. & Muris, P. (1997). Spider phobia in children: Disgust and fear before and after treatment. *Behaviour Research and Therapy, 35*, 559–562.

De Jong, P.J. & Merckelbach, H. (1998). Blood-injection-injury phobia and fear of spiders: Domain specific individual differences in disgust sensitivity. *Personality and Individual Differences, 24*(2), 153–158.

De Jong, P.J., Vorage, I. & Van den Hout, M.A. (2000). Counter-conditioning in the treatment of spider phobia: Effects of disgust, fear and valence. *Behaviour Research and Therapy, 38*, 1055–1069.

Denholz, M.S. (1975). An automated audiovisual treatment of phobias administered by non-professionals. *Journal of Behaviour Therapy and Experimental Psychiatry, 6*, 111–115.

Denholz, M.S., Hall, L.A. & Mann, E. T. (1978). Automated treatment for flight phobia: A 3–5 year follow-up. *American Journal of Psychiatry, 135*, 1340–1343.

Dewis, L.M, Kirkby, K.C, Martin, F. *et al.* (2001). Computer-aided vicarious exposure versus live graded exposure for spider phobia in children. *Journal of Behavior Therapy and Experimental Psychiatry, 32*, 17–27.

Eddie, S. (1984). Frequency of attendance in the General Dental Service in Scotland. A comparison with claimed attendance. *British Dental Journal, 157*, 267–270.

Edinger, J.D. & Radtke, R.A. (1993). Use of *in vivo* desensitization to treat a patient's claustrophobic response to nasal CPAP. *Sleep, 16*(7), 678–680.

Elkin, I. (1994). The NIMH treatment of depression collaborative research program: Where we begun and where we are. In A. Bergin & S. Garfield (eds), *Handbook of Psychotherapy and Behaviour Change.* New York: Wiley.

Forsyth, J.P. & Eifert, G.H. (1996). 'Cleaning-up cognition' in triple-response fear assessment through individualised functional behavioural analysis. *Journal of Behavior Therapy and Experimental Psychiatry*, 27, 87–98.

Fraser, J., Kirkby, K.C., Daniels, B. *et al.* (2001). Three versus six sessions of computer-aided vicarious exposure treatment for spider phobia. *Behaviour Change, 18*(4), 213–223.

Garcia-Palacios, A., Hoffman, H., Carlin, A. *et al.* (2002). Virtual reality in the treatment of spider phobia: A controlled study. *Behaviour Research and Therapy, 40*, 983–993.

Getka, E.J. & Glass, C.R. (1992). Behavioral and cognitive-behavioral approaches to the reduction of dental anxiety. *Behaviour Therapy 23*, 433–448.

Gilroy, L.J, Kirkby, K.C, Daniels, B.A. *et al.* (2000). Controlled comparison of computer-aided vicarious exposure versus live exposure in the treatment of spider phobia. *Behavior Therapy, 31*, 733–744.

Girodo, M. & Roehl, J. (1978). Cognitive preparation and coping self-talk: Anxiety management during the stress of flying. *Journal of Consulting and Clinical Psychology, 46*, 978–989.

Gladis, M., Gosch, E.A., Dishuk, N.M. & Crits-Christoph, P. (1999). Quality of life: Expanding the scope of clinical significance. *Journal of Consulting and Clinical Psychology, 67*, 320–331.

Green, R., Humphris, G., Lindsay, S. *et al.* (1997). Psychiatric distress, pain and fear in general dental practice. *Community Dentistry and Oral Epidemiology, 25*, 187–188.

Hallam, R.S. & Haffner, R.J. (1978). Fear of phobic patients: Factor analyses of self-report data. *Behaviour Research and Therapy, 16*, 1–6.

Hammarstrand, G., Berggren, U. & Hakeberg, M. (1995). Psychophysiological therapy vs. hypnotherapy in the treatment of patients with dental phobia. *European Journal of Oral Science, 103*, 399–404.

Harrison, J.A, Berggren, U. & Carlsson, S.G. (1989). Treatment of dental fear: Systematic desensitisation or coping? *Behavioural Psychotherapy, 17*, 125–133.

Haug, T., Brenne, L., Johnsen, B.H. *et al.* (1987). A three-systems analysis of fear of flying: a comparison of a consonant vs. a non-consonant treatment method. *Behaviour Research and Therapy*, 25, 187–194.

Heading, K., Kirkby, K.C., Martin, F. *et al.* (2001). Controlled comparison of single-session treatments for spider phobia: Live graded exposure alone versus computer-aided vicarious exposure. *Behaviour Change, 18*(2), 103–113.

Hellstroem, K. & Ost, L.G. (1995). One-session therapist directed exposure versus two forms of manual directed self-exposure in the treatment of spider phobia. *Behaviour Research and Therapy, 33*, 959–965.

Hillard, J.R. (1990). Severe claustrophobia in a patient requiring hyperbaric oxygen treatment. *Psychosomatics, 31*(1), 107–108.

Hofmann, S.G., Lehman, C.L. & Barlow, D.H. (1997). How specific are specific phobias? *Journal of Behavior Therapy and Experimental Psychiatry, 28*(3), 233–240.

Holloway, F. & Carson, J. (2002). Quality of life in severe mental illness. *International Journal of Psychiatry, 14*, 175–184.

Howard, W.A., Murphy, S.M. & Clarke, J.C. (1983). The nature and treatment of fear of flying, a controlled investigation. *Behaviour Therapy, 14*, 557–567.

Jacobson, N.S, Folette, W.C. & Ravensdorff, D. (1984). Psychotherapy outcome research: Methods for reporting variability and evaluating clinical significance. *Behaviour Research and Therapy, 15*, 336–352.

Jacobson, N.S. & Truax, F. (1991). Clinical Significance: a statistical approach to defining meaningful change in psychotherapy research. *Journal of Consulting and Clinical Psychology, 59*, 12–19.

Jerremalm, A., Jansson, L. & Oest, L.-G. (1986). Individual response patterns and the effects of different behavioral methods in the treatment of dental phobia. *Behaviour Research and Therapy, 24*(5), 587–596.

Kazdin, A.E. (1978). Evaluating the generality of findings in analogue therapy research. *Journal of Consulting and Clinical Psychology, 46*, 673–686.

Kazdin, A.E. (1994). Methodology, design and evaluation in psychotherapy research. In A. Bergin & S. Garfield (eds), *Handbook of Psychotherapy and Behaviour Change*. New York: Wiley.

Kazdin, A.E. (1999). The meanings and measurement of clinical significance. *Journal of Consulting and Clinical Psychology, 63*, 332–339.

Kirsch, I., Montgomery, G. & Sapirstein, G. (1995). Hypnosis as an adjunct to cognitive-behavioral psychotherapy: a meta-analysis. *Journal of Consulting and Clinical Psychology, 63*, 214–220.

Lambert, M.J. & Hill, C.E. (1994). Assessing psychotherapy outcome and process. In A. Bergin & S. Garfield (eds) *Handbook of Psychotherapy and Behaviour Change*. New York: Wiley.

Lindsay, S, Humphris, G. & Barnby, G. (1987). Expectations and preferences for routine dentistry in anxious adult patients. *British Dental Journal, 163*, 120–124.

Lindsay, S. & Jackson, C. (1993). Fear of routine dental treatment in adults: Its nature and measurement. *Psychology and Health, 8,* 135–154.

Magee, W.J, Eaton, W.W, Wittchen, H.-U. *et al.* (1996). Agoraphobia simple phobia and social phobia in the National Comorbidity Survey. *Archives of General Psychiatry, 53,* 159–168.

Makkes, P.C, Schuurs, A.H.B, Thoden van Velzen, S.K. *et al.* (1987). Effect of a special dental program upon extreme dental anxiety. *Community Dentistry and Oral Epidemiology, 15,* 173.

Maltby, N., Kirsch, I., Mayers, M. & Allen, G.J. (2002). Virtual reality exposure therapy for the treatment of fear of flying: A controlled investigation. *Journal of Consulting and Clinical Psychology, 70,* 1112–1118.

Marks, I. (1975). Behavioural treatment of phobic and obsessive-compulsive disorders: A critical appraisal. In M. Hersen, R. Eisler & P. Miller (eds), *Progress in Behavior Modification,* vol. 1. New York: Academic Press.

Marks, I. (1987). *Fears, Phobias and Rituals.* Oxford: Oxford University Press.

Mathews, A.M. & Rezin, V.A. (1976). Imaginal exposure with dental phobics. *Behaviour Research and Therapy, 15,* 321–328.

McCarthy, G.W. & Craig, K.D. (1995). Flying therapy for flying phobia. *Aviation Space and Environmental Medicine, 66*(12), 1179–1184.

McIsaac, H.K, Thordarson, D.S, Shafran, R. *et al.* (1998). Claustrophobia and the magnetic resonance imaging procedure. *Journal of Behavioral Medicine, 21*(3), 255–268.

McNally, R.J. & Louro, C.E. (1992). Fear of flying in agoraphobia and simple phobia: distinguishing features. *Journal of Anxiety Disorders, 6*(4), 319–324.

Merckelbach, H., De Jong, P.J., Muris, P. and Van den Hot, M.A. (1996). The etiology of specific phobias: a review. *Clinical Psychology Review, 16,* 337–361.

Miller, M.P, Murphy, P.J. & Miller, T.P. (1978). Comparison of EMG feedback and progressive relaxation training in treating circumscribed anxiety stress reactions. *Journal of Consulting and Clinical Psychology,* 46, 1291–1298.

Mogotsi, M., Kaminer, D. & Stein, D.J. (2000). Quality of life in the anxiety disorders. *Harvard Review of Psychiatry, 8,* 273–282.

Mollema, E.D, Snoek, F.J., Ader, H.J. *et al.* (2001). Insulin-treated diabetes patients with fear of self-injecting or fear of self-testing: psychological comorbidity and general well-being. *Journal of Psychosomatic Research, 51*(5), 665–672.

Moore, R., Abrahamsen, R. & Brodsgaard, I. (1996). Hypnosis compared with group therapy and individual desensitisation for dental anxiety. *European Journal of Oral Science, 104,* 612–618.

Moore, R., Brodsgaard, I., Berggren, U. & Carlsson, S.G. (1991). Generalization of effects of dental fear treatment in a self-referred population of odontophobics. *Journal of Behavior Therapy and Experimental Psychiatry,* 22(4), 243–253.

Muhlberger, A., Hermann, M.J., Wiedman, G. *et al.* (2001). Repeated exposure of flight phobics to flights in virtual reality. *Behaviour Research and Therapy, 39,* 1033–1050.

Muris, P., De Jong, P.J., Merckelbach, H. & Van Zuuren, F. (1993). Is exposure therapy outcome affected by a monitoring coping style? *Advances in Behaviour Research and Therapy, 15,* 291–300.

Muris, P. & Merckelbach, H. (1997). Treating spider phobics with eye movement desensitisation and reprocessing: A controlled study. *Behavioural and Cognitive Psychotherapy, 25,* 39–50.

Muris, P., Merckelbach, H. & De Jong, P.J. (1995). Exposure therapy outcome in spider phobics: effects of monitoring and blunting coping styles. *Behaviour Research and Therapy, 33,* 461–464.

Muris, P., Merckelbach, H., Holdrinet, I. & Sijsenaar, M. (1998). Treating phobic children: Effects of EMDR versus exposure. *Journal of Consulting and Clinical Psychology, 66,* 193–198.

Muris, P., Merckelbach, H., Schmidt, H. & Tierney, S. (1999). Disgust sensitivity, trait anxiety and anxiety disorders symptoms in normal children. *Behaviour Research and Therapy, 37*(10), 953–961.

Muris, P., Merckelbach, H., Van Haaften, H. & Mayer, B. (1997). Eye movement desensitisation and reprocessing versus exposure in vivo. A single-session crossover study of spider-phobic children. *British Journal of Psychiatry, 171,* 82–86.

Nathan, P.E. & Gorman, J.M. (eds) (2002). *A Guide to Treatments that Work* (2nd edn). New York: Oxford University Press.

Ning, L. & Liddell, A. (1991). The effect of concordance in the treatment of clients with dental anxiety. *Behaviour Research and Therapy, 29*(4), 315–322.

Ollendick, T.H, King, N.J. & Frary, R.B. (1989). Fears in children and adolescents: reliability and generalizability across gender, age and nationality. *Behaviour Research and Therapy, 27,* 19–26.

Ollendick, T.H, King, N.J. & Muris, P. (2002). Fears and phobias in children: phenomenology, epidemiology and aetiology. *Child and Adolescent Mental Health, 7,* 98–106.

Ost, L.-G. (1996). One-session group treatment of spider phobia. *Behaviour Research and Therapy, 34,* 707–715.

Ost, L.-G., Alm, T., Bandberg, M. & Breitholtz, E. (2001). One versus five sessions of exposure and five sessions of cognitive therapy in the treatment of claustrophobia. *Behaviour Research and Therapy, 39,* 167–183.

Ost, L.-G., Brandberg, M. & Alm, T. (1997). One versus five sessions of exposure in the treatment of flying phobia. *Behaviour Research and Therapy, 35*(11), 987–996.

Ost, L.-G. & Csatlos, P. (2000). Probability ratings in claustrophobic patients and normal controls. *Behaviour Research and Therapy, 38,* 1107–1116.

Ost, L.-G, Fellenius, J. & Sterner, U. (1991). Applied tension, exposure *in vivo* and tension-only in the treatment of blood phobia. *Behaviour Research and Therapy, 29,* 561–574.

Ost, L.-G, Ferebee, I. & Furmack, T. (1997). One-session group therapy of spider phobia: Direct versus indirect treatments. *Behaviour Research and Therapy, 35,* 721–732.

Ost, L.-G., Hellstrom, K. & Kaver, A. (1992). One versus five sessions of exposure in the treatment of injection phobia. *Behaviour Therapy, 23,* 263–282.

Ost, L.-G., Johansson, J. & Jerremalm, A. (1982). Individual response patterns and the effects of different behavioral methods in the treatment of claustrophobia. *Behaviour Research and Therapy, 20,* 445–460.

Ost, L.-G , Lindahl, I.L, Sterner, U. & Jerremalm, A. (1984). Exposure *in vivo* versus applied relaxation in the treatment of blood phobia. *Behaviour Research and Therapy, 22,* 205–216.

Ost, L.-G., Salkovskis, P. & Hellstroem, K. (1991). One-session therapist directed exposure versus self-exposure in the treatment of spider phobia. *Behaviour Therapy, 22,* 407–422.

Ost, L.-G., Sterner, U. & Fellenius, J. (1989). Applied tension, applied relaxation and the combination in the treatment of blood phobia. *Behaviour Research and Therapy, 27,* 109–121.

Ost, L.-G, Stridh, B.M. & Wolff, M. (1998). A clinical study of spider phobia: prediction of outcome after self-help and therapist-directed treatment. *Behaviour Research and Therapy, 36,* 17–35.

Page, A.C. (1994). Blood-injury phobia. *Clinical Psychology Review, 14*(5), 443–461.

Rachman, S. (1992). A psychological approach to the study of comorbidity. *Clinical Psychology Review, 11,* 461–464.

Rachman, S. (1997). Claustrophobia. In G. Davey (ed.) *Phobias: A Handbook of Theory, Research and Treatment.* London: Wiley.

Ritchie, E.C. (2001). Psychological problems associated with mission-oriented protective gear. *Military Medicine, 166,* 83–84.

Rose, M.P. & McGlynn, F.D. (1997). Toward a standard experiment for studying post-treatment return of fear. *Journal of Anxiety Disorders, 11,* 263–277.

Roth, A. & Fonagy, P. (2005). *What Works for Whom? A Critical Review of Psychotherapy Research* (2nd edn). New York: Guilford Press.

Rothbaum, B.O., Hodges, L., Smith, S., Lee, J.H. & Price, L. (2000). A controlled study of virtual reality exposure therapy for fear of flying. *Journal of Consulting and Clinical Psychology, 68,* 1020–1026.

Roy-Byrne, P.P, Milgrom, P., Khoon-mei, T. *et al.* (1994). Psychopathology and psychiatric diagnosis in subjects with dental phobia. *Journal of Anxiety Disorders, 8,* 19–31.

Sawchuk, C.N., Lohr, J.M., Westendorf, D.H. *et al.* (2002). Emotional responding to fearful and disgusting stimuli in specific phobics. *Behaviour Research and Therapy, 40*(9), 1031–1046.

Shaw, D.W. & Thoresen, C.E. (1974). Effects of modeling and desensitisation in reducing dentist phobia. *Journal of Counseling Psychology, 21,* 415–420.

Smith, K.L, Kirkby, K.C, Montgomery, I.M. & Daniels, B.A. (1997). Computer-delivered modeling of exposure for spider phobia: relevant versus irrelevant exposure. *Journal of Anxiety Disorders, 11,* 489–497.

Smits, J., Telch, M.J. & Randall, P.K. (2002). An examination of the decline in fear and disgust during exposure based treatment. *Behaviour Research and Therapy, 40,* 1243–1253.

Starcevic, V. & Bogojevic, G. (1997). Comorbidity of panic disorder with agoraphobia and specific phobia: Relationship with the subtypes of specific phobia. *Comprehensive Psychiatry, 38*(6), 315–320.

Stern, J.M. & Jones, R.J. (1997). Publication bias: Evidence of delayed publication in a cohort study of clinical research projects. *British Medical Journal, 315,* 640–645.

Thom, A., Sartory, G. & Joehren, P. (2000). Comparison between one-session psychological treatment and benzodiazepine in dental phobia. *Journal of Consulting and Clinical Psychology, 68*(3), 378–387.

Thorpe, S.J. & Salkovskis, P.M. (1995). Phobic beliefs: Do cognitive factors play a role in specific phobias? *Behaviour Research and Therapy, 33,* 805–816.

Thorpe, S. J. & Salkovskis, P.M. (1997). The effect of one-session treatment for spider phobia on attentional bias and beliefs. *British Journal of Clinical Psychology, 36,* 225–241.

Van Gerwen, L.J. & Diekstra, R.F.W. (2000). Fear of flying treatment programs for passengers: An international review. *Aviation Space and Environmental Medicine, 71*(4), 430–437.

Van Gerwen, L.J., Spinhoven, P., Dieskstra, R.F.W. & Van Dyck, R. (1997). People who seek help for fear of flying: Typology of flying phobics. *Behavior Therapy, 28*(2), 237–251.

Walder, C.P., McCracken, J.S., Herbert, M. *et al.* (1987). Psychological intervention in civilian flying phobia: Evaluation and a three-year follow-up. *British Journal of Psychiatry, 151,* 494–498.

Wilhelm, F.H. & Roth, W.T. (1997). Clinical characteristics of flight phobia. *Journal of Anxiety Disorders, 11*(3), 241–261.

CHAPTER 21

Social Anxiety Disorder

Winnie Eng
City University of New York, USA
and
Richard G. Heimberg
Temple University, Philadelphia, USA

DESCRIPTION OF THE DISORDER

Social anxiety disorder, also referred to as social phobia (Liebowitz *et al.*, 2000), has as its essential feature an extreme fear of appearing anxious or doing or saying something embarrassing in social or performance situations, accompanied by a fear of negative evaluation by others (American Psychiatric Association, 1994). For a diagnosis to be made in adults, the individual must recognize that the fear is excessive. Frequently feared situations include public speaking, going to parties, meeting strangers and talking to people in authority (Holt *et al.*, 1992). The individual becomes anxious in anticipation of feared situations and often avoids them, leading to significant distress and interference in the person's life. When the person's anxiety is experienced in most social situations, he or she is further described as having the generalized subtype of social anxiety disorder. The majority of persons presenting for treatment for social anxiety disorder are of the generalized subtype.

Findings from the National Comorbidity Survey rank social anxiety disorder as the third most prevalent psychiatric disorder in the general population of the United States, with a lifetime prevalence rate of 13.3 % and a 1-year prevalence of 7.9 % (Kessler *et al.*, 1994), and the prevalence of social anxiety disorder appears to be increasing (Heimberg *et al.*, 2000). More recent analyses suggest that the lifetime prevalence rate of clinically significant social anxiety disorder is closer to 4 % (Narrow *et al.*, 2002), a figure that is still substantial. This disorder is typically reported to begin in adolescence, with the mean onset age ranging from 13 to 20 years (Hazen & Stein, 1995). However, many patients report lifelong difficulties with social anxiety, and the distribution of age of onset of social anxiety disorder may actually be bimodal (Juster, Brown & Heimberg, 1996). While social anxiety disorder has been found to occur approximately 1.4 times more frequently in women than in men in epidemiological studies (Magee *et al.*, 1996), a slight preponderance of males is typically reported in treatment settings (Chapman, Mannuzza & Fyer, 1995; Stein, 1997). This discrepancy perhaps reflects cultural intolerance of socially anxious men, who experience greater interference in negotiating social situations in which they are expected to be outgoing and assertive (Weinstock, 1999).

Social anxiety disorder can be extremely debilitating. The majority of socially anxious individuals presenting for treatment report numerous problems of social adjustment, including impairment in school, work, family and romantic relationships and friendships (Bruch, Fallon & Heimberg, 2003; Schneier et al., 1994). Persons with social anxiety disorder tend to be less educated, less likely to be married and of lower socioeconomic status compared to those without social anxiety (Katzelnick et al., 2001; Magee et al., 1996; Schneier et al., 1992). Social anxiety frequently co-occurs with other psychiatric conditions (such as the affective disorders), most often with an earlier age of onset than the comorbid disorder (Magee et al., 1996; Schneier et al., 1992; Wittchen & Fehm, 2003). Individuals with social anxiety disorder are also more likely than persons without the disorder to abuse alcohol in efforts to reduce their discomfort (Amies, Gelder & Shaw, 1983; Kushner, Sher & Beitman, 1990; Wittchen & Fehm, 2003). The generalized form of social anxiety is highly familial (Stein et al., 1998), associated with greater comorbidity (Mannuzza et al., 1995), and generally has a more chronic and disabling course than other forms of the disorder (Chartier, Hazen & Stein, 1998; Reich et al., 1994). Despite its prevalence and associated impairment, many persons suffering from social anxiety disorder do not recognize that they have a condition for which effective treatments are available, with only 5.4 % seeking care from a mental health practitioner during their lifetime (Davidson et al., 1993; Schneier et al., 1992). In one study, one of the most frequently cited barriers to treatment for individuals with social anxiety was a fear of what others might think or say (Olfson et al., 2000).

COGNITIVE AND BEHAVIOURAL THERAPIES

Over the past decade, a number of studies have examined the efficacy of psychological (mostly cognitive-behavioural) treatments for social anxiety disorder. The most commonly investigated treatments have been in vivo exposure (with or without the addition of cognitive restructuring techniques), social skills training, and relaxation training. The International Consensus Group on Depression and Anxiety's 'Consensus Statement on Social Anxiety Disorder' concluded that there is good evidence for the efficacy of exposure-based cognitive-behavioural interventions for social anxiety (Ballenger et al., 1998). Accordingly, these interventions receive the bulk of our attention in this review.

Exposure Treatments

Exposure to feared situations is a central component of most treatments for social anxiety disorder. Exposure can be conducted either imaginally, in role plays or in vivo, to help clients habituate to anxiety-provoking situations and to provide an opportunity to gather disconfirmatory information and apply active coping skills. A substantial number of studies have demonstrated the superiority of exposure treatments to progressive relaxation training (Alström et al., 1984; Al-Kubaisy et al., 1992), pill placebo (Turner, Beidel & Jacob, 1994a), waiting-list controls (Butler et al., 1984; Newman et al., 1994) and a control therapy (Alström et al., 1984).

Combined Exposure and Cognitive Restructuring

Treatments that combine exposure techniques and cognitive restructuring are by far the most extensively researched psychosocial interventions for social anxiety disorder. Cognitive models of social anxiety disorder (see, for example, Beck, Emery & Greenberg, 1985; Clark & Wells, 1995; Rapee & Heimberg, 1997) suggest that the development and maintenance of social anxiety arises from distortions in the content of cognitions and in the way that individuals process information related to social-evaluative situations. Persons with social anxiety disorder experience anxiety in social situations because they evaluate their own performance in an excessively critical manner and believe that others hold excessively high standards for their behaviour, leading to negative expectations for social consequences (such as rejection or loss of social status). Avoidance of social situations often becomes a maladaptive learned response that effectively reduces anxiety in the moment but precludes the acquisition of adequate coping skills and the realistic appraisal of social outcomes. Thus, the vicious interaction of anxious arousal, negative thoughts and active behavioural avoidance provides the setting for the development of chronic problems with social anxiety. Most of the cognitive techniques employed in published studies of the treatment of social anxiety disorder are derived from the works of Aaron Beck (for example, Beck *et al.*, 1979, 1985) and Albert Ellis (for example, Ellis, 1962).

Heimberg's cognitive-behavioural group therapy (CBGT) (Heimberg & Becker, 2002) was initially derived from the Beckian tradition and serves as an example of a widely studied, empirically supported cognitive-behavioural treatment protocol for social anxiety disorder. In CBGT, the format of a small co-educational group of about six clients led by two therapists provides a 'built-in' exposure to social interactions. An initial psychoeducation component provides the client with accurate information about the cognitive, physiological and behavioural components of social anxiety and increases their awareness and understanding about their disorder. In teaching the skills of cognitive restructuring, self-monitoring is initiated to identify the thinking errors in clients' evaluations of social situations. Clients also learn an efficient routine for questioning the content of their anxiety-related thoughts. Before role-played exposures to simulated versions of personally feared situations, clients examine their negative anticipatory thoughts and substitute more evidence-based and less catastrophic alternative thoughts. During these role plays, clients practise their newly acquired views of feared situations and, at the same time, test the hypothesis that their anxiety will diminish with continued exposure to the feared situation. Thereafter, clients agree to expose themselves to feared situations between sessions and to practise cognitive restructuring skills as was done in session. Thus, CBGT employs both systematic therapist-directed in-session exposures and homework assignments for *in vivo* exposure and self-administered cognitive restructuring to address each client's individual fears.

Previous studies of CBGT have reported its superiority over a credible attention placebo control comprised of education and discussion regarding the nature of social anxiety and group support (Heimberg *et al.*, 1990). After 12 weeks of treatment both groups showed significant improvements, with the CBGT group rated as significantly less impaired than the control group by a clinical assessor. At a six-month follow-up, 81 % of CBGT patients were improved, compared to 47 % of controls. At a follow-up assessment four to six years post-treatment, 89 % of those who had received CBGT reported significant improvements in symptoms and impairment compared to 44 % of the control group, on several clinician-rated, self-report, and behavioural measures (Heimberg *et al.*, 1993).

In a comparative study of CBGT, exposure alone, and a waiting list, CBGT produced post-test results that were equivalent to those achieved by exposure, and both treatments were superior to the waiting list (Hope, Heimberg & Bruch, 1995a). Furthermore, Hope, Herbert & White (1995b) and Brown, Heimberg & Juster (1995) reported that CBGT was efficacious for the more severely impaired clients with the generalized subtype of social anxiety and/or comorbid avoidant personality disorder, although the group with generalized social anxiety disorder remained more impaired than the group with nongeneralized social anxiety disorder after treatment.

Lucas & Telch (1993) compared outcome across three treatment conditions: CBGT, an individual approach to CBT that used the same basic approach as the group treatment and educational supportive group therapy (the control condition used by Heimberg *et al.*, 1990). Clients in both the group and individual CBT conditions were significantly more improved than controls. There were no differences between the active treatments on clinical measures; however, the group was more cost-effective. A similar outcome was reported by Öst *et al.* (1995). In contrast, Stangier *et al.* (2003) reported that an individual CBT based on the model of social anxiety proposed by Clark & Wells (1995) was superior to group CBT on measures of social anxiety at post-treatment and at a six-month follow-up in a sample of clients with generalized social anxiety disorder. A controlled study of an individual CBT programme for social anxiety developed by Heimberg and colleagues (Hope *et al.*, 2000) was completed (Zaider *et al.*, 2003), and preliminary analyses suggested that this individual treatment may also be more efficacious than group treatment.

Component Analysis of Cognitive-Exposure Techniques

Research examining whether cognitive techniques enhance the efficacy of exposure has yielded mixed results. Hope *et al.* (1995a), Scholing & Emmelkamp (1993, 1996) and Taylor *et al.* (1997) reported that a combined exposure and cognitive restructuring package was not more effective than exposure alone, whereas Mattick & Peters (1988) and Mattick, Peters & Clarke (1989) found that a combined package was superior to exposure alone on certain measures of cognition, behaviour and end-state functioning. Some comparative studies found that only patients who received combined treatment showed continued improvement at follow-up (Butler *et al.*, 1984; Mattick *et al.*, 1989) while no differences at follow-up were reported by others (Hope *et al.*, 1995a; Taylor *et al.*, 1997). It is difficult to draw conclusions about the relative efficacy of 'cognitive restructuring combined with exposure' versus 'exposure alone' from this collection of studies and its often conflicting and equivocal results (but see the section on meta-analyses below).

It is important to note that, strictly speaking, exposure is rarely administered alone and therefore the question of whether exposure should or should not be combined with other techniques like cognitive restructuring may be off the mark. In fact, it may be difficult to tell the difference between the two, and this exercise may not be especially worthwhile (Rodebaugh, Holaway & Heimberg, 2004). Many exposure treatments, especially those in which exposure is therapist administered, include interactions over patient skill, visibility of anxiety, and coping strategies, either in getting the client ready for an exposure or in debriefing the exposure experience (Newman *et al.*, 1994; Turk, Fresco & Heimberg, 1999). If the combination of exposure and cognitive techniques is as effective as exposure alone, then only half the amount of exposure is necessary in combined treatments. Many mental health professionals may lack the resources for creating optimal exposure exercises (for example, providing an audience for a public speaking exposure), so techniques for cognitive restructuring may be applied as a practical and effective adjunct to systematized exposure exercises.

Social Skills Training

Cognitive-behavioural models of social anxiety suggests that distorted negative cognitions may lead to deficient social performance among persons with social anxiety but that many of these persons could perform adequately enough in the absence of anxiety (Clark & Wells, 1995; Rapee & Heimberg, 1997). However, others (Turner et al., 1994b) have suggested that the socially anxious person's negative expectancies may accurately reflect a history of poor performance and negative outcomes in social situations. From this perspective, actual deficits in social skills increase the probability of negative social outcomes and the individual's expectancies of future negative outcomes in social-evaluative situations lead to increased social avoidance, thereby further limiting the ability to develop social skills. The social skills model emphasizes the lack of effective social skills, whereas the cognitive-behavioural model suggests that social skills may be overshadowed by excessive and performance-impairing cognition and anxiety.

Social skills training (SST) is a structured therapy that involves training clients in interpersonal skills such as maintaining eye contact and active listening to enable effective performance in a variety of social situations. Techniques traditionally used in SST include therapist modelling, behavioural rehearsal, corrective feedback, social reinforcement and homework assignments. In one early controlled study of SST in clients with diagnoses of personality disorder or neurosis, Marzillier, Lambert & Kellet (1976) reported that 15 weeks of training produced improvements in social anxiety, social skills and clinical adjustment. However, these changes were not significantly different from those found in a wait-list control group. In several other uncontrolled studies, patients given social skills training demonstrated significant improvements in various aspects of social anxiety such as reductions in self-reported anxiety, depression and difficulty in social situations (Falloon, Lloyd & Harpin, 1981; Lucock & Salkovskis, 1988; Stravynski, Marks & Yule, 1982; Trower et al., 1978; Wlazlo et al., 1990). When CBGT was compared with a combination treatment of SST plus CBGT, significantly greater gains were demonstrated for the combined condition (Herbert et al., 2005). The efficacy data for SST are largely compromised by methodological problems such as lack of control groups and small sample sizes. Furthermore, the active component of these treatment-related changes is unclear, as SST includes inherent exposure opportunities.

A treatment combining exposure with SST has provided promising results. Social Effectiveness Training (SET) combines imaginal and therapist-directed exposure with SST and education in concurrent group and individual sessions (Turner et al., 1994b). A direct focus of SET is to teach clients to be aware of the social environment, through the instruction in and feedback on communication strategies, listening skills and presentation skills. Exposures in SET are longer than in CBGT, with the goal of habituation rather than active refutation of cognitions. Social effectiveness training is less well studied than CBGT. However, results of an uncontrolled pilot study with 13 persons with generalized social anxiety who completed SET showed significant improvements on self-report and clinician rated measures, as well as social skills effectiveness. At post-treatment, 84 % of completers were classified as having achieved either moderate or high endstate functioning. A two-year follow-up assessment of eight treatment completers indicated that all maintained their gains or showed additional improvement over time (Turner, Beidel & Cooley-Quille, 1995). Controlled treatment trials and dismantling studies of SET are needed to determine whether social skills training adds any benefit beyond that of exposure alone.

Relaxation Strategies

Applied relaxation training teaches the individual to identify anxiety immediately and to practise progressive muscle relaxation while in feared situations as a strategy for coping with social anxiety (Öst, 1987). The rationale for this treatment is that relaxation can help socially anxious persons to overcome excessive physiological arousal that can interfere with social performance. Öst, Jerremalm & Johansson (1981) randomly assigned 40 subjects to 10 individual sessions of SST or applied relaxation. The two types of treatments performed equally well on behavioural and self-report measures, although there seemed to be slightly better outcomes for applied relaxation among persons who showed the greatest physiological response in a behaviour test. A subsequent controlled study (Jerremalm, Jansson & Öst, 1986) found that applied relaxation appeared to be less effective than a cognitive treatment on self-report measures but superior to a waiting list on both behavioural and physiological indices. A more recent study comparing cognitive therapy (see Clark et al., 2003), exposure plus applied relaxation, and a wait-list control (Clark et al., 2006) showed a greater effectiveness of the cognitive therapy condition at post-treatment and one-year follow-up. Minimal improvements following the use of relaxation training without the applied focus (Al-Kubaisy et al., 1992; Alström et al., 1984) emphasize the importance of practising relaxation during in vivo exposure to feared situations.

COMPARISONS AND COMBINATIONS OF CBT AND MEDICATION

The few studies that have compared the efficacy of CBT to that of medication treatments have been difficult to interpret because of a variety of methodological problems. One study indicated that CBT was more effective than buspirone for socially anxious musicians (Clark & Agras, 1991) and another reported that combined imaginal and in vivo exposure was more effective than the beta-adrenergic blocker atenolol (Turner, et al., 1994a). However, neither atenolol nor buspirone has surpassed placebo in the treatment of social anxiety disorder (Liebowitz et al., 1992; van Vliet et al., 1997).

Other studies show that there were few significant differences in relative efficacy between CBGT and the high-potency benzodiazepine clonazepam (Otto et al., 2000), the high-potency benzodiazepine alprazolam, the monoamine oxidase inhibitor phenelzine, or placebo (Gelernter et al., 1991). In contrast, Clark et al. (2003) reported that individual CBT was superior to fluoxetine and placebo at post-treatment and one-year follow-up, although there was no difference between the fluoxetine or placebo. However, in these studies, instructions for self-directed in vivo exposure were included as part of the medication treatments.

Phenelzine has long been considered the best established pharmacological treatment for social anxiety, demonstrating the largest effect size across controlled trials (Blanco et al., 2003). However, it is not considered a first-line medication because of the risk of hypertensive reaction and the associated need for dietary restrictions. In a large, multisite collaborative study, Heimberg et al. (1998) examined the relative efficacy of CBGT, phenelzine (without exposure instructions), attention placebo, and pill placebo in 133 patients with social anxiety disorder. An important aspect of this study is that it controlled for the allegiance effect (the effect whereby more favourable results tend to be found for treatments conducted in settings of compatible theoretical orientation) by conducting all treatments at both a centre known for biological psychiatry and a centre known for cognitive-behavioural treatments. After the first six weeks of treatment, individuals receiving phenelzine were rated as more improved and less anxious than those in the other conditions. Following 12 weeks of treatment, CBGT and phenelzine were associated with similar rates of treatment response and were both superior to the control conditions. In a follow-up of post-treatment responders who received monthly maintenance treatment for six months followed by six months of follow-up, CBGT responders were less likely than phenelzine responders to relapse (Liebowitz et al., 1999). These results suggest that phenelzine may provide faster symptom relief, but CBGT may provide greater protection against relapse in the long term.

Empirical investigations of the efficacy of combined CBT and pharmacological treatment are limited and have yielded mixed results. Falloon et al. (1981) reported that the efficacy of social skills training was not enhanced by adding the beta-adrenergic blocker propranolol. Similarly, CBT plus buspirone was not more effective than CBT alone (Clark & Agras, 1991). Preliminary results from a multisite treatment outcome study suggest that the combination of phenelzine and group CBT was more likely to be superior to placebo than either CBGT or phenelzine alone (Heimberg, 2002). Pilot data also suggest that the combination of brief exposure therapy with the broad-band antibiotic D-cycloserine was superior to exposure plus placebo (Hofmann et al., 2006).

Initial results from a study conducted by Blomhoff and colleagues (2001) showed that the SSRI sertraline, exposure, and their combination were all superior to placebo after 12 weeks. The active treatments showed equivalent response after 24 weeks, although only the sertraline groups were significantly better than placebo. Follow-up one year after the beginning of treatment revealed, however, that patients who received exposure alone continued to improve whereas patients receiving sertraline alone or combined with exposure tended to deteriorate (Haug et al., 2003). Another multisite study examined the relative efficacy of group CBT, the SSRI fluoxetine, and their combination. The authors failed to find evidence for the enhanced efficacy of combined treatment compared to group CBT or fluoxetine alone, which also did not differ (Davidson et al., 2004).

META-ANALYSES

To date, there have been four peer-reviewed meta-analyses that have examined the relative importance of components of cognitive-behavioural treatments and compared cognitive-behavioural treatments to other interventions (Federoff & Taylor, 2001; Feske & Chambless, 1995; Gould et al., 1997; Taylor, 1996). In general, effect sizes tended to be moderate, with no differences in attrition across CBT variants. In Feske & Chambless' (1995) meta-analysis, treatments that integrated cognitive restructuring and exposure yielded effect sizes similar to exposure alone on both post-treatment and follow-up measures of social anxiety, cognitive symptoms, depression and general anxiety. Taylor (1996) compared the effect sizes of cognitive restructuring alone, exposure treatments, cognitive restructuring combined with exposure, and SST. Effect sizes for all interventions on measures of social anxiety were similar, and all surpassed those of waiting-list controls. However, only the combination of cognitive restructuring and exposure showed greater effect sizes than placebo controls. Furthermore, within-in group effect sizes for all active treatments tended to increase from post-treatment to follow-up assessment.

Two more meta-analyses examined the relative effectiveness of cognitive-behavioural treatments and pharmacotherapy for social anxiety disorder. After examining 24 studies, Gould *et al.* (1997) reported that both CBT (including cognitive restructuring, exposure, SST, systematic desensitization, flooding, and anxiety management) and pharmacotherapy were superior to control conditions and were associated with similar effect sizes on measures of social anxiety, cognitive change and depression. Treatments that included an exposure component also yielded significantly larger effect sizes than either cognitive restructuring alone or SST. For those studies reporting follow-up information (seven on CBT, one on pharmacotherapy), within-groups effects sizes revealed modest improvement after treatment. Although no differences were found for group versus individual treatment, CBGT was the most cost-effective intervention for social anxiety disorder, echoing the earlier finding of Lucas & Telch (1993).

Federoff & Taylor (2001) also provide evidence that pharmacotherapies and cognitive-behavioural therapies achieve similar effect sizes. In this meta-analysis of 108 outcome trials for social anxiety, benzodiazepines, but not the monoamine oxidase inhibitors or SSRIs, produced larger effects than CBT (including cognitive restructuring, exposure, combined cognitive restructuring and exposure, applied relaxation and SST) on self-report but not observer-rated, measures of social anxiety.

SOCIAL ANXIETY IN CHILDREN AND ADOLESCENTS

Social anxiety is often evident early in life and may be diagnosed in children as young as eight years old (Beidel & Turner, 1998). Furthermore, when the social fears of children continue to be expressed through late adolescence they are more likely to be associated with a poor prognosis for recovery (Davidson *et al.*, 1993; Mannuzza *et al.*, 1995). The clinical presentation of social anxiety in children is similar to that of adults, with comparable somatic symptoms and feared situations. However, because of the limited cognitive development of younger children, they may not report specific negative cognitions (Beidel & Turner, 1998). Social anxiety in children is also associated with significant distress and impairment, including poor school achievement, greater loneliness, and difficulties with social relationships (Albano, Chorpita & Barlow, 1996a). Socially anxious children and adolescents may also suffer from elevated rates of general anxiety, depression, and secondary alcohol abuse (Beidel, Turner & Morris, 1999). Although social anxiety is one of the more common principal diagnoses in children who present for treatment (Albano *et al.*, 1996b; Chapman *et al.*, 1995; Last *et al.*, 1992; Vasey, 1995), developmentally sensitive treatment programmes have only recently become a focus of empirical investigations.

Social Effectiveness Therapy for Children

An intervention called Social Effectiveness Therapy for children (SET-C) has been developed to treat socially anxious preadolescent children (ages 8 to 12) (Beidel, Turner & Morris, 1996). It was adapted from the adult SET programme (Turner et al., 1994b) and comprises separate group social skills training and individual exposure sessions for 12 weeks. A unique aspect of this treatment is that each child is paired with a non-anxious peer helper to assist in interactions in age-appropriate social outings. Parent involvement is limited to assistance with conducting the structured interaction homework assignments. Cognitive restructuring is not a fixed component of SET-C because the authors believe that children in Piaget's concrete operational stage may not endorse catastrophic negative thoughts during socially stressful situations.

A recent study compared SET-C with a nonspecific control intervention in 67 children (ages 8 to 12) with social anxiety (Beidel, Turner & Morris, 2000). Following 12 weeks of treatment, the SET-C group was significantly more improved than the control group on self-report and parent ratings of anxiety, as well as independent observers' ratings of skill and anxiety during behavioural tasks. Furthermore, 67 % of the children in the SET-C condition no longer met diagnostic criteria for social phobia at post-assessment compared with 5 % of those in the control group. Treatment gains were maintained at a six-month follow-up assessment of 73 % of the original SET-C group. Further, at three-year follow-up, post-treatment responders largely maintained their treatment gains and 72 % of children in the treatment condition no longer met diagnostic criteria (Beidel et al., 2005).

Cognitive-Behavioural Group Treatment for Adolescents

Cognitive-behavioural group treatment for adolescents with social anxiety disorder (CBGT-A) (Albano et al., 1995a) was first pursued with an adaptation of Heimberg's CBGT for adults. In addition to psychoeducation, cognitive restructuring, and exposure, CBGT-A incorporates social skills and problem-solving skills training to address specific concerns of socially anxious youth (Albano, 1995). Parents attend four key sessions involving psychoeducation, assessment of family interactions, exposure planning and the use of skills following treatment. Albano et al. (1995b) present data on the treatment of five adolescents who completed 16 sessions of CBGT-A. Three months after treatment, the social anxiety of four participants was reduced to subclinical levels. At a one-year follow-up the four adolescents showed no social anxiety or other mental disorder; the remaining adolescent reported subclinical social anxiety.

Hayward et al. (2000) compared CBGT-A with a no-treatment control condition for female adolescents with social anxiety (mean age = 15.8 years). Eleven participants who completed 16 weeks of CBGT-A showed greater reductions on self- and parent ratings of interference and on self-reported social anxiety than the 22 participants in the control condition. At post-treatment, 46 % (5/11) of the CBGT-A group no longer met criteria for social anxiety, compared to only 4.5 % (1/22) of the control group. However, at a one-year follow-up assessment, these differences were no longer significant. Additional analyses suggest that CBGT-A may reduce the frequency of major depression in participants with a previous history of major depression, with 17 % relapse in depression among CBGT-A participants with this history, compared to 64 % in the control group, over the course of the study.

The Coping Cat Programme

Other existing controlled trials examining the efficacy of cognitive restructuring and exposure therapy for anxious children have included mixed diagnostic samples, limiting the specificity of the results for social anxiety disorder. In the following studies, socially anxious children comprised 24 % to 33 % of the total samples. Kendall's (1994) Coping Cat programme combines relaxation training with exposure and cognitive restructuring to alleviate children's fears. This programme provides an age-appropriate format for leading younger children through cognitive restructuring steps. Parental involvement in therapy is mainly in a supportive role and collaboration within session is variable. After 16 sessions, this intervention was superior to a wait-list condition for children (ages 9 to 13) with either overanxious disorder, separation anxiety disorder or DSM-III-R (American Psychiatric Association, 1987) avoidant disorder of childhood, which was later subsumed under social anxiety disorder in the DSM-IV (American Psychiatric Association, 1994). Improvements were found on child self-report measures, parent ratings of their children's anxiety and social competence as well as observer ratings from a videotaped behavioural task. However, no changes were found on teacher ratings. Sixty-four per cent of the treated group no longer met criteria for their principal diagnosis at post-treatment. Results from a two- to five-year follow-up showed that treatment gains were maintained (Kendall & Southam-Gerow, 1996). Kendall *et al.* (1997) replicated these findings in another sample of 60 children (ages 9 to 13) with various anxiety disorders. More than half (53 %) of the treated children no longer met diagnostic criteria for their primary anxiety disorder compared with 6 % of the wait-list control group. Treatment gains were maintained at a one-year follow-up. There were no outcome differences by diagnostic group.

Because one of the hypothesized mechanisms of transmission for anxiety is observational learning and modelling within the family (Bruch, 1989; Bruch & Heimberg, 1994), additional involvement of the family in treatment may add to the efficacy of CBT. Barrett, Dadds & Rapee (1996) examined the efficacy of Kendall's intervention, alone or in combination with family anxiety management treatment (FAM), for 79 children with separation anxiety, overanxious disorder, or social anxiety disorder. FAM comprises strategies to support and encourage adaptive behaviour and to extinguish maladaptive behaviour, a component for the management of parental anxiety and training in problem-solving skills to extend the child's progress in treatment. The combined treatment was superior to child treatment alone on several clinical and self-report measures after treatment and at 12-month follow-up. Again, no differential response based on diagnosis was noted.

Since none of the studies of Kendall's treatment included specific measures of social anxiety, it is difficult to draw conclusions regarding its efficacy for children with social anxiety disorder. However, they seemed to fare as well as children with other diagnoses, calling into question the need for specialized social anxiety treatments for children. Further evaluation of the outcomes of this treatment for children with social anxiety disorder, in comparison to treatments focused specifically on social anxiety, in studies including specific measurement of social anxiety, appears to be warranted.

INTERPERSONAL PSYCHOTHERAPY

A review of the literature suggests that a small number of non-cognitive or behavioural treatment alternatives exist for the treatment of social anxiety (for a review see Lipsitz & Marshall, 2001). These studies show promising results but are limited by a lack of rigorous methodology, such as incorporation of control groups or larger sample sizes. Promising results come from a recent uncontrolled trial applying interpersonal psychotherapy (IPT) to nine individuals with social anxiety disorder (Lipsitz et al., 1999). IPT is a time-limited treatment approach that focuses on disruptions in the psychosocial and interpersonal context which may underlie psychological disorders. Treatment includes the identification and exploration of primary interpersonal problems, examination of communication styles, decisions analysis and role playing. Following 14 weeks of treatment, seven (78 %) clients were classified as responders by independent evaluators and general symptom improvement was found on several clinician-administered and self-rated measures of social anxiety. Further controlled evaluation in a larger sample is needed.

GAPS IN THE EVIDENCE BASE

An important issue in treatment outcome is that many clients do not achieve as much change as would be desirable, either in terms of symptoms or in terms of the impact of symptom change in other areas of life. Previous research on the clinical significance of symptom change immediately following a course of CBGT for social anxiety demonstrated a significant improvement in clients' self-perceived quality of life (Safren et al., 1997). Further, improvements from CBGT were shown to be maintained for several months after treatment (Eng et al., 2001). However, these improved ratings still fell below the normative average at post-test and follow-up.

Of major concern is the limited number of therapists who can recognize and effectively treat social anxiety disorder. Clinicians are most likely to recognize and diagnose a psychological problem in socially anxious persons who present with a comorbid condition – typically major depressive disorder or alcoholism – and are most likely to treat the comorbid condition before the social anxiety (Ballenger et al., 1998). In addition, studies have reported that, among the anxiety disorders, the most highly utilized psychosocial treatments are dynamic psychotherapy (Goisman, Warshaw & Keller, 1999) and supportive therapy (Rowa et al., 2000). There appears to be an underutilization of efficacious treatments in favour of those that have been less well studied. One promising study demonstrated that general practitioners may be trained successfully to provide brief exposure therapy (eight sessions of 15 to 20 minutes' duration) within a primary-care setting (Blomhoff et al., 2001; Haug et al., 2000; Haug et al., 2003).

One advantage of CBT for social anxiety is that its methods are manualized. However, there are not enough people who know how to administer these manuals effectively and manualized treatments are not always so simple to implement in the real world. A number of clients also have a complicated presentation that may require specific additional interventions targeted at depressive symptoms, anger management, or other adjustment difficulties. It is with these clients that there often appears to be a disconnect between the protocols described in the treatment outcome literature and the actual implementation of treatment in the real world.

Clinically relevant areas for future research also include expanding on the limited literature on treating social anxiety in children and adolescents. At the other end of the spectrum, the phenomenological experience of social anxiety in older adults has also not been adequately investigated. Mrozowski *et al.* (2001) found that older adults reported significantly lower levels of anxiety for most social situations but that their anxiety was less variable across situations on self-report measures in comparison to younger adults. Furthermore, Sheikh & Salzman (1995) suggest that social anxiety concerns of the elderly may be focused more on eating and writing in public because of the presence of dentures and tremors. Given the greater chance of medical problems and concurrent medications in the elderly, CBT may be an especially attractive alternative to pharmacological treatment (although the relative and combined effects of CBT and medications is another important area for research among clients of all ages). To our knowledge, there have not been studies that have investigated the effectiveness of specific treatments for social anxiety in the elderly. Similarly, we know little about the nature and treatment of social anxiety among persons who have been divorced or bereaved and who face new challenges in social interaction.

SUMMARY

Social anxiety is a problem of high prevalence, great chronicity, and substantial personal cost. It benefits most from exposure treatments, although there is some evidence that the use of cognitive restructuring techniques may enhance exposure outcomes. Treatment for clients with the generalized subtype of social anxiety disorder may be associated with poorer outcomes, despite a rate of improvement similar to that of clients with less pervasive fears, and these clients may require a longer course of treatment. There is limited evidence for the efficacy of social skills training, and there are differences among researchers regarding the central role of social skills deficits.

Pharmacological interventions may be associated with more rapid improvement but CBT may confer greater protection against relapse after treatment termination. Further controlled research studies are necessary for determining the efficacy of combined pharmacological and psychological treatments. These findings are tentative in light of the relatively short follow-up periods reported in the majority of studies. More intensive, controlled research into treatment outcome for socially anxious children and adolescents, as well as the elderly, is needed to address the different developmentally specific manifestations of social anxiety across the life span.

FURTHER READING

Beidel, D.C. & Turner, S.M. (1998). *Shy Children, Phobic Adults: The Nature and Treatment of Social Phobia*. Washington, DC: American Psychological Association.
Heimberg, R.G. & Becker, R.E. (2002). *Cognitive-Behavioral Group Therapy for Social Phobia: Basic Mechanisms and Clinical Strategies*. New York, NY: Guilford Press.
Hope, D.A., Heimberg, R.G., Juster, H.R. & Turk, C.L. (2000). *Managing Social Anxiety: A Cognitive-Behavioral Therapy Approach*. San Antonio, TX: Psychological Corporation.

REFERENCES

Albano, A.M. (1995). Treatment of social anxiety in adolescents. *Cognitive and Behavioural Practice,* 2, 271–298.

Albano, A.M., Chorpita, B.F. & Barlow, D.H. (1996a). Childhood anxiety disorders. In E.J. Mash & R.A. Barkley (eds), *Child Psychopathology* (pp. 196–241). New York: Guilford Press.

Albano, A.M., Chorpita, B.F., DiBartolo, P.M. & Barlow, D.H. (1996b). *Comorbidity in a Clinical Sample of Children and Adolescents with Anxiety Disorders: Characteristics and Developmental Considerations.* Unpublished manuscript, State University of New York at Albany.

Albano, A.M., DiBartolo, P.M., Heimberg, R.G. & Barlow, D.H. (1995a). Children and adolescents: assessment and treatment. In R.G. Heimberg, M.R. Liebowitz, D.A. Hope & F.R. Schneier (eds), *Social Phobia: Diagnosis, Assessment and Treatment* (pp. 387–425). New York: Guilford Press.

Albano, A.M., Marten, P.A., Holt, C.S. *et al.* (1995b). Cognitive-behavioral group treatment for adolescent social phobia: A preliminary study. *Journal of Nervous and Mental Disease, 183,* 649–656.

Al-Kubaisy, T., Marks, I.M., Logsdail, S. *et al.* (1992). Role of exposure homework in phobia reduction: a controlled study. *Behavior Therapy, 23,* 599–621.

Alström, J.E., Nordlund, C.L., Persson, G. *et al.* (1984). Effects of four treatment methods on social phobic patients not suitable for insight-oriented psychotherapy. *Acta Psychiatrica Scandinavica, 70,* 97–110.

American Psychiatric Association (1987). *Diagnostic and Statistical Manual of Mental Disorders* (3rd edn, revised). Washington, DC: APA.

American Psychiatric Association (1994). *Diagnostic and Statistical Manual of Mental Disorders* (4th edn). Washington, DC: APA.

Amies, P.L., Gelder, M.G. & Shaw, P.M. (1983). Social phobia: A comparative clinical study. *British Journal of Psychiatry, 142,* 174–179.

Ballenger, J.C., Davidson, J.R.T., Lecrubier, Y. *et al.* (1998). Consensus statement on social anxiety disorder from the International Consensus Group on Depression and Anxiety. *Journal of Clinical Psychiatry, 59* (suppl. 17), 54–60.

Barrett, P.M., Dadds, M.R., Rapee, R.M. & Ryan, S.M. (1996). Family intervention for childhood anxiety: a controlled trial. *Journal of Consulting and Clinical Psychology, 64,* 333–342.

Beck, A., Emery, G. & Greenberg, R.L. (1985). *Anxiety Disorders and Phobias: A Cognitive Perspective.* New York: Basic Books.

Beck, A., Rush, A., Shaw, B. & Emery, G. (1979). *Cognitive Therapy of Depression.* New York: Guilford Press.

Beidel, D.C. & Turner, S.M. (1998). *Shy Children, Phobic Adults: The Nature and Treatment of Social Phobia.* Washington, DC: American Psychological Association.

Beidel, D.C., Turner, S.M. & Morris, T.L. (1996). *Social Effectiveness Training for Children: A Treatment Manual.* Unpublished manuscript, Medical University of Charleston, South Carolina.

Beidel, D.C., Turner, S.M. & Morris, T.L. (1999). Psychopathology of childhood social phobia. *Journal of the American Academy of Child and Adolescent Psychiatry, 38,* 643–650.

Beidel, D.C., Turner, S.M. & Morris, T.L. (2000). Behavioral treatment of childhood social phobia. *Journal of Consulting and Clinical Psychology, 68,* 1072–1080.

Beidel, D.C., Turner, S.M., Young, B. & Paulson, A. (2005). Social effectiveness therapy for children: three year follow-up. *Journal of Consulting and Clinical Psychology, 73,* 721–725.

Blanco, C., Schneier, F.R., Schmidt, A. *et al.* (2003). Pharmacological treatment of social anxiety disorder: A meta-analysis. *Depression and Anxiety, 18,* 29–40.

Blomhoff, S., Haug, T.T., Hellstrøm, K. *et al.* (2001). Randomized controlled general practice trial of sertraline, exposure therapy, and combined treatment in generalised social phobia. *British Journal of Psychiatry, 179,* 23–30.

Brown, E.J., Heimberg, R.G. & Juster, H.R. (1995). Social phobia subtype and avoidant personality disorder: effect on severity of social phobia, impairment, and outcome of cognitive-behavioral treatment. *Behavior Therapy, 26,* 467–486.

Bruch, M.A. (1989). Familial and developmental antecedents of social phobia: Issues and findings. *Clinical Psychology Review, 9,* 37–47.

Bruch, M.A., Fallon, M. & Heimberg, R.G. (2003). Social phobia and difficulties in occupational adjustment. *Journal of Counseling Psychology, 50*, 109–117.

Bruch, M.A. & Heimberg, R.G. (1994). Differences in perceptions of parental and personal characteristics between generalized and nongeneralized social phobics. *Journal of Anxiety Disorders, 8*, 155–168.

Butler, G., Cullington, A., Munby, M. *et al.* (1984). Exposure and anxiety management in the treatment of social phobia. *Journal of Consulting and Clinical Psychology, 52*, 642–650.

Chapman, T.F., Mannuzza, S. & Fyer, A.J. (1995). Epidemiology and family studies of social phobia. In R.G. Heimberg, M.R. Liebowitz, D.A. Hope & F.R. Schneier (eds), *Social Phobia: Diagnosis, Assessment, and Treatment* (pp. 21–40). New York: Guilford Press.

Chartier, M.J., Hazen, A.L. & Stein, M.B. (1998). Lifetime patterns of social phobia: A retrospective study of the course of social phobia in a nonclinical population. *Depression and Anxiety, 7*, 113–121.

Clark, D.B. & Agras, W.S. (1991). The assessment and treatment of performance anxiety in musicians. *American Journal of Psychiatry, 148*, 598–605.

Clark, D.M., Ehlers, A., Hackman, A. *et al.* (2006). Cognitive therapy versus exposure plus applied relaxation in social phobia: A randomized controlled trial. *Journal of Consulting and Clinical Psychology, 74*, 568–378.

Clark, D.M., Ehlers, A., McManus, F. *et al.* (2003). Cognitive therapy versus fluoxetine in generalized social phobia: a randomized placebo controlled trial. *Journal of Consulting and Clinical Psychology, 71*, 1058–1067.

Clark, D.M. & Wells, A. (1995). A cognitive model of social phobia. In R.G. Heimberg, M.R. Liebowitz, D.A. Hope & F. R. Schneier (eds), *Social Phobia: Diagnosis, Assessment and Treatment* (pp. 69–93). New York: Guilford Press.

Davidson, J.R., Foa, E.B., Huppert, J.D. *et al.* (2004). Fluoxetine, comprehensive cognitive behavioral therapy, and placebo in generalized social phobia. *Archives of General Psychiatry, 61*, 1005–1013.

Davidson, J.R., Hughes, D.L., George, L.K. & Blazer, D.G. (1993). The epidemiology of social phobia: findings from the Duke Epidemiological Catchment Area study. *Psychological Medicine, 23*, 709–718.

Ellis, A. (1962). *Reason and Emotion in Psychotherapy*. New York: Lyle Stuart.

Eng, W., Coles, M.E., Heimberg, R.G. & Safren, S.A. (2001). Quality of life following cognitive behavioral treatment for social anxiety disorder: preliminary findings. *Depression and Anxiety, 13*, 192–193.

Falloon, I.R.H., Lloyd, G.G. & Harpin, R.E. (1981). The treatment of social phobia: Real-life rehearsal with nonprofessional therapists. *Journal of Nervous and Mental Disease, 169*, 180–184.

Federoff, I.C. & Taylor, S. (2001). Psychological and pharmacological treatments for social phobia: A meta-analysis. *Journal of Clinical Psychopharmacology, 21*, 311–324.

Feske, U. & Chambless, D.L. (1995). Cognitive behavioral versus exposure only treatment for social phobia: A meta-analysis. *Behavior Therapy, 26*, 695–720.

Gelernter, C.S., Uhde, T.W., Cimbolic, P. *et al.* (1991). Cognitive-behavioral and pharmacological treatments for social phobia: a controlled study. *Archives of General Psychiatry, 48*, 938–945.

Goisman, R.M., Warshaw, M.G. & Keller, M.B. (1999). Psychosocial treatment prescriptions for generalized anxiety disorder, panic disorder, and social phobia, 1991–1996. *The American Journal of Psychiatry, 156*, 1819–1821.

Gould, R.A., Buckminster, S., Pollack, M.H. *et al.* (1997). Cognitive-behavioral and pharmacological treatment for social phobia: a meta-analysis. *Clinical Psychology: Science and Practice, 4*, 291–306.

Haug, T.T., Blomhoff, S., Hellstrøm, K. *et al.* (2003). Exposure therapy and sertraline in social phobia: 1-year follow-up of a randomised controlled trial. *British Journal of Psychiatry, 182*, 312–318.

Haug, T.T., Hellstrøm, K., Blomhoff, S. *et al.* (2000). The treatment of social phobia in general practice. Is exposure therapy feasible? *Family Practice, 17*, 114–118.

Hayward, C., Varady, A., Albano, A.M. *et al.* (2000). Cognitive-behavioral group therapy for social phobia in female adolescents: Results of a pilot study. *Journal of the American Academy of Child and Adolescent Psychiatry, 39*, 721–726.

Hazen, A.L. & Stein, M.B. (1995). Clinical phenomenology and comorbidity. In M.B. Stein (ed.) *Social Phobia: Clinical and Research Perspectives* (pp. 3–41). Washington, DC: American Psychiatric Press.

Heimberg, R.G. (2002). Cognitive behavioral therapy for social anxiety disorder: current status and future directions. *Biological Psychiatry, 51*, 101–108.

Heimberg, R.G. & Becker, R.E. (2002). *Cognitive-Behavioral Group Therapy for Social Phobia: Basic Mechanisms and Clinical Strategies*. New York, NY: Guilford Press.

Heimberg, R.G., Dodge, C.S., Hope, D.A. *et al.* (1990). Cognitive behavioral group treatment of social phobia: comparison to a credible placebo control. *Cognitive Therapy and Research, 14*, 1–23.

Heimberg, R.G., Liebowitz, M.R., Hope, D.A. *et al.* (1998). Cognitive-behavioral group therapy versus phenelzine in social phobia: 12-week outcome. *Archives of General Psychiatry, 55*, 1133–1141.

Heimberg, R.G., Salzman, D.G., Holt, C.S. & Blendell, K.A. (1993). Cognitive-behavioral group treatment for social phobia: Effectiveness at five-year followup. *Cognitive Therapy and Research, 17*, 325–339.

Heimberg, R.G., Stein, M.B., Hiripi, E. & Kessler, R.C. (2000). Trends in the prevalence of social phobia in the United States: A synthetic cohort analysis of changes over four decades. *European Psychiatry, 15*, 29–37.

Herbert, J.D., Gaudiano, B.A., Rheingold, A.A. *et al.* (2005). Social skills training augments the effectiveness of cognitive behavioral group therapy for social anxiety disorder. *Behavior Therapy, 36*, 125–138.

Hofmann, S.G., Meuret, A.E., Smits, J.A.J. *et al.* (2006). Augmentation of exposure therapy with D-cycloserine for social anxiety disorder. *Archives of General Psychiatry, 63*, 298–304.

Holt, C.S., Heimberg, R.G., Hope, D.A. & Liebowitz, M.R. (1992). Situational domains of social phobia. *Journal of Anxiety Disorders, 6*, 63–77.

Hope, D.A., Heimberg, R.G. & Bruch, M.A. (1995a). Dismantling cognitive-behavioral group therapy for social phobia. *Behaviour Research and Therapy, 33*, 637–650.

Hope, D.A., Heimberg, R.G., Juster, H.R. & Turk, C.L. (2000). *Managing Social Anxiety: A Cognitive-Behavioral Therapy Approach*. San Antonio, TX: Psychological Corporation.

Hope, D.A., Herbert, J.D. & White, C. (1995b). Diagnostic subtype, avoidant personality disorder, and efficacy of cognitive behavioral group therapy for social phobia. *Cognitive Therapy and Research, 19*, 285–303.

Jerremalm, A., Jansson, L. & Öst, L.G. (1986). Cognitive and physiological reactivity and the effects of different behavioral methods in the treatment of social phobia. *Behaviour Research and Therapy, 24*, 171–180.

Juster, H.R., Brown, E.J. & Heimberg, R.G. (1996). Sozialphobie [social phobia]. In J. Margraf (ed.), *Lehrbuch der verhaltenstherapie [Textbook of Behaviour Therapy]* (pp. 43–59). Berlin: Springer-Verlag.

Katzelnick, D.J., Kobak, K.A., DeLeire, T. *et al.* (2001). Impact of generalized social anxiety disorder in managed care. *American Journal of Psychiatry, 158*, 1999–2007.

Kendall, P.C. (1994). Treating anxiety disorders in children: results of a randomized clinical trial. *Journal of Consulting and Clinical Psychology, 62*, 100–110.

Kendall, P.C., Flannery-Schroeder, E., Panichelli-Mindel, S.M. *et al.* (1997). Therapy for youths with anxiety disorders: a second randomized clinical trial. *Journal of Consulting and Clinical Psychology, 65*, 366–380.

Kendall, P.C. & Southam-Gerow, M. (1996). Long-term follow-up of treatment for anxiety disordered youth. *Journal of Consulting and Clinical Psychology, 64*, 883–888.

Kessler, R.C., McGonagle, K.A., Zhao, S. *et al.* (1994). Lifetime and 12-month prevalence of DSM-III-R psychiatric disorders in the United States: results from the National Comorbidity Survey. *Archives of General Psychiatry, 51*, 8–19.

Kushner, M.G., Sher, K.J. & Beitman, B.D. (1990). The relation between alcohol problems and the anxiety disorders. *American Journal of Psychiatry, 147*, 685–695.

Last, C.G., Perrin, S., Hersen, M. & Kazdin, A.E. (1992). DSM-III-R anxiety disorders in children: sociodemographic and clinical characteristics. *Journal of American Child and Adolescent Psychiatry, 31*, 1070–1076.

Liebowitz, M.R., Heimberg, R.G., Fresco, D.M., *et al.* (2000). Social phobia or social anxiety disorder: what's in a name? *Archives of General Psychiatry, 57*, 191–192.

Liebowitz, M.R., Heimberg, R.G., Schneier, F.R. *et al.* (1999). Cognitive-behavioral group therapy versus phenelzine in social phobia: Long term outcome. *Depression and Anxiety, 10*, 89–98.

Liebowitz, M.R., Schneier, F., Campeas, R. *et al.* (1992). Phenelzine versus atenolol in social phobia: a placebo-controlled comparison. *Archives of General Psychiatry, 49*, 290–300.

Lipsitz, J.D., Markowitz, J.C., Cherry, S. & Fyer, A.J. (1999). Open trial of interpersonal psychotherapy for the treatment of social phobia. *American Journal of Psychiatry, 156*, 1814–1816.

Lipsitz, J.D. & Marshall, R.D. (2001). Alternative psychotherapy approaches for social anxiety disorder. *Psychiatric Clinics of North America, 24*, 817–829.

Lucas, R.A. & Telch, M.J. (1993, November). *Group versus Individual Treatment of Social Phobia.* Paper presented at the annual meeting of the Association for Advancement of Behavior Therapy, Atlanta, GA.

Lucock, M.P. & Salkovskis, P.M. (1988). Cognitive factors in social anxiety and its treatment. *Behaviour Research and Therapy, 26*, 297–302.

Magee, W.J., Eaton, W.W., Wittchen, H.-U. *et al.* (1996). Agoraphobia, simple phobia, and social phobia in the National Comorbidity Survey. *Archives of General Psychiatry, 53*, 159–168.

Mannuzza, S., Schneier, F.R., Chapman, T.F. *et al.* (1995). Generalized social phobia: reliability and validity. *Archives of General Psychiatry, 52*, 230–237.

Marzillier, J.S., Lambert, C. & Kellet, J. (1976). A controlled evaluation of systematic desensitization and social skills training for socially inadequate psychiatric patients. *Behaviour Research and Therapy, 14*, 225–238.

Mattick, R.P. & Peters, L. (1988). Treatment of severe social phobia: effects of guided exposure with and without cognitive restructuring. *Journal of Consulting and Clinical Psychology, 56*, 251–260.

Mattick, R.P., Peters, L. & Clarke, J.C. (1989). Exposure and cognitive restructuring for social phobia: A controlled study. *Behavior Therapy, 20*, 3–23.

Mrozowski, K.O., Jeffery, S.E., Woodruff-Borden, J. & Meeks, S. (2001). *A Comparison of Social Anxiety in Older and Younger Adults with the SPAI.* Poster presented at the 34th Annual Meeting of the Association for the Advancement of Behavior Therapy, New Orleans, LA, November.

Narrow, W.E., Rae, D.S., Robins, L.N. & Regier, D.A. (2002). Revised prevalence estimates of mental disorders in the United States: Using a clinical significance criterion to reconcile 2 surveys' estimates. *Archives of General Psychiatry, 59*, 115–123.

Newman, M.G., Hofmann, S.G., Trabert, W. *et al.* (1994). Does behavioral treatment of social phobia lead to cognitive changes? *Behavior Therapy, 25*, 503–517.

Olfson, M., Guardino, M., Struening, E. *et al.* (2000). Barriers to the treatment of social anxiety. *American Journal of Psychiatry, 157*, 521–527.

Öst, L.-G. (1987). Applied relaxation: description of a coping technique and review of controlled studies. *Behaviour Research and Therapy, 25*, 397–409.

Öst, L.-G., Jerremalm, A. & Johansson, J. (1981). Individual response patterns and the effects of different behavioral methods in the treatment of social phobia. *Behaviour Research and Therapy, 19*, 1–16.

Öst, L.-G., Sedvall, H., Breitholz, E. *et al.* (1995, July). *Cognitive-behavioural Treatment for Social Phobia: Individual, Group, and Self-administered Treatment.* Paper presented at the World Congress of Behavioural and Cognitive Therapies, Copenhagen, Denmark.

Otto, M.W., Pollack, M.H., Gould, R.A. *et al.* (2000). A comparison of the efficacy of clonazepam and cognitive-behavioral group therapy for the treatment of social phobia. *Journal of Anxiety Disorders, 14*, 345–358.

Rapee, R.M. & Heimberg, R.G. (1997). A cognitive-behavioural model of anxiety in social phobia. *Behaviour Research and Therapy, 35*, 741–756.

Reich, J., Goldenberg, I., Vasile, R. *et al.* (1994). A prospective follow-along study of the course of social phobia. *Psychiatry Research, 54*, 249–258.

Rodebaugh, T.L., Holaway, R.M. & Heimberg, R.G. (2004). The treatment of social anxiety disorder. *Clinical Psychology Review, 24*, 883–908.

Rowa, K., Antony, M.M., Brar, S. *et al.* (2000). Treatment histories of patients with three anxiety disorders. *Depression and Anxiety, 12*, 92–98.

Safren, S.A., Heimberg, R.G., Brown E.J. & Holle C. (1997). Quality of life in social phobia. *Depression and Anxiety, 4*, 126–133.

Schneier, F.R., Heckelman, L.R., Garfinkel, R. *et al.* (1994). Functional impairment in social phobia. *Journal of Clinical Psychiatry, 55*, 322–331.

Schneier, F.R., Johnson, J., Hornig, C.D. *et al.* (1992). Social phobia: Comorbidity and morbidity in an epidemiologic sample. *Archives of General Psychiatry, 49*, 282–288.

Schneier, F.R., Martin, L.Y., Liebowitz, M.R. *et al.* (1989). Alcohol abuse in social phobia. *Journal of Anxiety Disorders, 3*, 15–23.

Scholing, A. & Emmelkamp, P.M.G. (1993). Exposure with and without cognitive therapy for generalized social phobia: Effects of individual and group treatment. *Behaviour Research and Therapy, 31*, 667–681.

Scholing, A. & Emmelkamp, P.M.G. (1996). Treatment of generalized social phobia: Results at long-term follow-up. *Behaviour Research and Therapy, 34*, 447–452.

Sheikh, J.I. & Salzman, C. (1995). Anxiety in the elderly: course and treatment. In M.H. Pollack & M.W. Otto (eds), *The Psychiatric Clinics of North America: Vol. 18. Anxiety Disorders: Longitudinal Course and Treatment* (pp. 871–883). Philadelphia: W.B. Saunders.

Stangier, U., Heidenreich, T., Peitz, M. *et al.* (2003). Cognitive therapy for social phobia: Individual versus group treatment. *Behaviour Research and Therapy, 41*, 991–1007.

Stein, M.B. (1997). Phenomenology and epidemiology of social phobia. *International Clinical Psychopharmacology, 12* (suppl. 6), S23–S26.

Stein, M.B., Chartier, M.J., Hazen, A.L. *et al.* (1998). A direct-interview family study of generalized social phobia. *American Journal of Psychiatry, 155*, 90–97.

Stravynski, A., Marks, I. & Yule, W. (1982). Social skills problems in neurotic outpatients: Social skills training with and without cognitive modification. *Archives of General Psychiatry, 39*, 1378–1385.

Taylor, S. (1996). Meta-analysis of cognitive-behavioral treatment for social phobia. *Journal of Behavior Therapy and Experimental Psychiatry, 27*, 1–9.

Taylor, S., Woody, S., Koch, W. *et al.* (1997). Cognitive restructuring in the treatment of social phobia. *Behavior Modification, 21*, 487–511.

Trower, P., Yardley, K., Bryant, B. & Shaw, P. (1978). The treatment of social failure: A comparison of anxiety-reduction and skills acquisition procedures on two social problems. *Behavior Modification, 2*, 41–60.

Turk, C.L., Fresco, D.M. & Heimberg, R.G. (1999). Social phobia: cognitive behavior therapy. In M. Hersen & A.S. Bellack (eds), *Handbook of Comparative Treatments of Adult Disorders,* 2nd edn (pp. 287–316). New York: John Wiley & Sons.

Turner, S.M., Beidel, D.C., Cooley *et al.* (1994b). A multicomponent behavioral treatment for social phobia: Social effectiveness therapy. *Behaviour Research and Therapy, 32*, 381–390.

Turner, S.M., Beidel, D.C. & Cooley-Quille, M.R. (1995). Two-year follow-up of social phobics treated with Social Effectiveness Therapy. *Behaviour Research and Therapy, 33*, 553–555.

Turner, S.M., Beidel, D.C. & Jacob, R.G. (1994a). Social phobia: a comparison of behavior therapy and atenolol. *Journal of Consulting and Clinical Psychology, 62*, 350–358.

Van Vliet, I.M., Den Boer, J.A., Westenberg, H.G. & Pian, K.L. (1997). Clinical effects of buspirone in social phobia: a double-blind placebo-controlled study. *Journal of Clinical Psychiatry, 58*, 164–168.

Vasey, M.W. (1995). Social anxiety disorders. In A.R. Eisen, C.A. Kearney & C.A. Schaefer (eds) *Clinical Handbook of Anxiety Disorders in Children and Adolescents* (pp. 131–168). Northvale, NJ: Jason Aronson.

Weinstock, L.S. (1999). Gender differences in the presentation and management of social anxiety disorder. *Journal of Clinical Psychiatry, 60* (suppl. 9), 9–13.

Wittchen H.-U. & Fehm L. (2003). Epidemiology and natural course of social fears and social phobia. *Acta Psychiatrica Scandinavica, 108*, 4–18.

Wlazlo, Z., Schroeder-Hartwig, K., Hand, I. *et al.* (1990). Exposure in vivo vs. social skills training for social phobia: Long-term outcome and differential effects. *Behaviour Research and Therapy, 28*, 181–193.

Zaider, T., Heimberg, R.G., Roth, D.A. *et al.* (2003). *Individual CBT for Social Anxiety Disorder: Preliminary Findings.* In D.A. Roth (chair) Cognitive Behaviour Therapy for Social Phobia: Recent Findings and Future Directions. Symposium conducted at the meeting of the Association for Advancement of Behavior Therapy, Boston, MA. November.

CHAPTER 22

Children and Adolescents

Alan Carr

University College Dublin, Ireland

INTRODUCTION

Major meta-analyses of trials of individual child psychotherapy (Weisz, 1998), cognitive-behaviour therapy for children (Durlak, Fuhrman & Lampman, 1991) and family therapy (Shadish *et al.*, 1993) have all yielded effect sizes of about 0.7 indicating that the average treated case fares better than approximately 76% of untreated cases after therapy. The results of these meta-analyses are important because they justify the use of psychological interventions for treating children's psychological problems. Broad-band meta-analyses have yielded an unequivocally positive answer to the big question – 'does child psychotherapy work?' In contrast, tightly focused narrative reviews and small meta-analyses that examine the effectiveness of specific interventions with specific problems have addressed the narrower question – 'what works for whom with children and adolescents?' (Carr, 2000a). The present chapter addresses this question with particular reference to a number of the more common conduct and emotional problems that occur during childhood and adolescence.

Space limitations restrict the range of problem areas addressed in this chapter. Among the more important psychological problems of children and adolescents not addressed in this review are developmental language delay (Whitehurst & Fischel, 1994); autism spectrum disorders (Howlin, 1998); intellectual disability (King & State, 1997; State & King, 1997); specific learning disabilities (Maughan, 1995), somatic conditions (Drotar, 1999; Lemanek & Koontz, 1999) and psychotic conditions (Clark & Lewis, 1998). Readers are referred to cited sources for reviews of psychological interventions with these conditions and elsewhere for guidelines on practice (Carr, 1999, 2000a, 2000b).

CONDUCT PROBLEMS

The effectiveness of psychological interventions for four distinct but related categories of conduct problems will be considered in this section. These are:

- oppositional behavioural difficulties;
- attentional and overactivity problems;

Handbook of Evidence-based Psychotherapies: A Guide for research and practice.
Edited by C. Freeman & M. Power. Copyright © 2007 John Wiley & Sons, Ltd.

- pervasive conduct problems in adolescence;
- adolescent drug abuse.

Oppositional Behavioural Difficulties

Preadolescent children who present with oppositional behavioural problems, temper tantrums, defiance and non-compliance confined largely to the family constitute a third to a half of all referrals to child and family mental health clinics. Prevalence rates for clinically significant levels of oppositional behavioural problems in the community vary from 2 % to16 % (American Psychiatric Association, 1994; Kazdin, 1995; World Health Organization). Oppositional behavioural problems are of particular concern because in the longer term they may lead to pervasive adolescent conduct problems and later life difficulties. Oppositional behavioural difficulties tend to develop gradually within the context of coercive patterns of parent-child interaction and a lack of mutual parental support (Patterson, 1982).

Serketich & Dumas (1996), in a meta-analysis of over 100 studies of behavioural parent training, concluded that for childhood oppositional behavioural problems it was a highly effective treatment. Behavioural parent training focuses on helping parents develop the skills to monitor specific positive and negative behaviours and to modify these by altering their antecedents and consequences (Forehand & Long, 1996; Forehand & McMahon, 1981). For example, parents are coached in prompting their children to engage in positive behaviours and preventing children from entering situations that elicit negative behaviours. They are also trained to use reward systems such as star charts or tokens to increase positive behaviours and time-out to reduce negative behaviours. Behavioural parent training is probably so effective because it offers parents a highly focused way to supportively co-operate with each other in disrupting the coercive parent-child interaction patterns that maintain children's oppositional behaviour problems. It also helps parents develop a belief system in which the child's difficult behaviour is attributed to external situational characteristics rather than to intrinsic characteristics of the child.

The impacts of a variety of formats on the effectiveness of behavioural parent training have been investigated and the results of these studies allow the following conclusions to be drawn. Behavioural parent training is most effective for families with children who present with oppositional behavioural problems when offered intensively over at least 20 sessions; exclusively to one family rather than in a group format; and as part of a multisystemic and multimedia intervention package that includes concurrent individual child-focused problem-solving skills training with video-modelling for both parents and children (Kazdin, Siegel & Bass, 1992; Webster-Stratton & Hammond, 1997). Such intensive, exclusive, multisystemic, multimedia programmes are more effective than less intensive, group-based, behavioural parent training alone, child-focused problem-solving skills training alone, or video modelling alone with minimal therapist contact. An argument may be made for offering more intensive treatment to cases with more severe difficulties. Where a primary caretaker (typically a mother) is receiving little social support from her partner, then including a component to enhance the social support provided by the partner into a routine behavioural parent training programme may enhance the programme's effectiveness (Dadds, Schwartz & Sanders, 1987).

Attentional and Overactivity Problems

Attention deficit hyperactivity disorder is now the most commonly used term for a syndrome characterized by persistent overactivity, impulsivity and difficulties in sustaining attention (American Psychiatric Association, 1994; Hinshaw, 1994; World Health Organization, 1992). The syndrome is a particularly serious problem because youngsters with the core difficulties of inattention, overactivity and impulsivity which are usually present from infancy may develop a wide range of secondary academic and relationship problems as they develop through the lifecycle. Available evidence suggests that vulnerability to attentional and overactivity problems, unlike oppositional behavioural problems discussed in the preceding section, is largely constitutional, although the precise role of genetic, prenatal and perinatal factors in the aetiology of the condition are still unclear. Using DSM IV criteria for attention deficit hyperactivity disorder, a prevalence rate of about 3 % to 5 % has been obtained in community studies (American Psychiatric Association, 1994).

Hinshaw, Klein & Abikoff (1998) and Barkley (1999), following extensive literature reviews, have concluded that family-based multimodal programmes are currently the most effective for children with attentional and overactivity problems. Multimodal programmes typically include stimulant treatment of children with drugs such as methylphenidate combined with family therapy or parent training; school-based behavioural programmes and coping-skills training for children. Family-based multimodal programmes are probably effective because they provide the family with a forum within which to develop strategies for managing a chronic disability. As in the case of oppositional behavioural problems discussed above, both behavioural parent training and structural family therapy help parents and children break out of coercive cycles of interaction and to develop mutually supportive positive interaction patterns. Both family therapy and parent training help parents develop benign belief systems where they attribute the child's difficult behaviour to either the disability (attention deficit hyperactivity disorder) or external situational factors rather than to the child's negative intentions. School-based behavioural programmes have a similar impact on school staffs' belief systems and behaviour. Stimulant therapy and coping skills training help the child to control both their attention to academic tasks and their activity levels. Stimulant therapy, when given in low dosages, helps children to both concentrate better and sit still in classroom situations. High dosage levels have a more marked impact on overactivity but impair concentration and so are not recommended. Coping-skills training helps children to use self-instructions to solve problems in a systematic rather than an impulsive manner.

In cases of attentional and overactivity problems, effective family therapy focuses on helping families to develop patterns of organization conducive to effective child management (Barkley et al., 1992). Such patterns of organization include a high level of parental co-operation in problem solving and child management; a clear intergenerational hierarchy between parents and children; warm supportive family relationships; clear communication and clear, moderately flexible rules, roles and routines.

Parent training, as described in the previous section on oppositional behavioural problems, focuses on helping parents develop the skills to monitor specific positive and negative behaviour and to modify these by altering those interactions and events that occur before and after them (see, for example, Barkley, 1987). School-based behavioural programmes, in cases of attentional and overactivity problems, involve the extension of home-based behavioural programmes into the school setting through home-school, parent-teacher liaison meetings (DuPaul & Eckert, 1997; Braswell & Bloomquist, 1991). Coping skills focus largely on coaching children in the skills required for sustained attention and systematic problem solving (Baer & Nietzel, 1991; Kendall & Braswell, 1985). These skills include identifying a problem to be solved; breaking it into a number of solvable subproblems; tackling these one at a time; listing possible solutions; examining the costs and benefits of these; selecting the most viable solution; implementing this; monitoring progress; evaluating the outcome; rewarding oneself for successful problem solving; modifying unsuccessful solutions; and monitoring the outcomes of these revised problem-solving plans.

Pervasive Conduct Problems in Adolescence

Pervasive and persistent antisocial behaviour, which extends beyond the family to the community, involves serious violations of rules or law-breaking and is characterized by defiance of authority, aggression, destructiveness, deceitfulness, cruelty, problematic relationships with parents, teachers and peers and typically leads to multiagency involvement is referred to as conduct disorder (American Psychiatric Association, 1994; World Health Organization, 1992). Conservative prevalence rates for conduct disorder range from 2 % to 6 % (Kazdin, 1995).

From a developmental perspective, persistent adolescent conduct problems begin during the preschool years as oppositional behavioural problems, described in an earlier section. For about a third of children these evolve into pervasive conduct problems in adolescence and antisocial personality disorder in adulthood (Loeber & Stouthamer-Loeber, 1998). Three classes of risk factors increase the probability that preschool oppositional behaviour problems will escalate into later life difficulties: child characteristics – notably impulsivity and learning problems, poor parenting practices and family organization problems (Lehmann & Dangel, 1998).

Kazdin (1998), in a review of empirically supported interventions for conduct disorders, concluded that functional family therapy and multisystemic therapy were among the more promising treatments available for adolescents with pervasive conduct problems. Chamberlain & Rosicky (1995) in a review of family-based interventions, concluded that treatment foster care may be the most effective intervention for cases of conduct disorder where outpatient family-based approaches have failed.

Functional family therapy aims to reduce the overall level of disorganization within the family and thereby modify chaotic family routines and communication patterns which maintain antisocial behaviour (Alexander & Parsons, 1973, 1982; Gordon et al., 1988; Parsons & Alexander, 1973). Functional family therapy focuses on facilitating high levels of parental co-operation in problem-solving around the management of teenagers' problem behaviour; clear intergenerational hierarchies between parents and adolescents; warm supportive family relationships; clear communication and clear family rules, roles and routines. Within functional family therapy it is assumed that if family members can collectively be helped to alter their problematic communication patterns and if the lack of supervision and discipline within the family is altered, then the youngsters conduct problems will improve (Alexander & Parsons, 1982). This assumption is based on the finding that the families of delinquents are characterized by a greater level of defensive communication and lower levels of supportive communication compared with families of non-delinquent youngsters (Alexander, 1973), and also have poorer supervision practices. With functional family therapy, all family members attend therapy sessions conjointly. Initially family assessment focuses on identifying patterns of interaction and beliefs about problems and solutions that maintain the youngsters conduct problems. Within the early therapy sessions parents and adolescents are facilitated in the development of communication skills, problem-solving skill and negotiation skills. There is extensive use of relabelling and reframing to reduce blaming and to help parents move from viewing the adolescent as intrinsically deviant to someone whose deviant behaviour is maintained by situational factors. In the later stages of therapy there is a focus on the negotiation of contracts in which parents offer adolescents privileges in return for following rules and fulfilling responsibilities.

Functional family therapy focuses exclusively on altering factors within the family system so as to ameliorate persistent conduct problems, but multisystemic therapy also addresses factors within the adolescent and within the wider social system. Effective multisystemic therapy, offers individualized packages of interventions that target factors that maintain conduct problems within the multiple social systems of which the youngster is a member (Henggeler, 1999). These multiple systems include the self, the family, the school, the peer group and the community. Multisystemic interventions integrate family therapy with self-regulation skills training for adolescents; school-based educational and recreational interventions; and interagency liaison meetings to co-ordinate multiagency input. In multisystemic therapy it is assumed that if conduct-problem maintaining factors within the adolescent, the family, the school, the peer group and the wider community are identified, then interventions may be developed to alter these factors and so reduce problematic behaviour (Henggeler & Borduin, 1990). Following multisystemic assessment where members of the adolescent's family and wider network are interviewed, a unique intervention programme is developed that targets those specific subsystems which are largely responsible for the maintenance of the youngster's difficulties. In the early stages of contact the therapist joins with system members and later interventions focus on reframing the system members' ways of understanding the problem or restructuring the way they interact around the problems. Interventions may focus on the adolescent alone; the family; the school; the peer group or the community. Individual interventions typically focus on helping youngsters develop social and academic skills. Improving family communication and parents' supervision and discipline skills are common targets for family intervention. Facilitating communication between parents and teachers and arranging appropriate educational placement are common school-based interventions. Interventions with the peer group may involve reducing contact with deviant peers and increasing contact with non-deviant peers.

In contrast to functional family therapy, which focuses exclusively on the family system, or multisystemic therapy, which addresses both individual factors and the wider social network in addition to family factors, treatment foster care deals with the problem of pervasive conduct problems by linking the adolescent and his or her family to a new and positive system: the treatment foster family. In treatment foster care, carefully selected and extensively trained foster parents in collaboration with a therapist offer adolescents a highly structured foster-care placement over a number of months in a foster-family setting (Chamberlain, 1990; Chamberlain & Reid, 1991; Kirgin et al., 1982). Treatment foster care aims to modify factors that maintain conduct problems within the child, family, school, peer group and other systems by placing the child temporarily within a foster family in which the foster parents have been trained to use behavioural strategies to modify the youngsters deviant behaviour (Chamberlain, 1994). Adolescents in treatment foster care typically receive a concurrent package of multisystemic interventions to modify problem maintaining factors within the adolescent, the birth family, the school, the peer group and the wider community. These are similar to those described for multisystemic therapy and invariably the birth parents complete a behavioural parent training programme so that they will be able to continue the work of the treatment foster parents when their adolescent visits or returns home for the long term. A goal of treatment foster care is to prevent the long-term separation of the adolescent from his or her biological family so, as progress is made, the adolescent spends more and more time with the birth family and less time in treatment foster care.

With respect to service development, it may be most efficient to offer services for adolescent conduct problems on a continuum of care (Chamberlain & Rosicky, 1995). Less severe cases may be offered functional family therapy. Moderately severe cases and those that do not respond to circumscribed family interventions may be offered multisystemic therapy. Extremely severe cases and those who are unresponsive to intensive multisystemic therapy may be offered treatment foster care.

Adolescent Drug Abuse

While experimentation with drugs in adolescence is widespread, problematic drug abuse is less common. A conservative estimate is that between 5 % and 10 % of teenagers under 19 have drug problems serious enough to require clinical intervention (Liddle & Dakof, 1995). Drug abuse often occurs concurrently with other conduct problems, learning difficulties and emotional problems and drug abuse is also an important risk factor for suicide in adolescence.

Liddle & Dakof (1995) and Waldron (1996) in literature reviews of a series of controlled clinical trials, concluded that family-based therapy (which includes both family therapy and multisystemic therapy) is more effective than other treatments in engaging and retaining adolescents in therapy and also in the reduction of drug use. From their meta-analysis of controlled family-based treatment outcome studies Stanton & Shadish (1997) concluded that family-based therapy is more effective in reducing drug abuse than individual therapy; peer group therapy; and family psychoeducation. Furthermore, family-based therapy leads to fewer dropouts from treatment compared with other therapeutic approaches. Their final conclusion was that family-based therapy is effective as a stand-alone treatment modality but it can also be combined effectively with other individually based approaches and lead to positive synergistic outcomes. Thus, family therapy can empower family members to help adolescents engage in treatment; remain committed to the treatment process; and develop family rules, roles, routines, relationships, and belief systems which support a drug free lifestyle. In addition family therapy can provide a context within which youngsters could benefit from individual, peer group or school based interventions.

Family systems theories of drug abuse implicate family disorganization in the aetiology and maintenance of seriously problematic adolescent drug taking behaviour and there is considerable empirical support for this view (Hawkins, Catalano & Miller, 1992; Szapocznik & Kurtines, 1989; Stanton, & Heath, 1995). Family-based interventions aim to reduce drug abuse by engaging families in treatment and helping family members reduce family disorganization and change patterns of family functioning in which the drug abuse is embedded.

Effective systemic engagement, involves contacting all significant members of the adolescent's network directly or indirectly, identifying personal goals and feared outcomes that family members may have with respect to the resolution of the adolescent's drug problems and the family therapy associated with this, and then framing invitations for resistant family members to engage in therapy so as to indicate that their goals will be addressed and feared outcomes will be avoided (Santisteban *et al.*, 1996; Szapocznik *et al.*, 1988). Once families engage in therapy, effective treatment programmes for adolescent drug abuse involve the following processes, which although overlapping may be conceptualized as stages of therapy: problem definition and contracting; becoming drug free; facing denial and creating a context for a drug-free lifestyle; family reorganization; disengagement and planning for relapse prevention (Stanton & Heath, 1995). The style of therapy that has been shown to be effective with adolescent drug abusers and their families has evolved from the structural and strategic family therapy traditions (Haley, 1980; Minuchin, 1974). Effective family therapy in cases of adolescent drug abuse helps family members clarify communication, rules, roles, routines hierarchies and boundaries; resolve conflicts; optimize emotional cohesion; develop parenting and problem-solving skills and manage lifecycle transitions.

Multisystemic ecological treatment approaches to adolescent drug abuse represent a logical extension of family therapy. They are based on the theory that problematic processes, not only within the family but also within the adolescent as an individual and within the wider social system including the school and the peer group may contribute to the aetiology and maintenance of drug abuse (Henggeler & Borduin, 1990). This conceptualization of drug abuse is supported by considerable empirical evidence (Hawkins, Catalano & Miller, 1992; Henggeler *et al.*, 1991). At a personal level, adolescent drug abusers have been shown to have social skills deficits, depression, behaviour problems and favourable attitudes and expectations about drug abuse. As has previously been outlined, their families are characterized by disorganization and in some instances by parental drug abuse. Many adolescent drug abusers have experienced rejection by prosocial peers in early childhood and have become members of a deviant peer group in adolescence. Within a school context drug abusers show a higher level of academic failure and a lower commitment to school and academic achievement compared to their drug-free counterparts. Multisystemic ecological intervention programmes for adolescent drug abusers, like those for adolescents with pervasive conduct problems described earlier, have evolved out of the structural and strategic family therapy traditions (Henggeler & Borduin, 1990). In each case treated with multisystemic therapy, around a central family therapy intervention programme, an additional set of individual, school-based and peer-group based interventions are offered that target specific risk factors identified in that case. Such interventions may include self-management skills training for the adolescent, school-based consultations or peer-group based interventions. Self-management skills training may include coaching in social skills, social problem-solving and communication skills, anger control skills and mood regulation skills. School-based interventions aim to support the youngsters' continuation in school, to monitor and reinforce academic achievement and prosocial behaviour in school, and to facilitate home-school liaison in the management of academic and behavioural problems. Peer group interventions include creating opportunities for prosocial peer group membership and assertiveness training to empower youngsters to resist deviant peer group pressure to abuse drugs.

With respect to service development, the results of controlled treatment trials suggest that a clear distinction must be made between systemic engagement procedures and the process of family therapy, with resources devoted to each.

EMOTIONAL PROBLEMS

The effectiveness of psychological interventions for anxiety disorders, depression and anorexia nervosa will be considered in this section.

Anxiety

While all children have developmentally appropriate fears, some are referred for treatment of anxiety problems when their fears prevent them from completing developmentally appropriate tasks such as going to school or socializing with friends. The overall prevalence for clinically significant fears and anxiety problems in children and adolescents is approximately 2 % to 9 % (Anderson, 1994; American Psychiatric Association, 1994; World Health Organization, 1992). With respect to age trends, simple phobias and separation anxiety are more common among preadolescents and generalized anxiety disorder, panic disorder, social phobia, and obsessive compulsive disorder are more common among adolescents (Klein, 1994).

In a review of evidence from experimental single-case designs and controlled outcome studies King & Ollendick (1997) concluded that exposure based procedures including systematic desensitization and flooding; modelling; contingency management and coping skills training are all effective treatments for childhood phobias. All of these elements have been incorporated along with psychoeducation into a comprehensive programme by Silverman & Kurtines (1999). Following psychoeducation, parents are coached in how to prompt and reinforce their children's courageous behaviour while not reinforcing anxious behaviour. Children are concurrently trained in relaxation and cognitive coping skills. Then children are prompted by parents to expose themselves to feared situations and reinforced by parents for courageous behaviour and for using cognitive coping skills and relaxation to manage their anxiety. Gradually, control over entry into anxiety-provoking situations and reinforcement for managing anxiety in these situations is transferred from the parents to the child who learns self-prompting and self-reinforcement skills. The programme concludes with relapse prevention training. Results of two controlled trials with anxious and phobic children support the efficacy of this treatment package (Silverman and Kurtines, 1999).

Elliott (1999) in a thorough literature review concluded that there is some evidence for the efficacy of behavioural and cognitive-behavioural approaches to school refusal, with effective programmes entailing a high degree of family involvement. For example, Blagg & Yule (1984) found that behavioural family therapy was more effective than a hospital-based multimodal inpatient programme and a home tuition and psychotherapy programme for the treatment of school phobia. Behavioural family therapy included detailed clarification of the child's problem; discussion of the principal concerns of the child, parents and teacher; development of contingency plans to ensure maintenance of gains once the child returned to school; a rapid return to school plan; and follow-up appointments with parents and teachers until the child had been attending school without problems for at least 6 weeks. A year after treatment, 93 % of children who received family-based behaviour therapy were judged to have been successful in returning to school compared with 38 % of children in the multimodal inpatient programme and 10 % of those from the home tuition and psychotherapy programme.

Barrett, Dadds & Rappee (1996) found that a family-based programme for children with severe generalized anxiety problems was more effective than an individual coping-skills training programme. In the family based programme both parents and children attended separate group sessions and some concurrent family therapy sessions and were coached in anxiety management, problem solving and communications skills and the use of reward systems. In the anxiety management sessions parents and children learned to monitor and challenge unrealistic catastrophic beliefs and to use relaxation exercises and self-instructions to cope with anxiety provoking situations. In the problem solving and communication skills sessions, coaching in speaking and listening skills occurred and families learned to manage conflict and solve family problems systematically. In the reward systems sessions, parents learned to reward their children's courageous behaviour and ignore their anxiety-related behaviours and children were involved in setting up reward menus. A year after treatment 90 % of those that participated in the family-based programme were recovered compared with 70 % of those in the individual programme.

Rapoport & Inoff-Germain (2000) concluded from an extensive literature review that cognitive-behavioural programmes, which include exposure and response prevention, relaxation training and coping skills training, especially when coupled with pharmacological intervention with serotonin reuptake inhibitors such as clomipramine hold particular promise for the treatment of obsessive compulsive disorder in children. For example, March, Mulle & Herbel (1994) found that 80 % of children with obsessive compulsive disorder (OCD) in a single group outcome study showed clinically significant improvement after treatment and this was maintained at follow-up following a family-based intervention programme and pharmacological treatment with clomipramine. The programme, *How I Ran OCD Off My Land* (March & Mulle, 1998), was based on Michael White's narrative therapy externalization procedure, exposure and response prevention, relaxation skills training and coping skills training. In the narrative therapy externalization component of the programme the child and parents were helped to view obsessive compulsive disorder as a medical illness separate from the youngster's core identity. Children were encouraged to externalize the disorder by giving it a nasty nickname and to make a commitment to driving this nasty creature out of their lives. They then were helped to map out a graded hierarchy of situations that elicited obsessions and led to compulsions of varying degrees and those situations in which the child successfully controlled these symptoms were noted. These situations were subsequently monitored on a weekly basis because increases in the number of these reflected therapeutic progress. In the behavioural family therapy component of the programme children were coached in coping with anxiety by using self-instruction and relaxation skills. Parents were coached to support and reward their children through the process of facing anxiety-provoking situations while avoiding engaging in compulsive anxiety reducing rituals.

Perrin, Smith & Yule (2000) in their review of the treatment of post-traumatic stress disorders in children and adolescents concluded that there is evidence from a small number of controlled trials for the effectiveness of cognitive behavioural programmes for this disorder. Such programmes begin with psychoeducation and goal setting, following which youngsters are trained in coping and relaxation skills that are subsequently used in exposure sessions. In these sessions therapists facilitate emotional processing of traumatic memories by helping youngsters recall vivid traumatic memories. Treatment programmes conclude with sessions on relapse prevention.

From this cursory review it is clear that effective psychological intervention programmes for anxiety disorders in children and adolescents are family based and include creating a context within family therapy that allows the child to eventually enter into anxiety provoking situations and to manage these through the use of personal coping skills, parental support and encouragement.

Depression

Major depression is a recurrent condition involving low mood, selective attention to negative features of the environment, a pessimistic cognitive style, self-defeating behaviour patterns, a disturbance of sleep and appetite and a disruption of interpersonal relationships (American Psychiatric Association, 1994; Harrington, 1993; Kovacs, 1997; Reynolds & Johnson, 1994; World Health Organization, 1992). In community samples prevalence rates of depression in preadolescence range from 0.5 % to 2.5 % and in adolescents from 2 % to 8 % while 25 % of referrals to child and adolescent clinics have major depression.

There is strong evidence that both genetic and family environment factors contribute to the aetiology of depression (Reynolds & Johnson, 1994). Parental criticism, poor parent-child communication and family discord have all been found to be associated with depression in children and adolescents. Integrative theories of depression propose that episodes occur when genetically vulnerable youngsters find themselves involved in stressful social systems in which there is limited access to socially supportive relationships.

Cognitive behaviour therapy, conjoint family therapy and concurrent group-based parent and child training sessions have all been found to be effective in the treatment of major depression (Harrington et al., 1998; Kazdin & Marciano, 1998). Effective cognitive behaviour therapy programmes include psychoeducation, self-monitoring, cognitive restructuring, coping and relaxation skills training, pleasant activity scheduling and problem-solving skills training. Effective family therapy and family-based interventions aim to reduce the family stress to which the youngster is exposed and enhance the availability of social support to the youngster within the family context. Core features of all effective family interventions include the facilitation of clear parent-child communication, the promotion of systematic family-based problem solving and the disruption of negative critical parent-child interactions.

Anorexia

The prevalence of anorexia nervosa – a syndrome where the central feature is self-starvation – among teenage girls is about 1 % (World Health Organization, 1992; American Psychiatric Association, 1994). Wilson & Fairburn (1998) in a recent extensive literature review concluded that family therapy and combined individual therapy and parent counselling with and without initial hospital-based feeding programmes are effective in treating anorexia nervosa (for example, Crisp et al., 1991; Eisler et al., 1997; Le Grange et al., 1992; Hall & Crisp, 1987; Robin & Siegal, 1999; Russell et al., 1987). They also concluded that in-patient refeeding programmes must be supplemented with outpatient follow-up programmes if weight gains made while in hospital are to be maintained following discharge. Key elements of effective treatment programmes include engagement of the adolescent and parents in treatment; psychoeducation about the nature of anorexia and risks associated with starvation; weight restoration and monitoring; shifting the focus from the nutritional intake to normal psychosocial developmental tasks of adolescence; facilitating the adolescent's individuation and increasing autonomy within the family; and relapse prevention. Structural family therapy (Minuchin, Rosen & Baker, 1978) and Milan systemic family therapy (Selvini Palazzoli, 1978) are the main treatment models that have influenced the types of therapies evaluated in these treatment trails. With respect to service development, available evidence suggests that for youngsters with eating disorders effective treatment involves up to 18 outpatient sessions over periods a long as 15 months. Initial hospitalization for weigh restoration is essential where medical complications associated with weight loss or bingeing and purging place the youngster at risk.

CLOSING COMMENTS

A number of comments may be made about the material reviewed in this chapter. First, well-articulated psychological interventions have been shown to be effective for a wide range of child-focused problems. Second, these interventions are brief and may be offered by a range of professionals on an outpatient basis. Third, for many of the interventions, useful treatment manuals have been developed which may be flexibly used by clinicians in treating individual cases. Fourth, the bulk of psychological interventions for which there is evidence of effectiveness have been developed within the cognitive-behavioural family-system psychotherapeutic traditions.

TREATMENT RESOURCES

Childhood behavioural problems

Forehand, R. & Long, N. (1996). *Parenting the Strong-Willed Child: The Clinically Proven Five Week Programme for Parents of Two to Six Year Olds*. Chicago: Contemporary Books.
Forehand, R. & McMahon, R. (1981). *Helping the Non-compliant Child: A Clinician's Guide to Parent Training*. New York: Guilford.
Webster-Stratton, C. (1987). *Parents And Children: A 10 Program Videotape Parent Training Series with Manuals*. Eugene, OR: Castalia Press.

Attentional and overactivity problems

Barkley, R. (1995). *Taking Charge of ADHD: The Complete Authoritative Guide for Parents*. New York: Guilford.
Barkley, R. (1999). *Attention Deficit Hyperactivity Disorder: A Handbook for Diagnosis and Treatment* (2nd edn). New York. Guilford.
Braswell, L. & Bloomquist, M. (1991). *Cognitive Behavioural Therapy for ADHD Children: Child, Family and School Interventions*. New York: Guilford.

Adolescent conduct problems

Alexander, J. & Parsons, B. (1982). *Functional Family Therapy*. Monterey, CA: Brooks/Cole.
Chamberlain, P. (1994). *Family Connections: A Treatment Foster Care Model for Adolescents with Delinquency*. Eugene, OR: Castalia.
Dishion, T. & Kavanagh, K. (1989) *The Adolescents Transition Programme* (manuals and accompanying video vignettes). Eugene, OR: Independent Video Services.
Henggeler, S. & Borduin, C. (1990). *Family Therapy and Beyond: A Multisystemic Approach to Treating the Behaviour Problems of Children and Adolescents*. Pacific Grove, CA: Brooks Cole.

Drug abuse

Szapocznik, J. & Kurtines, W. (1989). *Breakthroughs In Family Therapy With Drug Abusing Problem Youth*. New York: Springer.

Anxiety

Kendall, P., Kane, M., Howard, B. & Siqueland, L. (1990). *Cognitive-behavioural Therapy for Anxious Children. Treatment Manual.* Admore, PA: Workbook Publishing.
March, J. & Mulle, K. (1994). *OCD in Children and Adolescents: A Cognitive-Behavioural Treatment Manual*. New York: Guilford.

Depression

Clarke, G. & Lewinsohn, P. (1984). *The Coping with Depression Course – Adolescent Version: A Psychoeducational Intervention for Unipolar Depression in High School Students*. Eugene, OR: Peter Lewinsohn.
Lewinsohn, P. & Clarke, G. (1986). *The Coping with Depression course – Adolescent Version: Parent Manual*. Eugene, OR: Peter Lewinsohn.
Stark, K. & Kendall, P. (1996). *Treating Depressed Children: Therapists Manual for ACTION*. Ardmore, PA: Workbook Publishing.

Eating disorders

Woodside, B. & Shekter-Wolfson, L. (1991). *Family Approaches in Treatment of Eating Disorders*. Washington, DC: APA Press.

REFERENCES

Alexander, J. (1973). Defensive an supportive communication in normal and deviant families. *Journal of Consulting and Clinical Psychology, 40*, 223–231.
Alexander, J. & Parsons, B. (1973). Short-term behavioural intervention with delinquent families: Impact on family process and recidivism. *Journal of Abnormal Psychology, 81*, 219–225.
Alexander, J. & Parsons, B. (1982).*Functional Family Therapy*. Montereny, CA: Brooks Cole.
Anderson, J. (1994). Epidemiological Issues. In T. Ollendick, N. King & W. Yule (eds.), *International Handbook of Phobic and Anxiety Disorders in Children and Adolescents* (pp. 43–66). New York: Plenum.

APA (American Psychiatric Association). (1994). *Diagnostic and Statistical Manual of Mental Disorders* (Fourth Edition), (DSM IV). Washington, DC: APA.

Baer, R. & Nietzel, M. (1991). Cognitive and behaviour treatment of impulsivity in children: A meta-analytic review of the outcome literature. *Journal of Clinical Child Psychology, 20,* 400–412.

Barkley, R. (1987). *Defiant Children: A Clinician's Manual for Parent Training.* New York: Guilford Press.

Barkley, R. (1999). *Attention Deficit Hyperactivity Disorder: A Handbook for Diagnosis and Treatment* (2nd edn). New York: Guilford.

Barkley, R., Guevremont, D., Anastopoulos, A. & Fletcher, K. (1992). A comparison of three family therapy programs for treating family conflicts in adolescents with ADHD. *Journal of Consulting and Clinical Psychology, 60,* 450–462.

Barrett, P., Dadds, M. & Rappee, R. (1996). Family treatment of childhood anxiety: a controlled trial. *Journal of Consulting and Clinical Psychology, 64*(2), 333–342.

Blagg, N. & Yule, W. (1984). The behavioural treatment of school refusal: A comparative study. *Behaviour Research and Therapy, 2,* 119–127.

Braswell, L. & Bloomquist, M. (1991). *Cognitive Behavioural therapy for ADHD Children: Child, Family and School Interventions.* New York: Guilford.

Carr, A. (1999). *Handbook of Child and Adolescent Clinical Psychology: A Contextual Approach.* London: Routledge.

Carr, A. (2000a). *What Works for Children and Adolescents: A Critical Review of Psychological Interventions with Children, Adolescents and their Families.* London: Routledge.

Carr, A. (2000b). *Family Therapy: Concepts, Process and Practice.* Chichester: Wiley.

Chamberlain, P. (1990). Comparative evaluation of specialized foster care for seriously delinquent youths: A first step. *Community Alternatives: International Journal of Family Care, 2,* 21–36.

Chamberlain, P. (1994). *Family Connections: A Treatment Foster Care Model for Adolescents with Delinquency.* Eugene, OR: Castalia.

Chamberlain, P. & Reid, J. (1991). Using a specialized foster care treatment model for children and adolescents leaving the State mental hospital. *Journal of Community Psychology, 19,* 266–276.

Chamberlain, P. & Rosicky, J. (1995). The effectiveness of family therapy in the treatment of adolescents with conduct disorders and delinquency. *Journal of Marital and Family Therapy, 21,* 441–459.

Clark, F. & Lewis, S. (1998). Practitioner review: Treatment of schizophrenia in childhood and adolescence. *Journal of Child Psychology and Psychiatry, 39*(8), 1071–1081.

Crisp, A., Norton, K., Gowers, S. *et al.* (1991). A controlled study of the effect of therapies aimed at adolescent and family psychopathology in anorexia nervosa. *British Journal of Psychiatry, 159,* 325–333.

Dadds, M., Schwartz, S. & Sanders, M. (1987). Marital discord and treatment outcome in behavioural treatment of child conduct disorders. *Journal of Consulting and Clinical Psychology, 55,* 396–403.

Drotar, D. (1999). Psychological interventions for children with chronic physical illness and their families. In S. Russ & T. Ollendick (eds), *Handbook of Psychotherapies with Children and Families* (pp. 447–462). New York: Kluwer Academic/Plenum Publishing.

DuPaul, G. & Eckert, T. (1997). The effects of school-based interventions for attention deficit hyperactivity disorder: A meta-analysis. *School Psychology Review, 26,* 5–27.

Durlak, J., Fuhrman, T., Lampman, C. (1991). The effectiveness of cognitive behaviour therapy for maladapting children: A meta-analysis. *Psychological Bulletin, 110,* 204–214.

Eisler, I., Dare, C., Russell, G. *et al.* (1997). Family and individual therapy in anorexia nervosa: A 5-year follow-up. *Archives of General Psychiatry, 54,* 1025–1030.

Elliott, J. (1999). Practitioner review: school refusal: issues of conceptualization, assessment and treatment. *Journal of Child Psychology and Psychiatry, 40*(7), 1001–1012.

Forehand, R. & Long, N. (1996). *Parenting the Strong-Willed Child: The Clinically Proven Five Week Programme for Parents of Two to Six Year Olds.* Chicago: Contemporary Books.

Forehand, R. & McMahon, R (1981). *Helping the Non-compliant Child: A Clinician's Guide to Parent Training.* New York: Guilford.

Gordon, D., Arbuthnot, J., Gustafson, K. & McGreen, P. (1988). home-based behavioural systems family therapy with disadvantaged delinquents. *The American Journal of Family Therapy, 16,* 243–255.

Haley, J. (1980). *Leaving Home.* New York: McGraw-Hill.

Hall, A. & Crisp, A. (1987). Brief psychotherapy in the treatment of anorexia nervosa: Outcome at one year. *British Journal of Psychiatry, 151*, 185–191.

Harrington, R. (1993). *Depressive Disorder in Childhood and Adolescence.* New York: Wiley.

Harrington, R., Whittaker, J. & Shoebridge, P. (1998). Psychological treatment of depression in children and adolescents. A review of treatment research. *British Journal of Psychiatry, 173*, 291–298.

Hawkins, J. Catalano, R. & Miller, J. (1992). Risk and protective factors for alcohol and other drug problems in adolescence and early adulthood: Implications for substance use prevention. *Psychological Bulletin, 112*, 64–105.

Henggeler, S. (1999). Multisystemic therapy: An overview of clinical procedures, outcomes and policy implications. *Child Psychology and Psychiatry Review, 4*(1), 2–10.

Henggeler, S. & Borduin, C. (1990). *Family Therapy and Beyond: A Multisystemic Approach to Treating the Behaviour Problems of Children and Adolescents.* Pacific Grove, CA: Brooks Cole.

Henggeler, S., Borduin, C., Melton, G. *et al.* (1991). The effects of multisystemic therapy on drug use and abuse in serious juvenile offenders: A progress report from two outcome studies. *Family Dynamics Addiction Quarterly, 1*, 40–51.

Hinshaw, S. (1994). *Attention Deficits and Hyperactivity in Children.* Thousand Oaks: Sage.

Hinshaw, S., Klein, R. & Abikoff, H. (1998). Childhood attention deficit hyperactivity disorder: nonpharmacological and combination approaches. In P. Nathan & J. Gorman (eds), *A Guide to Treatments that Work* (pp. 26–41). New York: Oxford University Press.

Howlin, P. (1998). Practitioner review: psychological and educational treatments for autism. *Journal of Child Psychology and Psychiatry, 39*, 307–322.

Kazdin, A. (1995). *Conduct Disorders in Childhood and Adolescence* (2nd edn). Thousand Oaks, CA: Sage.

Kazdin, A. (1998). Psychosocial treatments for conduct disorder in children. In P. Nathan & J. Gorman (eds), *A Guide To Treatments That Work* (pp. 65–89). New York: Oxford University Press.

Kazdin, A. & Marciano, P. (1998). Childhood and adolescent depression. In E. Mash & R. Barkley (eds), *Treatment of Childhood Disorders* (2nd edn, pp. 211–248). New York: Guilford.

Kazdin, A., Siegel, T.C., & Bass, D. (1992). Cognitive problem solving skills training and parent management training in the treatment of antisocial behaviour in children. *Journal of Consulting and Clinical Psychology, 60*, 733–747.

Kendall, P. & Braswell, L. (1985). *Cognitive Behavioural Therapy for Impulsive Children.* New York: Guilford.

King, N. & Ollendick, T. (1997). Annotation: treatment of childhood phobias. *Journal of Child Psychology and Psychiatry, 38*, 389–400.

King, B. & State, M. (1997). Mental retardation: a review of the past 10 years, part 1. *Journal of the American Academy of Child and Adolescent Psychiatry, 36*, 1656–1663.

Kirgin, K., Braukmann, C., Atwater, J. & Wolf, M. (1982). An evaluation of teaching-family (achievement place) group homes for juvenile offenders. *Journal of Applied Behaviour Analysis, 15*, 1–16.

Klein, R. (1994). Anxiety disorders. In M. Rutter, E. Taylor & L. Hersov (eds) *Child and Adolescent Psychiatry: Modern Approaches* (3rd edn, pp. 351–374). London: Blackwell.

Kovacs, M. (1997). The Emanuel Miller Memorial Lecture 1994 – depressive disorders in childhood: An impressionistic landscape. *Journal of Child Psychology and Psychiatry, 38*, 287–298.

Le Grange, D., Eisler, I., Dare, C. & Russell, G. (1992). Evaluation of family treatments in adolescent anorexia nervosa: A pilot study. *International Journal of Eating Disorders, 12*, 347–357.

Lehmann, P. & Dangel, R. (1998). Oppositional defiant disorder. In B. Thyer & J. Wodarski (eds), *Handbook of Empirical Social Work Practice,* vol. 1. Mental Disorders (pp. 91–116). New York: Wiley.

Lemanek, K. & Koontz, D. (1999). Integrated approaches to acute illness. In S. Russ & T. Ollendick (eds), *Handbook of Psychotherapies with Children and Families* (pp. 463–482). New York: Kluwer Academic/Plenum Publishing.

Liddle, H. & Dakof, G. (1995). Efficacy of family therapy for drug abuse: Promising but not definitive. *Journal of Marital and Family Therapy, 21*, 511–543.

Loeber, R. & Stouthamer-Loeber, M. (1998). Development of juvenile aggression and violence: Some common misconceptions and controversies. *American Psychologist, 53*, 242–259.

March, J. & Mulle, K. (1998). *OCD in Children And Adolescents: A Cognitive-Behavioural Treatment Manual*. NewYork: Guilford.

March, J., Mulle, K. & Herbel, B. (1994). Behavioural psychotherapy for children and adolescents with OCD: An open trial of a new protocol-driven treatment package. *Journal of the American Academy of Child and Adolescent Psychiatry, 33*(3), 333–341.

Maughan, B. (1995). Long term outcomes of developmental reading problems. *Journal of Child Psychology and Psychiatry, 36*, 357–371.

Minuchin, S. (1974). *Families and Family Therapy*. Cambridge, MA: Harvard University Press.

Minuchin, S., Rosen, B. & Baker, L. (1978). *Psychosomatic Families*. Cambridge, MA: Harvard University Press.

Parsons, B. & Alexander, J. (1973). Short-term family intervention: a therapy outcome study. *Journal of Consulting and Clinical Psychology, 41*, 195–201.

Patterson, G. (1982). *Coercive Family Process*. Eugene, OR: Castalia.

Perrin, S., Smith, P. & Yule, W. (2000). The assessment and treatment of post-traumatic stress disorder in children and adolescents. *Journal of Child Psychology and Psychiatry, 41*(3), 277–291.

Rapoport, J. & Inoff-Germain, G. (2000). Practitioner review: Treatment of obsessive compulsive disorder in children and adolescents. *Journal of Child Psychology and Psychiatry, 41*(4), 419–431.

Reynolds, H. & Johnson, F. (1994). *Handbook of Depression in Children and Adolescents*. New York: Plenum Press.

Robin, A. & Siegel, P. (1999). Family therapy with eating disordered adolescents. In S. Russ & T. Ollendick (eds), *Handbook of Psychotherapies with Children and Families* (pp. 301 326). New York: Kluwer Academic/Plenum Publishing.

Russell, G., Szmukler, G., Dare, C. & Eisler, I. (1987). An evaluation of family therapy in anorexia nervosa and bulimia nervosa. *Archives of General Psychiatry, 44*, 1047–1056.

Santisteban, D., Szapocznik, J., Perez-Vidal, A. *et al.* (1996). Efficacy of intervention for engaging youth and families into treatment and some variables that may contribute to differential effectiveness. *Journal of Family Psychology, 10*, 35–44.

Selvini Palazzoli, M. (1978). *Self-starvation: From Individual to Family Therapy in the Treatment of Anorexia Nervosa* (translated by A. Pomerans). New York: Jason Aronson.

Serketich, W. & Dumas, J.E. (1996). The effectiveness of behavioural parent training to modify antisocial behaviour in children: a meta-analysis. *Behaviour Therapy, 27*, 171–186.

Shadish, W., Montgomery, L., Wilson, P. *et al.* (1993). The effects of family and marital psychotherapies: A meta-analysis. *Journal of Consulting and Clinical Psychology, 61*, 992–1002.

Silverman, W. & Kurtines, W. (1999). A pragmatic perspective toward treating children with phobia and anxiety problems. In S. Russ & T. Ollendick (eds), *Handbook of Psychotherapies with Children and Families* (pp. 505–521). New York: Kluwer Academic/Plenum Publishing.

Stanton, D. & Heath, A. (1995). Family treatment of alcohol and drug abuse. In R. Mikeselle, D. Lusterman & S. McDaniel (eds), *Integrating Family Therapy: Handbook of Family Therapy and Systems Theory* (pp. 529–541). Washington, DC: APA.

Stanton, M. & Shadish, W. (1997). Outcome, attrition and family-couples treatment for drug abuse: a meta-analysis and review of the controlled comparative studies. *Psychological Bulletin, 122*, 170–191.

State, M. & King, B. (1997). Mental retardation: a review of the past 10 years part 11. *Journal of the American Academy of Child and Adolescent Psychiatry, 36*, 1664–1671.

Szapocznik, J. & Kurtines, W. (1989). *Breakthroughs in Family Therapy with Drug Abusing Problem Youth*. New York: Springer.

Szapocznik, J., Perez-Vidal, A., Brickman, A. *et al.* (1988). Engaging adolescent drug abusers and their families in treatment: A strategic structural systems approach. *Journal of Consulting and Clinical Psychology, 56*, 552–557.

Waldron, H.B. (1996). Adolescent substance abuse and family therapy outcome: a review of randomised trials. *Advances in Clinical Child Psychology, 19*, 199–234.

Webster-Stratton, C. & Hammond, M. (1997). Treating children with early-onset conduct problems: A comparison of child and parent training interventions. *Journal of Consulting and Clinical Psychology, 65*, 93–109.

Weisz, J. (1998). Empirically supported treatments for children and adolescents: Efficacy, problems, prospects. In K. Dobson & K Craig (eds), *Empirically Supported Therapies: Best Practice in Professional Psychology* (pp. 66–92). Thousand Oaks, CA: Sage.

Whitehurst, G. & Fischel, J. (1994). Early developmental language delay: What, if anything should the clinician do about it. *Journal of Child Psychology and Psychiatry, 35*, 613–648.

Wilson, T. & Fairburn, C. (1998). Treatments for eating disorders. In P. Nathan & J. Gorman (eds). *A Guide to Treatments that Work* (pp. 501–530). New York: Oxford.

World Health Organization (WHO) (1992). *The ICD-10 Classification of Mental and Behavioural Disorders*. Geneva: WHO.

CHAPTER 23

Generalised Anxiety Disorder

Rob Durham
University of Dundee, UK
and
Peter Fisher
University of Liverpool

INTRODUCTION

Worry and anxiety are common features of all emotional and psychiatric disorder. They are also fundamental aspects of the human condition. It is part of our nature to be sensitive to threats to our physical and psychological wellbeing, to imagine ourselves and others in danger, to dwell on these situations with varying degrees of conscious awareness and sometimes to feel a paralysing sense of dread that there is really no escape from an unpleasant fate. Such experiences are a part of living for all of us and a way of living for some. Since the mid-1980s, chronic worrying and the effects of the chronic tension that accompanies this state have come to be the defining features of generalised anxiety disorder (GAD) which itself has assumed a much more important place in our understanding of psychopathology. How is GAD defined and conceptualised? How common is the disorder and what course does it tend to follow? How effective is psychological therapy for this condition and how can clinical effectiveness be improved? In this chapter we provide an overview of the rapidly growing clinical and research literature that addresses these questions.

DIAGNOSIS

Generalised anxiety disorder is defined in DSM-IV (American Psychiatric Association, 1994) as 'excessive anxiety and worry (apprehensive expectation), occurring more days than not for at least 6 months, about a number of events or activities (such as work or school performance).' In addition, three of six symptoms must be present (restlessness, excessive fatigue, poor concentration, irritability, muscle tension and sleep disturbance) with significant distress or impairment in functioning. Diagnostic criteria within ICD-10 (World Health Organization, 1993) are similar but more general in character. Generalised anxiety disorder is defined as a generalised and persistent state of free-floating anxiety over

Handbook of Evidence-based Psychotherapies: A Guide for research and practice.
Edited by C. Freeman & M. Power. Copyright © 2007 John Wiley & Sons, Ltd.

several months in which dominant symptoms are described as highly variable but with key symptoms of apprehension, motor tension and autonomic overactivity. Both classifications share exclusion criteria that involve determining that the focus of worry or apprehension is not a consequence of another disorder and is not related to organic causes such as hyperthyroidism or caffeine intoxication.

In general, establishing the presence and severity of somatic symptoms is usually straightforward and can be accomplished with standard questions of the kind: 'During the past six months how much have you been bothered by . . . feeling keyed up or on edge, being easily fatigued, muscle tension, and so forth?' Establishing the presence of excessive worry is less straightforward and requires persistence and careful probing for people whose style of worrying has an automatic quality that is felt to be natural and therefore less accessible to introspection. Useful questions to ask include:

• Are you a worrier?
• Do you think that you worry excessively?
• When things are going well do you still find things to be worried and anxious about?
• How long has this been a problem?
• How much does worry interfere with your work, or social activities or family life?

The main difficulty in establishing GAD as a primary or comorbid diagnosis is in distinguishing the worry and tension that are primary features of GAD from the worry and tension that frequently occur in adjustment disorders, anxious or avoidant personality disorders, other anxiety disorders, chronic medical disorder and, most commonly perhaps, depressive or dysthymic disorder. Structured interviews and questionnaires can be helpful in screening and assessing GAD and in monitoring progress during the course of treatment, and a useful review of relevant measures can be found in Antony, Orsillo & Roemer (2001).

Generalised anxiety disorder is highly comorbid with other mental disorders (Kessler *et al.*, 2001) and pure GAD is infrequently seen in clinical practice. Approximately 80 % of cases referred to mental health professionals comprise various combinations of GAD plus anxious personality disorders and other anxiety and depressive disorders (Maier *et al.*, 2000; Wittchen *et al.*, 1994). Comorbidity may be particularly high in clinical settings simply because it is the presence of other disorders that motivates GAD sufferers to seek help (Kessler, 2000). These complexities of clinical presentation are discussed at some length in Tyrer (1999) and may help to explain why GAD is often overlooked and undertreated (Ballenger *et al.*, 2001). Critical reviews of the reliability, validity and clinical utility of GAD as a diagnostic entity can be found in Andrews (2000) and Rickels & Rynn (2001).

In summary, GAD can be identified and diagnosed reliably provided that sufficient care is taken in asking the right questions and in establishing the presence of the disorder even when other disorders of a more obvious kind may also be present. It is important to bear in mind that GAD sufferers may lack insight into the problematic nature of their chronic tension and worrying and focus their attention instead on somatic symptoms or other disorders that are more easily recognised as pathological.

EPIDEMIOLOGY

Prevalence

The National Comorbidity Survey in the US, based on DSM-III-R, reported 12-month prevalence estimates of 3.1 %, and lifetime prevalence estimates of 5.1 % with women being twice as likely to suffer from GAD as men (Wittchen *et al.*, 1994). The recent Australian National Survey of Mental Health and Well Being used DSM-IV criteria and obtained a 12-month prevalence estimate of 3.6 % (Hunt, 2002). A survey using the broader criteria of ICD-10 reported lifetime prevalence rates of 8.9 % (World Health Organization, 1993). Looking at the evidence as a whole Tyrer (1999) concluded that around 10 % of the population have an anxiety disorder of some sort at any one time with GAD being the most common presentation. Subthreshold presentations of generalised anxiety are clearly much more common than episodes of disorder. It is also important to remember that anxiety disorders are amongst the most prevalent psychiatric disorders of childhood (Bernstein *et al.*, 1996) and there is evidence that GAD is the most prevalent of the anxiety disorders diagnosed later in life (Stanley & Novy, 2000).

Onset and Course

Age of onset may be as early as 13 years when presenting as a primary disorder and as late as 30 years when presentation is secondary to other disorders (Rogers *et al.*, 1999). The mean age of onset has been estimated at 21 years (Yonkers *et al.*, 1996) although the average age of referral to specialist services is in middle age (Ballenger *et al.*, 2001). Most cases are managed in primary care in which setting it is a common and often chronic disorder (Goldberg & Lecrubier, 1995; Noyes *et al.*, 1992). In a substantial proportion of those with GAD, chronic worry and tension are clearly lifelong problems with symptom severity waxing and waning in response to social and environmental stressors (Blazer *et al.*, 1987; Noyes *et al.*, 1992). The average length of particular episodes has been estimated to be 20 years (Yonkers *et al.*, 1996) which greatly exceeds the six-month duration required for DSM-IV.

There is growing evidence that chronic anxiety is associated with increased risk for medical illness (Greenberg *et al.*, 1999). Indeed, it may be a fundamental vulnerability factor in the aetiology of a range of psychiatric disorders but particularly depression and alcohol abuse (Fava *et al.*, 2000; Judd *et al.*, 1998). It is estimated to cause psychosocial disability of a similar magnitude to that of chronic somatic disease (Ormel *et al.*, 1994) and depression (Wittchen *et al.*, 2000). There is also evidence that comorbidity between GAD and other conditions increases the rate of attempted suicide (Lecrubier, 1998). In short, the overall evidence supports the view that GAD is a significant public health problem.

THEORETICAL FORMULATIONS

Current psychological formulations of GAD emphasise excessive worry as the core feature of the disorder and are concerned with understanding the nature of worry and the conditions under which it persists. A comprehensive overview of theory, treatment and research on worry can be found in Davey & Wells (2006). In this section we summarise the work of the most prominent theorists in the field. Borkovec and his colleagues have conducted extensive and influential research on the nature of worry (cf. Borkovec & Newman, 1999). Key findings are the predominance of verbal self-talk rather than imagery in worry, the inhibiting effect of worry on emotional processing of threat-related material and the significant connection between GAD and interpersonal factors. The relationships between these factors are quite complex but in essence worry is conceptualised as a form of cognitive avoidance that functions to decrease sympathetic arousal to perceived threat and to inhibit emotional processing thereby preventing extinction of the fear response (Borkovec, Ray & Stoeber, 1998). It is an attempt to avoid the anxious arousal or anticipated catastrophe associated with negative events or deeper level emotional concerns and to the extent that this succeeds its role as a coping response is strengthened through a process of negative reinforcement. The deeper level concerns are thought to be predominantly interpersonal in nature. Borkovec (1994) suggests that insecure attachments to primary caregivers, as well as psychosocial traumas in early childhood, may be strongly related to the sense of uncontrollability of negative events that is so characteristic of GAD.

The cognitive model of GAD developed by Adrian Wells is based on a distinction between two types of worry: Type 1 worries, which concern everyday events and bodily sensations, and Type 2 worries, which are focused on the act of worrying itself and reflect both positive and negative appraisals of worrisome activity (Wells, 1999). There is evidence that the content of Type 1 worries is very similar to normal worries (Craske et al., 1989) and that GAD is associated in particular with Type 2 worries. The theory proposes a particular sequence of events. Once triggered, the worry cycle persists initially through the activation of positive Type 2 worries (positive metacognitions such as 'worry helps me cope', 'worry prevents bad things happening'), which in turn increase the accessibility of, and sensitivity to, threat-related information and lead to more intense worrying. The balance of appraisal then shifts to predominantly negative Type 2 worries ('my worries are uncontrollable', 'I could go crazy with worrying'), which motivate attempts to reduce distress and regain control. These attempts may involve avoidance, reassurance seeking, suppression of upsetting thoughts or engagement in distracting activities all of which may, in fact, reinforce worry as a coping strategy rather than reducing it. Deliberate attempts to suppress unwanted thoughts, for example, may inadvertently lead to an increase in their intrusiveness (Clark et al., 1991).

The cognitive model of GAD developed by Dugas et al. (1998) consists of four components: intolerance of uncertainty, erroneous beliefs about worry, poor problem solving and cognitive avoidance. Clearly this draws on some of the same empirical and conceptual base as Wells and Borkovec. In addition, however, a distinction is made between worries that are amenable to problem solving and worries about situations that cannot be resolved or which may never occur. Cognitive exposure is thought to be ideally suited to the second but not the first type of worrying.

Although chronic worry is the primary focus of psychological theorising it is important to remember that this state of mind is not necessarily accompanied by the physiological symptoms of increased motor tension, vigilance and behavioural inhibition that are required for a diagnosis. Worry always carries some degree of emotional charge but it may be best viewed as a core feature of anxious temperament rather than as the core feature of GAD per se, that is, as a personality trait that results in an episode of GAD when somatic symptoms of arousal are added in response to a period of acute or chronic stress (cf. Akiskal, 1998; Rickels & Rynn, 2001). There are dangers of oversimplification, therefore, when GAD is seen as primarily a disorder of maladaptive cognitive processing in which worry is the essential defining feature, which drives the emotional response. Both somatic symptoms and chronic worrying are features of GAD, with varying emphases depending on the individual concerned. Theories of GAD need to account for both cognitive and biological maintaining factors and their joint relation to proximal environmental stressors and developmental vulnerabilities (Goldberg & Goodyear, 2005). Generalised anxiety disorder is a complex emotional response in which cognitive appraisal processes are likely to be one significant causal factor and associative learning processes linking events with anxious arousal another (cf. Power & Dalgleish, 1999).

PSYCHOLOGICAL TREATMENTS

Standard Treatment Strategies

Guidance for therapists on the psychological treatment of GAD can be found in a number of reviews and treatment manuals (Andrews *et al.*, 2002; Borkovec & Newman, 1999; Brown *et al.*, 2002; Clark, 1989; Wells & Butler, 1997). Guidance for sufferers can be found in sections of general self-help books (such as Butler & Hope, 1996), treatment manuals (Andrews *et al.*, 2002) and books focused solely on worry and how to cope with it (such as Hallowell, 1997). All of these sources adopt as their primary focus the broad 'coping skills' approach that is characteristic of cognitive behavioural therapy. Habitual, maladaptive cycles of worry and tension need to be reversed through systematic, repetitive focus on, firstly, understanding the personal triggers and patterns of thinking, behaving and feeling that underlie the disorder and, secondly, on acquiring active habits of reacting to these triggers with more balanced thinking, lower arousal, and active problem solving.

The standard therapies for GAD, evaluated in clinical trials from 1980 to 2000, have been broadly based on the procedures and principles of cognitive therapy as applied to the appraisal of threat (Beck, Emery & Greenberg, 1985) and behaviour therapy as applied to reducing muscle tension through relaxation training (Bernstein & Borkovec, 1973; Ost, 1987). These approaches will be familiar to therapists with a basic training in cognitive behaviour therapy (CBT). The primary emphasis is on a process of self-regulation in which the sufferer learns to understand and then interrupt his or her particular cycle of anxiety triggers, bodily responses and worries with coping strategies based on either reducing arousal and muscle tension or changing the beliefs, and appraisal processes that underlie worrisome thinking. Clinical and research evidence suggests that confidence in either approach can bring about significant reductions in the severity of GAD but confidence in both is probably most effective. As GAD sufferers are often socially anxious, lacking in self-esteem and demoralised by life circumstances, therapeutic strategies involving graded exposure, assertiveness training and problem solving may also be helpful.

At its most ambitious the overall goal of therapy is to bring about a fundamental shift in coping from an essentially passive, worried, inhibited reaction to potential threat to an active, problem-solving approach in which stressful events and emotional reactions are accepted and managed. For those GAD sufferers who accept worry and tension as an unchangeable aspect of their personality and have only limited insight into the maladaptive nature of the disorder, therapists face a considerable change in bringing about active engagement with the demands of therapy. Motivational issues are frequently complicated by the presence of comorbid disorders and effective therapy is likely to depend crucially on the collaborative development of a formulation that emphasises the central role of worry and tension in maintaining the problems perceived to be most distressing.

Evidence from Clinical Trials

More than 30 clinical trials of the efficacy of psychological treatments for GAD were published between 1975 and 2002, about half of which used DSM-defined diagnostic criteria from DSM-III onwards. The evidence is largely limited to CBT as this form of psychotherapy has been the main focus of evaluation in randomised controlled trials. A few non-CBT psychotherapies have been evaluated but only in the context of control conditions for testing the efficacy of CBT against non-specific treatment effects Most of the early trials compared 'cognitive-behavioural' therapies (cognitive restructuring, relaxation training, biofeedback, systematic desensitisation, anxiety management training) with no treatment, waiting list or psychological placebo. More recent trials have employed more complex and sophisticated combinations of behavioural and cognitive therapies with a more specific focus on worry. Direct comparisons of psychological therapy with pharmacotherapy are very few in number, most notably a comparison of diazepam, CBT and placebo, each alone and in combination (Power *et al.*, 1990), and a comparison of drug and psychological therapy for GAD, panic disorder and dysthymia (Tyrer *et al.*, 1993). Systematic reviews of these clinical trials have addressed a number of questions – the most important, for initial consideration, being whether or not treatment is more effective than no treatment.

A meta-analytic review by Gould and colleagues (Gould *et al.*, 1997) addressed treatment efficacy for 13 studies comparing psychological therapy with no treatment, wait-list or psychological placebo and 22 studies comparing pharmacotherapy with pill placebo. Both within- and between-group effect sizes were calculated for anxiety and depression measures at post-treatment and, where available, for follow-up. Length of treatment was fairly short (three to nine weeks for pharmacotherapy and six to 15 weeks for psychological therapy) and follow-up data limited to six months in six of the psychological treatment studies. The majority of studies allowed comorbid anxiety disorders as long as GAD was the primary disorder. The results indicated that, for severity of anxiety symptoms at post-treatment, both CBT and pharmacotherapy were superior to control conditions and of broadly similar efficacy with moderately large effect sizes (ES = 0.70 for CBT, ES = 0.61 for pharmacotherapy). For severity of depressive symptoms CBT was associated with a significantly greater antidepressant effect than pharmacotherapy (ES = 0.77 for CBT, ES = 0.46 for pharmacotherapy). Among CBT interventions there was evidence that the combination of cognitive and behavioural techniques was more efficacious than each used independently. The limited evidence on follow-up for CBT conditions suggested that therapeutic gains were largely maintained and the authors contrasted this finding with other evidence that the long-term efficacy of pharmacotherapy (mainly benzodiazepines in this review) was attenuated following medication discontinuation.

In the short term, therefore, it might be reasonable to conclude that CBT and pharmacotherapy are both efficacious but that CBT, importantly, may have the edge in the maintenance of treatment gains and in treating comorbid depression. Benzodiazepines, however, are no longer considered to be an appropriate first-line treatment for GAD because of dependency and withdrawal problems and an increased risk of sedation and industrial and road traffic accidents with prolonged treatment. In contrast, the newer antidepressants (such as the SSRI, paroxetine) can be effective with GAD and comorbid depression, in both the short and longer term, and carry a reduced risk of dependency and rebound withdrawal problems (Ballenger *et al.*, 2001; Davidson, 2001). The safest conclusion is that both CBT and antidepressants are broadly equivalent in efficacy and more effective than no treatment.

A more recent review by Borkovec & Ruscio (2001) analysed effect sizes for 10 of the same studies as in the previous review plus three studies not included, one of which compared CBT with psychoanalytic therapy (Durham *et al.*, 1994) and one of which evaluated CBT for GAD in older adults (Stanley *et al.*, 1996). This review is of interest in including a detailed breakdown of the methodological characteristics of the studies (described as generally rigorous) and in analysing effect sizes for four aggregated comparison groups: CBT, CT or BT, placebo or alternative therapies, wait list/no-treatment. Effect-size calculations were based on the five most commonly used outcome measures for anxiety (assessor rated severity of GAD on a 0–8 scale, Hamilton Rating Scale for Anxiety, and the Trait version of the State-Trait Anxiety Inventory) and depression (Hamilton Rating Scale for Depression and Beck Depression Inventory). The outcome of the analysis was consistent across studies with CBT clearly associated with the largest within-group and between-group effect sizes relative to all other comparison conditions. The absence of change in the wait-list/no treatment conditions is particularly striking in this review with mean within-group effect sizes on anxiety measures at post-treatment being 2.48 for CBT conditions and 0.01 for wait-list no treatment conditions. In the absence of treatment GAD shows little change and the spontaneous remission rate is estimated at around 20-25 % (Ballenger *et al.*, 2001).

Clinical Significance of Treatment Effects

Cognitive behaviour therapy is clearly established as an efficacious treatment for GAD (cf. Roth & Fonagy, 1996; Westen & Morrison, 2001), and is recommended as a first line treatment in the NICE guidelines (National Institute for Clinical Excellence, 2004), but what about the clinical significance of treatment effects? Fisher & Durham (1999) reviewed six clinical trials conducted between 1990 and 1998, all of which used rigorous selection criteria and employed the State-Trait Anxiety Inventory (STAI-T) (Spielberger *et al.*, 1983) as a common outcome measure. Jacobson's methodology for determining clinically significant change (Jacobson *et al.*, 1999) was applied to the STAI-T to allocate individual participants (total n = 404) to one of four categories: reliable deterioration, no change, reliable improvement within the dysfunctional population and recovery. A recovery rate of about 40 % was found for the sample as a whole with 12 of the 20 treatment conditions obtaining very modest recovery rates of 30 % or less. The best results were found with individual CBT and applied relaxation, which had recovery rates at six months follow-up of 50–60 %.

Evidence of treatment efficacy over the longer term (several years or more) is limited. Seivewright and colleagues conducted a five-year follow-up of a cohort of 210 psychiatric outpatients suffering from GAD, panic disorder or dysthymic disorder and randomised to medication, CBT or self help (Seivewright *et al.*, 1998). Sixty per cent had a broadly favourable outcome with the remainder handicapped either intermittently or continuously throughout the follow-up period. Of relevance to the current discussion is that neither initial diagnosis or treatment condition was found to be of predictive value. A 10 to 14 year follow-up of two clinical trials was recently completed in central Scotland using structured interview with an assessor blind to initial treatment condition (Durham *et al.*, 2003). One of the studies (Power *et al.*, 1990), had been based in primary care using DSM-III criteria, and had compared CBT with a benzodiazepine and placebo whereas the other (Durham *et al.*, 1994) had been based in secondary care and compared CBT with analytic psychotherapy. Follow-up samples were relatively low (30 % and 55 % of trial entrants respectively) but broadly representative of the original cohorts. Overall, 30 % to 40 % of participants were recovered (free of symptoms) and 30 % to 40 % did poorly. Outcome was significantly worse for the study based in secondary care in which the clinical presentation of participants was more complex and severe. Treatment with CBT was associated with significantly lower overall severity of symptomatology and less interim treatment, in comparison with non-CBT conditions, but there was no evidence that CBT influenced diagnostic status, probability of recovery or patient perceptions of overall improvement.

Treatment gains following CBT may, therefore, be less enduring than had been assumed from clinical trials with six- to 12-month follow-up periods. Sustained reductions in vulnerability to episodes of GAD, or other anxiety and depressive disorders, may occur in only a minority of people following a course of therapy. Some do well over the shorter term but relapse following stressful events and still others suffer a chronic course with continuing disability and distress. It seems reasonable to conclude that both CBT and the complexity and severity of presenting problems have a significant influence on the long-term outcome of GAD. This raises two important questions for the future: can we identify the characteristics of subgroups of people with GAD who do well and who do poorly and can we improve the power of current treatments and the quality of service delivery?

The Search for Moderating Variables

The search for reliable factors that moderate response to therapy is a natural step given the evidence of variable outcome and is of considerable theoretical importance. Unfortunately, small sample sizes and diverse measures, to name just two methodological difficulties, have limited growth of knowledge in this area (Durham, 2006). It is probably helpful at the outset to distinguish between general *prognostic factors* indicative of the overall likelihood of change for a person having GAD, irrespective of treatment received, and more specific *treatment response indicators,* reflecting that person's willingness and ability to engage with the demands of therapy. The former concern the complexity and severity of the person's presenting symptomatology and underlying vulnerability, the quality of their social adjustment and the severity of associated psychosocial stressors, whereas the latter concern the perceived suitability and power of the treatment being offered, the quality of the therapeutic alliance and the degree of engagement in therapeutic tasks.

A conceptual framework for outcome prediction along these lines has been described by Durham, Swan & Fisher (2000) who suggest that general prognostic factors will be most strongly related to outcome over the longer term and specific treatment response indicators will be most closely related to short- and medium-term outcome. They devised scales to reflect these two factors on the basis of both general research on prognostic factors in anxiety and depressive disorders and GAD clinical trial data (cf. Durham *et al.*, 1997). General prognostic indicators are reflected in the CASP index (Complexity and Severity of Presenting Problems) while treatment response indicators are reflected in the CAIR index (Collaborative Alliance and Initial Response). The CASP is a simple additive scale based on a yes/no rating of the following eight factors:

- axis 1 comorbidity;
- previous psychiatric treatment;
- single, widowed or divorced;
- significant relationship difficulties;
- low socioeconomic status;
- low self-esteem;
- high self-reported symptomatology;
- high clinician-rated clinical global severity.

Of these variables, the importance of comorbidity (axis 1 and 2), social adjustment/marital tension, global severity of disorder and, to a lesser extent, low socioeconomic status/unemployment, have received independent support (cf. Borkovec *et al.*, 2002; Yonkers *et al.*, 2000). The CASP index was used in a clinical effectiveness study to test whether or not more intensive CBT (15 versus nine sessions) was more effective with poor prognosis GAD patients (Durham *et al.*, 2004). A comparison group of good prognosis GAD patients (low scores on the CASP) was given brief CBT (five sessions). There were no differences in outcome between the levels of treatment for the poor prognosis patients and both did relatively poorly at post-treatment and six month follow-up. In contrast, the good prognosis condition did significantly better at six-month follow-up than poor prognosis patients despite receiving only brief treatment. This result lends some support for the validity of the CASP but further refinement and testing of the scale is clearly needed.

Enhancing Clinical Effectiveness

Generalised anxiety disorder is clearly a difficult condition to treat effectively on account of both its chronicity and complexity of presentation and our incomplete understanding of the essential vulnerabilities and psychological mechanisms that maintain the disorder. Although clinical trials have established that cognitive behavioural therapies, based on standard behavioural and cognitive strategies, are more efficacious than no treatment or alternative therapies, treatment effects are generally modest and may not be sustained over the longer term. Preliminary evidence on treatment efficacy in routine clinical practice suggests that recovery rates may be lower outside specialist treatment centres.

Three issues need to be addressed if we are to improve the effectiveness of psychological treatment. First, as argued persuasively by Ballenger *et al.* (2001), there is a need to increase awareness of the importance of the disorder as a potential source of long-term damage to physical and mental health, as well as quality of life, and as a suitable focus, therefore, for clinical assessment and intervention. Generalised anxiety disorder is frequently overlooked in healthcare settings, and consequently undertreated, either because presenting complaints such as fatigue or sleeping problems are given more weight than the underlying pattern of chronic worry and tension of which they are a part or because its presence is masked by other disorders, which are judged to be primary and which become the main focus of attention. The importance of GAD and the key questions required to make a diagnosis need greater emphasis in the education of healthcare professionals.

Second, it will be of value for both clinical and health economic reasons to develop prognostic indices that identify those people who are likely to respond positively to brief intervention and those who may require more intensive therapy and long-term management. Generalised anxiety disorder is a common condition, trained therapists are scarce and, for the large number of people with less severe or subthreshold forms of the disorder, self-help and brief CBT is likely to be the most effective and efficient clinical response. There are well-established programmes of this kind (White, 2000; Williams, 2003) that can be incorporated into a stepped care model of service delivery as advocated in the NICE guidelines (National Institute for Clinical Excellence, 2004). For those people whose prognosis is poor, or who fail to respond to brief intervention, more intensive therapy will be required. The exact nature of this more intensive therapy has yet to be established and this is the third issue that needs to be addressed.

The promise of theoretical advances in our understanding of the nature of chronic worry and tension is the development of treatment strategies that target more precisely those vulnerabilities and psychological processes that keep the disorder going. This has been one of the central themes of clinical researchers such as Adrian Wells and Tom Borkovec and there is no doubt that progress has been made. Candidates for future clinical trials include worry exposure and worry behaviour prevention (Brown, O'Leary & Barlow, 2002), cognitive therapy focussed on metacognition (Wells, 1999), therapy for interpersonal difficulties (Crits-Christoff et al., 1996; Newman et al., 2002), mindfulness training (Roemer & Orsillo, 2002) and a therapeutic focus on intolerance of uncertainty (Ladoucer et al., 2000). A recent analysis of the efficacy of those newer therapies by Fisher (2006) does suggest that they can deliver significantly higher recovery rates although large scale clinical trials have yet to be undertaken.

CONCLUSION

Our understanding of GAD has advanced significantly since the mid-1980s and there is no doubt that chronic tension and worry are both significant sources of human distress and important vulnerability factors for physical and psychiatric morbidity. Unfortunately, the presence of GAD is frequently overlooked in clinical settings and our current therapies are ineffective for a significant minority of sufferers. Future developments in enhancing treatment efficacy are likely to come from recent improvements to existing therapies that are promising but not yet fully tested and from flexible methods of service delivery that offer brief interventions emphasizing self-management as well as intensive therapy for those with complex presentations.

REFERENCES

Akiskal, H.S. (1998). Toward a definition of generalized anxiety disorder as an anxious temperament type. *Acta Psychiatrica Scandinavica, 98* (suppl. 393), 66–73.

Andrews, G. (2000). The anxiety disorder inclusion and exclusion criteria in DSM-IV and ICD-10. *Current Opinion in Psychiatry, 13*, 139–141.

Andrews, G., Crino, R., Hunt, C. *et al.* (2002). *The Treatment of Anxiety Disorders: Clinician's Guide and Patient Manuals* (2nd edn). Cambridge: Cambridge University Press.

Antony, M.M., Orsillo, S.M. & Roemer, L. (eds) (2001). *Practitioner's Guide to Empirically Based Measures of Anxiety*. AABT Clinical Assessment Series. New York: Kluwer Academic/Plenum Publishers.

APA. (1994). *Diagnostic and Statistical Manual of Mental Disorders* (4th edn). Washington DC: APA.

Ballenger, J., Davidson, J., Lecrubier, Y. *et al.* (2001). Consensus statement on generalised anxiety disorder from the international concensus group on depression and anxiety. *Journal of Clinical Psychiatry, 62* (suppl. 11), 53–58.

Beck, A.T., Emery, G. & Greenberg, R. (1985). *Anxiety Disorder and Phobias: a Cognitive Perspective*. New York: Basic Books.

Bernstein, D. & Borkovec, T.D. (1973). *Progressive Relaxation Training*. Champaign, IL: Research Press.

Bernstein, G., Borchardt, C.M. & Perwien, A.R. (1996). Anxiety disorders in children and adolescents: A review of the past 10 years. *Journal of American Academy of Child and Adolescent Psychiatry, 35*, 1110–1119.

Blazer, D.G., Hughes, D. & George, L.K. (1987). Stressful life events and the onset of a generalised anxiety syndrome. *American Journal of Psychiatry, 144*, 1178–1183.

Borkovec, T.D. (1994). The nature, function and origins of worry. In G. Davey & F. Tallis (eds), *Worrying: Perspectives in Theory, Assessment and Treatment* (pp. 5–34). New York: Wiley.

Borkovec, T.D. & Newman, M.G. (1999). Worry and generalized anxiety disorder. In P. Salkovskis (ed.), *Comprehensive Clinical Psychology. Adults: Clinical Formulation and Treatment*, vol. 6 (pp. 439–459). Oxford: Elsevier Science.

Borkovec, T.D., Newman, M., Pincus, A. & Lytle, R. (2002). A component analysis of cognitive be-havioural therapy for generalized anxiety disorder and the role of interpersonal problems. *Journal of Consulting and Clinical Psychology, 70*, 288–298.

Borkovec, T.D., Ray, W.J. & Stoeber, J. (1998). Worry: a cognitive phenomenon intimately linked to affective, physiological and interpersonal behavioural processes. *Cognitive Therapy and Research, 22*, 561–576.

Borkovec, T.D. & Ruscio, A. (2001). Psychotherapy for generalized anxiety disorder. *Journal of Clinical Psychiatry, 62* (suppl. 11), 37–42.

Brown, T.A., O'Leary, T.A. & Barlow, D.H. (2002). *Generalised Anxiety Disorder, Clinical Handbook of Psychological Disorders: A Step-by-Step Treatment Manual* (2nd edn). New York: Guilford Press.

Butler, G. & Hope, T. (1996). *Manage Your Mind: The Mental Fitness Guide.* New York: Oxford University Press.

Clark, D.M. (1989). Anxiety states: Panic and generalised anxiety. In K. Hawton, P. Salkovskis, J. Kirk & D.M. Clark (eds), *Cognitive Behaviour Therapy for Psychiatric Problems: A Practical Guide.* Oxford: Oxford Medical Publications.

Clark, D.M., Ball, S. & Pape, D. (1991). An experimental investigation of thought suppression. *Behaviour Research and Therapy, 29*, 253–257.

Craske, M.G., Rapee, R.M., Jackel, L. & Barlow, D.H. (1989). Qualitative dimensions of worry in DSM111-R: Generalised anxiety disorder subjects and nonanxious controls. *Behaviour Research and Therapy, 27*, 397–402.

Crits-Christoff, P., Connolly, M., Azarian, K. *et al.* (1996). An open trial of brief supportive-expressive psychotherapy in the treatment of generalized anxiety disorder. *Psychotherapy, 33*, 418–431.

Davey, G.C.L. & Wells, A. (2006). (Eds.) *Worry and its Psychological Disorders: Theory, Assessment and Treatment.* Chichester: John Wiley & Sons, Ltd.

Davidson, J. (2001). Pharmacotherapy of generalized anxiety disorder. *Journal of Clinical Psychiatry, 62* (suppl. 11), 46–50.

Dugas, M.J., Gagnon, F., Ladoucer, R. & Freeston, M.H. (1998). Generalised anxiety disorder: A preliminary test of a conceptual model. *Behaviour Research and Therapy, 36*, 215–226.

Durham, R.E. (2006). Predictors of treatment outcome. In G.C.L. Davey & A. Wells (Eds.) *Worry and its Psychological Disorders: Theory, Assessment and Treatment* (pp 379–397), Chichester: John Wiley & Sons, Ltd.

Durham, R.C., Allan, T. & Hackett, C. (1997). On predicting improvement and relapse in generalised anxiety disorder following psychotherapy. *British Journal of Clinical Psychology, 36*, 101–119.

Durham, R.C., Murphy, T.J., Allan, T. *et al.* (1994). A comparison of cognitive therapy, analytic psychotherapy and anxiety management training in the treatment of generalised anxiety disorder. *British Journal of Psychiatry, 165*, 315–323.

Durham, R.C., Chambers, J.A., Macdonald, R.R. *et al.* (2003). Does cognitive behavioural therapy influence the course of generalised anxiety disorder? 10–14 year follow-up of two clinical trials. *Psychological Medicine, 33*, 1–11.

Durham, R.C., Fisher, P.L., Dow, M.G.T. *et al.* (2004). Cognitive behaviour therapy for good and poor prognosis generalized anxiety disorder: A clinical effectiveness study. *Clinical Psychology and Psychotherapy, 11*, 145–157.

Durham, R.C., Swan, J.S. & Fisher, P.L. (2000). Complexity and collaboration in routine practice of CBT: What doesn't work with whom and how might it work better? *Journal of Mental Health, 9*, 429–444.

Fava, M., Rankin, M.A., Wright, E.C. *et al.* (2000). Anxiety disorders in major depression. *Comprehensive Psychiatry, 41*, 97–102.

Fisher, P.L. (2006). The efficacy of psychological treatments for generalised anxiety disorder. In G.C.L. Davey & A. Wells (Eds.). *Worry and its Psychological Disorders: Theory, Assessment and Treatment* (pp 359–377). Chichester: John Wiley & Sons, Ltd.

Fisher, P. L. & Durham, R. C. (1999). Recovery rates in generalised anxiety disorder following psychological therapy: An analysis of clinically significant change in STAI-T across outcome studies since 1990. *Psychological Medicine, 29*, 1425–1434.

Goldberg, D. & Lecrubier, Y. (1995). Form and frequency of mental disorders across centres. In T. Ustun & N. Sartorius (eds), Mental illness in general healthcare: an international study (pp. 323–334). New York: John Wiley & Sons.

Goldberg, D. & Goodyear, I. (2005). *The Origins and Course of Common Mental Disorders*. New York: Routledge.

Gould, R., Otto, M., Pollack, M. & Yap, L. (1997). Cognitive behavioural and pharmacological treatment of generalized anxiety disorder: a preliminary meta-analysis. *Behavior Therapy, 28*, 285–305.

Greenberg, P., Sisitsky, T., Kessler, R. *et al.* (1999). The economic burden of anxiety disorders in the 1990s. *Journal of Clinical Psychiatry, 60*, 427–435.

Hallowell, E. (1997). *Worry: Controlling it and Using it Wisely*. New York: Ballantine Books.

Hunt, C.J. (2002). The current status of the diagnostic validity and treatment of generalized anxiety disorer. *Current Opinion in Psychiatry, 15*, 157–162.

Jacobson, N.S., Roberts, L.J., Berns, S.B. & McGlinchey, J. (1999). Methods for defining and determining the clinical significance of treatment effects in mental health research: Current status, new applications and future directions. *Journal of Consulting and Clinical Psychology, 67*, 300–307.

Judd, L.L., Kessler, R.C., Paulus, M.P. *et al.* (1998). Comorbidity as a fundamental feature of generalized anxiety disorder: Results from the National Comorbidity Study (NCS). *Acta Psychiatrica Scandinavica, 98* (suppl. 393), 6–11.

Kessler, R. (2000). The epidemiology of pure and comorbid generalised anxiety disorder: A review and evaluation of recent research. *Acta Psychiatrica Scandinavica, 102*, 7–13.

Kessler, R., Keller, M.B. & Wittchen, H.-U. (2001). The epidemiology of generalized anxiety disorder. *Psychiatric Clinics of North America, 24*, 19–40.

Ladoucer, R., Dugas, M., Freeston, M. *et al.* (2000). Efficacy of a cognitive-behavioural treatment for generalized anxiety disorder: evaluation in a controlled clinical trial. *Journal of Consulting and Clinical Psychology, 68*, 957–964.

Lecrubier, Y. (1998). Risk factors for suicide attempts: Epidemiological evidence (abstract). *European Neuropsychopharmacology*, 8 (suppl. 1), S114.

Maier, W., Gansicke, M., Freyberger, H.J. *et al.* (2000). Generalized anxiety disorder (ICD-10) in primary care from a cross-cultural perspective: A valid diagnostic entity? *Acta Psychiatrica Scandinavica, 101*, 29–36.

National Institute for Clinical Excellence (2004). Clinical Guideline 22. Anxiety: Management of anxiety (panic disorder, with or without agoraphobia, and generalised anxiety disorder) in adults in primary, secondary and community care. http://www.nice.org.uk.

Newman, M., Castonguay, L., Borkovec, T. D. & Molnar, C. (2002). Integrative therapy for generalized anxiety disorder. In R. Heimberg, C. Turk & D. Mennin (eds), *Generalized Anxiety Disorder: Advances in Research and Practice*. New York: Guilford Press.

Noyes, R., Woodman, C., Garvey, M.J. *et al.* (1992). Generalised anxiety disorder vs panic disorder: Distinguishing characteristics and patterns of comorbidity. *Journal of Nervous and Mental Disorders, 180*, 369–379.

Ormel, J., VonKorff, M., Ustun, T. *et al.* (1994). Common mental disorders and disability across cultures: Results from the WHO Collaborative Study on psychosocial Problems in General Health Care. *Journal of the American Medical Association, 272*, 1741–1748.

Ost, L. (1987). Applied relaxation: Description of a coping technique and review of controlled studies. *Behaviour Research and Therapy, 25*, 397–409.

Power, K.G., Simpson, R.J., Swanson, V. *et al.* (1990). A controlled comparison of cognitive-behaviour therapy, diazepam, and placebo, alone and in combination, for the treatment of generalised anxiety. *Journal of Anxiety Disorders, 4*, 267–292.

Power, M.J. & Dalgleish, T. (1999). Two routes to emotion: some implications of multi-level theories of emotion for therapeutic practice. *Behavioural and Cognitive Psychotherapy, 27*, 129–141.

Rickels, K. & Rynn, M. (2001). What is generalised anxiety disorder? *Journal of Clinical Psychiatry, 62* (suppl. 11), 4–14.

Roemer, L. & Orsillo, S. (2002). Expanding our conceptualisation of and treatment for gener-alized anxiety disorder: integrating mindfulness/acceptance-based approaches with existing cognitive-behavioural models. *Clinical Psychology: Science and Practice, 9*, 54–68.

Rogers, M.P., Warshaw, M.G., Goisman, R.M., *et al.* (1999). Comparing primary and secondary generalized anxiety disorders in a long-term naturalistic study of anxiety disorders. *Depression and Anxiety, 10*, 1–7.

Roth, A. & Fonagy, P. (2005). *What Works for Whom? A Critical Review of Psychotherapy Research* (2nd edn). London: Guilford Press.

Seivewright, H., Tyrer, P. & Johnson, T. (1998). Prediction of outcome in neurotic disorder: A five-year prospective study. *Psychological Medicine, 28*, 1149–1157.

Spielberger, C.D., Gorsuch, R.L., Lushene, R. *et al.* (1983). *Manual for the State-Trait Anxiety Inventory (Form Y Self-evaluation Questionnaire)*. Palo Alto, CA: Consulting Psychologists Press.

Stanley, M.A., Beck, J.G. & Glassco, J.D. (1996). Treatment of generalized anxiety disorder in older adults: a preliminary comparison of cognitive-behavioral and supportive approaches. *Behaviour Therapy, 27*, 565–581.

Stanley, M. & Novy, D. (2000). Cognitive-behaviour therapy for generalized anxiety in late life: an evaluative overview. *Journal of Anxiety Disorders, 14*, 191–207.

Tyrer, P. (1999). *Anxiety: A Multidisciplinary Review*. London: Imperial College Press.

Tyrer, P., Seivewright, N., Ferguson, B. *et al.* (1993). The Nottingham study of neurotic disorder: Effect of personality status on response to drug treatment, cognitive therapy and self-help over two years. *British Journal of Psychiatry, 162*, 219–226.

Wells, A. (1999). A metacognitive model and therapy for generalized anxiety disorder. *Clinical Psychology and Psychotherapy, 6*, 86–95.

Wells, A. & Butler, G. (1997). Generalised anxiety disorder. In D.M. Clark & C.G. Fairburn (eds), *Science and Practice of Cognitive Behaviour Therapy*. Oxford: Oxford University Press.

Westen, D. & Morrison, K. (2001). A multi-dimensional meta-analysis of treatments for depression, panic and generalized anxiety disorder: an empirical examination of the status of empirically supported therapies. *Journal of Consulting and Clinical Psychology, 69*, 875–899.

White, J. (2000). *Treating Anxiety and Stress: A Group Psycho-educational Approach using Brief CBT*. Chichester: Wiley.

Williams, C.J. (2003). *Overcoming Anxiety: A Five Areas Approach*. London: Hodder Arnold.

Wittchen, H.-U., Carter, R., Pfister, H. *et al.* (2000). Disabilities and quality of life in pure and comorbid generalized anxiety disorder and major depression in a national survey. *International Journal of Clinical Psychopharmacology, 15*, 319–328.

Wittchen, H.-U., Zhoa, S., Kessler, R.C. & Eaton, W.W. (1994). DSM-IIIR generalised anxiety disorder in the National Comorbidity Survey. *Archives of General Psychiatry, 51*, 355–364.

World Health Organization (1993). *The ICD-10 Classification of Mental and Behavioural Disorders: Diagnostic Criteria for Research*. Geneva: World Health Organization.

Yonkers, K., Dyck, I., Warshaw, M. & Keller, M. (2000). Factors predicting the clinical course of generalised anxiety disorder. *British Journal of Psychiatry, 176*, 544–549.

Yonkers, K., Warshaw, M., Massion, A. & Keller, M. (1996). Phenomenology and course of generalised anxiety disorder. *British Journal of Psychiatry, 168*, 308–313.

CHAPTER 24

Adjuvant Psychological Therapy for Patients with Chronic Physical Illness

Tom M. Brown
Western Infirmary, Glasgow, UK
and
Siobhan MacHale
Royal Infirmary, Edinburgh, UK

INTRODUCTION

Despite the dominance of the biomedical model, there has been a huge amount of research into psychological aspects of medicine.

Alexander (1950), one of the great pioneers of psychosomatic medicine, attempted to apply psychoanalytic concepts to somatic medicine, hypothesising that psychological conflicts could alter the function of specific internal organs (he termed this 'specificity theory') and speculated that in a number of diseases psychological factors may be of aetiological importance, although he was clear that the aetiology of disease was multifactorial. He applied these concepts to diseases such as hypertension, rheumatoid arthritis, peptic ulcer and asthma.

The notion that psychological factors may be aetiologically important in either the genesis or the progression of physical illness persists. A full discussion of this is beyond the scope of this chapter, though we briefly discuss this particularly in relation to ischaemic heart disease and cancer.

There is a strong association between most chronic diseases and psychiatric disorder, especially depression (Katon & Sullivan, 1990). Increasing awareness of this has led to an upsurge in the literature assessing both pharmacological and psychological interventions in this area. For a review of the use of antidepressants the reader is referred to the review by Gill & Hatcher (2003).

For a comprehensive guide to the psychological assessment and practical management of patients with chronic physical illness the reader is referred to White (2001). Salmon (2000) provides an excellent account of how psychological principles can be applied to health care.

Handbook of Evidence-based Psychotherapies: A Guide for research and practice.
Edited by C. Freeman & M. Power. Copyright © 2007 John Wiley & Sons, Ltd.

Because of the volume of the literature in this area and constraints of space we have chosen to focus on eight large areas of medicine, namely ischaemic heart disease, stroke, hypertension, cancer, diabetes mellitus, rheumatoid arthritis, asthma and skin diseases. For the same reason we have looked principally at the literature in relation to adults and not children and adolescents.

CARDIAC DISEASE

Introduction

The important contribution of psychological factors to mortality and morbidity associated with ischaemic heart disease (IHD) is now well recognised. In a review of evidence-based cardiology, Hemingway & Marmot (1999) concluded that 'prospective cohort studies provide strong evidence that psychosocial factors, particularly depression and social support, are independent aetiological and prognostic factors for coronary heart disease.' The prevalence rates of major depressive illness in patients with IHD are three times that in the normal population. Cardiac mortality rates are increased by between three and four times for patients who are depressed post myocardial infarction (MI) compared with patients who have had a MI but are not depressed. Indeed the prognostic impact of depressive illness is comparable to that of degrees of ventricular dysfunction or coronary atherosclerosis in patients who have had a heart attack. Half of all cases of depression post-MI will remit spontaneously, with the other half either persisting or remitting followed by relapse within the year (Glassman, 2002).

Carney *et al.* (2002) has usefully summarised the literature with respect to the potential pathophysiological factors implicated. These can be separated into *indirect* (alterations in health-related behaviours such as compliance with treatments and smoking cessation) and *direct* mechanisms (including evidence of reduced heart rate variability in patients with IHD who are depressed, enhanced platelet reactivity and inflammatory processes). This suggests a plausible role for psychotherapy in helping to reduce the mortality and morbidity associated with cardiac disease, by focusing on behavioural interventions and/or the reduction of psychological distress.

Evidence for Psychotherapy

Prior to the eagerly awaited outcome of the Enhancing Recovery in Coronary Heart Disease Patients (ENRICHD) trial, detailed below, much of the literature had relied on cardiac nurse-led psychosocial interventions (often termed psychological interventions or counselling), with variable outcomes. This led to conflicting views about the efficacy of addressing psychological issues in cardiac patients. Linden's (2000) review of psychological treatments in cardiac rehabilitation programmes commented on the differing treatment approaches ranging from relaxation/breathing retraining, unstructured support or psychoeducation to improve compliance, to psychological interventions to reduce emotional distress. He concluded that critical differences in study outcomes can be explained by the finding that studies which failed to have an impact on levels of psychological distress also fail to have an impact on mortality or event recurrence.

Most of the reliable evidence for psychological interventions involves cognitive behavioural therapy (CBT) or behavioural therapy. However, even the CBT used was described as 'broadly defined' by Bennett & Carroll (1994) in a review of cognitive-behavioural interventions in cardiac rehabilitation. They commented on the difficulty of reaching definite conclusions in an area so beset by methodological weaknesses. These include problems with differing measures of psychological distress and variable outcomes, as well as the application of treatments irrespective of baseline measures of psychological distress – the so-called *floor effect*. The random assignment of all cardiac patients to psychological treatment without an assessment of actual psychological need is unlikely to be cost effective. It is also known that individually tailored treatment is more effective than standardised treatment packages.

Many studies include very small subject numbers, which are particularly unimpressive to cardiologists who are used to large international trials of thrombolysis incorporating 50 000 subjects. In an attempt to address this, there have been four notable meta-analytic reviews of efficacy of psychological interventions additional to usual treatment in patients with IHD.

- The focus of earlier studies in the 1980s was on Type A behaviour (TAB), a personality trait characterised by competitive, driven behaviour, hostility and impatience, as a risk factor for IHD. Nunes, Frank & Kornfeld (1987) carried out a meta-analysis of modification of TAB in 18 studies and noted that longer, more complex treatments produced more significant impact on mortality and morbidity rates up to three years after a MI. The most significant of these was the Recurrent Coronary Prevention Project (Friedman *et al.*, 1986), which randomly assigned patients to an educationally based cardiac counselling group (n = 270) or a Type A counselling group (n = 592). The Type A counselling, which combined didactic, CBT and existential humanistic components, resulted in a reduced coronary recurrence rate of 7 % compared to 13 % in the control group over a three-year follow-up. Of particular note was the finding that those who showed a reduction of TAB, irrespective of group allocation, had one-fifth of the cardiac recurrence rate of those who had no significant reduction in TAB. Subsequent studies have, however, failed to replicate this association, tending to focus instead on hostility as the pathogenic component of TAB.
- Linden, Stossel & Maurice (1996) then looked at psychological interventions (mainly 'broadly defined CBT') in a meta-analysis of 23 randomised controlled trials (RCTs) of cardiac rehabilitation and reported a positive impact on mortality and morbidity rates as well as a reduction in depression and anxiety levels.
- Dusseldorp *et al.* (1999) were less convinced by their further meta-analysis, based on 37 RCTs. However this included two large RCTs the first of which, by Jones & West (1996), involved 2 328 patients, most of whom were neither anxious nor depressed. The second, by Frasure-Smith *et al.* (1997) 1 376 patients were treated by cardiac nurses with no psychotherapy training using less sophisticated forms of psychological interventions with, not surprisingly, much less impact. Of particular relevance is the finding that mortality and MI recurrence rates were only reduced in those studies that also reduced levels of psychological distress.
- A Cochrane systematic review of the effectiveness of psychological interventions for patients with coronary heart disease has suggested that the reviews to date had not been fully systematic (Rees *et al.*, 2004). Some had included non-randomised trials and failed to differentiate sufficiently between types of psychosocial interventions. The Cochrane group

included 36 trials of psychological interventions in adults with coronary heart disease that had a minimum follow-up of six months, as well as identifying a subgroup of studies of 'stress management'. They noted extreme heterogeneity of the trials but were unable to carry out a planned stratified analysis of the data, due to a combination of insufficient trial information and numbers. Overall the outcomes of the 'stress management' subgroup were similar to all psychological interventions. They reported no evidence of reduced total mortality, but found some evidence of a reduction in non-fatal reinfarction in the intervention group. They caution that this apparent effect may be a result of ascertainment or publication bias, pointing out that the two largest studies (Berkman *et al.*, 2003; Jones & West, 1996) had shown no effect. Psychological outcomes were reported less often in the analysed trials. They concluded that there were small but significant effects on anxiety and a significant reduction in depression with psychological intervention.

The recently completed Enhancing Recovery in Coronary Heart Disease Patients (ENRICHD) trial is, however, at the forefront of current research in this area (Berkman *et al.*, 2003). The randomisation of 2 481 patients, enrolled within 28 days of acute myocardial infarction from eight clinical centres, into CBT versus usual care over six months makes it the largest controlled trial of psychotherapy ever completed. Patients (1 084 women, 1 397 men) were included if they met criteria for a DSM-IV diagnosis of depression or dysthymia ($\sim$ 75 %) or had low perceived social support (LPSS) ($\sim$ 25 %). To maximise cost-effectiveness, CBT and social learning interventions were given as a combination of individual (one hour weekly up to a maximum of six months) and group therapy (two hours weekly for 12 weeks). Treatment continued until the patient completed a minimum of six sessions, had developed self-therapy skills and had scored below seven on the BDI on two consecutive occasions. The ENRICHD counsellors were intensively trained in CBT and supervised weekly by experienced CB therapists. Although the therapy was manualised and standardised, a flexible approach was used to optimise recruitment and participation. This included 'taking the treatment to the patient', offering transport, conducting sessions over the telephone and motivational interviewing techniques. Adjunctive pharmacotherapy (generally sertraline) was used to treat patients with severe depression or slow to responders after five weeks of treatment.

The primary aim was to determine the impact of treating depression and low perceived social support on all-cause mortality and reinfarction rates. Secondary end-points included depression, LPSS and cardiac morbidity, and they achieved 93 % follow-up rates. Disappointingly, the intervention had no significant impact on recurrent MI or death at 29 months follow-up. There was an improvement on psychosocial outcomes at 6 months but this was not maintained at longer term follow-up.

Much debate has ensued to explain this negative outcome. The trial was initially designed in 1994, when the study of social support received as much attention as the impact of depression in the cardiac population. The ENRICHD trial involved the development of a new screening tool and CBT intervention for LPSS. It has been suggested in hindsight that there is as yet insufficient understanding of the impact of social support on cardiac prognosis to have targeted this (Frasure-Smith & Lesperance, 2003). Study power may have been reduced by the explicit inclusion of women (44 %) and minorities (34 %), unique to this cardiac study, with later subgroup analysis suggesting that white men alone may have benefited from the intervention. The study effect size, differentiating the outcomes between the intervention and standard care groups, was based on the assumption of no treatment of depression in the controls. There was a greater improvement in depression scores in the control group than expected, in part surely related to the finding at 36 months that 21 % of the controls had been prescribed antidepressants, compared to 28 % of the intervention group. On reflection, the study power, based on finding a 30 % difference in mortality and reinfarction between the groups, is also believed to have been unrealistic.

Finally, the significant but disappointingly small impact on depression scores is worth considering in the context of the other recent study looking at the effect of (pharmacological) treatment of depression post MI or unstable angina (Glassman *et al.*, 2002). The Sertraline Antidepressant Heart Attack Randomised trial (SADHART) of 369 depressed patients found no significant difference between 24 weeks double-blind treatment with sertraline and placebo. The authors recognised that screening patients soon after significant medical morbidity was likely to result in inclusion of milder, self-limiting depressive states, contributing to a significant placebo response. They therefore identified an *a priori* more severe depression group. Despite the smaller numbers, sertraline was found to be highly efficacious compared to placebo in this group. In an analysis of the ENRICHD study, Frasure-Smith & Lesperance (2003) suggest that a more aggressive, step-wise approach to treatment of patients who are depressed following MI may be necessary.

However this important study has proven that a large-scale multicentre trial of a standardised but individually tailored psychotherapy, requiring the close collaboration of psychologists, psychiatrists and cardiologists, is achievable. It has shown that most eligible patients can be successfully recruited with systematic screening and with little attrition on prolonged follow-up. Indeed, this trial is expected to remain a standard of comparison for many years (Frasure-Smith & Lesperance, 2003).

Although much of the research has focused on patients following MI, there is also some emerging evidence of benefit of CBT for patients with congestive cardiac failure, in reducing restenosis rates after angioplasty and in the treatment of recipients of implantable cardioverter defibrillators for ventricular dysrhythmias (Edelman & Lemon, 2003). A Cochrane systematic review attempting to assess the effects of psychological interventions for depression in patients with congenital heart disease failed to identify any RCTs in this area, despite evidence from cross-sectional studies of an association between congenital heart disease and depression (Lip *et al.*, 2003).

Conclusions

There is now considerable agreement, supported by robust research evidence, that psychological factors (particularly depression and poor social support) are associated with increased mortality and morbidity in patients with coronary artery disease. However, the pathophysiological mechanisms underlying this remain unclear and the evidence for psychotherapeutic interventions in reducing adverse clinical outcomes is equivocal.

In clinical terms, a stepped approach to patient care is advisable. The Scottish National Clinical Guidelines Network (SIGN) publishes evidence-based recommendations that have been extrapolated in a standardised format from meta-analyses, systematic reviews and/or RCTs. Their 2002 national clinical guideline on cardiac rehabilitation recommends that a comprehensive cardiac rehabilitation programme, including psychological interventions, is offered to all patients with significant angina, congestive cardiac failure or following a MI. In addition they advise appropriate treatment of patients with significant psychological distress diagnosed on routine screening. Of particular note are their recommendations that 'Rehabilitation staff should identify and address health beliefs and cardiac misconceptions in patients with CHD. (Lincoln & Flannaghan 2003). Patients with moderate to severe psychological difficulties should be treated by staff with specialist training in techniques such as CBT.'

The American College of Cardiology/American Heart Association have updated their guidelines for the management of patients with MI and recommend that the long-term management includes an evaluation of the patient's psychosocial status, with a particular emphasis on depression, anxiety and levels of social support (Antman *et al.*, 2004). They also recommend that treatment with CBT and selective serotonin reuptake inhibitors can be useful for patients who develop a depressive illness within a year of discharge from hospital.

STROKE

The psychological sequelae of stroke, particularly post-stroke depression, have been extensively detailed in the research literature. Up to 40 % of patients will suffer a depressive or anxiety disorder after stroke, with an associated negative impact on rehabilitation and increased mortality. Borrowing from the cancer literature, Lewis *et al.* (2001) found that fatalism and helplessness/hopelessness were associated with reduced survival after stroke. Lincoln's group has contributed most of the small evidence base currently available for the use of psychotherapeutic treatment (CBT) in depressed patients following stroke. Following an initial successful but non-randomised pilot study, they demonstrated negative cognitions in these patients that are qualitatively similar to those of non-stroke depressed patients, supporting the use of CBT as an appropriate treatment. They progressed to a RCT of 123 depressed patients following stroke, randomly allocating 1/3 of patients respectively to CBT (10 × one-hour sessions) given by a trained CPN, attention placebo (10 × one-hour sessions of general conversation) by the same CPN and a no intervention group. Although there was a significant improvement in mood over the six-month follow-up period, this was independent of the treatment given and the authors found no difference between the groups in levels of function or satisfaction with care. They suggest that future trials should increase the number of sessions to between 16 and 20, to allow appropriate comparison with other studies of the elderly, medically ill.

Using a different intervention, Clark, Rubenach & Winsor (2003) in Australia carried out a study of brief family counselling, along with an educational package, given to 32 families by a trained social worker over three sessions. They emphasise the importance of early treatment, within the first six months of the stroke, and reported a beneficial impact on family functioning and functional recovery when compared to a normal treatment control group. They found no impact on depression or anxiety, suggesting that the relatively low baseline scores for these measures may have explained this.

There are now two recent Cochrane reviews of relevance in this area. The first of these looks at the evidence supporting psychotherapeutic or pharmacological interventions to *prevent* depression after stroke, with the second focusing on *treating* depression after stroke. The reviewers considered inclusion of psychotherapeutic techniques only if there was 'a clearly defined psychological component' rather than just an educational package or general support.

• The review addressing prevention of depression included three RCTs of psychotherapeutic interventions (Anderson *et al.*, 2004) using problem-solving techniques taught by specialist nurses or a more broadly defined home-based intervention given by a mixed team of therapists. The Cochrane reviewers concluded there was a small but positive effect of psychotherapy on levels of mood but found no evidence for psychotherapy, or indeed pharmacotherapy, in reducing the number of cases of depression, levels of physical disability or other adverse effects after stroke.

- The latter Cochrane review addressed the evidence supporting treatment options (Hackett, Anderson & House, 2004). There were nine trials in total of which two looked at psychotherapeutic interventions. Despite some reduction of levels of depression on rating scales used, there was little evidence of complete remission of depression. The review concluded that there is as yet no evidence to support the routine use of either psychotherapy or medication to treat depression following stroke. However, the reviewers have reported elsewhere on the difficulty of the analysis due to the lack of standardised diagnostic, analytic or outcome measures and suggest this may be as relevant to their conclusions as any possible lack of efficacy of the proposed treatments.

HYPERTENSION

Some individuals are more susceptible to exaggerated cardiovascular changes, including blood pressure (BP) changes, in response to physical or psychological stress. The so-called 'reactivity hypothesis' suggests that such susceptibility contributes to cardiovascular pathology over time. Consistent findings in the literature on hypertension include greater cardiovascular responses to stress in hypertensive patients than normal controls and reports that the children of hypertensive parents respond to stress with greater elevations in blood pressure (Lane, Carroll & Lip, 2001).

The impact of antihypertensive medication on coronary heart disease has been less than expected, however, most likely because of the influence of adverse side effects and poor compliance. There has led to renewed interest in the non-pharmacological management of hypertension, with the aim of reducing stress by focusing on cognitive and behavioural stress coping strategies and reducing sympathetic arousal. Psychological interventions to date have tended to focus on either one or a combination of biofeedback, relaxation and stress-management techniques. An early meta-analysis purporting to assess the efficacy of cognitive behavioural techniques for hypertension included biofeedback, meditation and relaxation as forms of CB therapies, concluding that there was a lack of support for such interventions (Eisenberg et al., 1993). However, Linden and colleagues have suggested that there is such a varied interpretation of the term 'stress management', ranging from transcendental meditation to cognitive behaviour therapy that comparisons of such studies are not meaningful at present (Ong, Linden & Young, 2004). In a previous meta-analysis of hypertension treatments by Linden & Chambers (1994), the impact of individualised psychological therapy was found to match the effects of drug treatments on blood pressure. Similarly, a meta-analysis of behavioural interventions for hypertension found a beneficial impact of group counselling on blood pressure levels (Boulware et al., 2001) but has been criticised in a Cochrane structured review for a lack of clarity in the statistical methods and study designs included (Database of Abstracts of Reviews of Effects DARE-20012344).

It is worth looking in more detail at some selected studies such as that of Shapiro et al. (1997), albeit involving small numbers. They considered the impact of a true cognitive behavioural intervention as an adjunct to drug treatment of mild to moderate hypertension. Thirty-nine patients were randomised to either CBT (n = 22) administered by a clinical psychologist in six weekly group sessions lasting an hour-and-a half or an attention control group (n = 17), which had contact with a nurse practitioner. All patients were treated with a standardised antihypertensive drug regime, followed by gradual withdrawal of medication after the six-week period and follow-up to one year. The authors reported that the CBT intervention was twice as effective in reducing medication, with 73 % of the treatment group requiring lower levels of medication than at the start of the study, compared to 35 % of the control group at the one-year follow-up. They have usefully outlined the 10 components of their CBT intervention, including an emphasis on progressive muscle relaxation, cue-controlled relaxation and imagery and cognitive-behavioural techniques for stress and anger management. It is worth commenting that the positive effect of the intervention was achieved in this study despite a lack of impact on levels of anxiety, depression, health habits or quality of life. However reductions in hostility and defensiveness were significantly associated with reduction of medication in both the treatment and control groups and the authors suggest training in anger and hostility management may be of particular relevance in future treatment programmes.

Other studies have also considered the role of anger management training. A previous study of 97 patients compared cognitive group therapy for anger management with heart rate biofeedback and routine treatment control groups (Achmon et al., 1989). They found that both interventions significantly reduced blood pressure, with greatest impact on blood pressure from the biofeedback intervention and greatest anger control in the cognitive group.

Linden's group aimed to address a number of the potential weaknesses of previous research in this area (Linden, Lenz & Con, 2001). Their inclusion criteria of, firstly, ambulatory and, secondly, relatively high BP levels reduced the potential impacts of 'white-coat hypertension' and possible floor effects of low base-line blood pressure levels. They randomised 60 patients to a treatment group and offered 10 hours of an individualised cognitive-behavioural intervention or standard care. Their attention to the inclusion criteria was supported by the outcome finding that high initial BP levels were strongly predictive of degree of change. The study also emphasised the delivery of the intervention by psychotherapists with specific training in CBT for psychosomatic patients, using techniques of proven efficacy in general psychotherapeutic practice. The components of therapy used most frequently focused on management of anger/hostility, autogenic training and discussion of relationship/existential issues, with less use of cognitive therapy for anxiety or depression. Blood pressure was significantly reduced by the CBT, including the waiting list control group when subsequently offered treatment. Additionally, the impact of treatment increased during the six-month follow-up, with reduced psychological distress and improved anger management suggested as the likely mediators of improvement.

Blumenthal *et al.* (2002) have critically reviewed the current literature on non-drug treatments for hypertension, as well as suggesting some possible pathopyhsiological mechanisms of relevance. They comment that more recent studies of biofeedback therapy are less encouraging than those prior to the mid-1990s, with reductions of BP failing to show a significant difference for placebo or sham biofeedback therapy and that the literature supporting relaxation techniques is equally weak. However, they conclude that there is evidence of a significant impact of CBT if it is applied in an individualised multicomponent treatment package in the treatment of patients with hypertension.

CANCER

There is now a long history of using psychological therapies as adjunctive treatments for patients with cancer. There are several textbooks on the subject (for example, Holland,

1998) and an increasing number of dedicated journals. This has produced a body of evidence regarding the effectiveness of these therapies in cancer patients including a small number of high-quality RCTs and a few meta-analyses and systematic reviews. In this section we discuss these.

In addressing this literature it is important to highlight a number of issues:

- Cancer is not one disease. It should not be assumed, if there is a role for psychological treatments in cancer, that it will necessarily be the same or have the same effects for different cancer types. Greer (1999) discusses the successes of the biomedical model in the field of cancer and cautions us that to abandon this would be 'extremely foolish and damaging'. He acknowledges the evidence for the somatic mutation model for the initiation of cancer but suggests that this model alone does not explain the promotion and further progress of cancer. He cites evidence that cancer cells are not autonomous, that dormant cancer and spontaneous regression occur (albeit rarely), that some tumours are hormone dependent and that differentiation of leukaemia cell lines occurs after exposure to retinoids. These, he argues, indicate 'the probability of homeostatic controls that can restrain tumour growth and dissemination'. These homeostatic controls may well be influenced by psychological processes. Discussion of these processes is beyond the scope of this book. The interested reader is referred to Greer (1999) for a summary.
- Many cancers are now potentially curable and for many others survival has been significantly prolonged. For many patients, therefore, adjustment is more to do with living with a chronic disease with which they may survive for a considerable period of time rather than the harbinger of death in the near future.
- Psychological treatment can address many facets of cancer. These include coping with troublesome symptoms, adjusting to the impact of disease and its prognosis, adhering to and coping with cancer treatment and coping with comorbid psychological symptoms, for example depression and anxiety.
- If psychological interventions are effective in cancer it is far from clear as to the most effective timing of these interventions. Many if not most studies have looked at patients at different stages of the disease.

Fawzy (1999), in a review of psychosocial interventions for cancer patients, highlighted four categories for intervention used in clinical trials:

- education;
- interventions aimed at enhancing coping skills;
- provision of emotional support;
- formal psychotherapy.

This brief review focuses principally on formal psychotherapeutic interventions while acknowledging that there is some evidence base for other categories of intervention (Fawzy, 1999). Studies in this area have broadly speaking asked two questions each of which will be addressed in turn:

- Can psychological interventions improve quality of life for cancer patients?
- Can psychological interventions prolong survival in cancer patients?

QUALITY OF LIFE

Moorey & Greer (2002) provide an excellent summary of studies in this area. They highlight the fact that many trials have used measures of anxiety and/or depression as proxies for quality of life with relatively less attention being paid to social or interpersonal factors. They further note other important methodological and confounding issues including the following:

- Many studies use 'mixed' samples of cancer patients rather than focusing on one disease.
- Studies using single diagnostic groups, for example breast cancer, may not be generalisable to other patients.
- Some studies offered intervention to all cancer patients, others only to those with psychological distress such as depression and/or anxiety.
- The influence of side effects of treatment and/or stage of disease on outcomes may be considerable. It has not been clarified whether any benefits of treatment are for early disease, metastatic disease, terminal illness or all of these phases of cancer.

These are important issues and lead the authors to conclude 'because studies have taken various cancer diagnosis and intervened at different stages of the disease they cannot be compared easily and conclusions at the moment are tentative.'

Meyer & Mark (1995) carried out one of the first meta-analyses of psychosocial interventions in adult cancer patients. Forty-five studies were included, mostly from the US. They found an effect size of 0.24 for emotional adjustment measures, 0.19 for functional adjustment measures, 0.26 for treatment and disease related symptom measures and 0.28 for global measures. The effect size for medical outcome measures was non-significant. The effect size was not significantly different for different kinds of interventions, which included behavioural interventions, cognitive interventions, non-specific counselling, education and social support. This is a modest effect size and indeed Sheard & Maguire (1999) suggest this may be because the authors had cast the net too widely both in terms of the kinds of treatments that were included and in the outcomes used. Sheard & Maguire conducted their own meta-analysis focusing on studies of patients who either were psychologically distressed or at high risk of this. They identified four trials of cognitive behavioural therapy (CBT) (see Sheard & Maguire, 1999, for details), which had highly significant effects on outcome measures of both anxiety and depression. Group CBT was as effective as individual therapy. The authors concluded that psychological interventions were effective in anxiety but less so in depression.

A number of studies have looked at the efficacy of psychological interventions in patients with metastatic cancer. Most of these have been on patients with breast cancer. These were recently reviewed by Edwards, Hailey & Maxwell (2004) who identified five such studies, all group interventions. Two were cognitive behavioural and three supportive-expressive. They concluded that despite some short-term benefits and some improved psychological outcome measures there was insufficient evidence to suggest that either of these treatments be made routinely available.

The psychotherapeutic treatment modality for which there is most evidence in the oncology field is CBT. There are nine randomised controlled studies published and all except two favour CBT against the control condition (see Moorey & Greer, 2002, for a comprehensive account). Moorey & Greer have developed their own therapy, a specifically tailored

CBT for cancer patients. It is known as adjuvant psychological therapy (APT) and has been evaluated in three RCTs (Greer *et al.*, 1992; Moorey *et al.* 1998; Moynihan *et al.*, 1998). In the first study APT was compared with treatment as usual (TAU) in a group of 156 patients with various cancer types. Six sessions of APT were superior to TAU, with improvement maintained at one-year follow-up. In the second study, APT was compared to supportive counselling in patients with various cancers and was again superior. In the third study APT was evaluated in men with testicular cancer. In this study, the two main differences were firstly, the patients were from a single diagnostic group and secondly APT was offered to patients irrespective of the presence of psychological distress (the first two studies were of mixed cancer patients with psychological distress). This was a small study comparing APT with a no-treatment control group and after six sessions of APT no difference was demonstrated. At one-year follow-up change from baseline measures favoured the control group. This again highlights our earlier comments about psychological treatment being more effective when offered to those with measurable psychological distress.

In summary, most studies but particularly CBT studies in those who are psychologically distressed, confirmed the effectiveness of psychological treatments compared with TAU. Most studies have used mixed groups of cancer patients and have intervened with people at various different stages in their cancer. It is therefore unclear in which cancers and at what stage psychological treatment is of most benefit. Further, although there is most evidence for CBT, the superiority of CBT over other psychological treatments (as opposed to TAU) remains to be established.

Does Psychological Treatment Prolong Survival?

In 1989 David Spiegel and colleagues published in the Lancet, an RCT showing that group psychotherapy prolonged survival in patients with metastatic breast cancer (Spiegel *et al.*, 1989). This research came from a reputable source and was published in a reputable journal and therefore excited considerable interest. The therapy in question was 'supportive expressive' therapy, previously described by Spiegel (1985). Patients (n = 50) who received the treatment lived on average 18.9 months longer than controls (n = 36). Therapy was once a week for one year.

Subsequent studies by Fawzy *et al.* (1990, 1993) on patients with malignant melanoma, and Richardson *et al.* (1990) on patients with haematological cancers, have been similarly positive, showing prolonged survival in the intervention group (the treatments used in these studies could broadly be described as psycho-educational).

Not surprisingly, these studies have been the subject of much debate regarding both methodology and interpretation of the findings. Spiegel's study in particular has been criticised by Fox (1998). Moorey & Greer (2002) offer a fuller discussion of this debate.

Four other RCT have found no effect on survival for psychological interventions. These trials are summarised in Table 24.1. Chow, Tsao & Harton (2004) have recently conducted a meta-analysis of eight trials examining the effectiveness of psychosocial intervention in cancer patients in terms of prolonged survival. They concluded that 'psychosocial intervention does not prolong survival in cancer' but added the caveat that a small effect could not be ruled out on the grounds that trials were small in number and numbers of patients in each trial were small. Greer (1999) in an excellent reflection on the state of psycho-oncology states that even if future studies increased the evidence of prolonged survival, the results

Table 24.1 Randomised controlled trials of psychotherapy and survival in cancer patients

Author	Number	Cancer types	Treatment	Follow-up	Effect on survival
Spiegel et al. (1989)	86	Metastatic breast cancer	'Supportive-expressive group therapy'	10 years	+1
Fawzy et al. (1993)	68	Malignant melanoma	Psycho-educational groups	6 years	+6
Richardson et al. (1990)	94	Haematological cancers	Educational programme	5 years	+
Kuchler et al. (1999)	271	Gastro-intestinal cancers	Individual psychotherapy	2 years	+
Linn, Linn & Harris (1982)	120	Mixed cancers	Individual counselling	1 year	−
Ilnyckyj et al. (1994)	92	Mixed cancers	Group psychotherapy	11 years	−
Cunningham et al. (1998)	66	Metastatic breast cancer	CBT and supportive therapy and coping skills	5 years	−
Edelman et al. (1999)	124	Metastatic breast cancer	Group CBT and 'family night'	5 years	−
Goodwin et al. (2001)	235	Metastatic breast cancer	Supportive group Therapy and hypnosis and relaxation	6 years	−

'would be disbelieved and disregarded by the medical establishment until the biological pathways mediating such an effect were identified.'

DIABETES MELLITUS

Diabetes mellitus is a chronic disease caused by insulin deficiency, insulin resistance or both. It results in a hyperglycaemia. It is extremely common, affecting around two-and-a-half million people in the UK. It reduces life expectancy largely because of vascular complications resulting from macrovascular disease (ischaemic heart disease, stroke, peripheral vascular disease) and/or microvascular disease (retinopathy, nephropathy, neuropathy).

Optimal management of diabetes requires a significant degree of self-management from patients and sometimes support and assistance from families (especially for children with diabetes). This includes:

- lifestyle modification:
- diet;
- exercise;
- weight control;
- self-monitoring of blood glucose;
- adherence with medication and/or insulin (including administering of injections).

Moreover a variety of psychiatric disorders are associated with diabetes including depression (Lustman., 1997) and eating disorders (Herpetz, 2000). Other disorders, although not more prevalent, significantly interfere with self-management – for example, needle phobia.

For both of these reasons (need for self-management and increased prevalence of psychiatric disorder) there has long been interest in psychological interventions in patients with diabetes mellitus, both children and adults.

Bradley (1994) provides an excellent overview of the assessment and care of psychosocial problems in diabetes, which is beyond the scope of this chapter.

As has recently been pointed out by Ismail, Winkley & Rabe-Hesketh (2004) much of the early literature in this area failed to distinguish between educational and psychological interventions or between Type 1 and Type 2 diabetes. They highlight the resource and training implications of psychological therapy as opposed to education, emphasising the need, therefore, to establish the effectiveness and efficacy of the former.

The earliest interventions tended to be educational. These later evolved into self-management strategies and later still into formal psychotherapy (Steed, Cooke & Newhall, 2003).

As already highlighted in relation to cancer, outcome measures used have been variable. Improved glycaemic control has perhaps been most frequently used but some studies have also attempted to consider psychological variables such as depression, or quality of life.

Cognitive behavioural therapy (CBT) has been most frequently used of the psychological therapies but in a recent systematic review and meta-analysis (Ismail, Winkley & Rabe-Hesketh, 2004) also found RCTs using supportive therapy or counselling.

Two excellent recent systematic reviews provide a good summary of the literature in this area. Steed, Cooke & Newhall (2003) cover education, self-management and psychological interventions in both Type 1 and Type 2 diabetes in adults. Ismail, Winkley & Rabe-Hesketh (2004) confine themselves to psychological interventions in Type 2 diabetes.

Steed, Cooke & Newhall (2003) did not confine their review to randomised controlled trials looking at any intervention which assessed as a dependent measure, quality of life or psychological outcome measures.

The interventions themselves were broadly divided into three types, education, self-management and psychological therapies.

Fifteen studies specifically addressed improvement in depressive symptoms as an outcome measure. Seven of these were RCTs. Of these, four showed improvement for the intervention group and in three of these the intervention was a psychological therapy; in the other it was an education intervention (Piette et al., 2000).

Of the three psychotherapy studies, two used CBT (Henry, 1997; Lustman, 1998), and the third used distress reduction (Spiess, 1995). Negative RCTs used self-management or education interventions. Eight studies were reported as using a pre-post trial (PPT) design. Of these seven were positive, reporting benefits of the intervention over time. All the positive studies used a self-management intervention.

Studies looking at impact of interventions on anxiety were less positive. Of eight studies identified by the authors seven were RCTs, only two of which showed improvement for the intervention group compared with controls, one used CBT (Henry, 1997) and the other an education intervention Piette (2000). Negative studies included three using psychological treatments (relaxation and distress reduction), one educational intervention and one self-management.

A number of studies, none of them RCTs, have looked at generic quality-of-life measures (usually SF36). Overall these have not provided evidence for efficacy of any intervention although the poor nature of these studies limits the conclusions which can be drawn from them.

Diabetes-specific quality of life measures were assessed on five RCTs. None of these used specific psychological therapies. All used self-management and/or educational interventions (see Steed, Cooke & Newhall, 2003, for a summary).

Self-management interventions were more successful than educational interventions in producing improvements. The largest and longest of these studies (Trento *et al.*, 2001) showed advantages for a group self-management programme when compared with education and showed that these advantages were maintained at two-year follow-up.

Steed, Cooke & Newhall (2003) conclude that none of the interventions evaluated in the review have a negative impact on either physical wellbeing or quality of life measures. They are less clear on the impact of interventions on psychological wellbeing. As indicated above, depression seemed to respond better to interventions, particularly psychological therapies, than did anxiety. The authors point out, however, that positive studies on psychotherapy tended to be carried out on patients with high baseline levels of depression and that it is less easy to demonstrate positive effects of psychological intervention when these interventions are applied to diabetic populations in general irrespective of their level of psychological distress (this echoes the findings in the cancer and cardiac literature noted above).

The authors are unclear about the relationship of psychological wellbeing and adherence to self-management highlighting the complexity of the relationship between these two. They suggest that further studies need to compare the effects of psychological intervention on those with and without poor psychological wellbeing and those with and without poor self-management behaviour.

With regard to the impact of interventions on quality of life there is a difference between studies in which diabetes-specific quality of life measures have been used (generally positive) and those where generic quality of life measures have been used (generally negative) although, as indicated, the interventions in question have been self-management or educational interventions rather than psychotherapy.

Steed, Cooke & Newhall conclude by highlighting a number of methodological weaknesses in the studies including under-powering, measuring only change in negative aspects of wellbeing (depression and anxiety) and not positive aspects and, finally, the generally poor descriptions of interventions (see below for a further discussion of this). They do, however, argue that the review 'supports the use of both self-management and psychological interventions in diabetes care', suggesting the choice between these treatments may depend on the population of interest – psychological treatments probably benefit the more psychologically distressed. Importantly, they highlight the lack of evidence for didactic educational programmes.

The second major recent review (and meta-analysis) is that of Ismail, Winkley & Rabe-Hesketh (2004) who systematically reviewed 25 randomised controlled trials of psychological interventions aimed at improving glycaemic control in patients with Type 2 diabetes. This review looks specifically at psychological interventions classifying these as either supportive or counselling therapy, CBT, brief dynamic psychotherapy and interpersonal psychotherapy (see Ismail, Winkley & Rabe-Hesketh, 2004, for details). Simple educational interventions and self-management were not assessed although, in some studies, the control group received one of these interventions (usually education).

Most studies (10) used CBT, a further five used relaxation and others used problem-solving or behavioural methods. Four studies used counselling. No studies using IPT or dynamic therapy were found.

Within the review there was a meta-analysis of 12 studies. In this meta-analysis psychological therapies resulted in significantly better glycaemic control with a difference of 0.76 % in glycated haemoglobin (the difference increased to 1 % when 'less intensive' therapy studies were excluded). The authors state that the effect size is enough to reduce micro-vascular complications of diabetes. The meta-analysis also provided evidence of an effect of psychological therapy on psychological distress but not on weight control or blood glucose levels.

Like Steed, Cooke & Newhall (2003), Ismail, Winkley and Rabe-Hesketh highlight a number of issues including poor reporting of potential biases, poor description of psychological treatment, small sample sizes and poor distinction between psychological treatment and educational interventions. As in other areas, there were not enough studies to compare the relative benefits of different kinds of psychotherapy although, once again, the preponderance of cognitive behavioural interventions is noted.

In summary the available literature shows that adjuvant psychological therapies can improve glycaemic control, psychological wellbeing and quality of life in patients with diabetes, although we have noted a number of caveats. Further studies are required to clarify which therapies are most beneficial and for which subgroups of patients.

RHEUMATOID ARTHRITIS (RA)

Rheumatoid arthritis is a chronic polyarthritis of unknown cause affecting between 1 & and 3 % of the population. The term 'arthritis' is to some extent misleading as this disorder is a multisystem disease which can affect a number of other organs e.g. heart, nervous system, eyes, kidneys, lungs. It is a debilitating disorder in which drugs are helpful but not curative and patients often have to learn to cope with chronic or episodic pain, fatigue and psychological distress. Drug treatment both with non-steroidal anti-inflammatory drugs and disease-modifying anti-rheumatic drugs (such as sulphasalazine, methotrexate or gold) carries high side-effect levels, which can hugely affect adherence (Gotzche, 1989). For this and other reasons RA patients are high users of complementary therapies (Astin, 2002).

A substantial number of psychosocial interventions has been used in the management of RA patients. As in other areas these have included educational interventions, strategies to enhance self-management and more formal psychotherapies.

Riemsma (2002), in a Cochrane review on patient education in RA, include both counselling and behavioural treatment as well as information giving under the umbrella of 'patient education'. Note that this highlights a problem with terminology in this whole area of psychological medicine – the terms 'educational' and more commonly 'psycho-educational' are often used to describe activities as disparate as the handing out of leaflets and more formal CBT.

This review showed no significant effects for information-based education or for counselling (cf. diabetes) but showed significant effects for behavioural treatments with improvements in a range of outcome measures including depression, disability and patient-rated global assessment.

Disappointingly this review also concluded that any benefits appear to be short lived and their clinical significance unclear.

Astin (2002) provide the most recent and comprehensive meta-analysis of RCTs in this area. Twenty-five studies met their inclusion criteria. Thirteen of these were characterised as multimodel CBT studies; the others included group therapy, person-centred therapy, problem solving, narrative therapies and biofeedback (usually as part of a multimodel intervention). Significant but small pooled effect sizes were found at the end of the intervention for a number of outcomes including pain, functional disability, psychological status, coping skills and self-efficacy. At follow-up (which averaged 8.5 months) significant effect sizes were found for joint tenderness, coping skills and psychological status. As in other areas, the authors found it difficult to find differences in effect sizes for different kinds of intervention, although unlike the Riemsma review this was specifically a review of psychotherapies and did not include merely educational interventions. The authors tentatively conclude that adjuvant psychological interventions *may* be important in the management of RA. One potentially interesting conclusion of this meta-analysis concerns the timing of intervention. The findings suggest that intervention earlier in the course of the disease may produce more favourable outcomes. In one of the better quality studies included, Sharpe (2001) examined the efficacy of CBT in a group (n = 55) of patients with recent-onset seropositive RA. Cognitive behaviour therapy was effective in reducing both psychological and physical morbidity. Interestingly, the CBT group also showed reduction in its C reactive protein levels (an indicator of disease activity in RA).

The authors conclude that CBT when applied early in the course of RA may be a useful adjunctive therapy. This conclusion is also supported by the work of Sinclair & Wallston (2001), who looked at predictors of improvement with CBT in a group of women with RA and concluded that length of time since diagnosis (along with personal coping resources and pain coping behaviours) predicted response to intervention.

SKIN

Introduction

Skin, our largest sensory organ, plays a vital role in how we interface and communicate with the external world. It is integral to our body image and self-esteem, acting both as a protective barrier and a container. Given that foetal ectoderm gives rise to both the central nervous system (CNS) and the skin and that both systems share several hormones, neurotransmitters and receptors, it is not surprising that they are closely interlinked. However, despite long-held beliefs by doctors and patients alike that stressful events are linked with skin disease, it is only relatively recently that a small amount of research evidence has gradually emerged to support this. Many skin conditions are chronic and standard care is often unsatisfactory. The developing area of psychodermatology focuses on how an individual's emotional state impacts on diseases of the skin and how the skin can reflect a person's emotional world.

Emotional factors and the skin potentially interact in two directions. Psychological distress may trigger cutaneous dysfunction and the experience of chronic or disfiguring skin disease may have a profound emotional impact. The emerging area of psychoneuroimmunology explores the interrelationship between the CNS and endocrine and immune systems relevant to many physical disorders ranging from cancer to autoimmune diseases. There is now expanding evidence of pathophysiological mechanisms potentially bridging psychological stressors and skin conditions. For example, we now know that wound healing is slowed by psychological stress (Kiecolt-Glaser *et al.*, 1995) and that stress disrupts the epidermal permeability barrier implicated in inflammatory dermatoses such as psoariais and atopic dermatitis (Garg *et al.*, 2001). Corticotropin releasing hormone (CRH) acting locally on hair follicles has been implicated in alopecia areata triggered by acute stress (Katsarou-Katsari, Singh & Theoharides, 2001). Buske-Kirschbaum, Gelben & Helhammer (2001) and colleagues have summarised the area well with respect to atopic dermatitis, outlining a number of psychobiological pathways for stress-related modulation of symptoms of this disorder. Of course, the link between depression and reduced compliance with medical treatment is equally relevant for dermatology (Renzi, Picardi & Abeni, 2002) and non-dermatology patients.

Picardi & Abeni (2001) have carried out a thorough review of the area and are somewhat cautious in their conclusions. They report most support for links between stressful life events and four chronic skin conditions: psoriasis, alopecia areata, atopic dermatitis and urticaria. Depressive illness may act as a trigger or exacerbating factor for psoariasis, chronic urticaria, alopecia areata or idiopathic pruritis, whereas anxiety has been linked with atopic eczema, acne, seborrheoic dermatitis or rosacea presentations. However they note that the evidence cannot be considered to be conclusive due to problems with lack of control for confounding variables, acceptable measures of stress and a large majority of studies being retrospective.

Psychotherapy

The earliest case report of psychotherapy in the treatment of a chronic skin disorder dates back more than 1 200 years. In this, a Persian physician uses exploratory psychotherapy successfully to treat a patient's *psoriasis* by linking it to conflict with his father (Shafi & Shafi, 1979). Since then, much of the literature in this area has consisted of psychotherapeutic case reports. Fortune *et al.* (2004) have summarised the literature particularly with respect to group-based psychological interventions in the treatment of psoriasis, comprised of strategies ranging from hypnosis or meditation to stress management as an adjunct to standard medical care. Two of the four studies of CBT included had truly randomised patients to intervention or control groups: Zacharie *et al.* (1996) reported a moderate beneficial effect on psoriasis activity in 21 patients receiving seven individual sessions of stress management, guided imagery and relaxation compared to 23 patients given standard care, whereas Richards (1997) carried out an unpublished pilot study showing that a six-session psoriasis-specific CB symptom-management programme significantly reduced psoriasis-related stress at six weeks' follow-up compared to controls.

However, another of the CBT papers is worth commenting on in more detail. Fortune *et al.* (2002) offered patients with psoriasis a choice of a cognitive behavioural symptom-management programme or standard care. They argue that this patient-preference randomisation counterbalances the primacy of the RCT with a real-world benefit for routine clinical practice. There were no significant differences between the two groups on demographics, history or severity of psoriasis, although patients choosing standard care were more disabled. Six CB group sessions lasting two-and-a-half hours each were delivered by a multidisciplinary team of medical, nursing and psychology staff, based on the biopsychosocial model of pain management. Cognitive interventions included the management of appraisals, misinterpretations and maladaptive beliefs about psoriasis. Of 255 eligible patients, 40 chose the programme and 53 standard care. Those who declined to partici- pate scored lower on anxiety and depression ratings, which the authors interpreted as an appropriate self-identification of need. The intervention group showed significant improve- ments in severity of psoriasis, self-reported disability and psychological distress at six-week follow-up, compared with controls. There was continued improvement at six months re- view. However when they specifically explored the effects of the intervention they found that they had failed to shift patients' coping strategies including perceptions about re- currence, chronicity, physical causes or beliefs in cure or control (Fortune *et al.*, 2004). They did show a significant reduction in attributions for emotional causes of illness, ill- ness identity and perceptions of serious consequences, and suggested that the more deeply entrenched coping strategies may require more schema-based intervention for additional benefit.

Atopic dermatitis is a chronic skin disorder characterised by eczema, erythema and se- vere itch. Previous research has suggested possible benefits from relaxation training, stress management and habit-reversal training. Habit reversal is a behavioural intervention that involves self-monitoring for early cues of itching, and practising competing responses such as pressing the hands firmly on the area. Ehlers, Stangier & Gieler (1995) noted a lack of controlled trials in this area and so compared psychological interventions with a stan- dard medical care group, selected separately to avoid patients feeling a lack of additional treatment and hence minimise dropouts. Between five and seven patients in each group com- pleted 12 weekly group sessions, of between one-and-a-half and two hours. The main focus of the cognitive-behavioural group was to reduce scratching by self-control and increasing ability to cope with itching, as well as aiming to reduce overall stress levels by CBT and relaxation training. At one-year follow-up, patients in the relaxation training, cognitive- behavioural treatment or combined dermatological education (DE) and CB treatment had significantly improved skin condition compared to DE alone or standard care and required significantly less steroid therapy. The authors wondered if there might have been greater difference between the different groups if the CB programme had been spread out over more sessions and the small numbers in each group must also have limited inter- group differences. They also noted that the greatest impact of psychological interventions was on catastrophising rather than coping cognitions, suggesting that this may be a more appropriate focus of CB intervention.

Linnet & Jemec (2001) have more recently explored the impact of a brief dynamic psy- chotherapy in 32 patients with atopic dermatitis. They were randomly assigned in pairs to six months of psychodynamic psychotherapy or a control group receiving standard care. The psychotherapy focused on illness perception and illness-related conflicts, body image, feelings of rejection, and illness-related anxiety, aggression and depressive symptoms. Ini- tially they found no differences between the groups. Following a post hoc analysis, however, they concluded that AD patients with higher levels of anxiety were more likely to improve with psychotherapy but more likely to drop out of standard care. These findings support the previous work of Brown & Bettley (1971) who found most improvement in AD patients with acute emotional disturbances and a high motivation for psychological treatment compared with a similar group that did not receive such treatment, or a group receiving treatment and with low motivation and little emotional disturbance. Given the post hoc analysis, these finding await further replication.

A small RCT of CBT has also been shown to be effective in the treatment of *vitiligo*, a chronic skin condition characterised by areas of depigmentation and associated with a number of autoimmune diseases (Papadopoulos, Bor & Legg, 1999). As in much of the literature the study is limited by the small numbers (eight in each group of CBT or standard care) and lack of attention-control placebo. Nevertheless there was a substantial effect of treatment on self-esteem, quality of life and perceived body image, which was maintained at five-month follow-up. There was also objective evidence of a positive impact of treatment on the size of vitiligo lesions (the area was reduced in 3/6 of the treatment group but increased in 2/5 of the controls) although the numbers were too small to achieve significance.

Recognising the paucity of literature on psychological aspects of skin problems, White (2001) has outlined some general principles for CB assessment and interventions in dermatology, including specific guidance about how to approach the management of itch.

ASTHMA

Asthma is a disease characterised by chronic or recurrent airways obstruction. It affects around 5 million adults and children in the UK and is a significant cause of mortality and morbidity.

There has always been an awareness of the importance of psychological factors in asthma both in triggering acute attacks and in affecting adherence with medical treatment. The role of emotional factors in asthma has been well reviewed by Lehrer et al. (1993). More recently the British Thoracic Society, in its guidelines for asthma management, has recommended the use of strategies aimed at improving patients self-management skills (British Thoracic Society, 2003).

A number of psychological interventions have been tried in asthma including counselling (Bailey et al., 1990), autogenic training (Henry et al., 1993), relaxation and music therapy (Lehrer et al., 1994) and CBT (Kotses, 1995). In addition, education, medication management and hypnosis have been used. Doubt has been cast on the efficacy of education/self-management and hypnosis (Gibson, 2002; Hackman, 2000).

Fleming et al. (2004) have recently produced a systematic review of psychological interventions for adults with asthma. The most striking observation in this review concerns the paucity of available studies. This was so poor that the authors were unable to carry out a meta-analysis because of the quality of the data.

They found only 12 studies of sufficient quality to include in the review. The interventions used included relaxation, autogenic therapy, biofeedback, hypnosis, CBT and psycho-educational programmes. Many studies combined more than one of these techniques making it even more difficult to come to any conclusions about what might be helpful.

The assessed outcome measures most commonly related to frequency and severity of asthma symptoms and measures of psychological status. Other measures included use of medication, healthcare utilisation, pulmonary function and work absenteeism.

The authors conclude that psychological interventions do not decrease frequency or severity/duration of asthma symptoms or reduce healthcare utilisation.

Some studies showed some positive outcomes, however. Put et al. (2003) in a psycho-educational study (with significant cognitive and behavioural components) showed improvement in some asthma symptoms, lung function and psychological measures. As it was one of the better studies in the review this suggests that it is possible that psychological interventions may as yet have something to offer asthma patients, but further studies are awaited.

Fleming *et al.* (2004) could 'draw no conclusions as to the effectiveness of psychological techniques for adults with asthma'. Discussing the implications for future research they make the important observation that virtually all of the work in this area has been carried out by trialists who have done only one study. They note that this has led to a lack of clear direction in this area of research with no good programmes of research for evaluating psychological interventions in asthma (unlike many of the other areas we have reviewed such as cancer, heart disease, stroke, diabetes). They highlight the need for researchers to agree on common interventions and outcomes and to produce research which 'can be used in the real world with individual patients who have differing needs and get better at different speeds.'

CONCLUSION

There is a voluminous literature on the use of adjuvant psychological treatments in patients with physical illness. High-quality randomised controlled trials, systematic reviews and/or meta-analyses are, however, relatively small in numbers. From these, it is reasonable to conclude that there is evidence for efficacy of psychological interventions in most of the disease areas we have reviewed (asthma may be the major exception). Overall, the effect size of most studies has been clinically significant but modest.

Common themes in relation to the methodological quality of studies carried out to date are striking in all areas of the literature we have examined and include the following:

- Most studies have had small sample sizes.
- Interventions have often been poorly described making replication of studies difficult.
- Interventions have often been multifaceted and in positive studies it has therefore been difficult to be clear about which parts of the package are really important and which, if any, could be discarded.
- There is a real issue in many studies about treatment integrity. It was checked in only a very few studies. Training of therapists may also be an issue in this regard.
- There is considerable heterogeneity in the outcome measures that have been used. In more than one systematic review there were appeals to researchers in this area to work towards some kind of consensus with regard to what outcome measures should be used.

In addition to these issues of methodology, we are struck by one further commonly recurring theme across this literature. Psychological interventions appear to work best when applied to patients with psychological symptoms (usually depression or anxiety) rather than when applied across the board – for example, to all newly diagnosed breast cancer patients. Finally, the optimal timing for psychological interventions is far from clear and may indeed be different for different disorders.

We can make no conclusions as to which of the many kinds of intervention used (CBT, counselling, dynamic therapies) is best. Few head-to-head studies comparing therapies with each other have been found. Predictably there are more studies on CBT than any other psychotherapy and more have been positive than negative. Most compared CBT with treatment as usual, or waiting-list controls and not with another active psychotherapy. Cognitive behaviour therapy appears useful in a number of disease areas but it is not possible at this stage to conclude that it is better than other psychotherapies.

In summary, there is still much challenging work to be done in this area. Despite generally positive evidence for efficacy of adjuvant psychotherapy in physically ill populations the age old question of 'what works for whom and when?' remains unanswered.

REFERENCES

Achmon, J., Granek, M., Golomb, M. & Hart, J. (1989). Behavioural treatment of essential hypertension: A comparison between cognitive therapy and biofeedback of heart rate. *Psychosomatic Medicine, 51*, 152–164.

Alexander, F. (1950). *Psychosomatic Medicine*. New York: Norton.

Anderson, C., Hackett, M. & House, A. (2004). Interventions for preventing depression after stroke (Cochrane review). *The Cochrane Library,* Issue 3. Chichester: John Wiley & Sons.

Antman, E., Anbe, D., Armstrong, P. *et al.* (2004). ACC/AHA guidelines for the management of patients with ST-elevation myocardial infarction: Executive summary: a report of the ACC/AHA Task Force on Practice Guidelines on the Management of Patients With Acute Myocardial Infarction. *Journal of the American College of Cardiology, 44*, 671–719.

Astin, J.A. (2002). Arthritis and rheumatism. *Arthritis Care and Research, 47*(3), 291–302.

Bailey, W.C., Richards, J.M. & Brooks, M. (1990). A randomised trial to improve self-management practices of adults with asthma. *Archives of Internal Medicine, 150*, 1664–1668.

Bennett, P. & Carroll, D. (1994). Cognitive-behavioural interventions in cardiac rehabilitation. *Journal of Psychosomatic Research, 38*, 169–182.

Berkman, L., Blumenthal, J., Burg, M. *et al.* (2003). Effects of treating depression and low perceived support on clinical events after myocardial infarction: Enhancing recovery in coronary heart disease patients (ENRICHD). *Journal of the American Medical Association, 289*, 3106–3116.

Blumenthal, J., Sherwood, A., Gullette, E. *et al.* (2002). Biobehavioural approaches to the treatment of hypertension. *Journal of Consulting and Clinical Psychology, 70*, 569–89.

Boulware, L., Daumit, G., Frick, K. *et al.* (2001). An evidence-based review of patient-centred, behavioural interventions for hypertension. *American Journal of Preventive Medicine, 21*, 221–232.

Bradley, C. (1994). *Handbook of Psychology and Diabetes. A Guide to Psychological Measurement in Diabetes Research and Practice*. Chur: Harwood Academic Publishers.

British Thoracic Society (2003). The British Thoracic Society, Scottish Intercollegiate Guidelines Network (SIGN) British guidelines on the management of asthma. *Thorax, 8* (supplement) (1)1, 1094.

Brown, D. & Bettley, F. (1971). Psychiatric treatment of eczema: A controlled trial. *British Medical Journal, 2*, 729–734.

Buske-Kirschbaum, A., Geiben, A. & Hellhammer, D. (2001). Psychobiological aspects of atopic dermatitis: an overview. *Psychotherapy and Psychosomatics, 70*, 6–16.

Carney, R., Freedland, K., Miller, G. & Jaffe, A.J. (2002). Depression as a risk factor for cardiac mortality and morbidity. A review of potential mechanisms. *Psychosomatic Research, 53*, 837–902.

Chow, G., Tsao, M.N. & Harton, T. (2004). Does psychosocial intervention improve survival in cancer? A meta-analysis. *Palliative Medicine, 18*(1), 25–31.

Clark, M., Rubenach, S. & Winsor, A. (2003). A randomised controlled trial of an education and counselling intervention for families after stroke. *Clinical Rehabilitation, 17*, 703–712.

Cunningham, A.J., Edmonds, C.V.I., Jenkins, G.P. *et al.* (1998). A randomised controlled trial of the effects of group psychological therapy on survival in women with metastatic breast cancer. *Psycho-Oncology, 7*, 508–17.

Database of Abstracts of Reviews of Effects (DARE). 20012344 (structured abstract) (2004). *The Cochrane Library,* Issue 3. Chichester: John Wiley & Sons.

Dusseldorp, E., Van Elderen, T., Maes, S. *et al.* (1999). A meta-analysis of psycho-educational programmes for coronary heart disease patients. *Health Psychology, 18*, 506–519.

Edelman, S. Lemon, J., Bell, D.R. & Kidman, A.D. (1999). Effects of group CBT in the survival time of patients with metastatic breast cancer. *Psycho-Oncology, 5*, 474–481.

Edelman, S., Lemon, J. & Kidman, A. (2003). Psychological therapies for recipients of implantable cardioverter defibrillators. *Heart and Lung, 32*, 234–240.

Edwards, A.G.K., Hailey, S. & Maxwell, M. (2004). Psychological intervention for women with metastatic breast cancer. *The Cochrane Library,* Issue 3. Chichester: John Wiley & Sons.

Ehlers, A., Stangier, U. & Gieler, U. (1995). Treatment of atopic dermatitis: a comparison of psychological and dermatological approaches to relapse prevention. *Journal of Consulting and Clinical Psychology, 63*, 624–635.

Eisenberg, D., Delbanco, T., Berkey, C. *et al.* (1993). Cognitive behavioural techniques for hypertension: Are they effective? *Annals, Internal Medicine, 118*, 964–972.

Fawzy, F. (1999). Psycho-social intervention for patients with cancer, what works and what doesn't. *European Journal of Cancer, 35*, 1559–1564.

Fawzy, F., Fawzy, N.W., Hynn, C.S. *et al.* (1993). Malignant melanoma: effects of an early structured psychiatric intervention, coping and effective state of recurrence and survival 6 years later. *Archives of General Psychiatry, 47*, 729–735.

Fawzy, F., Kemeny, M.E., Fawzy, N.W. *et al.* (1990). A structured psychiatric intervention for cancer patients. I. Changes over time in methods of coping and affective disturbance. *Archives of General Psychiatry, 47*, 720–725.

Fleming, S.L., Pagliari, C., Churchill, R. *et al.* (2004). Psychotherapeutic interventions for adults with asthma (Cochrane Review). *The Cochrane Library.* Chichester: John Wiley & Sons.

Forster, A. & Young, J. (1996). Specialist nurse support for patients with stroke in the community: A randomised control trial. *British Medical Journal, 312*, 1642–1646.

Fortune, D., Richards, H., Griffiths, C. & Main, C. (2004). Targeting cognitive-behaviour therapy to patients' implicit model of psoriasis: Results from a patient-preference controlled trial. *British Journal of Clinical Psychology, 43*, 65–82.

Fortune, D., Richards, H., Kirby, B. *et al.* (2002). A cognitive-behavioural symptoms management programme as an adjunct in psoriasis therapy. *British Journal of Dermatology, 146*, 458–465.

Fox, B.H. (1998). A hypothesis about Spiegel et al.'s 1989 paper on psychosocial intervention and breast cancer survival. *Psycho-oncology, 7*, 361–370.

Frasure-Smith, N. & Lesperance, F. (2003). Depression – a cardiac risk factor in search of treatment. *Journal of the American Medical Association, 289*, 3171–3173.

Frasure-Smith, N., Lesperance, F., Prince, R.H. *et al.* (1997). Randomised trial of home-based psychosocial nursing intervention for patients recovering from myocardial infarction. *Lancet, 350*, 473–479.

Friedman, M., Thoresen, C., Gill, J. *et al.* (1986). Alteration of Type A behavioural and its effects on cardiac recurrences in post-myocardial infarction patients: Summary results of the Recurrent Coronary Prevention Project. *American Heart Journal, 112*, 653–665.

Garg, A., Chren, M., Sands, L. *et al.* (2001). Psychological stress perturbs epidermal permeability barrier homeostasis. *Dermatology, 137*, 53–59.

Gibson, P.G. (2002). Limited information (information only). Patient education programmes for adults with asthma (Cochrane Review). *The Cochrane Library,* Issue 2. Oxford, Update Software. CD001005.

Gill, D. & Hatcher, S. (2003). Antidepressants for depression in people with physical illness (Cochrane review). The Cochrane Library, Issue 2. Oxford Update Software.

Glassman, A., O'Connor, C., Califf, R. *et al.* (2002). Sertraline treatment of major depression in patients with acute MI or unstable angina for the SADHART Group. *Journal of the American Medical Association, 288,* 701–709.

Goldberg, S., Segal, M., Berk, S. *et al.* (1997). Stroke transition after inpatient rehabilitation. *Topics in Stroke Rehabilitation, 4*, 64–79.

Goodwin, P., Leszcz, M., Ennis, M. *et al.* (2001). The effect of group psychosocial support on survival in metastatic breast cancer. *New England Journal of Medicine, 345*, 1719–1726.

Gotzshe, P.C. (1989). Methodology and overt and hidden bias in reports of 196 double -blind trials of non-steroidal anti-inflammatory drugs in rheumatoid arthritis. *Controlled Clinical Trials, 10*, 31–56.

Greer, S. (1999). Mind-body research in psycho-oncology. *Advances in. Mind-Body Medicine, 15*, 236–244.

Greer, S., Moorey, S., Baruch, J.D.R. *et al.* (1992). Adjuvant psychological therapy for patients with cancer: A prospective randomised trial. *British Medical Journal, 304*, 675–680.

Hackett, M., Anderson, C. & House, A. (2004). Interventions for treating depression after stroke (Cochrane review). *The Cochrane Library*, Issue 3. Chichester: John Wiley & Sons.

Hackman, R.M. (2000). Hypnosis and asthma: A critical review. *Journal of Asthma, 37*(1), 1–15.

Hemingway, H. & Marmot, M. (1999). Evidenced based cardiology: Psychosocial factors in the aetiology and prognosis of CHD: systematic review of prospective cohort studies. *British Medical Journal, 318*, 1460–1467.

Henry, J.L. (1997). Cognitive-behavioural stress management for patients with non-insulin dependent diabetes mellitus. *Psychology Health and Medicine, 2*, 109–118.

Henry, M., De Rivera, J.L., Gonzales-Martin, I.J. & Abreu, J. (1993). Improvement of respiratory function in chronic asthmatic patients with autogenic therapy. *Journal of Psychosomatic Research, 37*(3), 265–270.

Herpetz, S. (2000). Relationship of weight and eating disorders in type 2 diabetic patients: A multi-center study. *International Journal of Eating Disorders, 28*, 68–77.

Holland, J.C. (ed.) (1998). *Psycho-Oncology.* New York: Oxford University Press.

Ilnyckyj, A., Farber, J., Cheang, M.C. & Weinerman, B.H. (1994). A randomised controlled trial of psycho-therapeutic intervention in cancer patients. *Annals of the RCPSC, 27*, 93–96.

Ismail, K., Winkley, R. & Rabe-Hesketh, S. (2004). Systematic review and meta analysis of randomised controlled trials of psychological interventions to improve glycaemic control in patients with type 2 diabetes. *Lancet, 363*, 1589–1597.

Jones, D.A. & West, R.R. (1996). Psychological rehabilitation after myocardial infarction: Multicentre randomised controlled trial. *British Medical Journal, 313*, 1517–1521.

Katon, W. & Sullivan, M.P. (1990). Depression and chronic medical illness. *Journal of Clinical Psychiatry, 51* (supplement 6), 3–11.

Katsarou-Katsari, A., Singh, L. & Theoharides, T. (2001). Alopecia areata and affected skin CRH receptor unregulation induced by acute emotional stress. *Dermatology, 203*, 157–161.

Kiecolt-Glaser, J., Malarkey, W., Marucha, P. *et al.* (1995). Slowing of wound healing by psychological stress. *Lancet, 346*, 1194–1196.

Kotses, H., Bernstein, L., Bernstein, D.I. *et al.* (1995). A self-management programme for adult asthma, part 1: development and evaluation. *Journal of Allergy and Clinical Immunology, 95*(2), 529–540.

Kuchler, T., Henne-Burns, D., Rappat, S. *et al.* (1999). Impact of psychotherapeutic support on gastro-intestinal cancer patients undergoing surgery: Survival results of a trial. *Hepato-Gastro-Enterology, 46*, 322–335.

Lane, D., Carroll, D. & Lip, G. (2001). Editorial comment: Cardiovascular and behavioural reactions to stress and cerebrovascular disease. *Stroke, 32*, 1718–1719.

Lehrer, P.M., Hochron, S.M., Mayne, T. *et al.* (1994). Relaxation and music therapies for asthma among patients prestabilised on asthma medication. *Journal of Behavioural Medicine, 17*(1), 1–24.

Lehrer, P.M., Isenberg, S. & Hochvon, S.M. (1993). Asthma and emotion: A review. *Journal of Asthma, 30*(1), 5–21.

Lewis, S., Dennis, M., O'Rourke, S. & Sharpe M. (2001). Negative attitudes among short-term stroke survivors predict worse long-term survival. *Stroke, 32*, 1640–1645.

Lincoln, N. & Flannaghan, T. (2003). Cognitive behavioural psychotherapy for depression following stroke: A randomised controlled trial. *Stroke, 34*, 111–115.

Linden W. (2000). Psychological treatments in cardiac rehabilitation: review of rationales and out-comes. *Journal of Psychosomatic Research, 48*, 443–454.

Linden, W. & Chambers, L. (1994). Clinical effectiveness of non-drug therapies for hypertension: A meta-analysis. *Annals of Behavioural Medicine, 16*, 35–45.

Linden, W., Lenz, J. & Con, A. (2001). Individualized stress management for primary hypertension: a randomised trial. *Archives of Internal Medicine, 161*, 1071–1080.

Sheard, T. & Maguire, P. (1999). The effect of psychological interventions on anxiety and depression in cancer patients: Results of two meta-analyses. *British Journal of Cancer, 80*, 1770–1780.

Sinclair, V.G. & Wallston, K.A. (2001). Predictors of improvement in a cognitive-behavioural intervention for women with rheumatoid arthritis. *Annals of Behavioural Medicine, 23*(4), 291–297.

Spiegel, D. (1985). Psychosocial interactions with cancer patients. *Journal of Psychosocial Oncology, 3*, 83–95.

Spiegel, D., Bloom, J.R., Kraemer, H.C. *et al.* (1989). Effect of psychosocial treatment on survival of patients with metastatic breast cancer. *Lancet, 2*, 889–891.

Spiess, K. (1995). A programme to reduce onset distress in unselected type 1 diabetic patients: Effects on psychological variables and metabolic control. *European Journal of Endocrinology, 132*, 580–586.

Steed, L., Cooke, D. & Newhall, S. (2003). A systematic review of psychosocial outcomes following education, self management and pschological interventions in diabetes mellitus. *Patient Education and Counselling, 51*, 5–15.

Trento, M. (2001). Group visits improve metabolic control in type 2 diabetes: A 2 year follow-up. *Diabetes Care, 24*, 995–1000.

White, C. (2001). *Cognitive Behaviour Therapy for Chronic Medical Problems: A Guide to Assessment and Treatment in Practice.* Chichester: John Wiley & Sons.

Zacharie, R., Oster, H., Bjerring, P. & Kragballe, K. (1996). Effects of psychologic intervention on psoriasis: A preliminary report. *Journal of the American Academy of Dermatology, 34*, 1008–1015.

PART III

Conclusions

Practice-based Evidence as a Complement to Evidence-based Practice: From Dichotomy to Chiasmus

Michael Barkham

University of Leeds, UK

and

Frank Margison

Gaskell Psychotherapy Centre, Manchester, UK

SECTION I: FROM DICHOTOMY TO CHIASMUS

INTRODUCTION

The aim of this chapter is to provide a context within which to place much of the current research work focusing on the psychological therapies and to do so in a way that is useful for researchers and practitioners alike. The preceding chapters in this volume as well as other major texts – for example, the fifth edition of *Bergin and Garfield's Handbook of Psychotherapy and Behavior Change* (Lambert, 2004) and the second edition of *What Works for Whom? A Critical Review of Psychotherapy Research* (Roth & Fonagy, 2005) – attest to the wealth of research evidence accrued over 50 years concerning the full spectrum of psychological therapies. This huge research activity can be viewed as occurring through a series of overlapping research generations originating with a response to Eysenck's (1952) classic critique of the effectiveness of psychotherapy. Since that time, research on the psychological therapies has been driven by key thematic questions. Table 25.1 presents a resumé of the themes and questions, methods and issues that have dominated research on the outcomes and processes of the psychological therapies since 1950. The specific

Handbook of Evidence-based Psychotherapies: A Guide for research and practice.
Edited by C. Freeman & M. Power. Copyright © 2007 John Wiley & Sons, Ltd.

components summarized in Table 25.1 are explored in detail elsewhere (see Barkham, 2002) and variations on these research generations can also be found in the literature (for example, Goldfried & Wolfe, 1996; Orlinsky & Russell, 1994) as well as other historical accounts (such as Lambert, Garfield & Bergin, 2004; Nathan, Stuart & Dolan, 2000; Wallerstein, 2002). Although time frames have been placed on each research generation in Table 25.1, it is clear that research characterized by each generation continues to the present day. Hence, they can be seen as providing a developmental account of psychotherapy research, giving the origins and context within which each research theme arises.

The overall yield of this research activity has been considerable. In particular, the cumulative body of findings arising from research generations I, II and III has provided the foundations for the influential standing of evidence-based practice. As such, the paradigm of evidence-based practice rests largely on the methodological strengths of efficacy studies (see Bower, 2003). Increasingly better designed studies have provided the basis for overviews of the healthcare literature through systematic reviews and meta-analytic studies (for example, Eggar *et al.*, 2001). This research effort has, in turn, delivered procedures aimed at driving up the quality of care provided via, for example, clinical guidelines for practitioners (such as Department of Health, 2001; Parry, Cape & Pilling, 2003). In this way, the research generations have moved forward to provide the foundations for best practice in response to the needs of policy makers. By contrast, research generation IV has shown developments that have placed individual clients and their context at the forefront. This has been reflected in a research focus on routine practice settings in which clients receive interventions within their national healthcare systems (e.g., Lambert, 2001; Stiles *et al.*, 2003) and via a range of statistical procedures which have centred on the individual client (Bryk & Raudenbush, 1987; Jacobson & Truax, 1991; Rogosa & Willett, 1985). This orientation is also reflected in methods and studies of the process of change through re-valuing qualitative and narrative approaches to therapy (McLeod, 1997, 2000; Stiles, Honos-Webb & Surko, 1998).

Dichotomies

However, even given the established evidence base, the glass can still be considered to be either half full or half empty (Shapiro, 1996). There is a considerable wealth of knowledge about the psychological therapies but there are many basic questions unanswered. The 'either-or' aspect of the glass phenomenon is reflected in the 'either-or' dichotomies that have bedevilled research at all levels into the psychological therapies. For example, this has occurred at the level of participants (client versus therapist), types of therapy (cognitive therapy versus interpersonal therapy), duration of therapy (brief versus long-term), effective components (specific techniques versus common factors), and therapy itself (process versus outcome). However, it has also impacted in areas germane to all aspects of psychological research methods (qualitative versus quantitative) and statistical outcomes (significant versus not significant).

One of the most enduring dichotomies throughout the past 50 years has been that between science and practice – the 'scientist-practitioner' debate (Hayes *et al.*, 1999) – as evidenced by a continuing focus on this issue in academic journals relating to clinical psychology (Lampropoulos *et al.*, 2002), counselling psychology (Chwalisz, 2003), and psychiatry (Bower & Gask, 2002) as well as in professional articles (Barkham, 2006; Charman & Barkham, 2005; Shapiro, 2002). This issue has become redefined in the area of research in

Table 25.1 Summary of research activity across four generations

	Research generations			
	I	**II**	**III**	**IV**
Time frame / **Theme**	1950s–1970s onwards / Justification	1960s–1980s onwards / Specificity	1970s–2000 onwards / Efficacy/cost effectiveness	1984– present / Effectiveness/clinical significance
OUTCOME				
Thematic question	Is psychotherapy effective?	Which psychotherapy is more effective?	How can treatments be made more (cost) effective?	How can the quality of treatment delivery be improved?
Methodologies	Control group comparisons; effect sizes; meta-analysis	Randomized control trial; factorial design; placebo group	Probit analysis; growth curves; structural modelling	Clinical significance
Key issues	Efficacy; spontaneous remission	What treatment, by whom, is most effective for this individual with that specific problem, and under which set of circumstances?	Dose-response; medical offset; health economics; evidence-based medicine; empirically validated treatments; practice guidelines	User perspectives; evidence-based practice; outcomes monitoring
PROCESS				
Thematic question	Are there objective methods for evaluating process?	What components are related to outcome?	How does change occur (via a quantitative approach)?	How does change occur (via a qualitative approach)?
Methodologies	Random sampling of sections of therapy; 'uniformity myth' assumed	Single-case methodologies	Taxonomies; linking process to outcomes	Qualitative methods; narrative approach; discourse analysis; descriptive studies; theory development
Key issues	Verbal & speech behaviours	Rogerian facilitative conditions (e.g. empathy)	Therapeutic alliance; verbal response modes	Events paradigm; single case approach; qualitative methods

Source: Methods, outcomes and processes in the psychological therapies across successive research generations, M. Barkham, in *Handbook of Individual Therapy* (4th edition), W. Dryden (Ed.), 2002. London: Sage Publications.

terms of *efficacy* versus *effectiveness* studies (Howard *et al.*, 1996; Lambert & Ogles, 2004; Nathan, Stuart & Dolin, 2000). Other writers have defined this issue slightly differently in terms of *treatment-focused* versus *patient-focused* research (Donenberg, Lyons & Howard, 1999). The former aims to provide an evidence base by focusing primarily on the efficacy and secondarily on the effectiveness of specific treatments at the level of either the clinical population (technology transfer studies) or individual cases (single case studies). By contrast, the latter focuses on the effectiveness and efficiency of mental health services at the level of the clinical population (health services research studies) or individual cases (case-based decision-support studies).

Within this context, researchers have coined terms denoting the applicability of science to practice. For example, Salkovskis (2002) writes about a multidimensional approach to *clinical science* while Lutz (2002) writes about the requirement for a *scientific groundwork for an empirically based clinical practice*. These calls reflect the desire to move towards a greater *relevance* of research to what actually occurs in clinical practice with the central axiom that any such procedures or approaches should be thoroughly *rigorous* (see Barkham & Mellor-Clark, 2000). However, the predominance of concepts such as 'clinical' and 'science' are not necessarily ones that best accommodate the contribution of more qualitative and narrative approaches to understanding the process of psychological therapies (McLeod, 1998). This is a key issue as these latter approaches have constant appeal and relevance to practitioners and which have been the focus of more recent attempts to facilitative their acceptance into mainstream journals via the development of publication guidelines (Elliott, Fischer & Rennie, 1999).

Chiasmus

As noted above, the dilemma of the scientist-practitioner has continued to impact on the activity of research in the psychological therapies in the guise of the debate between *efficacy* and *effectiveness* research. Efficacy research is viewed as the gold standard for building and promoting *evidence-based practice,* which has its origins in evidence-based medicine. Evidence based medicine has been defined as: ' . . . the conscientious, explicit, and judicious use of current best evidence in making decisions about the care of individual patients. The practice of evidence-based medicine means integrating individual clinical expertise with the best available external clinical evidence from systematic research' (Sackett *et al.*, 1996, p. 71).

However, the term *evidence based practice* – and its underlying principles and procedures – provides the potential for a complementary term using the concept of chiasmus. *Chiasmus* (ky-AZ-mus, *n.*) refers to a reversal in the order of words in two otherwise parallel phrases (OED). The reversal in order of words yields the term *practice-based evidence* and the resulting parallel phrases are *evidence-based practice* and *practice-based evidence*. Hence, this procedure provides us with a complementary paradigm and also the potential for a combined knowledge base arising from the contribution of both components. Our definition of practice-based evidence amends Sackett's definition as follows: 'Practice-based evidence is the conscientious, explicit, and judicious use of current evidence drawn from practice settings in making decisions about the care of individual patients. Practice-based evidence means integrating both individual clinical expertise and service-level parameters with the best available evidence drawn from rigorous research activity carried out in routine clinical settings.'

Accordingly, the emphasis is on acquiring evidence via rigorous research carried out in routine clinical practice. The term 'practice-based evidence' has appeared in the context of the psychological therapies (Barkham & Mellor-Clark, 2000, 2003), psychotherapy (Margison, 2001; Margison *et al.*, 2000), professional practice in the US (Pingitore *et al.*, 2001) and as applied to practice-based psychological interventions for specific disorders (such as depression – Ford *et al.*, 2002). It has also permeated other professional activities (such as education – Simons *et al.*, 2003). However, it is the combination of these two terms – the chiasmus – which provides the greatest potential for building a knowledge base of the psychological therapies that is both appropriately rigorous but also relevant to the practitioner and scientific communities.

The concept of practice-based evidence is crucial in three respects. First, it identifies an equally valued approach to evidence-based practice by reversing the order of words to achieve a 'bottom-up' approach originating with the practitioner in contrast to a 'top-down' approach in which evidence derived from randomized controlled trials are channelled down to practitioners in routine practice settings. Secondly, it draws on the broader concept that there is a greater value in drawing upon the parallelism – that is, the complementarity – of *both* approaches whereby the two parallel but reverse approaches of *evidence-based practice* and *practice-based evidence* can yield a greater product by their interplay than achieved by either approach alone. And thirdly, practice-based evidence provides the foundations for generating research questions, which are grounded in the practice context and for this reason are seen to be relevant to practitioners and the delivery of routine services. Such questions may be pragmatic or theory driven but have in common a fundamental relevance to practice. This approach contrasts with questions arising from academia, which contribute to an advanced understanding but may not directly inform practitioners on the delivery or implementation of clinical interventions.

Accordingly, in this chapter we set out the key research activities which are generic and which underpin quality research. We then set out the principles of practice based evidence as a complement to evidence-based practice. We then conclude by presenting the potential yield of this chiastic approach to evidence-based practice and practice based evidence in the hope that this provides a way of harnessing these complementary paradigms in service of building a rigorous and relevant knowledge-base for the psychological therapies.

SECTION II: EVIDENCE, RESEARCH AND PRACTICE

Psychotherapeutic Evidence

In scoping the activity defined by either evidence-based practice or practice-based evidence, a central component is the concept of *evidence* itself. Evidence-based healthcare derives primarily from the twin disciplines of clinical epidemiology and general internal medicine from which it has been transported to other disciplines. The literature on evidence-based practice in general is considerable (for example, Sackett *et al.*, 1996) and there are texts specifically addressing the evidence-base for counselling and the psychological therapies (Lambert, 2004; Parry, 2000; Roth & Fonagy, 2005, Rowland & Goss, 2000). The premise for this evidence base rests on specific assumptions as to what type of evidence is considered and how that evidence is then prioritized (appraised). Critically, the accumulated evidence is disseminated with the specific aim of moving clinical practice more in line with the evidence base via a range of procedures including, for example, clinical guidelines. There are two main aims: to drive up the quality of care provided and to lessen the variability of care received by clients in differing locations and service settings. In effect, the objective is to set and maintain the best possible standards of care that are achievable.

The evidence-based practice approach has not been without its critics within the health-care disciplines generally (Kerridge, Lowe & Henry, 1998), the psychological therapies specifically (Barkham & Mellor-Clark, 2000) and across other disciples. For example, in the field of education, Simons *et al.* (2003) have developed the idea of 'situated generaliza-tion', which refers to the process whereby practitioners (teachers) only accept evidence for change to practice if there is a clear connection with the situation in which the improvement takes place. In other words, evidence is not freestanding knowledge: it is inextricably bound up with the situation in which it is generated and will only be accepted – validated – by practitioners if they can recognize and connect to the evidence through a commonly held frame of reference.

However, the criticisms are not about having an evidence-based healthcare system *per se*, but rather with the limited definition of evidence employed. In the same way that issues arise in the transition between randomised controlled trials (RCTs) and effectiveness studies, is-sues arise in the transition of the concept of evidence from the areas of clinical epidemiology and medicine to the disciplines underpinning, in this instance, the psychological therapies. The research activities relating to health care comprise such diverse academic traditions, disciplines, and professions that it is implausible for a single concept of evidence to sustain credibility. However, the central tenet that evidence can be ranked hierarchically has been proposed to transcend these differences.

Qualitative studies do not fit neatly into the hierarchy. Qualitative studies address different types of underlying question about healthcare. In a world where context helps to shape evidence, researchers need to be aware of how evidence is collected and interpreted. Upshur, VanDenKerkhof & Goel (2001, p. 92) state: '. . . there is a need for an evidence synthesis that recognizes the interdependence of research methodologies, yet has a sufficient theoretical base that will allow it to have solid 'scientific' standing in the eyes of proponents of evidence-based care.'

Because the origins of evidence-based practice have been in clinical epidemiology, there has been a primacy of quantitative methods and approaches to healthcare questions through *measurement*. However, the need to take account of values, preferences, and perspectives of individual people and patients requires the approach to take account of *meaning* as well as measurement. A key aspiration in moving forwards, from this perspective, would be to discard hierarchical or linear models of evidence. For example, Upshur, VanDenKerkhof & Goel (2001) proposed a conceptual base for a taxonomy of evidence (see Figure 25.1) using two axes: method (with anchor points of meaning and measurement) and context (with anchor points of personal and social). In such a form, evidence can then be viewed as a function of the interface between the method by which it is procured and the context in which it arises.

Stricker (2000) has identified the need for the effective delivery of healthcare to rest on a foundation of evidence from which to derive clinical decisions. Clearly, the results of efficacy research should be part of the practitioner's knowledge base and effectiveness research should guide the hypotheses to be tested by the research scientist. A distinction between efficacy and effectiveness is a crucial implied difference between two approaches to philosophy: social constructionism and positivism. Social constructionism is implicit in the effectiveness approach and its refusal to adopt any singular version of reality. By

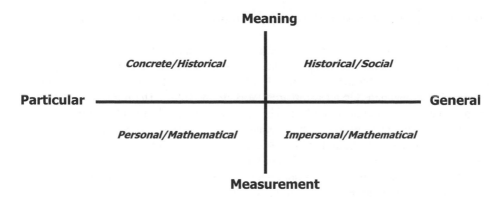

Meaning

Concrete/Historical   Historical/Social

Particular ———————————————————————— **General**

Personal/Mathematical   Impersonal/Mathematical

Measurement

Figure 25.1 Upshur model.
Source: Meaning and measurement: An inclusive model of evidence in health care, Upshur, R.E.G., VanDenKerkhof, E.G., & Goel, V., *Journal of Evaluation in Clinical Practice, 7*, 91–96. Blackwell Science, 2001.

contrast, positivist psychology could be identified with testing a specific and restricted range of hypotheses. With such a reading of contrasting philosophies, it is possible to reconcile both efficacy and effectiveness as different aspects of epistemology or *knowledge discovery*. Social constructionism leads to heuristic knowledge while positivism focuses on knowledge that can be refuted by observations or experiment.

The Landscape of Research Activity: Appropriate, Rigorous and Relevant Research

In attempting to move on from a hierarchical or structural view of evidence, we have construed research in terms of a landscape with contours rather than levels. Within this landscape view of research activity, three key requirements need to be met. First, the research activity (i.e., design, method and approach) needs to be *appropriate* to the question under investigation. Research methods are the equivalent of the artisan's tools in the sense that an artisan who only uses a hammer will see everything as a nail. Research needs to be driven by the question to be addressed and not defined by a restricted range of tools (i.e., methodologies). Secondly, research activity needs to be *rigorous* regardless of method. The advent of the *evidence-based practice* movement in the 1980s and the adoption of this paradigm as a driver within US and UK health policy have ensured that the key component of 'science' is a genuine force in delivering *rigorous* research within the area of the psychological therapies. However, the adoption of hierarchies of evidence has tended to cut across the issue of appropriateness by giving greatest weight to quantitative methodologies. In addition, the most valued methodologies have tended to be more distant from routine practice settings.

This has given rise to the third component regarding the *relevance* of such research to practitioners in routine clinical settings. Here, the drive towards enhancing treatment quality takes a quite different form, namely *practice-based evidence* (Barkham & Mellor-Clark, 2000; Margison *et al.*, 2000). Practice-based evidence has its roots – continuing the landscape analogy – in *routine* clinical settings and is a naturally occurring 'bottom-up' model of compiling evidence in contrast to a 'top-down' model driven by the valuing of RCTs and meta-analytic studies.

Towards a More Inclusive Research Strategy: Strategic Overview

A notable attempt to set out the range of research paradigms applicable to the mental health services that would influence the appropriate policy space was delivered in *Bridging Science and Service*, a report by the US National Advisory Mental Health Council's (NAMHC) Clinical Treatment and Services Research Workgroup (1999). The report – written under the auspices of both the National Institutes of Health and the National Institute of Mental Health – set out a clear vision of the role and kinds of research paradigms that would be most likely to deliver a relevant evidence-base for mental health services. Although some specifics of the US managed care system differ significantly from other countries, including the UK and continental Europe, this does not lessen the need for a strategic shift in the focus and orientation of research as stated in the report.

The NAMHC report set out four key domains of research activity: efficacy, effectiveness, practice, and service systems. The primary aims of each activity would be as follows:

- *Efficacy research* aims to examine whether a particular intervention has a specific, measurable effect and also to address questions concerning the safety, feasibility, side effects, and appropriate dose levels.
- *Effectiveness research* aims to identify whether efficacious treatments can have a measurable, beneficial effect when implemented across broad populations and in other service settings.
- *Practice research* examines how and which treatments or services are provided to individuals within service systems and evaluates how to improve treatment or service delivery. The aim is not so much to isolate or generalize the effect of an intervention but to examine variations in care and ways to disseminate and implement research-based treatments.
- *Service systems research* addresses large-scale organizational, financing and policy questions. This includes the cost of various care options to an entire system; the use of incentives to promote optimal access to care; the effect of legislation, regulation, and other public policies on the organization and delivery of services and the effect that changes in a system (for example, cost-shifting) have on the delivery of services.

From a conceptual viewpoint, we see efficacy research as underpinning the evidence-based paradigm while both effectiveness and practice research are components of practice-based evidence. Service systems research extends effectiveness of practice into the area of policy. These four types of research describe the domains of activity that are needed in order to provide a more comprehensive approach to the accumulation of evidence.

SECTION III: PRACTICE-BASED EVIDENCE

In the context of the four types of research activity outlined above, in this part of the chapter we set out the various components comprising practice-based evidence. Within our definition of practice-based evidence (see earlier) we subsumed the activities listed above (with the exception of efficacy research) – namely, research focusing on effectiveness, practice and service systems. In doing so, we set out the various components in the form of a stage-wise model in order to assist practitioners and researchers alike in viewing these components as a cohesive series of activities that have the potential for engaging practitioners and yielding research findings which have high salience to the field.

The seven sequential components, or stages, can be termed as follows. The first stage is the explication of the *practice-based paradigm*. This refers to the adoption of the philosophy and need for a complementary approach to evidence based practice. The second concerns the required *infrastructure* to support this approach whereas the third focuses on the role of *practice research networks* in being prepared to collect a large and centrally held data base. The fourth stage centres on the adoption of a *common approach to measurement and outcomes* – perhaps the heart of the approach – and the fifth stage involves the *application of measurement at individual and service levels* to enhance the evidence base in routine practice settings. The sixth stage involves using the resulting information in a reflective fashion to *enhance practice and clinical governance* whereas the seventh and final stage provides the critical *interface with evidence-based practice* by synthesizing findings from the practice-based paradigm with those derived from an evidence-based practice paradigm. These seven stages are built from the bottom upwards – a hallmark of the paradigm – and are set out in Figure 25.2.

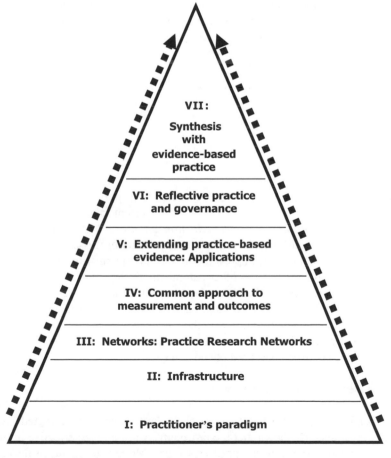

Figure 25.2 Building blocks of practice-based evidence.

Stage 1: Practice-based Evidence Paradigm

Towards a Practice-based Psychology

Fishman (2000) has drawn on the work of others to describe the basis upon which therapy, as an activity, is based and which he has termed 'pragmatic psychology' (Fishman, 1999). This has been referred to in terms of 'professional activity as disciplined inquiry' (Peterson, 1991), whereas others have referred to it as 'a human science of practice' (Hoshmand & Polkinghorne, 1992), 'reflective practice' (Schön, 1983), or 'local clinical practice' (Stricker & Trierweiler, 1995). Here we briefly explicate Peterson's (1991) notion of professional activity as disciplined inquiry as one example of the psychology underpinning practice-based evidence. The model is presented diagrammatically in Figure 25.3. The model is driven by the needs of the client rather than the need for general knowledge and the starting point is with the client, rather than with 'science' *per se*, and all associated knowledge whether it derives from a qualitative or quantitative approach. Within the disciplined inquiry model there is an emphasis on the importance of the practitioner's personal professional experience which results in the construction of an internal 'database' of accumulated case studies that then becomes a source for guidance and action in subsequent cases.

This model – and its variants – has its base in key clinical activities such as 'assessment' and 'formulation'. At this level, we can identify a series of additional procedures that have the explicit aim of improving practice. These procedures have been labelled *practice improvement methods* (Cape & Barkham, 2002) and the key components are their *intention* to change practitioner behaviour and that they are based *in practice*. The range of activities is presented in the top part of Figure 25.4 under the three headings of 'process guidance', 'process monitoring', and 'outcomes management' and these complement the model presented earlier by Peterson (1991) by focusing on the activities of the individual practitioner. However, to be able to engage in the development of data sets which relate to services and to delivery systems requires additional components in which the unit extends beyond the individual practitioner.

Crucial to the paradigm of practice-based evidence is the purpose of *predicting* processes and outcomes with the aim of impacting on past, present, and future behaviours. The long-term aim of this approach is to use *prediction and prevention* in support of improved quality patient care. This includes the prevention of contrary processes and outcomes within therapy as well as broader aspects of prevention based on a population approach. Hence, the paradigm draws on procedures from other naturalistic settings. For example, Sperry *et al.* (1996) draw on the parallel of predicting earthquakes while Lutz *et al.* (2005) use approaches employed in predicting avalanches. This approach contrasts with the central tenet of efficacy research which is to *replicate* findings with the aim of identifying causal mechanisms that will enable services subsequently to *react* in an informed and knowledgeable way based on lawful relationships between observed phenomena.

Practice-based Research Activity

A core principle of a practice-based approach is that evidence must indeed be *practice based* – that is, it must be shown that the procedures work and are effective in improving the quality of patient care in real-life practice settings. Moreover, *practice* is the core driver and assistance in case management is crucial to the utility of such approaches, particularly when a client shows a pattern of deterioration or of less-than-expected gains. A method used primarily in the treatment of eating disorders employs a decision-tree approach (e.g. Classification and Regression Tree; Breiman *et al.*, 1984) to assist decision making in a clinical context where the presence or absence of particular clinical features are used to assist decision making (Hannöver *et al.*, 2002). This procedure shows potential, at least in the research-friendly clinical settings where the method has been developed, but requires wider applications.

However, in practice, the situation is not always as clear as the above account suggests. There are two types of problem. First, reducing the data set, as above, to young, female, single patients with anxiety, depression and possible work-related problems will reduce the sample size dramatically so that the confidence intervals increase. However, Sperry *et al.* (1996) demonstrate that reasonable confidence limits can be obtained. The second and more profound difficulty is that the search for purely numerical case monitoring is likely to be a chimera. Even the strongest advocates of case monitoring would only claim that these methods are adjuncts to clinical methods of supervision and case reviews. They may have particular utility, however, where the clinician has an area of clinical practice that is usually kept from self-scrutiny. These 'special cases' are notorious for countertransferential re-enactments (Main, 1957).

Service Level Applications

At the service level, the focus moves to groups or clusters of clients rather than the individual client. Thus rather than feeding back results to the individual client, the focus is on feeding back findings on the service to managers and service providers in order to drive up the quality of the service delivery. Thus, the focus is on issues of context, therapist and client characteristics and how these variables mediate and moderate outcomes within a service setting. There have been calls for this form of research to more directly inform mental health decision making (for example, Newman & Tejeda, 1996).

The development of large naturalistic data sets (e.g., the CORE National Research Database) has enabled questions to be asked as to, for example, the effectiveness of mainstream therapies as delivered in routine practice settings. Stiles *et al.* (2006) reported on a client sample of 1 309 clients drawn from 58 primary and secondary UK NHS services where the treatment modality was identified by the practitioner (i.e., counsellor) as being either cognitive-behavioural, person-centred, or psychodynamic therapy. The three treatment approaches were found to be broadly equivalent with each other and did not become less effective when mixed with another approach. This finding is important as treatments delivered in routine settings are sometimes considered to be less effective than those in efficacy trials because they are less 'pure'.

One key component at a service level which has received relatively sparse attention until recently is that of the practitioner. Traditional treatment-focused research aims largely to make therapist contributions uniform in that the central interest is the treatment. Not surprisingly, therefore, efficacy studies have tended to report therapist effects to be small and non significant (e.g., Clark *et al.*, 2006). However, differing analyses of therapist effects in the NIMH Treatment of Depression Collaborative Research Program have yielded evidence for both the presence (Dong-Min, Wampold & Bolt, 2006) and absence of effects (Elkin *et al.*, 2006). But powering a study of therapist effects by the number of practitioners would require a huge study – an area ideally suited to the practice-focused research. Lutz *et al.* (in press) drew on data from 60 practitioners each treating between 10 and 77 clients and found practitioners to account for approximately 8 % of the total variance and 17 % of the variance in rates of client improvement. In line with this focus, there is an urgent need for addressing the issue of therapist effectiveness and this is wholly consistent with practice-based focused research. Okiishi *et al.* (2003), using a data base comprising 91 practitioners, found considerable variation around the outcomes to their clients with therapists whose clients reporting the fastest rate of improvement had an average rate of change 10 times greater than the mean. On the basis of these results, the authors argue the need for emphasising the notion of empirically supported practitioners rather than of therapies alone.

Another key component at the service level is that of benchmarking. Despite concerns about its use, benchmarking refers to 'the establishment of reference points that can be used to interpret data' (Sperry *et al.*, 1996, p. 143). The term derives from the practice by artisans of marking a workbench to make measurement of work in progress easier. Benchmarking systems are sometimes derided because of the simplicity of measures that are used. However, the use of consistent procedures within a culture that encourages 'error checking' can allow healthcare settings to learn from so-called 'high reliability' organizations that take a systemic view rather than an individual view of practice (Reason, 2000). Benchmarking at the level of services requires services to compare their effectiveness with other similar services. Benchmarks for primary care counselling services in the NHS have been established for a range of parameters including completion rates for outcome measures (Bewick *et al.*, 2006), client-initiated termination of therapy (Connell, Grant & Mullin, 2006), and rates for improvement and recovery (Mullin *et al.*, 2006). Similarity involves comparison of the service structure and function, but services also need to be able to consider their case mix. This means that information that might predict outcome, such as relapse history, severity, or co-morbidity, needs to be taken into account in any comparison between services. Such comparisons can, given an appropriate organizational framework, lead to improved practice and patient safety (Nolan, 2000). Benchmarking can also take the form of comparing effectiveness in a particular clinical setting against the outcomes obtained in efficacy studies (for example, Merrill *et al.*, 2003). This is a key component in bridge building between evidence-based practice and practice-based evidence. The aim should be to carry out benchmarking involving real world comparisons of services against specified benchmarks.

The service-level activity operates both within and across services and enables lawful relationships to be derived from very large datasets. An exemplar of this level of research has been the establishment of the dose-effect curve for psychotherapy (Howard *et al.*, 1986). This showed that the relationship between the number of sessions received by clients and the percentage of clients showing measurable improvement was best represented by a negatively accelerating curve. This means that while the curve 'accelerates' (the percentage of clients improving gets higher as a result of more sessions) it does so 'negatively' in that the greatest improvement occurs early in therapy and then there are diminishing returns thereafter such that smaller and smaller gains are made later on in therapy in response to the provision of more sessions. Hansen *et al.* (2002) reviewed the clinical trials literature and found that between 58 % and 67 % of patients improved within an average of approximately 13 sessions. The authors then calculated rates of improvement based on a large database drawn from routine service settings and found that rates of improvement and duration of therapy to be considerably less – around 20 % of clients showing improvement with a median of three sessions (Hansen *et al.*, 2002). In contrast, a study of 33 UK-based primary care services showed 56.5 % of 1 868 clients to meet criteria for reliable and clinically significant improvement (Barkham *et al.*, 2006b). When only those clients who were originally at or above the clinical cut-off score at intake, this rate rose to 71.7 %. Of particular note, however, the data suggested that the negatively accelerating curve previously reported in the literature may be a function of clients exiting therapy when they have achieved a good enough level of improvement. Clearly more research is required into this phenomenon but the contrasting evidence highlights the need both for research that is practice-based and also for an interface between results drawn from these routine settings with established findings derived from clinical trials.

Stage 6: Reflective Practice: Improving Practice and Providing Governance

Practice-based Evidence and Quality Assurance

Practice-based evidence can be used as a systematic approach to building and maintaining an effective service whether at the level of, for example, a UK NHS Trust (Lucock *et al.*, 2003) or US state (Brower, 2003). To the extent that results are fed back into the service system, the process might be considered to be a topic closely linked to audit. Conventionally, audit deals with the details of inputs, activities and outputs, setting desired standards and examining the potential steps that might lead to change. The whole process forms an iterative loop with the standards against which the service is to be assessed being, themselves, continually revised. To complement the audit approach, questions about quality improvement have focused mainly on the following: how comprehensive a service is intended to be? How relevant is the intervention? How acceptable is the intervention? How accessible and equitable is the service? How efficiently is the treatment delivered? Audit and evaluation of quality have been viewed with suspicion by clinicians. They may have concerns about confidentiality, freedom of clinical choice, untoward effects of the audit on the therapist-patient relationship; an excessive concern with costs, medico-legal fears and a lack of trust in how the information might be used (Margison *et al.*, 1998).

Notwithstanding such concerns, attempts to enhance the quality of services within a practice-based approach can be progressed by, for example, feeding back the performance of a service on key indicators (e.g., waiting times, premature endings, clinical outcomes, etc.) for which benchmarks have been established (see Stage 5). Evans *et al.* (2006) have reported on how, through data management workshops with the managers of services using the CORE System, they were able to work with them to help improve aspects of their service delivery. In this respect, inspection and interrogation of such data with service managers can be construed of as 'service supervision' and akin to the parallel process at an individual client level of 'clinical supervision' – an activity that is universally accepted as good practice.

Although the evidence derived from this practice approach is of value in and of itself, it carries with it the crucial component of situated generalization – the process whereby practitioners accept evidence for change to practice if there is a clear connection with the situation in which the improvement takes place. Hence, it contains the great potential for building reflective practice whereby practitioners can be the consumers of their – and other practitioners' – research. Lucock *et al.* (2003) describe building a service delivery system on a model of practice-based evidence and identified key components and reflections on this

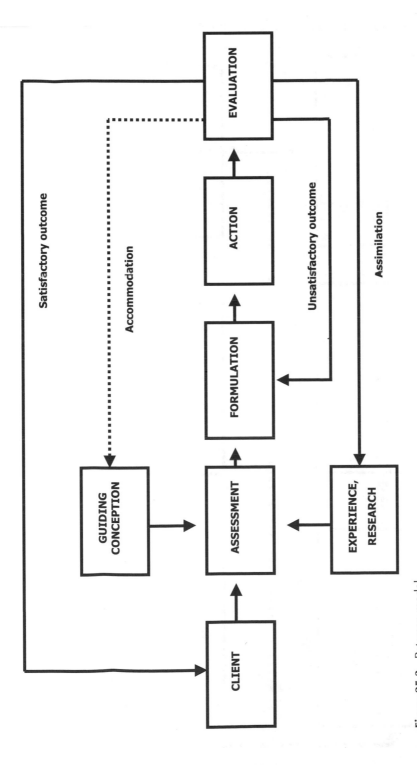

Figure 25.3 Petersen model.
Source: Connection and disconnection of research and practice in the education of professional psychologists, Peterson, D.R. *American Psychologist, 40*, 441–451, American Psychological Association, 1991.

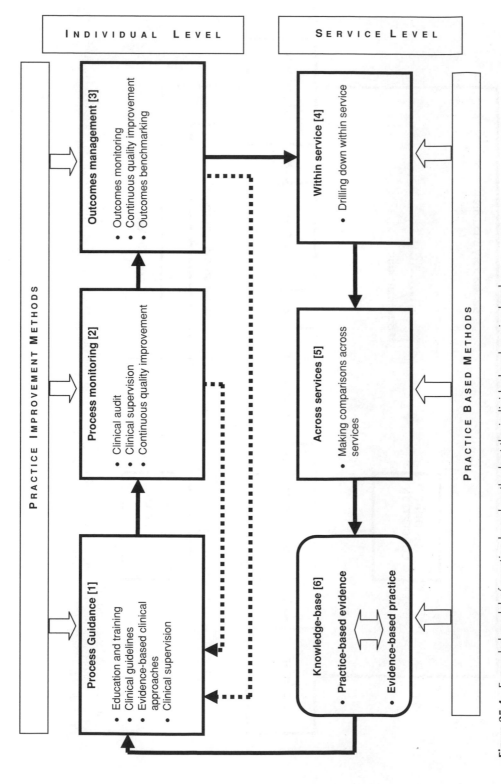

Figure 25.4 Expanded model of practice-based methods at the individual and service level.
Source: Practice Improvement Methods: Conceptual base, evidence-based research and practice based recommendations, Cape, J. & Barkham, M., British Journal of Clinical Psychology, 41, 285–307, British Psychological Society, 2002.

of the process – driven by practitioners' and managers' desires to provide a quality service to their clients. At this level, the issue of *ownership* of the research activity by practitioners becomes crucial as they strive to innovate and generate solutions to local issues.

Two key components are central to the practice-based paradigm: *effectiveness* and *practice* (Barkham & Mellor-Clark, 2003; National Advisory Mental Health Council, 1999). The *effectiveness* component addresses the generalizability of results *across* particular services and settings. For example, it is being viewed as increasingly important to be able to locate the activity of an individual service in the context of other services (see, for example, Evans *et al.*, 2003). The ability of a local service to profile itself against comparative national information across key delivery indicators provides invaluable information in terms of providing a fuller understanding of how a service is performing. The *practice* component addresses the analysis of results *within* a service or setting: That is, enabling services to 'drill down' in the data to ascertain individual differences and variations in relation to patient subgroups and according to which therapist carried out the treatment (for example, see Sperry *et al.*, 1996). The philosophy of practice-based evidence is aimed at enhancing the quality of the intervention or care provided by the practitioner rather than being a tool for service managers to plan their service. That is not to deny the legitimacy or necessity of this function but rather to note that it has a different rationale and process to it. Indeed, we might consider a number of levels of purpose here. For example, while the purpose of *practice improvement methods* is to enhance individual practitioner behaviour, the purpose of *practice-based evidence* is to enhance service-level activity both within and across services, at the level of individual practitioners, clinical units, or even whole services. While the top level within Figure 25.4 focuses on the individual level, the model is extended here to comprise both individual *and service* levels.

Stages 2 and 3: Infrastructure and Networks

Infrastructure

Practice-based evidence relies on there being an infrastructure and network of practitioners and associated researchers who are committed to the potential of the paradigm. The identification of issues concerning the development of a necessary infrastructure is relatively embryonic. A systematic review of the structures, process and outcomes from inter-organizational research highlighted the need for high quality studies to compare different network structures and processes, and to examine the impact of different structures and processes on the effectiveness of a network (Ruddy *et al.*, 2005). Several methods for studying networks were highlighted within this review. These included, for example, the mapping of co-author activity as a method for examining network structure (Newman, 2001). This principle could be used to compare different network structures and how they relate to research productivity. Questionnaires have been developed to determine what is and what is not acceptable within inter-group collaboration (Lucena *et al.*, 2002) and Provan provided an example of how to measure the effectiveness of a network using clinical outcomes (Provan & Milward, 1995; Provan & Sebastian, 1998). These methods provide tools that could be employed by future studies of mental health networks where establishing the effectiveness of the network is critical.

Practice Research Networks

Practice research networks (PRNs) provide and fulfil a central role within the practice-based evidence paradigm, building on the implicit infrastructure discussed above. The rise of PRNs has been in response to two major concerns. The first concern relates to constraints placed upon the generalizability of efficacy research and the second concern focuses on the issue of the lack of robustness of some effectiveness research whereby the possible explanatory accounts for results are so numerous as to undermine the whole activity (Borkovec et al., 2001). In light of these growing tensions, many researchers have moved to develop a body of activity that would help to bridge the external-internal validity issue. Borkovec et al. (2001, p. 155) state: 'one of the wisest approaches that the field of clinical psychology can take would involve the creation of clinical research programs that maximise both internal validity by their choice of rigorous scientific methodologies and external validity by conducting psychotherapy research in actual applied settings.'

In order to achieve this body of activity, Borkovec et al. (2001) set out two clear phases for the setting up of a PRN: the first focusing on issues of organization and infrastructure, and the second focusing on the development and conduct of research that was deemed to be internally valid and clinically relevant.

A PRN is defined as a 'network of clinicians that collaborate to conduct research to inform their day to day practice' (Audin et al., 2001) and involve '...a large number of clinicians who agree to collaborate to collect and report data...' (Zarin et al., 1996, p. 147). In contrast to most 'formal' research, PRNs use data gathered in 'real-world' practice settings rather than specifically orchestrated clinical trials. They have been described as naturalistic 'laboratories' for large-scale data collection (Hickner, 1993). Comparability is ensured by using the same data collection tools across the sites constituting the PRN enabling standard setting and outcomes benchmarking. Hence, the PRN is an appropriate mechanism for helping services to establish ongoing service evaluation and routine collection of effectiveness data. Data can also be collected prospectively to answer a particular research question of interest to the members.

Examples of PRNs in relation to the psychological therapies include the Pennsylvania PRN (Borkovec et al., 2001) in the US and the Psychological Therapies Research Network North (PsyReNN; Audin et al., 2001) and the CORE Network (Mellor-Clark et al., 2006) in the UK. The main strength of these PRNs is in the collection of very large data sets. This allows much better prediction at the level of the individual case (see Sperry et al., 1996). Many studies reported in the literature are of marginal power even for the main research hypothesis (Dar et al., 1994). Questions most relevant to clinicians are often very difficult to answer from the available efficacy research literature because there are insufficient data to answer detailed questions referring to variables such as ethnicity and co-morbid diagnosis.

Stage 4: Common Approach to Measurement and Outcomes

The Role of Measurement

Regardless of the paradigm or method adopted, measurement is the vehicle for transporting the phenomenon under investigation into data that yield information and ultimately knowledge. In terms of measures available, there are numerous texts summarizing methodological issues in outcome measurement (Hill & Lambert, 2004), specific outcome measures

(Maruish, 1999, 2001), and approaches to outcome evaluation (Speer, 1998). There is a parallel literature relating to process measures in terms of methodological issues (Hill & Lambert, 2004; Llewelyn & Hardy, 2001) and specific measures (Greenberg & Pinsoff, 1986; Hill et al., 1994). Regardless of the specific measure used, a key issue is that of retaining *meaning*. Too often, researchers in the field of the psychological therapies over-invest in one type of measurement at the expense of another. For example, many studies use multiple outcome measures that are all highly correlated with each other. It can be argued that such additional measures act as quasi-replications that help to determine the effect of measurement error, a process made far more difficult if only a single measure is used. However, there is a point at which this is outweighed by empirical redundancy and overburdening the client in return for only a low scientific yield. Rather than simply use overlapping and often redundant measures, it is possible to bring in a pluralistic design instead (Lambert et al., 2004).

A related issue in measurement has always been that of trading fidelity with 'bandwidth'. Fidelity refers to the purity (internal validity) and specific focus of a measure and is a dimension traditionally prized in research. By contrast, in this context, bandwidth refers to the 'range' of information collected. Practitioners prize multiple domains being measured (even though in practice there is often substantial common variance). Bandwidth also reflects a related concept of the scale covering a wide range of severity. But a logical consequence of greater bandwidth is likely to be a reduction in statistical power due to decreased purity in the measures and increased 'noise' in the sampling – and hence the requirement for larger samples to overcome the effects of this reduced efficiency.

A Core Approach to Measurement

In order for PRNs to deliver the large Ns required of the paradigm, there needs to be a common approach to measurement and the selection of measures. In many respects, this is the heart of a practice-based approach as without this the research activity immediately becomes fragmented and underpowered. Moreover, several reviews have drawn a rather disappointing picture of the impact on services of adopting routine outcome measures (Gilbody, House & Sheldon, 2001; Greenhalgh & Meadows, 1999). However, while the decision-making process involved in measurement selection within an efficacy trial is, if not easy, is at least contained within the specific purpose of the trial, the scenario is somewhat different in routine practice. While practitioners will diverge in terms of their specific interests, there needs to be an organizational commitment to the selection, adoption, and implementation of an agreed measurement approach. In its true sense, the aim would be to identify a core set of measures upon which all parties agree. Both the Pennsylvania and the PsyReNN PRNs used the notion of a core outcome battery to achieve this requirement.

Various approaches to a core outcome battery have been proposed. In order to build bridges between studies and across paradigms, attempts have been made both in the US (Strupp et al., 1997; Waskow, 1975) and the UK (Barkham et al., 1998) to devise a core outcome battery. The US attempts focused on three specific patient groups: anxiety disorders, mood disorders and personality disorders (Horowitz et al., 1997). This approach contrasted with parallel UK initiatives in which the vision was of developing a *generic* or 'core' outcome battery focused on what is core to the majority of clients presenting with psychological difficulties (Barkham et al., 1998). This resulted in the development of the Clinical Outcomes in Routine Evaluation – Outcome Measure (CORE-OM; for a summary see Barkham *et al.*, 2006a). However, more than applying a common core outcome measure, practice-based research has required the development of broader based management and information *systems* (Grissom, Lyons & Lutz, 2002). The Pennsylvania PRN (Borkovec *et al.*, 2001) adopted significant portions of the COMPASS system (Sperry *et al.*, 1996) in addition to the 64-item version of the Inventory of Interpersonal Problems (Alden *et al.*, 1990). The PsyReNN PRN (Audin *et al.*, 2001) adopted the CORE-OM (Barkham *et al.*, 2001; Cahill *et al.*, 2006; Evans *et al.*, 2002) with some participating sites also using components from the broader-based CORE System (Mellor-Clark & Barkham, 2000; Mellor-Clark *et al.*, 2006). Table 25.2 sets out the desiderata for a core outcome measure. These extend beyond the design stage to include the feasibility of implementation and also the resulting yield to clinical services.

A core approach to measurement has undeniable yield but it also presents the possibility of stifling measure development. Fundamental to research activity is the need continually to review measures to reflect current concerns. The trade-off here is between stability of use (ensuring comparability with prior research) *versus* responsiveness to new research findings and ideas. Conceptual and empirical mapping of measures is needed if there is to be a robust understanding of the relationship between measures. With these relationships established, then more appropriate decisions can be made as to whether a new measure can appropriately replace an earlier measure. For example, precise tables have been developed for transforming BDI-I scores into CORE-OM scores and *vice versa* based on large samples drawn from routine practice settings (Leach *et al.*, 2006). The yield of establishing these lawful relationships is considerable in terms of bridging the scientist-practitioner gap as the decision rules that determine choice of measures differ between research and practice settings. Hence, the BDI may be selected in efficacy trials due to it being viewed as the gold standard and because procurement costs of the measure for the required number of clients are carried by research funding. By contrast, procurement costs for such a measure make this impracticable for routine use, hence the adoption of other quality measures that carry no financial burden (for example, the CORE-OM or the Patient Health Questionnaire-9 (PHQ-9; Kroenke, Spitzer & Williams, 2001).

Analysing and Presenting Outcomes

As an adjunct to traditional procedures for determining the significance of outcomes, there has been a gradual move towards using procedures that are more sensitive to the phenomena under investigation. These include a range of procedures that address differing but interrelated issues, most of which are well-established in the literature. With studies in routine settings using increasingly large Ns, the meaning of significant differences becomes a concern. In response, greater use is made of effect sizes (ESs) that enable consumers of research to determine the magnitude of either the pre-post change for a single sample or the differential effect between two comparative samples (Cohen, 1977). Indeed, the Fifth Edition of the American Psychological Association (APA) Publication Guidelines (American Psychological Association, 2003) requires that ESs be stated as part of reporting results. Table 25.3 presents a guide to the interpretation of ESs between two comparative samples using guidelines from Cohen (1977, 1988).

Distinct from the use of ESs has been the application of meaningful categories of change and in particular that of determining *reliable and clinically significant change*, a concept

Table 25.2 Design, implementation, and yield criteria of a core outcome battery

Stage 1: Design

1. As far as possible, the measure should be pan-theoretical. If it is based on a specific theory, then it becomes a test of that one theory rather than being a more generic measure of change derived from an empirical base.
2. It should include items that assess patients' risk to themselves and to others.
3. It should be easy to score and interpret (i.e. it should not require specialist professional skills).
4. It should be relatively short.
5. It should show respectable reliability in a range of clinical and non-clinical samples (e.g., adequate internal consistency and test-retest reliability over short intervals).
6. Development work should establish any relationships to gender and age in both clinical and non-clinical samples.
7. Development work should have established convergent validating relationships with existing referential measures such as the BDI, PHQ-9, and SCL-90-R both at scale and at item level (as some items will not be expected to correlate with those more specific measures).
8. It should be clinically sensitive in that it will detect change when it has occurred.
9. Clinical and non-clinical samples should have established fairly precise estimates of the likely distributions in these populations. Together with the reliability data these should be sufficient to calculate clinically reliable and significant change in individuals (Jacobson & Truax, 1991).
10. Ideally, there should be data on possible differences in score distributions between ethnic and cultural groups (e.g. social class, level of education).
11. It should include shorter parallel forms for repeated administration within treatment.
12. It should also be backed by recommended extension measures for specific problem areas and also by more targeted versions for specific purposes (e.g. screening, weekly monitoring).

Stage 2: Implementation

13. The outcome measure should be part of a total systems approach which enables contextual data on the surface delivery system to be collected. Readable manuals should provide clear guidance on the use of the measures to maximize comparability of use.
14. The measure should be utilised by as wide a range of services as possible and their clinical data collated into a central, anonymized, national research database (NRD) database. Monitoring of psychometric properties and any "drift" in distributions should be continued and adjusted referential figures published if these parameters change.
15. The collation of a National Research Database should become a resource from which individual services can scrutinize their data and aggregate data can yield scientific articles.
16. Contributing services should, as far as possible, be encouraged to form peer review groups linking on geography, mode of therapy, specialist focus or other commonalities.
17. Similarly, contributing services would be encouraged to link with research units to form 'practice research networks' (PRNs) (Zarin *et al.*, 1996). Such networks already exist (e.g. Pennsylvania PRN; CORE PRN) and these serve to break down the separation of research from clinical practice.
18. A form of technical data processing should be made available (e.g. using the Internet) that provides calculation of reliable and clinically significant change.
19. The measure should be, effectively, in the public domain (i.e. there is no cost at the point of use).

Stage 3: Yield

20. The measure should become the basis for outcome benchmarking and service level monitoring and supervision.

Source: The rationale for developing and implementing core batteries in service settings and psychotherapy outcome research, Barkham, M. *et al., Journal of Mental Health, 7,* 35–47. Carfax Publishing, 1998.

Table 25.3   Guide to interpreting between-group effect sizes

Cohen's guidelines for interpreting effect sizes	Effect size (d)	Proportion of people in control condition who are below the mean of people in the treated condition
No effect	0.0	0.50
Small effect	0.1	0.54
	0.2	0.58
	0.3	0.62
	0.4	0.66
Medium effect	0.5	0.69
	0.6	0.73
	0.7	0.76
	0.8	0.79
Large effect	0.9	0.82
	1.0	0.84

originally proposed by Jacobson and colleagues (Jacobson, Follette & Revenstorf, 1984), modified (Christensen & Mendoza, 1986) and then consolidated in a series of articles (Jacobson *et al.*, 1986; Jacobson & Revenstorf, 1988; Jacobson & Truax, 1991). This concept has received considerable attention in some areas of the literature while being eschewed in others. For example, it has been the focus of historical (Ogles, Lunnen & Bonesteel, 2001; Wise, 2004), conceptual (Kendall *et al.*, 1999) as well as methodological and statistical (Bauer, Lambert & Neilsen, 2004) attention. Various modifications to the formulae have been proposed (for example, Hsu, 1989, 1996) but the procedures set out by Jacobson & Truax (1991) remain robust. Although the procedures are based on theories of distribution, they are accessible to practitioners because they are premised on two key clinical indicators: first, whether the change in a client's score is reliable and, second, where this change now places the client in terms of a given population (normal, clinical, and so forth). This is an example of the continuing trade-off between the fidelity, which is sought after in efficacy research and the practical approach – good enough – required in practice (Barkham, 2006). Within practice-based evidence, this procedure combines the ability of mapping the outcomes of large numbers of clients while at the same time enabling the practitioner to see that each individual dot represents a specific individual client.

Figure 25.5 (left portion) presents a reliable and clinically significant change plot of data reported by Lucock *et al.* (2003). Points below the main diagonal are those clients whose CORE-OM scores improved. Points outside the lines parallel to the diagonal are those clients who have reliably improved (bottom right triangle) or reliably deteriorated (upper left triangle) and those in the outlined boxes have shown reliable and clinical improvement (bottom box) or reliable and clinical deterioration. The plot shows a total of 42 % of clients achieving reliable and clinical improvement while none show reliable and clinical deterioration. A total of 58 % showed statistically reliable improvement and 3 % showed statistically reliable deterioration. The notched box-plot to the right of the figure shows the statistically reliable change information in a different form, slicing the data in the scatterplot diagonally across the plot. The 'notches' represent approximate 90 % confidence intervals for the median – noted by the centre point – with the central box comprising

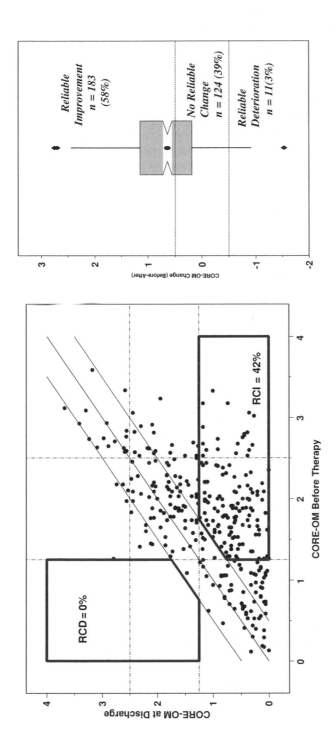

RCD = reliable and clinically significant deterioration.
RCI = reliable and clinically significant improvement.

Figure 25.5 Plots indicating reliable and clinically significant change and comparable notched box.
Source: Evaluating psychological therapies services: A review of outcome measures and their utility, Leach, C., Lucock, M., Iveson, S. & Noble R., *Mental Health and Learning Disabilities Research and Practice, 1,* 53–66, South West Yorkshire Mental Health NHS Trust/University of Huddersfield, 2004.

the middle 50 % of the data. Confidence intervals can be used to enable consumers of research to judge the range in which the true score lies (Wilson, 1927).

Outcomes that Cannot be Measured May Have Worth

There are important decisions to be made about the values underlying the evaluation of change data (Margison *et al.*, 2000). Some outcomes may be valued by both therapist and patient but still be difficult to summarize in words, let alone measure accurately (Holmes & Lindley, 1991). The difficulty in measuring a valued outcome does not make that outcome less desirable but it makes it less amenable to standardized assessment of change. Some models of change have emerged from qualitative research and may fit appropriately into a meaning or narrative framework.

> [A]gain and again defenders of such values are faced with a dilemma of either refusing to quantify the value in question, in which case it disappears from the equation altogether, or else of trying to attach some quantity to it, in which case they misrepresent what they are about, and also usually lose the argument, since the quantified value is not enough to tip the scale. (Williams, 1972 cited in Kerridge *et al.*, 1998, p. 1152)

This leaves the clinician researcher with a significant problem in using some practice-based evidence approaches. The reasoned argument that everything of value cannot be captured in a simple scale is turned into a counter-claim that using a numerical scale is reductionist and an affront to human values. This argument simply widens the scientist-practitioner divide. As we argue below, there are ways of narrowing the gap by focusing on actual practice rather than the highly controlled settings that characterize efficacy research. But, even with a pragmatic approach it is inevitable that some values cannot be put into unambiguous words and concepts and hence cannot be measured. We argue that attempts to improve standards of healthcare require at least a tentative system of definitions and measurement, and that the search for increasing effectiveness need not compromise high standards of ethical practice.

Stage 5: Extending Practice-based Evidence at Individual and Service Levels

Practice-focused Research

The drive to improve patient care in health settings has highlighted the potential gap between the complex and pressing demands on treatment as delivered in routine settings and the simple and fixed treatment models that are the focus of randomized controlled or clinical trials. However, potential ways of loosening the simple approach to RCTs have been proposed (TenHave *et al.*, 2003). Efficacy studies trade off contextual relevance for experimental control and seek to derive general causal principles. There is a more pragmatic approach in effectiveness research, but not necessarily less interest in possible underlying causes. Rather, the two models reflect different ways of looking at cause from a non-experimental, large scale population approach. However, as noted earlier, practice-based evidence is premised on client-focused research and within that there are two pragmatic levels of activity: individual case level and service level.

Individual Client-focused Applications

As noted earlier, in contrast to the dominance of treatment-focused research in evidence-based practice, practice-based evidence relies on client-focused research in which the individual client is central (Howard *et al.*, 1996; Lambert, 2001; Lueger, 2002). Much of this work aims to predict the course of individual clients' progress in psychotherapy based on their initial scores on a battery of measures. The predicted trajectory can be used for triage or compared with clients' actual progress as a basis for clinical decisions during treatment (Lambert *et al.*, 2003; Lutz, 2002). The approach has used large clinical data sets drawn from practice research networks (Barkham *et al.*, 2001; Borkovec *et al.*, 2001) or data from health insurance companies (Lyons *et al.*, 1997) to calculate the expected trajectories. The purpose of this approach is to provide a continuous reference point or benchmark against which to evaluate a patient's progress. This has been called the expected treatment response model (Lambert *et al.*, 2003b; Lueger *et al.*, 2001; Lutz *et al.*, 2006).

The ability to predict patient responses to psychological interventions has become a major focus for researchers and provides an exemplar of the use of increasingly sophisticated statistical analyses with the clinically grounded approach of practitioners. The use of 'nearest neighbours' provides a case in point in which the closest examples to the target case within a data set can be used to model the projected outcome (Lutz *et al.*, 2005). In effect, this parallels practitioners' use of tacit clinical information within their clinical expertise to draw upon in guiding them through successive clinical decision-making. Similarly, procedures have been developed to provide feedback to practitioners during the therapy on their patients' progress (Lambert *et al.*, 2005). Evidence suggests that feedback, supported by case discussion, on patient progress *during* therapy may improve eventual outcome by reducing the number of sessions to achieve equivalent outcomes to those who did not receive feedback and also by enabling therapists to sustain therapies and improve outcomes in those where treatment failure was predicted (Lambert *et al.*, 2001). More recently, Lambert *et al.* (2005) have reviewed for controlled studies in which clinical decision tools (i.e. feedback) provide therapists with signals for when a client's outcome is off target (i.e. not what would be expected from clients with similar presentations). They conclude that employing a feedback system enhances treatment outcomes for clients who show a negative response to treatment.

When conducting a particular type of therapy, a large database allows a comparison with appropriate confidence limits so that if the therapy is not showing improvement within the expected range, then the therapy is *flagged* for further scrutiny. Sperry *et al.* (1996) give a clinical example. They cite a 28-year old female patient with a two- to three-month history of anxiety and depression. She complained of diffuse difficulties, which were worse on workday mornings. The therapist provided five sessions of initial therapy looking for underlying causes. The case manager expressed alarm at the review point because of evident deterioration in her clinical scores. After a second opinion, and a revised focus on the underlying work issues, the patient's clinical state improved. At the review point when the case is 'flagged' it is possible to use more specific quality measures. Is the therapist following the procedures for this type of therapy? Is the formulation complete and of reasonable quality? Are there complicating factors (such as inter-current substance abuse) that have been overlooked?

In this example, the practitioner can discuss the case formulation in a peer group to identify any factors that can be remedied. This use of clinical support through supervision and assistance in case management is crucial to the utility of such approaches, particularly when a client shows a pattern of deterioration or of less-than-expected gains. A method used primarily in the treatment of eating disorders employs a decision-tree approach (e.g. Classification and Regression Tree; Breiman *et al.*, 1984) to assist decision making in a clinical context where the presence or absence of particular clinical features are used to assist decision making (Hannöver *et al.*, 2002). This procedure shows potential, at least in the research-friendly clinical settings where the method has been developed, but requires wider applications.

However, in practice, the situation is not always as clear as the above account suggests. There are two types of problem. First, reducing the data set, as above, to young, female, single patients with anxiety, depression and possible work-related problems will reduce the sample size dramatically so that the confidence intervals increase. However, Sperry *et al.* (1996) demonstrate that reasonable confidence limits can be obtained. The second and more profound difficulty is that the search for purely numerical case monitoring is likely to be a chimera. Even the strongest advocates of case monitoring would only claim that these methods are adjuncts to clinical methods of supervision and case reviews. They may have particular utility, however, where the clinician has an area of clinical practice that is usually kept from self-scrutiny. These 'special cases' are notorious for countertransferential re-enactments (Main, 1957).

Service Level Applications

At the service level, the focus moves to groups or clusters of clients rather than the individual client. Thus rather than feeding back results to the individual client, the focus is on feeding back findings on the service to managers and service providers in order to drive up the quality of the service delivery. Thus, the focus is on issues of context, therapist and client characteristics and how these variables mediate and moderate outcomes within a service setting. There have been calls for this form of research to more directly inform mental health decision making (for example, Newman & Tejeda, 1996).

The development of large naturalistic data sets (e.g., the CORE National Research Database) has enabled questions to be asked as to, for example, the effectiveness of mainstream therapies as delivered in routine practice settings. Stiles *et al.* (2006) reported on a client sample of 1 309 clients drawn from 58 primary and secondary UK NHS services where the treatment modality was identified by the practitioner (i.e., counsellor) as being either cognitive-behavioural, person-centred, or psychodynamic therapy. The three treatment approaches were found to be broadly equivalent with each other and did not become less effective when mixed with another approach. This finding is important as treatments delivered in routine settings are sometimes considered to be less effective than those in efficacy trials because they are less 'pure'.

One key component at a service level which has received relatively sparse attention until recently is that of the practitioner. Traditional treatment-focused research aims largely to make therapist contributions uniform in that the central interest is the treatment. Not surprisingly, therefore, efficacy studies have tended to report therapist effects to be small and non significant (e.g., Clark *et al.*, 2006). However, differing analyses of therapist effects in the NIMH Treatment of Depression Collaborative Research Program have yielded evidence for both the presence (Dong-Min, Wampold & Bolt, 2006) and absence of effects (Elkin *et al.*, 2006). But powering a study of therapist effects by the number of practitioners would require a huge study – an area ideally suited to the practice-focused research. Lutz *et al.* (in press) drew on data from 60 practitioners each treating between 10 and 77 clients and found practitioners to account for approximately 8 % of the total variance and 17 % of the variance in rates of client improvement. In line with this focus, there is an urgent need for addressing the issue of therapist effectiveness and this is wholly consistent with practice-based focused research. Okiishi *et al.* (2003), using a data base comprising 91 practitioners, found considerable variation around the outcomes to their clients with therapists whose clients reporting the fastest rate of improvement had an average rate of change 10 times greater than the mean. On the basis of these results, the authors argue the need for emphasising the notion of empirically supported practitioners rather than of therapies alone.

Another key component at the service level is that of benchmarking. Despite concerns about its use, benchmarking refers to 'the establishment of reference points that can be used to interpret data' (Sperry *et al.*, 1996, p. 143). The term derives from the practice by artisans of marking a workbench to make measurement of work in progress easier. Benchmarking systems are sometimes derided because of the simplicity of measures that are used. However, the use of consistent procedures within a culture that encourages 'error checking' can allow healthcare settings to learn from so-called 'high reliability' organizations that take a systemic view rather than an individual view of practice (Reason, 2000). Benchmarking at the level of services requires services to compare their effectiveness with other similar services. Benchmarks for primary care counselling services in the NHS have been established for a range of parameters including completion rates for outcome measures (Bewick *et al.*, 2006), client-initiated termination of therapy (Connell, Grant & Mullin, 2006), and rates for improvement and recovery (Mullin *et al.*, 2006). Similarity involves comparison of the service structure and function, but services also need to be able to consider their case mix. This means that information that might predict outcome, such as relapse history, severity, or co-morbidity, needs to be taken into account in any comparison between services. Such comparisons can, given an appropriate organizational framework, lead to improved practice and patient safety (Nolan, 2000). Benchmarking can also take the form of comparing effectiveness in a particular clinical setting against the outcomes obtained in efficacy studies (for example, Merrill *et al.*, 2003). This is a key component in bridge building between evidence-based practice and practice-based evidence. The aim should be to carry out benchmarking involving real world comparisons of services against specified benchmarks.

The service-level activity operates both within and across services and enables lawful relationships to be derived from very large datasets. An exemplar of this level of research has been the establishment of the dose-effect curve for psychotherapy (Howard *et al.*, 1986). This showed that the relationship between the number of sessions received by clients and the percentage of clients showing measurable improvement was best represented by a negatively accelerating curve. This means that while the curve 'accelerates' (the percentage of clients improving gets higher as a result of more sessions) it does so 'negatively' in that the greatest improvement occurs early in therapy and then there are diminishing returns thereafter such that smaller and smaller gains are made later on in therapy in response to the provision of more sessions. Hansen *et al.* (2002) reviewed the clinical trials literature and found that between 58 % and 67 % of patients improved within an average of approximately 13 sessions. The authors then calculated rates of improvement based on a large database drawn from routine service settings and found that rates of improvement and duration of therapy to be considerably less – around 20 % of clients showing improvement with a median of three sessions (Hansen *et al.*, 2002). In contrast, a study of 33 UK-based primary care services showed 56.5 % of 1 868 clients to meet criteria for reliable and clinically significant improvement (Barkham *et al.*, 2006b). When only those clients who were originally at or above the clinical cut-off score at intake, this rate rose to 71.7 %. Of particular note, however, the data suggested that the negatively accelerating curve previously reported in the literature may be a function of clients exiting therapy when they have achieved a good enough level of improvement. Clearly more research is required into this phenomenon but the contrasting evidence highlights the need both for research that is practice-based and also for an interface between results drawn from these routine settings with established findings derived from clinical trials.

Stage 6: Reflective Practice: Improving Practice and Providing Governance

Practice-based Evidence and Quality Assurance

Practice-based evidence can be used as a systematic approach to building and maintaining an effective service whether at the level of, for example, a UK NHS Trust (Lucock *et al.*, 2003) or US state (Brower, 2003). To the extent that results are fed back into the service system, the process might be considered to be a topic closely linked to audit. Conventionally, audit deals with the details of inputs, activities and outputs, setting desired standards and examining the potential steps that might lead to change. The whole process forms an iterative loop with the standards against which the service is to be assessed being, themselves, continually revised. To complement the audit approach, questions about quality improvement have focused mainly on the following: how comprehensive a service is intended to be? How relevant is the intervention? How acceptable is the intervention? How accessible and equitable is the service? How efficiently is the treatment delivered? Audit and evaluation of quality have been viewed with suspicion by clinicians. They may have concerns about confidentiality, freedom of clinical choice, untoward effects of the audit on the therapist-patient relationship; an excessive concern with costs, medico-legal fears and a lack of trust in how the information might be used (Margison *et al.*, 1998).

Notwithstanding such concerns, attempts to enhance the quality of services within a practice-based approach can be progressed by, for example, feeding back the performance of a service on key indicators (e.g., waiting times, premature endings, clinical outcomes, etc.) for which benchmarks have been established (see Stage 5). Evans *et al.* (2006) have reported on how, through data management workshops with the managers of services using the CORE System, they were able to work with them to help improve aspects of their service delivery. In this respect, inspection and interrogation of such data with service managers can be construed of as 'service supervision' and akin to the parallel process at an individual client level of 'clinical supervision' – an activity that is universally accepted as good practice.

Although the evidence derived from this practice approach is of value in and of itself, it carries with it the crucial component of situated generalization – the process whereby practitioners accept evidence for change to practice if there is a clear connection with the situation in which the improvement takes place. Hence, it contains the great potential for building reflective practice whereby practitioners can be the consumers of their – and other practitioners' – research. Lucock *et al.* (2003) describe building a service delivery system on a model of practice-based evidence and identified key components and reflections on this process. They deemed seven factors to be important in bringing about a change management consistent with practice-based evidence:

- ownership, especially in being party to decision making;
- training sessions to disseminate revised ways of working;
- clarity of written documentation to explain procedures;
- a range of forums for voicing and sharing concerns;
- clear lines of accountability;
- providing staff with a background – and context – to national policy drivers; and
- feedback of results to clinicians as a standard procedure.

While these factors are very closely related to organizational and management procedures that embed practice-based evidence within a service setting (see Stage 2), the key product of this cycle lies in the feedback provided to clients, practitioners, the service, and all other stakeholders.

Stage 7: Synthesizing Practice-based Evidence and Evidence-based Practice – The Yield of Chiasmus

The six stages above have outlined the components of the complementary term practice-based evidence. However, the danger of multiple paradigms is that they are seen as competitive or mutually exclusive: one paradigm is 'right' and the other 'wrong'. A move away from such a dichotomous position would be to construe each paradigm as occupying a space along a continuum. However, one component of a continuum is its linearity and this fuels the argument that a research question is first tested under one condition and then tested under the other. The usual direction is that from efficacy to effectiveness. Within this framework, several models have been presented: for example, a developmental model (Linehan, 1999) or an 'hour glass' model (Salkovskis, 1995). However, our view is that, rather than a continuum, there is a need for a cyclical process – inherent in the action of the hour glass (a reverse flow of ideas from practice to evidence as well as the more conventional direction) – which combines features of both paradigms.

The paradigm of practice-based evidence has previously been presented as complementary to evidence-based practice (e.g., Barkham & Mellor-Clark, 2000, 2003). As a consequence, this complementarity – or chiasmus – generates an evidence cycle between the rigours of evidence-based practice and the relevance of practice-based evidence. The two paradigms have the potential for feeding into each other to generate a model for the knowledge base of the psychological therapies that is both rigorous and relevant. This cyclical model is presented in Figure 25.6 to demonstrate the practical products, yields and activities arising from each paradigm.

The yield of this cyclical process can be seen in research on, for example, the general efficacy and effectiveness of the psychological therapies. The finding of broad equivalence in the effectiveness of the psychological therapies in routine practice (Stiles et al., 2006) can be placed against the yield from efficacy studies (see Lambert & Ogles, 2004) to help provide a fuller understanding of similarities and differences between performance within these two paradigms of research. The interface in this area is crucial because, for example, variability in therapist effects is reduced in efficacy studies in a way that does not occur in routine practice. Focusing research efforts in practice-based studies towards therapist effects

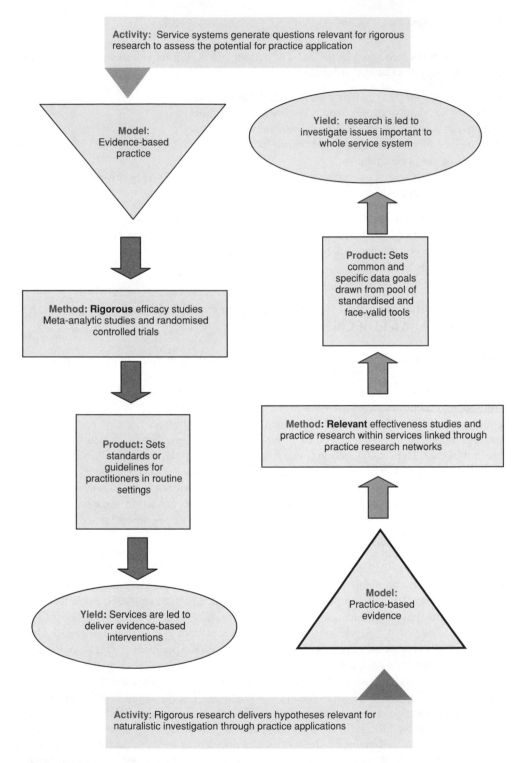

Figure 25.6 The cycle of rigorous and relevant research.
Source: Bridging evidence-based practice and practice-based evidence: Developing a rigorous and relevant knowledge for the psychological therapies, Barkham, M. & Mellor-Clark, J. *Clinical Psychology and Psychotherapy, 10*, 319–327, John Wiley & Sons Ltd, 2003.

(e.g., Okiishi *et al.*, 2003; Lutz *et al.*, in press) might help build an evidence base of practitioners that would, in turn, enhance the quality of service provision to clients and also provide the basis for more controlled studies of therapeutic interventions within specific treatment modalities.

A key principle in this cyclical model is that each component is equally valued in helping to deliver best practice and this, in turn, has important implications for the relationship between policy, practice, and research. The traditional linear direction is of RCTs informing policy, which in turn directs practice. The complement to this process is of practitioners developing and building an evidence base rooted in practice. This can then feed into and inform issues that can be shaped into more finely tuned tests of specific hypotheses through efficacy research. The yield of both these evidence bases can then better inform policy. Hence, in this cyclical and chiastic model, policy *per se* is not the driver for practice. Rather, policy is a product of knowledge informed by a combined evidence base. Hence, any specific policy will have a provenance that is grounded in both paradigms. The openness of researchers and practitioners to cycle through these differing paradigms may provide us with a more robust knowledge base about the process and outcomes of psychological interventions.

CONCLUSIONS: REQUIREMENTS FOR A COMPLEMENTARY EVIDENCE-BASED PRACTICE AND PRACTICE-BASED EVIDENCE

This chapter has dealt with an overview of the history and consequences of the forced dichotomy between practice and research. To overcome this artificial barrier we have presented a range of options for both clinicians and researchers. The *chiasmus* of the title refers to the concept of parallel but reversed and intersecting lines of travel, as denoted by the Greek letter Chi (χ). Our approach to the intersecting concepts of evidence based practice and practice based evidence is to develop an overarching system that sustains both. Such a system depends on three inter-linked requirements:

- The first requirement is for clinically and methodologically meaningful *critical questions* (see for example, Sackett *et al.*, 1996). Within the paradigm of evidence-based practice, these questions have traditionally been at the level of the individual case being treated by the clinician but it is useful to pose similar questions about the service delivery system and organization of care.
- The second requirement is a *system to measure change* before, during and following therapy. The system should be clinically appropriate and fulfil fundamental criteria for replicability, validity, reliability, and fidelity (Barkham *et al.*, 1998).
- The third and final requirement calls for systems to improve the delivery of effective psychological treatments via a good *infrastructure* (Audin *et al.*, 2001; Sperry *et al.*, 1996). This includes facilities and support to carry out focused literature reviews and critical appraisal. Also, clinicians need an infrastructure for collating and analysing outcome reports in a systematic way, preferably in ways that allow information to be managed intuitively and with minimal requirements for individual practitioners to manipulate data.

This combination of a system of critical questions arising from a good knowledge of the findings from efficacy studies and of underlying theory, with a system of measurement and a sound infrastructure provides the foundations for high quality practice based evidence, and in turn effective clinical practice. Beyond that, it requires an interface with research centres, national and research council funding agencies as well as policy makers to ensure that as broad an evidence base as possible is generated so that researchers and practitioners alike can contribute in equal measure.

REFERENCES

Alden, L.E., Wiggens, J.S. & Pincus, A.L. (1990). Construction of circumplex scales for the assessment of Interpersonal Problems. *Journal of Personality Assessment, 55*, 521–536.

American Psychological Association. (2003). *Publication Manual of the American Psychological Association* (5th edn). Washington, DC: American Psychological Association.

Audin, K., Mellor-Clark, J., Barkham, M. *et al.* (2001). Practice Research Networks for effective psychological therapies. *Journal of Mental Health, 10*, 241–251.

Barkham, M. (2002). Methods, outcomes and processes in the psychological therapies across successive research generations. In W. Dryden (ed.), *Handbook of Individual Therapy* (4th edn) pp. 373–433). London: Sage.

Barkham, M. (2006). Good enough science: The CORE-OM as a bridge between research and practice in the psychological therapies. *Psychotherapy Bulletin, 41*, 11–15.

Barkham, M., Evans, C., Margison, F. *et al.* (1998). The rationale for developing and implementing core batteries in service settings and psychotherapy outcome research. *Journal of Mental Health, 7*, 35–47.

Barkham, M., Margison, F., Leach, C. *et al.* (2001). Service profiling and outcomes benchmarking using the CORE-OM: towards practice-based evidence in the psychological therapies. *Journal of Consulting and Clinical Psychology, 69*, 184–196.

Barkham, M. & Mellor-Clark, J. (2000). Rigour and relevance: practice-based evidence in the psychological therapies. In N. Rowland & S. Goss (eds), *Evidence-based Counselling and Psychological Therapies: Research and Applications* (pp. 127–144). London: Routledge.

Barkham, M. & Mellor-Clark, J. (2003). Bridging evidence-based practice and practice-based evidence: developing a rigorous and relevant knowledge for the psychological therapies. *Clinical Psychology and Psychotherapy, 10*, 319–327.

Barkham, M., Mellor-Clark. J., Connell, J. & Cahill, J. (2006a). A CORE approach to practice-based evidence: A brief history of the origins and applications of the CORE-OM and CORE System. *Counselling and Psychotherapy Research, 6*, 3–15.

Barkham, M., Connell, J., Stiles, W.B., *et al.* (2006b). Dose-effect relations and responsive regulation of treatment duration: The good enough level. *Journal of Consulting and Clinical Psychology, 74*, 160–167.

Bauer, S., Lambert, M.J. & Neilsen, S.L. (2004). Clinical significance methods: A comparison of statistical techniques. *Journal of Personality Assessment. 82*, 60–70.

Bewick, B.M., Trusler, K., Mullin, T. *et al.* (2006). Routine outcome measurement completion rates of the CORE-OM in primary care psychological therapies and counselling. *Counselling and Psychotherapy Research, 6*, 33–40.

Borkovec, T.D., Echemendia, R.J., Ragusea, S.A. & Ruiz, M. (2001). The Pennsylvania Practice Research Network and future possibilities for clinically meaningful and scientifically rigorous psychotherapy effectiveness research. *Clinical Psychology: Science and Practice, 8*, 155–167.

Bower, P. (2003). Efficacy in evidence-based practice. *Journal of Clinical Psychology and Psychotherapy, 10*, 328–336.

Bower, P. & Gask, L. (2002). The changing nature of consultation-liaison in primary care: bridging the gap between research and practice. *General Hospital Psychiatry, 24*, 63–70.

Breiman, L., Freidman, J.H., Olshen, R.A. & Stone, C.J. (1984). *Classification and Regression Trees*. Monterey, CA: Wadsworth.

Brower L. (2003). The Ohio Mental Health Consumer Outcomes System: Reflections on a major policy initiative in the US. *Journal of Clinical Psychology and Psychotherapy, 10*, 400–406.

Bryk, A.S. & Raudenbush, S.W. (1987). Application of hierarchical linear models to assessing change. *Psychological Bulletin, 101*, 147–158.

Cahill, J., Barkham, M., Stiles, W.B. *et al.* (2006). Convergent validity of the CORE measures with measures of depression for clients in brief cognitive therapy for depression. *Journal of Counseling Psychology, 53,* 253–259.

Cape, J. & Barkham, M. (2002). Practice improvement methods: conceptual base, evidence-based research and practice based recommendations. *British Journal of Clinical Psychology, 41*, 285–307.

Charman, D. & Barkham, M. (2005). Psychological treatments: Evidence based practice and practice based evidence. *InPsych.* http://www.psychology.org.au/publications/inpsych/12.2_106.asp.

Christensen, L. & Mendoza, J.L. (1986). A method for assessing change in a single subject: An alteration of the RC index. *Behavior Therapy, 17*, 305–308.

Chwalisz, K. (2003). Evidence-based practice: A framework for twenty-first century scientist-practitioner training. *The Counseling Psychologist, 31*, 497–528.

Clark, D.M., Ehlers, A., Hackman, A. *et al.* (2006). Cognitive therapy versus exposure and applied relaxation in social phobia: A randomized controlled trial. *Journal of Consulting and Clinical Psychology, 74,* 568–578.

Cohen, J. (1977). *Statistical Power Analysis for the Behavioural Sciences.* New York: Academic Press.

Cohen, J. (1988). *Statistical Power Analysis for the Behavioural Sciences* (2nd edn). Hillsdale, NJ: Lawrence Erlbaum.

Connell, J., Grant, S. & Mullin, T. (2006). Client initiated termination of therapy at NHS primary care counselling services. *Counselling and Psychotherapy Research, 6,* 60–67.

Dar, R., Serlin, R.C., & Omer, H. (1994). Misuse of statistical tests in three decades of psychotherapy research. *Journal of Consulting and Clinical Psychology, 62,* 75–82.

Department of Health (2001). *Treatment Choice in Psychological Therapies and Counselling: Evidence Based Clinical Practice Guideline.* London: Department of Health.

Donenberg, G.R., Lyons, J.S. & Howard, K.I. (1999). Clinical trials versus mental health services research: Contributions and connections. *Journal of Clinical Psychology, 55,* 1135–1146.

Dong-Min, K., Wampold, B.E. & Bolt, D.M. (2006). Therapist effects in psychotherapy: A random-effects modelling of the National Institute of Mental Health Treatment of Depression Collaborative Research Program data. *Psychotherapy Research, 16,* 161–172.

Eggar, M., Davey Smith, G. & Altman, D.G. (2001). *Systematic Reviews in Health Care: Meta-analysis in Context.* London: BMJ Publishing Group.

Elkin, I., Falconnier, L., Martinovitch, Z. & Mahoney, C. (2006). Therapist effects in the National Institute of Mental Health Treatment of Depression Collaborative Research Program. *Psychotherapy Research, 16,* 144–160.

Elliott, R., Fischer, C.T. & Rennie, D.L. (1999). Evolving guidelines for publication of qualitative research studies in psychology and related fields. *British Journal of Clinical Psychology, 38,* 215–229.

Evans, C., Connell, J., Barkham, M. *et al.* (2002). Towards a standardised brief outcome measure: Psychometric properties and utility of the CORE-OM. *British Journal of Psychiatry, 180,* 51–60.

Evans, C., Connell, J., Barkham, M. *et al.* (2003). Practice-based evidence: Benchmarking NHS primary care counselling services at national and local levels. *Clinical Psychology and Psychotherapy, 10,* 374–388.

Evans, R., Mellor-Clark, J., Barkham, M. & Mothersole, G. (2006). Routine outcome measurement and service quality management in NHS primary care psychological therapy services: Reflections on a decade of CORE development. *European Journal of Psychotherapy and Counselling, 8,* 141–161.

Eysenck, H.J. (1952). The effects of psychotherapy: An evaluation. *Journal of Consulting Psychology, 16,* 319–324.

Fishman, D.B. (1999). *The Case for Pragmatic Psychology.* New York: NYU Press.

Fishman, D.B. (2000). Transcending the efficacy vesus effectiveness research debate: proposal for a new electronic journal of pragmatic case studies. *Prevention and Treatment, 3,* article 8, http://journals.apa.org/prevention/volume3/pre0030008a.html.

Ford, D.F., Pincus, H.A., Unutzer, J. *et al.* (2002). Practice-based interventions. *Mental Health Services Research, 4,* 199–204.

Goldfried, M.R. & Wolfe, B.E. (1996). Psychotherapy practice and research: Repairing a strained alliance. *American Psychologist, 51*, 1007–1016.

Greenberg, L.S. & Pinsoff, W. (eds). (1986). *The Psychotherapeutic Process: A Research Handbook.* New York: Guilford Press.

Greenhalgh, J. & Meadows, K. (1999). The effectiveness of the use of patient-based measures of health in routine practice in improving the process and outcomes of patient care: A literature review. *Journal of Evaluation in Clinical Practice, 5*, 401–416.

Gilbody, S.M., House, A.O. & Sheldon, T.A. (2001). Routinely administered questionnaires for depression and anxiety: systematic review. *British Medical Journal, 322*, 406–409.

Grissom, G.R., Lyons, J.S. & Lutz, W. (2002). Standing on the shoulders of a giant: Development of an outcome management system based on the dose model and phase model of psychotherapy. *Psychotherapy Research, 12*, 397–412.

Hannöver, W., Richard, M., Hansen, N.B. *et al.* (2002). A classification tree model for decision-making in clinical practice: an application based on the data of the German Multicenter study on eating disorders, Project TR-EAT. *Psychotherapy Research, 12*, 445–461.

Hansen, N.B., Lambert, M.J. & Forman, E.M. (2002). The psychotherapy dose-response effect and its implications for treatment delivery services. *Clinical Psychology: Science & Practice, 9*, 329–343.

Hayes, S.C., Barlow, D.H. & Nelson-Gray, R.O. (1999). *The Scientist Practitioner: Research and Accountability in the Age of Managed Care.* Boston: Allyn & Bacon.

Hickner, J. (1993). Practice-based network research. In M.J. Bass, E.V. Dunn, P.G. Norton & F. Tudiver (eds), *Conducting Research in the Practice Setting.* London: Sage Publications.

Hill, C.E. & Lambert, M.J. (2004). Methodological issues in studying psychotherapy processes and outcomes. In M.J. Lambert (ed.), *Bergin & Garfield's Handbook of Psychotherapy and Behavior Change* (5th edn; pp. 84–135). New York: Wiley.

Hill, C.E., Nutt, E. & Jackson, S. (1994). Trends in psychotherapy process research: Samples, measures, researchers, and classic publications. *Journal of Counseling Psychology, 41*, 364–377.

Holmes, J. & Lindley, R.L. (1991). *The Values of Psychotherapy*, Oxford: Oxford University Press.

Horowitz, L.M, Strupp, H.H, Lambert, M.J. & Elkin, I. (1997). Overview and summary of the Core Battery Conference. In H.H. Strupp, L.M. Horowitz & M.J. Lambert (eds), *Measuring Patient Changes in Mood, Anxiety, and Personality Disorders: Toward a Core Battery* (pp. 11–54). Washington, DC: American Psychological Association.

Hoshmand, L. T. & Polkinghorne, D. E. (1992). Refining the science–practice relationship and professional training. *American Psychologist, 47*, 55–66.

Howard, K.I., Kopta, S.M., Krause, M.S., Orlinsky, D.E. (1986). The dose-effect relationship in psychotherapy. *American Psychologist, 41*, 159–164.

Howard, K. I., Moras, K., Brill, P. L. *et al.* (1996). Evaluation of psychotherapy: Efficacy, effectiveness, and patient progress. *American Psychologist, 51*, 1059–1064.

Hsu, L.M. (1989). Reliable change in psychotherapy: Taking into account regression towards the mean. *Behavioral Assessment, 11*, 459–467.

Hsu, L.M. (1996). On the identification of clinically significant client changes: Reinterpretation of Jacobson's cut scores. *Journal of Psychopathology and Behavioral Assessment. 18*, 371–385.

Jacobson, N.S., Follette, W.C. & Revenstorf, D. (1984). Psychotherapy outcome research: Methods for reporting variability and evaluating clinical significance. *Behavior Therapy, 15*, 336–352.

Jacobson, N.S., Follette, W.C. & Revenstorf, D. (1986). Toward a standard definition of clinically significant change. *Behavior Therapy, 17*, 308–311.

Jacobson, N.S. & Revenstorf, D. (1988). Statistics for assessing the clinical significance of psychotherapy techniques: Issues, problems, and new developments. *Behavioral Assessment, 10*, 133–145.

Jacobson, N.S. & Truax, P. (1991). Clinical significance: A statistical approach to defining meaningful change in psychotherapy research. *Journal of Consulting and Clinical Psychology, 59*, 12–19.

Kendall, P.C., Marrs-Gracia, A., Nath, S.R. & Shedrick, R.C. (1999). Normative comparisons for the evaluation of clinical significance. *Journal of Consulting and Clinical Psychology, 67*, 285–299.

Kerridge, I., Lowe, M. & Henry, D. (1998). Ethics and evidence based medicine. *British Medical Journal, 316*, 1151–1153.

Kroenke, K., Spitzer, R.L. & Williams, J.B. (2001). The PHQ-9: validity of a brief depression severity measure. *Journal of General Internal Medicine, 16*, 606–613.

Lambert, M. (2001). Psychotherapy outcome and quality improvement: introduction to the special section on patient-focused research. *Journal of Consulting and Clinical Psychology, 69*, 147–149.

Lambert, M. (2005). Emerging methods for providing clinicians with timely feedback on treatment effectiveness: An introduction. *Journal of Clinical Psychology, 61*, 141–144.

Lambert, M., Harmon, C., Slade, K. *et al.* (2005). Providing feedback to psychotherapists on their patients' progress: Clinical results and practice suggestions. *Journal of Clinical Psychology, 61*, 165–174.

Lambert, M.J. (ed.). (2004). *Bergin and Garfield's Handbook of Psychotherapy and Behavior Change* (5th edn). New York: Wiley.

Lambert, M.J., Garfield, S.L. & Bergin, A.E. (2004). Overview, trends and future issues. In M.J. Lambert (ed), *Bergin and Garfield's Handbook of Psychotherapy and Behavior Change (5th edn)*, (pp. 805–821). New York: Wiley.

Lambert M.J. & Ogles, B. (2004). The efficacy and effectiveness of psychotherapy. In M.J. Lambert (ed.), *Bergin and Garfield's Handbook of Psychotherapy and Behavior Change (5th edn)*. (pp. 139–193). New York: Wiley.

Lambert, M. J., Whipple, J. L., Hawkins, E. J. *et al.* (2003). Is it time for clinicians to routinely track patient outcome? A meta-analysis. *Clinical Psychology: Science and Practice, 10*, 288–301.

Lambert, M.J., Whipple, J.L., Smart, D.W. *et al.* (2001). The effects of providing therapists with feedback on patient progress during psychotherapy: Are outcomes enhanced? *Psychotherapy Research, 11*, 49–68.

Lampropoulos, G.K., Goldfried, M.R., Castonguay, L.G. *et al.* (2002). What kind of research can we realistically expect from the practitioner? *Journal of Clinical Psychology, 58*, 1241–1264.

Leach, C., Lucock, M., Barkham, M. *et al.* (2006). Transforming between Beck Depression Inventory and CORE-OM scores in routine clinical practice. *British Journal of Clinical Psychology, 45*, 153–166.

Linehan, M.M. (1999). Development, evaluation, and dissemination of effective psychosocial treatments: Levels of disorder, stages of care, and stages of treatment research. In M.D. Glantz & C.R. Harte (eds). *Drug Abuse: Origins and Interventions* (pp. 367–394). Washington DC: American Psychological Association.

Llewelyn, S.P. & Hardy, G. (2001). Process research in understanding and applying psychological therapies. *British Journal of Clinical Psychology, 40*, 1–21.

Lucena, R.J.M., Lesage, A., Elie, R. *et al.* (2002). Strategies of collaboration between general practitioners and psychiatrists: a survey of practitioners' opinions and characteristics. *Canadian Journal of Psychiatry, 47*, 750–758.

Lucock, M., Leach, C., Iveson, S. *et al.* (2003). A systematic approach to practice-based evidence in a psychological therapies service. *Journal of Clinical Psychology and Psychotherapy. 10*, 389–399.

Lueger, R.J. (2002). Practice-informed research and research informed psychotherapy. *Journal of Clinical Psychology, 58*, 1265–1276.

Lueger, R.J., Howard, K.I., Martinovich, Z. *et al.* (2001). Assessing treatment progress with individualized models of predicted response. *Journal of Consulting and Clinical Psychology, 69*, 150–158.

Lutz, W. (2002). Patient-focused psychotherapy research and individual treatment progress as scientific groundwork for an empirically based clinical practice. *Psychotherapy Research, 12*, 251–272.

Lutz, W., Leach, C., Barkham, M. *et al.* (2005). Predicting rate and shape of change for individual clients receiving psychological therapy: using growth curve modeling and nearest neighbor technologies. *Journal of Consulting and Clinical Psychology, 73*, 904–913.

Lutz, W., Leon, S.C., Martinovitch, Z. *et al.* (in press). Therapist effects in outpatient psychotherapy: A three-level growth curve approach. *Journal of Counseling Psychology*.

Lutz, W., Sanders, S.M., Leon, S.C. *et al.* (2006). Empirically and clinically useful decision making in psychotherapy: Differential predictions with treatment response models. *Psychological Assessment, 18*, 133–141.

Lyons, J. S., Howard, K. I., O'Mahoney, M. T. & Lish, J. D. (1996). *The Measurement and Management of Clinical Outcomes in Mental Health*. New York: Wiley.

Main, T. (1957). The ailment. *British Journal of Medical Psychology, 30*, 129–145.

Margison, F. (2001). Practice-based evidence in psychotherapy. In C. Mace, S. Moorey & B. Roberts (eds), *Evidence in the Psychological Therapies: A Critical Guide for Practitioners* (pp. 174–198). London: Brunner-Routledge.

Margison, F., Barkham, M., Evans, C. *et al.* (2000). Measurement and psychotherapy: evidence-based practice and practice-based evidence. *British Journal of Psychiatry, 177*, 123–130.

Margison, F., McGrath, G. & Loebl, R. (1998). The Manchester Experience: Audit and psychotherapy services in North-West England. In M. Patrick & R. Davenhill (eds), *Reconstructing Audit: the Case of Psychotherapy Services in the NHS* (pp. 76–110). London: Routledge.

Maruish, M.E. (ed.) (1999). *The Use of Psychological Testing for Treatment Planning and Outcomes Assessment* (2nd edn). Mahwah, NJ: Lawrence Erlbaum.

Maruish, M.E. (ed.) (2000). *Handbook of Psychological Assessment in Primary Care Settings.* Mahwah, NJS: Lawrence Erlbaum.

McLeod, J. (1997). *Narrative and Psychotherapy.* London: Sage Publications.

McLeod, J. (1998). *An Introduction to Counselling.* Buckingham: Open University Press.

McLeod, J. (2000). The contribution of qualitative research to evidence-based counselling and psychotherapy. In N. Rowland & S. Goss (eds), *Evidence-based Counselling and Psychological Therapies: Research and Applications* (pp. 112–126). London: Routledge.

Mellor-Clark, J. & Barkham, M. (2006). The CORE System: Developing and delivering practice-based evidence through quality evaluation. In C. Feltham & I. Horton (eds), *Handbook of Counselling and Psychotherapy* (2nd edn). London: Sage.

Mellor-Clark, J., Barkham, M., Connell, J. & Evans, C. (1999). Practice-based evidence and the need for a standardised system: Informing the design of the CORE System. *European Journal of Psychotherapy, Counselling and Health, 3*, 357–374.

Mellor-Clark, J. Curtis Jenkins, A., Evans, R. *et al.* (2006). Resourcing a CORE Network to develop a National Research Database to help enhance psychological therapy and counselling service provision. *Counselling and Psychotherapy Research, 6*, 16–22.

Merrill, K.A., Tolbert, V.E. & Wade, W.A. (2003). Effectiveness of cognitive therapy for depression in a community mental health centre: A benchmarking study. *Journal of Consulting and Clinical Psychology, 71*, 404–409.

Mullin, T., Barkham, M., Mothersole, G. *et al.* (2006). Recovery and improvement benchmarks in routine primary care mental health settings. *Counselling and Psychotherapy Research, 6*, 68–80.

Nathan, P.E., Stuart, S.P. & Dolan, S.L. (2000). Research on psychotherapy efficacy and effectiveness: Between Scylla and Charybdis? *Psychological Bulletin, 126*, 964–981.

National Advisory Mental Health Council, National Institute of Mental Health (1999). *Bridging Science and Service: A Report by the National Advisory Mental Health Council's Clinical Treatment and Services Research Workshop* (NIH Publication No. 99-4353). Washington, DC: National Institute of Mental Health.

Newman, F.L. & Tejeda, M.J. (1996). The need for research that is designed to support decisions in the delivery of mental health services. *American Psychologist, 51*, 1040–1049.

Newman, M.E. (2001). The structure of scientific collaboration networks. *Proceedings of the National Academy of Sciences of the United States of America, 98*, 404–409.

Nolan, T.W. (2000). System changes to improve patient safety. *British Medical Journal, 320*, 771–773.

Ogles, B.M., Lunnen, K.M. & Bonesteel, K. (2001). Clinical significance: history, application, and current practice. *Clinical Psychology Review, 21*, 421–446.

Okiishi, J., Lambert, M.J., Nielsen, S.L. & Ogles, B.M. (2003). Waiting for supershrink: An empirical analysis of therapist effects. *Journal of Clinical Psychology and Psychotherapy, 10*, 361–373.

Orlinsky, D.E. & Russell, R.L. (1994). Tradition and change in psychotherapy research: notes on the fourth generation. In R.L. Russell (ed.), *Reassessing Psychotherapy Research* (pp.185–214). New York: Guilford Press.

Parry G. (2000). Developing treatment choice guidelines in psychotherapy. *Journal of Mental Health, 9*, 273–281.

Parry, G.D., Cape, J. & Pilling, S. (2003). Clinical practice guidelines in clinical psychology and psychotherapy. *Journal of Clinical Psychology and Psychotherapy, 10*, 337–351.

Peterson, D.R. (1991). Connection and disconnection of research and practice in the education of professional psychologists. *American Psychologist, 40*, 441–451.

Pingitore, D., Scheffler, R., Haley, M. *et al.* (2001). Professional psychology in a new era: Practice-based evidence from California. *Professional Psychology: Research and Practice, 32,* 585–596.

Provan, K.G. & Milward, H.B. (1995). A preliminary theory of interorganizational network effectiveness: A comparative study of four community mental health systems. *Administrative Science Quarterly, 40,* 1–33.

Provan, K.G. & Sebastian, J.G. (1998). Networks within networks: Service link overlap, organizational cliques, and network effectiveness. *Academy of Management Journal, 41,* 453–463.

Reason, J. (2000). Human error: models and management. *British Medical Journal, 320,* 768–770.

Rogosa, D.R. & Willett, J.B. (1985). Understanding correlates of change by modeling individual differences in growth. *Psychometrika, 50,* 203–228.

Roth, A. & Fonagy, P. (2005). *What Works for Whom? A Critical Review of Psychotherapy Research* (2nd edn). London: Guildford.

Rowland, N. & Goss, S. (eds) (2000). *Evidence-based Counselling and Psychological Therapies: Research and Applications.* London: Routledge.

Ruddy, R., Audin, K. & Barkham, M. (2005). How to develop inter-organisational research networks in mental health: a systematic review. *Journal of Mental Health, 14,* 7–23.

Sackett, D., Rosenberg, W., Gray, J. *et al.* (1996). Evidence-based medicine: what it is and what it is not. *British Medical Journal, 312,* 71–72.

Salkovskis, P.M. (1995). Demonstrating specific effects in cognitive and behavioural therapy. In M. Aveline & D.A. Shapiro (eds), *Research Foundations for Psychotherapy Research* (pp. 191–228). Chichester: John Wiley & Sons.

Salkovskis, P.M. (2002). Empirically grounded clinical interventions: Cognitive-behavioural therapy progresses through a multi-dimensional approach to clinical science. *Behavioural and Cognitive Psychotherapy, 30,* 3–9.

Schön, D. (1983). *The Reflective Practitioner: How Professionals Think in Action.* New York: Basic Books.

Shapiro, D.A. (1996). Forward. In A. Roth & P. Fonagy (eds). *What Works for Whom? A Critical Review of Psychotherapy Research* (pp. viii–x). London: Guilford.

Shapiro, D.A. (2002). Renewing the scientist-practitioner model. *The Psychologist, 15,* 232–234.

Simons, H., Kushner, S., Jones, K. & James, D. (2003). From evidence-based practice to practice-based evidence: The idea of situated generalization. *Research Papers in Education, 18,* 347–364.

Speer, D.C. (1998). *Mental Health Outcome Evaluation.* San Diego: Academic Press.

Sperry, L., Brill, P.L., Howard, K.I. & Grissom, G.R. (1996). *Treatment Outcomes in Psychotherapy and Psychiatric Interventions.* New York: Brunner-Mazel.

Stiles, W.B., Barkham, M., Twigg, E. *et al.* (2006). Effectiveness of cognitive-behavioural, person-centred, and psychodynamic therapies as practiced in UK National Health Service settings. *Psychological Medicine, 36,* 555–566.

Stiles, W.B., Honos-Webb, L. & Surko, M. (1998). Responsiveness in psychotherapy. *Clinical Psychology: Science and Practice, 5,* 439–458.

Stiles, W.B., Leach, C., Barkham, M. *et al.* (2003). Early sudden gains in psychotherapy under routine clinic conditions: practice-based evidence. *Journal of Consulting and Clinical Psychology, 71,* 14–21.

Stricker, G. (2000). The relationship between efficacy and effectiveness. *Prevention and Treatment,* Volume 3, Article 10, http://journals.apa.org/prevention/volume3/pre00300010c.html.

Stricker, G. & Trierweiler, S.J. (1995). The local clinical scientist: A bridge between science and practice. *American Psychologist, 50,* 995–1002.

Strupp, H.H., Horowitz, L.M. & Lambert, M.J. (eds). (1997). *Measuring Patient Changes in Mood, Anxiety, and Personality Disorders: Toward a Core Battery.* Washington, DC: American Psychological Association.

TenHave, T.R., Coyne, J.C., Salzer, M. & Katz, I.R. (2003). Research to improve the quality of care for depression: Alternatives to the simple randomized clinical trial. *General Hospital Psychiatry, 25,* 115–123.

Upshur, R.E.G., VanDenKerkhof, E.G. & Goel, V. (2001). Meaning and measurement: An inclusive model of evidence in health care. *Journal of Evaluation in Clinical Practice, 7,* 91–96.

Wallerstein, R.S. (2002). The generations of psychotherapy research: an overview. In M. Leuzinger-
    Bohleber & M. Target (eds), *Outcomes of Psychoanalytic Treatment: Perspectives for Therapists
    and Researchers* (pp. 30–52). London: Whurr Publishers.
Waskow, I.E. (1975). Selection of a core battery. In I.E. Waskow & M.B. Parloff (eds), *Psychother-
    apy Change Measures* (DHEW Pub. No (ADM) 74–120). (pp. 245–269). Washington, DC: US
    Government Printing Office.
Williams, B. (1972). *Morality.* Cambridge: Cambridge University Press.
Wilson, E.B. (1927). Probable inference, the law of succession, and statistical inference. *Journal of
    the American Statistical Association, 22*, 209–212.
Wise, E.A. (2004). Methods for analyzing psychotherapy outcomes: a review of clinical significance,
    reliable change, and recommendations for future directions. *Journal of Personality Assessment,
    82*, 50–59.
Zarin, D.A., West, J.C., Pincus, H.A. & McIntyre, J.S. (1996). The American Psychiatric Association
    Practice Research Network. In L.I. Sedderer & B. Dickey (eds), *Outcomes Assessment in Clinical
    Practice.* (pp. 146–155). Baltimore: Williams & Williams.

Author Index

Subject Index